Does God Suffer?

To St Edith Stein

Does God Suffer?

Thomas G. Weinandy, O.F.M., Cap.

UNIVERSITY OF NOTRE DAME PRESS
NOTRE DAME, INDIANA

Copyright © T&T Clark Ltd, 2000
Published in Great Britain by T&T Clark Ltd,
59 George Street, Edinburgh EH2 2LQ, Scotland

www.tandtclark.co.uk

This edition published under license from T&T Clark Ltd by
University of Notre Dame Press
Notre Dame, IN 46556

First published 2000

0–268–00890–6 (pb.)

Library of Congress Cataloging-in-Publication Data

Weinandy, Thomas G. (Thomas Gerard)
Does God suffer? / Thomas Weinandy.
p. cm.
Includes bibliographical references.
ISBN 0–268–00890–6 (pbk. : alk. paper)
1. Suffering of God.   2. Suffering of God—History of doctrines.
I. Title.
BT453. S8W45 1999
231'.4—dc21
99–39506

Contents

Preface   vii

1. The God Who Suffers   1
2. Theology – Problems and Mysteries   27
3. Yahweh: The Presence of the Wholly Other   40
4. Bridges to the Patristic Doctrine of God   69
5. The Patristic Doctrine of God   83
6. The Trinity's Loving Act of Creation   113
7. God's Love and Human Suffering   147
8. The Incarnation – The Impassible Suffers   172
9. The Redemptive Suffering of Christ   214
10. Suffering in the Light of Christ   243

Conclusion   287

Bibliography   288

Index of Names   305

Index of Subjects   309

Preface

I did not want to write this book. In August of 1975 I completed my doctoral dissertation on the relationship between God's immutability and the Incarnation – on how an unchanging God can actually *become* man.[1] In attempting to bring clarity to that issue I became acutely aware that the question of God's impassibility, particularly that God, within his divine nature, does not experience inner negative emotional states such as suffering, was indeed even more problematic. One of my supervisors, H.P. Owen (the other being E.L. Mascall) wrote at the time that the impassibility of God 'is the most questionable aspect of classical theism.'[2]

For approximately twenty years I tried to avoid the topic, even though it incessantly arose within lectures, tutorials, seminars, and even within 'pub' conversations. I was aware of what the majority of the contemporary theological community was teaching, and I knew what it had concluded – God is passible and so he suffers. I basically knew why such was proposed – because God, being personal, is loving and compassionate, he surely suffers in solidarity with those he loves. I too, obviously, held that God is loving, but I was not comfortable with the inference that he must therefore suffer. I was not convinced by the arguments, though I did acknowledge that they were intellectually and emotionally persuasive, and that I could not easily dismiss or refute them. While part of me wanted to throw myself into what I considered an exciting and significant philosophical and theological fray, another part of me fearfully refused to become engaged.

What frightened me was not simply the need to confront the biblical evidence where God, especially in the Old Testament, is said to experience differing emotional states, including suffering. I suspected that the truth of such statements needed to be interpreted from within a broader and deeper revelation of who God is. Nor was I particularly bothered by the historical questions. Because of my knowledge of the Fathers and Aquinas, who held God to be impassible, I instinctively knew that they could not possibly be guilty of all, though maybe of some, of the errors of which they were so frequently accused. Moreover, since I considered

---

[1] This was subsequently revised and published as *Does God Change?: The Word's Becoming in the Incarnation* (Petersham: St Bede's Publications, 1985).

[2] *Concepts of Deity* (London: Macmillan, 1971), p. 24.

myself an adequate philosopher, neither was I particularly timid in the face of the philosophical issues, though I knew that these would be the most knotty. I confidently trusted that, given some hard thought, I could satisfactorily address them. Nor was I put off by the doctrinal and theological concerns. I felt that I could ultimately address the trinitarian, incarnational and soteriological questions in quite a creative and insightful manner. While it would have required some effort on my part to address all of these concerns in a comprehensive and scholarly fashion, they did not frighten me.

No, what I feared most was Auschwitz – with all of its contemporary iconic meaning and pathos. With the Holocaust and similar events of horrendous human suffering as the existential backdrop, how could I write a book in which I would argue that God is impassible and so does not suffer? How could such a book, and it was this book that I knew I must write, even be contemplated? Within this contemporary setting, to write such a book would demand that it be not only academically sound, but also, and even more so, emotionally compelling. I feared that my book, should I ever choose to write it, would lack this latter virtue, and so for many years it never was attempted. To use a favorite phrase of one of my esteemed colleagues, Professor R. Swinburne, I refused 'to grasp the nettle.'

On 13 February 1995 Mrs Jane Williams, then of Darton, Longman and Todd, having read my book, *Does God Change?*, and finding it 'a breath of fresh air,' wrote to me asking if I would be interested 'in doing a more popular and accessible book in defence of impassibility.' I wryly smiled at the words 'popular' and 'accessible,' but I consented to 'give it a go.' I gave such consent aware that, because of the complexity of the topic, and more so because of my own need to work through all of the 'unpopular' academic questions that required attention, I would probably be unable to write such a 'popular' book. My suspicion was correct, and Darton, Longman and Todd, having considered some draft chapters, rightly turned it down. Nonetheless, it was Mrs Williams who compelled me to conquer my fear and to undertake, finally, the topic I had so long avoided. For this I owe her a great deal of gratitude.

In response to those who advocate a passible and so suffering God I endeavor, in this book, to accomplish two ends. First, I strive to refute what I consider to be the often erroneous arguments and assumptions that support the notion of a suffering God, and in so doing diminish the sincere but ultimately, I believe, often misconceived sentiments attached to them. Second, and more important, I offer a positive Christian view of God and of his relationship to humankind, with its history of grief, which, I trust, is more biblically authentic, more historically accurate, more philosophically convincing, more theologically persuasive, and so more emotionally gratifying.

I attempt the above by systematically, in the various chapters, addressing each of the issues concerning God and human suffering. I attempt to safeguard the logical progression of my arguments, both within the individual chapters and in the sequence of the chapters, so as to ensure that all the distinct elements are properly placed and related. In so doing I hope that the reader will be able to give assent at each critical juncture and so, in the end, concur with the whole. I normally limit the dialogue with my opponents to the footnotes so as not to detract from my own positive presentation within the body of the text.

Because the question of God's impassibility touches on so many issues, I desire in this book to be as comprehensive as possible so as to provide as complete as possible a theology of the Christian understanding of God and suffering. In Chapter 1 I present a thorough and, hopefully, accurate account of the arguments (with their various authors) in favor of a passible and suffering God. In Chapter 2 I articulate my own theological method in order to ensure that it is clear what I am and am not attempting to do in this book.

Chapters 3 to 7 examine the various topics that bear directly upon God's impassibility as God and to his relationship to the created order, especially to human beings. These include such topics as: the biblical understanding of God and his ability to act within history, and so relate to humankind; the patristic concept of God; the notion of God as Creator and the type of relationship the act of creation establishes with the created order; and what it means for God to be impassible, and yet be merciful, compassionate and loving.

In Chapter 8 I discuss the Incarnation, specifically the truth that the Son of God actually did suffer as man. Chapter 9 is an exposition of my understanding of New Testament soteriology, that is, what Jesus has accomplished through his suffering and death. Chapter 10, the final chapter, examines the Christian experience and interpretation of suffering in the light of Jesus and his work of redemption.

There are a few philosophical lacunae. I have not, for example, treated, in the light of his impassibility, God's eternity and omniscience in relationship to time and contingent events. I felt that to undertake these and similar topics, which are in themselves complex, would unnecessarily add to an already lengthy book. Moreover, from what I do say on other issues, one could surmise how I might approach these questions as well.

Many friends and colleagues have helped me in various ways in the writing of this book. First, I want especially to thank Professors David Burrell, Germain Grisez, Paul Helm, Keith Ward, and John Webster; Drs Mark Edwards, William Fey, Peter Hocken and Uwe Lang; and Mr Stephen Clark for reading various draft chapters of this work and offering many useful comments and criticisms. The reader should not assume, however, that all of the above agree completely, if at all, with my arguments and conclusions. I am also grateful to all those who helped me locate bibliography – Drs John Dillon and Norman Solomon; Messrs Patrick Hayes, Nicholas Healy, Mark Hutson, and Daniel Keating; and Miss Clodagh Brett, who also proofread almost the entire manuscript. Then there are those who offered their encouragement and much needed prayers – Mrs Kathleen Jones and Judith Virnelson, my Capuchin brothers Frs Robert McCreary and James Menkhus, and my good friend Fr James Overton, who, while ardently supporting my efforts, often 'devilishly' queried my 'indefensible' position. I also am grateful to Mr Stratford Caldecott of T&T Clark for guiding the co-publishing of this book with Notre Dame University Press. Last, I deeply appreciate the fraternal support of the Capuchin friars of my own province in the United States, especially those at Sacred Heart Friary in Washington, DC, and that of the friars here at Greyfriars in Oxford.

While I was reluctant to undertake the writing of this book, having done so, I am glad that I did. It has forced me to consider issues that are at the heart of the Christian gospel, and in so doing I have come to a greater love and appreciation of it. Moreover, the writing of this book has compelled me to consider what I feared the most – the authentic and impassioned human cry for a loving and just God in the midst of untold suffering. I never forgot, in the years of its making, that this book was being written in the shadow of Auschwitz and its like. As well as being a scholarly work, I hope, then, that this book meets, in some small way, the genuine emotional needs of a wounded world longing for a loving God.

The Feast of Mater Dolorosa, 1999

1

The God Who Suffers

'Theology has no falser idea than that of the impassibility of God.'[1]   This
severe judgment, first made by A.M. Fairbairn in 1893, is now shared, to
a greater or lesser degree, by many, if not most, contemporary theologians. Since the latter part of the nineteenth century, there has been a
growing consensus that the traditional claim, held to be axiomatic since
the Fathers of the church, of God's impassibility is no longer defensible.
Rather, to this growing consensus it has become obvious, seemingly so
obvious that one might wonder why it was not apparent from the start,
that God must be passible. This break with the past understanding of
God is so sharp and the new consensus is so strong that D.D. Williams
refers to this phenomenon as a 'structural shift' within theology.[2] R.
Goetz simply designates it 'the new orthodoxy.'[3] M. Sarot, who is
probably the most prolific advocate of divine passibility, maintains, and
rightly so, that 'during this present century the idea that God is
immutable and impassible has slowly but surely given way to the idea
that God is sensitive, emotional and passionate . . . . By now the rejection
of the ancient doctrine of divine impassibility has so much become a
theological common place, that many theologians do not even feel the
need to argue for it.'[4] So confident is Moltmann of the success of the
present consensus that he can write: 'The doctrine of the essential impassibility of the divine nature now seems finally to be disappearing from
the Christian doctrine of God.'[5]
   What has brought about such a radical reconception of God? How, in
only one hundred years, has the tradition of two thousand years, so
readily and so assuredly, seemingly been overturned? There are a multiplicity of factors, but they all cluster around three headings: the
prevailing social and cultural milieu, biblical revelation, and contem-

---

1 A.M. Fairbairn, *The Place of Christ in Modern Theology* (New York: Charles Scribner's
   Sons, 1893), p. 483.
2 D.D. Williams, *What Present-Day Theologians Are Thinking* (New York: Harper & Row,
   1952), p. 138.
3 R. Goetz, 'The Suffering God: The Rise of a New Orthodoxy,' *The Christian Century*
   103/13 (1986):385. However, it must be stated that Goetz is not in sympathy with 'the
   new orthodoxy.'
4 M. Sarot, 'Suffering of Christ, Suffering of God?', *Theology* 95 (1992):113. At my count,
   Sarot has written nine articles and a full-length book in support of divine passibility
   and suffering.
5 J. Moltmann, *History and the Triune God* (London: SCM, 1991), p. xvi.

porary philosophy. All three are intertwined and they all mutually
support one another. Using these three headings, I will in this chapter
summarize, as clearly and objectively as I can, the various arguments on
behalf of the passibility of God.[6] I will also allow, as much as possible, the
advocates to speak for themselves.

The Contemporary Milieu

The conviction that God is passible did not arise within a dispassionate
academic setting. Nor was it nurtured within the context of what it might
mean for God to be passible in various ways, that is: Is God passible in
his will, knowledge, love, joy, anger, sorrow, and suffering? Historically,
the question of God's passibility focused primarily and, at times almost
exclusively, upon the issue of whether God could suffer. The catalyst for
affirming the passibility of God, one that is still intensely operative, is
human suffering.[7] God must be passible for he must not only be in the
midst of human suffering, but he himself must also share in and partake
of human suffering. Succinctly, God is passible because God must suffer.

   The passibility of God was first advocated within an English Anglican
setting in the late nineteenth and early twentieth centuries. With the
demise of nineteenth-century optimism and in the face of the social
suffering caused by the Industrial Revolution and the agony of World
War I, the passibility of God found a cultural climate in which to sprout.
By 1928 Brasnett could clearly perceive the passionate drive within the

---

6 M. Steen also holds that the passibility of God has arisen 'under the impulse of three
   factors, which actually work in convergence.' They are 1. biblical and christological
   discourse, 2. the new metaphysical ideas of Process thought, 3. human suffering and the
   question of God. See M. Steen, 'The Theme of the "Suffering" God: An Exploration' in
   God and Human Suffering, eds J. Lambrecht and R.F. Collins (Louvain: Peeters Press,
   1990), pp. 71–78.
      P. Fiddes gives four factors: 1. the love of God, 2. The cross of Christ, 3. The problem
   of human suffering, 4. The world-picture of today. See *The Creative Suffering of God*
   (Oxford: Clarendon Press, 1988), pp. 16–45.
      R. Goetz gives slightly different reasons: 1. the decline of Christendom, 2. the rise of
   democratic aspirations, 3. the problem of suffering and evil, 4. the critical reappraisal of
   the Bible. See 'The Suffering God,' p. 386.
      For almost complete bibliographies on the issue of God's impassibility or passibility,
   see M. Sarot, 'De Passibilitas Dei in de Hedendaagse Westerse Theologie: Een
   Literatuuroverzicht,' *Kerk en Theologie* 40 (1989):196–206, and M. Sarot, *God, Passibility
   and Corporeality* (Kampen: Kok Pharos Publishing House, 1992), pp. 246–62. My own
   bibliography contains titles not found in either of Sarot's listings. I must admit that I
   have not read every book and article that advocates a passible God, but as this chapter
   should demonstrate, I have examined a great deal of the literature. Having read what I
   have, I am confident that what I have not read does not state anything radically new
   and different from what I have read.
      For an excellent brief survey of the history of, and the arguments for, the passibility
   of God, see R. Bauckham, ' "Only the Suffering God Can Help": Divine Passibility in
   Modern Theology,' *Themelios* 9 (1984:3):6–12. For the broader question of God's
   immutability, see S. Sia, 'The Doctrine of God's Immutability: Introducing the Modern
   Debate,' *New Blackfriars* 68 (1987):220–32.
7 P. Ramsey and W.F. May state in their Foreword to A. McGill's book *Suffering: A Test of
   Theological Method* (Philadelphia: Westminster Press, 1982) that 'suffering poses the
   fundamental test for theology in our day' (p. 7).

already cultural and intellectual groundswell for a passible God. 'Men feel, and perhaps will feel increasingly, that a God who is not passible, who is exempt from pain or suffering, is a God of little value to a suffering humanity.'[8]

Auschwitz, however, became the interpretative experience that advanced the phenomenal growth in and acceptance of the tenet that God is passible. No other event has so impacted the contemporary conception of God, especially concerning his passibility.[9] Again and again, in books and articles advocating God's passibility, E. Wiesel's horrific story is told.

> The SS hanged two Jewish men and a youth in front of the whole camp. The men died quickly, but the death throes of the youth lasted for half an hour. 'Where is God? Where is he?' someone asked behind me. As the youth still hung in torment in the noose after a long time, I heard the man call again, 'Where is God now?' And I heard a voice in myself answer: 'Where is he? He is here. He is hanging there on the gallows.'[10]

8 B.R. Brasnett, *The Suffering of the Impassible God* (London: SPCK, 1928), p. ix. See also the immensely important and influential work, commissioned by the Archbishops' Doctrine Commission, of J.K. Mozley, *The Impassibility of God: A Survey of Christian Thought* (Cambridge: Cambridge University Press, 1926). Besides discussing the entire theological history of God's impassibility, Mozley also presents those theologians who, in the previous sixty years, had advocated the passibility of God. See pp. 130–66.

    R. Bauckham proudly states: 'For once, English theology can claim to have pioneered a major theological development: from 1890 onwards, a steady stream of English theologians, whose theological approaches differ considerably in other respects, have agreed in advocating, with more or less emphasis, a doctrine of divine suffering' ('Only the Suffering God Can Help,' p. 6). Bauckham gives references to the English theologians. See p. 6, fn. 4.

    I would like to think, though, that the theological jury is still deliberating on whether or not the passibility of God is a 'true' development.

    For a defense of the impassibility of God given within the context of the then new drift toward a passible notion of God, see F. von Hügel, 'Suffering and God,' in *Essays and Addresses on the Philosophy of Religion*, second series (London: J.M. Dent & Sons, 1926), pp. 167–213.

9 Auschwitz has now become this century's icon, a century indelibly stained by genocide and 'ethnic cleansing.' It graphically portrays the radical evil humankind is capable of perpetrating. It depicts the inexpressible monstrous and morally intolerable suffering of the poor, the weak, and the innocent.

10 What I have quoted here is actually a summary given by Moltmann of Wiesel's own account, *The Crucified God* (London: SCM, 1974), pp. 273–74. Moltmann references E. Wiesel, *Night* (London: Fontana/Collins, 1972), pp. 76–77.

    Sarot notes that Moltmann 'introduced the story into theology. While suggesting that he quotes Wiesel, Moltmann gives a summary in his own words of Wiesel's story. Besides, Moltmann suggests that the event that is related happened at Auschwitz, whereas in fact it happened at Buna. Far worse, however, is the fact that Moltmann suggests that Wiesel in the story of the youth on the gallows relates a religious experience of the suffering God' ('Auschwitz, Morality and the Suffering of God,' *Modern Theology* 7/2 (1991):137). Sarot contends that 'in Buna Wiesel was not comforted by the presence of a suffering God; in Buna Wiesel rebelled against God because he could no longer believe in his justice. For Wiesel, it was not God who died on the gallows – "I did not deny God's existence" – but his faith in God, his concept of a loving, gentle, just God' (*ibid.*, p. 138). For Sarot it is therefore inappropriate for Christian theologians to use Wiesel's story to advocate a Christian notion of a suffering God. '*In short*, it is impossible to defend with integrity the claim that in this story Wiesel relates how he

Moltmann, who himself was a prisoner of war, wrote in response to Wiesel's story:

> Any other answer would be blasphemy. There cannot be any other Christian answer to the question of this torment. To speak here of a God who could not suffer would make God a demon. To speak here of an absolute God would make God an annihilating nothingness. To speak here of an indifferent God would condemn men to indifference.[11]

In a more recent study Moltmann further develops the need for a suffering God in the light of Auschwitz.

> There can be no theology 'after Auschwitz,' which does not take up the theology *in Auschwitz*, i.e. the prayers and cries of the victims. God was present where the Shema of Israel and the Lord's Prayer were prayed. As a companion in suffering God gave comfort where humanly there was nothing to hope for in that hell. The inexpressible sufferings in Auschwitz were also the sufferings of God himself.[12]

Moltmann is also concerned about the whole question of human suffering in relationship to God. 'The suffering of a single innocent child is an irrefutable rebuttal of the notion of the almighty and kindly God in heaven. For a God who lets the innocent suffer and who permits senseless death is not worthy to be called God at all.'[13] For Moltmann, only a God who suffers in solidarity with the innocent is worthy of the name God.

The passibility of God has also found support in the aftermath of Hiroshima. Kitamori, a Japanese Lutheran, wrote a very influential book in which he argued that only a God who suffers can theologically ground and make sense of the immense pain and suffering within the contemporary world. For Kitamori, the pain of God is the most central truth of

---

was comforted by the suffering of God. Nor is it possible without presumption to interpret this story as conveying the deeper meaning that what the Jews in Auschwitz needed was the Christian faith' (*ibid.*, p. 139).

    References to Wiesel's story are too numerous to note them all. J. Vanhoutte states that 'this account is to be found in at least twenty publications in the domain of pastoral and systematic theology' ('God as Companion and Fellow-Suffer,' *Arhivio di Filosofia* 56,1–3 (1988):193). Sarot notes that J. Vanhoutte, in another article, lists thirty titles, see 'Een Thematisch Overzicht van de Recente Literatuur over "God en het Lijden"' in J. Lambrecht (ed.) *Hoelang Nog en Waarom Toch? God, Mens en Lijden* (Leuven/Amersfoort: Acco, 1988), pp. 264–66). I am confident that I found further references to the story of which Sarot and Vanhoutte are unaware. Nonetheless, for a few examples, see B.R. Brinkmann, *To the Lengths of God* (London: Sheed & Ward, 1988), p. 138; Steen, 'The Theme of the "Suffering" God,' p. 77; K. Surin, 'The Impassibility of God and the Problem of Evil,' *Scottish Journal of Theology* 35 (1982):97–115.

11 Moltmann, *The Crucified God*, p. 274.

12 Moltmann, *History and the Triune God*, p. 29. Moltmann also speaks of Auschwitz and his own experience. For example, see *The Crucified God*, pp. 1, 277–78.

13 J. Moltmann, *The Trinity and the Kingdom of God* (London: SCM, 1981), p. 47. See also pp. 48–49.

The God Who Suffers

5

the gospel.[14] Equally, the North Korean theologian J.Y. Lee states that 'the concept of divine suffering is not only the core of our faith but the uniqueness of Christianity.'[15]

This same theme was taken up within the context of the suffering due to racial injustice and the struggle to assure racial equality. The black theologian, J. Cone, argued that God, as witnessed in the exodus event, identifies and suffers with the marginalized and the oppressed, such as the blacks of America.[16]

The experience of immense global human suffering – innocent, violent and unjust – of recent and present generations created a psychological climate and an emotional state that cried out for a God who not only witnessed it, but actually participated in it. The human experience demanded that its experience be God's experience.

An apathetic God who, staying in his own bliss, as the unmoved observer of misfortune 'is by contemporary man justly experienced as cynical and readily dismissed,' says Brantschen. So the idea catches on: God's response to suffering is to be found in his sympathizing and compassionate love. He heals our suffering by sharing in it.[17]

14 See K. Kitamori, *Theology of the Pain of God* (London: SCM, 1966), p. 19. See also p. 90.
15 J.Y. Lee, *God Suffers For Us: A Systematic Inquiry into a Concept of Divine Passibility* (The Hague: Martinus Nijhoff, 1974), p. 1.
16 See J. Cone, *God of the Oppressed* (London: SPCK, 1977). Because much of the suffering experienced in the modern world was and is due to social, political, racial, and economic injustice, the theology of the passibility of God, which developed in this milieu, for example that of Moltmann and Cone, is of a political nature, that is, God suffers on behalf of and for the sake of those who are socially, racially, politically, and economically abused. In so doing the suffering God brings about, in some fashion, 'salvation.' As W. McWilliams writes: 'Cone would concur with Moltmann's judgement that the theodicy issue in our time is political rather than naturalistic, i.e. he focuses on "moral evil" rather than "natural evil" ' ('Divine Suffering in Contemporary Theology,' *Scottish Journal of Theology* 33 (1980):39).
    Because the suffering of the innocent is so closely tied to political injustice, the suffering of God is also a theme within Liberation Theology. See for example, L. Boff, *Passion of Christ, Passion of the World* (Maryknoll: Orbis, 1987), pp. 102–16; G. Gutierrez, *On Job, God-Talk and the Suffering of the Innocent* (Maryknoll: Orbis, 1987); and J. Sobrino, *Christology at the Crossroads* (London: SCM, 1978), pp. 217–35. For a short exposition of the role that suffering plays in formulating the doctrine of God within Liberation Theology, including that of J.B. Metz, see L. Richard, *What Are They Saying About the Theology of Suffering?* (New York: Paulist Press, 1992), pp. 58–72, 89–103.
    F.J. van Beeck also rightly writes: 'It would seem to be no coincidence that some of the more creative attempts at reintegrating compassion into the conception of God's transcendence have come from women theologians.' ' "This Weakness of God's is Stronger" (1 Cor. 1:25): An Inquiry Beyond the Power of Being,' *Toronto Journal of Theology* 9/1 (1993):15. He notes: D. Sölle, *Suffering* (Philadelphia: Fortress Press, 1975); R. Haughton, *The Passionate God* (New York: Paulist Press, 1981); M. Hellwig, *Jesus, the Compassion of God: New Perspectives on the Tradition of Christianity* (Wilmington: Michael Glazier, 1983); C.M. LaCugna, 'The Relational God,' *Theological Studies* 46 (1985):647–63. One should also add: G. Jantzen, *God's World, God's Body* (London: Darton, Longman & Todd, 1984) and E. Johnson, *She Who Is* (New York: Crossroad, 1993). For a short discussion of Sölle's theology, see Richard, *What Are They Saying ...?* pp. 73–88.
17 Steen, 'The Theme of the "Suffering" God,' p. 76. Steen quoted J.B. Brantschen, 'Die Macht und Ohnmacht der Liebe. Randglossen zum dogmatischen Satz: Gott ist unveränderlich,' *Freiburger Zeitschrift für Philosophie und Theologie* 27 (1980):226.

Why did the impassible God give way to the passible God? 'The basic problem of traditional theism, with its purely active, impassible God, is the problem of theodicy: how can an all-powerful and invulnerable creator and ruler of the world be justified in the face of the enormity of human suffering?'[18] Such a question, many conclude today, can only be answered if one simply acknowledges that God is passible and so suffers.

Thus, that God is passible sprouted, took root and thrived within the religious and theological community – Jewish and Christian – immersed in the social and cultural environment just described. Bonhoeffer, who himself suffered and died in a Nazi concentration camp, pointedly expressed the exact sentiment of that community. 'Only the suffering God can help.'[19]

The Biblical Notion of God

The contemporary experience of human suffering, which seemed to demand a passible God, found a ready ally and firm warrant, it appeared, in the biblical revelation of God. Thus contemporary theologians, in turning to the Bible, saw the God portrayed within it as not only sanctioning their felt need for a God who suffered, but one that actually advocated what they had perceived. On the question of a passible God who suffered, the experience of present-day men and women and the revelation of the Bible appeared to be substantially the same. Thus contemporary experience and biblical interpretation mutually supported and promoted one another on this issue. But what is it that contemporary theologians found in the Bible that supported and nurtured their conviction that God is passible? We will first briefly examine the Old Testament and then, again briefly, the New Testament.

The Passionate God of the Old Testament
God revealed himself in the Old Testament as a living personal God who acted in time and history, and thus a God who can be experienced by human beings. He was intimately involved in the affairs of the Hebrew people. 'For what great nation is there that has a god so near to it as the Lord our God is to us whenever we call upon him'(Deut. 4:6). So familiar was God that he actually revealed to the Israelites his very name: Yahweh – I AM WHO AM (see Exod. 3:13–15). As the living God who truly is, he was ever active. He not only made the heavens and earth, but he also heard the cry of his enslaved people in Egypt. He suffered over their plight, and he determined, in his mercy, to rescue them (see Exod. 2:23–25; 3:7–8). He made convenants with his people, and so bound them to himself (see Gen. 17, Exod. 24). Yahweh will be with his people so that he will be their God and they shall be his people (see Lev. 26:12; Jer. 11:4, 30:22).

---

18 R. Bauckham, 'In Defence of *The Crucified God*' in *The Power and Weakness of God*, ed. N.M. de S. Cameron (Edinburgh: Rutherford House Books, 1990), p. 96. This article is also re-published in R. Bauckham, *The Theology of Jürgen Moltmann* (Edinburgh: T & T Clark, 1995), pp. 47–69.
19 D. Bonhoeffer, *Letters and Papers from Prison* (London: SCM, 1967), p. 197.

Has any people ever heard the voice of a god speaking out of a fire, as you have heard, and lived? Or has any god ever attempted to go and take a nation for himself from the midst of another nation, by trials, by signs and wonders, by war, by a mighty hand and an outstretched arm, and by terrifying displays of power, as the Lord your God did for you in Egypt before your very eyes? (Deut. 4:33–34).

The reason for all of this is simply that God 'loved your fathers and chose their children after them' (Deut. 4:37, see also Exod. 2:25, 3:1–6, 3:15–17). Thus God showed himself to be a God of compassion and, above all, a God of faithful love (*hesed*) (see Exod. 34:6–7; Is. 63:7–9).

Thus Yahweh is a God who is approachable. Not only does Abraham converse with him (see Gen. 15:1–6), but Moses is able to speak to God 'face to face' (Exod. 33:11). The Psalms are not only prayers of praise, thanksgiving, repentance and intercession, but they also proclaim God's mighty deeds – past and present. The Psalms declare that Yahweh is a God who delivers his people in times of distress (see Pss 18; 30; 40:9–10; 66:13–20). They affirm that Yahweh is a God who 'acts,' 'forgives,' 'heals,' 'redeems,' 'crowns,' 'satisfies' and 'works' (see Ps. 103:5–9). In all of these actions Yahweh again manifests his primary covenantal attribute – *hesed* – steadfast love (see Pss 59:10, 16–17; 119:41, 64, 76, 88, 124, 149, 159).

Moreover, Yahweh reveals himself, especially in the prophets, to be a God who grieves over the sin of his people. He is distressed by their unfaithfulness, and suffers over their sinful plight. Hosea, in words that attest to the great love and pathos of God, states that when Israel was a child, he loved him. He taught Ephraim how to walk and enfolded his people in his arms. He led them 'with cords of human kindness, with bands of love' (Hos. 11:1–4).

Yet Israel became disloyal. So disheartened was God by their hard-heartedness that he actually became angry. However, 'my heart recoils within me; my compassion grows warm and tender. I will not execute my fierce anger; I will not again destroy Ephraim; for I am God and not mortal; the Holy One in your midst and I will not come in wrath' (Hos. 11:8–9). While God's wrath, in the Old Testament, rises in justice, it is always tempered by his forgiving and compassionate love, a love that even moves God to repent of what he had intended to do (see Exod. 32:11–14; 1 Sam. 15:11).[20]

Because the Old Testament portrays God in such a manner as exemplified in the above, and in other numerous and similar passages,

---

20 For other Old Testament passages that speak of God repenting or changing his mind see, Gen. 6:6–7; Judg. 2:18; 2 Sam. 24:16; 1 Chr. 21:15; Ps. 106:45; Jer. 18:8; Amos 7:3 and 6; Joel 2:13; Jon. 3:10.

 These passages are seen by some theologians as expressing God's unquestionable passibility. He does change his mind and is affected by the intercession of others or by the repentance of his people. See L.J. Kuyper, 'The Suffering and the Repentance of God,' *Scottish Journal of Theology* 22 (1969):257–77.

 For an excellent and brief account of the notion of God in the Old Testament, see J.J. Scullion, *The Anchor Bible Dictionary*, Vol. 2, ed. D.N. Friedman (New York: Doubleday, 1992), pp. 1041–48.

contemporary theologians conclude that God, as found in the Old Testament, must be changeable and passible. M. Steen writes:

> In the biblical-theological movement a static concept of God has been exchanged for a dynamic perspective in which God is conceived as personal, loving, and history-making; as such, He is involved with his creation and his people. It is striking that God is represented in an 'anthropomorphic' manner in the Bible. Even such human feelings as love, anger and sorrowful regret are attributed to Him. Hence theologians increasingly wish to valorize the so-called 'anthropomorphic' and 'anthropopathic' God. So the living God of the Bible comes into focus.[21]

Moreover, it is the ability of God to suffer that captivates the minds and imagination of contemporary theologians. If God is truly involved in the lives of people, if he actually enters into and acts within time and history, and most of all, if he does so as the God of love, then such a God must, by necessity, experience suffering. As van Beeck writes: 'Since the faithful remainder of Israel was now a suffering nation, the conviction arose that God must be more, not less, closely involved with it. But this in turn meant that God must be in a real sense *suffering* as well.'[22] It is not only that God acts within history to change history, nor that he acts within the lives of human beings in order to affect them, but equally the course of history and the vicissitudes of human life affect and change him.

Heschel's book on the prophets has had an immense influence on contemporary theologians in their understanding of the Old Testament notion of God.[23] Heschel speaks of God's 'pathos' – a pathos that suffers in love. He suffers an anguish that penetrates his very being as God. Fiddes describes this divine pathos.

The sorrow of God because his people reject his loving care leads to

---

21 Steen, 'The Theme of the "Suffering" God,' pp. 71–72. K.J. Clark also expresses this sentiment well: 'While the Scriptural record can be made to fit the hypothesis of divine impassibility, the fit is at best forced and unnatural. There is a certain naturalness of the passibilist interpretation given Scripture. For the Christian philosophical theologian, one must always think with Scripture in the background.' 'Hold not Thy Peace at My Tears: Methodological Reflection on Divine Impassibility' in *Our Knowledge of God*, ed. K.J. Clark (Dordrecht: Klewer Academic Press, 1992), p. 186.
       See also L. Kolakowski, *Metaphysical Horror* (Oxford: Oxford University Press, 1988), pp. 87–91; H. Küng, *The Incarnation of God* (New York: Crossroad, 1987), pp. 533–37; J. Lucas, *The Future* (Oxford: Oxford University Press, 1989), pp. 214–15; C. Pinnock, 'The Need for a Scriptural, and Therefore a Neo-Classical Theism' in *Perspectives on Evangelical Theology*, eds K. Kantzer and S. Gundry (Grand Rapids: Baker, 1979), pp. 37–42; C. Pinnock, R. Rice, J. Sanders, W. Hasker, D. Basinger, *The Openness of God: A Biblical Challenge to the Traditional Understanding of God* (Carlisle: The Paternoster Press, 1994), pp. 11–38; Richard, *What Are They Saying …?* pp. 11–22; R. Swinburne, *The Coherence of Theism: Revised Edition* (Oxford: Clarendon Press, 1993), pp. 219–29.
22 van Beeck, 'This Weakness of God's is Stronger,' p. 13.
23 See A. Heschel, *The Prophets* (New York: Harper & Row, 1962). For examples of Heschel's influence on other theologians, see Bauckham, 'Only the Suffering God Can Help,' pp. 9–10; Lee, *God Suffers for Us*, p. 12; Moltmann, *The Crucified God*, pp. 270–73; *The Trinity and the Kingdom of God*, pp. 25–30; K. Ward, *Religion and Creation* (Oxford: Clarendon Press, 1996), pp. 19–24.

a unique kind of pain which is ascribed to God, a state of feeling which is characterized by the prophets as *a blend of love and wrath*. This is presented as a pathos which is God's own pathos.[24]

Similar to the prophet Hosea quoted above, Fiddes sees this pathos especially exemplified in the prophet Jeremiah. 'Is Ephraim my dear son? Is he the child I delight in? As often as I speak against him, I still remember him. Therefore I am deeply moved for him; I will surely have mercy on him' (Jer. 31:20). This pathos embodies God's empathy towards and his sympathy with his people. Because of God's pathos, he is willing to suffer because of, on behalf of and in union with his people.[25]

Love is the foundation of God's pathos, and thus the foundation of his suffering. Lee argues that because God's very nature is defined by love – *Agape* – then it follows that God must be passible.

Love is the fulfilment of suffering, and suffering is the enduring strength of love. Suffering is subsequent to love, and love is carried out by suffering. These two do not stand side by side and separate from one another, but are united together.[26]

For Moltmann, 'Were God incapable of suffering in any respect, and therefore in an absolute sense, then he would also be incapable of love.'[27] 'A God who cannot suffer cannot love either.'[28] Fiddes argues in a similar fashion: 'Now, if God is not less than personal, and if the claim that "God is love" is to have any recognizable continuity with our normal experience

24 Fiddes, *The Creative Suffering of God*, p. 20.
25 For a thorough examination of the suffering of God in the Old Testament see, T.E. Fretheim, *The Suffering of God: An Old Testament Perspective* (Philadelphia: Fortress Press, 1984). See also E. Jacob, 'Le Dieu souffrant, un thème théologique vétérotesta-mentaire,' *Zeitschrift für die Alttestamentliche Wissenschaft* 95 (1983):1–8.
   Fretheim argues that the anthropomorphic language in the Old Testament must be interpreted in accordance with the metaphor being used. 'The metaphors do reveal an essential continuity with the reality which is God' (p. 7). They are 'reality depicting.' Thus the Old Testament metaphors must be interpreted 'along the metaphorical grain' and not contrary to it. 'If one moves against the natural implication of the metaphor, one is misinterpreting it' (p. 8). Thus the metaphors and anthropomorphic language that depict the possibility and suffering of God must be interpreted in accordance with that grain and not against it.
   Fretheim has also discussed the suffering of God and his passible nature within the Old Testament in the following articles: 'Divine Foreknowledge, Divine Constancy and the Rejection of Saul's Kingship,' *Catholic Biblical Quarterly* 47 (1985):595–602; 'The Repentance of God: A Study of Jeremiah 18:7–10,' *Hebrew Annual Review* 11 (1987): 81–92; 'The Repentance of God: A Key to Evaluating Old Testament God-Talk,' *Horizons in Biblical Theology* 10 (1988):47–70; 'Suffering God and Sovereign God in Exodus,' *Horizons in Biblical Theology* 11 (1989):31–56.
   D.J. Hall states that the basic aim of his study is to give 'a reasoned elaboration . . . that the response to human suffering coming out of the tradition of Jerusalem is nothing less than the suffering of God.' *God and Human Suffering: An Exercise in the Theology of the Cross* (Minneapolis: Augsburg, 1986), p. 16. See especially pp. 93–121.
26 Lee, *God Suffers for Us*, p. 19. See also pp. 6–22.
27 Moltmann, *The Crucified God*, p. 230. See also p. 222.
28 Moltmann, *The Trinity and the Kingdom of God*, p. 38. See also pp. 21–60. See also *History and the Triune God*, pp. 29, 123.

of love, the conclusion seems inescapable that a loving God must be a sympathetic and therefore suffering God.'[29] F. Varillon asks: 'Comment croire que Dieu est Amour, s'il faut penser que notre souffrance ne l'etteint pas dans son être éternel?'[30] Even Galot, who is rather theologically cautious, argues that God's love cannot exclude suffering.

> Par contre, l'amour de Dieu pour l'humanité comporte nécessaire-ment le risque de souffrance. En effet, cet amour, en se portant vers de êtres libres de s'opposer à lui, ne peut prétendre, s'il veut être absolument sincère et logique avec lui-même, exclure toute possi-bilité de conflit et de douleur. Il serait impossible de concevoir un amour divin qui aurait respecté la liberté humaine et ne se serait pas exposé à souffrir du péché.[31]

29 Fiddes, *The Creative Suffering of God*, p. 17. T. Johannes Van Bavel argues in a similar vein. 'If God is love, then he must be involvement at its highest. If he is such, it is not odd that he is affected by human suffering, and that he shares in the legitimate joys and the suffering of innocent people.' 'Where is God When Human Beings Suffer?' in *God and Human Suffering*, p. 149.
   For a critique of Augustine's view of God and the necessity for God to suffer because he loves, see also N. Wolterstorff, 'Suffering Love' in *Philosophy and the Christian Faith*, ed. T.V. Morris (Notre Dame: University of Notre Dame Press, 1988), pp. 196–237.
   See also Bauckham, 'Only the Suffering God Can Help,' p. 10.
30 F. Varillon, *La Souffrance de Dieu* (Paris: Le Centurion, 1975), p. 14.
31 J. Galot, *Dieu Souffre-t-il?* (Paris: Editions P. Lethielleux, 1976), p. 172. See also pp. 212–14. For another more traditional theologian who also advocates the passibility of God, see T.F. Torrance, *The Christian Doctrine of God: One Being Three Persons* (Edinburgh: T & T Clark, 1996), pp. 235–56.
   For other authors, besides those already referred to, who hold that love demands that God suffer, see: E. Burnley, 'The Impassibility of God,' *The Expository Times* 67 (1955–56):90–91; B.P. Gaybba, 'God As Love' in *God and Temporality*, eds B.L. Clarke and E.T. Long (New York: Paragon House, 1984), pp. 15–35; L. Gillet, 'Le Dieu Souffrant,' *Contacts* 17 (1965):239–54; C. Grant, 'Possibilities for Divine Passibility,' *Toronto Journal of Theology* 4/1 (1988):8–14; F. House, 'The Barrier of Impassibility,' *Theology* 83 (1980):409–15; D.E. Jenkins, *Still Living with Questions* (London: SCM, 1990), pp. 15–27; J. Kamp, 'Présence du Dieu Souffrant,' *Lumière et Vie* 25 (1976):54–66; G. MacGregor, *He Who Lets Us Be: A Theology of Love* (New York: Seabury Press, 1975); H. Wheeler Robinson, *Suffering Human and Divine* (New York: Macmillan, 1939), pp. 155–56; K. Surin, 'Theodicy?', *Harvard Theological Review* 76 (1983):225–47; K. Surin, 'The Impassibility of God and the Problem of Evil,' *Scottish Journal of Theology* 35 (1982):97–115; W.H. Vanstone, *Love's Endeavour, Love's Expense* (London: Darton, Longman & Todd, 1977).
   Sarot rightly notes that Surin has modified his position. 'He [Surin] still thinks that God should be concerned about the travails of his creatures, but he now is inclined to think that his having this concern does not require us to say that he is a co-sufferer.' 'Auschwitz, Morality and God's Suffering,' *Modern Theology* 7/2 (1991):151, fn. 26). See also *ibid.*, p. 150, fn. 4. See K. Surin, *Theology and the Problem of Evil* (Oxford: Basil Blackwell, 1986).
   Sarot strongly argues as well that only the suffering love of God gives comfort to those who suffer. God's co-suffering with human beings 'opposes the de-humanizing influence of suffering and reinforces the self-esteem of the sufferer.' Moreover, co-suffering 'transforms the suffering from something entirely negative, humiliating and degrading into an in itself unpleasant experience which nevertheless contains the possi-bility of establishing and deepening fellowship.' 'Divine Suffering: Continuity and Discontinuity with the Tradition,' *Anglican Theological Review* 78/2 (1996):232. See also 'Divine Compassion and the Meaning of Life,' *Scottish Journal of Theology* 48/2 (1995):162–65 and 'Pastoral Counseling and the Compassionate God,' *Pastoral Psychology* 43 (1995):185–90.

Because God's very nature is love, many authors point out that God's suffering, and thus his passibility, is not something that is forced upon him, but something that he willingly assumes out of love.[32] His passibility is something that flows from his willingness to create human beings and to love them even if it means he must suffer with them and because of them. Steen comments that 'those who favour the notion of divine passibility refer to a distinction between suffering as a purely fatal, passive and paralysing event and suffering as a free, constructive act of solidarity and openness.'[33] In God then, according to Moltmann, we find exemplified to the supreme degree 'the voluntary laying oneself open to another and allowing oneself to be intimately affected by him; that is to say, the suffering of passionate love.'[34] For Pannenberg, God, because of the plenitude of his being, can freely open himself to new possibilities in which he himself is intimately involved.[35] Ward holds that in creating God freely opened himself up to the world.

> If God can experience the goods of creation, then God must also experience its sorrows. They must enter into God's experiential knowledge of created being. If one can properly speak of divine joy in the beauty of the universe, one must also speak of divine grief or pity at the sorrows.[36]

For Johnson, God does not suffer passively because of deficiency, but rather 'speech about Holy Wisdom's suffering with and for the world points to an act of freedom, the freedom of love deliberately and generously shared in accord with her own integrity.'[37] While Galot says that God is invulnerable in himself, yet he makes himself vulnerable in his relations with human beings. 'La Bible nous montre précisément comment par l'alliance il s'est rendu vulnérable. En établissant des relations amicales avec le peuple que lui-même a choisi, il s'est mis à son niveau, et volontairement a accepté d'avance toutes le souffrances qui pourraient en résulter pour lui.'[38]

---

32 Despite the fact that many theologians do so, Sarot holds that it is false to argue that, because there is suffering in the world, God, therefore, has a moral obligation to suffer. He believes that one could still argue that God is impassible even though there is human suffering. Rather, he believes that God's suffering must be founded upon his love. Because God is a God of love, he freely embraces the suffering of humankind. See 'Auschwitz, Morality and the Suffering of God,' *Modern Theology* 7/2 (1991):141–49; *God, Passibility and Corporeality*, pp. 80–91, 96–102.

33 Steen, 'The Theme of the "Suffering" God,' p. 80.

34 Moltmann, *The Trinity and the Kingdom of God*, p. 23. See also *The Crucified God*, p. 230.

35 See W. Pannenberg, 'The Appropriation of the Philosophical Concept of God as a Dogmatic Problem of Early Christian Theology' in *Basic Questions in Theology*, Vol. 1 (London: SCM, 1971), p. 161.

36 Ward, *Religion and Creation*, pp. 249–50. See also pp. 243–55.

37 Johnson, *She Who Is*, p. 266. See also pp. 224–45, 265–70.

38 Galot, *Dieu Souffre-t-il?*, p. 154. See also p. 155. Throughout his works Galot argues that while God is passible within his freely committed relations to human beings, he does not believe that this passibility disturbs his immutable and impassible 'inner' divine being.

> Une distinction doit être reconnue en Dieu entre l'être divin, qu'on peut appeler être nécessaire, et l'attitude adoptée envers l'humanité, où s'exprime la liberté et la

The arguments on behalf of a passible and suffering God based upon the Old Testament follow a very logical and compelling pattern. If God is living, personal and, above all, loving, and if this God acts in time and history and within the lives of human beings, then such a God must, it is argued, be passible and capable of suffering. Pollard is so confident that

---

gratuité des décisions divines. Vouloir les identifier, ce serait confondre avec l'être nécessaire ce qui est libre engagement. En raison de la distinction entre être divin et initiative gratuite, on comprend la distinction qui doit demeurer entre d'une part l'immutabilité et l'impassibilité de la nature divine, et d'autre part l'engagement dans de libres relations où se produit la souffrance. L'affirmation de la souffrance divine n'empêche donc pas de maintenir le principe de l'impassibilité. 'Le Mystère de la Souffrance de Dieu,' *Esprit et Vie* 100 (1990):265. See also pp. 261–68.

See also 'La Réalité de la Souffrance de Dieu,' *Nouvelle Revue Theologique* 101 (1979):224–45; 'Le Dieu Trinitaire et la Passion du Christ,' *Nouvelle Revue Theologique* 104 (1982):70–87; and 'La Révélation de la Souffrance de Dieu,' *Science et Esprit* 31 (1979):159–71; *Père, qui es-Tu?* (Versailles: Éditions Saint-Paul, 1996, pp. 77–79; and *Notre Père qui est Amour* (Saint-Maur: Parole et Silence, 1998) pp. 110–12.

A. Torrance believes that it is wrong to predicate suffering of God as if it were a necessary attribute of his being. Rather the suffering of God must be seen 'as a free act of love.' This he believes is in keeping with the thought of Barth, Moltmann, and Jüngel. See 'Does God Suffer? Incarnation and Impassibility' in *Christ in Our Place*, eds T. Hart and D. Thimell (Exeter: Paternoster Press, 1987), pp. 364–68.

It is impossible here to give a complete exposition of K. Barth's and E. Jüngel's thinking on divine mutability and passibility. Both strongly hold that our view of God cannot be predicated upon some preconceived philosophical position, but must be founded upon the event of God's revelation. Thus our notion of God must be thoroughly biblical. From this biblical perspective, Barth argues that God, in the vitality of his life and freedom, engages himself as Creator and Saviour, and thus he freely allows himself to be affected by such an engagement (see *Church Dogmatics* II/1 (Edinburgh: T & T Clark, 1957), pp. 495–99). If God were immutable, as traditionally understood, this would deny that God could participate in the created order and that the created order could participate in his divine life (see p. 501). If God is 'the pure *immobile*, it is quite impossible that there should be any relationship between himself and a reality distinct from himself – or at any rate a relationship that is more than the relation of pure mutual negativity, and includes God's concern for this other reality . . . . For we must not make any mistake: the pure *immobile* is – death. If, then, the pure *immobile* is God, death is God' (p. 494). God is immutable in the sense that he is constantly faithful to who he is as the living God of love. 'The immutable is the fact that this God is as the One he is, gracious and holy, merciful and righteous, patient and wise. The immutable is the fact that he is the Creator, Reconciler, Redeemer and Lord. This immutability includes rather than excludes life' (p. 495). Within the Bible 'God is certainly the immutable, but as the immutable he is the living God and he possesses a mobility and elasticity which is no less divine than his perseverance' (p. 496). See pp. 490–51. Thus J.M. Russell believes that Barth holds that God is impassible in the sense that he cannot, by necessity, be acted upon from without and, therefore, that he does not have 'sensational' passibility, that is, he is not liable to pleasure and pain caused by the action of another being. Nonetheless, Barth does propose that God possesses 'internal' passibility in that he can freely engage himself in the created order and in so doing he can freely change his emotions from within. See 'Impassibility and Pathos in Barth's Idea of God,' *Anglican Theological Review* 60/3 (1988):221–32. Scholars hold conflicting opinions as to what extent and degree Barth holds that God is passible. See Fiddes, *The Creative Suffering of God*, pp. 114–23; W. Loewe, 'Two Theologians of the Cross: Karl Barth and Jürgen Moltmann,' *The Thomist* 41/4 (1977):510–39; and M. Steen, 'Jürgen Moltmann's Critical Reception of K. Barth's Theopaschitism,' *Ephemerides Theolgicae Lovanienses* 67/4 (1991):278–311.

E. Jüngel argues that, because God is loving and so vulnerable, he freely associates himself with human sinfulness and weakness, and so suffers. See *The Doctrine of the*

the Old Testament bears witness to a passible and suffering God that he
states that if God cannot experience passion and suffering 'we have
either to re-write the Scriptures or treat them as a collection of books
embodying primitive anthropomorphic conceptions of God.'[39]

Trinity: God's Being is in Becoming (Grand Rapids: Eerdmans, 1976), pp. 83–88; *God as the Mystery of the World: On the Foundation of the Theology of the Crucified One in the Dispute Between Theism and Atheism* (Edinburgh: T & T Clark, 1983), pp. 184–225, 314–30; 'Humanity in Correspondence to God' in *Theological Essays* (Edinburgh: T & T Clark, 1989), p. 144. See also J. Webster, *Eberhard Jüngel: An Introduction to His Theology* (Cambridge: Cambridge University Press, 1986), pp. 20–22, 63–78.

For further discussions of Barth and/or Jüngel, see also Fiddes, *The Creative Suffering of God*, especially pp. 67–71, 114–23, 198–200, 210–25; Küng, *The Incarnation of God*, pp. 544–52; E.P. Meijering, *God Being History* (Amsterdam: North-Holland Publishing Company, 1974), pp. 149–51; and H.U. von Balthasar, *Theo-Drama V: The Last Act* (San Francisco: Ignatius Press, 1998), pp. 240–43.

Again, this is not the place to present H.U. von Balthasar's entire thought on divine impassibility and passibility. Yet, it should be noted here that, while he wishes to uphold the immutability and impassibility of God in himself, he also argues that, because of God's free and loving engagement with the world, he can be said to be mutable and passible in his relationship to the created order. His perfect immutable love allows him to be affected by the created order and so respond to it. Von Balthasar wishes to steer a position between the mythological notion of God's action in the world as, he believes, is found in Hegel, Moltmann, process theologians and others, and that of the traditional position, as found in Aquinas, where God appears to be disengaged from the vicissitudes of human life. He writes:

Accordingly, there is only one way to approach the trinitarian life in God: on the basis of what is manifest in God's kenosis in the theology of the covenant – and thence in the theology of the Cross – we must feel our way back into the mystery of the absolute, employing a negative theology that excludes from God all intramundane experience and suffering, while at the same time presupposing that the possibility of such experience and suffering – up to and including its christological and trinitarian implications – is grounded in God. To think in such a way is to walk on a knife edge: it avoids all the fashionable talk of 'the pain of God' and yet is bound to say that something happens in God that not only justifies the possibility and actual occurrence of all suffering in the world but also justifies God's sharing in the latter, in which he goes to the length of vicariously taking on man's Godlessness (*Theo-Drama IV: The Action* (San Francisco: Ignatius Press, 1994), p. 324).

For a further discussion of these issues in the context of an exposition and critique of some of the major contemporary theologians who espouse a passible God see his *Theo-Drama V*, pp. 216–50.

For a good exposition on how von Balthasar attempts to reconcile all of his concerns, see G.F. O'Hanlon, 'Does God Change? H.U. von Balthasar and the Immutability of God,' *The Irish Theological Quarterly* 53 (1987):161–83; and his *The Immutability of God in the Theology of Hans Urs Von Balthasar* (Cambridge: Cambridge University Press: 1990), especially pp. 110–44. See also T.R. Krenski, *Passio Caritatis. Trinitarische Passiologie im Werk Hans Urs von Balthasar* (Freiburg: Johannes Verlag, 1990), pp. 348–61; S. Lösel, 'Murder in the Cathedral: Hans Urs von Balthasar's New Dramatization of the Doctrine of the Trinity,' *Pro Ecclesia* 5/4 (1996):427–39; and M. Ouellet, 'The Message of Balthasar's Theology to Modern Theology,' *Communio* 23 (1996):286–99.

For other authors who hold that God willingly makes himself vulnerable to suffering out of love, see Bauckham, 'Only the Suffering God Can Help,' pp. 7–8; Brasnett, *The Suffering of the Impassible God*, p. 12; R. Cantalamessa, *The Power of the Cross* (London: Darton, Longman & Todd, 1996), pp. 114–16; I.A. Dorner, *Divine Immutability: A Critical Reconsideration* (Minneapolis: Fortress Press, 1994), pp. 161–95; Lee, *God Suffers for Us*, pp. 10, 12, 41, 44; J. Macquarrie, *In Search of Deity: An Essay in Dialectical Theism* (London: SCM, 1984), pp. 179–80; Mozley, *The Impassibility of God*, pp. 145, 152–53, 163; C. Taliaferro, 'The Passibility of God,' *Religious Studies* 25/2 (1989):217–24.
39 T.E. Pollard, 'The Impassibility of God,' *Scottish Journal of Theology* 8 (1955):360.

Creel summarizes the logic and the arguments on behalf of the passibility of God very well.

> All of these rejections of divine impassibility seem to be motivated by a clash between the conviction that God should be thought of as a loving person and the further conviction that an impassible being cannot be a loving person.... Hence, for biblical theists, if there is a conflict between God being loving and being impassible, it is impassibility that must be modified or ejected. To go at the point another way, it is conceivable that one could affirm that God is love and deny that God is impassible yet remain a Christian, but it is inconceivable that one could affirm that God is impassible and deny that God is love, yet remain a Christian .... Hence, whether God is impassible is negotiable (for biblical theists), but whether God is love is not.[40]

While it is the Old Testament that lays the groundwork for subscribing to a passible God, it is the New Testament's proclamation that the Son of God has become man and died on the cross that brings the notion of a passible and suffering God to its full and complete resolution.

The Suffering of the Crucified God

The heart of the Christian kerygma is that the Son of God became man and lived a true and full human life. Within that human life the Son's death on the cross stands as the consummate event. From the Incarnation and the cross theologians argue for God's passibility on three interconnected levels. The first pertains to God in himself, the second pertains to the Son as man, and the third pertains to the Father's and Son's relationship.

First, so great was God's love for us that he sent his Son into the world (see Jn 3:16). Thus the Incarnation is the supreme paradigm and exemplification of God's passible pathos towards and empathy with humankind.

> Divine passibility was not the consequence of incarnation but the Incarnation was the consequence of divine passibility .... The Incarnation is certainly not the beginning of divine passibility but the continuation of it with an intensification in time and space.[41]

Moreover, those who argue for the passibility of God find, especially in the cross, their conclusive and decisive argument. The cross expresses fully the eternal nature of the suffering God. 'God suffers on the cross in *oneness* with the person of Christ; God suffers *eternally* in the cross;

40 R. Creel, *Divine Impassibility* (Cambridge: Cambridge University Press, 1986), p. 2.

41 Lee, *God Suffers for Us*, p. 56. See also, pp. 52–55. On the importance of the Incarnation for revealing a suffering God, see also S. Bulgakov, *Agniec Bozij* (Paris: YMCA Press, 1933), published in French as *Du Verbe Incarné* (Paris: Aubier, 1943); W. Hryniewicz, 'Le Dieu Souffrant?: Réflexions sur la notion chrétienne de Dieu,' *Eglise et Théologie* 12 (1981):333–56; H. Mühlen, *Die Veränderlichkeit Gottes als Horizont einer zukünftigen Christologie* (Münster: Aschendorff, 1969). Hryniewicz stresses the paradoxes that must be held within the nature of God, for example, his transcendence and yet his ability to suffer.

God is most *Godlike* in the suffering of the cross.'[42] Following the Johannine principle that he who sees Jesus sees the Father (see Jn 14:9), Moltmann argues, 'that the historical passion of Christ reveals the eternal passion of God, then the self-sacrifice of love is God's eternal nature.'[43] E. Jüngel states that the cross 'has destroyed the axiom of absoluteness, the axiom of apathy, and the axiom of immutability, all of which are unsuitable axioms for the Christian concept of God.'[44] The Incarnation and the cross are the fullest disclosure of the passible God, already witnessed to in the Old Testament, and thus the supreme verification that what was partially revealed in the Old Testament is eternally true.

Second, the Father's sending of his Son not only reveals the passible, suffering love of God in himself, but it equally manifests the possibility of his divine Son. Jesus manifests his great love for us on the cross where he dies to obtain salvation for the whole of humankind. Now if it is truly the Son of God who exists as man and, as man, dies on the cross, then it must be the Son of God who experiences all that human life entails and, most importantly, he must experience suffering and even death itself.

The christological tradition, inherited from the Fathers and the Scholastics, held that the Son of God did suffer, but *as man and not as God.* As God, the Son remained impassible, but as man he was passible. The illogic of this position arises, it is argued, because the tradition, as will be shown shortly, was shackled by the Platonic notion of God's impassibility and the two-nature model of the Incarnation that resulted from it.[45] However, if the Son of God did actually become man then it would seem, by necessity, that the Son suffered not only in his humanity but in his divinity as well. For Pollard, to ascribe impassibility to God renders the Incarnation impossible, or at the very least makes for Docetism, that is, God only *appears* to be man. 'To say that the Son of God, as divine, is impassible is to assert that the divine in Christ was unaffected by the human; and therefore that there is no real Incarnation, or if there is an Incarnation, it is meaningless.'[46] If Christ is one then what pertains to the humanity pertains also to the divinity.

Moltmann argues that the traditional use of the communication of idioms, that is, the predicating of divine and human attributes to the one

---

42 Fiddes, *The Creative Suffering of God*, p. 31. Lee states that 'The Cross of Calvary *always* points to the eternal Cross.' *God Suffers for Us*, p. 59.

    Brasnett also writes: 'We agree with those who would see in the Incarnation a revealing glimpse of the life of God; a manifestation, if we like to put it so, in time and space of the eternal life of Deity. And as there was pain for God in the Incarnation, so we hold there is pain for God when not incarnate.' *The Suffering of the Impassible God*, p. 36.

43 Moltmann, *The Trinity and the Kingdom of God*, p. 32. He also states that 'When the crucified Jesus is called the "image of the invisible God", the meaning is that *this* is God, and God is like *this*. God is not greater than he is in this humiliation.' *The Crucified God*, p. 205.

44 Jüngel, *God as the Mystery of the World*, p. 373.

45 See Brasnett, *The Suffering of the Impassible God*, p. 38; Fiddes, *The Creative Suffering of God*, pp. 26–28; Moltmann, *The Crucified God*, pp. 227–35.

46 Pollard, 'The Impassibility of God,' p. 363. See also pp. 361–62. See also B. Vawter, *This Man Jesus* (London: Geoffrey Chapman, 1975), pp. 145–71.

person of Christ, cannot be seen merely as abstract or as the ascribing of attributes to one or other of the natures, but must be ascribed to the whole Christ. Thus what pertains to the humanity of Christ must also affect his divinity as well. The oneness of Christ makes it possible 'to ascribe suffering and death on the cross to the divine-human person of Christ. If this divine nature in the person of the eternal Son of God is the centre which creates a person in Christ, then it too suffered and died.'[47]

T.F. Torrance likewise believes that the suffering of Christ must be ascribed to his 'divine-human Person.' Therefore, 'what Christ felt, did and suffered in himself in his body and soul for our forgiveness was felt, done, and suffered by God in his innermost Being for our sake.'[48]

Moreover, theologians see the misplaced attribute of divine impassibility giving rise to an exaggerated fear of *patripassianism*, that is, the early church's concern that not adequately distinguishing the person of the Son from the person of the Father would demand that the Father as

---

47 Moltmann, *The Crucified God*, p. 234. Moltmann is here following Luther's christological position. See pp. 232–34. Brasnett as far back as 1928 expressed a similar view. 'On our own view (to express ourselves in terms of the orthodox theology) both natures suffered; suffering smote upon the one Person in his humanity and in his Deity.' *The Suffering of the Impassible God*, p. 38.

48 T.F. Torrance, *The Christian Doctrine of God*, pp. 247, 249. See also p. 252. See also D.G. Attfield, 'Can God Be Crucified? A Discussion of J. Moltmann,' *Scottish Journal of Theology* 30 (1977):47–56; M. Deneken, 'God at the Heart of Hell: From Theodicy to the Word of the Cross' in *Concilium: The Spectre of Mass Death*, eds N. Power and F.K. Lumbala (London: SPCK, 1993), pp. 52–64; Wheeler Robinson, *Suffering Human and Divine*, pp. 156–59, 163–84; A. Torrance, 'Does God Suffer? Incarnation and Impassibility', pp. 345–68.

   Some authors cite G. Vann as an example of someone who espouses the suffering of God as God within the Incarnation, for example, Sarot. However, Vann actually holds the traditional view that the Son of God actually does suffer as man, but that he does not suffer as God. While God does not suffer within his divine nature, Vann does emphasize that the suffering of Jesus reveals the immense pity and compassion which God has for humankind. See *The Pain of Christ and the Sorrow of God* (London: Blackfriars, 1947), pp. 62–79.

   Sarot maintains that there are actually two arguments for the passibility of God stemming from the Incarnation. The first is founded upon the traditional understanding of the Incarnation. If the Son of God actually became man, then when the humanity suffers so too does the divinity. Nonetheless, Sarot believes that the traditional argument that the Son only suffers as man and not as God could be maintained. He therefore prefers the second argument, that is, 'the suffering of Christ reveals to us the suffering and therewith the passibility of God. This argument does not presuppose the reality of the Incarnation; it works just as well when one holds that Christ was a human being and nothing more than that. It presupposes something else, something which – just like the reality of the Incarnation – is deeply rooted in the Christian faith: that Christ is the ultimate and most perfect revelation of God' ('Suffering of Christ, Suffering of God?', *Theology* 95 (1992):116).

   Moreover, if one accepts this second argument, that Christ's suffering reveals the suffering of the Father, then 'we therewith leave behind us the problem of how the impassible Logos may have suffered during the Incarnation. If the Father is passible, the Logos will be passible as well. This means that, in that case, we may still accept the rationality of the doctrine of the *communicatio idiomatum*, but we will have no need for it any more' (*ibid.*, p. 118). Sarot argues in a similar fashion in *God, Passibility and Corporeality*, pp. 91–96, and in 'Divine Suffering: Continuity and Discontinuity with the Tradition,' *Anglican Theological Review* 78/2 (1996):233–34.

well as the Son suffered.[49] However, if one maintains a proper under-standing of the Trinity, and so avoids *patripassianism*, one can nonetheless say that while the Son suffers on the cross, the Father also suffers *as the Father* in the death of his Son.[50]

This leads to the third manner in which the Incarnation and cross bear upon the passibility of God. The cross is not merely the experience of a passible divine Son. The suffering and pain of the cross rather is the experience of both the Father and the Son. Moltmann, who initiated and has most fully developed this point, argues that Jesus' cry of dereliction upon the cross was not just the cry of a man being abandoned by God nor even the cry of the Son *as man* experiencing abandonment. Rather the cry of abandonment was the cry of the Son as God experiencing the loss of the Father. The cry of dereliction was a cry being experienced within the very depths of God's nature.

> The rejection expressed in his [Jesus'] dying cry, and accurately inter-preted by the words of Ps. 22, must therefore be understood strictly as something which took place between Jesus and his Father, and in the other direction between his Father and Jesus, the Son – that is, as something which took place between God and God. The abandon-ment on the cross which separates the Son from the Father is something which takes place within God himself.[51]

On the cross then it is not only the Son who suffers the loss of the Father, it is equally the Father suffering the loss of the Son. 'In the passion of the Son, the Father himself suffers the pains of abandonment. In the death of the Son, death comes upon God himself, and the Father suffers the death of his Son in his love for forsaken man.'[52] For Moltmann the suffering

---

49   J.Y. Lee holds that resistance to *patripassianism* actually gave rise to the two-nature model of the Incarnation. Since the Father could not suffer, then the Son, who was also God, could not suffer. Thus a distinction had to be made between the divine nature in Christ, which could not suffer, and the human nature of Christ which could suffer. See *God Suffers for Us*, pp. 36–38.

  Sarot is not always happy with how those who advocate the passibility and suffering of God use such terms as 'patripassianism' and 'theopaschitism.' He attempts to clarify, and so limit, the use of such terms. See 'Patripassianism, Theopaschitism and the Suffering of God: Some Historical and Systematic Considerations,' *Religious Studies* 26 (1990):363–75.

50   See Moltmann, *The Crucified God*, p. 243. See also Fiddes, *The Creative Suffering of God* were he comments on Moltmann's understanding of *patripassianism*, pp. 196–98. See also J.J. O'Donnell, *Trinity and Temporality* (Oxford: Oxford University Press, 1983), pp. 49–50, and Pollard, 'The Impassibility of God,' pp. 358–59.

  B.P. Gaybba holds that the Christian belief that God suffered for us was 'effectively anesthetized by affirming that he [the Son] suffered only in his human nature. Within the divinity he experienced no suffering. Christians also held that the Father experi-enced no suffering. But if the Father did not pay any personal price in sending us his Son, and if the Son did not really, as a divine person, experience pain, rejection, and crucifixion, then the Christian praise of such great love on God's part is nonsense.' 'God As Love' in *God and Temporality*, p. 25.

51   Moltmann, *The Crucified God*, pp. 151–52.

52   Moltmann, *The Crucified God*, p. 192. See also *History and the Triune God*, pp. 51, 47, 172. In *The Way of Jesus Christ* (London: SCM, 1990) Moltmann states:

  > Yet here we have to make a clear distinction: in the surrender of the Son the Father surrenders himself too – but not in the same way. The Son suffers his dying in this

experienced by the Father and Son, due to the cross, is even formative and constitutive of their being the Father and the Son.[53]

Galot agrees that resistance to *patripassianism* often led in the past to the denial of the Father's suffering. Nonetheless, while not agreeing with Moltmann that the Father's suffering is constitutive of the Trinity, he does affirm that the Father does suffer in solidarity with the Son.

> Only the Son suffers on the Cross, but the Father, a distinct divine person and intimately united to the Son, suffers with him. The Father's is a suffering of compassion, of exceptional intensity because of their complete oneness .... In the suffering face of the Savior we must also see the suffering face of the Father. Jesus' human suffering enables us to enter into the mystery of the Father's divine suffering.[54]

What the Old Testament revealed about God then finds its completion in the Incarnation and, especially in the cross. Both reveal that God is indeed passible, and thus the divine Son, within his incarnate state, does suffer as God. Moreover, the cross, and so suffering, reaches into the very depths of the Father's and the Son's relationship.

We have now briefly examined the cultural milieu out of which the theology of God's passibility sprung as well as the biblical evidence that

---

forsakenness. The Father suffers the death of the Son. He suffers it in the infinite pain of his love for the Son. The death of the Son therefore corresponds to the pain of the Father. And when in this descent into hell the Son loses sight of the Father, then in this judgement the Father also loses sight of the Son. Here what is at stake is the divine consistency, the inner life of the Trinity. Here the self-communicating love of the Father becomes infinite pain over the death of the Son. Here the responding love of the Son turns into infinite suffering over his forsakenness by the Father. What happens on Golgotha reaches into the very depths of the Godhead and therefore puts its impress on the trinitarian life of God in eternity. In Christian faith the cross is always at the centre of the Trinity, for the cross reveals the heart of the triune God, which beats for his whole creation (p. 173).

53 See *The Crucified God*, pp. 244–47. Moltmann also states:

To understand what happened between Jesus and his God and Father on the cross, it is necessary to talk in trinitarian terms. The Son suffers dying, the Father suffers the death of the Son. The grief of the Father here is just as important as the death of the Son. The Fatherlessness of the Son is matched by the Sonlessness of the Father, and if God has constituted himself as the Father of Jesus Christ, then he also suffers the death of his Fatherhood in the death of the Son. Unless this were so, the doctrine of the Trinity would still have a monotheistic background (p. 242).

For a clear exposition and defense of Moltmann's position see Bauckham, 'In Defence of *The Crucified God*,' pp. 93–118. See also his 'Only the Suffering God Can Help,' pp. 11–12, and Richard, *What Are They Saying ...*? pp. 42–57.

54 J. Galot, *Abba, Father* (New York: Alba House, 1992), pp. 138–39. See also p. 140. Galot develops his notion of the suffering of the Father in union with the crucified Son in *Dieu Souffre-t-il?*, pp. 63–137. For his critique of Moltmann see 'Le Dieu Trinitaire et la Passion du Christ,' *Nouvelle Revue Théologique* 104 (1982):70–87.

For the notion that the Father suffers with Christ on the cross see also T.F. Torrance, *The Christian Doctrine of God*, pp. 252–53, and A. Torrance, 'Does God Suffer? Incarnation and Impassibility', pp. 345–68.

It can also be noted that the Russian theologian N. Berdyaev believes that the cross brings suffering to God. For a short summary of his thought see K.J. Woollcombe, 'The Pain of God,' *Scottish Journal of Theology* 20 (1967):133–35.

nurtured this theological development. We must now turn to the final factor that contributes to the notion of a possible God – contemporary philosophy.

From the God of the Greeks to the God of Process

The influence of Greek philosophy, especially Platonism, is the main reason why it has taken almost two thousand years to develop the notion of God's passibility. *All* theologians, who advance the idea that God is passible, agree on this judgment. The static, self-sufficient, immutable, and impassible God of Platonic thought hijacked, via Philo and the early church Fathers, the living, personal, active, and passible God of the Bible.

The Impassible God of Greek Philosophy
Philo (c. 20 BC–c. AD 50), the Jewish-Platonic scholar of Alexandria, in attempting to reconcile the Hebrew scriptures with Platonic philosophy, forced the living God of Israel into the procrustean bed of the immutable God of Greek thought. Significantly he is the first to write a treatise entitled *Quod deus immutabilis sit (On the Unchangeableness of God)*.[55]

The controlling principle of Platonic theodicy, and its subsequent developments within Middle and Neoplatonic thought, was that God is a completely self-sufficient, all-perfect, transcendent, and unchanging substance. Thus God could not be affected by anything outside himself. He possessed the attribute of impassibility (*apatheia*) for to be passible (*patheia*) would mean that he would be under the control of something other than himself in his all-perfect and unchanging reason, and thus manifest weakness, passion, and emotion. As Bauckham writes:

> For the Greeks, God cannot be passive, he cannot be affected by something else, he cannot (in the broad sense) 'suffer' (*paschein*), because he is absolutely self-sufficient, self-determining and inde-pendent.... To be moved by desire or fear or anger is to be affected by something outside the self, instead of being self-determining. Again this is weakness and so God must be devoid of emotion. To suffer or to feel is be subject to pain or emotion and to the things that cause them. God cannot be *subject* to anything.... Since he is self-sufficient, he cannot be changed. Since he is perfect, he cannot change himself. Thus suffering and emotion are both incompatible with the nature of a God who never becomes, but *is*.[56]

---

55 For comments and critiques of Philo, see Bauckham, 'Only the Suffering God Can Help,' p. 7; J. Hallman, *The Descent of God: Divine Suffering in History and Theology* (Minneapolis: Fortress Press, 1991), pp. 23–29; Pannenberg, *Basic Questions in Theology*, Vol. 1, p. 167; Pollard, 'The Impassibility of God,' p. 356; J. Sanders, *The Openness of God*, pp. 69–72.

56 Bauckham, 'Only the Suffering God Can Help,' pp. 7–8. Fiddes, commenting on the Greek notion of God, states: 'God as Absolute Being, either at the top of the pyramid or beyond it altogether (depending upon the particular school of Platonism in vogue), must therefore be absolutely unmoving, unchanging, and unaffected by the world of Becoming.' *The Creative Suffering of God*, p. 37.

For similar assessments of Greek Platonic theodicy, see C. Cain, 'A Passionate God?', *Saint Luke's Journal of Theology* 25 (1981):52–57; K.J. Clark, 'Hold not Thy Peace at My

Historically, it is the Greek Platonic notion of God that Christianity practically inherited. The Fathers of the church too uncritically accepted the immutable and impassible God of the Greeks and in so doing distorted the Christian God of revelation. This cancer was transmitted to the Scholastics and thus deformed the whole body of Christian theology.

Thus, while Pollard acknowledges that the Fathers had to make use of the philosophy of their day, yet, in so doing, 'much that was distinctive in Christianity was either lost or falsely expressed, and alien elements which they imported into Christian thought have cursed theological thought ever since their time.' This is especially so with regard to God's impassibility. 'Brought into the Christian tradition from Greek philosophy, it has brought with it far greater and more serious difficulties than those which it was originally designed to obviate.'[57]

Pannenberg is a little more nuanced in his judgment. He denies that the Christian faith was hellenized, as Harnack and Ritschl maintained, but he nonetheless believes that the Greek notion of God's immutability has retarded and arrested a proper Christian understanding of God and his relation to the world, especially within christology. Divine immutability does not allow adequate scope to the living God's 'inner plenitude,' 'creative activity,' 'freedom,' 'spontaneous act,' and 'acts in history.'[58]

In contrast to this, the concept of a God who is by nature immutable necessarily obstructs the theological understanding of his historical action, and it has done so to an extent that can hardly be exaggerated. It indeed constitutes the background for the ideal of the impassibility of God which so fatefully determined the Christology of the early church right down to the theopaschite controversy. Above all,

---

Tears,' pp. 178–80; Deneken, 'God at the Heart of Hell,' pp. 57–58; Dorner, *Divine Immutability*, pp. 82–130; Rem B. Edwards, 'The Pagan Dogma of the Absolute Unchangeableness of God,' *Religious Studies* 14 (1978):305–13; C. Grant, 'Possibilities for Divine Passibility,' *Toronto Journal of Theology* 4/1 (1988):6–8; Küng, *The Incarnation of God*, pp. 518–25; Lee, *God Suffers for Us*, pp. 28–32, 40; W. Maas, *Unveränderlichkeit Gottes: Zum Verhältnis von griechisch-philosophischer und christlicher Gotteslehre* (München: Schönigh, 1974); Moltmann, *The Crucified God*, pp. 214–15, 267–70; Pannenberg, *Basic Questions in Theology*, Vol. 1, pp. 117–83; Pollard, 'The Impassibility of God,' pp. 353–64; H. Wheeler Robinson, *Suffering Human and Divine*, p. 144; D. Soelle, *Suffering* (Philadelphia: Fortress Press, 1975), pp. 35–45; Swinburne, *The Coherence of Theism*, pp. 219–23; A. Torrance, 'Does God Suffer?' pp. 348–49; and Ward, *Religion and Creation*, pp. 192–214.

57 Pollard, 'The Impassibility of God,' p. 354. Pollard states that 'So alien is this idea [impassibility], so foreign is it to Hebraic-Christian thought, that it makes nonsense of the revelation of God in the Old Testament, it makes the Incarnation no real Incarnation, and it reduces the sufferings and death of Christ to a purely human work' (p. 356). Pollard's entire article attempts to demonstrate how the Greek notion of impassibility has adversely affected the theology of the Fathers.
    Moltmann holds that the early Church Fathers attempted to combine two incompatible principles – divine immutability and impassibility with the central gospel message of God's involvement in the world in all that this entails. He concludes: 'The contradiction remains – and remains unsatisfactory.' *The Trinity and the Kingdom of God*, p. 22. See also p. 23.

58 Pannenberg, *Basic Questions in Theology*, Vol. 1, pp. 160, 162, 164, 165. See also pp. 119–20.

however, the concept of the immutability of God necessarily leads to the consequence that the transition to every innovation in the relationship between God and man has to be sought as much as possible on the side of man. Thus, the idea of God becoming man has to recede into the background behind that of God assuming human nature.[59]

Lee argues that Aquinas, in maintaining that God is pure act (*actus purus*) brings the philosophical principle of God's impassibility to its logical conclusion. 'This static notion of divine perfection as the immovable and unchanging Being is based on the idea that in God there is no potentiality or receptivity to be affected from without or actualized from within but is *"actus purus"*.'[60] Dorner, in his classical critique of divine immutability, argues that, because God is loving and merciful, the traditional understanding of divine immutability must be radically modified. God is not ontologically immutable, but ethically immutable for he possesses a living relationship with the humanity which changes not only humanity but himself as well. 'Without reciprocity between God and world such vital relations would have no authentic reality.'[61]

Because the notion of God which has dominated Christian theology for almost its entire history has been so heavily formed within the foreign mould of Greek philosophy, it is not truly the authentic God of the Bible. Many theologians would then agree with Moltmann's judgment that 'the God of theism is poor. He cannot love nor can he suffer.'[62]

The Passible God of Process Theology
In response to this inherited tradition of the impassible God, theologians, as we have seen above, have argued for a more living, personal, active, and dynamic God. As Blocher points out: 'The epithet "static", which suits Being, has become distinctly pejorative. Dynamically to be on the move now holds supreme value.'[63] Nowhere is this more clearly seen and

---

59 Pannenberg, *Basic Questions in Theology*, Vol. 1, p. 162. For similar criticisms, see Forster, 'Divine Passibility,' pp. 23–51, especially p. 28, and Bauckham, 'In Defence of *The Crucified God*,' p. 94; Steen, 'The Theme of the "Suffering" God,' pp. 82–83, and Van Bavel, 'Where is God When Human Beings Suffer,' p. 149; Fiddes, *The Creative Suffering of God*, pp. 37–38; O'Donnell, *Trinity and Temporality*, pp. 24–25, 44–52; and T.F. Torrance, *The Christian Doctrine of God*, pp. 239–40. Pannenberg also believes that God's immutable nature inevitably leads to Pelagianism since all change must take place 'from man's side' (p. 163).

It should be noted here as well that the impassibility of God influences the Fathers' understanding of redemption. Since God is impassible and since to be saved is to become God-like, then human beings should become less and less passible, that is, under the control of their emotions and passions. *Apatheia* becomes the supreme human virtue. See Bauckham, 'Only the Suffering God Can Help,' p. 8; and Moltmann, *The Trinity and the Kingdom of God*, p. 23.

Hallman, in *The Descent of God*, contends that, while almost all of the Fathers take as axiomatic the immutability and impassibility of God, there are some texts which diverge from this view (see p. xii). We will examine Hallman's work more closely later in this study.

60 Lee, *God Suffers for Us*, p. 40. See also pp. 30–32.
61 Dorner, *Divine Immutability*, p. 110.
62 Moltmann, *The Crucified God*, p. 253.

more consistently, systematically and philosophically proposed than among the process theologians. It is process thought that has given the philosophical and metaphysical impetus to the notion of God's passibility. This is acknowledged even by those who do not fully subscribe to it.[64] We will therefore briefly outline the process notion of God.

Process theology receives its philosophical inspiration from Whitehead and Hartshorne.[65] Their philosophy grew out of the basic principle that change is the universal element of reality, and so were influenced by such philosophers as Hegel and Leibnitz, and they equally found support from the scientific theory of biological evolution.[66]

Consequently, process theologians level similar criticisms against classical theism as the ones we saw above. For them the supernaturalistic notion of God makes him completely unrelated to the world and unconcerned with the cares of this world. Ogden believes that the Greek God inherited by Christianity forces God to be 'as Camus has charged, the eternal bystander whose back is turned to the woe of the world.'[67] Pittenger argues that because classical theism sees God as all-powerful, almighty and all-perfect, 'the usual picture has been of an external ruler who pushes, thrusts, twists, and moves his subjects at will, with little or no regard for their own self-realisation. God is a dictator.'[68] Moreover, he is an 'aloof and distant deity ... [the] static Absolute and the all-powerful

63 H. Blocher, 'Divine Immutability,' p. 1.
64 For example, see Fiddes, *The Creative Suffering of God*, pp. 44–45. While not everyone who advocates the passibility of God does so under the auspices of process theology, because it has been primarily responsible for setting the philosophical tone for much of the philosophical and theological advocacy of a passible and suffering God, I believe it important to present its position in some detail. Actually, process philosophy and theology, as a viable and coherent system, appears to be waning, and has for some time now, among scholars.
65 See A.N. Whitehead, *Religion in the Making* (London: Cambridge University Press, 1926); *Process and Reality* (New York: Free Press, 1979); and C. Hartshorne, *The Divine Relativity* (New Haven: Yale University Press, 1948).
66 For introductions to process theology, see J.A. Bracken and M.H. Suchocki, eds, *Trinity in Process: A Relational Theology of God* (New York: Continuum, 1997); J.B. Cobb, *A Christian Natural Theology* (London: Lutterworth Press, 1966); J.B. Cobb and D. Griffin, *Process Thought: An Introductory Exposition* (Philadelphia: Westminster Press, 1976); E.H. Cousins, ed., *Process Theology* (New York: Newman Press, 1971); R. Mellert, *What is Process Theology?* (New York: Paulist Press, 1975); D. Pailin, 'The Utterly Absolute and the Totally Related: Change in God,' *New Blackfriars* 68 (1987):243–55; S. Ogden, *The Reality of God* (New York: Harper and Row, 1961); N. Pittenger, *God in Process* (London: SCM, 1967) and *Process Thought and Christian Faith* (New York: Macmillan, 1968).
    For brief accounts of process theology, see Fiddes, *The Creative Suffering of God*, pp. 37–45; C. Gunton, 'Process Theology's Concept of God,' *The Expository Times* 84 (1972–73): 294–96; Vanhoutte, 'God as Companion and Fellow-Sufferer,' pp. 191–252; and Weinandy, *Does God Change?*, pp. 125–53. Some of what I say below is an abbreviated version of this account.
67 S. Ogden, *The Reality of God*, p. 51. Ogden also states:

    He [God] is said to be a reality which is in every respect absolute and whose only relations to the world are purely nominal or external relations of the world to him ...: Accordingly, the attributes or perfections by which the nature of God is classically defined – pure actuality, immutability, impassivity, aseity, immateriality, etc. – all entail an unqualified negation beyond his own wholly absolute being (*ibid.*, pp. 48–49).

68 N. Pittenger, *Christology Reconsidered* (London: SCM, 1970), p. 137.

monarch.'[69] Whitehead concludes that 'the Church gave unto God the attributes which belonged exclusively to Caesar.'[70]

In contrast to the classical notion of God and his relationship to the world, process theologians champion a much more dynamic view of reality and of God within it. Within process theology, the whole cosmos is made up of 'actual entities' or 'actual occasions' which are moments of experience. Each actual occasion 'prehends,' that is, each actual occasion takes into itself previous actual occasions and adds its own new subjective novelty in the prehension. It is this successive prehension of past actual occasions by present ones, who are in turn prehended by future actual occasions, that gives rise to and constitutes the continual creative process of on-going reality. Prehension is what makes reality dynamic and inter-relational. It is within this basic philosophical cosmology that God is grasped and understood. As Whitehead noted: 'God is not to be treated as an exception to all metaphysical principles, invoked to save their collapse. He is their chief exemplification.'[71]

Within process thought God is dipolar, that is, he has a primordial or abstract pole and a consequent or concrete pole. The abstract pole of God is God in his pure potential – not what God actually is, but what God actual could come to be. It gives God the ability to prehend all events and so relate himself to all other actual realities in the world, especially human persons. God is, in his primordial pole, unchangeable and absolute, for he is forever potentially and supremely related to all. Because God can be related to all, all is related to God. As God prehends all, so all else, especially human beings, prehends God. Likewise, since God is all good, he strives to lure, persuade and encourage all reality to fulfil the perfect goodness that potentially lies within him.

God in his concrete pole is God as he actually exists at any given time in the process. Pittenger concludes: 'Therefore time – or succession as the world exemplifies it – is real to God.' God constantly changes with each successive prehension of all actual occasions. He ever increases and actualizes his abstract potential in the course of history. Thus, literally, '*What happens matters to God* .... History, historical occurrence in time, are real to him, for him and in him.'[72]

Process theologians classify their notion of God as panentheistic, that is, while God is always potentially more, yet as concrete, the world is in God, not in its subjective immediacy, but in its objective past. Griffin states: 'The world is in God, but only in his experience, not in his essence. Hence God includes everything, but everything is not God.'[73]

69 Cousins, 'Process Models in Culture, Philosophy, and Theology' in *Process Theology*, p. 15.
70 Whitehead, *Process and Reality*, p. 404.
71 Whitehead, *Process and Reality*, p. 405.
72 Pittenger, *Process Thought and Christian Faith*, pp. 29 and 30.
73 D. Griffin, *A Process Christology* (Philadelphia: Westminster Press, 1973), p. 188. While Moltmann would not be classified as a process theologian, he nonetheless sees his own view of God's relationship to the world as panentheistic. See *The Crucified God*, p. 277; *The Trinity and the Kingdom of God*, pp. 106–8; and *God in Creation: An Ecological Doctrine of Creation* (London: SCM, 1985), pp. 90–103. For comments on Moltmann's panentheism and its relationship to process thought, see W. McWilliams, *The Passion of God: Divine Suffering in Contemporary Protestant Thought* (Macon: Mercer University Press, 1985), pp. 45, 48–49.

Process theology admits an easy grasp as to how and why God is
passible. He takes into himself all that has happened within the world,
and so is not only affected but is also actually constituted by it. Thus, all
of the joy, pain and suffering which occurs within the world and the lives
of human beings becomes the tangible experiences of God. Hallman
writes:

> On the physical or consequent side, God receives all from the world
> of change, shares or inherits everything which occurs. Temporal
> entities inherit their limited pasts from those concrete past entities
> which precede them; God inherits the totality of past entities. They
> become the divine experience of the temporal world and are woven
> together with the conceptual experience of eternal objects which
> precede concrete experience.[74]

Because God's very being is constituted by the experiences of the
world and humankind, he is, according to Hartshorne 'infinitely passive,
the endurer of all change, the adventurer through all novelty, the
companion through all vicissitudes.'[75] Whitehead, in his celebrated

74 Hallman, *The Descent of God*, p. 139. Hallman sees in Hegel and Whitehead a positive, if
    only partial, Christian alternative to the impassibility of God. See pp. 125–45. Fiddes
    writes in a similar vein.

    While his [God's] primordial nature is independent of the world, he also has a
    'consequent nature' corresponding to his physical aspect, by which he himself
    prehends the world. That is, he absorbs influence from the world, receiving the
    effects of worldly action and decision into himself. In feeling the world like this he
    suffers, for while all entities contribute value to God they also actualize both good
    and evil through the choices they make, and God receives the effect of these; he also
    feels their experience of suffering. *The Creative Suffering of God*, p. 41.

75 C. Hartshorne, *Man's Vision of God and the Logic of Theism* (Hamden: Archon Books,
    1964), p. 298. Sarot demonstrates that, for Hartshorne, God must be corporeal if he is to
    be passible (see *God, Possibility and Corporeality*, pp. 210–19). While Sarot is somewhat
    critical of Hartshorne's understanding of God's corporeality, he himself, nonetheless,
    argues that God's passibility demands that God be corporeal. He finds in Aquinas'
    denial that God is passible because he is incorporeal the basis for his own argument
    that God must be corporeal.

    We have seen that there is a very close connection between emotion and corpore-
    ality: without corporeality no emotion. We have also seen that Aquinas poses the
    question whether God can have emotions and that the corporeality needed for
    emotions is an important reason for him to answer the question negatively .... Thus
    one of the reasons Aquinas provides for rejecting divine passibility is the fact that
    passibility is incompatible with incorporeality. *Ibid.* 118–19.

    Sarot agrees with the logic of Aquinas, but turns it around. Because he believes, for
    biblical, philosophical and theological reasons, that God is passible, he argues that God
    must be corporeal (see *ibid.*, pp. 160–208). In basic agreement with Jantzen (see *God's
    World, God's Body*) Sarot argues that only a corporeal God allows God to feel the world,
    and to be active and present in the world (see *ibid.*, pp. 219–27). For Sarot's complete
    understanding of God's corporeality, see *ibid.*, pp. 209–43.

    While the vast majority of those who argue for the passibility of God would not wish
    to hold Sarot's position that God is, therefore, corporeal, yet, I suspect, that Sarot has
    merely allowed the passibilist position to run its course and so come, as Aquinas was
    well aware, to its logical conclusion.

    S.A. McFague also holds that the world is God's body. See 'Imaging a Theology of
    Nature: The World as God's Body' in *Liberating Life: Contemporary Approaches to
    Ecological Theology*, C. Birch, ed. (New York: Orbis, 1990), pp. 201–27. For a critique of
    such a view see J. Milbank, *The Word Made Strange: Theology, Language and Culture*
    (Oxford: Blackwell, 1997), pp. 257–67.

observation, simply states that God is 'the greatest companion – the fellow sufferer who understands.'[76]

This finds its greatest expression in Jesus. Jesus embodies (prehends) God's lure or aim for his life most fully and completely (this constitutes him as God's Son or Logos) and so God, in turn, prehends all of Jesus' human experiences – all his suffering and even his death on the cross. Jesus, then, is the supreme paradigm of God's relationship to world and humankind. According to Pittenger, Jesus is 'the chief exemplification ... of those "principles" which are required to explain, make sense of, and give the proper setting for whatever goes on in the entire process of God in relationship to man and man in relation to God.'[77] If Jesus is the chief exemplification, then 'the Incarnation is not confined only to the historical person of Jesus Christ, but is also the manner and mode of all of God's work in the world. That is to say, God is ever incarnating himself in his creation.'[78] Thus the relationship between Jesus and God is the same as our relationship with God, and as God participates in the life of Jesus so too does he participate in ours – in all of its joy and suffering.

Despite its very metaphysical nature, process theologians believe that their thought is thoroughly biblical in inspiration and content. It once more captures in a philosophically consistent manner the personal, living, relational, loving and active God of the Bible.

The Passionate God Who Loves and Acts

I have attempted in this opening chapter to present, as clearly, as objectively, and as strongly as possible, the arguments on behalf of the passibility of God.[79] I have done so primarily through the words of the many advocates themselves. I hope that I have been just to their concerns, thoughts, and arguments.

The arguments presented in this chapter are intellectually and, even more so, emotionally compelling. They possess an earnestness and integrity that is beyond doubt. I, obviously, am in sympathy with many of the concerns they raise and the theological issues they confront and attempt to resolve. Unquestionably God, as revealed in the Bible, is a personal, loving and dynamic God who acts in history and in the lives of human beings. Moreover, he is not indifferent to the horror of Auschwitz, nor to the injustice which inflicts the lives of the oppressed, nor to the sufferings within our own lives. Likewise, the early Fathers did struggle with Greek philosophical thought and not always with complete success.

---

76 Whitehead, *Process and Reality*, p. 351.
77 Pittenger, *Christology Reconsidered*, p. 68.
78 Pittenger, *God in Process*, p. 19. For complete expositions of process christology, see D. Griffin, *A Process Christology*; S. Ogden, *The Reality of God*; N. Pittenger, *The Word Incarnate* (Welwyn: James Nisbet and Co., 1959) and *Christology Reconsidered*. For an introductory essay, see J.R. Baker, 'The Christological Symbol of God's Suffering' in *Religious Experience and Process Theology*, eds H.J. Cargas and B. Lee (New York: Paulist Press, 1976), pp. 93–105.
79 For a very readable and competent presentation of many of the theologians treated in this chapter, see W. McWilliams, *The Passion of God*. In this work he treats such theologians as Moltmann, Cone, Kitamori, and Lee.

However, while I want to uphold much of what the theologians in this chapter advocate, I do not believe that one must conclude that God is, therefore, passible. I believe a passible God is actually less personal, loving, dynamic and active than an impassible God. The remainder of this study will attempt to demonstrate this, seemingly, paradoxical thesis.

2

Theology – Problems and Mysteries

To take up the topic of God's impassibility is to address not simply the mystery of God in himself, but also, and maybe even more so, his relationship to the created order, especially his relationship with human persons and their history. As is clearly evident from the previous chapter, it is a theological issue that is not only on the minds of theologians, but also in the hearts of many Christian faithful.

Before we begin to examine the question of God's impassibility it is, I believe, imperative that I first articulate what I consider the precise nature of the theological enterprise, for this will govern my whole approach to the issue at hand. The questions are: What is the theologian attempting to achieve when he or she does theology? More specifically, what is the *Christian* theologian hoping to achieve when he or she is pondering, in the light of reason, the revealed truths of the gospel and the received tradition and doctrines of the Christian faith? In the present case, when we wish to examine whether God is passible or impassible and the impact that the alternatives have on God's relationship to the created order, to human history, and to individual human beings, what is it that we are theologically trying to accomplish? Moreover, what attitude of faith should we possess and what theological disposition should we embrace in pursuing this topic?[1] In this chapter I will address these issues.

Theology and the Development of Doctrine

I want first to articulate briefly some of the ingredients that foster and encourage the theological enterprise, and so help define the task of the theologian. Moreover, in so doing we will also see more clearly how this study of God's impassibility is theologically situated.

---

1 For a different, but very compatible, approach to the one that I will present here on the nature of theology and the craft of the systematic theologian, see R.W. Jenson's excellent preparative chapters to his *Systematic Theology, Volume 1: The Triune God* (Oxford: Oxford University Press, 1997), pp. 3–41. For other fine introductory essays on the same subjects, see C. Gunton, 'Historical and Systematic Theology,' pp. 3–20; G. Loughlin, 'The Basis and Authority of Doctrine,' pp. 41–64; and F. Watson, 'The Scope of Hermeneutics,' pp. 65–80, all in *The Cambridge Companion to Christian Doctrine*, ed. C. Gunton (Cambridge, Cambridge University Press, 1997); and J. Webster, *Theological Theology: An Inaugural Lecture* (Oxford: Clarendon Press, 1998).

First, inherent within the very nature of Christian revelation is the principle that faith seeks understanding.[2] Precisely because rational persons are the beneficiaries of this revelation, they are eager, impelled by the Spirit of truth, to deepen their understanding of what they believe. Such searching and querying is a sign, not of a lack of faith, but of an authentic spiritual vibrancy. Thus, it is characteristic of believers to wish to grow, for example, in their understanding of what it means for Jesus to be the Son of God or to discern more deeply the importance of his resurrection. Christian theology cultivates this growth in the understanding of revelation, and so discloses its deeper significance.

Christian theologians, their reason guided by faith and the light of the Holy Spirit, clarify and advance what has been revealed by God, written in the scriptures, and believed by their fellow Christians. In so doing Christian theologians wish to make what has been revealed more intelligible, lucid, and relevant to the Christian community. This present study exemplifies that Christian theologians and the Christian body at large are presently searching, in faith, for a clearer perception of the nature of God and his attributes, specifically whether or not reason and revelation demand that God be impassible or passible – 'Does God Suffer?'.[3]

Second, Christian theology also wishes to defend, by reasoned argument, what has been revealed against those who question, distort, or attack it. However, not all questioning and dissent are in bad faith. Today, for example, many Christians, theologians and faithful alike, argue and believe that revelation and reason necessitate that God be passible and so suffer. I am not of that mind, but it is precisely this

---

2 St Augustine was the first to articulate this principle. He wrote 'Understanding is the reward of faith. Therefore do not seek to understand in order to believe, but believe that you may understand.' *Tractatus in Joannis Evangelium*, 29,6. He also wrote: 'For although no one can believe in God unless he understands something, nonetheless the faith by which he believes, heals him, so that he may understand more fully. For there are some things which we believe only if we understand and other things which we understand only if we believe.' *Enarrationes in Psalmos*, 119. [Unless otherwise stated all translations of the works of the Fathers in this book are taken from *The Ante-Nicene/Nicene and Post-Nicene Fathers*, ed. P. Schaff, reprinted by T & T Clark and Eerdmans, 1989.] Also see, Augustine's sermon on Isaiah 7:9 and *De Trinitate*, 1,1–2 and 5,2,2. St Anselm articulated the principle more succinctly. 'For I do not seek to understand in order to believe but I believe in order to understand. For I believe even this: that I shall not understand unless I believe.' *Proslogion*, 1.

3 I hope that this doctrinal and systematic study will, in some small way, faithfully actualize Pope John Paul II's grand vision of the true and fruitful relationship between faith and reason, that is, of faith seeking understanding. See the whole of his *Fides et Ratio* (1998).

> For its part, *dogmatic theology* must be able to articulate the universal meanings of the mystery of the One and Triune God and of the economy of salvation, both as a narrative and, above all, in the form of argument. It must do so, in other words, through concepts formulated in a critical and universally communicable way. Without philosophy's contribution, it would in fact be impossible to discuss theological issues such as, for example, the use of language to speak about God, the personal relations within the Trinity, God's creative activity in the world, the relationship between God and man, or Christ's identity as true God and true man. Ibid., n. 66

> The question of God's impassibility demands that all of the above examples given by John Paul be examined, in the light of faith and philosophy, during the course of this study.

climate of controversy that has compelled me and others to address newly the nature of God in the light of these contemporary issues.

This relationship between controversy and growth should not surprise us. The principle that faith seeks understanding is often, historically, most clearly observed when theologians were forced to clarify the truths of faith, not simply for the edification of believers, but in order to protect and demonstrate the reasonableness of what had traditionally been believed. In the fourth century it was in the midst of defending the divinity of the Son and of the Holy Spirit that the church came to a new clarity about the Trinity. Theological controversy by its very nature forces theologians and the church to address pressing questions, and so reasonably to justify anew what has been revealed. This fresh theological clarity will, it is hoped, lead all believers to a deeper and more committed faith, and aid those who find it difficult to believe.

Third, Christian theology also wishes to demonstrate the inter-relationship between the various truths of faith. This too clarifies and expands the understanding of the truths related. For example, in clarifying the relationship between the Father and Jesus one not only acquires a better understanding of their relationship, but also what it means for the Father to be the Father and the Son to be the Son. In this study, issues concerning the nature of God and his impassibility must be related to the notion of creation, to the manner of God's presence and activity in the world and in human history, and to the salvation that comes through Jesus. Our study of the inter-relationship between all of these topics will shed light on them both individually and collectively.

Fourth, the work of individual theologians is not done in isolation. Theologians work within an historical context and within the Christian community. Clarity and understanding grow within the history of the Christian church and within the context of the community of believers. What may come to greater clarity in one historical era will differ from what becomes clearer in another. Again, for example, the early church experienced a growth in understanding with regards to the Incarnation and the Trinity. During the Reformation the church's recognition of the nature and importance of faith and justification increased.

This does not mean that these issues were never addressed previously nor does it imply that they will cease to be addressed in the future, as if all has now been concluded. Rather, this only specifies that certain key theological questions or issues were raised and certain important communal concerns for the church were addressed at specific times, and that through this historical and communal process, with the help of theologians and church authorities, a new clarity was achieved.

This study concerning the impassibility of God exemplifies a concern that is presently challenging Christian theologians of all denominations and their respective communities. The issues have been discussed, as we will see, in the past, but today they have come to the fore with new intensity arising out of contemporary concerns, and so innovative arguments and fresh clarity are demanded in our day.

Fifth, personal prayer and communal worship likewise foster theological understanding. Liturgy is a living expression of what is believed, and so through participation in it one grows in an understanding of the

faith. Historically, liturgy at times expressed an intuitive apprehension of
the faith that actually preceded and exceeded the later explicit intellectual exposition. For example, the baptismal formula and the doxologies
clearly expressed the church's belief that the Father, the Son, and the
Holy Spirit were all equally God. When some in the early church
doubted or denied that the Holy Spirit was God equal to the Father and
the Son, one of the principal arguments on behalf of the Spirit's divinity
was the church's ancient liturgical practise.[4] Here we not only see that
liturgical prayer and practise fostered the faith, but also that it later
became a primary source for theological reflection and argument. This
illustrates the well-known formula: *lex orandi, lex credendi* (the law of
prayer is the law of belief) – as the church prays, so the church believes.

Prayer and liturgical practise embody and express then the Christian
understanding of God, his attributes and his relationship to believers.
Thus the question of God's impassibility must be examined in the light
of how Christians pray and how the church worships. Does Christian
prayer and worship entail and manifest belief in God's impassibility or
passibility?

All of these various ingredients, which advance the growth of theological understanding, contribute then, to what John Henry Newman
was first to call, the development of doctrine.[5] The Christian
community's understanding of the truths of revelation grows and
develops. These components, which make up the theological enterprise
of the entire church body, testify that the knowledge of faith is not static.
Faith, in constantly seeking to be more deeply understood and ardently
lived, by different Christians at different times and in different cultures,
evolves. As the Christian church progresses through history and
confronts, thoughtfully and prayerfully, the problems and issues of its
particular time, its understanding of what God has revealed develops
and matures. The question of God's impassibility and all its theological,
spiritual, and practical ramifications is presently a case in point.

Problems and Mysteries

Having briefly enunciated some of the ingredients which cultivate theological understanding and doctrinal growth, it is now important to
examine how theologians, in the light of these elements, should approach
and foster such understanding and development. What is it that the theologian does, as a believer seeking understanding within the historical
and communal setting, to help bring about new theological focus and
advance authentic development? It is here that I believe there is a great
deal of confusion among theologians, and the issue of God's impassibility illustrates this confusion.

Gabriel Marcel, in his Gifford Lectures of 1949 and 1950, and later
Jacques Maritain, who borrowed the distinction from Marcel, spoke of two

---

4 See, for example, Basil the Great's treatise *On the Holy Spirit* where he argues for the
   divinity of the Holy Spirit from the church's doxological practise.
5 See John Henry Newman, *Essay on the Development of Christian Doctrine* (Harmondsworth: Penguin, 1974).

contrasting attitudes a person may possess when approaching questions. Marcel pointed out that we can approach a field of inquiry as either a *problem* or as a *mystery*.[6] He was critical of the modern mentality which approached every intellectual endeavor under the rubric of *problem*, that is, as if one were always examining some detached state of affairs which could be coldly dissected and systematically analyzed so as to produce complete and comprehensive knowledge. This was being done, he believed, not only within the natural sciences, where it may be legitimate, but also within the humanities, specifically within his own discipline – that of philosophy.[7] Marcel argued that some fields of human enquiry cannot be properly understood, and in actual fact they become distorted, when approached as problems. Rather, they must be approached under the rubric of *mystery*, which 'by definition, transcends every conceivable technique.'[8] Human beings are, for Marcel, a mystery and the fundamental concerns of human beings are mysteries – personhood, identity, friendship, family, good and evil, etc. By mystery then Marcel meant that while one could say a great deal about human beings and the central issues that surround them, yet no matter how much one said and no matter how true it may be, there is always more to be understood and articulated. There is no comprehensive, complete, and final answer. We may come to a greater understanding of the mystery of human life, but we never come to a complete comprehension of it. Maritain states that where there is mystery 'the intellect has to penetrate more and more deeply the *same* object.'[9] The mystery, by the necessity of its subject matter, remains.

While Marcel and Maritain were primarily concerned with distinguishing the problems of scientific enquiry from the mysteries of philosophic enquiry, I believe that such a distinction between problem and mystery is relevant to how theologians ought to approach issues of faith and theology.

Marcel and Maritain were well aware that, arising out of the Enlightenment, there grew the mentality that intellectual advancement

---

6 See Gabriel Marcel, *The Mystery of Being, I, Reflection and Mystery* (London: The Harvill Press, 1950), pp. 204–19.

7 Jacques Maritain states: 'The problem aspect naturally predominates where knowledge is least ontological, for example, when it is primarily concerned with mental constructions built around a sensible datum – as in empirical knowledge, and in the sciences of phenomena.' *A Preface to Metaphysics* (London: Sheed & Ward, 1939), p. 6.

8 Marcel, *The Mystery of Being, I*, p. 211.

9 Maritain, *A Preface to Metaphysics*, p. 7. Maritain also states:

Where the problem aspect prevails one solution follows another; where one ends, the other begins. There is a rectilinear progress of successive views . . . . Where the problem aspect predominates I thirst to know the answer to my problem. And when I have obtained the answer I am satisfied: *that particular* thirst is quenched. . . . In the second case where the mystery aspect predominates I thirst to know reality, *being* under one or other of its modes, the ontological mystery. When I know it I drink my fill. But I still thirst and continue to thirst for the same thing, the same reality which at once satisfies and increases my desire. Thus I never cease quenching my thirst from the same spring of water which is ever fresh and yet I always thirst for it. *A Preface to Metaphysics*, pp. 7–8.

For Maritain God is the fundamental mystery, and our thirst can only be satiated when we see him face to face. See *ibid.*, pp. 5 and 8–9.

consisted in solving problems that had hitherto not been solved. The former 'mysteries' of the physical universe were being resolved by approaching them as scientific problems to be decoded and unraveled. The scientific and physical laws of nature became transparent and unmistakable. The new enthusiasm and success of the scientific method was the major contributing factor to this mentality. Science became the means of resolving all kinds of problems and issues concerning nature and how nature worked. All this was done in a concise, rational, mathematical, and experiential fashion. It was equally eminently practical. Scientific knowledge could solve a host of practical problems, and everyone gloried in its success. This mentality is illustrated in the contemporary belief that technology, one of the fruits of science, can solve almost any problem. In the realm of science and technology this mentality, that intellectual advancement consists in solving theoretical and practical problems, may be legitimate.[10] However, I want to argue that this mentality, to disastrous effect, has coloured how many philosophers and theologians approach questions of faith and theology.

Many theologians today, having embraced the Enlightenment presuppositions and the scientific method that it fostered, approach theological issues as if they were scientific problems to be solved rather than mysteries to be discerned and clarified. However, the true goal of theological inquiry is not the resolution of theological *problems*, but the discernment of what the *mystery* of faith is. Because God, who can never be fully comprehended, lies at the heart of all theological enquiry, theology by its nature is not a problem solving enterprise, but rather a mystery discerning enterprise.

This can be seen already in the early stages of God's revelation of himself to the Jewish people. God manifested himself to Moses in the burning bush (see Exod. 3). Moses, in the course of the conversation, asked God: 'What is your name?' Since names, for the Israelites, both revealed the character of the person so named and allowed the knower of the name to call upon the person so named, Moses, in asking God to tell him his name, wanted to know God as well as have the power to call upon him. Moses was attempting to solve, what was for him, a theological problem. God must have chuckled[11] to himself as he replied to Moses: 'I Am Who Am' or 'I Am He Who Is.'[12]

God did reveal to Moses his name and so Moses now knew more about God than he knew before. He now knew that God is 'He who is.' However, Moses must have quickly realized that, in knowing God more

---

10 However, even in the field of science there remains a sense of 'mystery' and, I believe, many scientists are coming to this awareness. The more science unlocks the 'mysteries' of the universe, the more mysterious it becomes. New knowledge always leads to new and baffling questions. Science may solve *problems*, but its solutions often create even greater *mysteries*.

11 It was, obviously(?), an 'impassible' chuckle!

12 Scholars debate as to the exact translation of the name *Yahweh*. Scholars agree that it comes from the Hebrew root word meaning 'to be.' Some translate it in the causative sense of 'he causes to be,' but the more likely and traditional translation is 'I am who am' or 'I am the one who exists,' or 'I am he who is.' For a concise treatment, see *The New Jerusalem Bible* (London: Darton, Longman & Todd, 1985), Exodus 3:13 fn. g.

fully, God had become an even greater mystery (problem) than he was before. Previously Moses in calling God, for example, *El Shaddai* – God of the Mountain – may not have known a great deal about God, but the little he did know was at least somewhat comprehensible. God was he who dwelt on the mountain, which was the home of the gods. However, Moses now knew much more about God. He actually knew that God is 'I Am Who Am,' but what it means for God to be 'He Who Is' is completely incomprehensible. Moses, nor we today, can comprehend that God's very nature is 'to be,' that he is the one who is the fulness of life and existence.

Here we learn a primary lesson concerning the nature of revelation and theology. The more God reveals who he is and the more we come to a true and authentic knowledge of who he is, the more mysterious he becomes. Theology, as faith seeking understanding, helps us come to a deeper and fuller understanding of the nature of God and his revelation, but this growth is in coming to know what the mystery of God is and not the comprehension of the mystery.[13]

Examples from the History of Theology

Let me further illustrate the difference between approaching questions of revelation as problems to be solved rather than as mysteries to be clarified by examining a couple of theological controversies that arose within the early church.

In the early fourth century, Arius, a priest in Alexandria, took up the issue of how God could be one and how simultaneously the Son could be God. This is an authentic theological concern, and one that had been percolating in the early church for a long time. Arius, having examined all of the previous attempts at explaining this 'problem' concluded that there was no way to resolve the issue rationally. If God was one, then the Son, Arius concluded, could not possibly be God and, therefore, he must be a creature. Arius resolved the 'problem' of how God could simultaneously be one and the Son be God by denying one of the truths that the church had previously held, that is, the divinity of the Son. Arius provided an answer. It was very clear and understandable. The problem was solved. However, in solving this theological 'problem' Arius also dissolved the faith of the church which believed that not only was the Father God but also equally the Son.

In response to Arius, the church held its first ecumenical council at Nicea in 325. The majority of the church Fathers probably did not know how to answer fully or satisfactorily Arius' arguments, but they did know what the church believed, and so proclaimed that Jesus is God as the Father is God and that he was *homoousion* (one in being) with the Father.

---

13 Christians believe that Jesus revealed God to be a trinity of persons – the Father, the Son and the Holy Spirit. Christians now know more about God than did Moses, but in coming to a greater knowledge of God, God has become even more mysterious than he was for Moses.

It was Athanasius, in the ensuing controversy after the council, who grasped the real significance of Nicea's *homoousion* doctrine. Athanasius reconceived what it meant for God to be one. Where in the past all Christian theologians conceived the one God to be the Father (this understanding included Arius), and then attempted to show how the Son shared in the one nature of God, an attempt that Arius realized was doomed to failure, Athanasius recognized that Christian revelation completely shattered this view of God. Athanasius' great insight was to perceive that the one God is not just the Father, but rather that the one God is the Father begetting the Son. This is the very nature of the one God. This is what God is. What the one nature of God is is the Father eternally begetting the Son. Therefore, the Father and Son are the one God, one in being, for the one God is the dynamic inter-relationship between Father and the Son.

Athanasius approached the issue of how God can be one and the Son be God not as a problem to be solved, but as a mystery to be discerned. With Arius all becomes comprehensible. With Athanasius a new clarity is achieved as to what the mystery is, but the mystery itself does not become completely comprehensible. We know more precisely and clearly what the mystery is, that is, that the one God is the Father begetting the Son, but we do not comprehend the mystery, that is, we do not fully grasp how the one being/nature of God is the Father eternally begetting the Son. That remains a mystery and has become, in a sense, even more a mystery, but one that has obtained new depth of clarity.[14]

---

14 One could also cite the example found in the fifth century with regards to the Incarnation. The Council of Nicea had proclaimed the full divinity of the Son, and equally the church later condemned Apollinarius for denying the full humanity of Jesus. There then arose, with greater intensity, the question of how the one Jesus could be both fully God and fully man. Nestorius upheld the full divinity and the full humanity. The problem for him was how to conceive of them as one without jeopardizing either the humanity or the divinity. He rightly argued that some in the past, for example Apollinarius, in order to make Jesus one denied the full humanity of Jesus. Apollinarius denied the human soul of Jesus, and thus the divinity was united to the body alone so as to form the one reality of Jesus, after the manner of the human soul and body forming the one reality of man. Apollinarius had resolved the problem of Jesus' oneness by denying the full humanity. Nestorius knew that this was erroneous. The incarnation demanded the fulness of divinity and the fulness of the humanity. However, Nestorius himself solved the problem by ultimately denying the ontological union between the humanity and the divinity, that is, that Jesus is really one. The divinity and the humanity were only united by a moral union, that is, the Son assumed the humanity in love or by 'good pleasure.' Nestorius proposed this because he could not conceive how God and man could be truly one without destroying either the divinity or the humanity. Nestorius solved the theological problem, but again he equally dissolved the mystery. The mystery of the Incarnation is that the Son of God, in the fulness of his divinity, did actually, *come to exist* as a full man.

Cyril of Alexandria, Nestorius' arch-opponent, who himself had some of his own theological ambiguities, nonetheless realized that the Son of God did actually become man. He began to discern, what the Council of Chalcedon in 451 would later affirm, that the Incarnation is not the union of natures, which would demand that either or both the humanity and the divinity be transformed in the process and so produce some third kind of being which was neither God nor man, but rather that in the Incarnation it is the *person* of the Son who takes on an entirely new mode of existence. He comes to exist as man. Thus Jesus is the one person of the Son existing as God and as man. The Council

An example of a more contemporary nature may be also helpful. Kenotic christologists ask the question: How can a God who is almighty, all-knowing, and all-powerful become man, and so take on human limitations – weakness, lack of knowledge, etc.? It would appear that we are faced, within the Incarnation, with contrary and irreconcilable attributes. Kenotic christology, both past and present, solves *the problem* by having the Son of God either give up (empty himself – *kenosis*) those divine attributes which would be incompatible with his human limitations, or holding them in abeyance or restraint. The problem is solved. However, again the mystery is also equally dissolved. No longer is the Son of God, in the fulness of his divinity, existing as man. Rather, a truncated and lesser 'humanized' form of divinity now exists as man. Kenotic christology always proposes that someone less than fully God exists as man and not that God, in all his wholly otherness, exists as man.

Kenotic christology misconceives the nature of the Incarnation. It is not a union of incompatible natures with the ensuing conflict of incompatible attributes. Rather, within the Incarnation the person of the eternal Son, while remaining fully divine, takes on a new life as man, and so assumes a fully human life in all its human frailty and weakness. The mystery is that one and the same person or subject, who actually is all-powerful as God, is equally weak and frail as man, for it is in that manner that the same Son now also exists.[15]

The Contemporary Theological Mindset

Examples of how theologians have treated theological questions as either problems to be solved or mysteries to be clarified could be multiplied throughout the history of theology. Hopefully, the above examples make it evident that true Christian theology has to do with clarifying, and so developing, the understanding of the mysteries of faith and not the dissolving of the mysteries into complete comprehension. The point at issue here is that this distinction between solving problems and elucidating mysteries has, since the Enlightenment, become almost

---

of Chalcedon declared that Jesus is one and the same Son existing as fully God and fully man without destroying either the divinity or the humanity. Within the Incarnation the identity of Jesus, who he is, is the eternal divine Son but the manner of the Son's identity is as man. Again, Cyril and Chalcedon did not solve a theological problem. What they did was clarify the mystery of the Incarnation. We now know more clearly that the mystery of the Incarnation is that the one person of the eternal Son actually exists as a complete man, but we do not comprehend the mystery. That remains, and is, in a sense again, even more mysterious.

For a fuller account of the controversies surrounding Arius, Apollinarius and Nestorius see A. Grillmeier, *Christ in Christian Tradition*, Vol. 1 (London: Mowbrays, 1975); J.N.D. Kelly, *Early Christian Doctrines* (London: Adam & Charles Black, 1968), chapters 4–6, 9–12; B. Studer, *Trinity and Incarnation* (Collegeville: The Liturgical Press, 1993); J. Pelikan, *The Christian Tradition: A History of the Development of Doctrine 1: The Emergence of the Catholic Tradition (100–600)* (Chicago: University Press of Chicago, 1971), chapters 4–5; and T. Weinandy, *Does God Change?*, chapters 1–2.

15 For a further examination of kenotic christology and its refutation see T. Weinandy, *Does God Change?*, chapter 4, and *In the Likeness of Sinful Flesh: An Essay on the Humanity of Christ* (Edinburgh: T & T Clark, 1993), pp. 8–13.

completely lost within theology. While multiple examples again could be given to illustrate this, the question of God's impassibility is the subject of this book, and itself well exemplifies the point.

As we saw in the first chapter, many theologians argue that God's impassibility, as traditionally believed by Christians through the centuries, cannot be compatible with his being a loving person who cares for and interacts with human beings within time and history. Thus, they deny that God is impassible, and instead assert that he must be passible, and so suffers. Again, the problem is solved, but is it solved at the expense of maintaining the great mystery of God and of his relationship to the world and human beings? An affirmative answer to this question will be given in the course of this study. However, this study will not solve this theological *problem*. This study only hopes to clarify the *mystery* of God's impassibility in relationship to the passible lives of human beings within the ever-changing world of history. In so doing the mystery, it is hoped, will come into sharper focus and so become more deeply known and appreciated, but it will not become comprehensible. As Pope John Paul II has stated: 'In short, the knowledge proper to faith does not destroy the mystery; it only reveals it the more, showing how necessary it is for people's lives.'[16]

Openness to Further Development

Before concluding this chapter, I would like to make two final points. Firstly, it should be noted, as alluded to above, that when theological issues are treated as problems to be solved, once the seeming solution has been found, usually by denying one of terms of the problem, the issue becomes completely closed. The problem is solved. The complete answer has been given. There is no longer any further need for clarification or development. One can move on to the next problem.

This is not the case with true theological and doctrinal development. While the mystery has been clarified, it has not become fully comprehensible, and so it remains open to further clarification and development. The depth of the mystery can still be plunged further. True development is an impetus to further development.[17]

The reason for the open-ended nature of true theological and doctrinal development is that we are ultimately engaged with the mystery of God in himself and with his actions in time and history. God, in himself, is incomprehensible, and thus his relationship to the created order and his actions within that order throughout history and in the lives of human beings can never be fully comprehended.[18] We can come to know who the mystery of God is, and we can come to know the mysteries embodied in his dealings with human persons, but we will never be able to fully comprehend him or his actions – not even in heaven. In heaven the

---

16 *Fides et Ratio*, n. 13.
17 This is one of the most insightful points that Cardinal Newman makes in his *Essay on the Development of Christian Doctrine.*
18 This is the point Maritain makes, see n. 8 above.

mystery of God will become crystal clear for we will see God face to face, but in seeing him face to face the incomprehensibility of God will equally become luminously evident.[19]

It must be remembered too that our guiding principle that faith seeks understanding does not mean that faith seeks comprehension. Precisely because it is the faith – the mystery of God and all his words and deeds – that we are attempting to understand more fully, we will never be able to comprehend it entirely. Faith by its very nature is 'the assurance of things hoped for, the conviction of things not seen' (Heb. 11:1). Here 'we see in a mirror dimly' (1 Cor. 13:12).

The Compatibility of Truths

Second, as was briefly noted above, one of the primary reasons theological issues become problems is that two or more 'truths' are seen as seemingly incompatible. God cannot be one and the Son be God. Jesus cannot be both God and man. God cannot be impassible and yet loving. Some would solve the problem, as we saw, by denying one of the truths. This is often seen as the most rational way forward, but I believe it is the all too easy way forward, and one that ultimately comes to a dead end.

Others, who seek less radical solutions to theological problems, propose that such incompatible 'truths' must be held dialectically, that is, that even though they are incompatible, yet both must nonetheless be maintained. The opposition is between truths that are held together for the sake of preserving 'the mystery.' Thus, for example, despite the fact that God's impassiblity does conflict with his being loving, yet both must be held because there is a 'mystery' present. I do not subscribe to, as will become evident in this book, a dialectical approach to theological issues. I believe that such a proposal still approaches theological issues as problems or riddles, but now ones that cannot be solved.

To address the mysteries of faith as true mysteries is to clarify why two or more seemingly incompatible truths are not incompatible, and why they actually complement one another.[20] Thus, this book wishes to demonstrate not that *despite* God's impassibility he is nonetheless loving and kind, but rather precisely *because* he is impassible that he is loving and kind. I want to argue in this study that *only* an impassible God, and not a passible God, is truly and fully personal, absolutely and utterly loving, and thoroughly capable of interacting with human persons in

---

19 This is in keeping with the writings of the great Christian mystics of the East and the West who maintain that the more one grows in union with God, and so comes to know him ever more intimately, the more incomprehensible he becomes. The mystics are fond of such phrases as 'luminous darkness' and 'the rays of divine darkness.' Besides the standard introductions and histories of eastern and western spirituality and mysticism see also O. Clément, *The Roots of Christian Mysticism* (London: New City, 1993); and A. Louth, *The Origins of the Christian Mystical Tradition* (Oxford: Clarendon Press, 1981).

20 I attempted to demonstrate this principle in my book *Does God Change?*. There I argued that the immutability of God is not in opposition to the Incarnation, but rather that *only* an immutable God can actually come to exist as man.

time and history.[21] This is the great challenge of this study. This is the awesome mystery that ultimately needs to be clarified and developed. Whether this book meets this challenge, can be judged at the end.

Definition of Terms

Before proceeding it would be helpful to define briefly the terms 'impassibility' and 'passibility.' *The Oxford Dictionary of the Christian Church* states:

> There are three respects in which orthodox theology has traditionally denied God's subjection to 'passibility', namely (1) external passibility or the capacity to be acted upon from without, (2) internal passibility or the capacity for changing the emotions from within, and (3) sensational passibility or the liability to feelings of pleasure and pain caused by the action of another being.[22]

It is this understanding of impassibility that is employed throughout this study, and it is this understanding of impassibility which I will be defending. God is impassible in the sense that he cannot experience emotional changes of state due to his relationship to and interaction with human beings and the created order. This understanding of impassibility

---

21 In this chapter I have attempted to describe the nature of the theological enterprise and the work of Christian theologians in a manner that would be 'ecumenical,' that is, in a manner that theologians of all Christian denominations might affirm; although I realize that some, and maybe many, might not. Nonetheless, while I have made appeal to the received Christian tradition, the early ecumenical councils, and to the church's teaching authority, I, consciously, did not specifically mention doctrines and dogmas that would be peculiar to specific Christian denominations. Nor did I specify any particular form of ecclesial teaching authority other than the ancient councils. It is this 'ecumenical' understanding of the theological enterprise which will govern this work. However, in honesty, I should say that, being a Roman Catholic, the tradition and magisterial teaching of my own denomination has also guided my thinking from the onset of this undertaking. While the common Christian tradition has, from the patristic age, upheld the impassibility of God in himself, and therefore is obliged, I believe, to continue to do so, I also believe that I must do so in order to be faithful to the tradition and teaching of the Roman Catholic Church. I do not think that such an obligation has constrained either my freedom or my creativity as a theologian. Rather, it has forced me and freed me to be more creative, as this book will hopefully demonstrate, than the vast multitude of contemporary theologians who argue that God is passible.
22 *The Oxford Dictionary of the Christian Church*, 3rd edition edited by E.A. Livingstone (Oxford: Oxford University Press, 1997), p. 823. R. Creel discusses eight different, but interconnected, understandings of what it means for God to be impassible which result in a choice of sixteen permutations. While such a detailed discussion may be useful for the sake of clarity, the clarity can easily become lost in the complexity. See *Divine Impassibility*, pp. 3–12.
    H.P. Owen states that impassibility 'means particularly that he [God] cannot experience sorrow, sadness or pain' (*Concepts of Deity*, p. 23). M. Sarot defines impassibility as *'immutability with regard to one's feeling, or the quality of one's inner life.'* 'Patripassianism, Theopaschitism and the Suffering of God: Some Historical and Systematic Considerations,' *Religious Studies* 26 (1990):368.
    It should also be noted that divine impassibility is a logical consequence of divine immutability. If God is ontologically unchangeable, then, by definition, he is equally ontologically impassible, for to undergo inner emotional changes of state would render him ontologically mutable.

does not imply, as this study will demonstrate, that God is not utterly passionate in his love, mercy and compassion.

For God to be 'passible' then means that he is capable of being acted upon from without and that such actions bring about emotional changes of state within him. Moreover, for God to be passible means that he is capable of freely changing his inner emotional state in response to and interaction with the changing human condition and world order. Last, passibility implies that God's changing emotional states involve 'feelings' that are analogous to human feelings. Thus one can speak, for example, of God's inner emotional state as changing from joy to sorrow, or from delight to suffering. It is this notion of passibility – that God experiences inner emotional changes of state, either of comfort or discomfort, whether freely from within or by being acted upon from without – that will be denied in this study.

3

Yahweh: The Presence of the
Wholly Other

In the first chapter I presented the case for the passibility of God and thus for his suffering. In the remainder of this study I wish to argue against such a notion and to demonstrate instead that God is impassible and so does not suffer. I want to show why the impassibility of God is absolutely essential if we are to embrace and to defend the biblical revelation of God as lovingly present and dynamically active in our midst, even to the point of his becoming man.

The notion of God's impassibility is a piece of a whole theological puzzle (mystery), and before we place this particular piece in its proper place we first must place some (many) other essential pieces in their proper place, otherwise the puzzle (mystery) will become distorted and the picture will never take its true configuration.[1] In this chapter I will focus almost exclusively on the Old Testament notion of God and the types of relationships he formed with the Hebrew people, and only then, from within this perspective, address the question of God's impassibility.[2] As the first chapter demonstrated, one of the primary arguments for a passible God is its biblical warrant. It not only appears to bear strong witness to a passible God, but it also poses some of the greatest challenges to the traditional claim for God's impassibility.[3]

---

1 I believe this is one of the major weaknesses of those who propose a passible God. They do so without first adequately considering the more central issues of God's nature and of his relationship to the created order. Thus, while their affirmation of a passible God seems clear, yet it ultimately throws into disarray the whole mystery of God and of his relationship to the created order.

2 I will make reference to the New Testament only in so far as it illustrates or furthers a particular point from the Old Testament. I will treat the question of the Incarnation and redemption as they bear on the impassibility or passibility of God in later chapters.

3 The Old Testament never actually addresses the question of whether God is impassible or passible. This is a philosophical question that arises out of the Old Testament revelation. In this chapter I wish first to discern the Old Testament notion of God, and then address the question of God's impassibility and passibility from within this scriptural context.

For brief accounts of God in the Old Testament, see J.J. Scullion, 'God in the Old Testament' in *The Anchor Bible Dictionary*, ed. D.N. Freedman (New York: Doubleday, 1992), Vol. II, pp. 1041–48; and M. Rose, 'Names of God in the Old Testament', *ibid.*, Vol. IV, pp. 1001–11; Kleinknecht, Quell, Stauffer, Kuhn, 'Theos' in *Theological Dictionary of the New Testament*, Vol. 3, ed. G. Kittel (Grand Rapids: Eerdmans, 1965), pp. 65–123; and Quell, Foerster, 'Kyrios', *ibid.*, pp. 1039–98. For the New Testament understanding of God, see J.M. Bassler, 'God in the New Testament,' *The Anchor Bible Dictionary*, Vol. II, pp. 1049–55.

Moreover, since the Bible is not a work of philosophy, I will not, as far as possible, take up the philosophical issues that arise from the scriptural revelation. While interpretation of the biblical data is necessary, I will attempt to let the Bible speak for itself, from within its own Hebraic thought-forms and Semitic concepts. These tend to be more functional and relational in character than ontological, that is, the Bible tends to speak in terms of how God and persons function and inter-relate rather than what they are ontologically in themselves. However, it is from within these relational concepts that we will discover the biblical notion of God, for by discerning the types of relationships God has with the created order, we will detect who God *is*.[4]

Similarly, inherent within the Bible's Hebraic thought-forms and concepts lie principles or notions – ontological in nature – which pertain to a philosophical understanding of who God is and how he relates to what is other than himself. One of the goals of this chapter, having ascertained the biblical understanding of God and his relationships, is to discern what philosophical notion of God best upholds, clarifies, and enhances our understanding of the biblical truth of who God is and the manner in which he relates to the created historical order. In Chapter 6 I will propose a philosophical understanding of God and of his relationship to the created historical order which, I believe, underlies the biblical revelation, and thus necessarily flows from it.

Transcendence and Immanence

God's impassibility or passibility revolves around the question of God's transcendence and immanence. What is the nature of God's transcendence? In what way(s) does God transcend the created order – the cosmos and all that it contains? Does his transcendence demand that he be impassible? What is the nature of God's immanence? How does he relate to and act within the created order – the cosmos and all that it contains? Does his immanence demand that he be passible?

The Old Testament does not answer these questions in a speculative and systematic manner. The theology of the Hebrew people arises out of their experience of God as he is present in their midst and acts within their history. They experience his immanent working and in so doing simultaneously perceive that God is, in some sense, transcendent.[5] Thus the words and actions by which and in which Yahweh revealed his immanent presence are the very same words and actions by which and in which Yahweh revealed his transcendence, and thus ultimately whether or not he is impassible or passible.

---

4 In his excellent little book R. Bauckham argues that the Old Testament, especially the Second Temple theology, speaks not so much about the nature of God but of the revelation of God's identity – who God is. See *God Crucified: Monotheism and Christology in the New Testament* (Carlisle: Paternoster Press, 1998), pp. 1–22.

5 It will only be toward the end of this chapter that we will be able to say in what sense God is transcendent and immanent within the Hebrew scriptures. Therefore, I will avoid the use of the terms 'transcendent,' 'transcendence,' 'immanent,' and 'immanence' until I have clarified their true biblical meaning.

From within biblical revelation then, the immanence of God takes epistemological precedence. It is only because God first revealed himself within the created order, within time and history, that he came to be known as someone who, in some sense, is transcendent. However, because it is the transcendent God whom the Jewish people came to know through his immanent presence and action, it is his transcendence which takes ontological precedence. God revealed himself within time and history, and thus came to be known, only because he is the kind of God he is, that is, as one who is transcendent, and yet, capable of acting within the historical lives of persons and nations. The nature of God's immanence is thus dependent upon the nature of his transcendence, and the Hebrew people came to know the nature of God's transcendence only through his immanent presence and action. While there is an epistemological priority in the manner in which God is known and an ontological priority in the manner in which God is, and so can be known, the God who is transcendent is the same God who is immanent and vice-versa.[6] What then do the immanent words and actions of Yahweh reveal about his transcendence? Or, what kind of God has Yahweh, through his immanent words and actions, revealed himself to be?

While it is not possible here to give a detailed account of the historical and theological development of the entire Old Testament understanding of Yahweh, it is necessary for our purposes to illustrate some of its distinguishing features. These will provide us with the necessary basis upon which we can biblically, and subsequently philosophically, address the issue of God's impassibility or passibility.

Yahweh: The One God of the Covenant

While the Israelites believed that God first intervened in their history through the call of Abraham and the patriarchs, the experience which defined them as a distinct people was God saving them from the slavery of Egypt. It was here that they initially experienced the presence, the power, the love, and the faithfulness of God. In his compassion and mercy God saw their plight and heard their cry (see Exod. 2:24–25). He raised up Moses and revealed to him his very own name (see Exod. 3:1–17). He rescued them through his mighty deeds (see Exod. 7–12) and acted so as to assure their escape (see Exod. 14). He provided for them in the desert (see Exod. 16–17) and made a covenant with them, giving them his own commandments (see Exod. 19–20). They would be his people and he would be their God (see Exod. 6:7; Deut. 26:17–19). This defining experience was appealed to and reshaped throughout the history and the writings of the Old Testament. It became the basis for the prophetic call to repentance and a return to faithfulness. It was seen as the hope in new and present crises. It became the assurance of present and future actions of God. What is it that the Israelites learned about God

---

6 It should be noted that the Hebrew people believed that the God whom they experienced, who related to them and acted in their midst, was God as he actually is, and not some abridged revelation of God tempered for human consumption.

and his relationship to them from this defining experience and from subsequent experiences similar to it?

First, the exilic covenant formed the experiential context from which the Old Testament understanding of God as Yahweh was formed and nurtured. This is so precisely because it was not the Hebrew people who initiated the covenant, nor did their notion of God arise out of abstract philosophical speculation, but rather Yahweh himself had intervened in their midst and bound himself to them in a unique manner different from that of any other nation. 'Now therefore, if you obey my voice and keep my covenant, you shall be my treasured possession out of all the peoples. Indeed, the whole earth is mine, but you shall be for me a priestly kingdom and a holy nation' (Exod. 19:5, see Deut. 7:6, 10:14–15). Thus, whatever else Yahweh might be, he is primarily experienced, and so known, as a God capable of establishing imminent and intimate relationships, and he does so at his own initiative. Only because of his love and faithfulness, and not out of any merit of their own, did Yahweh separate the Israelites from the other nations, and make them his own (see Deut. 7:7–11; 9:4–6).

Second, it was from within this covenantal experience that the distinguishing characteristic of the Hebrew people took shape and was fostered – their belief in one God. However, this monotheistic faith did not come easy to the Israelites. In the early history of the Hebrew people this monotheistic faith did not exclude a belief in the existence of other gods, as their infidelity shows (see Deut. 9:7–21). 'They had worshipped other gods and walked in the customs of the nations whom the LORD drove out before the people of Israel' (2 Kgs 17:7–8, see 9–18).[7] The one God of the Hebrews may have been the highest of deities, but he was not the only deity. Gradually, as monotheism rooted itself more deeply within the religious traditions, worship, and life of the Israelites, it excluded, despite their continued infidelity, belief in other deities. Yahweh, God of Israel, was not only the supreme god, he was also the only God. 'Yahweh our God is one, the only Yahweh' (Deut. 6:4, NJB).

Third, this covenantal relationship bore witness to a specific type of monotheism. The covenant manifested that the one God was not an impersonal power or a distant deity, but a personal God who, because of his compassion, manifested the supreme covenantal virtue of faithful love (*hesed*). This faithful love guaranteed that Yahweh would be continually present to his people and would act in their midst on their behalf. 'For what other great nation has a god so near to it as the LORD our God is whenever we call to him' (Deut. 4:7; see 32–34). The covenant revealed the personal, close, and familiar relationship which Yahweh had with his people.

Before proceeding in our examination of the Old Testament notion of God, I wish to pause for a moment and interpret more fully what we have just seen. It abundantly illustrates the intimate nature of Yahweh's

---

7 Since I am using almost exclusively either the *Revised Standard Version* or the *New Revised Standard Version* of the Bible, the Hebrew name for God – Yahweh – is rendered in small capitals and translated as LORD.

personal presence and activity. He is a personal, loving God who acts in time even to the extent of making a covenant. His personal relationship to the world and its history is without question.

What equally needs to be grasped is that, while an intimate covenantal relationship was made with the Israelites, which specified his loving presence and commitment, yet it was *the one God* – Yahweh – who established such a covenant. There may be many other gods, but they are all generically the same – gods of fertility and war, etc. Yahweh in his oneness is unique, and because he is the one God, the Israelites ultimately came to believe that he is the only God. Moreover, being the one God radically differentiates him from all else, even from the false and specious gods. While the Old Testament never treats the issue of 'the One and the Many' in a philosophical manner, nonetheless the more the unique oneness of God became manifest to the Israelites the more he was differentiated from all else – the many.[8] To say that God is one not only specified that there is numerically only one God, but also that, being one, he is distinct from all else.

The intimate, personal covenant, which bound the Israelites to Yahweh, was unique therefore not only because it was with the one and only God Yahweh, but also because it was initiated by him, and he was able to initiate such a covenant precisely because he, as the one God who is distinct from all else, possessed the ability to do so. We see here that the covenantal relationship reveals the type of God Yahweh is. It is precisely his otherness, as the one and only God, distinct from all else, which allowed Yahweh to choose to bind the Hebrew nation to himself, and so to live in intimacy with it.[9]

---

8 The pagan Greek gods, like the pagan gods encountered by the Israelites, while superior to human beings and so transcending them, lived and acted solely within the confines of history and time. However, as Greek philosophical thought developed and matured, the notion of there being only one God was established. Interestingly, similar to the growth in the Hebrew understanding of one God, the Greek philosophical notion more and more concluded that the one God was distinct from all else – the many. He was outside the confines of time and history and the finite order. However, in confirming this notion of one God, distinct from all else, the Greek philosophers also believed that he must be apart from all else. God, they believed, could only maintain his transcendent nature, and thus his true divinity, if he remained apart from and inaccessible to the finite realm. Thus, the one God of Greek philosophy either did not know that anything else existed and so never acted within the cosmos (Aristotle), or only related to it through lesser intermediaries – the *Demiurge, Nous,* or *Logos* (Platonism) – and so protected his transcendence. This Greek view of the one God's transcendence never entered into the Hebrew understanding precisely because their understanding of God's otherness arose from their experience of him actually acting in their midst, within time and history. It first entered into Jewish thought when contact was made with Greek philosophy. Having contaminated Jewish (and subsequently Christian) theology, it would take centuries to eradicate it completely, as the critics, seen in the first chapter, have zealously recorded. However, as I will argue at the appropriate places, the contamination was not as sweeping as they would suggest. To my mind the precise nature of the problem and the appropriate solution to it radically differ from their interpretation.

9 Despite the christological context of the New Testament, it affirms the reality of the one and only God, who is the God of Israel. See, for example, 1 Cor. 8:4–6; Eph. 4:6; 1 Tim. 1:17, 2:5, 6:15; Rom. 3:30, 16:27; Jas 2:19; Jude 25. The God and Father of Jesus is the God of Abraham, Isaac and Jacob. This continuity is seen in that 'Theos,' as is well known,

At least three other essential attributes of Yahweh, which were also revealed within the covenantal relationship, nurtured and clarified his singularity, that is, that he is the Savior, the Creator, and All Holy. We will now examine each of these in turn.

Yahweh: God the Savior

Because of Yahweh's personal loving care, the Hebrew people learned that God is in their midst as the one who possesses the power to rescue and to save. Yahweh is God the Savior (see Is. 63:8). The very exodus event, within which the covenant was first established, proved this.

> We were Pharaoh's slaves in Egypt, but the LORD brought us out of Egypt with a mighty hand. The LORD displayed before our eyes great and awesome signs and wonders against Egypt, against Pharaoh and all his household. He brought us out from there in order to bring us in, to give us the land that he promised on oath to our ancestors. Deut. 6:21–23; see 7:7–9.

Unlike the pagan gods, who are dead and lifeless and cannot save (see Is. 44:9-20, Jer. 10:3-5), Yahweh is the living God who acts in time and history, freeing his people from evil and distress (see Judg. 8:19, 1 Kgs 17:1). As Moses sang: 'Who is like you, O LORD, among the gods? Who is like you, majestic in holiness, awesome in splendor, doing wonders?'(Exod. 15:11, see 1–18). He fights with them in battle and delivers them from their enemies. 'Know then today that the LORD your God is the one who crosses over before you as a devouring fire; he will defeat them and subdue them before you' (Deut. 9:3). He gives victory to David (see 2 Sam. 8:7,14). He is able to save those who are incapable of defending themselves – the poor, the needy and the oppressed (see Ps. 18:27). Thus he is the Lord of history and of all the events which take place within history. 'For dominion belongs to the LORD, and he rules over the nations' (Ps. 22:28). Therefore, 'The LORD will reign forever and ever' (Exod. 15:18). The Old Testament abundantly testifies that no historical situation is outside Yahweh's providential care nor immune from his saving action.

Here again, it was in these intimate saving actions, where Yahweh marches with their armies, protects them from enemies mightier than themselves (2 Kgs 19:34, 20:6), that the Israelites found Yahweh to be other than the pagan gods and mightier than all human and natural powers. God is not seen as one among many saviors. He is not even seen as the mightiest of the mighty. As Savior, Yahweh stands unique and independent. 'I have been the LORD your God ever since the land of Egypt; you know no God but me, and besides me there is no saviour'

---

is applied almost exclusively to the Father. In affirming the one God of the Hebrew tradition, the New Testament equally affirms that he is distinct from all else that is. The coming of the kingdom in the person and action of Jesus is not due to human effort or the evolution of history, but, like the covenant of old, is due to the initiative, and so inbreaking, of God into time and history. Thus the New Testament strongly confirms the Old Testament belief that the one and only God who is immanent in time and history is equally distinct from time and history.

(Hos. 13:4). He is the sole Savior because he is the one and only God, and equally he is the sole God because he is the one and only Savior. No worldly power, no historical crisis, no natural threat is beyond him for he is other than them, and so can act in a manner that is in keeping with his unique distinctiveness. Because he is outside their parameters, Yahweh's will and action is not frustrated by worldly power and might, nor hampered by the vicissitudes of history. The term Savior itself, a term that distinguished a specific relationship between Yahweh and his people, equally then identified his otherness. Yahweh could be the mighty Savior he was only because he surpassed all other-worldly and cosmic forces. The covenantal relationship which reveals Yahweh to be Savior is the same relationship which reveals that he is singular in his otherness as Savior.[10]

Yahweh: God the Creator

This loving and compassionate experience of Yahweh as the one God who is the sole Savior, nurtured the belief that he is likewise the Creator of all that is. While God is first Creator before he is Savior, yet experientially it was only as the Israelites encountered God as Savior that they came to realize that the God who has the power to save also possessed the unique power to create. Within the Hebrew scriptures the notion of Yahweh as Creator again expresses both the intimate presence of God and his radical otherness. It is his being the Creator that ultimately founds the close presence of Yahweh as the Wholly Other.[11]

10 For a brief account of God as Savior in the Old Testament, see C. Westermann, *What Does the Old Testament Say About God?* (London: SPCK, 1979), pp. 25–38.
11 I am not entirely pleased with designating Yahweh as 'the Wholly Other.' First, it is not a biblical term, and so I hesitate to insert a non-biblical term within a biblical exegetical context in order to explain the biblical notion of God. Second, it could give the impression that I am inserting then some alien philosophical notion of God that is non-biblical. Third, designating Yahweh as 'the Wholly Other' could also give the impression that I mean that he is completely unlike everything else in every respect. This would be false since creation does testify to the existence of God (see Wis. 13:1–9; Sir. 17:8; Rom. 1:19–20), and human beings are created in God's image and likeness (see Gen. 1:26–27). I have decided, nonetheless, to designate Yahweh as 'the Wholly Other' because I could find no other designation which clearly, succinctly, and singularly expressed the biblical notion that God cannot be numbered among the things created. In this sense, and in this sense only, do I mean that Yahweh is completely and absolutely other. As Creator Yahweh is not a creature, and so he is wholly other than the things created. To say that Yahweh is 'the Wholly Other' does not mean then, as I am using the phrase, that God is 'other' in the sense that he cannot be known, or that he is so 'other' that we cannot make true statements about him, or that he is so 'other' that he has no relationship with the created order. Nor do I want to imply that in calling God 'the Wholly Other' that he is impersonal. I merely wish to highlight the biblical teaching that God is unique because he exists, and so relates to the created order, in a manner that distinguishes and demarcates him from everything else. His singular identity is defined by his otherness from what he has created. G. Grisez states that if the term 'wholly other,' when applied to God, means that God *cannot* be said to be whatever contingent entities are said to be, this expression is appropriate, but nothing is affirmed.' *Beyond the New Theism* (Notre Dame: University of Notre Dame Press, 1975), p. 249. M. Henry also stresses that what distinguished the Israelites' understanding of God from the polytheism of their Mesopotamian neighbors was his otherness from all else. See *On Not Understanding God* (Dublin: The Columba Press,

The first creation story illustrates that Yahweh is distinct from all else that exists for he, in an orderly systematic manner, calls into existence the cosmos and all that it contains (see Gen. 1). Thus neither the cosmos nor anything within it is divine. Moreover, unlike the Babylonian gods, Yahweh does not form the world by doing battle with other cosmic deities, but rather he simply calls forth creation through his mere word (see Gen. 1; Pss 104, 148:8).[12] 'By the word of the LORD the heavens were made, and all their host by the breath of his mouth' (Ps. 33:6). The pagan idols are dead, but Yahweh is the living God who made the earth and all that lives therein (see Jer. 10:1–16). The fact that all is dependent upon Yahweh manifests that he is everlasting. 'Before the mountains were brought forth, or ever you had formed the earth and the world, from everlasting to everlasting you are God' (Ps. 90:2; see Ps. 93:2).[13]

Yahweh being the Creator of all, and thus distinct from what he has made, means that he cannot be depicted. Only human persons are made in his image and likeness (Gen. 1:26–27), yet they too are creatures (see 2 Macc. 7:48). All idols depicting God are forbidden for as such they would misrepresent and so corrupt his complete otherness (Exod. 20:4–6, Deut. 5:8–10). 'To whom then will you liken God, or what likeness compare with him?' (Is. 40:18; see 40:25).

On the one hand, the notion of Yahweh as Creator, who is distinct from all that he creates, and so can neither be depicted in any fashion nor numbered as one of the things created, radicalizes more completely the integral otherness of the one God who is Savior. Yet, simultaneously it is this same Creator God who is the Savior and who remains most intimate with his creation. Though not a creature, God, nonetheless, remains lovingly present to what he has made, especially to human beings, made in his own image and likeness, and with whom he communes (see Gen. 3:8). Psalm 139 gives beautiful expression to this truth.

> O Lord, you have searched me and known me. You know when I sit down and when I rise up; you discern my thoughts from far away.... Where can I go from your spirit? Or where can I flee from your presence? If I ascend to heaven, you are there; if I make my bed in Sheol, you are there. If I take the wings of the morning and settle at the farthest limits of the sea, even there your hand shall lead me, and your right hand shall hold me fast.... For it was you who

---

1997), pp. 79-85. Equally, R. Bauckham argues that the Hebrew notion of God as Creator, unlike non-Jewish thought which sees God as 'the summit of a hierarchy' or 'the original source of a spectrum of divinity,' accentuates 'the absolute distinction between God and all else.' *God Crucified*, p. 16. See also pp. 9–17.

12 The Hebrew *bārā* (word) appears forty-nine times in the Old Testament and is used exclusively for God. Eight of those times are within Genesis 1.

13 While God as Creator is seen as distinct from all that he creates, only once does the Old Testament allude to the concept of *creatio ex nihilo.* 'I beg you, my child, to look at the heaven and the earth and see everything that is in them, and recognize that God did not make them out of things that existed' (2 Macc. 7:28). Nonetheless, such a notion lies within the Old Testament account of Yahweh creating all else, and thus, that there was nothing out of which God could fashion all else. Moreover, the emphasis on the creative capacity of God's word specifies that it was by his will and power alone that all else came to be.

formed my inward parts; you knit me together in my mother's womb. I praise you, for I am fearfully and wonderfully made. Wonderful are your works; that I know very well. Ps. 139:1–2, 7–10, 13–14.

The psalmist cannot escape the love and care of God precisely because, as other than creation, he is present everywhere and at all times. As Creator, he is in no way limited. Again, we see that the term Creator specifies both the relationship between Yahweh and his creation and simultaneously his radical distinctiveness from creation. It is the very otherness of God, as Creator, which allows him to be so close and intimate.[14]

14 For a brief account of God as Creator in the Old Testament see C. Westermann, *What Does the Old Testament Say About God?*, pp. 39–52. B.S. Childs speaks of the distinction between God and creation when he states: 'To say that God reveals himself in his creation is not to say that God is known through nature. To try to discover God by scanning the sun and the moon can just as easily lead to idolatry and superstition. Rather, the confession of the biblical writer is that God reveals himself as creator.' *Old Testament Theology in a Canonical Context* (London: SCM, 1985), p. 31.
    The New Testament also speaks of God as Creator (see Mk 13:19; Rom. 11:36; Eph. 3:9; 1 Tim. 6:13; and Rev. 4:11, 10:6, 14:7), and in so doing distinguishes him from all else that is. Bassler points out that God as Creator is especially evident in the prayers (see 4:24) and the speeches within Acts (see 14:15–17, 17:22–31). The speeches were primarily attempts at evangelizing the Greeks, and so attempting to confirm that the one God of the Greeks was also the Creator God who has now brought salvation in Jesus (see *The Anchor Bible Dictionary*, Vol. II, p. 1051).
    The New Testament has two unique emphases concerning God as the Creator. Both are founded upon and anticipated within the Old Testament. The first is that the Father created through the Word/Son (see Jn 1:2–3; 1 Cor. 8:6; Col. 1:15–20; Heb. 1:1–3) and that the Father manifests his lifegiving power in the raising of Jesus from the dead by the Holy Spirit (see Acts 2:23, 32, 36; 3:13–17; 4:10; 5:30–31; 7:52; 10:39–40; 13:27–30; 17:31; 1 Thes. 1:10; 1 Cor. 6:14, 15:15; 2 Cor. 4:14; Gal. 1:1; Rom. 4:24, 10:9; 1 Pet. 1:21). Thus the Father will also raise to glory all who believe in his Son (see Rom. 6:5, 8:11; 1 Cor. 6:14, 15:20ff.; 2 Cor. 4:14, 13:4; Eph. 2:6; Col. 1:18; 2:12ff.; 1 Thes. 4:14; 2 Tim. 2:11). Christians, then, participate in a new birth (see 1 Pet. 1:3), a new creation (see 2 Cor. 5:17), a new life (see Rom. 6:4, Col. 2:12–13; Eph. 2:1), and so become a new man (see Eph. 2:15). This all finds its completion when the Father creates a new heaven and a new earth with the return of Jesus in glory (see Rev. 21:1–22:5). We see here that God as Creator and God as Savior are intimately intertwined in the New Testament, and that this unity finds its source in the unique person of Jesus and his saving work. We will discuss later the whole question of christology. Here I wish only to note again that all these historical saving actions of God through Jesus, especially in the resurrection, manifest his complete otherness, for no one from within the created order could do what God does, especially raise someone into glory and bring about a whole new created order at the end of time. The New Testament corroborates and enlarges the Old Testament notion that the God who creates and acts within the created order is completely other than the created order.
    The Old and New Testament notion of God as active within the created order is utterly foreign to Greek theodicy. There are two reasons why Greek philosophy isolated God in his transcendence. The first, which is foundational, is that it had no perception of God as Creator. Not being Creator, God had no 'natural' bond to the finite realm. Within Neo-Platonic thought all emanated out from God, and while human beings therefore contained a 'seed' or 'spark' of God within them (the soul), yet the very notion of emanation meant that there was a constitutional gulf or chasm between God and that which emanated out from him. Second, Platonic thought viewed the finite realm itself as evil because it was mired in matter and so never fully conformed to the true good of the immutable ideal forms. God, therefore, needed to remain aloof from the finite lest he be contaminated by the depravity of matter. The biblical notion of

Yahweh: God the All Holy

The experience of the Creator and Savior God of the covenant equally and simultaneously nurtured the notion that Yahweh was the All Holy God. For example, through his theophanies and mighty works Yahweh showed forth his holiness (see Exod. 19:3–20; Num. 20:1–13). Yahweh's holy presence was both terrifying to approach (see 1 Sam. 6:19–21), and yet protective (see 2 Sam. 6:7–11). Yahweh, in the splendor of his holiness, took possession of the Tent of Meeting (see Exod. 40:34–35) and filled the temple with his glory (see 1 Kgs 8:10–11), and so dwelt in the midst of his people. The most sacred inner part of the temple, a specific place, literally secured within the earth, and so fixed in time and history, was called the Holy of Holies, for it was here that Yahweh specifically abided. Within the temple Isaiah experienced the thrice-holy presence of God (see Is. 6:1–5).

The temple strikingly expresses both Yahweh's presence and yet his complete otherness as All Holy, for within the Holy of Holies, this earthly place where Yahweh dwelt, there was no depiction of him – neither image or idol. As the All Holy wholly other, Yahweh could only be worshiped in awe and reverence. He could not be depicted. The very material splendor and grandeur of the temple itself accentuated the sacredness and the otherness of the one who abided therein.

Moreover, Solomon's prayer dedicating the temple equally manifests the complete otherness of Yahweh as the All Holy God. He acknowledges that his 'name' will be present in the temple and so affirms that Yahweh himself will abide there, and yet, since he is present in his 'name,' that he is not solely confined to the temple (see 1 Kgs 8:16, 29). His otherness exceeds and cannot be confined to his presence in the temple. Thus the constant refrain within Solomon's prayer is that, when the people come to the temple to ask for forgiveness, or to seek favorable weather, or to be freed from famine and plague, or to win victory in battle, or even when the foreigner comes to the temple because he hears of Yahweh's great name, Yahweh would 'hear in heaven' and answer their pleas (see 1 Kgs 8:30–53). The people come to the temple, for it is there that Yahweh abides, but it is from heaven that he hears and answers their prayers for, as the Wholly Other, his existence exceeds the limits and confines of this world. It is precisely because he does surpass this realm as the Wholly Other that he is able to do what they request of him concerning forgiveness, weather, plagues, and war.

Only because Yahweh is holy in himself, dependent upon no other for his holiness, is he also able to sanctify those with whom he is covenanted. He was the one who brought the Israelites out of the desecration of slavery and made them his holy nation (see Lev. 11:44–5, 20:8, 22:32). God gave to his people the commandments so that in keeping them they

---

creation, in contrast, confirmed both the otherness of God from creation and simultaneously his 'natural' bond with creation since he was its Creator and Sustainer. Moreover, since it was the good God who is Creator, the whole of creation was created good, even matter. Clearly, the notion of God as Creator is absolutely crucial for confirming both the otherness of God from the created order and his indispensable intrinsic relationship to it.

might be as holy as he is holy (see Lev. 19:2, 20:7, 26). All the minute
details of the law and worship had but one purpose – that of separating
the Israelites from all defilement, so that they might embrace the holiness
of God (see Lev. 17–26). 'Thus you shall keep my commandments and
observe them: I am the LORD. You shall not profane my holy name, that I
may be sanctified among the people of Israel: I am the LORD; I sanctify
you' (Lev. 22:31–32).

The sin of the Israelites, their infidelity to the covenant, defiled them
and so separated them from the All Holy God (see Is. 5:24). This caused
God to grieve over his people (see Ps. 73:21) and even to become angry
with them, expelling them from his holy presence (see 2 Kgs 24:20). Yet,
because of his faithful love and compassion, God sent forth the prophets
to call the people to repentance and to a recommitment to the holy and
faithful life of the covenant. Even though they had profaned his holy
name among the nations, he would manifest the power of his holiness by
purifying them of their uncleanness, making them once more holy (see
Ezek. 36:16–36).

The above can be summarized in the declaration that Yahweh is 'the
Holy One of Israel' (Is. 10:20, 17:7). Yahweh is 'the Holy One,' and so
dissimilar to Israel. Yet he is the Holy One 'of Israel' and so present to
Israel making it holy. 'I am God and no mortal; the Holy One in your
midst' (Hos. 11:9). This is Israel's glory. 'Then you shall rejoice in the
LORD; in the Holy One of Israel you shall glory' (Is. 41:16; see 41:14–23;
Ps. 71:22).

Holiness, within the Hebrew scriptures, then, is not just one of many
divine attributes, but rather characterizes Yahweh's very identity (see Ps.
33:21; Am. 2:7). It identifies Yahweh's moral goodness and perfection as
well as his mighty and awesome power. It characterizes all that Yahweh
is as God in majesty and glory. It evokes wonder, reverence, fear, and
praise. It distinguishes him from all else. The very Semitic word, *qōdes*,
(holiness) derives from the root meaning 'to cut off' or 'to separate,' and
thus Yahweh, as holy, is other than all that is profane or sinful.
Nonetheless, this identity of Yahweh as holy again illustrates the same
pattern discerned with regard to his being One, Savior and Creator.
Yahweh's holiness was only manifested within the covenantal relationship, as he revealed himself in the midst of his people. The theophanies,
the sanctification of his people, and especially his abiding presence in the
temple, portrayed then that the one who was present as the All Holy was
indeed the same one who was wholly other as the All Holy.[15]

The Mature Proclamation of Deutero-Isaiah

In examining the Hebrew understanding of Yahweh as One, Savior,
Creator and All Holy, I have purposely tried to avoid quoting from
Deutero-Isaiah. The reason is that he expresses the mature Hebrew

15 For a similar interpretation of the biblical notion of God's holiness see: W. Pannenberg,
   Basic Questions in Theology, Vol. 1, pp. 154–55; and his *Systematic Theology*, Vol. 1 (Grand
   Rapids: Eerdmans, 1991), pp. 398–400. Nonetheless, Pannenberg equally, and I think
   inconsistently, espouses that the All Holy God is mutable and passible.

understanding of Yahweh, and so I would now like to use his prophetic words to summarize what we have learned thus far.

Deutero-Isaiah adamantly proclaims that the pagan idols are merely the handiwork of men. They are crafted out of wood, silver and gold. Their eyes are shut. Their ears are closed. They are mindless. They are lifeless and are actually nothing at all. 'No, they are all a delusion; their works are nothing; their images are empty wind' (Is. 41:29).[16] In contrast to the many lifeless idols, Yahweh is the one and only God who is alive and active. 'I am the LORD, and there is no other; besides me there is no god' (Is. 45:5).[17] His singularity is highlighted by the repeated phrases 'I, I am He,' and 'I am Yahweh' (see Is. 43:13, 15, 25; 45:3–7; 48:12; 49:23; 51:15). This singularity denotes the complete otherness of Yahweh. It attests that Yahweh is not only numerically one, but also that he is singular in his mode of existence. He cannot be numbered among the gods or anything else that exists.

The singularity of Yahweh is re-enforced within the proclamation that he alone is the Savior, Creator, and Holy One of Israel. All of these cluster around and so amplify the understanding of the one God, Yahweh.

Yahweh is with his people and thus they need not be afraid for he will help and uphold them with his 'victorious right hand' (Is. 41:10; see v. 13; 43:5). He has redeemed Israel and called her by name (see Is. 43:1). 'I will help you, says the LORD, your Redeemer is the Holy One of Israel' (Is. 41:41; see 43:3, 44:6, 48:17). Yahweh's salvation is everlasting and for all peoples (see Is. 45:17, 22). 'There is no other god besides me, a righteous God and a Savior, there is no one besides me' (Is. 45:21).

Deutero-Isaiah closely aligns Yahweh as Savior and Yahweh as Creator. 'Thus says the LORD, your Redeemer, who formed you in the womb: I am the LORD, who made all things' (Is. 44:24). As Creator he is awesome in majesty and can be compared with nothing. 'Who has measured the waters in the hollow of his hand and marked off the heavens with a span, enclosed the dust of the earth in a measure and weighed the mountains in a scales and the hills in a balance' (Is. 40:12; see v. 22, 42:5). Because of this, his wisdom and knowledge are unsurpassable (see Is. 40:13–14). Because he is the author of all 'The LORD is the everlasting God, the Creator of the ends of the earth. He does not faint or grow weary, his understanding is unsearchable' (Is. 40:28; see v. 26). All that is seen, 'the Holy One of Israel has created it' (Is. 41:20). He created human beings for his glory (see Is. 43:7). As the Creator he is 'the first' and 'the last' (Is. 41:4).

As the above quotations already note, Yahweh creates and saves as 'The Holy One of Israel.' After contemplating all that was made, 'To whom then will you compare me, or who is my equal? says the Holy One' (Is. 40:25). In all danger and peril the people can trust in Yahweh. 'For I am the LORD your God, the Holy One of Israel, your Saviour' (Is.

16 For descriptions of the lifelessness and nothingness of idols and false gods, see Is. 40:19–20; 41:6–7, 23–24; 42:17; 43:10–13; 44:9–20; 46:1–13; 48:5. The New Testament has a similar understanding (see 1 Thes. 1:9; Acts 14:15; Rom. 1:23; 1 Cor. 8:4–6).

17 The refrain 'I am the LORD, and there is no other' pervades throughout the whole of Chapter 45. See 45:6, 14, 21, 22; also 46:9.

43:3). Because Yahweh is the Holy One, 'I, I am He who blots out your transgressions for my own sake, and I will not remember your sins' (Is. 43:25; see 42:6). As the Redeemer and the Holy One of Israel, Yahweh will raise up his chosen people even though they are despised by the nations and rulers (see Is. 49:7) for he 'makes the rulers of the earth as nothing' (Is. 40:23).

The whole of Deutero-Isaiah can be summed up in this verse. 'I am the LORD, your Holy One, the Creator of Israel, your King' (Is. 43:15).

Nowhere in the Old Testament do we find the confirmation of Yahweh's activity in time and history so majestically and ardently proclaimed. The terms Creator, Savior, and Holy One all testify to Yahweh's presence and activity as the one and only God of whom there is no other. They are all relational concepts which express the activity and closeness of Yahweh to his people. Yet, within these very relation-ships, the singularity of Yahweh, as wholly other, is simultaneously evident and transparently manifest.[18] It is here that I must draw some conclusions, some of which should be already apparent.

---

18 While I have focused on Yahweh being One, Savior, Creator and All Holy, there are other aspects which re-enforce the understanding expressed here. For example, while the Psalms extol the mighty and loving works of Yahweh and praise him for them, yet these reveal his singular greatness (see Ps. 77:11–15). The Book of Job portrays Yahweh as the fount of wisdom and knowledge. As the author of all he needs no counsel or teaching (see Job 38–41). The Wisdom literature equally asserts that wisdom finds its source in God alone. Moreover, the names ascribed to God in the Old Testament also manifest his uniqueness. El-Elyôn (God Most High), El-'Olam (Everlasting God), Shaddai (Almighty), Abir (Mighty One), Adônai (Lord), Yahweh Sabaoth (LORD of Hosts) all denote Yahweh's otherness from the created order and simultaneously his presence and activity within it. This is especially seen in the divine name Yahweh.

   As I noted earlier Moses' request that God reveal his name served a twofold purpose. Since names were indicative of one's 'nature,' to know God's name was to obtain a knowledge of him. Moreover, it allowed the knower of the name to call upon him and so have access to him. God in revealing his name to Moses and the Hebrew people granted them privileged knowledge of him and the ability to call upon him. Scholars debate the exact meaning of the name Yahweh, but they are agreed that it derives from the Hebrew verb 'to be' (*hawah*). *'ehyeh 'asher 'ehyeh* can then be translated as either 'I am he who is' or 'I am the one who exists.' The Greek Septuagint translated it as 'I am who am' (*ego eimi ho on*). Thus, God in revealing his name Yahweh, manifests both that he is with his people, since they know his name, and that he is present as the unknowable or unnameable. As 'He who is' God remains 'the mystery' – the Wholly Other – in their midst. S. Terrien prefers to translate the divine name as 'I shall be whoever I shall be', but concludes:

   According to this interpretation, the name indeed carries the connotation of divine presence, but it also confers upon this presence a quality of elusiveness. The God of biblical faith, even in the midst of a theophany, is at once *Deus revelatus atque abscon-ditus*. He is known as unknown. *The Elusive Presence: Toward a New Biblical Theology* (San Francisco: Harper & Row, 1978), p. 119. See pp. 106–19.

   J.C. Murray in his classic study on the divine name argues that the Hebrew people themselves would have understood the name 'Yahweh' to mean: 'I shall be there as who I am shall I be there.' 'The text, thus understood, contains a threefold revelation – of God's immanence in history, of his transcendence to history, and of his transparence through history.' *The Problem of God* (New Haven: Yale University Press, 1964), p. 10. See pp. 5–30.

   For other studies see, 'YHWH' in *The Theological Dictionary of the Old Testament*, eds.

Yahweh: Present and Active as the Wholly Other

I have briefly summarized four major aspects of the Hebrew under-standing of Yahweh – that he is One, Savior, Creator and All Holy. I have tried to accentuate the relational character of God in the Old Testament. Yahweh is the One All Holy Creator God who, in his love and compassion, made a covenant with his people and was personally present to and acted within their midst, within time and history, as Savior. I have equally argued that in so doing Yahweh simultaneously manifested his complete otherness. Within the Hebrew scriptures, to say that Yahweh is One, Savior, Creator and All Holy is to say, at one and the same time, within the same concepts, that he is present and active as the one who is wholly other, and that he is present and active in time and history, as the Wholly Other without jeopardizing his total otherness in so doing. The words and actions by which and in which Yahweh revealed his presence are the very same words and actions by which and in which Yahweh revealed his wholly and complete otherness.

That God is able to be present and active as the Wholly Other, and is present and active only because he is the Wholly Other is, I believe, the primary, central and pivotal mystery of biblical revelation and of the Jewish/Christian faith. There is no mystery that is more remarkable or more fundamental. It is the Mystery. To state this mystery more philo-sophically: While God, in his complete otherness, is ontologically distinct from the created order, and thus from all other beings, yet he is able to bring into existence, be present to, and act within the created order as one who is ontologically distinct from the created order, and he is able to do so only because he is ontologically distinct. Moreover, he is able to do so, in his wholly otherness, without forfeiting his wholly otherness in so doing.[19] All other mysteries are founded upon and give expression to this

---

G.J. Botterwick and H. Ringgren (Grand Rapids: Eerdmans, 1986), Vol. 5, pp. 500–21; 'Names of God in the Old Testament' in *The Anchor Bible Dictionary*, Vol. 4, pp. 1602–11; W. Kasper, *The God of Jesus Christ* (New York: Crossroad, 1984), p. 148.

The New Testament takes up similar names for God. He is almighty (see Rev. 1:8); the Lord of Hosts (see Rom. 9:29, Jas 5:4); the Most High (see Lk 1:32, 35, 76, 8:28; Mk 5:7); the Sovereign (see 1 Tim. 6:15; Rev. 6:10); the Mighty One (Lk 1:49); Lord of lords and King of kings (see 1 Tim. 1:17; 6:15; Rev. 15:3); the Lord of heaven and earth (see Rev. 11:4; Mt 11:25). As with the names and titles for God in the Old Testament so these too highlight both his relationship to the created order and his distinctiveness from it.

19 The philosophical issue of divine causality will be treated in Chapter 6. However, it would be good to state here that the biblical notion of Yahweh and of his relationships to the created order as Creator, Savior, and Sanctifier demand an understanding of causality that is unique to him. Actually, it is this unique causality of Yahweh which establishes him relationally as Creator, Savior and Sanctifier. Yahweh is Creator precisely because he is not a cause within the created realm, for he establishes the existence of the created order, and thus is necessarily related to it as one who is not of it. Moreover, his actions as Savior manifest that he is not wholly determined or causally constrained and restrained by physical/natural laws, or political conditions, or economic circumstances, but rather, being free from such constraints, he is able to act independently of them and so save and redeem even in the midst of such laws, conditions, and circumstances. Likewise, he is able to sanctify as the All Holy God, for, while he abides in the midst of a sinful people and world, he is not enmeshed within it.

mystery. For example, as we will examine in Chapter 8, in the Incarnation, the Son of God, in the fulness of his divinity, actually comes to exist as man and so be man, in time and history, without mitigating his full divinity in so doing and existing. The incarnation is but an example of this fundamental mystery expressed in its most pure and intense form. How such an understanding of God and his ability to be present to and act within the created order of time and history can be sustained philosophically will be treated in Chapter 6. Here I wish to emphasize, resolutely and clearly, that this is the biblical and revelational mystery that must be philosophically sustained, clarified and amplified. This understanding of the mystery of God's otherness and his presence to and activity within the created order is absolutely central to this study concerning the question of God's impassibility.

I believe then that any understanding of God's activity in time and history which undermines his total otherness is not in keeping with biblical revelation. This is so not just for the sake of defending the otherness of God as God, but more importantly to uphold the significance of his activity within the created order. It is of no advantage to uphold the complete otherness of God if it is not the wholly other God who is present to and acts within the created order. Equally, and this point many contemporary theologians fail to grasp, it is of no advantage to uphold the intimate presence and activity of God within the created order if it is not the wholly other God who is so present and active. The whole significance of Yahweh's presence and activity, expressed in his love, care, and compassion, is predicated precisely on the truth that it is actually God, in his wholly otherness as God, who is present and active. To make God less than wholly other in order to promote or protect his presence and activity is to undermine the very importance of his presence and activity. If it is not the wholly other God who is acting in time and history and forming personal relationships with his people, then the whole significance of this activity and these relationships is lost.

Moreover, God is able to establish such intimate relationships only because he is the Wholly Other. To make God less than wholly other does not make him more personal, loving, and compassionate, but rather he would be less personal, loving and compassionate.[20] If God were not the Wholly Other, he could not be the Creator, the Savior, and the Holy One capable of the intimate presence and the dynamic actions that these designations disclose.

It is this singular causal ability as Creator, Savior and Sanctifier that constitutes Yahweh's immanent presence and activity as the Wholly Other. While the Hebrew scriptures (and the New Testament) testify to such causality, they, somewhat surprisingly, never comment on it other than to assume that Yahweh does what he does because he is God and so can do it. But are not the scriptures a narration of God's revelation, and not a philosophical treatise on it? He leaves it up to us to figure out, philosophically, *how* he does what he does, and it would be philosophically erroneous to conclude, in attempting to grasp *how* God acts, that he cannot do what the Bible reveals that he does.

20 How this is philosophically the case will be demonstrated in Chapters 6 and 7.

Transcendence and Immanence Revisited

While I briefly stated, at the onset of this chapter, that the notion of God's transcendence and immanence is pivotal to the discussion of his being impassible or passible, I have, as I stated I would, avoided the use of the terms 'transcendent,' 'transcendence,' 'immanent,' and 'immanence' in describing who God is in relationship to all else. The reason is that these terms, when describing God and his relationship to all else, are I believe, often misconceived. It is only now, having examined the Hebrew under-standing of God and his relationship to the created order that it is possible to discern clearly the biblical notion of God's transcendence and immanence.

From the biblical perspective, as witnessed in the Hebrew scriptures, for God to be transcendent does not mean that there are certain aspects of God's being or nature which are distinct from those aspects of God's nature which allow him to be immanent. To say that God transcends the created order of time and history does not mean that there are properties within God which make him unlike the created order and which then differ from those properties which allow him to act within the created order. If one understands God to be transcendent in this manner, as possessing qualities which differ from those qualities which make him immanent, this would mean that those qualities which make him tran-scendent are the divine peculiarities which make him inaccessible, separate, or apart from the created order of time and history. This is precisely how many theologians today, as witnessed in the opening chapter, conceive God's transcendence. Transcendence specifies those qualities in God which not only make him distinct from all else, but also make him disassociated, and so disconnected, from all else. Thus, many theologians today, who conceive God's transcendence in this manner, argue that God's transcendence, that is, those qualities which make him isolated and aloof, must be diminished in some manner and/or that the qualities which make him more accessible be amplified in some manner so as to make it possible for him to be immanent.[21] However, this under-

<hr>

21 Despite all of the criticism of Greek philosophy, those theologians who conceive God's transcendence in opposition to his immanence and so wish to deprive God of some of his transcendence in order to make him immanent are actually working from within a Greek understanding of transcendence. Within Platonic thought, for God to be tran-scendent meant that he was not only other than the created order, but also far from it. God could not be both transcendent and immanent simultaneously for to be immanent would jeopardize his transcendence. While many contemporary philosophers and theologians rightly wish to make God immanent, in contrast to the Platonic under-standing, they are nonetheless still working from within the Platonic understanding of transcendence in that they believe God cannot be wholly transcendent and yet immanent at the same time. Their solution is to make God less transcendent and therefore more immanent, but in so doing they do what the Greeks feared – make God less than God. It is not surprising, as we already saw, that in their attempt to make God more immanent many contemporary theologians argue for a panentheistic notion of God which, in the end, differs little from pantheism itself. This is hardly the biblical view of God. As J.C. Murray states: 'The Israelite world-view was never touched by any taint of pantheism. However seductive to the philosopher, pantheism was no tempta-tion to the people whose sense of God as the Holy One made pantheism unthinkable' (*The Problem of God*, p. 20). What many contemporary theologians have not grasped,

standing of God and of his transcendence and immanence is completely
contrary to biblical revelation.

The Old Testament never conceives of God's transcendence in opposition to his immanence, as if that which makes God wholly other is
different from that which allows him to be a personal God who lovingly
acts in time and history. For the Bible, transcendence and immanence do
not describe two divine modes of being or two sets of distinguishing
qualities – one as God is apart from the created order and another as he
is in relation to the created order. For God to be transcendent in the
biblical understanding means that he is wholly other than the created
order but not apart from the created order. That which makes him divine,
and thus wholly other and so transcendent, is that which equally allows
him to be active within the created order and so be immanent. There is
no opposition between God's transcendent being and his immanent
activity.[22] As I have argued throughout, to say that Yahweh is the One
All Holy Creator and Savior is to express his immanent activity as the
Wholly Other. To use present-day jargon, the biblical understanding of
God's transcendence is precisely what makes him 'user friendly' or
'creation order compatible.'[23] The biblical notion of transcendence is not
then a description of how God exists in himself as isolated from the

---

which is the central issue of this chapter, is that the biblical understanding demands
that God be present to and active within the created order as he truly is, as the Wholly
Other, and that he be present and active precisely because he is the Wholly Other. For
the Bible, God is transcendent not in the sense that he is far away from or inaccessible
to the created order, but only that he is wholly other than the created order and is
related to and active within the created order as the Wholly Other. M. Henry writes:

> It is because his [God's] otherness from his creation is of such a unique kind that he
> can be present to, or immanent in, his creation in a unique way.... In other words,
> it is actually – paradoxical though it may sound – God's transcendence that makes
> him relevant to the world rather than remote from the world. It is his transcendence
> that allows him to overcome and not be restricted by the world's differences, and to
> be present to, or immanent in, creation in a unique way. *On Not Understanding God,*
> p. 91.

22 Using the notion of holiness as an example, T.E. Fretheim writes concerning God's
immanence and transcendence:

> Perhaps the phrase, 'in your midst is the Holy One' (Is. 12:6; Hos. 11:9) can assist us
> here. This phrase indicates that holiness, one important biblical word for speaking
> of transcendence, and presence do not stand opposed to one another. It is probably
> also true to say that the language of polarity does not capture the sense either, as if
> holiness and presence stood in some tension with each other. Rather, it is *as* the
> Holy One that God is present.... The transcendence of God is thus manifested by
> the *way in which* God is present among his people. It is not just that any God or God
> in some attenuated form is present among the people, it is the Holy God, a God who
> does great things.... And this God *is* present – not some emanation of God, nor
> some bits and pieces of God, but God in all of God's Godness is present. *The
> Suffering of God: An Old Testament Perspective,* pp. 70–71. See also p. 38.

   While I agree with Fretheim here, he does, nonetheless argue throughout his book
that God does change and is passible. As I will argue later, this does seem to undermine
the 'Godness' of God and so the significance of the one who is truly in our midst.

23 B.S. Childs writes: 'His [God's] transcendence does not undercut his immanence, nor
his mysterious otherness his gracious presence'. *Old Testament Theology in a Canonical
Context,* p. 41.

created order, but rather how he exists in relation to the created order. For God to be transcendent means that he intimately relates to, is lovingly present to, and dynamically acts within the created order as the one who is ontologically wholly other than the created order.

Actually, God in himself is neither transcendent nor immanent. He is just God. Transcendence, by its very nature, only expresses who God is in relation to what he is not, that is, that he is not 'a part' of the created order and therefore, as such, transcends it. God's mode of being God differs then in kind and not just in degree from all else that exists. Equally, to speak of God's immanence is not to speak of God in himself as if there were aspects of him which are part of the created order, but rather 'immanence' specifies that he who is not 'a part' of the created order is nonetheless present to and active within it.[24]

As I stated above, this is the great mystery of the Judeo-Christian tradition. It is a mystery precisely because, while we may know that this is what God has clearly revealed about himself and about his relationship to the created order, we can neither thoroughly comprehend nor adequately explain it. The reason for this is simply put – we are dealing with the incomprehensible God. If we did believe that we could comprehend and explain it fully, we would no longer be dealing with God, and so, whatever answer we arrived at, it could not possibly be true.[25] In this chapter I have merely attempted to clarify and to state exactly what the mystery is. In Chapter 6 I will try to give philosophical warrant for this mystery, and so hopefully provide greater clarity and exactness, but it will still remain a mystery.

---

24 Some scripture scholars speak of God's revelation of himself in the Old Testament in terms of 'disclosure' and 'hiddenness' rather than in terms of 'transcendence' and 'immanence.' While God discloses who he is, yet he does so as to remain hidden for he is always more than contained in the revelation of himself. As B.S. Childs states: 'God both reveals and conceals his identity to Israel. What first seems to be the divine form itself soon emerges as only his outward manifestation: his "glory", "messenger" or "face",' *Old Testament Theology in a Canonical Context*, p. 41. S. Terrien's entire study, *The Elusive Presence: Toward a New Biblical Theology*, develops this theme. 'The reality of the presence of God stands at the center of biblical faith. This presence, however, is always elusive' (p. xxvii). He continues:

> Alone in their cultural milieu, the Hebrews developed a unique theology of presence. They worshipped a God whose disclosure or proximity always had a certain quality of elusiveness. Indeed, for most generations of the biblical age, Israel prayed to a *Deus Absconditus*.

Terrien notes that the Hebrew original of this expression means 'a self-concealing God' (Is. 45:15), (p. 1). To speak of God's 'disclosure' and 'hiddenness' may be more in keeping with biblical language, yet I believe such terms are not contrary to speaking of God's transcendence and immanence. If properly understood, the later terms give more philosophical clarity to the biblical proclamation.

25 To attempt to make the mystery of God's transcendence and immanence comprehensible is to transform it into a problem as I described in the second chapter. This, I believe, is one of the mistakes made by those theologians who argue for God's passibility. They may make the mystery comprehensible, but in so doing destroy the mystery itself and thus distort both God and his relationship to the created order.

That the incomprehensibility of God, and so his mystery, is the basis for any authentic discussion of impassibility, see P. Groves' D.Phil. dissertation, *Ineffability and Divine Impassibility* (University of Oxford, 1995).

The Passion of Yahweh

Having examined the Hebrew understanding of God and of his relationship to the created order, it is now possible to address the question of
whether or not the Old Testament conceives Yahweh as impassible or
passible. This question, by necessity, entails philosophical issues, issues
that the Hebrew scriptures do not address. Because of this a full answer
to the question cannot be given at this juncture, but must await the
following chapters. Nonetheless, some biblical insights can be obtained.

We saw in Chapter 1 that many contemporary theologians argue that
the Hebrew scriptures bear copious and even undeniable witness to
God's passibility. Heschel's concept of 'divine pathos' seems to articulate
well the whole of Yahweh's character and bearing. However, does this
'divine pathos' reveal a passible God?[26] We must consider some of the
key texts.

First, there are passages where Yahweh suffers on behalf of, with, or
because of his people, and so grieves with or over them.[27] As Yahweh
witnessed the suffering of his people in Egypt and delivered them (see
Exod. 3:7–12), so he raised up judges and rescued his people from their
enemies 'for the LORD would be moved to pity by their groaning' (Judg.
2:18). The sin of his people caused Yahweh to suffer and grieve most.
'How often they rebelled against him in the wilderness and grieved him
in the desert!' (Ps. 78:40). For forty years Yahweh 'loathed that generation
and said, "They are a people whose hearts go astray, and they do not
regard my way." Therefore in my anger I swore, "They shall not enter
my rest"' (Ps. 95:10–11). Even though his people acted as an adulterous
prostitute and so suffered the consequences, yet Yahweh cleansed his
people from all defilement. 'I will take you for my wife forever; I will take
you for my wife in righteousness and in justice, in steadfast love, and in
mercy. I will take you for my wife in faithfulness; and you shall know the
LORD' (Hos. 2:19–20). From Israel's infancy Yahweh loved him and
taught him to walk. Yahweh led his people 'with cords of human
kindness and with bands of love' (Hos. 11:4). Despite their wayward
ungratefulness and obstinacy of heart, Yahweh could not give his people
up. 'My heart recoils within me; my compassion grows warm and tender.
I will not execute my fierce anger ... for I am God and no mortal, the
Holy One in your midst, and I will not come in wrath' (Hos. 11:8–9; see
Jer. 31:20). The Book of Isaiah recalls all 'the gracious deeds of the LORD'
because of 'his mercy' and 'the abundance of his steadfast love.' Yahweh
did not save them by a 'messenger or angel, but his presence saved them;
in his love and in his pity he redeemed them' (Is. 63:7–9). Isaiah assures
the people that if they seek Yahweh, who is ever near, and forsake their
wickedness and return to him, then he will show them great mercy and
abundant pardon. 'For my thoughts are not your thoughts, nor are your
ways my ways, says the LORD. For as the heavens are higher than the

26 For an exposition and critique of Heschel's understanding of divine 'pathos,' see the
Addendum to this chapter.
27 See Fretheim, *The Suffering of God*, pp. 107–48.

earth, so are my ways higher than your ways and my thoughts above your thoughts' (Is. 55:6–9). Indeed the passion – the pathos – of Yahweh is nowhere more ardently and fervently expressed than in these and similar passages.

The traditional defense for God's impassability is simply to argue that the Bible in such passages is using anthropomorphic language, and so cannot be taken literally. Therefore, it is argued, God does not actually 'groan' or 'suffer,' nor does his heart 'grow warm.' Undoubtedly, the Bible is using anthropomorphic language, but it, nonetheless, is attempting to say something that is actually true about God. Many contemporary theologians emphasize the latter, and so argue that God must be passible if his groaning, suffering and love are to be actual and genuine. What both sides of the debate miss in the interpretation of these passages is that the one who is so filled with passion is the Wholly Other. It is Yahweh, 'the Holy One in your midst.' The very superlative, extravagant, and even excessive, expression of the love, the compassion, the forgiveness and, indeed, the anger, accentuates that the one who displays all of this intense passion is someone who transcends what is beyond the merely customary and human. This is why Yahweh 'is God and no mortal.' What makes Yahweh's thoughts so different from our own and what makes his ways so different from our own is that he is so different from us. The difference is far greater than is the distance 'between heaven and earth.' Yes, Yahweh is passionate but it is the passion of the Wholly Other, and he is able to express such depth of passion only because he is the Wholly Other. Therefore, there is a legitimate literalness to what is being said, but it is a literalness that must be interpreted from within the complete otherness of God, for this is the manner in which this passion is expressed. If God were not wholly other, he would not be able to be as passionate as he is. Therefore, if one were to conceive of God's love, suffering and groaning in such a manner as to undermine his complete otherness, then his love, suffering and groaning would be diminished, and thus the significance of his love, suffering and groaning would be completely lost. How God can be wholly other and yet love, suffer and groan is a philosophical issue. Here I wish only to assert emphatically, on biblical grounds, that Yahweh is passionate as the Wholly Other and that his passion can in no way diminish his wholly otherness for it is the wholly otherness of his passion which allows for and confers upon it its true divine significance and singular definition.[28]

Does Yahweh Change His Mind?

Even if one grants that it is Yahweh, as the Wholly Other, who is passionate, it does seem that he is nonetheless changeable and, therefore,

---

28 Heschel makes the same point. See *The Prophets*, pp. 270–72. I discuss this in the Addendum. S.D. Goitein argues that the divine name Yahweh should actually be translated as: 'I shall love passionately whom I love.' See 'YHWH The Passionate: The Monotheistic Meaning and Origin of the Name *YHWH*,' *Vetus Testamentum* 6 (1956):1–9.

passible. Does not his compassion '*grow* warm and tender' as if he had been 'cool' towards his people and now has aroused his love anew? Does he not say, 'I will not execute my fierce anger,' as if he had changed his mind? This arousal of love and this cooling of anger appear to express change in Yahweh, and one that is founded upon the possibility of his passionate nature.

In the Hebrew scriptures Yahweh appears to change his mind quite frequently. For example, Yahweh, in seeing how wicked the human race had become, was 'sorry that he had made humankind on the earth, and it grieved him to his heart' (Gen. 6:6–7). Or again, Moses implores Yahweh to 'change your mind and do not bring disaster on your people,' and 'the LORD changed his mind about the disaster that he planned to bring on his people' (Exod. 32:12, 14). Moreover, on seeing the repentance of the Ninevites, 'God changed his mind about the calamity that he had said he would bring upon them; and he did not do it' (Jon. 3:10). This is precisely what upset Jonah. He knew God would, in his graciousness and kindness, 'relent' (Jon. 4:2; see Joel 2:13). Yahweh hopes that his people will reform their lives, so that 'I may change my mind about the disaster that I intend' (Jer. 26:3).

However, there are equally numerous passages about Yahweh not changing his mind. 'God is not a human being, that he should lie, or a mortal, that he should change his mind' (Num. 23:19). 'The LORD has sworn and will not change his mind' (Ps. 110:4). Yahweh swore an oath to David 'from which he will not turn back' (Ps. 132:11). Because of the sin of his people Yahweh promised: 'I have not relented nor will I turn back' (Jer. 4:28). Equally Ezekiel states: 'I the LORD have spoken; the time is coming, I will act. I will not refrain, I will not spare, I will not relent. According to your ways and your doings I will judge you, says the LORD God' (Ezek. 24:14; see Zech. 8:14).

The classic passage, which brings into relief the whole discussion, is 1 Samuel 15. Here Yahweh 'regrets' and 'is sorry' that he had made Saul king, for he has turned away (1 Sam. 15:11, 35). And yet, in the very same chapter, Samuel states: 'Moreover the Glory of Israel will not recant or change his mind; for he is not a mortal, that he should change his mind' (1 Sam. 15:29).

I have quoted these passages not just to highlight the biblical dilemma over Yahweh's impassible or passible nature, but more to illustrate that there needs to be an interpretative or hermeneutical tool for bringing consistency to them. To interpret these statements on the same level, that is, to say that God, in one and the same manner, does and does not change his mind is to predicate of God something which necessarily demands an irreconcilable contradiction. However, if the seemingly contradictory statements are attempting to say different things about God on different levels then both could be true without contradiction.

In the passages that speak of Yahweh changing his mind, the first thing to notice is that this is predicated upon or conditioned by a change in the people involved. God is sorry because the human race or Saul have become sinful. He relents because the Ninevites or the Hebrew people have repented. One could argue then that the change takes place in others – their sin or repentance – but that a change does not take place in

God. He remains unchanging and unchangeable.[29] However, this does not arrive at the heart of the matter, for Yahweh, in his holiness, truly does 'react' to sin, and in his mercy, he does 'respond' to repentance. The question is: Does this 'reaction' necessarily imply that he passibly changes?

Is not the 'reaction' an expression of a deeper truth – that of his unchanging and unalterable love for his people and of his demand for moral rectitude? In a sense God is said 'to change his mind' precisely because, as the Wholly Other, 'he does not change his mind.' The interpretative tool here is the same as that articulated throughout. The very language that is used, being 'sorry,' 'relenting,' 'repenting,' and 'changing' of mind seeks to express Yahweh's unswerving and unalterable love which is expressed in his compassion, mercy and forgiveness, and equally, that he is adamant in his demand for goodness and justice. Yahweh then is sorry that he appointed Saul not just because Saul had changed, but he is equally sorry because he, as God, has not changed. The sorrow is an expression of the fact that 'the Glory of Israel will not recant or change his mind; for he is not a mortal, that he should change his mind.' The All Holy God consistently demands righteousness and this very consistency is expressed in his sorrow. Thus the statement that God does not change his mind is an expression of God's total otherness, and the statement that God does change his mind expresses this unchangeable mind of God under circumstances which, under ordinary human conditions (if God were man), would demand that a change of mind take place, but in actual fact need not, because God, as the Wholly Other, is constant in his love, forgiveness, righteousness and justice. 'God is not a human being, that he should lie, or a mortal, that he should change his mind' (Num. 23:19).

Ontological or Ethical Immutability?

The crucial question at this juncture is: Have I shown, from biblical evidence, that God is ontologically immutable or ethically immutable? That is, is God ontologically incapable of undergoing passionate changes, such as going from anger to repentance, grieving to joy, sorrow to forgiveness? Or, is God ethically immutable, in that he is consistently true to himself and to his perfect love and justice, and this is manifested in his changeable and passible actions and reactions to our various human conditions? Thus, while God may be ethically unchangeable in his moral rectitude, is he ontologically changeable as witnessed by his changing passible states, such as, anger, repentance, forgiveness, grieving, joy and suffering?[30]

---

29 R. Rice criticizes such an interpretation as being unfaithful to the intent of the texts, that is, that God does actually change his mind (see *The Openness of God*, pp. 26–29. Also see p. 33 for Rice's interpretation of what it means for God not to change his mind.

30 In his *Divine Immutability: A Critical Reconsideration*, I.A. Dorner may have been the first theologian to argue that the biblical notion of God expresses an ethical understanding of his immutability and not an ontological understanding. God remains immutable in his self-identity as the all-loving God and changes in his vital and active relationship to human history.

I obviously have been arguing for the former, and I have been arguing for it from within a biblical setting. I believe that the singular passion of God's love, compassion, mercy, forgiveness, anger, etc., as witnessed in the Hebrew scriptures, demands that his passionate love, compassion, mercy, forgiveness, anger, etc. be that of the Wholly Other, for these passions themselves arise out of and testify to his total otherness. To

> *This self-identity and ethical immutability are precisely the reason that he does not always behave in a simply identical way toward mutable humankind,* but that change enters both into his act and even into his attitude toward humanity. According to the Old Testament (as well as to the New Testament), it is not that through sin only the relation of men to God is altered while God's relation to men remains simply the same. To be sure, the latter has a self-identity in that it contains the purely ethical character; but this ethical immutability, in its living relation to each moment of creaturely life, to its value or disvalue, is the basis of continual alterations in the way in which God is disposed toward mutable man (p. 180). See also pp. 160–95.

Many others have since followed Dorner's lead. For example, K. Barth acknowledges his indebtedness to him (see *Church Dogmatics* II/1, p. 493). Barth argues at length that God's immutability consists in his constancy in that God is always faithful to who he is in his divine freedom, love and life. Thus the biblical notion of God portrays God as constantly changing in accordance with historical and human situations – he becomes angry and repents – and yet all of these changes bear witness to his constancy and faithfulness. 'His constancy consists in the fact that he is always the same in every change' (*ibid.*, p. 496). Thus 'God's constancy – which is a better word than the suspiciously negative word "immutability" – is the constancy of his knowing, willing and acting and therefore of his person' (*ibid.*, p. 495). See *ibid.*, pp. 490–512.

Similarly, Rem B. Edwards states: 'There is an infinite conceptual difference between the claim that (1) God does not change *with respect to his goodness or righteousness* (which was the Biblical view of the perfection and unchangeableness of God) and the claim that (2) God does not change *in any conceivable respect whatsoever* (which was the Greek view of the nature of divine perfection),' 'The Pagan Dogma of the Absolute Unchangeableness of God', *Religious Studies* 14 (1978):306.

See also Brasnett, *The Suffering of the Impassible God*, pp. 6, 14, 18, 91–98; Fretheim, *The Suffering of God*, p. 31; Küng, *The Incarnation of God*, p. 533; Pannenberg, *Basic Questions in Theology*, Vol. 2, pp. 161–62, 180, and his *Systematic Theology*, Vol. 1, pp. 436–38; Pollard, 'The Impassibility of God,' 360; Rice, *The Openness of God*, pp. 46–50; Swinburne, *The Coherence of Theism*, pp. 219–23; T.F. Torrance, *The Christian Doctrine of God*, pp. 235–46; van Beeck, 'This Weakness of God's is Stronger,' p. 11; and Ward, *Religion and Creation*, pp. 186–91.

The obvious motivation behind these theologians is to maintain both God's goodness and love, and his vital interaction with and in the world. Ethical immutability seems to allow both and there is no doubt that Yahweh is revealed within the Hebrew scriptures as ethically immutable. However, by making God merely ethically immutable, it is difficult to see what is the metaphysical foundation for his immutable goodness and love. These are merely posited because God always acts in a perfectly good manner; but why does he always so act? By denying the ontological unchangeable perfection of God, his goodness and love are no longer truly rooted in what God actually *is*. While I will discuss this more fully later, must he not be ethically immutable in his love and goodness, because he is ontologically unchangeable in his perfection? As von Balthasar has stated:

> Such forms of the eternal divine life as mercy, patience, and so on, can be understood on the analogy of human emotions, but this must not involve attributing 'mutability' to God. Nor is it correct – and many Catholic theologians have followed Protestant theologians in this – to restrict God's immutability to his attitude of covenant faithfulness within the dispensation he has established: the Bible, in both Old and New Testaments, looks *through* his attitude and discerns beyond it a quality of the Divinity as such. *Theo-Drama V*, p. 226.

make God passible in his passion, I believe, undercuts the wholly otherness of God, and so diminishes the biblical, and so divine, significance of his passion or pathos (to use Heschel's term). However, because the Bible does not address the philosophical issues which now loom large, a complete and thorough demonstration has not been possible.[31] Nonetheless, I believe the biblical foundation which I have laid, that is, that Yahweh is present and active within the created order as the Wholly Other without diminishing his wholly otherness, actually leads to and demands a philosophical argument for the ontological impassibility of God.

Moreover, to make God ontologically mutable may disallow him to do things that he also is revealed to do – like being the All Holy Creator and Savior. As we will see, by making God merely ethically immutable, these and similar theologians cannot adequately address other philosophical and revelational issues involving God.

It should also be noted that I have not discussed the two classic references to God's unchangeability – Malachi 3:6 ('I the LORD do not change') and James 1:17 ('Every generous act of giving, with every perfect gift, is from above, coming down from the Father of lights, with whom there is no variation or shadow due to change.') The reason is that I did not wish to base my argument, as has been done in the past, on a couple of 'proof texts,' but rather on the whole of the Old Testament revelation of who God is. Moreover, these texts could be interpreted, as is now normally the case, as expressing God's ethical goodness, that is, his unchanging faithfulness. This may be the correct interpretation, but the real issue is not just how these passages are interpreted, but rather what is the ground in which God's unchanging faithfulness is rooted.

It should be noted as well that those who argue for a passible understanding of God have their own set of biblical 'proof texts.' The problem is that they also interpret these texts too narrowly and so do not interpret them within the context of the whole of biblical revelation of who God is. By attempting to place the biblical notion of God within the entire context of the Bible, I have tried to avoid this narrow interpretation of 'proof texts' as has been done in the past for the impassibility of God and is now being done in the present for his passibility.

31 My biblical interpretation has consistently pushed the argument for supporting the ontological impassibility of God to the limits, but I have tried hard not to allow my interpretation to exceed the biblical warrant and so slip into philosophy. Because of this, while my biblical arguments, I believe, lead to, support, and will ultimately demand a God who is ontologically impassible and not just ethically unchangeable, they do not absolutely prove this. The reason is simply that, while biblical revelation cannot be contradicted and while it can govern, support, and even demand specific philosophical orientations and interpretations, of itself it cannot answer the philosophical issues that arise from but are not fully addressed by it.

Addendum: A. Heschel
and Divine 'Pathos'

As was noted in Chapter 1, Heschel's exposition of divine 'pathos' within the writings of the Hebrew prophets has greatly influenced many contemporary theologians who espouse a passible and suffering God. Because of this, and because I do not think that these theologians have interpreted Heschel in an entirely correct manner, I wish to present here a brief addendum and critique of his thought.

Heschel, throughout his study, stresses that the prophetic knowledge of God was not abstract, philosophic, syllogistic, or speculative. Rather, the prophets obtained their knowledge of God through their interaction and fellowship with the living God.[32] Within this relationship 'pathos' became the central category for their understanding God. Thus Heschel can describe divine pathos as follows:

> He [God] is also moved and affected by what happens to the world, and reacts accordingly. Events and human actions arouse in him joy or sorrow, pleasure or wrath. He is not conceived as judging the world in detachment. He reacts in an intimate and subjective manner, and this determines the value of events. Quite obviously in the biblical view, man's deeds may move him, affect him, grieve him or, on the other hand, gladden and displease him. This notion that God can be intimately affected, that he possesses not merely intelligence and will, but also pathos, basically defines the prophetic consciousness of God.[33]

It would appear that Heschel is here advocating a passible understanding of God. While he emphasizes, as do many others, that human deeds and situations do not necessitate God's pathos, but only offer the occasion for God freely to bestow his pathos, yet he equally emphasizes that 'the predicament of man is a predicament of God who has a stake in the human situation.'[34] Heschel clearly contrasts this biblical view of

---

32 For example, see *The Prophets*, pp. 221–23, 231.
33 *The Prophets*, p. 224.
34 *The Prophets*, p. 226. See p. 225. Because of God's intimate relationship to humankind, Heschel is critical of referring to God as 'the Wholly Other.' He interprets such a designation as implying a 'strange, weird, uncanny Being, shrouded in unfathomable darkness.' Such a God would be 'the Remote One' and 'the Silent One' (pp. 226–28).

God's pathos with that of the Greek philosophical notion of God's self-sufficiency and apathy, which, he believes, has come to dominate both Jewish and Christian thought down to the present.[35] Divine pathos, for Heschel, demands that 'the grandeur of God implies the capacity to experience emotion. . . . It [pathos] finds its deepest expression in the fact that God can actually suffer. At the heart of the prophetic affirmation is the certainty that God is concerned about the world.'[36]

It is this understanding of divine pathos that many contemporary theologians embrace. However, it is at this point in Heschel's exposition that a shift occurs, a shift that theologians have failed to acknowledge or appreciate. Indeed, even Heschel himself may have failed fully to consider its significance.

Heschel rightly maintains that the prophets, the psalmists and the authors of the Wisdom literature show no apprehension that their portrayal of divine pathos in any way jeopardizes the one, unique and transcendent God. This fear has arisen because divine pathos has been understood in an anthropomorphic or anthropopathic sense, that is, that God can actually be conceived in literal human terms. However, such an interpretation, Heschel argues, was utterly foreign to the biblical mentality. 'Since the human could never be regarded as divine, there was no danger that the language of pathos would distort the difference between God and man.'[37] Therefore, according to Heschel, the term 'anthropopathy' should not be applied to the prophetic understanding of divine pathos.

> The term applies properly to religions in which there is no discrepancy between imagination and expression: the gods are conceived of as human beings and described as human beings – in their appearance, their way of life, their passions, their occupations. These are myths and images. In contrast, the biblical man's imagination knows nothing about God, how he lives and what occupies him. He is God and not man (Hos. 11:9, Is. 31:3).[38]

Here we discern the shift in Heschel's exposition. Yes, God does

---

While I agree that such an interpretation can be given to the phrase 'the Wholly Other,' yet I do not think that such an interpretation is necessitated by the concept itself. I too would want to exclude from this designation those characteristics that Heschel gives to it. I have attempted to use it only to specify that God is distinct from, and so other than, the created order, something that Heschel would himself uphold.

35 See *The Prophets*, pp. 232–35, 247–67. It should be said that much of Heschel's critique of the various Greek philosophical understandings of God and their notion of apathy is not only correct but also insightful. The difficulty is in his not properly discerning how Christian and Jewish theologians, while using the same 'Greek' vocabulary, have radically transformed the meaning of such words in the light of the biblical revelation. I will attempt to demonstrate this in subsequent chapters.

In the light of the Hebrew understanding of divine pathos, Heschel is equally critical of other non-biblical notions of God, such as the Tao, Karma, Moira, and the Greek pagan gods. See pp. 235–46.

36 *The Prophets*, p. 259. This biblical notion of God is incompatible with the conception of God as a Supreme Being who is unmoved and unchangeable. See pp. 260–67.

37 *The Prophets*, p. 270.

38 *The Prophets*, p. 270.

possess pathos, but it cannot be conceived in any anthropomorphic or anthropopathic manner. 'The error in regarding the divine pathos as anthropomorphism consisted in regarding a unique theological category as a common psychological concept. This was due to the complex nature of prophetic language, which of necessity combines otherness and likeness, uniqueness and comparability, in speaking about God.'[39] The difficulty is that human beings more easily perceive the similarities between divine and human pathos rather than being cognisant of the radical dissimilarities. However, to conceive God's pathos in such a manner is 'a form of humanization of God, [and so] the profound significance of this fundamental category is lost.'[40] The true significance of divine pathos lies precisely, for Heschel, in its dissimilarity for this is what makes God's pathos truly divine and unique. Statements of divine pathos must not be lowered to the human level, but raised to a 'super-human' level. Words expressing divine pathos, while psychological in nature, are 'endowed with a theological connotation. In the biblical expressions of divine emotions ... the religious consciousness experiences a sense of superhuman power rather than a conception of resemblance to man.'

> The idea of the divine pathos combining absolute selflessness with supreme concern for the poor and the exploited can hardly be regarded as the attribution of human characteristics. Where is the man who is endowed with such characteristics? Nowhere in the Bible is man characterized as merciful, gracious, slow to anger, abundant in love and truth, keeping love to the thousandth generation. Pathos is a thought that bears a resemblance to an aspect of divine reality as related to the world of man. As a theological category, it is a genuine insight into God's relatedness to man, rather than a projection of human traits into divinity, as found for example in the god images of mythology.[41]

For Heschel, one must neither anesthetize God as did Greek philosophy, nor must one humanize God through anthropomorphism. This is why Heschel, concerning the latter, emphasizes that God's pathos is not man's pathos. It is here that many contemporary theologians fail to recognize the significance of what Heschel is actually saying. They consistently interpret Heschel's idea that God's pathos is not human pathos as indicating the similarity between God and man. Both God and man are characterized by pathos. In actual fact, Heschel uses the idea to emphasize the dissimilarity between God and man. God's pathos *is not* man's pathos, and therefore God is different from man. 'The prophets had to use anthropomorphic language in order to convey his nonanthropomorphic Being. . . . It is precisely the challenge involved in using inadequate words that drives the mind beyond all

---

39 *The Prophets*, p. 270.
40 *The Prophets*, p. 270.
41 *The Prophets*, p. 271. See pp. 272–74.

words. Any pretension to adequacy would be specious and a delusion.'[42]

While I believe that there are ambiguities and tensions within Heschel's understanding of divine pathos which allow contemporary theologians to use him for their own purposes, I also believe that the heart of what he wishes to say can be discerned, and that it is logically coherent. On the one hand, Heschel wishes to uphold the true biblical notion that God is attentive to human history and is intimately involved within the lives of human beings. He is not like the God of Greek philosophy. His pathos is expressed in his love, kindness, mercy and compassion – even to the point of speaking, as Heschel and the Bible do, of his grief and suffering. On the other hand, Heschel, equally faithful to biblical revelation, does not want such pathos to be conceived in an anthropomorphic manner, as if to attribute such characteristics of God, one were saying that God's pathos – his love, compassion, grief and suffering – could be conceived in a psychological manner similar to that of humans. For Heschel, it is precisely the otherness of God's pathos which gives it its true and full significance. This, I believe, is quite in conformity with what I have attempted to articulate in the present chapter. Through his immanent activity as the Creator, the Savior and the Sanctifier, God reveals, in these very immanent actions, that he is the One, All Holy God who transcends, and so is other than, the created and historical order. It is precisely the utterly transcendent component contained within these immanent actions that confers upon them their unique and unparalleled significance. Moreover, similar to Heschel, I stated in the body of the chapter that it is precisely the extravagant nature of God's passion/pathos which reveals its transcendent, divine origin. Heschel, in his turn, is but using the prophetic concept of divine pathos as the heuristic tool for discerning and articulating this same understanding. It is the immanent expression of divine pathos that manifests its transcendent ('superhuman' and 'nonanthropomorphic') nature.[43]

While I am confident that this is Heschel's true position, he is inconsistent in the manner in which he expresses it. The tension within Heschel resides in his often speaking, despite his later disclaimers, as if God's pathos is similar to human pathos, that is, his pathos is not merely experienced by humans in a psychological and emotional manner, but it is also experienced within himself in a psychological and emotional manner, as if God undergoes psychological and emotional changes. Thus God psychologically and emotionally experiences suffering and grief. It is this that contemporary theologians have borrowed from Heschel, but it is an appropriation that I am not convinced he would, in the end, wholeheartedly approve. While Heschel and I may have some disagreements, in intent and even content, I believe that, on the whole, I have more in common with him than do those who employ him to espouse a passible notion of God.

---

42 *The Prophets*, p. 276. See pp. 274–78.
43 H.U. von Balthasar interprets Heschel in a similar manner. He states that Heschel's understanding of divine pathos has 'nothing whatever to do with any mythological suffering, dying and rising God' (*Theo-Drama IV: The Action*, pp. 343–44, fn. 20)

The heart of the problem is that Heschel does not possess, and so does not provide, a consistent philosophical account for how God's pathos can be expressed within the created and historical order without it ceasing to be truly divine. I hope to provide such a philosophical account.

4

Bridges to the Patristic Doctrine of God

In the previous chapter we examined the biblical, primarily the Hebrew, notion of God. We stressed that the Hebrew scriptures portray Yahweh as the All Holy Creator and Savior. As such he is wholly other than all else that exists, and yet, precisely because he is the Creator and Savior, he is present to the created order and active within time and history. In this chapter we will examine two 'bridges' to the Fathers and to the subsequent Christian tradition, that is, (1) those passages about God within the New Testament which contain within them a philosophical character; and (2) Philo of Alexandria's understanding of God. This chapter will then set the religious context and philosophical milieu out of which the early church developed its own doctrine of God and of his relationship to the created order.

New Testament Bridges

The New Testament is not devoid of words and concepts that are also common among ancient philosophy. Grant notes that the New Testament contains '"bridges" toward philosophical doctrines of God.'[1]

These 'bridges' cluster around the New Testament's evangelistic and apologetic appeal to the Gentiles that the true God is the One Creator God. Echoing the Book of Wisdom, Paul states that the pagans have no excuse for not knowing God. 'Ever since the creation of the world his eternal/everlasting (ἀίδιος) power (δύναμις) and divine nature (θειότης), invisible (ἀόρατα) though they are, have been understood and seen through the things he has made' (Rom. 1:20; see Wis. 13:1–9; Sir. 17:8). Visible creation itself testifies to the power of the everlasting divine nature both of which are invisible. The pagans had 'exchanged the glory of the immortal (ἀφθάρτου) God for images resembling a mortal (φθαρτοῦ) human being' (Rom. 1:23). In the Pauline First Letter to Timothy, God is called 'the King of the ages, immortal (ἀφθάρτῳ), invisible (ἀοράτῳ), the only God' (1 Tim. 1:17). Equally in Acts, when the Lycaonians declared

---

1 R. Grant, *The Early Christian Doctrine of God* (Charlottesville: University Press of Virginia, 1966) p. 5. Grant refers to some of the Greek and Roman authors to which the New Testament may allude. See pp. 3–14. While I will be drawing somewhat different, but not contrary, conclusions than Grant, I am indebted to him for specifying the following New Testament texts.

Paul and Barnabas to be gods (Zeus and Hermes respectively), due to the healing of a cripple, Paul protested that they were only mortal, and that the people should instead 'turn from worthless things to the living God, who made the heaven and the earth and the sea and all that is in them' (Acts 14:15). Moreover, it is this living God who governs the heavens and the seasons of the year (see Acts 14:16). Similarly, in Paul's famous speech in the Areopagus he declared to the Athenians a knowledge of 'an unknown god' who 'made the world and everything in it, he who is Lord of heaven and earth' and so does not live in shrines made by human hands, nor then, 'is he served by human hands, as though he needed anything, since he himself gives to all mortals life and breath and all things' (Acts 17:23–25). Moreover, in 1 Corinthians 8:4–6, Paul contrasts the unreality of the many pagan gods with the reality of the one God. While he quotes the *Shema* of Deuteronomy 6:4, the one God of the Judeo/Christian faith is nonetheless a 'bridge' to the one God of contemporary Greek philosophy. This one God is the Father 'from whom are all things and for whom we exist, and one Lord, Jesus Christ through whom are all things and through whom we exist.' Romans 11:36 also declares that all things are 'from,' 'through' and 'to' God. It is as Creator that God manifests his inscrutable wisdom and knowledge, and therefore no one can give to him something that he does not already possess (see vv. 33–35). Equally, God has given us 'all things that pertain to life and godliness,' and in contrast to the perishability of this life, Christians come to share in the divine nature, which, it is presumed, is imperishable (2 Pet. 1:4, see 1 Pet. 1:3–6).

Even the Gospels seem to appeal to a common cultural philosophic view of God. Only the one God is good (see Mk 19:18; Mt 19:17; Lk 18:19). Human beings are called to be perfect as God himself is perfect (see Mt 5:48); the implication being that God is all perfect.

The above passages are attempting to do a number of things simultaneously, some stressing one aspect more than another. First, there is the contrast between the many 'dead' and 'unreal' gods with the one living God of the Judeo/Christian tradition. This contrast not only undercuts the popular Greco-Roman pagan religion, but simultaneously provides a 'bridge' to Platonic and Aristotelian philosophy. It is an apologetic appeal which severs what is utterly false and, simultaneously, provides a link with what is basically true – there are not many gods, but only one God.

Before proceeding to the second point, I would like to make a small digression. Since we will be noting some of the similarities and dissimilarities between the scriptural and Greek notions of God and of his relationship to the world, both in this and later chapters, it would be good at this point to outline briefly their respective understandings of God and of his relation to the world.

Scholars debate whether or not Plato conceived God as personal. 'The Good' is at the apex of his metaphysical hierarchy, and it would seem to denote the supreme metaphysical principle rather than a personal being. The 'Demiurge', on the other hand, is often spoken of in personal terms. He is perfect in every way (and so unchanging, for to change would be change for the worse), and is the intermediary between the Good (and the realm of the ideal Forms) and the finite realm. As such he can be seen as Plato's 'God'. However, he is not the Creator, but 'the Maker' or 'Reason' who orders and fashions pre-existent chaotic matter so as to conform it to the eternal Forms or Ideas. At times then the Demiurge is seen almost as impersonal Reason (Nous) immanent within the world conforming it to the ideal Forms. Whether the Demiurge is envisaged as a personal being or as an impersonal metaphysical principle, he is nonetheless, as an intermediary, subject to and controlled by both the eternal Good (and all lesser Forms and Ideas) and by pre-existent matter. (On the above see Plato's *Timaeus*.) Because Plato perceives matter as 'evil,' since it never conforms fully to the transcendent Forms or Ideas (the Good), and thus to the Truth, there is a chasm between 'God' or 'the Good' and everything else, that is, between the realm of immutable Goodness and Truth and the ever-changing realm of becoming. The relationship between the unchanging ideal realm of the eternal Forms and the changing world of matter is, therefore, always problematic for Plato.

For Aristotle God is absolutely perfect, and so unchanging since he need not change for the better and cannot change for the worse. He is defined as 'Self-Thinking Thought' for 'thinking' is the highest expression of being and the most perfect thing he could think about is himself. Thus God knows nothing outside of himself since he would then be thinking of that which is imperfect, which would be unbecoming of the most perfect being. Aristotle never addressed the question of creation, but he was concerned about how pre-existent matter could be set in motion since it is mere potency. How does the process of going from potency to act begin and continue? Matter is set in motion, and so actuates its potential, by being attracted by the immutable perfection of God. God is the Unmoved Mover in that he sets in motion all else, not by an action on his part, but by his mere perfect and unchangeable presence as the Final Cause, the perfect attraction which draws all else to become as he is. He is like a transcendent 'Big Mac' that attracts the hungry (the world) into action so as to obtain it. Being the Final Cause, God is present to the world, but only as that which attracts the world. He himself is not conscious of the world nor does he act within the world for to do so would jeopardize his immutable perfection. (On the above see Aristotle's *Metaphysics*, Book XII.)

While the Neoplatonism of Plotinus (c. AD205–70) comes after the period we are considering here in this chapter, it would be good, for the sake of completeness, to briefly summarize it as well. Plotinus sees the One as the unknowable source of all else. The Νοῦς (Intelligence) and Soul emanate out from the One as do all the lesser beings. Thus, while all other beings are related to the One in so far as they emanate out from the One, nonetheless, precisely because they do emanate out from the One, there is a chasm or gulf between the One and the lesser emanations.[2]

---

2 For studies on Plato's, Aristotle's, and Plotinus' understanding of God see the standard histories of Greek Philosophy, such as F. Copleston, *The History of Philosophy*, Vol. 1 (New York: Doubleday, 1962); and M.J. Walsh, *A History of Philosophy* (London: Geoffrey Chapman, 1985), pp. 23–74. See also C. Stead, *Philosophy in Christian Antiquity* (Cambridge: Cambridge University Press, 1994), pp. 14–39, 54–75; and G. Watson, *Greek Philosophy and the Christian Notion of God* (Dublin: The Columba Press, 1994), pp. 18–87.

As we will see Philo and the Fathers also maintain that God is other than all else (transcendent), that he is unchanging in his absolute perfection, and therefore, that he cannot undergo passionate changes, such as sorrow, anger, and suffering. However, Philo and, to a greater degree, the Fathers (some more than others) will radically transform this Hellenic view of God. The catalyst for this 'baptism,' as will become evident, is the biblical view of the act of creation. As Creator, God must be personal and have a relationship to the world and, being perfectly good, he must be concerned about and active within his creation. How God can be unchangeable and impassible in his perfection, and yet be the Creator in all that this entails is obviously the question at hand.

Second, the vocabulary and concepts that are used to form the bridge between the Christian proclamation of the one God and that of philosophy are often similar. Akin to much Greek philosophical thought, the Christian God is one, invisible, imperishable, all powerful, all perfect, all good, and everlasting or eternal.[3]

However, third, it is precisely the notion of God as being the Creator that sets the Judeo/Christian God apart from traditional Hellenic philosophy. In contrast to Plato and Aristotle, the one God of the Judeo/Christian faith is the Father, 'from whom are all things and for whom we exist, and one Lord, Jesus Christ, through whom are all things and through whom we exist' (1 Cor. 8:6). Unlike any Greek philosophy, God the Father is the Creator from whom all receive their existence, and this existence comes through Jesus Christ. Moreover, as Creator, the Father is neither far from nor disinterested in the finite realm, nor is Jesus then the cosmic intermediary who unites the cosmos to the divine realm. Rather, Jesus is the Word through whom and in whom the Father calls creation into existence (see Jn 1:1–5; Heb. 1:1–3; 1 Cor. 8:6; Col. 1:15–20).

Fourth, all the attributes predicated of God focus on his being the Creator. It is because he is the invisible Creator that he possesses imperishability, absolute perfection and goodness, and all power; and he needs to possess them if he is to be the Creator. There is here a significant difference between the Greek view of God and his attributes and the Christian view of God and his attributes. Within Greek thought these attributes constitute God as one who is removed from, even if related to, all else that is. They constitute him as transcendent in the sense of not only making him other than the cosmic order, but also as often being incapable of actively relating to the cosmic order. Within the Judeo/Christian tradition these attributes do constitute God as wholly other than all else, but they equally constitute him as Creator and so immediately related to all else that is.

Thus, in contrast to creation, God is all-powerful, invisible, everlasting, and imperishable. In the light of these attributes these passages note that God is therefore in need of nothing since all depend on him for

---

3 R. Grant even sees James' appeal that within God 'there is no variation or shadow due to change' (Jas 1:17) as 'influenced by Hellenistic rhetoric' (*The Early Christian Doctrine of God*, p. 10). If Grant is correct, the Letter of James would not just be proposing the ethical immutability of God, but rather his ontological unchangeableness.

their very existence and all the gifts that flow from it. It is only a small philosophical step to conclude that God is therefore absolutely perfect in his goodness, but his perfection is founded not upon his withdrawal from the world, but upon his ability to create as found in the Hebrew tradition. Here we find both a contrast and a 'bridge' to Greek philosophy. While both the New Testament and Platonic/Aristotelian philosophy would hold that God is perfect, the New Testament upholds this attribute because God must be perfect as the Creator of a good world, whereas Greek philosophy tends to hold that God is perfect because he is removed from the imperfect world of materiality. Equally, while both Platonic and Aristotelian thought would agree that God and his power are everlasting and invisible, what is different is that what is invisible (the everlasting God and his power) is manifested in the visible effects of God's power – creation.

It is the concept of creation then, with its one Creator God, that separates Christianity from popular pagan religion, and offers a bridge to Greek philosophy, but a bridge that simultaneously conveys the Greek God from Athens to Jerusalem and, in the crossing, baptizes him into the likeness of the God of Israel.

Finally, there is one further significant point that must be grasped. The New Testament proclaims that Jesus, the Son, is also the Creator along with the Father. Moreover, it intrinsically joins the notion of Jesus as Creator with that of his equally being the supreme revelation of the Father. Jesus himself, as Creator and Revealer, can be seen, not as a linguistic or conceptual 'bridge' to Greek philosophy, but as a personal 'bridge.'

> In the beginning was the Word [Logos], and the Word was with God, and the Word was God. He was in the beginning with God, and without him not one thing came into being. . . . And the Word became flesh and lived among us, and we have seen his glory, the glory as a father's only son. . . . No one has ever seen God. It is God the only Son, who is close to the Father's heart, who has made him known. Jn 1:1–3, 14, 18.

The eternal Son, as the Logos of God, is the one through whom the Father creates. Like the Father he is then other than the world, yet as man he is the supreme revelation of the Father. The Son, through whom God has now spoken is the same one 'through whom he also created the world. He is the reflection of God's glory and the exact imprint of God's very being, and he sustains all things by his powerful word' (Heb. 1:1–3).

Jesus, the 'image of the invisible God' (Col. 1:15), who, as the Logos, is 'co-Creator' with the Father, appropriates to himself then all the attributes of the Father – power, goodness, imperishability, invisibility, eternity – that is, all of which is common to much of the Greek understanding of God and so offers a 'bridge,' and simultaneously a 'correction,' for as Creator he is present to creation and as Revealer he is visibly active within time and history. Jesus, as Creator and Revealer, unites within his very person the understanding of God as wholly other than the world and yet one who acts within the world in his wholly otherness. Jesus is the ultimate bridge to Greek philosophy, but one that radically transforms it.[4]

Philo of Alexandria

Philo (c. 20BC–c. AD40), the Alexandrian Jewish philosopher, had an immense formative influence on the early patristic tradition. He was fundamentally an interpreter of the Hebrew scriptures, primarily the Pentateuch. Moreover, he philosophically exemplifies what many scholars today refer to as Middle Platonism; though he was also influenced by Aristotelianism and Stoicism.[5] It was within this philosophical context that he interpreted the Hebrew scriptures, and so he may also be considered a 'bridge' between the biblical and Greek notions of God.[6] As a 'bridge' between biblical revelation and Greek philosophy, Philo also became a 'bridge' to the Fathers, for they attempted to emulate his example and further his rapprochement in the light of the gospel.

For many contemporary theologians, however, his is a counterfeit and deceptive 'bridge,' for he built his bridge, they claim, not from the scrip-

---

4 What is evident here is that the New Testament notion of revelation, surprisingly, also offers a 'bridge' to Greek philosophy. Greek philosophy was ultimately concerned about knowledge of God and humankind's relationship to God. However, because God is transcendent he cannot be present to or act within the world. Whatever knowledge of God humans are able to obtain is from their own philosophical efforts. The Christian notion of revelation supports the transcendence of God since what is revealed is from God himself, who is other than all else. Yet, while what is revealed is from the transcendent God and so not of human origin and so not a human philosophy (see 1 Thes. 1:4-5; 1 Cor. 1:17—2:16; 2 Cor. 5:16–19), it is nonetheless truly revelation for God reveals it to humankind through the words and actions of his Son, Jesus Christ, within time and history. The New Testament notion of revelation, in contrast to its understanding of creation, does not offer words and concepts that might be philosophical 'bridges,' but rather it offers a person, Jesus – the supreme revelation of God – as a bridge to Greek philosophy and its concerns. As R. Grant states:

> We conclude that for the theologians of the earliest church all cosmological statements are ultimately Christological, the knowledge of God that man can infer from the cosmos by itself is inadequate and, apart from God's self-revelation in Christ, bound to lead to idolatry. *The Early Christian Doctrine of God*, p. 13.

The Apologists, such as Justin Martyr, would develop this idea. While the Greeks may have had some knowledge of God through the *logos spermatikos* (the seed of the word), Christians have the full knowledge of God for the Logos himself has become man and revealed it to them.

5 For studies of Philo and Middle Platonism see: H. Chadwick, 'Philo' in *The Cambridge History of Greek and Early Medieval Philosophy*, ed. A.H. Armstrong (Cambridge: Cambridge University Press, 1970), pp. 135–57; J. Dillon, *The Middle Platonists: A Study of Platonism 80 B.C.–A.D. 220* (London: Duckworth, 1977); E.R. Goodenough, *An Introduction to Philo Judaeus* (Oxford: Basil Blackwell, 1962); Hallman, *The Descent of God*, pp. 23–31; S. Sandmel, *Philo of Alexandria* (New York: Oxford University Press, 1979); J. Sanders, 'Historical Considerations' in *The Openness of God*, pp. 69–72; Stead, *Philosophy in Christian Antiquity*, pp. 54–62; Watson, *Greek Philosophy and the Christian Notion of God*, pp. 52–67; H.A. Wolfson, *Philo*, 2 Vols (Cambridge, MA: Harvard University Press, 1947).

6 Following the philosophical tradition of interpreting Homer allegorically, Philo introduced the allegorical interpretation of the Pentateuch. In this he hoped to harmoniously synthesize biblical revelation with Greek philosophy, believing that the truth discovered in each finds its source in one and the same God.

tures to philosophy, but from philosophy to the scriptures. They maintain that he was the first to be seduced by the Platonic understanding of God and so defiled the biblical notion.[7] This adulterated understanding was inherited by the Fathers and the subsequent Christian tradition to our day.

For Philo, there is a hierarchy of being at the summit of which is God who, as the active Creator cause of all, is 'the intellect of the universe, thoroughly unadulterated and thoroughly unmixed, superior to virtue and superior to science, superior even to abstract good or abstract beauty.'[8] He is self-existent, superior to the Good, more simple than the One, and more primordial than the Monad.[9] Since no name can ultimately be ascribed to 'the truly Existent,' Philo saw the divine name 'Yahweh' as a concession to human beings, and, relying on the Septuagint, understood it to mean: 'It is my nature to be, not to be described by name.'[10]

Philo, as is well known, is the first to write a treatise on the immutability of God. There he argued that unlike unstable creation, 'the Existent' is 'firm' in his existence. He is 'incorruptible,' 'imperishable,' 'everlasting,' 'endowed with all the virtues, and with all perfection, and with all happiness.'[11] Because God dwells 'in pure light,' he sees and comprehends all, 'even the future.'[12] God, as the 'creator of time' in so far as he is the creator of the world, exists outside time, and 'in eternity nothing is past and nothing is future, but everything is present only.'[13] He is 'uncreated, and the Being who has brought all other things to creation.'[14] The God who truly exists then cannot be compared

7 For a few of many examples, see R.E. Edwards, 'The Pagan Dogma of the Absolute Unchangeableness of God,' *Religious Studies* 14 (1978):305–13; Hallman, *The Descent of God*, pp. 23–29; Pollard, 'The Impassibility of God,'pp. 355–57; Sanders, *The Openness of God*, pp. 69–72.

8 Philo, *De Opificio Mundi*, 8. Translation from *The Works of Philo*, C.D. Yonge (Peabody: Hendrickson Publishers, 1993). J. Hallman in his historical study of the impassibility of God – *The Descent of God* – provides almost all of the relevant passages from Philo and the Fathers. While I am greatly indebted to his research, I have also found a few other relevant passages. For another survey of the scriptural, Jewish/Hellenic, and patristic thought on God's impassibility one should consult Mozley's classic study: *The Impassibility of God: A Survey of Christian Thought*.

9 See Philo, *De Vita Contemplativa*, 2. In saying that God was 'beyond the Monad,' Philo did not want to make God abstract and impersonal or even beyond being, but rather he wanted to ensure that God was not 'numbered' as the first in a series and so part of that series. As the Creator, God cannot be numbered with or placed within that which is created.

10 *De Mutatione Nominum*, 11, see 12–14. Yonge translates τὸ ὂν 'the living God.' I prefer the more literal and accurate translation – 'the Existent.'

11 *Quod Deus Immutabilis Sit*, 4, 18, 26, 32, and 142.

12 *Quod Deus Immutabilis Sit*, 29.

13 *Quod Deus Immutabilis Sit*, 30 and 32.

14 *Quod Deus Immutabilis Sit*, 56. God brought the universe 'out of non-existence (ἐκ μὴ ὄντων)' (*Legum Allegoriae*, III, 10). See also *De Fuga et Inventione*, 46 and *De Vita Mosis*, II, 267.

There has been much discussion among scholars as to whether or not Philo actually taught *creatio ex nihilo*. For a brief account of this discussion see E.F. Osborn, *The Philosophy of Clement of Alexandria* (Cambridge: Cambridge University Press, 1975), pp. 34–35; and G. May, *Creatio Ex Nihilo: The Doctrine of 'Creation out of Nothing' in Early Christian Thought* (Edinburgh: T & T Clark, 1994), pp. ix, 9–26.

to any species of created beings; but, dissociating it with any idea of distinctive qualities (for this is what most especially contributes to his [man's] happiness and to his consummate felicity, to comprehend his [God's] naked existence without any connection with figure or character), they, I say are content with the bare conception of his existence, and do not attempt to invest him with any form.'[15]

Thus, for Philo, it is the greatest 'wickedness' to think that 'the unchangeable God can be changed.'[16] God does not repent or become angry, or undergo emotional and passionate changes. 'God is utterly inaccessible to any passion whatever. For it is the peculiar property of human weakness to be disquieted by any such feelings, but God has neither the irrational passions of the soul, nor the parts and limits of the body in the least belonging to him.'[17] God is only said to become angry and to show passion for our instruction and correction.[18]

Obviously, Philo wants to uphold the complete wholly otherness of God. But has he gone too far? Has he made God and the world inaccessible to one another? Let us first enumerate his strengths and then his weaknesses.

First, some scholars have criticized Philo for translating God's name, Yahweh, in the impersonal neuter – τό ὄν ('That Which Is'). This appears to undermine the personalism of the biblical notion of God.[19] While there is some validity to this criticism in that it would have been biblically more sound to retain the ὁ ὤν ('He Who Is'), I do not believe that Philo necessarily wanted to weaken the personalism of the Hebrew and Septuagint rendering. Rather he wanted to intensify the biblical truth

---

May argues that Philo did not teach *creatio ex nihilo*.

He is so strongly dependent on the Platonist ontology that he cannot think of the creation of the world without the presupposition of a pre-existent material. He has not grasped the biblical conception of creation in its uniqueness, and therefore he cannot undertake the task of mediating it philosophically and fundamentally setting aside the Platonist doctrine of 'first principles.' p. 24.

May puts forth a very strong case. Nonetheless, while Philo may not have used that exact wording – *creatio ex nihilo* (in Greek, obviously), and while he is clearly ambiguous at times, I believe it is precisely this idea that he is striving to express. He argues, contrary to the philosophies of his day, that the world (and so, it would seem, matter) is not eternal. In contrast Philo maintains that the world was brought into existence by God. See for example, *De Opificio Mundi*, 7 and 8, 170 and 171; *De Confusione Linguarum*, 114; *De Somniis*, II, 283. In his treatise *De Aeternitate Mundi* Philo first sets forth the arguments for the creation of the world (13–19) and then gives all the arguments for its eternity (20–149). He concludes by stating that in a further work he will refute these last arguments (150). Unfortunately, he either never wrote this treatise or it is now lost.

15 *Quod Deus Immutabilis Sit*, 55.
16 *Quod Deus Immutabilis Sit*, 22. See 26. For further references to God's unchangeableness see, *De Cherubim*, 19; *Quaestiones et Solutiones in Genesin*, I, 93; *De Somniis*, II, 220.
17 *Quod Deus Immutabilis Sit*, 52. For Philo, we must take from our minds all that is created, mortal, changeable, and unconsecrated when 'regarding the uncreated God, immortal, unchangeable, and holy, the only God, blessed for ever.' *De Sacrificiis Abelis et Cain*, 102.
18 See *Quod Deus Immutabilis Sit*, 53.
19 For example see, Sanders, *The Openness of God*, p. 69 and fn. 31.

that God is the one who truly is, the 'living' God.[20] By naming God as τό ὄν Philo could more precisely accent that God was 'the Existent,' that is, that his very nature is 'to be,' and so more clearly designate him, in accordance with the Hebrew scriptures, as the Creator who is the author of all else that exists, and equally then that he cannot be placed among nor numbered with all else that exists.[21]

Second, by grasping that God could not be placed within a species, Philo rightly saw that God cannot be named among the things created and so, unlike all else, he cannot be fully comprehended. God's name reveals or 'names' him as the 'unnameable' or 'unknowable,' again in accordance with the scripture. 'His [God's] existence, indeed, is a fact which we do comprehend concerning him, but beyond the fact of his existence, we can understand nothing.'[22] God is comprehensible only to himself.[23]

Third, when speaking of God's immutability, Philo used this term to say more what God is not than what he is. It is an expression of his apophatic theology. It needs to be emphasized that all of Philo's examples of how God is unchangeable and impassible are in contrast to the created order and to human beings, and not positive statements of what God is in himself. The greater portion of his treatise on the unchangeability of God enumerates the ways in which human beings undergo passion and change, only then to differentiate these from the unchangeability of God. For example, human beings are fickle in their relationships, at one moment fervent friends only later to separate. Human beings are unable 'steadily to adhere to the professions which we originally made; but God is not so easily sated or wearied,' and thus, in his faithfulness, he could never have actually 'repented' of or 'regretted' creating humankind (see Gen. 6:50).[24] Moreover, unlike plants, God does not grow nor change with the seasons.[25] Furthermore, God created human beings with the dignity of a soul, and so with intelligence and freedom. Yet they are composed of parts which are in need, but God 'inasmuch as he is uncreated, and the Being who has brought all other things to creation, stood in need of none of those things which

---

20 Those who criticize Philo and the Septuagint for rendering the name 'Yahweh' as 'I Am Who Am' or 'He who/that Is' fail to grasp that to be the fulness of being does not render God immutably 'lifeless,' but immutably 'life-full.' This is what Philo believes is revealed and the Septuagint has rightly understood. We will discuss this more fully when we treat Aquinas' notion of God.

21 Philo's use of τὸ ὄν may be similar to my refering to God as 'the Wholly Other.' In calling God 'the Wholly Other,' I do not wish to undermine his personal nature, but to stress that he is completely distinct from, and so other than, all else that exists. He cannot be placed within the created order and so exists in a singular manner, that is, in an ontological order of his own.

22 *Quod Deus Immutabilis Sit*, 62. Also see *De Mutatione Nominum*, 7. While saying that we can know nothing of God beyond the fact of his existence, Philo does not mean that we literally know nothing other than that he exists. Rather he is emphasizing that we cannot comprehend what it means for God to exist. Through creation and especially through revelation we can obtain some knowledge of God. See Chadwick, *The Cambridge History of Later Greek and Early Medieval Philosophy*, pp. 148–50.

23 See *Legum Allegoriae*, III, 206, and *De Posteritate Caini*, 16 and 168.

24 *Quod Deus Immutabilis Sit*, 28. Also see *Quaestiones et Solutiones in Genesin*, I, 93.

25 See *Quod Deus Immutabilis Sit*, 37–40.

are usually added to creatures.'[26] Human beings not only become physically ill, but they also, in misusing their reason and freedom, have fallen prey to sin – 'anger,' 'intemperance,' 'cowardice,' 'injustice,' and 'impiety.'[27] Not only does God not participate in these corruptible and sinful attributes, but he rather is unchangeable in his goodness, love and mercy.

> God remembering his own perfect goodness in every particular, even if the whole or the greater part of mankind fall off from him by reason of the abundance and extravagance of their sins, stretching forth his right hand, his hand of salvation, supports man and raises him up, not permitting the whole race to be utterly destroyed and to perish everlastingly [for God] mingles mercy with his justice, which he exercises towards the good actions of even the unworthy; and he not only pities them while judging, but judges them while pitying them, for mercy is older than justice in his sight.[28]

Fourth, what we find in Philo, as the above exemplifies, is a denial of negative attributes in order to accentuate what is positive. God is immutable only in the sense that he does not undergo the changes that are inherent within the created order, and he is impassible only in the sense that he is not subject to or controlled by the appetites of a body and the sinful passions of the heart and mind as are human beings.[29] By disavowing of God all the negative changes within the world and all unreasonable and sinful passions of humankind, thus making him immutable and impassible, Philo has not made God aloof, static, unloving, and impersonal, which is the common cry of many contemporary theologians. Rather, such a denial actually allows him to intensify God's mercy, love, and providence as unchangeable in its utter perfection – this is why God does not 'regret' having made humankind.

What we see here is the birth of a distinction, unarticulated by Philo and probably unconscious, between the impassibility of God and what might be called the passion of God. Philo states that unlike the human race, which is subject to sorrow, grief and fear over present and expected evil, 'God is free from grief, and exempt from fear, and enjoys immunity from every kind of suffering, and is the only nature which possesses

---

26 *Quod Deus Immutabilis Sit*, 56, see 57. In *De Mutatione Nominum* Philo states that God, 'in as much as he is living, ... is full of himself, and is sufficient for himself, and he existed before the creation of the world, and equally after the creation of the universe; for he is immovable and unchangeable, having no need of any other thing or being whatever, so that all things belong to him, but, properly speaking, he does not belong to anything.' 27–8.

27 See *Quod Deus Immutabilis Sit*, 63–66, 70–71, and 112.

28 *Quod Deus Immutabilis Sit*, 73 and 76.

29 Almost as a refrain Philo states that 'God is not as man,' see *Quod Deus Immutabilis Sit*, 53, 62. It is sometimes argued that Philo, having been influenced by Stoicism, has a very negative view of human emotion and passion. There may be some truth to this, but it must be remembered that in this treatise he is discussing the negative aspects of human change and passion in order to show that God does not possess these. It is interesting that, while Philo denies the negative aspects of human emotion and passion, he nonetheless attributes to God those 'human' passions and emotions (virtues) which are good, such as mercy, justice and love.

complete happiness and blessedness.' And yet, Philo immediately continues: 'God is merciful, and compassionate, and kind, driving envy to a distance from him.'[30] God is impassible in that he does not undergo change of emotional states as do humans, but he is nonetheless utterly passionate in his love, mercy and goodness because, as the eternal and self-existing God, he is all perfect and unchanging in these attributes.[31] Implicitly for Philo, the attributes which establish that God is immutable and impassible – being imperishable, incorruptible, eternal, self-existent, and all perfect – are the same attributes which allow him to be the living, merciful, loving and providential Creator. As Philo states:

> But God has given nothing to himself, for he has no need of anything; but he has given the world to the world, and its parts he has bestowed on themselves and on one another, and also on the universe, and without having judged anything to be worthy of grace, (for he gives all his good things without grudging to the universe and to its parts), he merely has regard to his own everlasting goodness, thinking the doing of good to be a line of conduct suitable to his own happy and blessed nature; so that if any one were to ask me, what was the cause of the creation of the world, having learnt from Moses, I should answer, that the goodness of the living God, being the most important of his graces, is in itself the cause.[32]

These are not the words of a Platonist nor of an Aristotelian. They are the words of a faithful Jew who knew his scriptures. While God is wholly other than all else that exists, he is the good Creator who is present to and active within his good creation without ceasing to be the wholly other in so doing. Thus, as we saw in the Old and New Testaments, it is the notion of God as Creator, for Philo, which founds both the otherness of God from the created order and his intimate presence to and activity within the created order. What is becoming ever more evident is that the

---

30 *De Abrahamo*, 202 and 203.
31 J. Hallman notes that 'In spite of his adherence to the Hellenistic understanding that God is impassible and without emotion, not once in his entire corpus did Philo connect the technical term *apathes* or *apatheia* to God.' *The Descent of God*, pp. 23–24. The reason Philo never used these technical Greek terms may lie precisely in that, while he wanted to deny of God the negative changes and passions exemplified in the created order and human life, he did not want to deny the perfect passion of God. God may be impassible, but he is not completely devoid of passion, that is, he is not *apatheia*.

Most critics of Philo's treatise on God's unchangeability so completely miss this aspect of his thought that one wonders at times whether they have read anything other than the title and each others' criticisms. Hallman is aware that Philo allows for God to be loving, kind, and merciful. However, he wishes to interpret this as either Philo being inconsistent or that he allows for some possibility in God. What Hallman misses is that God's passionate love and mercy, for Philo, are not inconsistent with his being impassible. Actually, for Philo, God is supremely passionate in his love, because he is impassible with regards to all that would negate this love – such as emotional and passionate changes. See Hallman, *The Descent of God*, pp. 23–29, and also Sanders, *The Openness of God*, pp. 70–1.
32 *Quod Deus Immutabilis Sit*, 108. See also *De Mutatione Nominum*, 46; *Legum Allegoriae*, III, 68; and *De Opificio Mundi*, 23. What Philo fails to address is the deeper philosophical issue of what founds God's impassible passion, that is, his immutably perfect love and mercy. As we will see none of the Fathers addresses this issue either.

act of creation is developing into a hermeneutical principle for defining the nature of God and his relationship to the created order. Nonetheless, Philo is not without tensions and weaknesses.

Despite the above defense of Philo, there is tension within his thought concerning God's transcendence and immanence, and it is due to the influence of Platonism. While Philo emphasized the presence and activity of God, founded upon the fact that God is Creator, yet he states in numerous places that God creates and acts within the created order through the Logos and Sophia. Commenting on the three strangers who visited Abraham (see Gen. 18), Philo states:

> The one in the middle is the Father of the universe, who in the sacred scriptures is called by his proper name, I am that I am; and the beings on each side are those most ancient powers which are always close to the living God, one of which is called his creative power, and the other his royal power. And the creative power is God, for it is by this that he made and arranged the universe; and the royal power is the Lord, for it is fitting that the Creator should lord it over and govern the creature.[33]

Scholars debate whether Philo understands the Logos of God to be an actual personal being or the personification of God's power immanent within the world. The above text illustrates this problem. While the Logos is depicted as a distinct 'person,' yet Philo refers to 'him' as God's creative power. If the Logos is God's immanent power and activity, this would be more in accordance with the Hebrew view found in Genesis 1, the prophets, and the Wisdom literature. Contemporary Platonic thought, especially later Neoplatonism, would see the Logos as a distinct being. The Logos here would be understood to be an intermediary interposed between the transcendent God and the created order. For example, Philo states that 'the word of God is over all the world, and is the most ancient, and the most universal of all the things that are created.'[34] He is 'the Son of God, the being most perfect in all virtue.'[35] The Logos is also called 'the divine reason, which is the helmsman and governor of the universe.'[36] Here the Logos appears to be a created personal being and not the divine power of God through which he creates and governs the world.

Because of Philo's hierarchical order, an order where God is beyond 'the One' and beyond 'the Monad,' his understanding of the Logos can,

---

33 *De Abrahamo*, 121; see also 122. Christians have been fascinated by Philo's 'trinitarian' interpretation of this passage. In *De Cherubim*, Philo also states that God 'is the cause of it [the world], by whom it was made. That the materials are the four elements, of which it is composed; that the instrument is the word [logos] of God, by means of which it was made; and the object of the building you will find to be the display of the goodness of the Creator.' 127.

See also *Quod Deus Immutabilis Sit*, 57, and *De Opificio Mundi*, 72–75 where Philo discusses the phrase of Genesis 1:26: 'Let *us* make ... ,' and *De Somniis*, I, 137–59 for his interpretation of Jacob's ladder.

34 *Legum Allegoriae*, III, 175.
35 *De Vita Mosis*, II, 134.
36 *De Cherubim*, 36.

at times, appear to act as a 'spatial' semi-divine intermediary or principle between God and the created order. God would then be not only other than the created order, but also apart from the created order.[37] This is the real ambiguity of Philo's thought and it will be a weakness that is inherited by many of the early Fathers.[38]

This ambiguity and tension may be clarified if one bears in mind Philo's use of allegorical interpretation. Thus, when Philo designates the Logos as a being in his own right, as for example, when he portrays the Logos as one of the angels who appeared to Abraham, or as the governor, the helmsman, the most ancient one, and the Son of God, he is allegorizing, and so personifying the Logos as God's immanent power and activity. This is similar to the way in which the Wisdom literature personifies 'Wisdom.' If this interpretation is correct, then Philo does not necessarily place God apart from the created order, but rather he is present to and active within the created order through the Logos. The Logos becomes the immanent expression of the transcendent Creator.

In conclusion, what has been said here hopefully clarifies and demonstrates that Philo's thought is an authentic 'bridge' between the biblical and Greek notions of God. He is not a Jew who became a Greek, as his critics charge, though he may be a Jew who spoke with a Greek accent.[39] While there may be some ambiguities and weaknesses, yet Philo founded his understanding of God upon the biblical, and not Greek, truth that God is the Creator. That God is the Creator determined, for Philo, that he

---

37 On this point, H. Chadwick writes:

> Philo also has a developed notion of the great chain of being: the cosmos is a continuum of grades of being, filled out to the maximum possible plenitude, the diversity of which is held together by the immanent power of the Logos.... The Logos is God immanent, the vital power holding together the hierarchy of being, who as God's viceroy mediates revelation to the created order so that he stands midway on the frontier between creator and creature. Like the manna he is God's heavenly food to man, and the high priest who intercedes with God for frail mortals. The supreme God is too remote to have direct contact with this world, and it was the Logos who appeared, e.g., at the burning bush. The Logos dwelt especially in Moses, who was thereby virtually deified. By those less than enlightened the Logos is taken to be God, though in reality he is God's image.... On the other hand, the actual function of Logos in Philo's thought points to the conclusion that the impetus is coming not so much from the Jewish side as from that of late Platonist philosophy, where the remote transcendent God requires a second, metaphysically inferior aspect of himself to face towards the lower world. *The Cambridge History of Later Greek and Early Medieval Philosophy*, pp. 142–43, 144, 145.

> Chadwick may overstate the Platonism within Philo for he, like Philo himself, sometimes refers to Philo's notion of the Logos as 'the immanent power of God' active within the universe, and at other times as a distinct subject in his own right. The former would be in keeping with the Hebrew understanding of the Word of God, the latter would be the more Platonic understanding.

38 Only at the Council of Nicea, where the Logos, as a distinct eternal divine subject in his own right, is proclaimed *homoousion* with the Father, will this Platonic influence be broken. For now the one who is God as the Father is God, and so transcendent as he is transcendent, is the same one who became man and dwelt in our midst. Nicea firmly established the biblical notion of God's transcendence as the Wholly Other in our midst.

39 M. Edwards states that we must take Philo 'at his own word as a pious intellectual, who expressed in Greek the spirit of a Jew.' 'Justin's Logos and the Word of God,' *Journal of Early Christian Studies* 3/3 (1995):264.

is truly the living God who is the author of all that is. As such, God is wholly other than all else, and it is this very wholly otherness which empowers him to create and so manifest his immutable and impassible love, mercy and providence in all their passionate perfection.

5

The Patristic Doctrine of God

Because the early Fathers lived and worked within the environment of the New Testament and Jewish/Hellenic 'bridges,' they did not think it inappropriate to use language and concepts that were prevalent among their contemporary philosophical colleagues, even though they wished to be faithful to the Jewish and Christian revelation. They too, following the example of Philo and the apostles, especially Paul, saw themselves as apologetic and evangelistic 'bridges' to the pagan and philosophical world in which they lived. They instinctively did what they believed the New Testament did, and they did so by design.[1] The question is: Did they do so without any, or little, gospel discernment and theological discrimination?

Many contemporary theologians, as we have seen, argue that the Fathers too easily succumbed to the dominant Greek philosophical notion of God.[2] In so doing they transformed the living, loving and active

---

1 R.L. Wilken writes: 'In restating the Christian doctrine of God within the Graeco-Roman world, Christian thinkers sought out points of contact between biblical language of God's transcendence and Greek philosophical conceptions of the nature of God.' *Remembering the Christian Past* (Grand Rapids: Eerdmans, 1995), p. 38.

2 A couple of theologians, who espouse a passible God, do note that there are differences between the Greek philosophic notion of God's impassibility where God is unsympathetic, apathetic and static, and the Judeo-Christian notion of God's impassibility espoused by the Fathers where God is alive and active. See Sarot, *God, Passibility and Corporeality*, pp. 44–48, and his 'Divine Suffering: Continuity and Discontinuity with the Tradition,' *Anglican Theological Review*, 78/2 (1996):226. F.J. van Beeck writes:

Hermeneutically speaking, therefore, it is unwise and superficial for contemporary theologians to hint that the massive patristic affirmation of *apatheia* as a divine attribute is simply an example of the Church making common cause with Greek philosophy as well as protecting its socio-political privilege by projecting status and stoicism onto Christ and the Father by way of a divine attribute. The patristic tradition's indubitable respect for Greek philosophy was exceeded only by its eclectic use of it. If anything, its sheer consistency on the subject of divine impassibility was theological. We are well advised, therefore, to be careful in treating the subject – more careful, in fact, than some of the otherwise commendable theologians mentioned above have been. 'This Weakness of God's is Stronger,' p. 18.

G. Hanratty, who defends God's impassibility, equally claims that the charge leveled against the Fathers of succumbing to Greek philosophy is without foundation. See 'Divine Immutability and Impassibility Revisited' in *At the Heart of the Real*, ed. F. O'Rourke (Dublin: Irish Academic Press, 1992), pp. 146–48. See also Henry, *On Not Understanding God*, pp. 94–113.

God of the Bible into the immutable, impassible and inert God of
Hellenic philosophy. They maintain that only a changeable and passible
God can philosophically account for the biblical data.

However, I believe that this is a large component of the problem.
Contemporary theologians have not come to the Bible and the Fathers
philosophically neutral, but rather already convinced that an impassible
and immutable God will not do. Thus, their interpretation of the Old
Testament and the Fathers is driven, at least in part, by an already
preconceived understanding of the philosophical issues involved and the
philosophical answers that must be given.[3]

In this chapter I wish to demonstrate that, on the whole (but not
without mistakes), the Fathers, in their account of the impassibility of
God, were more influenced by and more faithful to biblical revelation
than those contemporary theologians who champion God's passibility. I
want to maintain that the philosophical notion of God and of his relationship to the world, which grew up within and gave expression to the
patristic tradition, finds its source, its inspiration, and its impetus from
within the Bible itself. Thus, it is not the Fathers' teaching on God's
impassibility which was and is imposed upon the Bible, but rather the
contemporary theological currents concerning God's passibility.

However, merely to present here the patristic tradition, and later the
Scholastic teaching, concerning God's impassibility will far from suffice.
It would be unjust and irresponsible to write off, in the name of the
tradition, the issues raised and the answers proffered within contemporary theology. The contemporary issues that have been raised
rightfully demand of the tradition further clarification, greater refine-
ment, and more creative development. Hopefully then, this chapter will
freshly and creatively, yet critically, examine the teaching of the Fathers
in the light of the scriptures and the contemporary philosophical and
theological questions, and provide answers that are more theologically
convincing and more religiously compelling than those of the past.[4] I
wish to do this in such a manner so as to establish not only that the
Fathers affirmed God's wholly otherness, but equally to substantiate that
they both maintained and even enhanced the early church's understanding of his personal, loving, compassionate presence to and activity
within the world.

In the light of the previous chapter we will now examine the patristic
understanding of God and of his relationship to the created order. We
will focus exclusively on the teaching of some of the significant second-
and third-century Greek and Latin Fathers since it is within their early
apologetic defence of Christianity that the church's more philosophical

---

3 The heart of the difficulty may be that many contemporary theologians, as we will see,
   have failed to understand correctly the philosophical tradition supporting the impassibility of God. They misconceive and so misinterpret and misrepresent the Fathers
   and Aquinas. This failure has forced them to jettison the tradition and to search
   instead for something more philosophically persuasive.
4 While, in examining the patristic tradition, I will argue for the impassibility of God,
   the full and complete arguments will have to await the next chapter when the even
   deeper philosophical issues raised within the patristic tradition are examined and
   addressed by Aquinas.

understanding of God, both in contrast to and in comparison with the pagan and Greek tradition, was initially formulated.[5]

Our starting point must be Pelikan's correct assessment that 'the early Christian picture of God was controlled by the self-evident axiom, accepted by all, of the absoluteness and impassibility of the divine nature.'[6] The question is: Why is this so? What confirmed the early church in this axiom? Was it due to philosophy or to scripture?

Justin Martyr

We will first consider Justin Martyr (c. AD100–165) since, of all the early Apologists, he provides the most philosophic and systematic defense of Christianity. Justin's apologetic for Christianity was written within the Middle Platonic and the Hellenistic Judaic (Philonic) tradition of his academic environment.[7] He zealously upholds the transcendence of God, and so he is other than the finite order. God in his goodness to man is the provider of all things. Therefore it is an insult to God's 'ineffable glory' to worship idols.[8] God is above all names and the names that are given to him, such as Father, Creator and Lord, are due to his 'good deeds and functions.'[9] He is 'unbegotten and incorruptible, and therefore he is God, but all other things after him are created and corruptible.'[10] God is 'unchangeable and eternal,'[11] and therefore, 'God, the Creator of all things, is superior to the things that are to be changed.'[12] Therefore, Christians dedicate themselves 'to the unbegotten and impassible God.'[13] When asked what he calls God, Justin responded: 'That which always

5   The early Fathers, more than the later, engaged in discussion with the then dominant pagan culture and philosophical tradition. From within this apologetic dialogue they defended and promoted the intellectual integrity of the gospel, and so were primarily responsible for originating and developing the Christian doctrine of God and of his relationship to the created order. Also, because of this intense colloquy with the Greek philosophical tradition, we will be able to discern more clearly whether or not the early Fathers were more faithful to the scriptures or to the philosophy of their age. Therefore, this chapter will only address these early issues. The concerns of the later Fathers focused more on specific Christian issues, such as the Trinity and the Incarnation, and so I will not treat here the patristic understanding of the Incarnation and its doctrinal formulation within the early councils. How the Son of God, who is God as the Father is God, experiences a full human life – birth, suffering and death – will be the subject of a later chapter.

6   Pelikan, *The Christian Tradition I*, p. 229 Also see Grant, *The Early Christian Doctrine of God*, pp. 10, 13–15, 21, 111–14.

7   See C. Andresen, 'Justine und die mittlere Platonismus,' *Zeitschrift für die neutesta- mentliche Wissenschaft* 44 (1952–53):157–95; M. Edwards, 'On the Platonic Schooling of Justin Martyr,' *Journal of Theological Studies* 42 (1991):17–34; E.R. Goodenough, *The Theology of Justin Martyr* (Jena, 1923; and reprinted Amsterdam: Philo Press, 1968), pp. 1–56; R. Holte, 'Spermatikos Logos,' *Studia Theologica* 12 (1958):123–18 and 147–48; D.T. Runia, *Philo in Early Christian Literature* (Assen: Van Gorcu, 1993), pp. 97–105.

8   *Apologia*, 1, 9. See also 10.

9   *Apologia*, 2, 6.

10 *Dialogus cum Tryphone*, 5.

11 *Apologia*, 1, 13.

12 *Apologia*, 1, 20. Justin refutes Stoic pantheism by arguing that such a notion of God implies change and corruptibility which is impossible for God to undergo. See *Apologia*, 2, 7 and *Dialogus*, 127.

13 *Apologia*, 1, 25.

maintains the same nature, and in the same manner, and is the cause of all other things – that, indeed, is God.'[14]

It is evident that Justin, like Philo, in ascribing to God the attributes of unchangeability, impassibility, unutterability, and unbegottenness, was stating what God is not, rather than what he is. He was protecting the transcendent otherness of God by denying of him those aspects – changeability, passibility – which would place him within the created order. He did not wish to deny, in so doing, God's providential goodness and love.[15] The main concern here is the implications that Justin, nonetheless, drew from what he taught about God. It must be admitted that he did what contemporary critics argue must be the case if one conceives God as immutably and impassibly perfect.

In order to uphold the otherness of God, Justin felt compelled to deny that God has any direct contact with the created order. L.W. Barnard states that, for Justin, God is 'the eternal, immovable, unchanging Cause and Ruler of the Universe, nameless and unutterable, unbegotten, residing far above the heavens, and is incapable of coming into immediate contact with any of his creatures, yet is observant of them although removed from them and unapproachable by them.'[16] While God cannot have any spatial character, yet Justin states that 'he remains in his own place, wherever that is.'[17] Wherever God may exist, either above the heavens or in the heavens, he is far removed from the created order.[18] Thus God cannot be the subject of the Old Testament theophanies. Rather, only the Logos, who comes forth from him at creation, has immediate contact with creation and the affairs of human beings.[19] 'He who has but the smallest intelligence will not venture to assert that the Maker and Father of all things, having left all supercelestial matters, was visible on a little portion of the earth.'[20]

Justin has given to God the Hellenistic notion of transcendence where God must not only be other than the created order, but also removed from it. In so doing, even though God loves and cares for human beings, his activity within the created order is always one step removed. The immediate love and immanent activity is always that of the Logos, who while divine, is necessarily subordinate to the one who is truly and fully God.[21]

There is necessarily then a tension within Justin's thought. While he upholds the perfect goodness and love of God, yet, in wanting to uphold

---

14 *Dialogus*, 3.
15 Justin speaks of God's solicitude and even sorrow over humankind's sinful plight. See *Apologia*, 1, 28 and 44; *Dialogus*, 1.
16 L.W. Barnard, *Justin Martyr: His Life and Thought* (Cambridge: Cambridge University Press, 1967), p. 81. See also pp. 75–84. Also see Hallman, *The Descent of God*, pp. 31–32.
17 *Dialogus*, 127.
18 See *Dialogus*, 56 and 127.
19 See *Dialogus*, 56, 58, and 126.
20 *Dialogus*, 60. Because Justin conceives the Logos as emanating out from the Father, he holds that the Logos is divine. However, since he does emanate out from the Father, as the spatial intermediary between the Father and the created order, he is not as divine as the Father is divine. See *Dialogus*, 56 and *Apologia*, 1, 63.
21 It would seem, for Justin, that the Logos must be less divine than the Father not only because he emanates out from the Father, but also because he is 'in touch' with the created order. If the Logos embodied the whole of the Godhead, he too would be unable to be present to and immanently active within time and history.

the godness of God, God himself is never actually permitted to express directly his godly love on behalf of the world.[22]

The reason why Justin isolated God from the world, and so making him incapable of directly acting within it, may lie in his ambiguous notion of creation. He seems to have held that Plato, Moses, and Christians equally believed that God, through the Logos, 'altered matter which was shapeless ... (and so) the whole world was made out of the substance spoken of before by Moses.'[23] It is unclear whether Justin held, along with Plato, that this pre-existent matter was eternal. He does not address this issue.[24] Nonetheless, if Justin had had a clear concept of

---

For fuller studies of Justin's understanding of God and the Logos, see Barnard, *Justin Martyr*; M. Edwards, 'Justin's Logos and the Word of God,' *Journal of Early Christian Studies* 3/3 (1995):261–80; Goodenough, *The Theology of Justin Martyr*; R. Grant, *Greek Apologists of the Second Century* (Philadelphia: Westminster Press, 1988), pp. 57–64; E.F. Osborn, *Justin Martyr* (Tübingen: Mohr, 1973).

Edwards argues that Justin's understanding of the Logos is primarily founded upon the scriptural tradition and not upon Platonic thought. I believe Edwards is correct, but this does not seem to have mitigated his subordinationism nor his understanding that the Logos acts as an intermediary who bridges the gap between God and the world.

22 L.W. Barnard states:

Our conclusion is that two conceptions of the Deity existed in Justin's mind. On the one hand was his acceptance of the biblical and Christian idea of God as a living Creator, a compassionate Father who in Christ had drawn near to men and who was concerned with the welfare of each soul. On the other hand Justin retained the Middle Platonist emphasis on God as the unknowable and transcendent Cause far removed from the world and disconnected from it.... Justin had no real theory of divine immanence to complement his emphasis on divine transcendence ... it was not given to him ... to unite transcendence and immanence in a system at once rational and biblical. *Justin Martyr*, pp. 83–84.

E.R. Goodenough more positively comments upon this tension within Justin:

His very inconsistencies are those of the Hellenistic Jews who had long been trying to do what Justin was forced to attempt, to justify their faith by the help of philosophy. Like them Justin taught at one time that God was transcendent, unbegotten, impassive, perfect, self-contained, unmoved, unchanging, unnamed, the First Cause; at another time that he was the personal creator and sustainer of the universe; at another time he was the kind merciful Father who led errant individuals into faith and saved them by his grace, or the dread God of righteousness whose final judgement awaited all men. Such a many-sided God was the God of the Wisdom Literature of the Hellenistic Jewish philosophers, and such a God Hellenistic Jews would have brought with them into Christianity. *The Theology of Justin Martyr*, p. 138.

23 *Apologia*, 1, 59.
24 For a discussion of the scholarly opinions of whether or not Justin believed in the eternal pre-existence of matter, see Goodenough, *The Theology of Justin Martyr*, pp. 206–11; and May, *Creatio Ex Nihilo*, pp. 120–33. May writes:

The conception so emphatically declared by Justin of the unlimited creative power of God and the thought that God, as the sole unoriginate being stands over against the originate, the creation, are mutually supportive in their bearing and seem to urge the doctrine of *creatio ex nihilo*. But Justin did not take the last step towards its formulation; in that he was obviously hindered by the Platonist preconceptions of his thinking. In Justin's philosophical theology two things can be observed: on the one hand that the dynamic of the Christian concept of God practically compelled acceptance of the doctrine of *creatio ex nihilo*, on the other hand how monstrously difficult it was for thought stamped with the philosophical tradition to take in the biblical idea of creation in its full implications (p. 132).

creatio ex nihilo, he would never have conceived God as being distant, and so disassociated, from creation. Here we again see the importance of the concept of creation. It not only guarantees the otherness of God, but it also safeguards his immediate presence to what is created. Thus, while those who argue that an immutable and impassible God cannot be present to and active within the created order can find some justification for such an accusation in the theology of Justin, the fault lies not in his notion of God, but in his dubious and faulty notion of the act of creation.

Aristides, Athenagoras, Theophilus

Three lesser Apologists, while not as comprehensive as Justin in their philosophical approach to Christianity, nonetheless exemplify the early patristic understanding of God and of his relationship to the world and humankind.

Aristides (early second century) contrasts the true understanding of God with that of the pagan gods and the created order. The pagans worship 'creation more than their Creator.'[25] 'God is not born, not made, an ever-abiding nature without beginning and without end, immortal, perfect and incomprehensible.'[26] He is above all passions and infirmities.[27] The elements out of which the world is made are not gods for they are 'perishable and mutable, and produced out of that which did not exist at the command of the true God, who is indestructible and immutable and invisible; yet he sees all things and as he wills modifies and changes things.'[28] God is not like man who is 'subject to anger and jealousy and desire and change of purpose and has many infirmities.'[29] Human beings should not worship pagan gods who are not God at all, but 'one ought to reverence the invisible and all-seeing and all-creating God.'[30]

Athenagoras (second century) argued in a similar fashion. Unlike the false gods and created things which are composed of parts, God is 'uncreated, and impassible, and indivisible.'[31] Christians are not atheists for they acknowledge that God is 'uncreated, eternal, invisible, impassible, incomprehensible, illimitable, who is apprehended by the understanding only.'[32] The false gods are subject to time and so change with the elements and the seasons, but the true God is 'immortal, and immovable, and unalterable.'[33] The gods are subject to emotional fits, to immorality and to sin, but the true God is 'in want of nought, and is superior to carnal desire.'[34]

---

25 *Apologia*, 2.
26 *Apologia*, 1.
27 See *Apologia*, 1.
28 *Apologia*, 4.
29 *Apologia*, 7.
30 *Apologia*, 13.
31 *Legatio pro Christianis*, 8.
32 *Legatio pro Christianis*, 10. See also 16.
33 *Legatio pro Christianis*, 22.
34 *Legatio pro Christianis*, 29. See 13, 21 and 30.

Of all of the Apologists, Theophilus (late second century) presents one of the most comprehensive statements about God and his attributes.

> The appearance of God is ineffable and indescribable, and cannot be seen by eyes of flesh. For in glory he is incomprehensible, in greatness unfathomable, in height inconceivable, in power incomparable, in wisdom unrivalled, in goodness inimitable, in kindness unutterable.... [Theophilus then proceeds to say what it means for God to be named Light, Word, Mind, Spirit, Wisdom, Strength, Power, etc. and continues:] You will say, then, to me, 'Is God angry?' Yes; he is angry with those who act wickedly, but he is good, and kind, and merciful to those who love and fear him; for he is a chastener of the godly and the father of the righteous; but he is a judge and punisher of the impious.
>
> And he is without beginning, because he is unbegotten; and he is unchangeable, because he is immortal. And he is called God on account of his having placed all things on security afforded by himself; and on account of [θέειν], for θέειν means running, and moving, and being active, and nourishing, and foreseeing, and governing, and making things alive. But he is Lord, because he rules over the universe; Father, because he is before all things; Fashioner and Maker, because he is creator and maker of the universe; the Highest because of his being above all; and Almighty because he himself rules and embraces all.[35]

Unlike matter, which is not uncreated and therefore mutable and alterable, God, who is uncreated, 'is immutable and unalterable.'[36]

Three comments can be made concerning the thought of the above three Apologists. First, it should be noted that God's immutability and impassibility are primarily founded upon what he is not and not upon what he is. The line of demarcation is that between Creator and creature.[37] As Creator God cannot possess those attributes which are constitutive of being a creature nor those vices to which humankind have fallen prey. To say that God is immutable and impassible is to deny of him those attributes that would make him like the fickle and sensuous pagan gods or like sinful and corruptible humankind. Therefore, God is not perishable, changeable, alterable, and subject to infirmities or to sinful and carnal passions. More positively, the attributes of immutability and impassibility, in denying of God all that is changeable and corruptible, assure that he possesses those attributes that constitute his divinity – uncreated, immortal, eternal, perfect, indestructible. The attributes of immutability and impassibility then free God from all that is

---

35 *Ad Autolycum*, I, 3 and 4.
36 *Ad Autolycum*, II, 4.
37 G. May argues that neither Aristides nor Athenagoras hold *creatio ex nihilo*, but rather that God is seen in the Platonic manner of the former of the world out of pre-existent matter (see *Creation Ex Nihilo*, pp. 118–20 and 137–39). However, he maintains that Theophilus of Antioch was the first to clearly formulate the full doctrine of *creatio ex nihilo*. The catalyst for this theological breakthrough, as May argues throughout his study, is the confronting of the philosophical issues raised by Gnosticism (see pp. 156–63).

not divine and simultaneously guarantee all that is divine, his eternal and unchanging perfection.

Second, and following from this, to say that God is immutable and impassible, is not to say that he is lifeless and inert. Rather, as Theophilus strongly argues, the immutable and impassible perfection of God attests that he is truly the living, active and dynamic God who is the sole source of all that lives and is active. He governs and cares for his creation in all his goodness and love.

Third, Theophilus even states that God is angry. What needs to be noted is that this anger is not predicated upon some negative emotional state, but rather upon his unchangeable goodness and love. Anger is more an expression of God's perfect goodness, than an expression of some emotional change of state within God himself. While the philosophical implications of this are not worked out by Theophilus, the inference is that it is because of God's unchangeable and perfect goodness that one can predicate anger of God. Sin and evil confront the perfect and unchanging goodness of God and therefore the wicked come under God's righteous judgment.[38]

Irenaeus

The Gnostics held that everything which exists, including God, formed one continuous whole. There was one contiguous chain of being which included the immutably perfect God at the apex and the passibly corrupt matter at the bottom. Between God and matter were placed a whole myriad (depending on the various schools) of lesser beings or aeons. While God was transcendent for the Gnostics, in that he was remote from the created realm (which he himself did not create but some lesser being, since for him to do so would have jeopardized his perfect transcendence) and could have no direct contact with it, he was, nonetheless, only relatively transcendent since he too was part of the whole.[39] By conceiving reality as such, the Gnostics could maintain both the unchangeable perfect transcendence of God and yet his, even if remote, relationship to it.[40]

In contradistinction to the Gnostic view of God and the pleroma of various aeons, Irenaeus (c. AD130–200) enunciated his Christian notion of God. While he was acquainted with the philosophy of his day, Irenaeus was far more the biblical theologian than the philosopher. It was with a

---

38 For brief accounts of and bibliography on the thought of Aristides, Athenagoras, and Theophilus, see Grant, *Greek Apologists of the Second Century*.

39 D. Minns clearly points out the dilemma faced by the Gnostics. 'On the one hand, God must be utterly transcendent, unchanging, incorporeal, invisible, beyond the grasp and description of created intellect, and so on. But, as God is also thought of as the provident, benign creator and ruler of all that is good, the question arises.' How does one reconcile this dilemma? 'The solution to this problem was to suggest that a subordinate god (or gods) effects the saving will of the first God for creation.' *Irenaeus* (London: Geoffrey Chapman, 1994), p. 24. Minns also notes that because God is part of a continuous chain of being, he ultimately is responsible, as Irenaeus himself argued, for the evil that exists in the world. See pp. 30–31.

40 For brief expositions of Gnosticism see: *Encyclopedia of Early Christianity*, ed. E. Ferguson (London: Garland Publishing, 1990); and *Encyclopedia of the Early Church*, ed. A. Di Berardino (Cambridge: James Clarke & Co., 1992).

mind and heart steeped in the Bible that Irenaeus forged his refutation of Gnosticism and equally his positive contribution to the Christian tradition. Thus, if we are to understand Irenaeus properly, we must grasp that the act of creation was for him the pivotal event which allowed him both to counter the gnostic teaching on God and to assert his own conception. The act of creation became, for Irenaeus, the fundamental hermeneutical principle which governed his conception of God and of God's relation to the created order.

Having given an account of the various gnostic teachings in Book 1 of *Adversus Haereses*, he writes at the onset of Book 2:

> It is proper, then, that I should begin with the first and most important head, that is, God the Creator, who made the heaven and the earth, and all things that are therein (whom these men blasphemously style the fruit of a defect), and to demonstrate that there is nothing either above him or after him; nor that, influenced by any one, but of his own free will, he created all things, since he is the only God, the only Lord, the only Creator, the only Father, alone containing all things, and himself commanding all things into existence.[41]

Placing the notion of creation at the centre of his theology allowed Irenaeus to do two absolutely essential things. First, as in the Hebrew scriptures, it establishes the wholly otherness of God in a manner that is far more radical than that of the Gnostics. God is not part of a contiguous whole, but absolutely (ontologically) distinct from all else that exists. Second and simultaneously, it establishes, as also found in the Bible, God's immediate relationship to the created order.[42] We need to examine these two aspects more closely, if we are to appreciate what Irenaeus stated concerning God's impassibility and his passionate love and goodness.

To say, as some Gnostics did, that angels created the world would imply, for Irenaeus, that they were more powerful than God. God needs no help in creating. Rather the pre-eminence of God is manifested precisely in that he himself summoned all into existence out of

---

41 *Adversus Haereses*, 2, 1, 1. G. May emphasizes that 'the contribution made by Irenaeus and Theophilus must not be underestimated: they developed the doctrine of *creatio ex nihilo* with such convincing stringency that from the end of the second century it becomes with astonishing speed the self-evident premise of Christian talk of the creation. We have to see in Theophilus and Irenaeus the specific founders of the church doctrine of *creatio ex nihilo*'. *Creatio Ex Nihilo*, pp. 177–78.

42 D. Minns writes: 'Paradoxically, just because God's transcendence over creation is absolute, he is immediately present to his creation in a way impossible within the Valentinian scheme.' *Irenaeus*, p. 33.
    R. Norris also writes: 'What makes God *different* from every creature – his eternal and ingenerate simplicity – is thus, for Irenaeus, precisely what assures his direct and intimate *relation* with every creature. In this way Irenaeus reaches for a solution to the problem which Justin had encountered when he defined the transcendence of God in terms of the opposition between Being and Becoming.' *God and World in Early Christian Theology* (London: Adam & Charles Black, 1966), p. 70.
    G. May also sees the doctrine of *creatio ex nihilo*, in contrast to Gnosticism, as arising out of the desire to 'express and safeguard the omnipotence and freedom of God acting in history.' *Creatio Ex Nihilo*, p. 180.

nothing.[43] 'God has pre-eminence, who alone is uncreated, the first of all things, and the primary cause of the existence of all.' Human beings are to grow into the perfection of God, 'for the Uncreated is perfect, that is, God.'[44] Because God is the uncreated Creator, he 'ought not to be counted with other productions.' Unlike all else then, God is 'incomprehensible' and 'without figure' and 'shape.' As Creator, God is then 'distinct' from all else, and unlike them, he is 'both without beginning and end, and lacking nothing. He is himself sufficient for himself; and still further, he grants to all others this very thing, existence.'[45] God, therefore, is 'truly and for ever the same, and always remaining the same unchangeable Being.'[46] Moreover, since he cannot be 'reckoned with an Aeon,' which is 'subject to passion, God is impassible.'[47]

The Gnostics distance God from the world and refuse to allow him to be Creator lest he entangle himself in evil. They limit the knowledge of God to the few, and yet 'they endow him with human affections and passions.' If the Gnostics had known the scriptures, they would have comprehended that God is not as men are (Is. 55:8).

> The Father of all is at a vast distance from those affections and passions which operate among men. He is a simple, uncompounded Being, without diverse members, and altogether like and equal to himself, since he is wholly understanding, and wholly spirit, and wholly thought, and wholly intelligence, and wholly reason, and wholly hearing, and wholly seeing, and wholly light, and the whole source of all that is good.[48]

Despite this grand description of God, Irenaeus next states that God 'is, however, above [all] these properties, and therefore indescribable.'[49] While he may understand and be light, he is so in a way that is unlike human understanding or created light. All of these attributes 'are names of those perfections which always exist in God, so far as it is possible and proper for men to hear and to speak of God. For with the name of God the following words will harmonize: intelligence, word, life, incorruption, truth, wisdom, goodness, and such like.'[50]

The above passages clearly testify that Irenaeus, unlike Justin, is utterly imbued with the biblical tradition. In arguing against Marcion and the Gnostics, he is defending what he believes is the correct biblical view of God. We perceive Irenaeus following the now common tradition, found in the Bible itself, of negating of God anything that would place him within the created realm.[51] He transcends all that he makes, and thus

43 See *Adversus Haereses*, 2, 2, 1; 2, 2, 4 and 5; 2, 9, 1; 2, 10, 2 and 4.
44 *Adversus Haereses*, 4, 38, 3.
45 *Adversus Haereses*, 3, 8, 3.
46 *Adversus Haereses*, 2, 34, 2.
47 *Adversus Haereses*, 2, 12, 1. See 2, 17, 3 and 8.
48 *Adversus Haereses*, 2, 13, 3.
49 *Adversus Haereses*, 2, 13, 4.
50 *Adversus Haereses*, 2, 13, 9.
51 For the emergence of negative descriptions of God within Hellenistic Judaism, Middle Platonism, Gnosticism, and Christianity, see J. Daniélou, *Gospel Message and Hellenistic Culture*, Vol. 2 (London: Darton, Longman & Todd, 1973), pp. 323–43.

he cannot be numbered among them. It is for this reason that Irenaeus denies of God changeability and passibility. Unlike creatures, who grow in perfection or suffer the desires and passions of sin, God is wholly perfect in himself and so is immutable and impassible in his perfection. As we saw in previous authors, to state, as Irenaeus does, that God is unchangeable and impassible, does not then tell us what God is, but what God is not. He is not like changeable and passible creatures because he is perfect in his eternal goodness and love.

This is why Irenaeus does not give any indication that such a view of God disallows him from simultaneously professing that God is equally all good, loving, and merciful. Nor does he evidence any concern that God's immutability and impassibility might jeopardize his action in the world on behalf of humankind. This lack of concern on Irenaeus' part is not due to an absence of philosophical sophistication, but rather to his innate grasp of the Bible and the philosophy inherent within it. For Irenaeus, the Creator, who is wholly other than all else that is, is precisely the same Creator who is all good and loving. What holds the transcendent otherness of God and the immanent presence and action of God together is the act of creation. Unlike the Gnostics, who denied that God was the Creator and so held him to be infinitely distant from the corruptible world, unable to be present to it and forbidden to act within it, Irenaeus stressed that the good God brought into existence a good creation, and so he and what he had made were thoroughly compatible. He providentially cares for and loves what he has made.[52]

Thus Irenaeus can write that 'God formed man at the first, because of his munificence.'[53] Moreover, 'the love of God, being rich and ungrudging, confers upon the suppliant more than he can ask from it.'[54] God had need of nothing, but granted 'communion with Himself to those who stood in need.'[55] God 'is rich in all things, and all things are his. It is fitting, therefore, that the creation itself, being restored to its primeval condition, should without restraint be under the dominion of the righteous.'[56] The compatibility between God as the wholly other Creator and God as the providential provider is witnessed when Irenaeus writes:

> With God there are simultaneously exhibited power, wisdom, and goodness. His power and goodness [appear] in this, that of his own will he called into being and fashioned things which had no previous existence; his wisdom [is shown] in his having made created things parts of one harmonious and consistent whole; and those things which, through his super-eminent kindness, receive growth and a long period of existence, do reflect the glory of the uncreated One, of that God who bestows what is good ungrudgingly.[57]

---

52 D. Minns rightly notes that Irenaeus, unlike the Gnostics, is enamoured with the reality – the material earthiness – of creation. Irenaeus' 'religious awe of and love for the Creator God went hand in hand with a religious awe of and love for the world he believed that God to have created.' *Irenaeus*, p. 25.
53 *Adversus Haereses*, 4, 14, 2.
54 *Adversus Haereses*, 3, preface.
55 *Adversus Haereses*, 4, 14, 2.
56 *Adversus Haereses*, 5, 32, 1.
57 *Adversus Haereses*, 4, 38, 3.

Unlike Marcion, who speaks of two Gods, one just and the other loving, Irenaeus holds that the one God must be good, just and wise. 'For he is good, and merciful, and patient, and saves whom he ought: nor does goodness desert Him in the exercise of justice, nor is his wisdom lessened; for he saves those whom he should save, and judges those worthy of judgement. Neither does he show himself unmercifully just; for his goodness, no doubt, goes on before, and takes precedence.'[58] The eternally perfect God, who is incorruptible, ultimately gives to those who are faithful to him his very own incorruptibility and immortality.[59]

While, for Irenaeus, God is immutable and impassible in that he does not undergo the negative changes and inimical passions which are the lot of the created order, he is nonetheless passionate. Hallman notes that Irenaeus held that we obtain some knowledge of God 'by comparing the divine with human personality. If one pursued this line of reasoning, is God not also total receptivity, total sympathy, and total love? Although it is a possible consequence of his argument, Irenaeus does not see this important application.'[60] Hallman not only misrepresents Irenaeus, as the above texts show, but he also completely misses his logic. God is, for Irenaeus, 'total sympathy, and total love' precisely because his mercy and love are not predicated of a changeable being. For God to be impassible and immutable is not to deny love and compassion of him, but to establish in his unchangeably perfect being a love that is absolutely and utterly passionate.[61]

Hallman exemplifies here a common mistake made by many contemporary critics of God's impassibility. They consistently argue that for God to be impassible means that he is unloving. This is not so. They forget that to say that God is impassible does not tell us something positive about God – that he is inert, static and lifeless and so not loving, kind and compassionate. Rather, to say that God is impassible, as Irenaeus does, is to deny of God all those characteristics and properties of the created order which would render him less than perfectly good, loving, and merciful.

In summary, God as the Creator, for Irenaeus, is the one who truly *is*, for he brings all else into existence. As such, in accordance with the Hebrew scriptures, he is both absolutely other than all else and simultaneously and immediately present to and active within creation. Because God is the one who truly *is*, unlike the changing order of creation, he is impassibly flawless and abidingly perfect in his passionate love. Irenaeus' view of God and of his relationship to the created order is then quite the antithesis to that of Greek philosophy, his gnostic

---

58 *Adversus Haereses*, 3, 25, 3.
59 See *Adversus Haereses*, 4, 38, 2–3.
60 Hallman, *The Descent of God*, p. 35.
61 J. Hallman also wants God to be 'total receptivity.' Irenaeus would agree with this if what is meant is that God is completely cognizant of all that is happening within the created order – the joys and sufferings of humankind. However, Irenaeus would not accept that God is 'total receptivity' in the sense that he is changed by all that is taking place in the created realm, which is the primary meaning that Hallman wishes to give to this phrase.

opponents having much in common with it. Rather, Irenaeus, while frequently employing words prevalent within the Hellenic philosophical tradition, such as immutability and impassibility, radically altered their signification so as to conform them to and to give affirmation of the Hebraic and Christian truth about God and his love and goodness.[62]

Clement of Alexandria

The Christian philosopher Clement of Alexandria (c. AD150–215) exemplifies and intensifies much of what we have already found in Justin Martyr, and therefore I will only briefly consider him here. Influenced by Philo and Middle Platonic thought Clement, conceptually and linguistically, offers an even more radically negative notion of God's transcendence. This is coupled with his Stoic ethic which negatively regards passions and desires as the source of all evil. However, what saves Clement from completely hellenizing the Gospel is his belief that God is the good Creator, who possesses a wise and providential love and care for humankind.[63] This is especially manifested in the Incarnation.[64]

For Clement then, God is 'one, indestructible, unbegotten' with an existence that is 'true and eternal.'[65] As the Creator, God is 'unborn,' 'immortal,' and in want of nothing for he neither grows nor changes.[66] Since God is the 'first principle' and 'cause of all other things,' he is 'neither genus, nor difference, nor species, nor individual, nor number; nay more, is neither an event, nor that to which an event happens. No one can rightly express him wholly.' We may refer to him as 'One, or the Good, or Mind, or Absolute Being, or Father, or God, or Creator, or Lord,' yet 'each one by itself does not express God; but all together are indicative of the power of the Omnipotent.' In the end God cannot be 'apprehended by the science of demonstration' since God is beyond all conception.[67] So transcendent is the one God that he is 'beyond one and above the Monad itself.'[68]

Such a negative view of God may seem to place him beyond the reach of humankind, existing in a realm that is utterly devoid of contact with the created order. However, when Clement asserts that God is beyond the One and the Monad in his transcendence, he wishes only to emphasize that God cannot be classified. He cannot be numbered among all else that exists. No concept can contain him. He is incomprehensible. Nonetheless, with such an understanding of God, Clement, not surpris-

---

62 R. Norris states that 'it is impossible not to recognize, in Irenaeus' polemic against Gnosis, a conscious attempt to fuse the idea of God as incorruptible Being with the doctrine that God is unlimited creative Power, intimately present *in* the finite world without in any sense being a part *of* it' (*God and World in Early Christian Theology*, p. 134–35).
63 See *Protrepticus*, 5.
64 See *Paedagogus*, 1, 8.
65 *Protrepticus*, 6.
66 *Stromata*, 5, 11.
67 *Stromata*, 5, 12.
68 *Paedagogus*, 1, 8.

ingly, insists particularly that God, unlike human beings, is immutable and impassible.[69]

What may be surprising is Clement's equal insistence on God's love, goodness, and compassion. He hates nothing that he has made, but 'loves them.'

> Much more than the rest, and with reason, will he love man, the noblest of all objects created by him, and a God-loving being. Therefore God is loving; consequently the Word is loving. But he who loves anything wishes to do it good. And that which does good must be in every way better than that which does not good. But nothing is better than the Good. The Good, then does good. And God is admitted to be good. God therefore does good. And the Good, in virtue of its being good, does nothing else than good. Consequently God does all good.[70]

While Clement denies that we can ascribe human passions and affections to God, he continues to state that if we pity one another, how much more does God show pity to us.

> God being by nature rich in pity, in consequence of his own goodness, cares for us, neither through portions of himself, nor by nature of his children. And this is the greatest proof of the goodness of God: that such being our relation to him, and being by nature wholly estranged, he nevertheless cares for us.

Animals care for their offspring, and human beings have a natural affinity for one another, but 'the mercy of God is rich toward us, who are in no respect related to him; I say either in our essence or nature, or in the peculiar energy of our essence, but only in our being the work of his will.'[71] God's love for us is 'ineffable.'[72]

Again with Clement, even within his negativity, we recognize that he maintains the passionate goodness and compassion of God. God's immutability and impassibility only tell us what God is not. His passionate love, compassion and goodness tell us what God is.[73] However, we apprehend these, not by reason, but 'by divine grace, and by the Word alone that proceeds from him.'[74] While Clement may at

---

69 See *Stromata*, 2, 11; 4, 23; 6, 7; 7, 3; 7, 6; 7, 13. Clement carries over his understanding of impassibility into the Incarnation and the life of Christians. Due to the influence of Stoicism, Clement tends to see all passion and desire in a negative light. Jesus, therefore, was devoid of human passion, and the Christian life is one of growing into an impassible state. See *Stromata*, 6, 9; 5, 11; 7, 11.

70 *Paedagogus*, 1, 8.

71 *Stromata*, 2, 16.

72 *Protrepticus*, 10. See *Paedagogus*, 1, 8 and 12.

73 J. Hallman again misses the point when he states: 'Coupled with the most extreme statement of God's transcendence in early Christian theology, however, are other texts that show that in some way, even for Clement of Alexandria, God is passible.' *The Descent of God*, p. 39. For Hallman, any statement that speaks of God's love or compassion means that he is passible and changeable. This is not true. God can be, as he is for Clement, impassible in that he does not undergo changeable and negative emotional states, such as human beings undergo, but he can also be immutably passionate in that he is absolutely good and perfectly loving.

74 *Stromata*, 5, 12.

times portray God and the Christian life in a rather grim and unattractive light, yet he does so only to emphasize that God and our life with him stand on a unique plain.[75]

Origen

Of much greater interest is Origen (c. AD185–254) for he gives more explicit scope to the passion of God, and so could be seen to undermine the tradition of his impassibility.[76] Origen wished to be both a faithful man of the church and a reconciler of the gospel with his inherited Middle Platonic tradition and the nascent Neoplatonism of his day. His understanding of God bears the marks of all of these.

Since both are spiritual, Origen holds that there is 'a certain affinity between the mind and God,' and thus humankind 'is able to have some perception of the divine nature.'[77] While God, like the sun, cannot be perceived in the fullness of his glory and so is incomprehensible, yet his works portray, as rays, his splendor.[78]

> God therefore must not be thought to be any kind of body, nor to exist in a body, but to be simple intellectual existence, so that he cannot be believed to have in himself a more or a less, but is Unity (*Monas*), or if I may so say, Oneness (*Henas*) throughout, and the mind and fount from which originates all intellectual existence or mind.[79]

Because he, unlike creation, does not partake of movement or change, '*God does not even participate in being*. For he is participated in, rather than participates.'[80]

Origen, in these passages, is emphasizing that God cannot be placed within or numbered among all else that exists, and therefore he does not 'participate' in their being. Rather, he is the source of all that exists, and thus all that does exist participates in his being. Here again we see Origen establishing the otherness of God on the act of creation.

Because he is wholly other, one must not take literally those passages of scripture which speak of God being angry or repenting, or subject to any other human emotion, for 'God must be believed to be entirely

---

75 For more complete studies of Clement of Alexandria see: C. Brigg, *The Christian Platonists of Alexandria* (Oxford: Clarendon Press, 1913); S.R.C. Lilla, *Clement of Alexandria: A Study in Christian Platonism and Gnosticism* (Oxford: Oxford University Press, 1971); Osborn, *The Philosophy of Clement of Alexandria.*

76 H. Crouzel notes that 'while Clement always speaks of *apatheia* as an essential virtue of the spiritual man, occurrences of *apatheia* and *apathes* in Origen's writings can be counted on the fingers of one hand and his teaching is nearer to *metriopatheia*, the restraint to be imposed on the passions, rather than *apatheia* itself.' *Origen* (Edinburgh: T & T Clark, 1989), p. 7.

77 *De Principiis*, 1, 1, 7. The translation is taken from *Origen: On First Principles*, trans. G.W. Butterworth (Gloucester, MA: Peter Smith, 1973).

78 See *De Principiis*, 1, 1, 6.

79 *De Principiis*, 1, 1, 6.

80 *Contra Celsum*, 6, 64. The translation is taken from *Origen: Contra Celsum*, trans. H. Chadwick, (Cambridge: Cambridge University Press, 1953). See also *Comment. in Joh.*, 19, 6.

without passion and destitute of all these emotions.' Passages in the Old or the New Testament which speak of God's anger or emotion must be given 'the spiritual meaning in them, endeavouring to understand them in a way that is worthy of God.'[81]

While Origen frequently speaks of the anger of God, he consistently interprets it, not as something God actually possesses in reaction to sin, but as a means of correcting the sinner. 'We do not attribute human passions to God, nor do we hold impious opinions about him.'[82] 'God's anger is not to be considered a passion. How can an impassible being have a passion? God does not suffer, he is immutable.'[83]

Arguing against the materialism of the Stoics, where God is corruptible and alterable, Origen states that 'the doctrine of Jews and Christians preserves the unchangeable and unalterable nature of God.'[84] Against the claim of Celsus that if God comes down from heaven and enters into the affairs of man, he must undergo change, Origen maintains in accordance with scripture (Ps. 101:28 and Mal. 3:6) that, 'while remaining unchanged in essence, he comes down in his providence and care over human affairs' for the true conception of God's nature is that he is 'entirely incorruptible, simple, uncompounded and indivisible.'[85] While the scriptures portray God as seeing, hearing and with bodily parts, it would be foolish to take these literally, for no 'change takes place in God either in action or in thought.'[86]

In contrast to this strong defense of God's immutable and impassible nature, Origen can also speak with great conviction about the passion of God. Origen believes that if one begs a human person for pity, if he is not callous of heart, but suffers on account of one's need, then he will respond in compassion.

> Something of this sort I would have you suppose concerning the Saviour. He came down to earth in pity for human kind, he endured our passions and sufferings before he suffered the cross, and he deigned to assume our flesh. For if he had not suffered he would not have entered into full participation in human life. He first suffered, then he came down and was manifested. What is that passion which he suffered for us? It is the passion of love. The Father himself and the God of the whole universe is 'long-suffering, full of mercy and pity' (Ps. 86:15). Must he not then, in some sense, be exposed to suffering? So you must realize that in his dealing with men he suffers human passions. 'For the Lord thy God bore thy ways, even as a man bears his own son' (Deut. 1:31). Thus God bears our ways, just as the son of God bears our 'passions'. The Father himself is not impassible. If he is besought he shows pity and compassion; he feels, in some sort, the passion of love, and is exposed to what he cannot be

81 *De Principiis*, 2, 4, 4.
82 *Contra Celsum*, 4, 72. See also 6, 64.
83 *Fragment on John*, 51. Translation taken from Hallman, *The Descent of God*, p. 43.
84 *Contra Celsum*, 1, 21.
85 *Contra Celsum*, 4, 14.
86 *Contra Celsum*, 6, 62. See *De Principiis*, 2, 8, 5.

exposed to in respect of his greatness, and for us men he endures the passion of mankind.[87]

Clearly Origen is here asserting that not only does the Son of God suffer as man, but also that the motivation for becoming man was precisely in the suffering he experienced in his divine state prior to becoming man. Equally, and of even greater significance, Origen affirms that the Father too suffers and that he is not impassible.

In another homily Origen also notes that God and heaven rejoice over the repentant sinner and so 'as our good actions and our progress in virtue produce gladness and rejoicing for God and the angels, so I feel does our evil way of life bring about lamentation and mourning not only on earth but also in heaven; and it may well be that men's sins afflict with grief even God himself.' Origen continues by graphically depicting God lamenting and crying over sinful man, yet he concludes: 'Now all of these passages where God is said to lament, or rejoice, or hate, or be glad, are to be understood as spoken by Scripture in metaphorical and human fashion. For the divine nature is remote from all affection and of passion and change, remaining ever unmoved and untroubled in its own summit of bliss.'[88]

While Origen can sometimes be inconsistent in what he says, his inconsistency is normally found within his speculative theology. Being the pre-eminent scripture scholar that he was, he habitually interpreted the Bible in a consistent fashion. What then are we to make of Origen's seeming inconsistency when it comes to the question of God's impassible or passible nature? Mozley holds that ultimately Origen retreats 'within the fortifications of the allegorical method of Scripture,' and so his statements concerning divine passibility cannot be taken seriously.[89] Hallman believes that Origen is just plain inconsistent, but that his inconsistency is significant in itself.[90]

What these scholars fail to recognize is that Origen is attempting to make, maybe for the first time explicitly, the distinction that we have seen made implicitly throughout this chapter. Origen upholds both the impassibility of God and the passion of God. To say that God is impassible is to deny emotional change of states within God. It is a negative way of upholding the absolute otherness of God and of his radical perfection. Thus, while God does not undergo any passible change of

87 *In Ezech. Hom.*, 6, 6. Translation is from *The Early Christian Fathers*, H. Bettenson (Oxford: Oxford University Press, 1956).
88 *In Num. Hom.*, 33, 2. Translation is from Bettenson. J. Hallman gives two further passages where Origen speaks both of God's passibility and impassibility. One is from *Selecta in Ezekiel*, 16, 8. There Origen insists that 'God is impassible, just as he is immutable and uncreated,' and yet concludes that 'God feels compassion for the one to be pitied; for God is not heartless.' The other passage is from Origen's *Homily on Exodus* where he discusses God's jealousy. He states: 'God does and suffers all things for us that we may be able to learn; he expresses notable and useful affections for us.' 8, 5; see *The Descent of God*, pp. 41–42. See also J. Hallman, 'Divine Suffering and Change in Origen and *Ad Theopompum*,' *The Second Century* 7 (1989–90):92–94.
89 Mozley, *The Impassibility of God*, p. 63.
90 See Hallman, *The Descent of God*, p. 46. For other opinions, see p. 41. Hallman states the same in 'Divine Suffering and Change in Origen,' pp. 89–94. See also Grant, *The Early Christian Doctrine of God*, pp. 28–36.

emotional states, yet, because of his immutable perfection, he is perfect in his passionate love for humankind. Note that Origen states twice that the suffering that God endures over the fallen condition of man is 'the passion of love.' The Father is 'not impassible,' not in the sense that he changes from not suffering to suffering, but in the sense that, in his unchangeable love, he passionately grieves over his people. The suffering that God endures is not due to a change in his love, but is subsumed by and predicated upon his impassible and unchangeable perfect love. This is why Origen insists that the scripture passages which speak of God's emotions must be interpreted metaphorically, and yet without denying the reality of which they speak. The emotions ascribed to God in the Bible are metaphorical in that they do not predicate of him states of emotional change as is universally the case with humans, but rather they predicate aspects of God's immutable passionate love for humankind.[91]

Tertullian

Until now we have studied only Greek Fathers. (Irenaeus, though Bishop of Lyon, grew up in the East and wrote in Greek.) Before we conclude this chapter, we need briefly to examine a few of the early Latin Fathers – Tertullian, Novatian, and Lactantius. We will find in them the same basic concerns and issues that we have met within the early Greek Fathers.

Concerning the passibility and impassibility of God, scholars find in Tertullian's (c. AD160–240) thought similar tensions (inconsistencies) to those found in Origen's. To grasp the logic of Tertullian's teaching on the passibility and impassibility of God, we must place it within his understanding of God's goodness.

Tertullian sets out what he calls the 'rules for examining God's goodness.' The first is that God does not become good by doing good things. Rather it is because he is good that he does good things, such as create. God's goodness is constitutive of who he is as God and so is an eternal attribute. 'In God, therefore, goodness is required to be both perpetual and unbroken, such as, being stored up and kept ready in the treasures of his natural properties.'[92] God's goodness must not only be an eternal property of who he is, but it must also be rational, that is, it must be used in a rational manner.[93] Moreover, because God is good and rational, 'so, I think, he is perfect in all things.'[94] It is only in the light of this understanding of God's goodness that we can properly discern Tertullian's rendering of God's 'passibility.'

Now Marcion wished to attribute only goodness, and not anger, to the God of the New Testament. However, Tertullian argues that for God to be simply good without possessing the other sensations and attributes

---

91 For further studies of Origen, see Brigg, *The Christian Platonists of Alexandria*; Crouzel, *Origen*; Daniélou, *Origen*; J.W. Trigg, *Origen: The Bible and Philosophy in the Third-century Church* (London: SCM, 1983).

92 *Adversus Marcionem*, 1, 22.

93 *Adversus Marcionem*, 1, 23.

94 *Adversus Marcionem*, 1, 24.

would mean that God is not good at all. God's goodness demands that he be angry over sin and that he judges evil. Such emotions are not incompatible with God's nature because they are constitutive of what it means for God to be eternally, rationally, and perfectly good.[95]

For Tertullian, while God is good in himself, this goodness expresses itself then in accordance with the changing created order. 'Up to the fall of man, therefore, from the beginning God was simply good; after that he became a judge both severe and, as the Marcionites will have it, cruel.'[96] For Tertullian God's justice directs his goodness 'according to men's application for it.'

> And this is the result; the divine goodness, being interrupted in that free course whereby God was spontaneously good, is now dispensed according to the deserts of every man; it is offered to the worthy, denied to the unworthy, taken away from the unthankful, and also avenged on all its enemies. Thus the entire office of justice in this respect becomes an agency for goodness: whatever it condemns by judgement, whatever (to use your phrase) it ruthlessly pursues, it, in fact, benefits with good instead of injuring.[97]

What must be grasped here is that, for Tertullian, goodness is the primary and foundational attribute of God. It is what makes God truly God. All other emotions or attributes are simply expressions of his goodness administered in various ways to meet various situations. Does this mean that God, for Tertullian, changes emotional states? On one level, the simple answer is yes. Depending upon the changing circumstances of human life, God's goodness will be expressed and experienced in different manners – anger toward the sinner, mercy toward the repentant. On another level, and I believe the deeper level, the answer is no. The differing expressions are but the expressions of the one constitutive attribute of God – his unchanging rational and perfect goodness. Thus, while God himself does not change – he is eternally and perfectly good – yet the mode of the expression of his goodness changes and the experience of his goodness changes in accordance with the change in the human situation and circumstance. It is because of this twofold reality – the unchangeableness of God's goodness and the various expressions of it – that Tertullian qualified what it means for God to exhibit different emotional states.

In *Adversus Marcionem*, 2, 16 Tertullian argues that while Marcion would hold that such emotions as anger imply that God is corruptible and mortal, he maintains that, while this may be true of human beings, it is not true of God. The nature of man and the nature of God are radically different. Therefore we must 'discriminate between the natures, and assign to them their respective senses, which are as diverse as their natures require.' While the Bible attributes to God hands, eyes and feet, what they designate about God is far different from what they designate about human beings. Similarly, while we can speak of God's sensations

---

95 See *Adversus Marcionem*, 1, 25.
96 *Adversus Marcionem*, 2, 11.
97 *Adversus Marcionem*, 2, 13.

and emotions, they too designate something radically different of God from what they designate of humankind. 'These sensations in the human being are rendered just as corrupt by the corruptibility of man's substance, as in God they are rendered incorruptible by the incorruption of the divine essence.' Because God is God 'he is undoubtedly diverse from every sort of human condition.' This does not mean that God is without emotion. Rather it means that God possesses emotions in a divine manner. It is not that God possesses human emotions, but rather that man possesses divine emotions. It is 'palpably absurd of you to be placing human characteristics in God rather than divine ones in man, and clothing God in the likeness of man, instead of man in the image of God. And this, therefore, is to be deemed the likeness of God in man, that the human soul has the same emotions and sensations as God, although they are not of the same kind; differing as they do both in their conditions and their issues according to their nature.' Goodness is 'the very parent' of all sensations and therefore God is not only meek, patient, and merciful, but he can also be angry. Being perfectly good, God possesses all of these perfectly. Moreover, unlike us, God's anger is subsumed into his happiness. 'God alone is truly happy, by reason of his property of incorruptibility. Angry he will possibly be, but not irritated, nor dangerously tempted; he will be moved but not subverted.' God must exhibit the full range of emotions in order to cover all the contingencies of the world and human life –

> anger because of the wicked, and indignation because of the ungrateful, and jealousy because of the proud, and whatsoever else is a hindrance to the evil. So, again mercy on account of the erring, and patience on account of the impenitent, and pre-eminent resources on account of the meritorious, and whatsoever is necessary to the good. All these affections he is moved by in that peculiar manner of his own, in which it is profoundly fit that he should be affected; and it is owing to him that man is also similarly affected in a way which is equally his own.[98]

Once more we need to ask the question: Does Tertullian want to hold that God merely exhibits different emotional states which spring from his unchangeable and perfect goodness but which do not actually bring about a change in himself, or does he want to say that God actually undergoes diverse emotional states? It appears that he has not fully worked out a complete philosophical answer. Tertullian realized from scripture that anger, justice, and judgment have real meaning when predicated of God. Yet he equally does not wish these 'emotions' to jeopardize God's perfect unchanging goodness, and even his happiness. This is why he consistently states that God possesses them in accordance with his perfect nature, and even that they must be attributed to God in a manner similar to the way 'hands' and 'feet' are attributed to God. While Tertullian does not explicitly state it, this seems to imply that, while they do predicate something true of God, they do so metaphorically.

---

98 All of the above quotations are from *Adversus Marcionem*, 2, 16.

Tertullian is able to state more clearly how these 'emotions' do not apply to God than how they positively do apply to him. While he wishes to predicate them of God in some true manner, he positively predicates them of God by rejecting false manners of predication. This is another example of attempting to state something positive about the nature of God, but doing so through negation. The real problem is that Tertullian does not clearly state what it means for God to possess them in accordance with his nature, but it does at least mean that he does not possess them in a human manner, which does betoken change. Moreover, this is also why Tertullian can insist that, despite God's seemingly differing emotional states, he is immutable.

Against Hermogenes, Tertullian argues that, unlike temporal matter which is mutable, God is eternal and 'eternity, however, cannot be lost, because it cannot be eternity, except by reason of its immunity from loss. For the same reason also it is incapable of change, inasmuch as, since it is eternity, it can by no means be changed.'[99] Moreover, while God cannot change for the worse by loss of his perfection, so neither can he change for the better, being eternally perfect. 'God is the great Supreme, existing in eternity, unbegotten, unmade, without beginning, without end.'[100] Eternity places God outside time and therefore outside the realm of change. 'Eternity has no time. It is itself all time. It acts; it cannot then suffer.'[101] God acts. He is not acted upon, and therefore he does not suffer change. For Tertullian, because God is eternally and perfectly good, he cannot suffer the changing and debilitating vicissitudes of time.

Despite the ambiguity of expression and the unresolved philosophical issues, what Tertullian wishes to uphold has become quite clear. Because of God's eternal, rational and perfect goodness, Tertullian believes that God, being eternal and so outside of time, is ontologically immutable and impassible (in the sense that he does not change emotional states). Moreover, he also wants to give true expression to God's anger and justice for they are expressions of his perfect and unchanging goodness. What he has not been able to do is positively to conceive, philosophically, how both of these truths can be harmoniously reconciled. Again, as with previous Fathers, it is not that Tertullian is inconsistent, as if he were attempting to uphold two incompatible and irreconcilable truths, one scriptural and the other philosophical, and that a choice must be made between them, the right choice being that scripture teaches that God is changeable and passible. Rather, Tertullian very clearly grasped that two truths, both of which are scriptural, must be upheld – the complete otherness of God and the passionate vitality of his goodness – and he was desperately attempting to hold them together conceptually.[102]

99 *Adversus Hermogenem,* 12.
100 *Adversus Marcionem,* 1, 3.
101 *Adversus Marcionem,* 1, 8.
102 J. Hallman is correct when he states that Tertullian, in speaking of God's 'emotion' was attempting to be 'more biblical.' However, he again misses the true logic of Tertullian's concerns and simply concludes that he was inconsistent, and he was inconsistent because his Greek philosophical presuppositions would not allow him to be thoroughly biblical. See *The Descent of God,* p. 62; and also his 'The Mutability of God: Tertullian to Lactantius,' *Theological Studies* 42 (1981):385. R. Norris makes a similar

Novatian

Novatian (c. AD210–280) stressed God's immutability and impassibility
without wishing to deny his passion and vitality. In his work *De Trinitate*
he systematically sets forth his arguments.

---

judgment. See *God and World in Early Christian Theology*, p. 112. See also Wilken,
Remembering the Christian Past, p. 77.

While it is somewhat of a digression from our present concerns, it must be noted,
for Tertullian's sake, that Hallman, both in his book (pp. 62–66) and in his article (pp.
382–86), argues that Tertullian is equally inconsistent in his understanding of the
Incarnation.

In his work, *De Carne Christi*, Tertullian places these words in the mouth of
Marcion: 'But the reason why I deny that God really and truly changed into man, in
the sense of being both born and corporated in flesh, is that he who is without end
must of necessity also be unchangeable: for to be changed into something else is an
ending of what originally was: therefore change is inapplicable to one to whom ending
is inapplicable.' In response to this argument Tertullian admits that such is the case on
the finite level – things that change into something else cease to be what they were.
However, 'nothing is on equal terms with God: his nature is far removed from the
circumstances of all things whatsoever.' If God would change into something in the
same manner as creatures, then there would be no difference between God and all
else. But 'the contrary obtains, namely that God can be changed into anything whatsoever, and yet continue such as he is.' If the angels who appeared to Abraham
remained who they were and yet 'changed into human shape, and that the bodies they
were clothed with were of such verity that Abraham washed their feet, ... will you
deny this to the more mighty God, as though his Christ had not the power, when truly
clothed with manhood, of continuing to be God?' All the quotations are from *De Carne
Christi*, 3 taken from E. Evans' translation *Tertullian's Treatise on the Incarnation*
(London: SPCK, 1956). Hallman believes that Tertullian is here espousing a mutable
understanding of God. While God can remain who he is, he can nonetheless 'change
into' something else and so, within the Incarnation, become man. This then allows,
Hallman believes, Tertullian rightly to predicate human passions and suffering to the
Son not just in so far as he is man, but also in so far as he is God. For Hallman this is
the right and proper understanding of the communication of idioms.

While it was infelicitous for Tertullian to continue to use the Marcionite language
that God, within the Incarnation, 'changed into man' (*deum in hominem vere conversum*),
yet the point that Tertullian wished to make is precisely the opposite of that proposed
by Hallman. First, Tertullian obviously did not hold that in the Incarnation God
actually 'changed into man' in that sense that he ceased being God and was transformed into a man similar to a caterpillar changing into a butterfly. The whole point
of Tertullian's stress that he 'continues as he is' is to assure that it is really and truly
God who is man. Second, it must remembered that Tertullian was arguing against the
Marcionite Docetism. Thus, his primary concern is to uphold the reality of the Son's
humanity. We see this in his use of the example of the angels appearing to Abraham –
their flesh was so real that Abraham could wash their feet. For Tertullian the Son was
truly 'clothed with manhood.' Third, in the light of this anti-docetic concern, Tertullian
was not then saying that somehow God, while maintaining his identity, 'changed into
man' in the sense of being mutable, but that God could actually become man without
changing. This is why Tertullian insists that 'change into,' when applied to the
Incarnation, assumes a radically different meaning than when applied to creatures.
When applied to creatures it denotes mutability, but when applied to the Incarnation
– God becoming man – it does not. This is precisely why God remains as he is even
though he has become man. For Tertullian the 'changing into' is not predicated of God
as if he changed in becoming man, but rather 'changing into' refers to the new mode
of existence he has assumed, that is, to the fact that Son was 'truly clothed with
manhood.' The 'changing into' is Tertullian's way of emphasizing the actual reality of
the Son's manhood and not a designation of divine mutability. It is fascinating that the
words Tertullian attributes to Marcion when defining what 'change into' means are

The *Regula Fidei* (Rule of Faith) 'requires that we should first of all believe in God the Father and Lord Omnipotent; that is, the absolutely perfect Founder of all things.'[103] The complete otherness of God is grasped from the fact that he is the Creator and so is radically different from all else that is. He is beyond all else. He has no beginning and no end. He is immortal and eternal and so does not exist within time. He is incomprehensible and so cannot be named.[104] God is perfectly good and thus the author of good.

> He, then, is always like to himself; nor does he ever turn or change himself into any forms, lest by change he should appear to be mortal . . . . Thus there is never in him any accession or increase of any part or honour, lest anything should appear to have ever been wanting to his perfection. . . . But what he is, he always is; and who he is, he is always himself; and what character he has he always has.[105]

Novatian makes reference to Malachi 3:6 and Exodus 3:14 both of which he believes uphold the fact that God truly is the 'one who is' and thus does not change. Because he is immutably perfect in every way he is 'immortal and incorruptible.'[106]

Novatian is here clustering arguments that are now part of the patristic tradition. He wishes to uphold the absolute uniqueness and perfection of God, and he does so by asserting positive and negative

---

these: 'God was really and truly changed into man, *in the sense of being both born and corporated in flesh*' (*ita ut et nasceretur et carne corporaretur*). I believe Tertullian here has written his own gloss into his adversary's words. For Marcion 'change into' meant ceasing to be one thing and coming to be another, but for Tertullian 'change into,' when applied to the Incarnation, denoted not change but simply the ability to take on flesh, and thus actually being born. Again it is the true reality of Jesus' humanity that most concerned Tertullian. Moreover, Hallman misrepresents Tertullian's understanding of the communication of idioms. Divine and human attributes are predicated of the same Son, but 'that these two sets of attributes, the divine and the human, are each kept distinct from the other, is of course accounted for by the equal verity of each nature' (*De Carne Christi*, 5). For Tertullian, it is truly the Son who suffers, but he truly suffers, not as God, but as man.

Because Tertullian advocated, according to Hallman, a mutable and passible God in *De Carne Christi*, Hallman holds that in his later work, *Adversus Praxean*, he reneged on this position and so becomes inconsistent. Here Tertullian asks: 'How did the Word become flesh, – whether it was by having been transfigured (*transfiguratio*), as it were in the flesh, or by having really clothed himself in flesh? Certainly it was by a real clothing of himself in flesh. For the rest, we must needs believe God to be unchangeable and incapable of form, as being eternal. But transfiguration is the destruction of that which previously existed' (*Adversus Praxean*, 27). This can now be interpreted in a manner that is totally consistent with, and obviously clarifies, Tertullian's earlier position. In the Incarnation the Son is not 'changed into' flesh, in the sense of being transfigured into flesh for God cannot cease to be who he is and, moreover, if he was so transfigured, it would no longer be God who is man. All that would now exist would be the present reality of 'his' transfigured state – the man Jesus – just as only the butterfly exists after the metamorphosis. Tertullian may have been struggling with finding the proper concepts and language, but inconsistent and illogical he was not.

103 *De Trinitate*, 1. See also 3.
104 See *De Trinitate*, 2.
105 *De Trinitate*, 4.
106 *De Trinitate*, 4.

attributes of him, which together complement and clarify one another. As the Creator God is wholly other than what he creates and thus he is positively all-perfect, all-good and eternal. In order to accentuate these positive attributes and to give more precise meaning to them, Novatian denies of God all that is constitutive of the created order. In contrast to the changeable, finite, and temporal creation, God is infinite, immutable, immortal, and incorruptible. These negative attributes then not only differentiate God from all that he created, but they also enhance his absolute and unchanging perfection. For Novatian, they in no way jeopardize his dynamic vitality, but rather they assure it. To say that God is immutable is to attest that God is eternally who he is in all his absolute goodness and love.

Novatian uses this same line of argument when it comes to God's anger. Yes, God can be angry and indignant, 'yet we are not to understand these to be asserted of him in the sense in which they are human vices.' These may corrupt man, they 'cannot corrupt the divine power.' The reason is that God is angry for our good. His anger is medicinal.[107] For Novatian then, God's anger is not an indication of God's mutability or passibility, but an expression of his immutable perfection and passionate goodness. We see here as well that Novatian is acutely aware that biblical language cannot always be taken literally even though the truth of what is said must be maintained. God does not really possess eyes, ears, or hands, yet God sees all, hears all and works ceaselessly.[108] Ultimately Novatian acknowledges that all human language and concepts fail to grasp the whole of who God is.[109]

Lactantius

Lactantius (c. AD240–320) was an ardent defender of the reality of God's anger, so much so that he wrote a treatise entitled *De Ira Dei*. However, because his treatise is primarily pastoral rather than philosophical and because he presents similar arguments to those of Tertullian, though in a much more developed and systematic manner, he does not significantly advance the discussion.

He states that many, for example, the Epicureans and the Stoics, deny anger of God either because God is beneficent and therefore anger would be inconsistent with his goodness, or because he does not take any notice of human affairs and therefore is not aroused to anger over human misdeeds.[110] However, Lactantius argues, to deny anger of God is to deny his goodness as well. God is not 'inactive' nor 'at rest' nor 'unmoveable.' Rather he is ever active in his care and governance of the world.[111]

> For if God is not angry with the impious and the unrighteous, it is
> clear that he does not love the pious and the righteous.... Thus he
> who loves the good also hates the wicked, and he who does not hate

---

107 *De Trinitate*, 5.
108 See *De Trinitate*, 6.
109 See *De Trinitate*, 7.
110 See *De Ira Dei*, 1 and 2.
111 *De Ira Dei*, 4. See also 17.

the wicked does not love the good; because the loving of the good arises from the hatred of the wicked, and the hating of the wicked has its rise from the love of the good.[112]

Echoing earlier authors, Lactantius states that without divine anger there would be no righteous fear of God.[113] God's anger is an exercise of his divine authority.[114] While God has the affections, emotions, and attributes that befit his divine power, such as kindness, pity and anger, he does not possess those that are contrary to his nature, such as fear, want, injury, carnal passion, envy, infirmity, and death.[115] Because God is eternally perfect and virtuous, so too is his anger eternally perfect, but it is an anger that is completely under the control of his perfect will.[116] Therefore it is wrong 'to represent God as being without emotions.'[117]

Here, as with Origen and Tertullian, we find God's anger to be an expression of the more basic divine attributes, that of God's goodness and love. What Lactantius fails to do, unlike Origen and Tertullian, is to grapple with the philosophical issues involved. His is a pastoral concern, and while he states that God exhibits anger in keeping with his perfect nature, he does not address the manner in which God is able to do this. This is especially significant since he equally wishes to uphold the tradition of God's immutability and impassibility. There is one God 'in whom complete energy and power can neither be lessened nor increased.'[118] He writes similarly in *Divinae Institutiones* that God 'who is the Eternal Mind, is undoubtedly of excellence, complete and perfect in every part' and, therefore, cannot be diminished or enhanced in any way.[119] Moreover, because God is the highest power, 'he must be incorruptible, perfect, incapable of suffering, and subject to no other being.'[120] Likewise, because God is uncreated and the Creator of all, 'that which is in him will always be permanent. . . . He is of himself . . . and therefore he is such as he willed that he should be, incapable of suffering, unchangeable, incorruptible, blessed, and eternal.'[121]

Lactantius exemplifies once again the common tradition that while God is immutable and impassible, this in no way denies that he is equally passionate – even in his anger. Implicit within his teaching is the notion that it is precisely the perfect and unchangeable goodness and love of God that allows him to be perfectly and eternally passionate even in his anger.

---

112 *De Ira Dei*, 5. See also 6 and especially 16. Lactantius distinguishes between just and unjust anger. God only exercises just anger against what is wicked for the benefit of the good. See *De Ira Dei*, 17.
113 See *De Ira Dei*, 11 and 12.
114 See *De Ira Dei*, 23.
115 See *De Ira Dei*, 15 and 16.
116 See *De Ira Dei*, 21.
117 *De Ira Dei*, 22.
118 *De Ira Dei*, 11.
119 *Divinae Institutiones*, 1, 3.
120 *Divinae Institutiones*, 1, 3.
121 *Divinae Institutiones*, 2, 9.

Conclusions

In closing this chapter on the early patristic doctrine of God and of his relationship to the created order, we can now draw together a number of conclusions. We want specifically to discern whether or not the early Greek and Latin Apologists were faithful to the Hebrew and Christian revelation of who God is in relation to the question of his impassibility or passibility. The conclusions will summarize and highlight what we have learned as a whole from our survey of the early patristic period, and will not, for the most part, retrace specific differences between and criticisms of the various Fathers.

To read those contemporary theologians who criticize the patristic understanding of God, one would imagine that the Fathers were better acquainted with and faithful to Greek philosophy than to the Bible. The Fathers, as our survey shows, would be rightly puzzled at such a critique. While they evidently did use words and concepts taken from philosophy, they did so primarily, as our examination illustrates, either to show that biblical revelation was compatible with some of what philosophy taught, or to defend Christianity against philosophical attacks, or to demonstrate that Christianity actually provided better philosophical answers to the questions at hand. What the Fathers brought to the philosophical conversation, a conversation that had been in progress for centuries, was precisely the new data of the Christian faith – the revelation of the Hebrew and Christian scriptures. Whatever they said that was new was not due to their faithfulness to some philosophy, but to their fidelity to the scriptures. They were not philosophical innovators. They were theological innovators and their innovation was founded upon the Bible.

Nonetheless, it is true that theological error and even heresy (in the case of Marcion and the Gnostics) came about precisely because the newness of Christian revelation did not adequately alter and satisfactorily reshape philosophical presuppositions and concepts. The philosophical conversation, which the early church joined, was not without its dangers. The present-day critics have adequately enumerated the pits into which the Fathers could and sometimes did fall. However, this chapter manifests that they, on the whole, did not fall into all the pits that they are alleged to have fallen into, nor then did they, on the whole, innocently, but nonetheless erroneously, abandon the God of Israel for the God of the Greeks.

All of the early Fathers were concerned with upholding the complete otherness of the one God in relationship to the created order. In this they were true to the Hebrew and Christian revelation, and they professed this in a number of ways. First, they denied existence, on scriptural and philosophical grounds, to the anthropomorphic and mythological gods of the pagans and the Gnostics. They, in accordance with scripture and 'true' philosophy, insisted that there is but one God who transcends all else. Second, on behalf of this one transcendent God, they also argued, by stressing (with the exception of Justin Martyr), in accordance with the scriptures, that God was the Creator of all else that exists. They gave philosophical depth to the biblical notion of creation by clarifying, in opposition to 'false' Greek philosophy, that God created all out of nothing – *creatio ex nihilo*. God did not just form or order pre-existent matter, as in Platonic thought or set it in motion as in Aristotelianism, but was actually responsible for the existence of all that is. The notion of God as Creator then radically distinguished him from all else, and in a manner that was even more radical than that of Greek philosophy or gnostic thought. He did not just relatively transcend all else in that he was the pinnacle of a contiguous chain of being, but rather he transcended creation in that he constituted a distinct ontological order all his own, and so was not one of the things made. Thus he could not be numbered among them, nor could he then be contained in any species or genus. His mode of existence was entirely unique and distinct from that of the created order.

For the early Fathers, the biblical and philosophical notion of God as Creator carried with it a number of consequences with regard to his attributes. Because God is the Creator, the Fathers positively held that he was outside of time and so eternal, without beginning or end. In accordance with scripture, and in contrast to the Gnostics and Marcion, he is the all perfect and all good God who created everything good by his almighty power. Moreover, because he is the all perfect author of all life and existence, he is the one who truly exists or is. This is the ultimate reason for his total perfection, his consummate goodness, and his almighty power. This, the Fathers believed, was in accordance with biblical revelation, especially as regards his revealed divine name, Yahweh – He Who Is.

In order to accentuate these positive biblical attributes which accrued to God as Creator, the Fathers attributed to him a whole cluster of negative attributes some of which are directly biblical in origin and some of which stem more from philosophical reflection. For the Fathers, these negative attributes served a twofold purpose. They primarily were used to distinguish God from the created order, but in so doing they equally gave more noetic content to the positive attributes.[122]

In contrast to the world and to the anthropomorphic gods of the pagans, God is incorporeal. This not only helped distinguish him from the created order, it also denied of God all that is constitutive of bodily existence – literally having eyes, ears, hands, etc., and possessing physical feelings, passions, and needs, such as pain, lust, and hunger. It equally accentuated his spiritual nature, and thus, in whatever ways God

---

122 G.L. Prestige significantly comments:

> In point of fact, though the Fathers in speaking of the ineffable being of God tended to use abstract forms which are outwardly expressive of a negative meaning, nevertheless their minds were far from being bounded by merely negative conceptions. The negative forms are enriched with an infinite wealth of positive association.
>
> This may be realised when it is seen that the negative prefixes so widely employed in words intended to describe the divine nature really testify to divine freedom and independence. When it is asserted that God is free from various limitations and controls, the effect is to assert his entire freedom to be himself and to act according to his own nature and will. His absolute independence is a corollary to his absolute goodness and wisdom, as well as to his absolute capacity to create. *God in Patristic Thought* (London: SPCK, 1952), p. 4.

may be like human beings, since he created them in his image and likeness, he is so only in a manner that is appropriate to and in conformity with his spiritual (divine) character. Moreover, because God, as Creator, could not be numbered among the things created and because he is all perfect, he is incomprehensible, and so could not be fully known nor named as are creatures. This, again, they believed to be in accordance with his revealed name, Yahweh – 'I Am Who Am.' God revealed his name as the one who could not be named. God is also infinite in the negative sense that he is in no way finite, that is, he does not possess any of the attributes which limit creatures, such as location, growth, development, imperfection, contingency, and time. To call God infinite also intensified more positively that, as Creator, he possesses unlimited power and life, and is omnipresent. As Creator, unlike creatures, he is also unbegotten and uncreated. This accentuated the eternal nature of God's existence for it is constitutive of creaturely existence to come to be, to grow and develop, and to cease to be. God, as unbegotten and uncreated, in contrast, eternally is. Equally, because God is eternally the one who truly is, he, unlike creatures, is incorruptible and immortal. The unqualified nature of God's existence is underlined in these two negative attributes. Nothing can corrupt the absolute perfection and power of the truly living God nor bring about his demise.

In the light of this complementary and reciprocal interplay between these positive and negative attributes, the early Fathers insisted that God was immutable and impassible. Negatively, God is immutable in the sense that he does not change as do creatures, but he does not change for positive reasons. For the Fathers, and this is essential to understanding their doctrine of God, God's immutability radically affirms and profoundly intensifies the absolute perfection and utter goodness of God, who as Creator, is the one who truly lives and exists. Thus, to say that God is immutable tells us, in the first instance, primarily what God is not. He, unlike creatures, does not change, in that, he can neither diminish in his goodness and perfection, nor can he increase in his goodness and perfection. Moreover, to say that God is immutable, again, accentuates that he is distinct from the changeable created order and so outside of time which marks these changes. But, the attribute of immutability equally affirms, in its denial, that God is then eternally the living God who is utterly dynamic in his goodness, love and perfection. There is no fluctuation or change within God which could in any way alter his comprehensive goodness and consummate love.

Thus, there is little, if any, ground for the familiar criticism that the attribute of divine immutability transformed, within the teaching of the Fathers, the living and dynamic God of the Bible into the static and inert God of Greek philosophy. The problem is that contemporary critics of the Fathers consistently give to the attribute of divine immutability the positive noetic content of being static, lifeless and inert, something which the Fathers never argued for nor even contemplated. The Fathers grasped, as the contemporary critics do not, that to say that God is immutable is to deny those aspects of his nature – changes of a diminishing or of a developmental kind – which would jeopardize or render less than perfect his dynamic vitality as the one who truly is. While the

Fathers may have snatched the attribute of immutability from the Greek philosophical vocabulary and tradition, they radically altered it so as to assert, in a philosophical manner, God's unconditional goodness and unqualified love as revealed in the scriptures.

Similarly, for the early Fathers (we see this especially in Irenaeus, Origen and Tertullian), while the divine attribute of impassibility primarily tells us what God is not, it does so for entirely positive reasons. God is impassible in that he does not undergo successive and fluctuating emotional states; nor can the created order alter him in such a way so as to cause him to suffer any modification or loss. Nor is God the victim of negative and sinful passions as are human beings, such as fear, anxiety, and dread, or greed, lust, and unjust anger. For the Fathers, to deny that God is passible is to deny of him all human passions and the effects of such passions which would in any way debilitate or cripple him as God. Thus, to say that God is impassible is again to ensure and to accentuate his perfect goodness and unalterable love. As I have argued throughout, the Fathers, almost universally, Justin and Clement being somewhat the exceptions, attributed impassibility to God in order to safeguard and enhance his perfect and dynamic passion – his all-consuming goodness and ardent love. Even those Fathers who argued, on biblical and pastoral grounds, for the reality of God's anger did so from the perspective of his goodness and love. Anger, when applied to God, was not seen as a separate passion or an intermittent emotional state within God, but constitutive of his unchanging perfect goodness and providential care, and so must be predicated of God in a manner suitable to divine nature.

As we have noted throughout this chapter, the contemporary critics invariably accuse those Fathers who uphold the impassibility of God as well as his love, compassion, mercy and anger of being inconsistent. This accusation is founded upon the false premise that to be impassible is to be devoid of passion. This, again, the Fathers never argued for nor even countenanced. The Fathers denied of God those passions which, they believed, would imperil or impair those positive attributes which were constitutive of his divine nature – his goodness and love. And equally then, such a denial amplified the intensity of these same unchangeably perfect passions.[123] The Fathers wished to preserve the wholly otherness

---

123 G.L. Prestige's comments are again appropriate:

> It is clear that impassibility means not that God is inactive or uninterested, not that he surveys existence with Epicurean impassibility from the shelter of a metaphysical isolation, but that his will is determined from within instead of being swayed from without. It safeguards the truth that the impulse alike in providential order and in redemption and sanctification come from the will of God. *God in Patristic Thought*, p. 7.

Or again:

> As has been stated already, there is no sign that divine impassibility was taught with any view of minimising the interest of God in his creation or his care and concern for the world that he made. In fact, any such theory is manifestly absurd. Impassibility, though affording an obvious line of approach to the wider doctrine, is a department of the larger question of self-consistency. God is, in the fullest sense, the same yesterday, today, and for ever. *God in Patristic Thought*, p. 11.

Even someone as critical as J.K. Mozley could write: 'To suppose that Christian

of God, as found in scripture, and equally, also in accordance with scripture, to profess and enrich an understanding of his passionate goodness and love that was truly in keeping with his wholly otherness.[124]

Lastly, it cannot be over-emphasized that it is the act of creation that scripturally and philosophically grounded the early Christian understanding of God and distinguished its doctrine of God from that of the Greek philosophical tradition. While it established the inherent ontological otherness of God, in a manner far more radical than that of the Greek philosophical and gnostic traditions, yet it simultaneously fixed his immediate and unmediated presence to the created order. Thus, for the Fathers, God, in accordance with the scriptures, could act within the created order as the wholly other without losing his wholly otherness in so doing.

Consequently, the early patristic doctrine of God was fundamentally faithful to the biblical notion of God and of his relationship to the created order, and this was so precisely because they took as their source and inspiration, not Greek philosophy, but the Bible itself. They maintained the biblical mystery of who God is while attempting to clarify and to enhance it through the use of philosophy.

However, the early Fathers left a few important questions unanswered. They did not fully treat, philosophically, what it is about the very being of God which allows him to create. Yes, he is all powerful, eternal, perfectly good and loving. But what is it that constitutes him as all powerful, eternal, perfectly good and loving? What, philosophically, establishes the complete otherness of God, and simultaneously allows him to act within and interact with the created order, especially in relation to human beings, as the wholly other without losing his wholly otherness in so doing? What founds God's immutable and impassible perfect nature, and simultaneously founds his ability to relate to the changeable created order with all of his passionate goodness and love? These, and similar questions will be discussed and, it is hoped, answered in the next chapter.

---

thinkers carelessly passed over all that seems to us involved in our belief in God's loving care, his fatherly providence, and his moral purposefulness, would be the greatest injustice both to their words and their thought.' *The Impassibility of God*, p. 46.

124 Similar to Prestige, F.S. van Beeck holds that the patristic notion of *apatheia* ensures the freedom of God. He writes that '*apatheia* safeguards God's transcendent freedom to be God-in-self-manifestation – that is, to communicate the divine Self to the world in wholly self-initiated love, irrespective of human or cosmic readiness or response.' He also notes that within the patristic monastic spiritual tradition the human virtue of *apatheia* is not seen in any Stoic ideal of impassiveness, 'but as the patient pursuit of love, just as the attribution of *apatheia* to God had served to affirm the divine mercy and love.' 'This Weakness of God's is Stronger,' 20 and 22.

6

The Trinity's Loving Act
of Creation

Thus far I have argued that God has revealed himself, as witnessed in the biblical account, to be completely other than the created realm, and yet capable of relating to and acting within it without losing his total otherness in so doing. The acts which reveal God to be the Savior and Creator, and so related to the created order as the One All Holy God, are the very same acts that reveal him to be, as the Savior and Creator, wholly other than the created realm. Indeed, God could not be the Savior, Creator and Sanctifier that he is unless he were the Wholly Other. The immanent activity of God in the created order, and his intimate relationship with human beings are predicated upon his absolute transcendent otherness. The philosophical question of God's impassibility or passibility must be answered from within this biblical doctrine of God, and as I argued, the biblical evidence, while not addressing the philosophical issues, strongly points to God being impassible.

I have also argued that Philo and the early Apologists attempted, each individual with greater or lesser success, to uphold the biblical account of both God's transcendence and his immanence. For the early Fathers the act of creation which manifests and establishes the complete otherness of God, and thus his eternal, all-powerful and unchanging nature, is the very same act which relates him to the created order and so founds his loving and salvific relation to it. Moreover for the Fathers, the attributes which define God as completely other – eternal, all-powerful, incorruptible, infinite, immutable, impassible, etc. – are equally the very same attributes assuring that he is the living, dynamic, all good, loving, kind, merciful and compassionate God.

We have now reached the stage in our study when we must establish more fully and systematically the theological and philosophical basis of God's all-powerful, eternal, incorruptible, immutable and impassible nature. It is one thing to say, as the Fathers did, that because God is Creator he must be all-powerful. It is quite another to found this attribute philosophically, that is, to conceive the precise nature of his power which allows him to create. One can also hold that, because God is other than the created order, and thus eternal and therefore outside time, he must be immutable and impassible. Yet, one must demonstrate the theological and philosophical justification for this. Above all it is necessary to give a theological and philosophical account of God which justifies his absolute otherness, and, equally and simultaneously, his intimate loving relationship to the world and human beings. In this chapter I wish to offer such an account.

Here I want to present my theological and philosophical understanding of God and of his relationship to the created and human order, especially as it concerns his impassible nature and, equally, his ability to love and care for human beings. While this chapter is the heart of this study, it will not address the key issue of whether or not God, in his compassion and love, suffers in himself on behalf of and with humankind, nor will I address the christological issue concerning the manner of the Son's suffering as man. These issues will be examined in the following two chapters, and this chapter will simply, but necessarily, lay the crucial foundation for such a discussion. All the proper philosophical and theological pieces must first be precisely placed before such a discussion can be undertaken, and this is the objective of this chapter.

In order to approach these concerns properly I wish to treat them both by way of Christian revelation and by way of philosophical enquiry. While some of the arguments presented in this chapter will be founded upon philosophical reasoning alone, apart from Christian revelation, other arguments will be primarily founded upon Christian doctrine and interpreted and elucidated through philosophical reasoning. Such an approach will not only help establish the primacy of biblical revelation and Christian doctrine, but also help to thwart the frequent criticism that the God of traditional Christian philosophy differs from, and often is in conflict with, the God of Christian revelation. I wish to found my arguments on the inter-relationship between doctrine and philosophy, and so demonstrate that the interplay between them helps to reinforce and clarify both, thus providing answers that are theologically orthodox and philosophically sound.[1]

Because this chapter is composed of many inter-related components, it is rather lengthy. However, the argument of the chapter, as a whole, is one. This must be kept in mind as each component is examined and interconnected with the others. Hopefully, at the end, the inner logic of the whole argument will then be clearly discerned and easily grasped.

The Persons of the Trinity: Subsistent Relations

I wish to begin then by examining the nature of the Trinity. This may appear an improbable place to begin since the question of God's immutability and impassibility is normally read under the philosophical rubric concerning the nature of the one God and his attributes. This, as we saw, was the primary context within which the Fathers argued, and it was equally the context from which Aquinas approached the issue. However, by opening our enquiry with an examination of the Trinity we not only locate it within the environment of Christian doctrine, but also

---

1 Throughout this chapter Aquinas will be my primary, but not exclusive guide. I use the word 'guide' with regards to Aquinas purposefully. While I will be in basic agreement with much of what Aquinas teaches, I will also attempt to clarify, correct, and even, at times, go beyond what he proposes.

within the foundational mystery of the Christian faith. It would seem appropriate that the Trinity itself should bear primary witness to the attributes of either immutability and impassibility or mutability and passibility.

This study is not the place to recount the development of the doctrine of the Trinity as it arose out of scripture and found expression in the early church.[2] I take as my starting point the Christian trinitarian tradition, founded upon the councils of Nicea and Constantinople I, which professed that the Son and the Holy Spirit are *homoousioi* (one in being) with the Father, and thus that the one God is a trinity of co-equal persons or subjects. Equally, following the tradition initiated by Gregory of Nazianzus and developed by Augustine and Aquinas, I hold that what distinguishes the persons of the Trinity is their relationships, that is, that they subsist as distinct subjects or are defined as distinct persons only in relationship to one another.[3] I first wish to examine more fully the significance and implications of the persons of the Trinity being subsistent relations.

Human persons are partially defined by their relationships and so cannot be fully understood apart from their relationships. A father is a father only because he begets a child and so is related to his child as father. A woman is a wife only because she has a husband. Children are sons or daughters only because they are related to their parents who begot them. However, human persons are not entirely constituted by their relationships. Relationships can cease (a parent, a child, or a spouse can die), and yet the person continues to live.[4] A human person can also make new relationships (one can marry or make a new friend). Human persons then possess relational potential which can be actualized, and in so doing they are defined as who they are. While human persons cannot

---

2 See the standard histories on the development of the doctrine of the Trinity. For example: S.G. Hall, *Doctrine and Practice in the Early Church* (London: SPCK, 1991); J.N.D. Kelly, *Early Christian Doctrines*; Pelikan, *The Christian Tradition 1*; Studer, *Trinity and Incarnation*; A.W. Wainwright, *The Trinity in the New Testament* (London: SPCK, 1962).

3 Gregory of Nazianzus wrote that 'the difference of manifestation, if I may so express myself, or rather of their mutual relations one to another, has caused the difference of their names' (*Oratio*, 31, 9). See Augustine, *De Trinitate*, VI: 6, 9, 11, 14; VII, 9. Aquinas defines a divine person as 'a relation as subsisting' (*Summa Theologica* [hereafter, *ST*], I, 29, 4). Also see I, 40. For the *ST* I am using the translation by the Fathers of the English Dominican Province (New York: Benziger Brothers, 1947).

  Aquinas notes that, unlike other genera such as quantity and quality which signify something inherent in a subject, the notion of relation 'in its own proper meaning signifies only what refers to another' (*ST*, I, 28, 1). Thus 'relation' signifies 'a way of being *towards*.' As subsistent relations the persons of the Trinity are completely and solely defined insofar as they 'are for' one another. W. Kasper writes: 'The three persons of the Trinity are pure relationality; they are relations in which the one nature of God exists in three distinct and non-interchangeable ways. They are subsistent relations.' *The God of Jesus Christ*, p. 309. See also pp. 279–81, 289–90.

  See also W. Hill, *The Three-Personed God* (Washington, DC: Catholic University of America Press, 1982), pp. 71–73; L. Boff, *Trinity and Society* (New York: Orbis, 1988), pp. 57, 92, 127, 138; and Pannenberg, *Systematic Theology*, Vol. 1, pp. 322–25, 428–31.

4 Of course a parent or a child remains such even after death and so continues to be related in this sense. However, because human persons are not totally defined by their relationships, a child can remain alive even if its parents die, or vice-versa.

exist without relationships, yet they are always more than the sum total of their relationships.[5]

For human beings not to be completely constituted by their relationships may first appear to be a good thing. Human persons possess an independent integrity apart from their relationships. However, it is precisely this independent integrity which does not allow a human person to be given completely to another, but he or she must do so only through mediating words (words of kindness and love) and actions (hugs, kisses, sexual relations, etc.) which express only a partial giving of oneself even if one's intention is to give the whole of oneself.[6] This is not the case within the Trinity.

The persons of the Trinity are eternally constituted in their own singular identity only in relation to one another, and thus they subsist as who they are only within their mutual relationships. In their relationships to one another each person of the Trinity subsistently defines, and is equally subsistently defined by, the other persons. Thus the persons of the Trinity are subsistent relations. These mutual subsistent relationships, which constitute and define the identity of the persons of the Trinity, are founded upon origin and action.[7]

The Father subsists eternally as Father only in relation to the Son and to the Holy Spirit, for his very identity as Father is predicated upon his being the origin of the Son and of the Holy Spirit, and so he is constituted as Father in the one eternal act of begetting the Son and spirating the Holy Spirit.[8] The Father then only subsists as Father in and by giving

---

5 J. Galot argues that the very nature of being a person is to be relational. Thus he proposes that human persons, as well as divine persons, are subsistent relations, that is, our relations constitute who we are – our identity. Nonetheless, as human persons we only form relationships through our nature as human beings, and so, while our relationships define who we are, we always have further relational potential to be actualized. While Galot emphasizes the similarity between divine and human persons, an emphasis I would agree with, here I wish to highlight the dissimilarity. See J. Galot, *The Person of Christ* (Rome: Gregorian University Press, 1981 and Chicago: Franciscan Herald Press, 1983); and *Who is Christ?* (Chicago: Franciscan Herald Press, 1981), pp. 279–313.

6 Of course there can be hostile relations mediated through words of anger and hatred or through actions of spitefulness and fighting.

    There is also one exception to what has just been stated. While the inter-relationship between human persons only partially defines each human person, a human person is entirely defined as 'a creature' in relationship to God as Creator. This relationship, unlike other relationships, cannot be broken for if it were broken, the human person would cease to exist. What makes the Creator–creature relationship unique will be discussed later in this chapter.

7 See Aquinas, *ST*, I, 28, 4; I, 29, 4; I, 36, 2, ad 7; I, 40, 2; I, 40, 4. Aquinas states: 'Now the divine persons are multiplied by reason of their origin; and origin includes the idea of someone from whom another comes, and of someone that comes from another, and by these two modes a person can be known' (*ST*, I, 32, 3). Or again: 'In the divine persons distinction is founded on origin. But origin can be properly designated only by certain acts. Wherefore, to signify the order of origin in the divine persons, we must attribute notional acts to the persons' (*ST*, I, 41, 1). See also Gregory of Nyssa, *Quod non sint tres*, and Gregory of Nazianzus, *Oratio*, 29, 2 and 31, 8–9.

8 Aquinas states that it is better to say that the Father is the principle rather than the cause of the Son and the Holy Spirit since 'cause seems to mean diversity of substance, and dependence of one from another; which is not implied in the word *principle*. For in all kinds of causes there is always to be found between the cause and the effect a distance

himself wholly as Father in the begetting of his Son. He gives himself wholly in the begetting of the Son through the Holy Spirit. The Father then equally and simultaneously gives himself wholly in spirating the Holy Spirit for the Holy Spirit proceeds from the Father as the fulness of his fatherly love in and by whom the Father begets the Son.[9] Thus, the Son and the Holy Spirit are fully divine only because the Father has given himself wholly as Father, and the Father is Father only because his whole identity is founded upon the action of his complete giving of himself. The Father only subsists as Father in relation to the Son and the Holy Spirit.

The Son subsists eternally as Son only in relation to the Father and to the Holy Spirit, for his very identity is predicated upon his being begotten of the Father from whom he takes his origin and upon his being conformed by the Holy Spirit, in whom he is begotten, to be the Son of and for the Father. As the Son, he in turn gives himself completely to the Father as Son in the same Spirit who conformed him to be Son of and for the Father. Thus, the Holy Spirit proceeds from the Son as the act of the Son's total giving himself in love for the Father who begot him in the same Holy Spirit of love. Therefore, the Son is Son only because he is begotten by the Father in the Holy Spirit and in the reciprocal giving of himself completely to the Father in the same Spirit in whom he was begotten. There is nothing which constitutes the Son as Son other than his being begotten of the Father in the Spirit and in the act of giving himself as Son to the Father in the same Spirit, and thus he subsists as Son only in relationship to them.

The Holy Spirit subsists eternally as the Holy Spirit only in relation to the Father and to the Son, for his identity as the Holy Spirit is predicated upon his coming forth from the Father as the one in whom the Father begets the Son and as the one in whom the Son, having been begotten in the Spirit, in turn completely gives himself, in the Spirit, to the Father as Son. Thus, while the Spirit comes forth from the Father as the Father's love in whom the Son is begotten and proceeds from the Son as the Son's love of the Father, the Holy Spirit equally only subsists, as the Holy Spirit, in the act of conforming the Father to be Father of and for the Son, and in the simultaneous act of conforming the Son to be Son of and for

---

of perfection or of power; whereas we use the term *principle* even in things which have no such difference, but have only a certain order to each other' (*ST*, I, 33, 1, ad 1).

Moreover, unlike the causal temporal act of human begetting which becomes a 'finished' or 'completed' act, the eternal act of begetting does not cease, and therefore it is more a continuous principle rather than a finished cause. Likewise, for the Father to be the origin of the Son and the Holy Spirit does not then imply a causal precedence, priority, or sequence. See D. Braine, *The Reality of Time and the Existence of God* (Oxford: Clarendon Press, 1988), p. 122.

9 The conception of the Trinity that I am both summarizing and further developing here is the one I put forth in my book *The Father's Spirit of Sonship: Reconceiving the Trinity* (Edinburgh: T & T Clark, 1995). There I argued for the thesis that the Father begets the Son in or by the Holy Spirit. The Son is begotten in the Spirit, and thus the Spirit simultaneously proceeds from the Father as the one in whom the Son is begotten. This conception of the Trinity, I argue, gives to the Holy Spirit a proper defining active role within the Trinity, and in so doing not only gives greater symmetry to the Trinity, but also better accounts for why the Holy Spirit is a person, that is, an active member along with the Father and the Son in the constituting of the trinitarian relationships.

the Father. There is nothing which constitutes the Holy Spirit as Holy Spirit other than his proceeding from the Father and the Son and so conforming the Father to be Father of and for the Son and the Son to be the Son of and for the Father, and thus he subsists as the Holy Spirit only in relation to them.[10]

A number of important conclusions must now be drawn. First, because the persons of the Trinity only subsist as distinct subjects in relationship to one another, they are fully, completely, and absolutely relational. Each distinct person is defined as who he singularly is, and so subsists as who he is, only in relation to the other two. The Father, the Son and the Holy Spirit solely and completely are who they are only in relation to one another.

Second, because the persons of the Trinity subsist only in relation to one another, they are relations in act and only relations in act. As designating subsistent relations or relations fully in act, the terms 'Father,' 'Son,' and 'Holy Spirit' are therefore *verbs*, for they refer to, define, and name, solely and exclusively, the *interrelated acts* by which all three persons are who they are.[11] The Father is not 'someone' who possesses fatherhood. The term 'Father' designates that the Father is completely and solely 'fatherhood in act' and nothing more. The Son is sonship itself for he is begotten by the Father in the Spirit and so gives himself in the same Spirit to the Father as Son. The Holy Spirit has no specific name because the Holy Spirit is solely defined as the one who proceeds from the Father and the Son and in so doing is the act which conforms the Father to be Father of and for the Son and the Son to be Son of and for the Father.[12] Put succinctly and boldly, the persons of the Trinity are not

10 In my book *The Father's Spirit of Sonship* I argued that, while Aquinas emphasized that the Father, the Son, and the Holy Spirit subsist as relations of opposition, they equally subsist as relations of complementarity to one another.

> The Father is Father not only in opposition to the Son and the Son is Son not only in opposition to the Father, but they also, in their relatedness complement one another as being, respectively, Father for the Son and Son for the Father. This complementarity of the persons as subsistent relations is due again to the Holy Spirit. By being the one in whom the Father begets the Son and so is Father for the Son, and by being the one in whom the Son is begotten and so is Son for the Father, the Holy Spirit subsists as the source of their complementarity. The Trinity of persons then subsists in opposition to one another only as complementary relations. Pp. 82–83.

11 In *The Father's Spirit of Sonship* I emphasize that there is a '*perichoresis of action.*'

> While, in both the East and the West, the *perichoresis* or circumincession has been seen as *the result* of the begetting and the spirating, I have emphasized the *perichoresis* of the actions themselves. Because the Father spirates the Spirit as he begets the Son, for it is in the Spirit that the Son is begotten, there is a *perichoresis* of action – the acts of begetting and spiration co-inhere in one another and thus account for why the persons themselves co-inhere. Actually, the persons themselves are the co-inhering acts. This *perichoresis* of the trinitarian act gives an unprecedented dynamism to the persons and to their life within the Trinity. Pp. 79–80.

12 Aquinas holds that the Holy Spirit does not possess a proper name, but can appropriately be called Holy Spirit because he is spirated and, like the Father and the Son, he is both spirit and holy. See *ST*, I, 27, 4, ad 3; I, 28, 4; I, 36, 1. Aquinas based this idea on Augustine, *De Trinitate*, V, 12.

nouns; they are verbs and the names which designate them – Father, Son and Holy Spirit – designate the acts by which they are defined.

By stating that the persons of the Trinity are verbs and not nouns does not mean that they are not acting subjects or persons, as if one needs a noun (a subject or person) in order to perform an action. Because the acts (the verbs) that completely define and constitute the Father, the Son and the Holy Spirit are personal or subjective acts (and not impersonal acts), the very acts themselves constitute the subjectivity or personhood of the Father, the Son and the Holy Spirit. Within the Trinity the action (the verb) constitutes the subject and the subject is a verb – the action by which he is so constituted.

The Trinity: Immutable and Impassible

The conclusion to which all of this leads is that the Father, the Son and the Holy Spirit, as subsistent relations fully in act, are immutable and impassible. They are immutable not because they are static or inert in their relationships, but precisely for the opposite reason. Because they are subsistent relations fully in act, because the terms 'Father,' 'Son,' and 'Holy Spirit' designate pure acts (and thus are pure verbs and nothing other than verbs), they do not have any relational potential which would need to be actualized in order to make them more relational – more who they are. As subsistent relations fully in act, the persons of the Trinity are utterly and completely dynamic and active in their integral and comprehensive self-giving to one another, and could not possibly become any more dynamic or active in their self-giving since they are constituted, and so subsist, as who they are only in their complete and utter self-giving to one another.

Moreover, they are impassible not because they lack passion, in the sense of being fully loving and completely self-giving, but again precisely for the opposite reason. As subsistent relations fully in act, the persons of the Trinity are completely and utterly passionate in their self-giving to one another and cannot become more passionate for they are

---

In *The Father's Spirit of Sonship*, I state:

The Holy Spirit does not have a distinct name because he subsists precisely as the one in whom the Father and the Son are named. The Father subsists in relation to the Son (and so is named Father) only in the Holy Spirit by whom he begot the Son. The Son subsists in relation to the Father (and so is named Son) only in the Holy Spirit who conformed him to be Son. The Spirit subsists as a pure relation together with the Father and the Son in that he sustains their relationship and so imparts or manifests their names. The Holy Spirit is the hidden or unnamed person or 'who' because the very nature of his subjectivity as a subsistent relation is to illuminate or, more deeply, to substantiate or person the Father and the Son for one another. . . . This is in keeping with the Holy Spirit's economic mission. The role of the Spirit in the economy of salvation is not to make himself known, but to manifest the love of God the Father and Jesus as Son. Pp. 84–85.

See also, C. Gunton, *The One, the Three and the Many* (Cambridge: Cambridge University Press, 1993), p. 190; Kasper, *The God of Jesus Christ*, pp. 198, 223; and H.U. von Balthasar, *Explorations in Theology III: Creator Spirit* (San Francisco: Ignatius Press, 1993), pp. 114–15.

constituted, and so subsist, as who they are only because they have absolutely given themselves completely to one another in love.[13]

Thus we see that the Trinity itself demands that the divine persons be immutable and impassible, and it does so for unconditionally positive reasons. If the divine persons were not immutable and impassible, they would not be subsistent relations fully in act, and so their absolute dynamic intimacy as distinctly related subjects would be shattered.[14]

God as *Actus Purus*

Having just argued that the Christian doctrine of the Trinity demands that the divine persons be immutably and impassibly who they are, not in a stagnant or inert manner, but in a way that is supremely dynamic and supremely relational, I now want to put forth the purely philosophical reasons for why God is immutable and impassible. Because these arguments are solely philosophical in nature, and thus according to reason, and not founded upon revelation, they will concern the one God rather than the Trinity since reason alone cannot establish that God is a trinity of persons. However, as we will see, what is established through revelation and doctrine is reinforced and in accord with what can be grasped by reason, and vice-versa.

The Christian biblical and patristic tradition holds that God is almighty, all-powerful, all-perfect, eternal, immutable, and impassible. But what is it about the very nature of God which demands that he possess these and similar attributes? Here I would argue, in accordance with Aquinas, that God's nature is 'to be', that he is *ipsum esse* (to-be itself) and thus, *actus purus* (pure act).[15] In order to understand what it means for God to be 'to-be itself' it is first necessary to discern the meaning of *esse* (to be) with regards to finite beings.[16]

In finite beings Aquinas makes a distinction between what something

---

13 See M. Dodds, 'St Thomas Aquinas and the Motion of the Motionless God,' *New Blackfriars* 86 (1987):238–39 and G. Hanratty, 'Divine Immutability and Impassibility Revisited' in *At the Heart of the Real*, ed. F. O'Rourke (Dublin: Irish Academic Press, 1992), p. 155.

14 As we will see, Aquinas argues that God, as *ipsum esse*, cannot be placed within a genus for he has no substantial quiddity by which to classify him. What Aquinas and the tradition failed to discern is that the persons of the Trinity, as subsistent relations, are also placed outside the order of genus. As relations fully in act, they cannot be classified for they too are signified and designated by verbs. Thus the Trinity itself demands that there be an ontological distinction between itself and all else. The very character of the Trinity specifies its radical mode of transcendence, in that it be wholly other than and so totally distinct from the created order.

15 A great deal has been written concerning Aquinas' notion of God. For example see: D. Burrell, *Aquinas: God and Action* (London: Routledge & Kegan Paul, 1979); B. Davies, *Thinking About God* (London: Geoffrey Chapman, 1985); B. Davies, *The Thought of Thomas Aquinas* (Oxford: Clarendon Press, 1992); M. Dodds, *The Unchanging God of Love* (Fribourg: Editions Universitaires Fribourg Suisse, 1985); E. Gilson, *God and Philosophy* (New Haven: Yale University Press, 1941); E. Gilson, *The Christian Philosophy of St Thomas Aquinas* (London: Gollancz, 1957); E.L. Mascall, *He Who Is* (London: Libra Books, 1966); E.L. Mascall, *Existence and Analogy* (London: Libra Books, 1966); Owen, *Concepts of Deity*.

16 In the following I am further developing what I wrote in *Does God Change?*, pp. 74–82.

is, its essence or quiddity, and that something is. 'I can know, for instance, what a man or a phoenix is and still be ignorant whether it has being or reality. From this it is clear that being is other than essence or quiddity, unless perhaps there is a reality whose quiddity is its being.'[17] Thus, for Aquinas, *esse* is that act by which something actually does exist. *Esse* (to be) is a verb and as such does not possess any quiddity, but purely specifies the act by which something exists and so is the foundation of all subsequent actions performed by the existing being.[18] While *esse* (to be) and *essentia* (quiddity) are distinct in that *esse* possesses no quiddity and *essentia* possesses no *esse*, yet they are not realities in themselves.[19] Rather, only beings actually exist and so *esse* and *essentia* are related to one another, for Aquinas, in an act–potency relationship. *Esse* makes *to be* what potentially is and potentially *what is* only *is* because of *esse*.[20]

Because *esse* and *essentia* are distinct within finite reality, no finite being, whether it be a man, dog, or star, is of such a nature that its nature demands that it be. Therefore, Aquinas argues that the *esse* of finite creatures must come from an extrinsic cause.[21] 'There must be a reality that is the cause of being for all things, because it is pure being (*esse*

---

17 *De Ente et Essentia*, 4, 6. Translation from *On Being and Essence*, A. Maurer (Toronto: Pontifical Institute of Mediaeval Studies, 1968).

    E. Gilson writes: 'The definition of no empirically given thing is existence; hence its essence is not existence, but existence must be conceived as distinct from it.' *God and Philosophy*, p. 71.

18 Because *esse* has no quiddity it cannot be conceptualized by the mind. Being a verb, *esse* designates action as do all verbs, but here it specifies that act by which a being is and without which it would not be. For Aquinas 'a being is said to be in as much as it possesses being (*esse*)' (XII *Metaphysica*, lect. I, 2419). Thus *esse* is the basis of all subsequent actions. See *De Potentia*, 7, 2, ed. 9, and *De Anima*, 6.

    G. Phelan writes:

> Things which 'have being' are not 'just there' (*Dasein*) like lumps of static essence, inert, immovable, unprogressive, and unchanging. The act of existence (*esse*) is not a state, it is an act, the act of all acts, and therefore, must be understood as act and not as any static and definable object of conception. *Esse* is dynamic impulse, energy, act – the first, the most persistent and enduring of all dynamisms, all energies, all acts. 'The Existentialism of St Thomas,' *Selected Papers*, ed. A.G. Kirn (Toronto: Pontifical Institute of Mediaeval Studies, 1967), p. 77.

19 See *De Veritate*, 27, 1; and *Super Libros Sententiarum*, I, d 13, q 1, a 3.

20 Aquinas states: 'That in which act is present is a potentiality, since act, as such is referred to potentiality. Therefore, in every created substance there is potentiality and act'. *Summa Contra Gentiles* [hereafter, *SCG*], II, 53, 3. Trans. *On the Truth of the Catholic Faith*, eds J. Anderson, A. Pegis, V.J. Bourke, J. O'Neil (Garden City: Image Books, 1955–57). See also *De Ente et Essentia*, 4, 8.

    For a discussion of Aquinas' distinction between *esse* and *essentia* and its importance see D. Burrell, *Knowing the Unknowable God* (Notre Dame: University Press of Notre Dame, 1986), pp. 19–34; and J.B. Reichmann, 'Immanently Transcendent and Subsistent Esse: A Comparison,' *The Thomist* 38/2 (1974):335–43, and 'Aquinas, God and Historical Process,' in *Tommaso d'Aquino nel suo settimo centenario*, Vol. 9, (Naples: Edizioni Domenicane Italiane, 1978), p. 428.

    For a contemporary exposition of the *esse–essentia* distinction see D. Braine, *The Reality of Time and the Existence of God*, pp. 138–61.

21 Aquinas states:

> Whatever belongs to a thing is either caused by the principles of its nature . . . or comes to it from an extrinsic principle. . . . Now being itself cannot be caused by

tantum). If this were not so, one would go on to infinity in causes, for everything that is not pure being has a cause of its being.' This being who is pure *esse* is 'the first cause or God.'[22] Aquinas' understanding of God as pure *esse* is founded upon what *esse* is in creatures. God must be pure *esse* for this is what finite beings lack, and what they must be given if they are to be. If God were not pure *esse*, he would be in the same situation as creatures and so be in need of *esse* himself. While finite beings are composite beings in which their essence and *esse* are in an act–potency relationship, God, whose very nature is to be, *ipsum esse*, is not composite, and 'therefore his essence is his existence,' that is, his very nature or quiddity is *'to-be'* and nothing more.[23]

What must be grasped and remembered, something which Aquinas' critics never seem to do, is that *esse* is an act, that *esse* is a verb. As *ipsum esse* God's very nature, as with the persons of the Trinity, is not then designated or signified by a noun, but by a verb.[24] Being pure act (pure verb) as *ipsum esse* does not mean that God is *something* fully in act, such as a creature might actualize its full potential, but rather that God is act pure and simple. Because God is *ipsum esse* he has no self-constituting potency which needs to be actualized in order for him to be more fully who he is, not because he is *something* fully in act, but again, because he is act pure and simple. God is *actus purus.*[25]

---

the form or quiddity of a thing (by 'caused' I mean by an efficient cause) because that thing would then be its own cause and it would bring itself into being, which is impossible. It follows that everything whose being is distinct from its nature must have being from another. *De Ente et Essentia,* 4, 7. See also *ST*, I, 3, 4, and *SCG,* I, 22, 6.

22 *De Ente et Essentia,* 4, 7.

23 *ST*, I, 3, 4. See also I, 3, 1–3. Aquinas' arguments that God is *ipsum esse,* as they appear in his early work *De Ente et Essentia* and the two *Summae,* could be interpreted as proofs for the existence of God. However, their primary focus, especially in the *Summae,* seems to be that of establishing what the nature of God is and not that God is. Obviously, if God is *ipsum esse,* then for Aquinas the question whether God is and the question what God is become one and the same question, but only after they have been treated separately. See *SCG*, I, 22, 6 and *ST*, I, 3, 4.

24 D. Burrell states that to say God is *ipsum esse* or *actus purus* is to say that 'God's essence is to exist, more precisely as: "to be God is to be to-be".' *Aquinas: God and Action,* p. 42. See also pp. 115–19. See also his *Knowing the Unknowable God,* pp. 42–50.

25 Aquinas argues that his understanding of God as *ipsum esse* and *actus purus* is totally in keeping with the biblical revelation that God is 'He Who Is' (Exod. 3:14). 'He Who Is' is the most proper name of God 'For it does not signify form, but simply existence itself. Hence since the existence of God is his essence itself, which can be said of no other, it is clear that among the other names this one specially denotes God, for everything is denominated by its form.' *ST*, I, 13, 11. See also *SCG,* I, 22 and *De Potentia,* 2, 1. Because God's name is 'He Who Is' and thus specifies that his essence is 'to be,' he is unknowable for human beings cannot conceive what pure being is. To know that the proper name of God *is to-be (ipsum esse)* is different from knowing *what* to be *to-be* is or means. Thus Aquinas' understanding of God is totally in keeping with the biblical understanding. For God in revealing his name as 'He Who Is,' has also revealed that he is unknowable. See Burrell, *Aquinas: God and Action,* p. 42; E. Gilson, *The Spirit of Mediaeval Philosophy* (London: Sheed and Ward, 1936), chapters 3 and 4; Mascall, *Existence and Analogy,* pp. 12–15; Murray, *The Problem of God,* pp. 5–30, 66–76; Reichmann, 'Aquinas, God and Historical Process,' pp. 429–31; Reichmann, 'Immanently Transcendent and Subsistent Esse: A Comparison,' pp. 344–60.

God: Immutable and Impassible

Because God is *actus purus* it is evident why God is all-perfect, and thus immutable. If '*esse* is the actuality of all acts, and on account of this is the perfection of all perfections,' then God as *actus purus* 'must needs be most actual, and therefore most perfect; for a thing is perfect in proportion to its state of actuality, because we call that perfect which lacks nothing of the mode of its perfection.'[26] God is then perfect not because he has perfected all his potential, but, being *ipsum esse*, he is perfection itself.

This is why God is immutable. Because God is pure act it is impossible for him to acquire more perfection through some change which would make him more actual. 'Everything which is in any way changed, is in some way potentiality. Hence it is evident that it is impossible for God to be in any way changeable.' Being pure act God possesses 'all the plenitude of perfection of all being. He cannot acquire anything new' through change, that is, by actualizing some potential.[27] While the attribute of immutability is a negative attribute, it is founded on something that is entirely positive – God being pure act or being itself. God is immutable not because he is static, inert, or inactive, but precisely because he, as pure act, is supremely active and dynamic and cannot ontologically become more in act. As M. Dodds states:

> The true significance of the attribute of divine immutability in the theology of St. Thomas consists, not in the fact that it indicates the invariable self-identity of God, but in the fact that it indicates the dynamic and boundless perfection of God as *ipsum esse subsistens*. . . . Far from implying, therefore, that God may be somehow static or inert, the attribute of immutability directly signifies that God, as pure *esse*, is pure dynamic actuality.[28]

God then is supremely immutable because he is supremely in act.

The problem is that all critics of Aquinas and the Christian tradition consistently interpret divine immutability in a positive manner, as if to say that God is immutable is to conceive him as static and inert. As was noted earlier, Barth gives one of the most striking accounts of this understanding when he states that if God were absolutely immutable, he would be utterly immobile and lifeless, and thus God would be death.[29]

Dodds, in what is by far the best comprehensive study on Aquinas' understanding of divine immutability, comments on this misinterpretation by noting that 'it is quite possible for us to assume that when immutability is predicated of God, it is that creaturely sort of

---

26 *De Potentia*, 7, 2, ad 9 and *ST*, I, 4, 1. See also *SCG*, I, 28.

27 *ST*, I, 9, 1. Aquinas also writes: 'All motion or mutation, in whatever way it is predicated, results from some potentiality since motion is the act of something existing in potency. Therefore, since God is pure act, having no admixture of potency, there cannot be any change in him.' I *Sent.*, 8, 3, 1. See also the Papal International Theological Commission's document, *Theology, Christology, Anthropology* (1983), II, B, 4.1.

28 Dodds, *The Unchanging God of Love*, p. 227. Dodds footnotes Aquinas *De Veritate*, 21, 4, ad 7. See also M. Dodds, 'St Thomas and the Motion of the Motionless God,' *New Blackfriars* 68 (1987):233-42, especially 235–38.

29 See *Church Dogmatics* II/1, p. 494.

immutability, whose image is present in our imagination, which is intended. The result of such an assumption is, as we have seen, usually a monstrous image of the unchanging God'.[30]

G. Grisez argues that because one holds that God is immutable, it does not follow that he is 'standing still, fixed, inert, or rigid.' Moreover, to say that God 'is not affected by man's suffering and stops with this negation, one strongly suggests that he is cold and unconcerned about evil. One must negate of God *everything* descriptive of entities given in experience.'[31]

I state in *Does God Change?*:

One should not be misled into thinking that God's immutability is like the immutability of a rock only more so. What God and rocks appear to have in common is only the fact that they do not change. The reason for their unchangeableness is for polar-opposite reasons. . . . God is unchangeable not because he is inert or static like a rock, but for just the opposite reason. He is so dynamic, so active that no change can make him more active. He is act pure and simple.[32]

This should be kept in mind when one considers process theology or any other theology that predicates change in God in order to make him more dynamic. In making God mutable, process theology's notion of God has more in common with rocks than does Aquinas' notion of God.

What the critics consistently fail to grasp is that God's immutability is not opposed to his vitality. Nor need one hold together in some dialectical fashion his immutability and his vibrancy, as if in spite of being immutable he is nonetheless dynamic. Rather, it is precisely God's immutability as *actus purus* that guarantees and authenticates his pure vitality and absolute dynamism. Thus, when the critics assert that because Aquinas and the tradition believe God to be immutable they espouse a static and inert conception of God, they but demonstrate their own lack of understanding.[33]

Aquinas did not treat impassibility when considering the various attributes of God within his two *Summae*. It arises primarily in the context of discussing God's willing and loving. The objection is raised: 'It seems

---

30 *The Unchanging God of Love*, p. 221. See also 211–15.
31 *Beyond the New Theism*, pp. 245–46. See also pp. 264–65.
32 Pp. 78–79.
33 For further studies on or arguments on behalf of Aquinas' notion of divine immutability see: Burrell, *Aquinas: God and Action*, pp. 15–38; Davies, *Thinking About God*, pp. 161–65; Davies, *The Thought of Thomas Aquinas*, pp. 101–63; L.B. Gillon, 'Dieu Immobile Et Dieu en Mouvement,' *Doctor Communis* 29 (1976):135–45; Hanratty, 'Divine Immutability and Impassibility Revisited', pp. 148–57; T.J. Kondoleon, 'The Immutability of God: Some Recent Challenges,' *The New Scholasticism* 58/3 (1984):293–315; H. McCabe, *God Matters* (London: Geoffrey Chapman, 1987), pp. 39–46; Owen, *Concepts of Deity*, pp. 22–23; S. Sia, 'The Doctrine of God's Immutability: Introducing the Modern Debate,' *New Blackfriars* 68 (1987):224.

      P. Helm places God's immutability within God's eternity. See *Eternal God: A Study of God Without Time* (Oxford: Clarendon Press, 1988), especially p. 90. W.E. Mann argues for the immutability of God from his simplicity. See 'Simplicity and Immutability in God' in *The Concept of God*, ed. T.V. Morris (Oxford: Oxford University Press, 1987), pp. 253–67.

that love does not exist in God. For in God there are no passions. Now love is a passion. Therefore love is not in God.'[34] Obviously, Aquinas wants to hold that God does love and does so supremely. He therefore distinguishes between passion and love within human beings and love (without passibility) within God.

In response to the above objection Aquinas argues that passion in human beings pertains to the will and to the objects toward which the will tends. The will tends toward the good as an object known and so loved.[35] In human beings the knowledge of a thing as good arouses the sensitive appetite (pertaining to the senses) with its concomitant sensible emotion, which in turn motivates the will to desire and obtain the good as loved. For example, I come to know someone and in so doing I find him or her to be good and attractive. This knowledge arouses within me thoughts and feelings of love and affection and so my will desires to express this love in the hope of becoming friends with the person. For Aquinas, this process, this arousal of the sensitive appetite through sensitive knowledge with its concomitant sensible emotion by a known and loved good is passion. 'Therefore acts of the sensitive appetite, inasmuch as they have annexed to them some bodily change, are called passions.'[36] In human beings then passion denotes a twofold change. First, through knowledge of a known good the sensitive appetite is aroused, which carries with it a sensible bodily emotional change; and second, the will is thus motivated and moved to desire and obtain the good as loved.[37]

In contrast God does not undergo this passible process. God is not corporeal and so does not possess sensitive knowledge or a sensitive appetite. 'Therefore, there is no passion in God.'[38] However, God does possess intellect and will. God, being pure act, knows and wills in the one act that he himself is.[39] While God does not then possess a sensitive intellect and a sensitive appetite, both of which pertain to human

34 *ST*, I, 20, 1, obj. 1. This is similar to the objections raised against Aquinas and the tradition. If God is not passible, he cannot love.
35 See *ST*, I, 20, 1 and I, 82, 2, ad 1.
36 *ST*, I, 20, 1, ad 1.
37 Since this process is the activating of the intellect and the will to desire and obtain a known good as loved, it exemplifies, for Aquinas, an act–potency relationship which therefore marks a change. See *ST*, I, 82, 3, ad 2.

    M. Dodds notes that in human love there is, for Aquinas, both motion and stability (a type of immutability). The human person is moved, and so changed, by the desire to possess the loved known good. However, in possessing what is loved, the lover comes to rest. 'That ultimate union and rest is found only in the real union of lover and beloved.' *The Unchanging God of Love*, p. 279. See also pp. 277–80.

    Similarly for human knowledge, as for love, there is 'motion and stability' – a searching for the truth and a resting in the possession of it. For Aquinas 'certainty' (*certitudo*) refers to this 'rest' – in the union of the knower and the known. I am grateful to W. Fey for pointing this out to me.
38 *SCG*, I, 89, 2. See also I, 89, 1–7. Aquinas further states:

> Moreover, every passion of the appetite takes place through some bodily change, for example, the contraction or distension of the heart, or something of the sort. Now, none of this can take place in God, since he is not a body or a power in a body. . . . There is, therefore, no passion of the appetite in him. ST, I, 89, 3.

39 See *ST*, I, 14, 1–4 and I, 19, 1.

knowing and willing as a corporeal being, God does possess an intellectual appetite in that his will is focused on the known good and so loved.
Therefore, 'there are certain passions which, though they do not befit
God as passions, do not signify anything by the nature of their species
that is repugnant to the divine perfection.'[40] What Aquinas means here is
that there are human passions which are not contrary to the nature of
God but, because he possesses them not through a passible process but
as part of his unchanging nature, they are not passions, strictly speaking,
within him.

> From this it is manifest that joy and delight is properly in God. For
> just as the apprehended good and evil are the object of sensible
> appetite, so too, are they of intellective appetite. . . . Hence, there are
> found in the intellective appetite, which is the will, operations that in
> the nature of their species are similar to the operations of the
> sensitive appetite, differing in that in the sensitive appetite there are
> passions because of its union to a bodily organ, whereas in the intel-
> lective appetite there are simple operations. . . . Since, then, joy and
> delight are not repugnant to God according to their species, but only
> in so far as they are passions, and since they are found in the will
> according to their species but not as passions, it remains that they are
> not lacking even to the divine will.[41]

Aquinas can equally state that 'Love, therefore, and joy and delight are
passions, [but] in so far as they denote acts of the intellective appetite,
they are not passions. It is in this latter sense that they are in God.'[42]
    What has become evident from the above discussion is that Aquinas,
in denying passion in God, is simply denying of God the passible, and so
changing, process which is inherent within human passion. Thus there is
no passion in God, not in the sense that he does not love, but because,
being pure act, there is no need for an arousal of his will to love the good
and so to come to desire the good and rejoice in it. God's arousal to the
good as loved, and so rejoicing and delighting in it, is eternally and
perfectly in act.[43] If there were changeable and passible passions within
God, as these are found in human beings, it would mean that he is not
fully loving for he would have to actualize further 'loving' potential. This
is why Aquinas states that God 'loves without passion.'[44] This only
means that he loves without undergoing the passible processes and
changes that are inherent within human love. While God is not
passionate in the sense that there are passible passionate changes within
him, he can be said, although Aquinas does not say this, to be passionate
in the sense that his will is fully and wholly fixed on the good as loved.

40 *SCG,* I, 90, 1.
41 *SCG,* I, 90, 3.
42 *ST,* I, 20, 1, ad 1. See also *SCG,* I, 91. D. Braine writes concerning God's love: 'Love does
    not essentially consist in imaginable feelings, but in dispositions and activities of heart
    and will, wherein something is sought or delighted in.' *The Reality of Time and the
    Existence of God,* p. 133.
43 In the *Summa Contra Gentiles* Aquinas states that 'there must be love in God according
    to the act of his will' (I, 91, 1).
44 *ST,* I, 20, 1, ad 1.

Being fully in act his love is fully in act and therefore his passion is fully in act. God cannot become more passionate or loving by actualizing, as human beings do, some further potential and so become more passionate or loving. God is supremely passionate because he is supremely loving and he is both because both are fully in act since God as *ipsum esse* is pure act. This is why 'God is love' (1 Jn 4:6). God would not be simply love if he were not pure love in act, and thus absolute passion in act. God is impassible precisely because he is supremely passionate and cannot become any more passionate.[45] God simply loves himself and all things in himself in the one act which he himself is.[46]

At this juncture we need to interconnect and develop what we have achieved thus far.

The Trinity as the One God is Utterly Relational

From our doctrinal examination of the persons of the Trinity as subsistent relations and from our philosophical study of God as *ipsum esse* what we have discovered is that both converge upon the notion of 'pure act.' As subsistent relations, the Father, the Son, and the Holy Spirit are fully in act in that they are constituted and defined only in the act of being inter-related to one another. Because the persons of the Trinity are subsistent relations fully in act they are verbs (pure acts) and not nouns (substances). Equally, the nature of God, as conceived philosophically, is pure act – *ipsum esse* or *actus purus* – and so is a verb as well. While Aquinas does not bring out this relationship, in that he never addresses the relationship between God being *ipsum esse* and being a trinity of persons, yet he does state that 'relation really existing in God has the existence of the divine essence in no way distinct therefrom. . . . Thus it is clear that in God relation and essence do not differ from each other, but are one and the same.'[47]

Therefore, it is *ipsum esse* which grounds the trinity of persons as being subsistent relations fully in act – pure verbs, and likewise, it is the trinity of persons as subsistent relations fully in act which grounds their being *ipsum esse* – pure verb. There is an inherent ontological reciprocal constitutive relationship, or better, a reciprocal constitutive ontological oneness, between being *ipsum esse* and being subsistent relations (and vice-versa) for both express 'being' as *actus purus*. What we see then from the convergence of our doctrinal and philosophical study is that to be fully 'to-be' (*ipsum esse*) is 'to be fully relational' (a subsistent relation).[48]

---

45 M. Dodds speaks of 'the dynamic stillness' of God's immutable love. See *The Unchanging God of Love*, pp. 280–82.

46 See *ST*, I, 14, 5 and I, 20, 2.

47 *ST*, I, 28, 2.

48 W. Hill argues that because God is *ipsum esse* and thus *actus purus*, his pure dynamism cannot be 'chaotic, unintelligible, utterly without meaning.' He concludes that God as pure being must give rise to intentionality and thus knowing himself as truth, and also to love and thus loving himself as good. 'The import of these intelligible emanations is that they posit *relationality* at the core of existence.' He concedes that a trinity of persons cannot be deduced from such 'an analysis of pure actuality,' but it 'can afford to theological reason, working under the light of faith . . . an a posteriori analogy for talking

For our present study a very important point must now be grasped. God, whether considered under the philosophical rubric of *ipsum esse* or under the doctrinal rubric of a trinity of persons as subsisting relations fully in act, has no self-constituting relational potential which needs to be actualized in order to make him/them more relational. Since the persons of the Trinity are immutable as subsistent relations fully in act in accordance with their being pure being, they do not have any self-constituting relational potential which needs to be actualized in order to make them more relational. This lack of any self-constituting relational potential, since they are subsistent relations fully in act, gives to the persons of the Trinity absolute positive relational potential, that is, they have the singular ability to establish relationships with others other than themselves whereby the persons of the Trinity can relate others to themselves as they are in themselves as a trinity of persons.

Because human beings are not fully relational, they must relate and be related to one another through mediating actions – hugs and kisses. They must actualize their latent and inert relational potential and so positively become related to one another through their actions. This brings about change in human beings. The persons of the Trinity need not, and cannot, do this.

The persons of the Trinity, being fully actualized relations in accordance with being pure being, contain no potency which needs to be actualized or overcome through new actions in order to establish new relations. Because the persons of the Trinity are subsistent relations fully in act, and so are entirely related to one another as they are in themselves, whatever is related to the persons of the Trinity is, in some manner, related to them as they are in themselves. No mediating actions, actions which would involve change on the part of the persons of the Trinity, lie between or establish the relations between the persons of the Trinity and the one(s) to whom they are related. The only change is in the other who is related to the persons of the Trinity, for the other is, in some manner,

---

about the Trinity.' *The Three-Personed God*, pp. 261, 263 and 264. Hill gives a good account, something which Aquinas did not do, of the relationship between God being *ipsum esse* and being a trinity of persons. See pp. 259–68.

While I agree with Hill that pure actuality or pure being does give rise to relationality, I would not want to understand this as implying that the oneness of God as *ipsum esse* has priority over his being a trinity of persons. Rather I would argue that there is a mutual complementarity between God being pure being and being a trinity of persons. God is a trinity of subsistent relations because he is pure being and he is pure being because he is a trinity of subsistent relations. Neither has ontological precedence or importance. This further grounds the truth that pure being must be absolutely relational and that subsistent relations must be fully in act as pure being. Actually, it is not the one being of God as pure being that makes God one, but rather the oneness of God resides in the inter-relatedness of the three persons. What makes the persons three is the very same thing that makes them one, that is, subsisting as pure relations fully in act in accordance with their being pure being. They only subsist as three distinct subjects in their oneness, and they only exist as one in their specific threeness. See Weinandy, *The Father's Spirit of Sonship*, p. 83.

D. Braine appears to have a similar view to my own with regards to the actuality of God and the persons of the Trinity as subsistent relations fully in act. See *The Reality of Time and the Existence of God*, pp. 162–64.

newly related to the persons of the Trinity as they exist in themselves and is so changed in being so related. Thus, and this is absolutely essential to our present study, to be related to the Trinity, in whatever manner, is to be related in the most intimate and dynamic manner. No other relationships could exceed their intimacy and vitality. Let us examine then the Creator–creature relationship both to exemplify this and to lay more of the foundation for discussing further God's relationship with human beings.

God and the Act of Creation

The act of creation establishes the foundational relationship between God and creatures. Because of this it forms the type of relation God has with creatures and the type of relation creatures have with God. Thus it is essential that this relationship be understood properly if we are to assess correctly whether or not God loves his creation, especially human beings, and in so doing is compassionate and merciful towards them, and ultimately whether or not he suffers with them and on their behalf. Again I wish to build upon what we have discovered thus far about the persons of the Trinity being subsistent relations and about the nature of God, as a trinity of subsistent relations, being *ipsum esse* or *actus purus*.

Normally when considering the act of creation, philosophy and theology have focused almost exclusively upon the oneness of God. This is so for a twofold reason. First, the act of creation is seen primarily as springing from the fact that God is *ipsum esse* and as such gives being (*esse*) to creatures. Creation is understood more in the light of philosophy, from what we can learn from reason about God and his creative relationship to his creatures, than from what has been revealed about God as a trinity. Second, especially within the western tradition founded upon Augustine and developed by Anselm and Aquinas, it has been stressed that all acts of God outside of himself are done as one. The Council of Florence affirmed that, where there is no opposition of relation among the persons of the Trinity, all is done as one. Thus the trinity of persons are 'not three principles of creation, but one principle.'[49] While I do not want to deny the truth contained in the above, I believe that too narrow a reading diminishes the Christian understanding and significance of creation, and can even distort the tradition, especially the teaching of Aquinas. However, for the sake of clarity and order, and therefore, hopefully, ease of understanding, I will first examine and develop Aquinas' philosophical understanding of the Creator–creature relationship, and then place it within the context of the

49 *Enchiridion Symbolorum*, eds H. Denzinger, A. Schönmetzer (Friburgi Brisgoviae: Herder, 36 ed, 1976), 1331, see also 1330. See also the Fourth Lateran Council, Denzinger-Schönmetzer, 804. See also Augustine, *De Trinitate*, V, 14, 15; Anselm, *De Processione Spiritus Sancti*, chap. 1.

Aquinas states: 'Now the creative power of God is common to the whole Trinity; and hence it belongs to the unity of the essence, and not to the distinction of the persons.' *ST*, I, 32, 1.

Trinity, something which Aquinas intimated but never fully developed.[50]

For Aquinas relations are of three types.[51] First, there are mutual logical relations or relations according to reason (sometimes also referred to as 'unreal' relations). These relations are made by and in the mind, such as relating Fido to the canine species. Since the relation is mental, neither term is changed or affected by the relation. Second, there are real relations. These relations are founded upon something that is real within the two terms, such as the relation between a parent and a child, or a husband and a wife. Normally considered these relationships bring about a change or effect within the terms for they are established by some mediating action between the two terms.[52] Third, there are relations where the relation is real in one term and logical in another. These mixed relations occur when the terms are not in the same ontological order, such as that between a knower and the known, the Creator and the creature, and the Son of God and his humanity. In such a relationship the real term is affected or changed (the knower, the creature, and Christ's humanity), but the logical term (the known, the Creator, and the Son of God) are not changed by the relationship.[53] It is this mixed relation, as exemplified in the Creator–creature relation, that we must examine more closely for it is pivotal for the validity of the present argument.

For Aquinas, 'Creation signified actively means the divine action, which is God's essence, with a relation to the creature. But in God, relation to the creature is not real, but only a relation of reason; whereas the relation of the creature to God is a real relation.'[54] At first sight, as Aquinas' critics are incessantly pointing out, this appears to mean that while creation is related to God, God is not related to the creature. If this interpretation were correct, it would not only disavow and exclude God's love for and care of creation, but it would even more critically

50 I could have first examined creation in the light of the Trinity, and this might have been more theologically correct since philosophy must be in accord with revelation. However, I thought it would be best to treat first the philosophical issues since they are more complex, more difficult to grasp, and the most controversial. Having first sorted out the philosophical issues, it would then be easier to perceive and understand the significance of the Trinity within the act of creation.

51 I will be summarizing and developing here what I wrote in *Does God Change?*, pp. 88–96. See also A. Krempel, *La Doctrine de la Relation chez Saint Thomas* (Paris: J. Vrin, 1952); M. Henninger, *Relations: Medieval Theories 1250–1325* (Oxford: Clarendon Press, 1989), pp. 13–39; and E. Muller, 'Real Relations and the Divine: Issues in Thomas's Understanding of God's Relation to the World,' *Theological Studies* 56 (1995):673–95.

   W. Pannenberg believes that the notion of relation as applied to God is one of the crucial theological tasks of contemporary theology. He holds that such a notion cannot fall into the pantheism of Spinoza, nor the divine process of Hegel and Whitehead (see *Systematic Theology*, Vol. 1, p. 367). Hopefully, the following investigation will contribute to the contemporary discussion.

52 Real relations can also be founded upon quality or quantity, such as weight or color. While the relation is founded in reality, it need not bring about a change, for example, in what is termed a 'Cambridge change' where two terms are newly related because a change takes place in only one of the terms, such as one man being now shorter than another because the other man grew. There is a change in the relationship, but not a change in the man who is now shorter. See P.T. Geach, 'God's Relation to the World,' *Sophia* 8/2 (1969):1–4. Time and space can also found real relations.

53 See *ST*, I, 13, 7; also I, 28, 1 and *De Veritate*, 1, 5, ad 16.

54 *ST*, I, 45, 3, ad 1.

repudiate that God was actually the Creator. Such a position would be sheer nonsense and, moreover, one that Aquinas would hardly espouse.

To interpret him properly what must first be grasped is that, for Aquinas, 'to create' is to bring something into being and so pertains, not so much to what a thing is, but more specifically to that it is.[55] Thus the act of creation does not imply motion, change, or succession, for motion, change, and succession only take place in previously existing beings. The act of creation is something much more radical and even more dynamic than any possible change which may occur among existing beings, that is, the establishment of the creature itself as existing. The effect of the act of creation in the creature is the existence of the creature itself.[56] 'Creation is not a change, but the very dependence of the created act of being upon the principle from which it is produced.'[57] This is why the relation between the Creator and creature is real in the creature.[58] It is more real and more dynamic than any mutually real relation among creatures for it is a relationship that establishes and sustains the very existence of the creature. If the relationship ceased to be, the creature would cease to be.[59] As Aquinas states: 'Creation places something in the thing created according to relation only, because what is created, is not made by movement, or change. . . . Creation in the creature is nothing but a certain relation to the creator as to the principle of its being.'[60] The act of creation then is a relation fully in act in that it is only by continuously being related to God that the creature exists.

55 For Aquinas, to create is 'to produce being absolutely, [and] not as this or that being' (*ST*, I, 45, 5). See also I, 45, 4, ad 1 and I, 45, 6.
56 See *SCG*, II, 17, 4; II, 19; and *De Potentia*, 3, 1. Creation does bring about a change, but the change is not in the creature but simply in that the creature now is and was not. As E. Mascall writes: 'Creation does indeed "make a difference" to the creature, and the most radical of all differences, since were it not for creation there would be no creature at all; nevertheless, were it not for creation there would be no creature to which the difference could be made.' *Existence and Analogy*, p. 145.
        While we speak of 'before creation,' as if creation brings about a change, we do so only figuratively. This is why one cannot speak literally of 'before creation' since there is *no-thing* before creation to which creation can be before. See *ST*, I, 45, 1–3; *SCG*, II, 11; and *De Potentia*, 3, 1. This is also why creation is *ex nihilo* since there is *no-thing* out of which creation can be made. The act of creation is God simply bringing into existence that which never existed. While God brings something into existence and so uses his divine power, creation is not made *from* his 'divine substance.' See also J.F. Anderson, 'Creation as a Relation,' *New Scholasticism* 24 (1950):263–83.
57 *SCG*, II, 18, 2.
58 E. Muller correctly states that 'one can dispense with this relational asymmetry only by rejecting the transcendence of God.' 'Real Relations and the Divine,' *Theological Studies* 56 (1995):678.
        For the complete dependancy of the creature upon the Creator see also R. Neville, *God the Creator: On the Transcendence and Presence of God* (Chicago: The University of Chicago Press, 1968), pp. 61–119.
59 That creation and preservation are one and the same see *ST*, I, 8, 1; I, 9, 2; I, 104, 1 and *De Potentia*, 3, 4. D. Braine creatively constructs a 'proof' for the existence of God based upon the continuous existence of composite beings. The continuous existence of composite beings existing in time demands an incomposite being existing in himself as pure actuality eternally. See *The Reality of Time and the Existence of God*. See also D. Bradshaw, '"All Existing is the Action of God": The Philosophical Theology of David Braine,' *The Thomist* 60/3 (1996):379–416. See also G. Grisez's detailed argument for the existence of God based upon contingency (*Beyond the New Theism*, pp. 36–91, 261–66).
60 *ST*, I, 45, 3 (author's translation).

Second, 'to create,' as Aquinas states, signifies action on the part of God. God truly acts, but since he is pure act, the act of creation signifies no other action than the pure act that God is.[61] God can act in no other way, not to his detriment and to our disadvantage but to his capability and to our benefit, for the act of creation itself demands that God act by

61 While we must conclude that God acts in the act of creation by no other act than the pure act that he is, we cannot conceive the nature of such an act since it is completely beyond the realm of the created order. As D. Burrell writes: '[I]t makes no sense to ask *how* pure-act acts, since it is *ipso facto* in act. So God's acting involves no mechanisms, no process (from potency to act), no *powers* by which divinity acts.' 'Divine Practical Knowing: How an Eternal God Acts in Time' in *Divine Action*, pp. 93–94. See also his *Freedom and Creation in Three Traditions* (Notre Dame: University of Notre Dame Press, 1993), p. 70; R. Sokolowski, *The God of Faith and Reason* (Notre Dame: University of Notre Dame Press, 1982), p. 33; and T. Tracy, 'Narrative Theology and the Acts of God' in *Divine Action*, eds B. Hebblethwaite and E. Henderson (Edinburgh: T & T Clark, 1990), pp. 177 and 179.

G. Grisez states that the act of creation is 'unintelligible' in that it 'cannot be placed in some familiar category. Creation, being unique, cannot be placed in any of the other modes of causality, and so creation is not intelligible by assimilation to anything else' (*Beyond the New Theism*, p. 267). This is an excellent example of knowing *what* the mystery is but being unable to comprehend the mystery.

It is not possible here to elucidate an entire theory of 'how' God acts. However, it would be good to state briefly the notion of God's action that is presupposed in this study.

Many contemporary theologians argue against what is now termed an 'interventionist' view of God acting, that is that God acts in time and history in a manner that is peculiar and singular to himself, and so the action cannot be accounted for by the laws of nature and human freedom. Traditionally understood this would be a denial of God's 'supernatural acts,' that is those acts of God which go beyond what can be accounted for merely from within the created order. Rather, many theologians today argue that God is limited to some generic (not 'act' specific) providential will and care, and that this is accomplished solely from within the created order by those who exist within that order. See, for example, M. Wiles, *God's Action in the World* (London: SCM, 1986), and 'Divine Action: Some Moral Considerations,' in *The God Who Acts*, ed. T. Tracy (University Park, PA: The Pennsylvania State University Press, 1994), pp. 13–29.

I would argue that God does act in time and history in an 'interventionist' or 'supernatural' sense. I am thinking of such acts as the making of a covenant with the Jewish people, the Incarnation, the bodily resurrection of Jesus, the action of the Holy Spirit in the work of grace, the sacramental actions, as well as the miracles performed by Jesus during his earthly life and those which occur today. When God acts, as he does in the act of creation, he acts by no other act than the pure act that he is. Thus an action is predicated of God not because he has undergone some change, but because the thing or person acted upon is changed, and the change is such that it cannot be accounted for from within the causality of the created order (the instantaneous changing of water into wine) and/or is beyond the causality of the created order (the bodily resurrection). Now when God acts, he newly or differently relates the thing or person to himself as he is, and it is this new relation which brings about the change in the thing or person so related. In the resurrection, the humanity of Jesus is related to God (the Trinity) so as to be a glorified humanity. In the work of grace the person is related to the Trinity so as to be 'adopted' into the very trinitarian life. It is only because God is pure act, and so acts by no other act, that such relations and so changes can take place within the created order. Such an 'interventionist' or 'supernatural' view of God's action should not, therefore, be understood in the sense that he acts within the created order as a temporary meddler within that order, as if he becomes another acting member within the created order, performs his intervention, and then leaves having 'done his thing.' Since God would be acting as a member of the created order, such a view would demand that he changes in so acting. Rather, the 'interventionist' or 'supernatural' view of God's action must be understood as God, who remains ontologically distinct from

no other act than the pure act that he is as *ipsum esse* for no other act is capable of such a singular effect.[62] If God were to change in the act of creation, it would mean that he acted by some other act than the pure act that he is, but this is impossible both because God is pure act and because creation itself demands an immutably pure act.[63] The immutability of

---

the created order as the Wholly Other, bringing about a change in the created order by relating a thing or person to himself as the Wholly Other in a new manner. Thus to speak of 'The intervention of God' is to designate an effect brought about by God in the created order and not to designate that God himself entered into the created order as another acting member of that order.

On the nature of God's actions, besides the references given above, see also R.M. Adams, 'Theodicy and Divine Intervention,' pp. 32–40; W. Alston, 'Divine Action: Shadow or Substance?', pp. 41–62; T. Tracy, 'Divine Action, Created Causes, and Human Freedom,' pp. 77–102; and D. Burrell, 'Divine Action and Human Freedom in the Context of Creation,' pp. 103–9; all in *The God Who Acts?*. Also see W. Alston, 'How to Think About Divine Action' in *Divine Action*, pp. 51–71.

62 See *ST*, I, 45, 5; *SCG*, II, 21; and *De Potentia*, 3, 4. While Creel presents an ardent and often insightful defense of God's impassibility, his understanding of the act of creation is so flawed that it undermines the credibility of his entire book. Creel believes that *creatio ex nihilo* means that God either uses his own being to create others, which would be pantheism, or that God 'creates out of nothing,' not even himself, which is an 'absurdity'. Thus Creel feels compelled to posit an eternally pre-existent uncreated 'plenum' which contains all the possibilities that God could create. The absolute is God plus the plenum (*Divine Impassibility*, pp. 68–69). See pp. 64–79. While such a view is reminiscent of Plato's world of forms or ideas, it is hardly in conformity with the Judeo-Christian tradition. More to the point there is no sufficient reason to account for the plenum's existence. Moreover, if God cannot bring it into existence and it 'contains' only what could possibly exist, how can one speak of it as 'something' that does exist, since in itself, it is 'nothing.' The real difficulty is that Creel does not grasp the true meaning of *creatio ex nihilo*. It does not mean that God creates by using his own being as the 'stuff' out of which others are made (pantheism), but that God, as existence itself, simply brings into existence others with their own created act of existence. He needs nothing other than himself to perform this singular act.

63 R. Swinburne maintains that for God to be the Creator means that he 'either himself brings about or makes or permits some other being to bring about . . . the existence of all things that exist.' He continues: 'It would hardly seem to matter for theism if God on occasion permitted some other being to create matter. He would hardly be less worthy of worship if he did. I shall therefore understand the doctrine that God is the Creator of all things as the doctrine that God himself either brings about or makes or permits some other being to bring about the existence of all logically contingent things that exist (i.e. have existed, exist, or will exist), apart from himself.' *The Coherence of Theism: Revised Edition*, p. 131. See also pp. 134, 232–33. He imagines, for example, that God could give a human being the power to 'produce a sixth finger or a new fountain-pen (not made out of pre-existing matter)' (pp. 142–43). What Swinburne fails to grasp is that God could not permit, even if he wanted to, others, whether they be angels or human beings, to bring things into existence because it is not a matter of just having God's permission, but a matter of possessing the ability. Only God has the ability to bring things into existence because he is the only one who is existence itself, which the act of creation demands. For God to permit others to create he would not just have to give them a certain amount of power, but a specific kind of power, that is the power that accrues to being pure act as *ipsum esse*, which is impossible since it would demand that those beings would have to exist in and of themselves as *ipsum esse* and so be eternally God. Aquinas writes: 'Because no creature has simply an infinite power, any more than it has an infinite being . . ., it follows that no creature can create.' *ST*, I, 45, 5, ad 3. See the whole of article 5.

D. Braine also argues that God cannot 'deputize' the power to create. See *The Reality of Time and the Existence of God*, pp. 16, 21, 24, 191–96, 345, 349, 352.

God as pure act, far from being an impairment to creating, is the absolute prolegomenon and, literally, *sine qua non* for creating.[64]

Third, we must clearly grasp the full significance of what it means for God to be the logical term in the Creator–creature relationship. For God to be the logical term is not something negative in God as if he were not closely related, and least of all does it mean that his relation is 'unreal' in the sense that his relationship to creation is non–existent. Rather, to be the logical term specifies and clarifies the exact nature of the real relation in the creature, that is a relatedness to God as he is in himself which establishes the very being and continued existence of the creature, and in so doing it clarifies and specifies the exact nature of God's relation to the creature, that is a relatedness to the creature as the creature is. For God to be the logical term means then that he is supremely related in the most intimate and dynamic manner, for if God creates by no other act than the pure act that he is, and if the creature only is by being related to the pure act that God is, then God is actually related to and present in the creature by his very essence, that is by the pure act that he is. Aquinas writes:

> God is in all things; not, indeed, as part of their essence, nor as an accident; but as an agent is present to that upon which it works. . . . Now since God is very being by his own essence, created being must be his proper effect. . . . Now God causes this effect in things not only when they first begin to be, but as long as they are preserved in being. . . . Therefore as long as a thing has being, God must be present to it; according to its mode of being. But being is innermost in each thing and most fundamentally inherent in all things since it is formal in respect of everything found in a thing. Hence it must be that God is in all things, and innermostly.[65]

64 P. Helm rightly points out that only an immutable God can actually do the things the Bible claims that he does. See *Eternal God*, pp. 21–22.

In treating the question of whether there is power in God, Aquinas distinguishes between passive and active power. Passive power pertains to one's potential and is 'the principle of being acted upon by something else.' In contrast active power pertains to one's perfection. The more one is in act, the more one can act. Since God is pure act, it 'most fittingly belongs to him to be an active principle, and in no way whatsoever to be passive.' Therefore, 'in God there is active power in the highest degree' (*ST*, I, 25, 1 and ad 1). This is in keeping with what we stressed above that God/Trinity possess no self-constituting potential that needs to be actualized in order for them to be more who they are. God as a trinity of persons is fully actualized and so in perfect act. It is this unchanging fully actualized power as pure act that allows God to create.

65 *ST*, I, 8, 1. See also I, 8, 3, ad 1. M. Dodds writes:

> As the source of created being, God is most intimately present to each creature. His presence is far more intimate than the sort of presence which is possible for the terms of a mutually real relation among creatures. For in a mutually real relation of cause and effect, the created agent is related to the effect through the medium of the motion which it produces and which is distinct from its essence. God, however, as the cause of *esse* in creatures, is present to each one by his very essence. And because *esse* is the innermost actuality of the creature, God is most intimately present to each thing. *The Unchanging God of Love*, pp. 239–40.

See also Burrell, 'Divine Practical Knowing' in *Divine Action*, pp. 96, 101; Davies, *The Thought of Thomas Aquinas*, pp. 98–101; L.B. Gillon, 'Dieu Immobile et Dieu en Mouvement,' *Doctor Communis* 29 (1976):139–40; and Reichmann, 'Immanently Transcendent and Subsistent Esse: A Comparison,' pp. 339–47.

Now relationships between, for example, human beings are radically different from the Creator–creature relationship for they are always established through or by some mediating act (a hug or a kiss). The relation is established, by what I would call, 'act' to 'act,' that is both persons are engaged in the *act* of kissing and so are related, but because the relationship is established through some mediating act (a kiss) the two people are never related to one another as each fully is. However, this is not the case in the Creator–creature relationship. While the relationship between God and creatures is equally 'act' to 'act,' it is not mediated nor is it a partial expression of their being, but rather the complete and utter expression of their being. The 'act' (the *esse*) by which the creature is a creature only is 'act' because it is related to the 'act' by which God is (*ipsum esse*).[66] The Creator–creature relation is an unmediated relationship between the pure act of God as *ipsum esse* and the act, the *esse*, by which the creature is.[67] The creature is totally defined as a creature in this relation for it establishes the creature as created.[68] Moreover, unlike relations between human beings, the Creator–creature relation is perpetual and uninterrupted. Thus, this relation is absolutely immediate (no mediating action), supremely dynamic (pure act to created act), utterly intimate (a relation between God as he is in himself

---

It should be noted that even pantheism and panentheism fall short of such a close relationship, for in both God is never fully related as he is in himself, by his very being, but always by some lesser expression, either by way of emanation or by some divine spark of his being.

66 D. Braine states a similar view, but not, I think, as clearly. See *The Reality of Time and the Existence of God*, pp. 204–5.

67 Aquinas states: 'God however does not act through a mediating action which is understood as proceeding from God and terminating in the creature. But his action is his substance, and whatever is in it is altogether outside the genus of created being through which the creature is referred to God.' *De Potentia*, 7, 9, ad 4.

K. Tanner states that 'non-divine being must be talked about as always and in every respect *constituted* by, and therefore *nothing apart from*, an immediate relation with the founding agency of God.' *God and Creation in Christian Theology* (London: Blackwell, 1988), p. 84. See also her 'Human Freedom, Human Sin, and God the Creator' in *The God Who Acts*, pp. 111–35.

D. Braine also emphasizes the immediacy of God's relationship to creation. 'He is as immediate to each thing as each thing is to itself, and to its action. It is not that God is all things, but that He is in all things.' *The Reality of Time and the Existence of God*, p. 20. See also pp. 24, 105, 189, 286, 304, 338, 347–49, 357–58, 363. He therefore argues that God is not 'metaphorically' present to creation, but 'literally present' (see pp. 129–33).

See also Burrell, *Knowing the Unknowable God*, pp. 34, 49, 93–99; and Gillon, 'Dieu Immobile et Dieu en Mouvement,' p. 140.

68 We can grasp now why the two terms in a mixed relation are in distinct ontological orders. They are in distinct ontological orders because the one term, God, establishes the existence of the other term (the other ontological order), creation. The relation is a kind of 'subsistent relation' in that creation only 'is' by being totally dependent upon being related to God for its existence. It is not as if both terms existed and then were related through some mediating action. Rather the relationship itself establishes the existence of creation. The relationship is real in the creature for it establishes the creature's existence. It is logical in God for the creature only comes to be by being related to God as he is in himself.

G. Grisez holds a similar view of the Creator–creature relationship, *Beyond the New Theism*, pp. 261–66, as does G. Hanratty, 'Divine Immutability and Impassibility Revisited' in *At the Heart of the Real*, pp. 155–57.

and the creature as it is in itself), and unbreakably enduring (it can never be severed).[69]

Fourth, it is now also evident why God the Creator, as pure act, is not

---

69 As I argued in my book, *Does God Change?* (pp. 93–95), there is ambiguity in Aquinas' exposition of a mixed relation which has caused much confusion and misunderstanding, and so much criticism, especially among those who wish to predicate change in God through his relationships with the created order. Aquinas frequently uses the example of a man being on the right or the left of a column to illustrate a mixed relation (see *ST*, I, 13, 7; III, 16, 6, ad 2). The relation is real for the man and thus he is changed, but it is logical in the column, and so it is not changed. Moreover, the relation is made in the human mind, and thus the column, in reality, is not truly related. This is really a variation of a 'Cambridge change' for the column is only newly related to the man because the man has changed. This is why Aquinas uses this illustration. It is not really an example of a mixed relation, but an illustration of how the logical term of a relation can be related to another term without changing even though the other term does. It illustrates then how God can be related without changing. Nonetheless, it is an ambiguous illustration under the present circumstances. Furthermore, Aquinas consistently states that the relation between the Creator and the creature 'is not really in God, but only in our way of thinking' (*ST*, I, 13, 7). See also III, 2, 7, ad 1; *SCG*, II, 13, 4; *De Veritate*, 3, 2, ad 8; and *De Potentia*, 7, 8–11. If Aquinas means by this that God is not actually related to creatures in reality but only related in our way of thinking, then, as I stated above, no relation exists between God and creatures, and thus God could not actually be the Creator. This is how Aquinas' critics consistently interpret him. However, the above examination clarifies and demonstrates that this cannot possibly be what Aquinas means. He himself states: 'It cannot be said, however, that these relations exist as realities outside God' (*SCG*, II, 13, 1), and he further gives this interpretation as an objection to his own position (see *ST*, I, 13, 7, obj. 5 and *De Veritate*, 3, 2, obj. 8). The point that Aquinas is making is that God is actually related, in reality, to the creature, not because of some change in him, but only because the creature is really related to him as he exists in himself as *ipsum esse*. It is because the creature is really related to God that we come to understand God in a new way as Creator. Thus God is in reality Creator and is actually related to the creature, but only because the creature is related to him as he is. In discussing the title 'Lord' Aquinas writes: 'Since God is related to the creature for the reason that the creature is related to him; and since the relation is real in the creature, it follows that God is Lord [and thus Creator also] not in idea only but in reality, for he is called Lord according to the manner in which the creature is subject to him.' *ST*, I, 13, 7, ad 5. See also *SCG*, II, 11, 2, and Burrell, *Aquinas: God and Action*, pp. 84–87. The confusion lies in that Aquinas did not realize how radically he had altered Aristotle's notion of a mixed relation when treating the Creator–creature relation, something Aristotle never dealt with, and thus he never adequately distinguished between what it means to be a 'logical term' within a mutually logical relation and within a mixed relation. In the first the terms are related solely in the human mind. In the latter God, as the logical term, is not related to the creature solely in the human mind, but rather, because the creature is really related to God as he is in himself and not through some mediating action, he is actually related to the creature. God, then, as the logical term is truly understood in a new way, not because he has changed, but because the creature is related to him in a new way as the Creator. What is needed is a new word to express the full truth of being a 'logical term' within a mixed relation. I have spoken of it as being an 'actual relation' both because it is a relation founded within reality and one founded upon the pure act of God and the act of existence which establishes the creature as existent. Henninger states that Aquinas transforms 'yet another doctrine of Aristotle, that of the category of relation, in the light of his metaphysics of the act of existence.' *Relations: Medieval Theories 1250–1325*, p. 33. See also pp. 34–39.

Because of the confusion contained within Aquinas and because of the criticism leveled against him, many scholars of Thomist background have attempted, in various ways, to clarify, re-interpret, or develop Aquinas' position. For example see: Burrell, *Aquinas: God and Action*, pp. 82–7, 135–45; W. Norris Clarke, 'A New Look at the Immutability of God,' *God Knowable and Unknowable*, ed. R.J. Roth (New York: Fordham University Press, 1973), pp. 43–72; W. Norris Clarke, *The Philosophical Approach to God:*

one of many beings nor can he be numbered as one of many beings. God as pure *esse* ontologically transcends the order of created beings because he does not have a quiddity other than his *esse*, and thus unlike finite beings, he does not have an essence that would place him within a genus.[70] Moreover, it is the act of creation which both establishes and

---

A Neo-Thomistic Perspective (Winston-Salem: Wake Forest University Press, 1979), pp. 66–109; J. Galot, *Vers une Nouvelle Christologie* (Paris: Duculot-Lethielleux, 1971); Galot, *Dieu Souffre-t-il?*; Galot, *Who Is Christ*; Galot, *The Person of Christ*; Galot, *Abba Father*; Grisez, *Beyond the New Theism*, pp. 256–66; W. Hill, 'Does the World Make a Difference to God?', *The Thomist* 38 (1974):146–64; W. Hill, 'Does God Know the Future? Aquinas and Some Moderns,' *Theological Studies* 36 (1975):3–18; W. Hill, 'In What Sense is God Infinite? A Thomistic Perspective,' *The Thomist* 42 (1978):14–27; W. Hill, 'The Historicity of God,' *Theological Studies* 45 (1984):320–33; W. Hill, 'Does Divine Love Entail Suffering in God?' in *God and Temporality*, eds B.L. Clarke and E.T. Long (New York: Paragon House, 1984), pp. 55–71, especially pp. 65–9; A.J. Kelly, 'God: How Near a Relation?', *The Thomist* 34 (1970):191–229; A.J. Kelly, 'Trinity and Process: Relevance of the Basic Christian Confession of God,' *Theological Studies* 30 (1970):393–414; T. Kondoleon, 'The Immutability of God: Some Recent Challenges,' *The New Scholasticism* 58/3 (1984):293–315; E.L. Mascall, *Whatever Happened to the Human Mind?* (London: SPCK, 1980), pp. 64–96; J.H. Wright, 'Divine Knowledge and Human Freedom: The God Who Dialogues,' *Theological Studies* 38 (1977):450–77.

There is a similar theme in Clarke, Galot, Hill and Wright: while God is ontologically immutable, and therefore cannot be 'really related' to the created order, yet he can intentionally be actually and personally related through his knowledge and love. This can be called a 'real' relation. What these authors fail to realize is that God's immutability is not a detriment which must be held in dialectic with his relatedness nor an 'evil' that must be overcome in order for God to be 'actually' related to the created order: rather, as I have argued, the immutability of God is the primary presupposition for his dynamic and intimate actual relation to the created order. See my *Does God Change?*, fn. 110, pp. 95–96, 174–86.

70 See *De Potentia*, 7, 3; *SCG*, I, 25, 5 and I, 25, 9–10; *ST*, I, 3, 5. E.L. Mascall writes:

> We cannot lump together in one genus God and everything else, as if the word 'being' applied to them all in precisely the same sense, and then pick out God as the supreme one. For if God is the Supreme Being, in the sense in which Christian theology uses the term, 'being' as applied to him is not just one more instance of what 'being' means when applied to anything else. So far from being just one item, albeit the supreme one, in a class of being, he is the source from which their being is derived; he is not *in* their class but *above* it. *He Who Is*, p. 9.

That God does not belong to a genus is of the utmost importance for it establishes the radical and irreducible ontological difference between God and all else. It manifests that God is the Wholly Other and gives precision to the nature of God's transcendence. Unlike the gods of the pagans, or even the God of Aristotle, who were the most perfect being(s) within a continuum of beings, this notion of God as Creator establishes that he is absolutely distinct from all else. R. Sokolowski perceptively refers to this as 'the Christian distinction' and sees the preserving of this distinction as fundamental in all theological issues. 'The Christian understanding of God and the world is not an inert background for more controversial issues; it enters into their formulation and helps determine how they must be decided.' *The God of Faith and Reason*, p. 34. See also pp. 12, 15–16, 21–34. See also R. Sokolowski, 'Creation and Christian Understanding' in *God and Creation: An Ecumenical Symposium*, eds D. Burrell and B. McGinn (Notre Dame: University of Notre Dame Press, 1990), pp. 179–81. D. Burrell has also emphasized Sokolowski's 'distinction.' See his *Knowing the Unknowable God*, pp. 2, 7, 17–18, 46–47, 64–65, 75–79, 89; 'Divine Practical Knowing: How an Eternal God Acts in Time' in *Divine Action*, pp. 93–101; *Freedom and Creation*, pp. 9, 14, 22, 25, 61, 91, 97, 128, 164–65, 169–71, 174. See also Neville, *God the Creator*, pp. 94–119.

The reason this 'distinction' is of absolute importance for this study is, as we will see, that to make God changeable and possible is to destroy the distinction, and so make

manifests God's ontological distinctiveness and so his transcendence, and simultaneously his relation to the created order and so his immanence.[71]

The Trinity and the Act of Creation

In order to appreciate the full significance of what we have just philosophically established concerning the Creator–creature relationship, we must now place it within the context of the Trinity.[72] While the Trinity does act *ad extra* as one, as the tradition demands, God never acts generi-

---

God just the most perfect being among many beings. Moreover, and most importantly, to dissolve the distinction is to undermine the dynamic intimacy which God must have with all else, especially with human beings.

71 D. Braine correctly emphasizes that the proper understanding of God's transcendence and immanence is founded upon the act of creation.

What allows God to be immediate to every creature is a mode of existence which makes Him at the same time unlike every creature in nature. . . . We establish in one act [of creation] both the immediacy of God to creature, with their immediacy in respect of dependence on Him for their existence, and the gulf between creatures and God in respect to their manner of existence inasmuch as God is involved in doing something, *viz.* communicating existence, vigour, life, or actuality, which they are in themselves impotent to do. . . . Thus, the notion of God's transcendence in nature and God's immediacy or immanence are explained in one and the same act. *The Reality of Time and the Existence of God*, pp. 23, 24, and 349. See also pp. 25, 338, 357, 363.

R. Neville also writes:

The speculative theory of creation *ex nihilo* is committed to both the extreme transcendence and extreme presence. A theory that lies in between would not be able to say that all depends on the free grace of God. That is, if God were not so transcendent, his creative grace would be necessitated by the world; and if he were not so present, not all of the world would be dependent. Although the speculative arguments given above should be the philosophic reasons for holding our theory, its religious consequences should not be lost on the theologian. *God the Creator*, p. 119.

J. Quinn also writes:

Transcendence and immanence are not contradictorily but only relatively opposed. Indeed so closely do they comport with one another that in the line of causation God is most immanent in things because he is absolutely transcendent. Immanence does not cancel out but depends on transcendence. . . . Since God properly causes the existence that we may take as the most radical, the most formal determination or principle in a thing, he is most intimately present, most formally immanent, in the being and operation of all created things. 'Triune Self-Giving: One Key to the Problem of Suffering,' *The Thomist* 44 (1980):182.

W. Hill notes that the common solution to the problem of God's immanence is to make him less transcendent. This is a false and deceptive solution for in making God less transcendent he immediately becomes less immanent. Hill correctly stresses that it is precisely God's utter transcendence which allows for his intimate involvement within the world. 'The ground of God's immanence then is precisely his transcendence.' 'Does Divine Love Entail Suffering in God?' in *God and Temporality*, p. 56. See also Mascall, *He Who Is*, p. 126.

72 While I am developing my own thoughts and arguments in this section, I am indebted to B. de Margerie's work on the Trinity and creation. See his *The Christian Trinity in History* (Petersham: St Bede's Publications, 1981), pp. 186–93.

cally as the one God, for the one God is a trinity of persons and must act as such. It must be remembered that, for Aquinas, 'Creation signified actively means the divine action, which is God's essence,' and that God's essence is the same as the trinity of persons.[73] Therefore, God never acts as *ipsum esse* or *actus purus* apart from doing so as a trinity of persons. Moreover, while the Hebrew tradition sees the one God as Creator, in the light of subsequent Christian revelation the act of creation must be conceived as the act of God in so far as the one God *is* a trinity of persons.[74] The act of creation is common to all three persons and as such it is the act of the one God, but this one act must be predicated of them in a manner that is appropriate to each person. Aquinas argues that creation cannot be said properly of any one of the three persons singularly 'since it is common to the whole Trinity.' However, it is not common to the Trinity generically as the one God.

> The divine persons, according to the nature of their procession, have a causality respecting the creation of things. . . . Hence God the Father made the creature through his Word, which is his Son; and through his Love, which is the Holy Spirit. And so the processions of the persons are the type of the production of creatures inasmuch as they include the essential attributes, knowledge and will.[75]

---

73 *ST*, I, 45, 3, ad 1. See I, 39, 1.
74 While the Hebrew scriptures obviously do not speak of God as a Trinity creating the world, yet, in the light of Christian revelation, clues and intimations are present, as the early Fathers were quick to discern. For example, in the opening verses of Genesis, God is seen calling forth his creation through his word, as his breath (spirit) hovers over the water (see Gen. 1:1–3). Psalm 33:6 proclaims: 'By the word of the LORD the heavens were made, and all their host by the breath of his mouth.' That God creates through his word and wisdom see for example: Prov. 8:27–31; Wis. 9:9; Sir. 24:5. This is followed up in the New Testament by God creating through his Word (see Jn 1:1–2; 1 Cor. 8:6; Col. 1:15–20; Heb. 1:1–3). That the breath/spirit of God in the Hebrew scriptures is the Spirit of life see for example Gen. 2:7, 6:3; Job 33:4, 34:14–15; Ps. 104:27–31; Ezek. 37:7–10. The Holy Spirit, as instrumental in creation, is not as developed in the New Testament as that of the Word, but he is nonetheless seen as the Spirit of life, especially as the agent of new life in Christ (see for example, Jn 3:5–8; Rom. 8; Gal. 4:29).
     See Y. Congar, *The Word and the Spirit* (London: Geoffrey Chapman, 1986), pp. 15–41; de Margerie, *The Christian Trinity in History*, pp. 3–56; A. Heron, *The Holy Spirit* (Philadelphia: Westminster Press, 1983), pp. 3–60; J. McIntyre, *The Shape of Pneumatology* (Edinburgh: T & T Clark, 1997), pp. 29–73.
75 *ST*, I, 45, 6. The Council of Rome (AD 382) condemned those who deny that the Father created all, visible and invisible, through his Son and Holy Spirit. See Denzinger-Schönmetzer, 171. Likewise, even Augustine wrote: 'What things the Father does, these also the Son does: The Father made the world, the Son made the world, the Holy Spirit made the world. If three Gods, then three worlds; if one God, the Father, the Son, and the Holy Spirit, then one world was made by the Father, through the Son, in the Holy Spirit' (*In Joannis Evangelium Tractatus*, 20, 9).
     I would argue as well that only a God who is a trinity of persons could create. If God were a solitary monad existing in complete self-isolation, the 'thought' of creating something other than himself could never arise. It would be ontologically impossible for the thought of 'another' to arise, for there would be no ontological ground upon which this thought of 'another' could arise. Being the sole being that existed, it would be impossible for a single-person God to conceive of anything other than himself. Actually, I do not think it would be possible for a 'single-person' God to exist for the very notion of 'person' implies relationality. This is why some philosophers would hold that a non-trinitarian 'personal' God creates by necessity. He must do so in order to

Further for Aquinas, while all three persons share in the divine nature, they do so 'in a kind of order.' The Son receives his divinity from the Father and the Holy Spirit receives it from the Father and the Son, and therefore this same order is maintained within the act of creation. The term Creator is attributed to the Father for he receives his power to create from no other, but he creates through the Son, his Word, and through the Holy Spirit, his goodness and love.[76]

Now, what Aquinas does not fully articulate is that the Trinity–creature relationship is a mixed relation. Since the persons of the Trinity share in the pure act of divine being as subsistent relations fully in act, they possess no self-constituting relational potential and so they embrace the singular ability to relate, in the act of creation, the creature to themselves as they are, and are therefore related to the creature as who they are in themselves. The Trinity is the 'logical term' of the relationship in that the creature only comes to be and so is 'really related' to the Trinity as the Trinity is. Thus, as we saw above in our philosophical inquiry, the Trinity–creature relation is equally absolutely immediate (no mediating action between the Trinity and the creature), supremely dynamic (the persons of the Trinity fully in act related to the created act by which the creature is), utterly intimate (a relation between the trinity of persons as they truly exist in themselves and the creature as it is in itself), and unbreakably enduring (it can never be severed). Moreover, if we now add to this that the creature involved in this relationship is a human person, it means that the trinity of persons are actually and fully related to the human person as they are in themselves, for the human person is related to them as they are. The relation between the Trinity and a human person is absolutely relational and utterly personal, for the human person (the human 'I') only exists as a human person (a human 'I') by being related to the persons (the divine 'I's') of the Trinity in a personal manner – the human 'I' to the 'I' of each divine person.

In this regard one further very significant point must be made more explicit. Each creature, and more importantly, each human person, is related to each person of the Trinity in a singular manner or according to the proper order within the Trinity, that is, the creature or human person is related to the Father as the Father is, to the Son as the Son is, and to the Holy Spirit as the Holy Spirit is.

This is why Aquinas could state that the name 'Word' signifies a relation to creatures:

---

have something to which he can relate. In contrast, the persons of the Trinity are defined entirely by their relations to one another, and are not defined by something that is self-defining which is independent of their mutual relations. Who they are as distinct persons is only established in relation to one another. Only from within this ontological grounding could the idea of creation arise. It is only because the persons of the Trinity eternally gaze upon *one another* in the fulness of life and love that they could conceive of creating *another* other than themselves who could share in their life and love. On this and related points see von Balthasar, *Theo-Drama V*, pp. 61–92.

76 See *ST*, I, 45, 6, ad 2; *Super Libros Sententiarum*, I, Prologue and I, d 10, q 1, a 1 sol.; and *Super Boethium 'De Trinitate'*, Prologue. For an excellent discussion of how Aquinas conceives creation in relation to the distinct persons of the Trinity see the reference to von Balthasar above.

Word implies relation to creatures. For God by knowing himself, knows every creature. Now the word conceived in the mind is representative of everything that is actually understood. Hence there are in themselves different words for different things which we understand. But because God by one act understands himself and all things, his one only Word is expressive not only of the Father, but of all creation. And as the knowledge of God is only cognitive as regards God, whereas as regards creatures, it is both cognitive and operative, so the Word of God is only expressive of what is in God the Father, but is both expressive and operative of creatures; and therefore it is said (Ps. 33:9): 'He spoke, and they were made'; because in the Word is implied the operative idea of what God makes.[77]

God the Father is the author of creation not only because he knows the whole of creation in his Word, but also because he creates what is known in the Word through the Word. Thus creation is related to the Father not only as known in the Word, but it is also related to the Father through the Word. Moreover, then, the Word is related to creation not only as the one in whom the Father knows creation, but also as the one through whom creation comes to be. Thus creation is related to the Word not only as the one in whom it is known by the Father, but also as the one through whom it is created. The Father's knowledge of creation is the most thorough, dynamic and intimate, for he knows creation in the very act of begetting his Son or speaking his Word. Thus he knows creation in the very same act by which he knows himself – through the Word.[78]

Aquinas similarly states concerning the Holy Spirit:

The Father loves not only the Son, but also himself and us, by the Holy Spirit. . . . Hence, as the Father speaks himself and every creature by his begotten Word, inasmuch as the Word *begotten* adequately represents the Father and every creature; so he loves himself and every creature by the Holy Spirit, inasmuch as the Holy Spirit proceeds as the love of the primal goodness whereby the Father loves himself and every creature.[79]

As the Father knows the whole of creation in the Word and so creates through the Word, so the Father loves not only his Son but also the whole of creation in the Holy Spirit, and it is because of this love (in this Spirit) that he creates it through his Word. As the Father lovingly begets his Son in the Spirit so the Father lovingly creates, in the same Spirit, through his Word. Thus creatures participate in the same intimate, passionate, divine

---

77 *ST*, I, 34, 3.
78 This is why Aquinas holds that God's knowledge is the cause of all things and that his knowledge extends as far as his causality extends. God does not know things apart from his causality but within his causality, for it is through his Word that he equally knows and causes the whole of creation to come to be and to continue to be (see *ST*, I, 14, 8 and 11). Again this expresses the depth of the Father's knowledge of creation since he is present to and knows creation by his very Word through whom he creates and in so doing relates creation to himself through his Word and so knows it in his Word.
79 *ST*, I, 37, 2, ad 3.

love of the Spirit in which the Father and Son love one another, and so are related to the Father and to the Son in the same passionate love of the Spirit.

We clearly perceive now the awesome truth that because creatures, especially human persons, are in the act of creation related to the persons of the Trinity as they are in their own subsistent relations, and so are related to each person of the Trinity in a specific and proper manner, they are assumed into the very mystery of the Trinity itself. Thus the act of creation mirrors, though imperfectly, the processions within the Trinity.[80] 'It is evident that relation to the creature is implied both in the Word and in the proceeding Love, as it were in a secondary way, inasmuch as the divine truth and goodness are a principle of under-standing and loving all creatures.'[81]

To confirm the absolute love of God for creation one further point must be made concerning the Trinity. Aquinas states that there are two reasons why knowledge of the divine persons is necessary.

> [Firstly,] it was necessary for the right idea of creation. The fact of saying that God made all things by his Word excludes the error of those who say that God produced things by necessity. When we say that in him there is a procession of love, we show that God produced creatures not because he needed them, nor because of any

---

80 See *ST*, I, 45, 6, obj. 1. This is in keeping with the principle that the Trinity acts outside of itself in a manner consistent with the acts within itself. With regards to revelation the principle is stated that the manner in which the Trinity reveals itself in the economy is in keeping with the manner it is in itself. The economic Trinity is the immanent Trinity.

   However, while it is true that the act of creation mirrors the processions within the Trinity, this does not mean that the Trinity is fully revealed and so knowable in the act of creation. Reason alone can only grasp that God created the world, it cannot perceive, without the aid of revelation, its trinitarian implications. This 'mirroring' is only discerned in the light of the full revelation of the Trinity.

   It should also be noted that while the Trinity–creature relationship is fully relational, dynamic, intimate and enduring, it is such only by way of establishing the existence of the creature as a creature. The human person is related to the Trinity insofar as the human person exists as a creature and so is distinct, but not apart, from the Trinity. It is not a 'graced' relationship in the sense that it does not interiorly conform human beings into the likeness of the Son and so transform them into children of the Father through the Holy Spirit. The reason is that in the Trinity–creature relationship the relationship is primarily founded upon the Trinity as the author(s) of existence, and therefore insofar as the Trinity is *ipsum esse* or *actus purus*. This is why the act of creation only 'mirrors' in an imperfect or secondary manner the processions within the Trinity. In the 'graced' relationship, the relationship is primarily founded upon the Trinity as subsistent relations. The human person is related to and taken into the Trinity, not only insofar as the human person exists, but also insofar as the human person now fully shares in and so is interiorly conformed by the mutual relations shared by the divine persons themselves. This is why the 'graced' relationship divinizes the human person, for now the human person not only exists in relation to the Trinity as an existing being, but also shares in the life of the Trinity itself as the persons of the Trinity themselves live it. This distinction is made not to denigrate or disparage the Trinity–creature relationship, but to highlight that, even though such a relationship is itself extraordi-nary, the 'graced' relationship is even more relational, dynamic and intimate for now the human person is not related to the Trinity solely as a creature, but adopted into the very life of the Trinity as the persons actually live it themselves.

81 *ST*, I, 37, 2, ad 3.

other extrinsic reason, but on account of the love of his own goodness.[82]

That we needed a knowledge of the Trinity in order to have a proper understanding of creation seems, at first sight, a rather strange argument, yet it is one of Aquinas' great insights. The lack of such knowledge and its consequences were readily exemplified in the various pagan traditions and Greek philosophies. The pagan gods needed creatures for their own happiness, and even within Platonic emanationism and Stoic pantheism the world was a necessary correlative to God.[83] Even the Jewish people, despite their belief in the One Creator God, were not immune from pagan influences, as their history manifests. However, the revelation that God is a Trinity establishes the ontological independent transcendence of God in that God as a trinity of persons is already self-fulfilled both by way of knowledge and of love. The Father knows himself perfectly in his Word and loves himself perfectly in the Holy Spirit. This does not imply a selfish, self-centered and self-contained deity, but the exact opposite. The transcendent independence of the Trinity, as Wholly Other, allows the act of creation to be a sheer act of the Trinity's loving goodness and freedom. Because they possess no self-fulfilling needs, they are motivated solely by their beneficent and altruistic love to bring others into existence and so bestow upon them their goodness. Commenting on Dionysius, Aquinas states:

> Divine love did 'not' allow 'him to remain in himself without fruit,' that is, without the production of creatures, but love 'moved him to operate according' to a most excellent mode of operation according as he produced all things in being (*esse*). For from love of his goodness it proceeded that he willed to pour out and to communicate his goodness to others, insofar as it is possible, namely by way of similitude, and that his goodness did not remain in him, but flowed out into others.[84]

82 *ST*, I, 32, 1, ad 3. The second reason Aquinas gives is the much more obvious one: 'and in another way, and chiefly, that we may think rightly concerning the salvation of the human race, accomplished by the Incarnate Son, and by the gift of the Holy Spirit.' It is interesting that while this is the 'chief' reason for the revelation of the Trinity, it also, as we saw above, follows the pattern already established in creation, that is, that creation follows the order of the processions within the Trinity.

83 W. Hill writes that Plato's gods 'are subjects who act for their own enrichment quite as do other particular existents, even if on a heroic scale.' 'Two Gods of Love: Aquinas and Whitehead,' *Listening* 14 (1979):254). See also Hill, 'Does Divine Love Entail Suffering in God?', p. 58. Equally within Plotinus the universe necessarily emanates out from the One. See Burrell, 'Creation or Emanation: Two Paradigms of Reason', pp. 27–37, especially p. 29.

   R. Sokolowski writes: 'Over against this pagan and spontaneous understanding, Christian belief distinguishes the divine and the world in such a way that God could be, in undiminished goodness and greatness, even if everything else were not. . . . For the pagan the whole is essentially prior to both the divine and the rest of being, but for the Christian the divine could be the whole, even if it is not, since it is meaningful to say, in Christian belief, that God could be all that there is.' 'Creation and Christian Understanding', pp. 182 and 183.

84 *De Divinis Nominibus*, IV, lect. 9 (§409). Translation is from Dodds, *The Unchanging God of Love*, p. 287. W. Hill states that 'Divine loving cannot be conceived as an accidental or

Summary and Conclusions

In order to pull together all the components of this chapter, I will first summarize the main points. I have argued, from revelation, that the persons of the Trinity are subsistent relations fully in act, and therefore are immutable and impassible, not in the sense of being static and inert, but as being unconditionally active and supremely passionate. I have equally argued, from reason, that God is pure act, and therefore consummately dynamic in his immutability and wholly passionate in his impassibility. Moreover, I proceeded to demonstrate that because the persons of the Trinity are subsistent relations fully in act, in that they share the one pure act of divine existence, they possess no self-constituting relational potential, and therefore, they are fully relational. This allows the divine persons to relate others to themselves as they are in themselves. The act of creation exemplifies this. The act of creation, as a mixed relation, specifies that the persons of the Trinity relate the creature to themselves as they are, and so, reciprocally, are actually related to the creature as the creature is. Thus, this relationship is immediate, dynamic, intimate, and enduring. Moreover, because the Father knows and so creates through his Word and because he loves and so creates in the Holy Spirit, the creature is thoroughly known through the Word and fully embraced in the love of the Spirit. When the creature is a human person, this relationship acquires as well an altogether dynamic and a totally intimate personalism.

I will now draw a number of conclusions. First, I have argued throughout this study that any theological or philosophical understanding of God must explicate, sustain and confirm the biblical notion

---

contingent accretion; it is rather constitutive of God's very being in its pure actuality and so cannot be thought of as enhancing his own being intrinsically. The sole beneficiaries of such love are creatures loved for their own sakes.' 'Two Gods of Love: Aquinas and Whitehead', p. 256.

R. Sokolowski also states:

Finally, it should be apparent that what seemed like a kind of indifference of God toward the world, in the claim that God is not perfected by creation, is really the condition for a greater generosity and benevolence in creation. If God is not perfected by creating, then he does not create out of any sort of need, and his creating is all the more free and generous. There is no self-interest and no ambiguity in the goodness and benevolence of creation. And the pure generosity of creation tells us about the nature of the giver of this gift. The nature of the action tells us what the agent is like, and along with the generosity of redemption, it establishes the context for our own response in charity, first toward God and then toward others. . . . Because of the abundance of the life of the Trinity, God becomes even more independent in his nature of any involvement with anything that is not divine. This independence of nature, of course, does not become indifference; rather it defines both creation and redemption as all the more generous and unnecessitated. 'Creation and Christian Understanding,' pp. 184 and 186.

G. Grisez refers to God's unnecessitated loving act of creation as 'an act of play.' *Beyond the New Theism*, p. 271. See also Burrell, *Aquinas: God and Action*, p. 160, and his *Freedom and Creation*, p. 96; Dodds, *The Unchanging God of Love*, pp. 282–87; Gillon, 'Dieu Immobile et Dieu en Mouvement,' pp. 141–42; J. Quinn, 'Triune Self-Giving,' *The Thomist* 44 (1980):188; Reichmann, 'Aquinas, God and Historical Process,' pp. 434–35; and Sokolowski, *The God of Faith and Reason*, pp. 12–20.

of God, that is that God is wholly other than the created realm, and yet simultaneously is present to and active within the created realm as the Wholly Other, without losing his total otherness in so doing. In other words, the proper and authentic biblical notion of divine transcendence and immanence must be theologically elucidated and philosophically maintained. I believe I have done so on both accounts. 1) The persons of the Trinity are wholly other than the created order in that they are subsistent relations fully in act sharing the one pure act of *ipsum esse*. Their mode or manner of existence is ontologically distinct from all else, and in this sense they are absolutely transcendent. Yet, it is this very mode or manner of utter transcendence which allows the persons of the Trinity, as Creator, to be equally present to and active within the created order in all their complete otherness without losing their wholly otherness in so being related. 2) Philosophically, I have argued that the act of creation demands that God be *ipsum esse*, and so creates by no other act than the pure act that he is. This establishes and confirms, philosophically, the total otherness of God and the ontological distinction between God and the order of creation. Simultaneously, it clarifies and equally confirms that God as the Wholly Other, in that he is *ipsum esse*, is immediately related and so present to the created order as the Wholly Other without losing his complete otherness in so being present, in that the created order is related to him as he is in himself and so is. It is precisely this understanding of God, both by way of revelation and reason, that the Bible demands, and only this biblical notion of God as absolutely transcendent allows for the corresponding biblical notion of radical divine immanence.

Second, I have tried to clarify, but not render comprehensible, a number of fundamental mysteries of the Judeo-Christian faith.[85] Hopefully, our understanding of the persons of the Trinity as subsistent relations fully in act and the nature of God as pure act (and the significant consequences that flow from these) are now more intelligible and evident. Yet, it is impossible to comprehend either. We just cannot comprehend what it means to be a subsistent relation fully in act nor what it means to be pure act. Moreover, the trinitarian act of creation is also, hopefully, more intelligible. Yet again, we cannot comprehend how the persons of the Trinity act as pure act in creating. Nor then, can we comprehend how the Trinity can be wholly immanent as the Wholly Other without losing its wholly transcendent otherness in so being. This too is in keeping with the biblical understanding of God and his actions. He reveals himself and so makes himself known, through word and action, as the unknowable and the incomprehensible. It is here that the mind must bow in adoration and the heart burst forth in praise.

Third, what holds the entire argument of this chapter together, in all of its inter-related components, is the notion of 'act' – which, it must be remembered, is a verb. It is the persons of the Trinity as subsistent relations fully in act, sharing in the pure act of divine being (*ipsum esse*),

---

85 Remember that I stated in Chapter 2 that to make a mystery of the Christian faith fully comprehensible is a sure sign that one has articulated a heresy. The task of Christian theology is to identify and so articulate more clearly what the mystery is.

which makes possible, establishes, and grounds the Trinity–creature relationship and all that flows from it – its immediacy, dynamism, intimacy, and persistency. Ultimately, it is this notion of 'act' that both renders more intelligible the mysteries of faith that we have examined, and yet simultaneously, preserves and sustains their mystery, for we cannot comprehend that which is a pure verb (pure act) and nothing more.

Fourth, the divine attributes of immutability and impassibility are thus essential to the above understanding of 'act' for they insure both that the trinity of persons, as subsistent relations, are fully in act and cannot become any more in 'act' through change and mutation, and that God, considered as *ipsum esse*, is pure act and cannot become any more in act through change and mutation. Far from designating the Trinity or God as static and inert, these attributes affirm, protect, and sustain the absolute dynamism and pure passion of God's divine nature as a trinity of persons. Thus, there is no dialectic opposition between the Trinity's immutability and impassibility and its ability to love and to relate. Rather, as I have argued, these attributes, far from being a detriment or a hindrance to the Trinity's ability to love and to relate to others other than itself, are actually the presuppositions and prolegomena for its so doing in a singular divine manner. To imperil or discard the attributes of immutability and impassibility would thus disfigure the beauty and nullify the truth of the Creator–creature relationship. To conceive God or the Trinity as mutable and passible is to proffer a relationship with creatures that is literally impotent and thoroughly impoverished.

Last, I believe I have given theological clarity and philosophical precision to the teaching of the Fathers. I have theologically and philosophically clarified and developed their teaching on why God is immutable and impassible, and equally I have demonstrated, hopefully more clearly and consistently than they did, why God is yet supremely active and loving. Thus, I have confirmed their basic theological teaching and exploited their philosophical instincts, and in so doing I have attempted to locate these on a more stable theological and philosophical footing.

There is yet one more issue, one more piece of the puzzle, that needs to be examined before we take up the topic of whether or not God in himself suffers, that is, the nature of evil as the cause of suffering. In the next chapter, we will discuss this topic and then, in the light of it, turn to the question of whether God, as loving, merciful and compassionate, suffers with and on behalf of human beings.

7

God's Love and Human Suffering

In the previous chapter we saw that divine immutability and impassibility, when properly understood, far from implying that God is static, inert and remote, denote that the persons of the Trinity, as the one God, are supremely dynamic in their ability to act and absolutely passionate in their ability to love. This was founded upon and exemplified in the act of creation where an immediate, dynamic, intimate, and enduring relationship is established between God as a trinity of persons and the created order. In the case of human beings this relationship also acquired an inherent personalism.

This chapter will now examine three areas of concern: 1) Sin is the cause of evil and so of human suffering. 2) Sin and human suffering do not cause God to suffer. 3) The relationship between sin as the cause of human suffering and God's love. The next chapter will treat the suffering of the Son of God within the Incarnation, followed by a chapter on how and why his human suffering is redemptive. The final chapter will then examine human suffering in the light of Jesus' redemptive suffering.

Sin and Its Effects

When antiquity, whether within pagan religion and/or philosophical thought, confronted the reality of evil and the suffering that it wrought, it sought a solution primarily from within the ontological constitution of the cosmos. The culprit invariably indicted was 'matter.' The world was composed of defective 'stuff' at its origin, and humanity suffered the consequences. This is exemplified in the Babylonian creation myths of the *Enuma Elish* and the *Epic of Gilgamesh*, as well as in the more sophisticated dualism within the varieties of mystery religions, Gnosticism, and Manichaeism. Within Platonism, which had a great deal of philosophical influence, changeable, and so evil, matter is seen as that which hinders the immutable eternal Ideas or Forms from being properly and fully expressed in this world, and thus unchanging truth cannot be known through this material world but only in the contemplation of the Ideal World. For Plotinus matter holds the lowest and, therefore, meanest place within his emanationist hierarchy of beings. The religious and philosophical tenets of the ancients thus resolved the problem of evil, and the suffering that ensued from it, by positing an ontological dualism – that which is spiritual or immaterial is good and that which is material

147

is evil. Human beings, enmeshed in both, fall prey to the material world of evil and suffering, and so strive to extricate themselves from this world by advancing in the realm of the spiritual.

In contrast, the Judeo-Christian tradition held that the whole of creation is good, including matter, for it was created by the all-good God (see Gen. 1:1–31). There is then no ontological principle inherent within the created order which is the cause of evil. Ontologically the whole of the created order is entirely good.

Within the Judeo-Christian tradition evil, and the suffering that stems from it, is founded upon the misuse of what is ontologically good. In creating human beings in his own image and likeness (see Gen. 1:26–7), God gave to humankind the ability to live and act in a godlike manner, such as to know the truth and to act virtuously.[1] Freedom is essential to this manner of life for freedom is constitutive of virtues, such as love. Love is only love if it is freely given.[2] According to the Genesis account, Adam and Eve misused the good gift of freedom by which, instead of being faithful to God in obedience, they rebelled against him expecting to become gods themselves (see Gen. 3:4–5). It is the free misuse of God's good gifts that is called sin.[3] Sin, a concept not found within the dualisms

---

1 In the book of Wisdom the everlasting and immortal nature of human beings also testifies to their being in God's image and likeness. See Wis. 2:23. Frequently in the past 'to be in the image and likeness of God' has been limited to the spiritual qualities of the human person; those that are proper to 'the soul,' such as intellect and will. This emphasis grew out of the philosophical body–soul distinction. Biblically, I do not think this is entirely correct. The Bible does not make the philosophical body–soul distinction. In both the Old and New Testament the word 'flesh' (*basar* in Hebrew and translated as *sarx* in Greek) designates the whole human being in its creatureliness with an emphasis on its frailty, weakness and sinfulness. Equally, the Hebrew word *nepes* (translated by *psyche* in Greek) designates not the 'soul' as such but the complete human being as 'living,' and that one is only 'alive' in relation to God. These terms then emphasize not a division within the human being but the manner in which he is seen in relation to God. As a creature, in comparison to God, he is weak, frail and sinful, but nonetheless, because he is created by God, he is alive. In both instances, however, it is the whole human person, including the body, that is created in God's image and likeness. Pauline theology also speaks of *pneuma*, but again this designates the whole human person now living and acting under the new authority, power, and life of the Holy Spirit which comes through living in Christ. The biblical dichotomy then does not refer to a division within human beings, but to a divide between being either 'of the world' or 'of God.' For a discussion of these various biblical notions see the appropriate entries in the standard biblical dictionaries: *The Theological Dictionary of the Old Testament*, *The Theological Dictionary of the New Testament*, and *The Anchor Bible Dictionary*.

　　It should also be noted that it is only through the bodily senses that one obtains knowledge and expresses the truth, and equally, it is only through the body that one expresses love and kindness to others. Therefore, even within the body–soul distinction, the whole human being shares in the divine-like characteristics. Moreover, it is often through a holy person's face or countenance that the glory and love of God shines forth. The face can be an *icon* of God.

2 This is true of all virtues. One can be courageous, kind, generous, etc. only if one performs such actions freely.

3 Sin is always the free misuse of some good. Gluttony is the misuse of the good gift of food; lust the misuse of sex; lying the misuse of speech; and so on. For a good contemporary psychological, philosophical and theological account of the nature of sin, see C. Gestrich, *The Return of Splendor in the World: The Christian Doctrine of Sin and Forgiveness* (Grand Rapids: Eerdmans, 1997).

of the ancient world, designates moral evil freely committed and not an ontological evil.[4]

Moreover, according to the Judeo-Christian tradition, it is sin then which has brought the evil of suffering into the world. This suffering is fourfold as witnessed already in the Genesis account of 'the Fall.' First, as we see exemplified in Adam and Eve hiding from God (see Gen. 3:8), humankind's relationship with God is broken, not on an ontological level for human beings continue to exist, but on a moral level. Because humankind has rendered itself unholy through sin, it can no longer be properly related to the all-good and loving God.[5] In the act of free rebellion humankind has constituted itself as an unrighteous enemy opposed to God. It is not that God has changed. He has not become humankind's enemy, but rather humankind has changed. It has become God's enemy.[6] Because the human mind is now infected and the human heart hardened by sin, no longer then can human persons properly or easily know God and experience his love. Equally, human beings, according to the Judeo-Christian tradition, having separated themselves through sin from the God of life, die (see Gen. 3:2–3).[7] The chief cause

---

4 K. Rahner, while he rejects the notion that suffering is the natural side-effect of an evolving world, does not believe that the misuse of human freedom sufficiently addresses the question of why there is suffering. Since human freedom is ultimately dependent upon God, he argues that the reason for, but not the source of, human suffering is hidden within the incomprehensibility of God, and so itself remains incomprehensible. See 'Why Does God Allow Us To Suffer?', *Theological Investigations*, Vol. 29 (New York: Crossroad, 1983), pp. 194-208.

5 This is exemplified in that sinful human beings cannot see the face of the all-holy God and live. See Exod. 19:21, 33:18–23; Lev. 16:2; Num. 4:20; Is. 6:1–7. The whole point of the covenant was to once more consecrate the people in holiness so that they might keep the commandments and thus live a holy and god-like life. Only then could they worthily live in the presence of the all-holy God. See Exod. 19:6; Lev. 11:44–45, 19:2; Deut. 7:6.

6 It is fascinating that within the Genesis narrative, while obviously not a literal account, after Adam and Eve have sinned and then hear God walking in the garden, they hide, and do so successfully. God is forced to search for Adam by calling out his name. The author(s) of this tradition obviously realized that God, being God, would know where Adam and Eve were. Why then does the story depict God as ignorant of their whereabouts? It seems to me that it does so precisely to show that, while sin has changed Adam and Eve into fearful enemies of God, sin has not so changed God. He does not know where they are because he has not been affected by their sin. God is still the same loving and ever-present God who continues to want to take his neighbourly late afternoon stroll with Adam and Eve in the garden. It is only after God realizes that they are hiding from him that it dawns on him that something is amiss – the neighbourhood has changed. They have rebelled against him and so have made him into an enemy that must now be feared and avoided.

   While it is impossible to found a philosophical principle on one story from scripture, it seems evident here that God is portrayed as not being affected by human sin. It does not cause him to suffer any change, and this is to his advantage for he remains the ever-loving God even in the face of sin and evil.

7 The reality of death, as a necessary consequence of sin, becomes then the real symbol of the deeper death that has occurred, that of spiritual death (a life lived without God). Moreover, for Jews and Christians alike, death is seen as an evil because it is destructive of God's good creation and contrary to everything God, as the living God, stands for. It is an insult to the author of life. Likewise, since the whole of the human being, including the body, reflects the image and likeness of God, bodily death shattered this image and likeness. However, even within early Judaism death was not seen as the

then of human suffering within the Judeo-Christian tradition lies in the division wrought by sin between God – the author, sustainer and provider of all good – and humankind. Because of sin, humankind has rendered itself incapable of being the full beneficiary of God's bounty and so suffers its loss.

Second, as exemplified in Adam's accusation against Eve and in their mutual embarrassment over being naked, as well as in Cain's murder of Abel, sin has devastated human relationships (see Gen. 3:6–7,11–12; 4:8). Human beings suffer at the sinful hands of one another. They sin and are sinned against, and sin wreaks havoc upon sinner and victim alike. Greed, hatred, lust, pride, deceitfulness, etc. not only inflict immense suffering upon their victims, but they equally dehumanize the greedy, the avenger, the lustful, the arrogant, and the liar thus causing self-imposed suffering.[8] The litany of past and present atrocities, perpetrated by individuals, nations, and various racial and economic groupings testify to the degradation into which humanity has fallen and the horrendous and hideous suffering spawned by such degradation. No one is immune either from being a perpetrator of sin and so a cause of suffering, or from being a casualty of sin and so a victim of suffering. We are all both – often more so of the first than we care to admit.

Third, within the biblical perspective, sin also affects the whole of God's good creation. God declared: 'Cursed is the ground because of you [Adam]'(Gen. 3:17). No longer do Adam and Eve (and their descendants) live in the lush bounty of the Garden of Eden, but now man must toil for food and woman give birth in pain (see Gen. 3:17–19). Not only does the physical order cause its human inhabitants to suffer, but it equally groans for its own liberation from the effects of human sin (see Rom. 8:18–25).[9]

---

complete annihilation of the human person. While there was no clear belief in an afterlife, yet the concept of Sheol testifies to some shadowy existence after death. This is important for while death bore witness to humankind's moral separation from God, it did not shatter its ontological relationship with God. Death could defile God's good creation and render it corruptible, but it could not completely obliterate it. We see here why sin must be dealt with and why the resurrection of the body is important within Christianity. Only if sin is overcome will death be overcome. And death is only conquered if humankind is completely restored to God's image and likeness, which demands the restoration of the body.

This is in contrast to the ontological dualisms of the ancient (and even contemporary) world. Death is the final evil matter inflicts on the spiritual soul. Once free the soul lives unencumbered. This is why the Platonists of the Areopagus mocked Paul when he proclaimed 'the good news' of the resurrection of the body (see Acts 17:22–34). For the Platonists of Athens 'the good news' was 'bad news.' The last thing they wanted returned to them was their bodies.

8 This last point should not be forgotten. One never finds a happy tyrant, pornographer, abortionist, money-grubber, or power-mogul. The cunning seductiveness and disingenuous allurement of sin always exacts its own traitorous revenge.

9 The question of the suffering caused by natural 'disasters' – floods, drought, earthquakes, hurricanes, and tornadoes – can be seen as part of this biblical perspective. While such physical phenomena in one sense are not evil, since they are, as least in our present universe, but the result of the laws of nature, yet, because they cause destruction and human suffering, they are nonetheless rightly perceived as threats and the causes of suffering. Whether such natural phenomena would occur in a perfect non-sinful world is difficult to surmise. It would seem that they would not. What

Fourth, not only are human beings' relationships with God, others, and the world devastated by sin creating an environment of suffering, but human beings themselves, through sin, have become morally depraved. Sin has contaminated and infected man's very nature. While human beings remain ontologically good in that they remain human beings, they are now sinners and are thus predisposed by an inner compulsion to sin. This does not make sin any less serious for, as the whole history of humankind bears witness and as St Paul testifies, human beings have freely enslaved themselves to their sinful passions and drives and so rendered themselves less and less free (see Rom. 6:17, 7:14). Every human being finds his or her personal history told in the words of St Paul:

> I do not understand my own actions. For I do not do what I want, but I do the very thing I hate. . . . For I know that nothing good dwells within me, that is, in my flesh. I can will what is right, but I cannot do it. For I do not do the good I want, but the evil I do not want is what I do (Rom. 7:15, 18–19).[10]

There is one philosophical conclusion I wish to draw from this brief account of sin and the suffering it entails. Because God created every-thing good, the nature of everything, along with its ability to act in accordance with what it is, is good. Rocks, in so far as they are rocks, are good. Dogs are good and their ability to act in a 'dog-like' manner is good. Human beings are good and their ability to freely perfect them-selves physically, intellectually, and morally is good. Evil then, founded upon the reality of sin, is by necessity a privation of good – of some good given to it by God as Creator. Evil, while a reality, is not something then that exists in itself (as within the philosophical ontological dualisms), but

---

complicates the issue is the scientific theory of the 'big bang' with its resulting evolution which sees the massive convulsions at the dawn of the universe as part of the formative processes of the universe. Here such things as earthquakes are but the remaining 'after-shocks' of such a formative process and not the result of the universe being infected by sin. While such scientific theories may be true, one can still question whether the universe would not be more 'stable' and 'peaceful' had man not sinned. From the biblical perspective man, as the pinnacle of creation and for whom creation was made, is creation's steward, and so what affects man affects the whole of which he is a part.

10 Traditionally within Catholic theology, stemming from Augustine and developed by Aquinas, this compulsion or inordinate desire to sin is known as concupiscence and is seen as a consequence of original sin. While concupiscence in itself is not sinful, contrary to Luther and Calvin, yet because it is a disorder within humanity due to sin, it must be overcome and healed through grace.

Within the Eastern Orthodox tradition mortality or corruptibility is seen as the consequence of sin. Unlike the West, which emphasizes that humankind inherits the guilt of Adam's sin with its consequences, the East emphasizes that humankind inherits simply the consequence of Adam's sin – death. Humankind shares a solidarity in death and not a solidarity in guilt. Because humankind is now corruptible it is prone to sin, and can only be healed of sin by once more taking on the divine life of incorruptibility. While there is a difference of emphasis between the East and the West, both nonethe-less see sin and its consequences as the corruption of God's good creation. See J. Meyendorff, *Byzantine Theology: Historical Trends and Doctrinal Themes* (New York: Fordham University Press, 1974), pp. 143-46.

is always attached to some good as the corruption of that good.[11] For example, for human beings sight is a good, but blindness, while a reality, is the absence of the good of sight and so the partial corruption of the good of being human. Virtues are positive moral goods which perfect human beings – e.g., courage, kindness, and love. Vices – e.g., cowardice, callousness, and selfishness, while realities, are the absence of these goods and so the partial corruption of the good of being human.[12] What must be grasped is that it is the absence of some good then that is the cause of suffering. Sin, as the source of evil, deprives human beings of the goods proper to being human. It is this deprivation of good which, by necessity, causes suffering. Human beings suffer because, through sin, they are deprived of their proper relationships with God and others. They suffer because the cosmos itself is in some way contaminated by sin. Moreover, sin has corrupted reason and so deprived it of its full intellectual ability to know the truth (including a knowledge of God), and it has corrupted the will and so deprived it of its full freedom to choose the good. Human beings, spiritually, intellectually, morally, physically, and emotionally, suffer from these deprivations.[13]

God Does Not Suffer

It is at this precise juncture that we can now (finally) adequately address the question of whether or not God suffers. As with a jigsaw puzzle all of the relevant and necessary philosophical and theological pieces are now in their proper places so as to link correctly with them the question of

---

11 Aquinas states that 'being and perfection of any nature is good. Hence it cannot be that evil signifies being, or any form or nature. Therefore it must be that by the name of evil is signified the absence of good.' *ST*, I, 48, 1. See also ad 2 and 4.

   Pope John Paul II states:

   Man suffers on account of evil, which is a certain lack, limitation or distortion of good. We could say that man suffers *because of a good* in which he does not share, from which in a certain sense he is cut off, or of which he has deprived himself. He particularly suffers when he 'ought' – in the normal order of things – to have a share in this good, and does not have it. *Salvifici Doloris* (1984) n. 7.

   See also G. Grisez, *Beyond the New Theism*, pp. 295-96.

12 See *ST*, I, 48, 2 and 3.

13 It should be noted that because evil is always attached to some good and the corruption of a good, 'evil cannot wholly consume good,' in other words, something cannot be absolutely and totally evil in itself (*ST*, I, 48, 4). There cannot be something that is ontologically evil in itself for evil must be attached to something that exists and existence, by its very nature, is a good. This is even true of Satan and the other fallen angels. They are not ontologically evil as such. While they seek only to do what is evil, and so have become totally depraved morally, yet they do so by freely misusing the good of their intellect and will (see *ST*, I, 63 and 64). The good of their intellect and will remains even if they use these goods only to do evil.

   It should be noted as well that pain and suffering are good in so far as they make us aware of the presence, and so repugnance, of sin and evil. For example, the experience of physical pain is good because it alerts us to an immediate or pending evil. The pain caused by a burn allows us to pull our hand away from the fire. However, while the pain may be good, it is good because it is alerting us to the danger of losing some good, and for that reason alone it is good. While pain and suffering allow us to respond properly to evil, they are not good in themselves.

God's suffering and so allowing a precise and accurate answer to be given.

The simple answer to the question: 'Does God suffer?' is: No, God in himself as God does not suffer. To say that God does not suffer means not only that he does not feel any physical pain, since he is not corporeal, but also that he does not undergo some passible changes of state whereby he experiences some form of divine emotional agitation, anguish, agony, or distress. God is never in a state of inner *angst*.[14]

All that has been set out in the previous chapter concerning God's immutable and impassible nature as the one God who is a trinity of persons demands that God be immune from suffering. Nonetheless, following upon the conclusions of the last chapter and from the nature of sin and evil, I want to accentuate two inter-related reasons why God cannot suffer.

Reason One: The Creator–Creature Distinction

First, we must remember that God and all else are in distinct, but not unrelated, ontological orders. This distinction and relation is founded, as we saw, upon God's act of creation. The act of creation establishes that God is distinct, as Creator, from what is created and so cannot be numbered as one of the things created, and he is equally and simultaneously related, as Creator, to what is created. The act of creation actually brings into existence the created ontological order, and so an order that is by necessity, while related to God, ontologically distinct from God.

Moreover, because God is perfectly good and the source of all good, he could not create what is ontologically evil, but only what is ontologically good. 'To be' is 'to be good' for existence in itself is good. Nor then could God do anything that is evil which would cause himself or others to suffer. Thus, evil, for it to exist, must be caused by sin, a free misuse of what is good, and so evil is a deprivation of good. It is this deprivation which causes suffering.

The conclusion to be drawn is that, because the source of evil (and so suffering) is located not in the ontological constitution of 'things' – that is, not insofar as they are created and so exist in relation to God as the Creator, but rather in the free sinful misuse of the goods endowed to human beings as created – evil is contained within and confined to the created order. While God keeps the created order in existence, he is not of the created order in which sin and suffering take place. As Creator he is related to the created order as the one who is not of the created order. Thus evil does not and cannot reverberate back into the uncreated order where God alone exists as absolutely good. The ontological distinction between God and the created order, a distinction which establishes the

---

14 By stating here that God does not suffer I am simply and only denying of God what most contemporary theologians, who espouse a suffering God, wish to assert. However, it must be asserted as well that this does not mean, as we will see, that God does not grieve over sin and evil, and the suffering that these cause. In a true and authentic sense God does grieve and sorrow over sin and evil, but he does so in a manner that is in keeping with his impassible nature.

existence of the created order and so its ontological goodness, prevents God from being infected by the evil that takes place within the created order, and so renders him immune to suffering. The ontological distinction between Creator and creatures is, therefore, the fundamental positive reason for why God does not suffer.

In the light of this, what would be the repercussions if God did suffer? Are there disqualifying reasons for not allowing God to suffer? If God suffered, this would demand that something other than himself caused him to suffer, that is, that the evil of human sin would not only affect humankind causing it to suffer, but that it would also affect God causing him to suffer. At first sight this might appear to be good since, as all those who propose a suffering God argue, it would appear to allow God to share lovingly and compassionately in our suffering and grief. However, such divine suffering would demand that God and all else exist in the same ontological order, for only if he existed in the same ontological order in which the evil took place could he then suffer. This also might appear to be good. Again, many if not most, theologians who argue for a suffering God (process theologians and Moltmann being the prime, but not exclusive, examples) readily admit, and rightly so (and those who do not miss the logic of their stance), that their theodicy is panentheistic.[15] Since panentheism holds that, while God's being is more than all else and is not exhausted by all else, his being includes all else, these theologians clearly perceive that if God is to suffer he must share in the same ontological order as everything else.[16] However, to place God and all else in the same ontological order has disastrous philosophical and theological consequences.

---

15 J. Moltmann holds that his view of God is panentheistic. See *The Trinity and the Kingdom of God*, pp. 106–8; *God in Creation*, 90–103; and *The Crucified God*, p. 277. See also Johnson, *She Who Is*, pp. 231–33.

   While Moltmann is critical of process thought, his own version of panentheism, nonetheless, leaves him open to the criticisms I am about to make. For critiques of Moltmann's view of a suffering God within the context of panentheism, see D. Attfield, 'Can God be Crucified? A Discussion of J. Moltmann,' *Scottish Journal of Theology* 30 (1977):47–57; D.B. Farrow, 'Review Essay: In the End Is the Beginning: A Review of Jürgen Moltmann's Systematic Contributions,' *Modern Theology* 14/3 (1998):425–47; J. Galot, 'Le Dieu Trinitaire et la Passion du Christ,' *Nouvelle Revue Theologique* 104/1 (1982):70–87; J. McIntyre's review of Moltmann's *God in Creation* in *Scottish Journal of Theology* 41 (1988):267–73; P. Molnar, 'The Function of the Trinity in Moltmann's Ecological Doctrine of Creation,' *Theological Studies* 51 (1990):673–97; P. Molnar, 'Moltmann's Post-Modern Messianic Christology,' *The Thomist* 56/4 (1992):669–93; O'Donnell, *Trinity and Temporality*, pp. 109–10, 119–20; B. Walsh, 'Theology of Hope and the Doctrine of Creation: An Appraisal of Jürgen Moltmann,' *Evangelical Quarterly* 59 (1987):53–76; J. Webster, 'Jürgen Moltmann: Trinity and Suffering,' *Evangel* Summer (1985):4–6.

16 Panentheists could argue that, due to God's being in more than all else and not exhausted by all else, he 'transcends' all else and so is ontologically different from all else. However, God's transcendence is only relatively, and not absolutely, ontologically different. Since God does not wholly exist in a distinct ontological order from all else, he must exist within the same ontological order as all else. In reality there is only one ontological order which contains both God and all else, and God is different only to the extent that his existence is not entirely exhausted by all else that exists in that one ontological order.

First, the act of creation (*creatio ex nihilo*) is rendered impossible since God is now numbered among the things 'created.' This is why many theologians who argue for divine suffering are either ambiguous about the act of creation or willingly opt, by philosophical necessity, for some form of eternal ontological monism, process thought again being the principal, but not exclusive, example of this.[17] Process theology sees the entire ontological cosmic process, which contains God himself, not as something brought into existence but simply as having no beginning nor end. Thus, the question why anything actually exists, including God, is left unanswered. Like the ancients' pre-existent matter, the whole monistic system is now just taken as 'a given,' but 'a given' that cries out that it cannot be taken as 'a given' but demands a reasonable philosophical explanation.[18]

Moreover, to say that God and all else are in the same ontological order, and thus that God suffers along with everything else, demands that evil becomes once more ontological in nature as in the ancient religious and philosophical dualisms. Since the whole ontological order is infected with evil so that everything within it suffers, including God, then merely to exist within that order is to exist in an evil ontological state. Within Christianity one is born into a state of original sin whereby one's existential or ontological goodness is only morally impaired. To be

17 P. Fiddes and K. Ward are critical of process thought in that they wish to uphold God as Creator, and argue that God suffers by his free loving choice and not, as in process thought, by necessity. Nonetheless, they too see God as constantly changing and so perfecting himself, and thus experiencing temporality, through his relationship to world history and human events. (See Fiddes, *The Creative Suffering of God*, pp. 46–143 and Ward, *Religion and Creation*, pp. 159–284.) They rightly perceive, as does process thought, that if God is to suffer as God, he must be ontologically ensconced within the created order, in that his being or nature (who he is) is partially determined or established by the created, historical and temporal order. He relates to and interacts with the created order not as one who is ontologically distinct from the created order, but as one who ontologically exists within that order and so relates to and interacts with the created order from within the created order, and so is changed and perfected by so doing. However, because God is now, at least partially, only truly who he is because of his existence within the created order it is impossible to uphold the biblical notion that God is wholly other than the created order. What Fiddes and Ward forget is that if God is wholly other than the created order, and he must be if he is to be its Creator, it is metaphysically impossible for him to become an ontological member of that order. God can, and does, relate to and interact with the created order, and he does so in a most intimate and immediate manner (as I have argued), but he does so as the one who is completely other than the created order without losing his complete otherness in so doing. As I have stressed previously, and will do so again when discussing the Incarnation, this is the Judeo-Christian mystery.

18 The fundamental philosophical defect of such a monistic system as exemplified in process philosophy (one that would apply to Hegel's philosophy as well) is that it is impossible to account for why anything *exists*, including God. It can account for why God is the way he is and how he works, and why the world is the way it is and how it works, but why God or the world exist at all is completely unaccounted for. Nothing accounts for the existence of the process for nothing is outside the process, and to claim that the process is eternal simply begs the question for there must be something within the process that accounts for its eternal *existence*, and there is none. God, as in Plato's demiurge, is creative only in the sense that he orders and influences the process, but he does not bring the process into existence since his own existence is entirely dependent upon the process.

born into a panentheistic or monistic system infected by evil means that one is ontologically impaired. Just 'to be' is, at least in part, 'to be evil,' and so to suffer. Again, process theologians readily admit this.[19] Evil, and

---

19 An excellent example of this is found in D. Griffin's book *God, Power, and Evil* (Lanham, MD: University of America Press, 1991). Here Griffin states:

> The general thesis of the process theodicy which follows is that the possibility of genuine evil is rooted in the metaphysical (i.e., necessary) characteristics of the world. In Whitehead's words: 'The categories governing the determination of things are the reasons why there should be evil' (*Process and Reality*, p. 341). P. 276.

Since God, out of his own goodness, does not create the world (*creatio ex nihilo*) to be good in itself, but rather, because he too is subject to the metaphysical principles contained within the cosmic process of which he is a part, he merely attempts to bring order and harmony to an already pre-existing primordial 'state of absolute or near chaos' (p. 286). Because God is limited both by the philosophical principles contained within the process of which he is a part and because the process is metaphysically chaotic at the onset, evil within the whole cosmic process must be 'metaphysical and not moral' (p. 276). Since God did not freely establish the metaphysical principles, he cannot be blamed for the evil within the world. 'Since the metaphysical principles have no conceivable alternative, they are not "given," not "arbitrary," and hence should not be thought of as resulting from a volition' (p. 299), and thus they do 'not result from a divine decision' (p. 300). See pp. 277–310.
    We have obviously returned to the pagan religious and Greek ontological dualisms of the past. In his early works Griffin, as well as other process theologians such as Pittinger and Ogden, criticized the early church Fathers for being unfaithful to biblical revelation by allowing Platonism to disfigure it. In response to this accusation, I argued that it is was process theology that was more faithful to Platonism both in its view of God and as to the cause and nature of evil (see Weinandy, *Does God Change?*, pp. 140–53). It is fascinating that more recently Griffin criticizes, and I believe now rightly so from a process perspective, the early church for not being faithful to Platonism in that it espoused the concept of *creatio ex nihilo*, and so affirmed a 'supernaturalistic version of theism.' If Christianity had been faithful to what Griffin now believes is its Platonic heritage, it would have realized that 'God cannot create a universe such as ours instantaneously, unilaterally prevent evil events, infallibly reveal divine truth, or inerrantly inspire sacred scripture' ('A Naturalistic Trinity' in *Trinity in Process*, pp. 23 and 24). While Griffin may still hold a very dubious version of Christianity, he has at least got it right that process thought has more in common with Platonism than it has with traditional Christian doctrine.
    Moreover, while Griffin and other process theologians hold that God continuously 'lures' or 'persuades' all other realities, such as human beings, to actualize 'the good' within the cosmic process, and so overcome evil, there is no metaphysical grounding for this. Since God is not ontologically ultimate within process thought, containing all good and perfection in his immutable actualized self, there is no reason to presume that he 'contains all goods' nor that 'good' will ultimately triumph. There is simply no ontological foundation for such goods and values as justice and love. They exist in an ontological vacuum and so to assert their existence is completely gratuitous.
    Last, to speak of God suffering, as process philosophers and theologians glory in doing, is at best a euphemism. All God does, within his concrete or consequent nature, is to record that a human person has suffered. The suffering is not present to him as the contemporary suffering of a person, but merely the objective past idea. C. Gunton correctly states that, within process thought, God 'plays the essentially passive role as a cosmic memory.' 'Process Theology's Concept of God,' *The Expository Times* 84 (1973):294.
    For critiques of process thought other than my own, see the authors mentioned in Weinandy, *Does God Change?*, pp. 140–53. See also N. Frankenberry, 'Some Problems in Process Theodicy,' *Religious Studies* 17 (1981):179–97; W. Hill, 'The Historicity of God,' pp. 320–33; J. McIntyre, *The Shape of Christology* (Second Edition) (Edinburgh: T & T Clark, 1998), pp. 177–255; M. Rousseau, 'Process Thought and Traditional Theism: A Critique,' *The Modern Schoolman* 62 (1985):45–64; H. Smith, 'Has Process Theology

so suffering, is constitutive of the eternal process of 'becoming' whereby everything may be becoming 'better' (logically everything could be becoming worse) but is never actually able to obtain perfection, and so evil and suffering will never be wholly eradicated. But if the whole onto-logical system, which includes God, is impaired by evil, then there is no one, including God, who can repair it and make it right. Salvation – freedom from evil and suffering – becomes a false hope for it will never be obtained.[20] The consequences of a suffering God are dire indeed.

Reason Two: The Perfection of God as a Trinity of Persons

There is also a second related positive reason why God cannot suffer. Because evil, due to the reality of sin, is a privation of some good or perfection which in turn causes suffering, God as pure act, and thus pure goodness itself in act, can never be deprived of a good or perfec-tion which would cause him to suffer. Since God is pure good in perfect act, nothing can impair God's goodness so as to inflict a loss of some good which would then entail God suffering.[21] Negatively, if God

---

Dismantled Classical Theism?', *Theological Digest* 35/4 (1988):303–18; Vanhoutte, 'God as Companion and Fellow-Sufferer', pp. 191–225; J.H. Wright, 'The Method of Process Theology: An Evaluation', *Communio*, 6/1 (1979):38–55.

20 R. Goetz believes that 'any concept of a limited deity finally entails a denial of the capacity of God to redeem the world and thus, ironically, raises the question of whether God is in the last analysis even love, at least love in the Christian sense of the term.' 'The Suffering God: The Rise of a New Orthodoxy,' p. 388.
J. Selling states:

In the end, the image of a God who suffers along with creation is incapable of chal-lenging the tragedy of human suffering itself.... For if God *suffers* – experiencing pain without meaning or justification – then we are more alone and hopeless than our fear and anxiety could imagine. 'Moral Questioning and Human Suffering' in *God and Human Suffering*, p. 170.

In response to Moltmann and others, K. Rahner states: 'To put it crudely, it does not help me to escape from my mess and mix-up and despair if God is in the same predicament.' *Karl Rahner in Dialogue: Conversations and Interviews 1965–1982*, eds P. Imhof and H. Biallowons (New York: Crossroad, 1986), p. 126. Moltmann responded to Rahner's rejection of a suffering God by saying that such comments sound as if they come from a person whose life was 'unloved and incapable of love,' a life that was 'frozen' and 'fossilized', and 'one which is already dead.' He asks: 'Are these the pains of being cut off from natural relationships which celibacy imposes on a young man enthused by God?' *History and the Triune God*, p. 123. To disagree with Rahner is legit-imate. To accuse him of being incapable of loving due to his vow of celibacy is, well, a punch that is a little below the belt.

In agreement with Rahner, J.-B. Metz, on a number of occasions, has adamantly rejected the notion of a suffering God. He argues that a suffering God merely duplicates human suffering and powerlessness, but now hopelessly eternalizes them within God. See 'Suffering Unto God,' *Critical Inquiry* 20 (1994):618–20, and *A Passion for God: The Mystical-Political Dimension of Christianity* (New York: Paulist Press, 1998), pp. 69–71 and 116–20.

M. Steen expresses similar sentiments about the hopelessness of the human situation in the face of a suffering God. See 'The Theme of the "Suffering" God: An Exploration' in *God and Human Suffering*, pp. 90–93.

21 G. Hanratty forcefully argues that God cannot suffer because he cannot be deprived of any good. See 'Divine Immutability and Impassibility Revisited' in *At the Heart of the Real*, pp. 157–59. M. Rousseau argues in a similar manner. See 'Process Thought and Traditional Theism: A Critique,' p. 53.

did suffer, it would mean that he was deprived of a good, but if he were deprived of a good, he would not be fully in act, for he would now be in potency to obtaining or re-obtaining the good, and if he were not fully in act, as *ipsum esse*, then he could not create, and if he could not create, then he could not possess the absolutely immediate, supremely dynamic, utterly intimate, and unbreakably enduring relationship with creation and with human persons that the act of creation establishes.

A similar argument applies equally to God as a trinity. Because the persons of the Trinity are subsistent relations fully in act, and so are ontologically the one God in their mutual, reciprocal, and perfect love and goodness, they cannot be deprived of this perfect fully actualized love and goodness. Moreover, as we saw in the previous chapter, for the persons of the Trinity to be subsistent relations fully in act means that they possess the singular ability, complementary to being *actus purus*, to relate, in the act of creation, creatures to themselves as they are in their mutual and reciprocal love and goodness, and thus in an immediate, dynamic, intimate and unbreakable manner. Negatively, if the persons of the Trinity were infected with suffering, it would mean that they were deprived of some good, and so enmeshed in sin and evil. Thus they would no longer be subsistent relations fully in act possessing fully actualized love and goodness, but would now be in potency to obtaining or re-obtaining the good they did not possess. However, this loss would render them impotent to create, and thus to relate creatures to themselves in the fulness of their love and goodness in an immediate, dynamic, intimate, and unbreakable manner.

While a suffering God may have some intellectual and emotional appeal (often more emotional than intellectual), such an understanding of God is philosophically and theologically disastrous in its consequences. It may give the appearance of providing consolation to the innocent victims of sin and evil, but ultimately it throws into complete disarray the whole philosophical and theological structure upon which an authentic biblical understanding of God and of his loving relationship to creation and to humankind is based.[22] Thus, one must conclude that a suffering God is not only philosophically and theologically untenable; the concept is also religiously devastating, for it is at least emotionally disheartening if not actually abhorrent.[23]

22　P. Helm states:

> Since there is nothing morally wrong or intellectually incoherent with emotional change *per se*, the reason for not ascribing it to God must be that it is incompatible with other, more deeply entrenched (in terms of the biblical data) divine attributes and powers. 'The Impossibility of Divine Impassibility,' p. 130.

　　See also Davies, *Thinking About God*, pp. 156–57.

23　R. Creel admirably argues for why suffering within God debilitates him and makes him the one to be most pitied. See *Divine Impassibility*, pp. 121–26. D. Cook emphasizes that for those who espouse a suffering God it appears that suffering is more important than its cure. See 'Weak Church, Weak God' in *The Power and Weakness of God*, pp. 77, 86, 88–89.

The God of Love

Having argued that God does not suffer, I obviously do not want in any way to reject or even to diminish the truth that God is a God of love. Actually, I want to contend, as I have throughout, that a God who does not suffer is more loving, compassionate, and merciful than a God who does.

The whole Bible proclaims and the entire Christian tradition teaches that God is loving, compassionate, and merciful. We saw previously in the chapter on God in the Old Testament that Yahweh reveals himself to be a God of compassion, love, mercy, and forgiveness (see Exod. 34:6–7). The First Letter of John simply states that 'God is love' (4:8 and 16). Jesus counsels his disciples that, if they are to be perfect, they must 'Be merciful, just as your Father is merciful' (Lk 6:36). But how can a God who does not suffer be compassionate and merciful? Does not, as so many claim, the absence of suffering render God indifferent to evil and the immense suffering that arises from it? Does God not grieve over sin and the injustice perpetrated upon the innocent? If God does not suffer, is he not absent from the Auschwitzes of history? In order to address such legitimate questions and authentic concerns, we must first briefly examine the character of compassionate love among human persons and then discern from this the nature of God's compassionate love.

The bond of human friendship is love, the giving of ourselves to one another, not for our own good (although we may benefit as well), but for the other's good.[24] Within the present 'fallen' condition human beings attempt to live out and express this altruistic love within a milieu of sin and evil. This means that complete love is rarely achieved for human love is often marred by sinful selfish desires and ends. In relationships we seek not only the good of the other but frequently our own. Moreover, and more importantly for our present discussion, love is expressed in situations where, due to sin and evil, suffering is present. Love, in the midst of personal sin and the evil caused by sin, must risk suffering. Actually, love is often tested, fostered, and most fully expressed in the midst of suffering. We grow in love and manifest the full extent of our love by our willingness to suffer with and on behalf of the person we love. We suffer when someone we love is sick or dying. We suffer in love over the injustice perpetrated against the innocent, and we risk our own well-being when we stand against such injustice. It is this willingness to take action against the evil that is the cause of suffering and so restore the good that manifests most fully one's love. Moreover, when the person we love injures us by sinning against us, we are even willing, or should be willing, to suffer because of the person we love.

---

24 It is not necessary here to delineate the various types of love, e.g., *eros* and *agape*, other than to say that within the New Testament and the Christian tradition *agape* came to be seen as the fullest expression of selfless love first founded within God himself and then infused or given to creatures by the grace of the Holy Spirit. For Aquinas *amicitia* (friendship) is the most perfect aspect of love (*caritas*) for it implies intensity and fervour. For a study on the relationship between love and friendship in Aquinas, see Dodds, *The Unchanging God of Love*, pp. 287–92.

Two points can be drawn from this brief analysis of human love. First, love is defined by and manifested in the giving of ourselves – in thought, word, and deed – for the good and well-being of another. Second, while love in the present world of sin and evil entails the willingness to suffer and is most fully manifested in suffering, suffering itself is not a constitutive element of love. To do away with sin and evil, and thus suffering, would not in any way do away with nor lessen love.[25] The reason is that love is a good in itself. Suffering is not a good in itself, but rather an evil. It is not a good in itself for suffering is always caused by the absence of some good, and suffering love is always caused by the absence of some good that the one we love (even if the one we love is ourselves) should possess – health, justice, etc. Suffering then, as evil, is never sought for its own sake, and if it is, it is rightly seen as an aberration. Suffering is an evil even when attached to the good of love, for love rightly cries out in suffering at the absence or loss of some good, and seeks, if possible, to restore it. The reason human beings willingly suffer is for the good of love and so the suffering entailed in love is seen as good, but it is precisely the love that is good and not the suffering itself.[26]

We have previously argued that God cannot suffer because he cannot be deprived of any aspect of his fully actualized goodness which would cause him to suffer. Moreover, since suffering is not constitutive of love, we can also perceive why the absence of suffering in God does not necessarily imply the absence of love and thus divine indifference. Actually, since God does not suffer, his love becomes absolutely free in its expression and supremely pure in its purpose. If God did suffer, it would mean that God would need not only to alleviate the suffering of others, but also his own suffering, and thus there would be an inbuilt self-interest in God's love and consolation. However, since God does not suffer, his care for those who do suffer is freely given and not evoked by some need on his part.[27] His love is freely expressed entirely for the sake

25 In many situations it is precisely sin and the prospect of suffering that hinders the full development and expression of love. A person may desire, on one level, to love someone wholly and entirely, but be incapable of doing so because of the sinfulness which resides within his/her own person causing fear of the sacrifices required of such love. Selfishness, pride, etc. hinder the full growth and expression of love.

26 Aquinas states that all sorrow in itself is an evil, but that 'it is a sign of goodness if a man is in sorrow or pain on account of this present evil. For if he were not to be in sorrow or pain, this could only be either because he feels it not, or because he does not reckon it as something unbecoming, both of which are manifest evil. Consequently it is a condition of goodness, that, supposing an evil to be present, sorrow or pain should ensue' (*ST*, I–II, 39, 1). Sorrow, then, as the perception and rejection of evil is a virtuous good (see *ST*, I–II, 39, 2).

M. Dodds notes that those who propose that God suffers tend equally to hold that suffering is only 'seemingly' an evil. In reality it is actually a good. He quotes F. von Hügel: 'Suffering is intrinsically an Evil. It is impossible to read much of the literature which insists upon the presence of Suffering in God, without being struck with the trend – I believe the inevitable trend, once Suffering has been admitted into God – to treat that Suffering as but a seeming Evil.' *Essays and Address on the Philosophy of Religion: Second Series*, p. 199. See *The Unchanging God of Love*, pp. 441–42, n. 80. D. Cook concurs: 'The charge against those who embrace the ideas of the weakness and suffering of God is that they have omitted any adequate treatment of the nature and seriousness of sin.' 'Weak Church, Weak God,' p. 72. See also p. 88.

27 Aquinas states that God does not act for the acquisition of something, that is, he never

of those he loves. For Aquinas, moreover, what God does to alleviate suffering is done solely for the good and benefit of those suffering and not his own.[28] But if God's love does not involve suffering, what is the relationship between the suffering encountered by human beings and the love of God?

Again we must first recall that God as pure act and, correlatively, the trinity of persons as subsistent relations fully in act means that the divine attribute of love is fully in act. The trinity of persons subsist in relation to one another, as the one God, with their love for one another fully and completely actualized. They are immutable and impassible in their love for one another, not because their love is static or inert, but because it is utterly dynamic and totally passionate in its self-giving. It is impossible for the Trinity to be more loving for the persons of the Trinity possess no self-actualizing potential to become more loving. This is not only in keeping with the biblical proclamation that 'God is love,' but it actually gives to it befitting, exact, and even literal philosophical and theological depth. God '*is*' love because God's love, as reciprocally expressed within the Trinity, is fully in act.[29] Two extraordinary and marvellous conclu-

---

acts in order to acquire some good for himself. Rather, God acts 'only to communicate his perfection, which is his goodness.' *ST*, I, 44, 4. Obviously, God is able to act in such a totally unselfish manner only because, as pure act, he is in need of nothing.

In response to Moltmann, M. Dodds rightly perceives that a suffering God who, by necessity, is an ontologically imperfect being, 'will inevitably seek his own perfection and try to overcome his own deficiency. Only an entirely perfect being, subject to no defect and lacking in nothing, is able to love with a fully gratuitous love.' 'Thomas Aquinas, Human Suffering, and the Unchanging God of Love,' *Theological Studies* 52 (1991):333. See also p. 332.

W. Hill likewise states:

It is this uniqueness of divine being, whereby God does not and cannot suffer in himself, that explains why he can love unfathomably, in a totally altruistic way, why divine love can be what the New Testament calls *agape* rather than only the self-fulfilling *eros* of Greek rational thought. 'Does Divine Love Entail Suffering in God?' p. 64.

Hill further develops the difference between the philosophical notion of *eros* and the Christian understanding of *agape* in his article 'Two Gods of Love: Aquinas and Whitehead,' pp. 252–57.

On the free liberality of God's love, see also Blocher, 'Divine Immutability,' p. 21; and Cook, 'Weak Church Weak God,' p. 76, both in *The Power and Weakness of God*; Burrell, *Aquinas: God and Action*, pp. 87–89; and N. Kretzmann, *The Metaphysics of Theism: Aquinas's Natural Theology in* Summa Contra Gentiles *I* (Oxford: Clarendon Press, 1997), pp. 250–54.

28 See *Scriptum Super Libros Sententiarum*, IV, 46, 2, 1, 1.

29 God's love as fully actualized in the pure act that he is as a trinity of persons accounts for the all-consuming passion of God expressed in the Old Testament.

It should be noted that to say that God's love is fully in act in no way implies that we can fully grasp what it means to say such. We can know that the trinity of persons love one another fully and completely, but we cannot fully comprehend what such a loving relationship is like. For God to be love fully in act is beyond human comprehension. Again we can know what the mystery is, but we cannot comprehend the mystery.

Moreover, we now can grasp why God cannot merely be 'ethically immutable' as I.A. Dorner, K. Barth, K. Ward, R. Swinburne and others have proposed. If God is not pure goodness and love ontologically in act, and thus ontologically immutable, then there is no philosophical or theological ground upon which one can claim that God will

sions can be drawn from this which bear upon God's love and human suffering.

First, God as a trinity of persons, in their love for human beings, never needs to actualize some aspect of love in order to become more loving.[30] God's love possesses, as does human love, many different facets and expressions. His love embraces goodness, commitment, affection, joy, kindness, generosity, strength, courage, power, and passion (see 1 Cor. 13:4–7). Because sin affects human beings and their relationship to him, God's love, as does human love, also embraces mercy, compassion, patience, forgiveness and even sorrow and grief. At times it equally, again as does human love, entails justice, anger, admonition, correction, rebuke, and even condemnation. Within human beings all these various aspects of love are actualized at various times under various circumstances, and so human beings express compassionate love at one time and admonish in love at another. The various aspects of love are never in contradiction to one another, but they are actualized at disparate times depending upon which aspect of love is appropriate given the circumstances. In his relationship to the created order and to human beings in particular, because God's love is fully in act, he need not actualize, depending upon the changing situations and circumstances, these various facets of love. All of these facets of love are fully actualized and wholly contained within the one fully actualized love of God as a trinity of persons. When a human person repents of sin, God need not change the manner of his love within himself from being that of an admonishing love to that of being a forgiving love. When an innocent person suffers an injustice, God need not adapt himself so as to express compassionate love toward the person so injured and simultaneously adapt his love so as to reprove the perpetrator of the injustice. Eternally God is immutably and impassibly adapted to every situation and circumstance, not because his love is indifferent and unresponsive, but because his love, with all its facets, is fully in act, and so he is supremely and utterly responsive to every situation and circumstance. God is unconditionally adaptable in

---

always be ethical and faithful. Only an ontologically immutable God, in the pure act that he is, embraces, fully in act, goodness itself and love itself. Only as such is he always assured to act ethically in his dealings with human beings and to remain faithful to his promises. The 'ethical immutability' of the Bible (if that is in fact only what the Bible actually asserts) testifies to and mandates the 'ontological immutability' of God.
R.A. Muller writes:

Ethical, intentional constancy . . . must have an ontological basis. The constancy of the divine purpose, the consistency of the God who is what he is and will be what he will be, must also indicate a consistency, an immutability of the divine being. . . . The issue is not so much whether Scripture declares ontological immutability, but that this concept is strongly implied. 'Incarnation, Immutability, and the Case for Classical Theism,' *Westminster Theological Journal* 45 (1983):32.

30 J. Quinn argues that it is the love expressed within the Trinity that is the basis for the Trinity's love for human beings. As the persons of the Trinity give themselves entirely to one another in love so they give themselves entirely to human beings in love. It is this complete self-giving love of the Trinity, especially witnessed within the Incarnation, which is the Trinity's answer to human suffering. See 'Triune Self-Giving,' pp. 194–202.

his dynamic and passionate love because his love is immutably and impassibly in act.[31] If God did need, sequentially in a potency/act manner, to adapt and re-adapt and re-adapt himself again to every personal situation in every momentary instance, he would be conceived as an infinite mega-computer (PC, obviously, and user-friendly) continuously and simultaneously processing trillions of conflicting bits of emotional data. He would then be seen to be perpetually entangled in an unending internal emotional whirligig.[32]

Correlatively, because all of the facets of God's love are fully actualized within the love of God, human persons are able to know in faith, and even experience, that love in accordance with their personal situation at any one time. If a person sins, he or she knows and experiences God's love as a rebuke and as an admonishment. If the person repents, he or she knows and experiences God's love as compassionate and forgiving, and

31 In Chapter 1, fn. 38 I noted that, while J. Galot and H.U. von Balthasar (and maybe K. Barth as well) hold that God is immutable and impassible in himself, yet in their own distinctive manner, they feel obliged to argue that, in his freely constituted relationship with humankind, he is indeed passible. The reason for proffering such a position lies in their belief that God's immutability and impassibility are incompatible with his engaging in a loving relationship with humankind, a relationship in which he is compassionate and merciful, and even suffers. What they have failed to grasp is the argument that I have just offered. They do not perceive that God's immutability and impassibility do not make him less loving toward humankind, but actually guarantee that his love contains all its various attributes fully and perfectly in act. Immutability and impassibility must never be perceived, as Galot and von Balthasar do, as stumbling blocks that need to be overcome, as if, despite being immutable and impassible, God is nonetheless, in a dialectic fashion, still loving and merciful. Rather, God's immutability and impassibility are the absolute presuppositions and prolegomena for ensuring that he is perfectly loving. Moreover, by attempting to distinguish between God-in-himself and God-for-us, a distinction that is highly dubious in itself, they have placed a breach between God as he truly is and God who relates to us. Such a chasm is not only philosophically unwarranted, but it is also theologically detrimental to biblical revelation and the Christian tradition, which glories in the fact that God actually interacts with and relates to us as he truly is in the fullness of his divinity. God need not 're-fashion' himself in order to interact with us.

For further critiques of Galot, see J.-H. Nicolas, 'La Souffrance de Dieu?', *Nova et Vetera* 53 (1978):56–64; 'Aimante et Bienheureuse Trinité', *Revue Thomiste* 73 (1978):271–87; E.L. Mascall, *Theology and the Gospel of Christ* (London: Darton, Longman & Todd, 1977), pp. 182–84; *Whatever Happened to the Human Mind?*, pp. 94–95; and Weinandy, *Does God Change?*, pp. 174–86.

32 P. Helm argues that if God's love is seen as dispositional in a human manner, then we might think of God as exercising this disposition depending upon the need of creatures. 'Once the need vanishes, the disposition is no longer exercised.'

But this is altogether the wrong way of thinking about the character of God; for it supposes that there are occasions when God is less than wholly active, and moreover that these are the typical conditions of his existence. So that while it may be helpful to think of God's moral attributes as dispositions, in that they have the stability and uniformity that dispositions in general have, unlike human dispositions they are dispositions that are always/eternally exercised. They are maximally active; that is, there is no actual situation in which God requires to exercise a given disposition in which that disposition is not exercised, every disposition that comprises the divine character is exercised, and each is exercised without any limitation or conditionality. So that, for example the love of God is never not exercised where it is appropriate for it to be exercised. 'The Impossibility of Divine Passibility,' pp. 124–25.

so rejoices in his merciful love.[33] If a person suffers due to injustice, he or she knows, in faith and sometimes by experience, that God's lovingkindness and consolation are present. God's love as fully actualized is 'ready made' to meet any situation, and human beings are able to know and experience this love in all its varied actualized fulness.

Therefore, not only are joy, kindness, and generosity truly contained within the fully actualized love of God, but also compassion, mercy, grief, and even anger are also truly subsumed within his perfect love.[34] Aquinas states that 'God takes pity (*miseretur*) on us through love alone, in as much as he loves us as belonging to himself (*tanquam aliud sui*).'[35] While some facets of love within human beings entail suffering, such as compassion and grief, they are subsumed and contained within the perfectly actualized love of God, but now devoid of the suffering which would render his love less than perfectly actualized. While compassion is defined as 'suffering with,' the heart of compassion is the love expressed within the suffering and not the suffering itself. Thus God is perfectly compassionate not because he 'suffers with' those who suffer, but because his love fully and freely embraces those who suffer. What human beings cry out for in their suffering is not a God who suffers, but a God who loves wholly and completely, something a suffering God could not do.[36]

While such facets of love as compassion, mercy, grief, and sorrow are ascribed to God, in one sense, metaphorically, in so far as they predicate within human beings changeable and passible emotional states as well as suffering, yet they are truly and really facets of God's fully actualized love and are experienced as such by human beings. God truly grieves over sin and actually is sorrowful over injustice not because he has lost some good (which would imply a self-centred grief and sorrow) and so

---

33 R. Creel states that 'if I repent and consequently experience God's forgiveness, it is not because God has responded to my repentance that I feel forgiveness; rather it is the case that by my repentance I have put myself in the stream of his forgiveness.' *Divine Impassibility*, p. 30. While I basically agree with Creel, I would want to say that God does respond to 'my repentance' though he does so in a manner that does not imply a change in him since his forgiveness is a facet of his fully actualized, and so unchanging, love.

34 This notion of God's fully actualized love as containing all the various facets and expressions of love provides theological depth and philosophical precision to the patristic understanding which equally subsumed God's anger under the rubric of God's love.

35 *ST*, II–II, 30, 2, ad 1. Since compassion in God pertains to his love, it is not a passion, in Aquinas' understanding of passion, but 'simple an act of the will' (*Scriptum Super Libros Sententiarum*, IV, 46, 2, 1, 1).

36 M. Dodds states:

> If it were my friend's compassionate suffering itself that brought me consolation, then I would be in the peculiar situation of reacting in quite the opposite way to my friend's suffering from the way that he reacts to mine. For I would be taking some sort of joy in his suffering while he reacts rather with sadness at my own.
>
> Compassionate suffering is both a consequence of love and a sign of love. But it is love rather than suffering that we truly admire in the compassionate person, and it is love rather than suffering that brings healing and comfort to the person for whom we have compassion. *The Unchanging God of Love*, p. 300.

See also Davies, *Thinking About God*, p. 156.

suffers, but rather because, in his love, he knows that the one he loves is suffering due to the absence of some good. Sadness and grief do not spring from or manifest suffering within God, but rather they spring from, manifest and express the fulness of his completely altruistic, all-consuming and perfect love for his creatures.

Aquinas consistently states that such things as anger, sadness and mercy are predicated of God metaphorically.[37] With regards to mercy Aquinas states:

> Mercy is especially to be attributed to God, as seen in its effects, but not as an affection of passion. In proof of which it must be considered that a person is said to be merciful (*misericors*), as being, so to speak, sorrowful at heart (*miserum cor*); being affected with sorrow at the misery of another as though it were his own. Hence it follows that he endeavours to dispel the misery of this other as if it were his; and this is the effect of mercy. To sorrow, therefore, over the misery of others belongs not to God; but it does most properly belong to him to dispel that misery, whatever be the defect we call by that name. Now defects are not removed, except by the perfection of some kind of goodness; and the primary source of goodness is God.[38]

While Aquinas wants to uphold that God is merciful, he does not want his mercy to be seen as a passion, that is as an emotional change of state within God, and one moreover, that implies an evil since evil can in no way reside in God.[39] Thus Aquinas limits the mercy of God to his ability to dispel the effects of evil and to restore the good. I do not wish to deny any of what Aquinas here proposes. However, what Aquinas may fail to appreciate is that mercy arises out of the reality of God's love and so, while not a negative passion, gives expression to the reality of God's passionate love. Thus God may not sorrow over the misery of others in the sense that he experiences a negative passible state due to his own suffering, yet it can reside in God, and reside in him in a more perfect state, because of the lack of suffering, as a positive facet of his perfectly actualized, and so completely altruistic, love.[40]

In the *Summa Contra Gentiles* Aquinas would seem to agree. Here he states that love and joy are said properly of God, but that some affections, attributed to him in scripture, are metaphorical 'because of a likeness either in effects or in some preceding affection,' sadness being one of them.[41] However, Aquinas holds that sadness proceeds from the affection of love, and 'God, then is said to be saddened in so far as certain things take place that are contrary to what he loves and approves; just as we experience sadness over things that have taken place against our will.'[42]

---

37 For 'anger' see *ST*, I, 19, 11; II–II, 162, 3, and *SCG*, I, 89, 14; I, 91, 16.
38 *ST*, I, 21, 3.
39 See *SCG*, I, 89, 8 and 9.
40 G. Grisez, in a personal letter, emphasizes that, because God is all loving and good and because he is aware of sin and evil, he finds sin and evil 'repugnant.' To speak of God grieving over sin is to specify the truth that, due to God's goodness and love, sin and evil are repugnant to him.
41 *SCG*, I, 91, 15.
42 *SCG*, I, 91, 17. See Kretzmann, *The Metaphysics of Theism*, pp. 226–54.

Likewise, Aquinas does not wish to attribute anger to God in so far as it is a passion, in that human sin cannot deprive God himself of something that would cause anger at such a loss, but in so far as a person injures himself or another through sin, this 'injury redounds to God, in as much as the person injured is an object of God's providence and protection.'[43] Here we see that sadness, and even anger, are realities within God, not as passible emotional states (and so are predicated, in this sense, metaphorically of God), but as subsumed within the reality of God's providential love. But it is this love that bears upon the reality and truth of God's anger, mercy, and sadness. This notion then of God's fully actualized love as containing all the various facets and expressions of love provides theological depth and philosophical precision to the patristic understanding which equally subsumed God's anger under the rubric of God's love.

While J. Maritain maintains that God does not suffer, he also wishes to uphold the realism of God's compassion and mercy within his perfect love. It is not solely or simply metaphorical when applied to God. Commenting on Aquinas' statement that God's mercy is seen in its effects and not as a passion, he writes:

L'amour n'est pas seulement attribué à Dieu parce qu'il est cause du bien dans les êtres, *creans et infundens bonum in rebus*. L'amour, non pas seulement selon ce qu'il fait, mais selon ce qu'il est, est une perfection de Dieu, et est Dieu même.

N'en va-t-il pas de même de la miséricorde? Dieu est Pitié comme il est Amour et parce qu'il est Amour. Ne devrait-on donc pas dire de la miséricorde qu'elle se trouve en Dieu selon ce qu'elle est, et non pas seulement selon ce qu'elle fait, mais à l'état de perfection *pour laquelle il n'y a pas de nom*: gloire ou splendeur innominée, n'impliquant aucune imperfection, à la différence de ce que nous appelons la souffrance ou la tristesse, et pour laquelle nous n'avons aucune idée, aucun concept, aucun nom qui soit applicable en propre à Dieu. C'est seulement en raison de l'effet produit par elle, oui, que pour la miséricorde il y a dans notre bagage un concept et un nom applicables en propre à Dieu, mais ça ne veut pas dire que nous devions en rester là. Dans l'infinité de perfection, qui, derrière les concepts par où nous connaissons en propre les perfections de Dieu, reste encore *quelque chose d'innominé et d'innominable*, d'inconnaissable en propre par aucun de nos concepts, doit exister la splendeur innominée à quoi correspond, non seulement quant à son effet mais quant à son essence, ce que la miséricorde est en nous. Que dire alors, sinon qu'il s'agit là de la perfection, irreprésentable en propre par aucun de nos concepts, dont, en Celui qui nous a faits et qui nous aime, ce qui selon son consitutif propre s'appelle miséricorde en nous (le *passionis affectus* si bien marqué par l'expression biblique *viscera misericordiae*) est un reflet ou une participation mais scellée dans notre imperfection quant à sa notion même, et qui nous laisse aveugles lorsque nous

---

43 *ST*, I–II, 47, 1, ad 1.

cherchons à discerner, sinon métaphoriquement, ce que son exemplaire est en Dieu?[44]

There is one further important aspect of God's love that bears directly upon his compassion and mercy. We have already noted that Aquinas is insistent that God's mercy and compassion 'is seen in its effect, but not as an affection of passion.'[45] This means that while mercy cannot be attributed to God in so far as it is a passible emotional state as in human beings, it can properly be attributed to him in so far as his love moves him to dispel the evil which is the cause of suffering. It is in the dispelling of the evil and so the suffering that God properly manifests his compassion and mercy.[46] Thus God's compassion and mercy is of far greater consequence than human compassion and mercy. We may suffer in love with those who are suffering, but often we are incapable of relieving the evil that is causing the suffering.[47] This is not the case with God. Because God is ontologically distinct from the created order, and thus is not entrapped within the evil and suffering contained within that order, and because his goodness and love are fully actualized, he is able to act compassionately within the created order so as to dispel the evil and suffering within it. Aquinas holds that mercy can be seen as the greatest virtue for 'it belongs to mercy to be bountiful to others.' Moreover, 'to succour others in their want . . . pertains chiefly to one who stands above. Hence mercy is accounted as being proper to God: and therein his omnipotence is declared to be chiefly manifested.'[48] God's

---

44 'Quelques Réflexions sur le Savoir Théologique,' *Revue Thomiste* 69/1 (1969):17. See also pp. 16–27. See also J.-H. Nicolas, 'La Souffrance de Dieu?', *Nova Et Vetera* 53 (1978):60; and Burrell, *Knowing the Unknowable God*, pp. 59–61.

45 *ST*, I, 21, 3. See also *SCG*, I, 91, 16.

46 Aquinas states:

> In anything that is said of God and of man, it is understood of each one according to his mode. Therefore, when compassion is said of God, it is taken according to the mode of God, and in man, according to the mode of man. Compassion is in man when he suffers (*compatitur*) at the distress of another. . . . But it is not in God in this way. For God is impassible and does not suffer. . . . Compassion is in God when he repels the distress of any particular thing. *In Psalmos*, xxiv, 8; translation from Dodds, *The Unchanging God of Love*, p. 301.

47 W. Hill points out that true human compassion, which entails suffering, 'is an attempt to alleviate his or her pain.' Thus 'the core reality of love' is not in the suffering, but is the attempt to alleviate the cause of suffering as much as possible. 'Only when its resources are exhausted due to its finitude, is it [love] content with compassion for the friend in a loving endeavour to lessen this misery by sharing it in a vicarious and sympathetic way. Compassion, then (as opposed to mere pity) characterizes love, not as such but in its finite modes.' 'Does Divine Love Entail Suffering in God?' p. 64.

While I agree with Hill, I would not want to limit compassion to human beings. God is compassionate, not in the sense that he suffers, but in so far as his all-consuming love goes out to those who suffer and in so doing acts to dispel the evil which is the cause of suffering.

48 *ST*, II–II, 30, 4. J. Quinn argues that those who pit God's love against his power, as if an all-powerful God would be an unloving tyrant, entirely miss the point of their relationship. His almighty power and perfect love are simply attributes of who God is. Thus, it is because God is all-loving that he can use his divine power to do loving deeds, and because he is all-powerful he is actually capable of doing them. See 'Divine Self-Giving,' pp. 184–85.

mercy is most fully manifested by his dispelling evil and in his restoring good through his almighty power.[49]

This understanding of God's love as fully actualized in all its various facets brings a new realism and intensity to his love that often appeared to be, or actually was, lacking within the Christian tradition. All aspects of love are truly and really actualized within the perfect actualized love of God. Thus, in accordance with the biblical proclamation, God, as the Wholly Other, is present to and active within the created order as the Wholly Other – in the fulness of his wholly-other love – without losing his complete otherness, and so his wholly-other love, in so doing. Or, to put it another way, emphasizing this time God's love, it can be stated that, since God's love is immutably and perfectly actualized in his total otherness, God's wholly-other love is present to and active within the created order in all its wholly fully actualized otherness without losing its wholly fully actualized otherness in so doing. If God's love was not fully actualized, in all of its various facets, within his total otherness, then it would mean that his love would not be present to and active within the created order in all its total otherness, but only in some mediated and, thus, lesser manner. The absence of suffering in God, therefore, not only preserves the wholly otherness of God, but it also simultaneously preserves the full reality of his wholly-other love, and it does so not solely for his own sake, but also for the sake of the created order, particularly and especially for the sake of human beings.

The Suffering of God

Before concluding, there is one question that could be raised. Having argued that grief and sorrow can be truly predicated of God, is it possible, in a similar manner, to predicate suffering of God? Could 'suffering' be considered as a facet or aspect of God's fully actualized love and goodness? I am very reluctant to say 'yes,' since 'suffering' when applied to God has traditionally meant, especially now within the contemporary theological context (and as it has been used throughout this study and will continue to be used after this section), that God undergoes some passible change of state and that, as a consequence, he experiences some inner emotional distress or anguish. Moreover, suffering normally implies that some event outside of God has caused him to suffer. All of this I deny. If one did predicate suffering to God, it would need to be in a manner radically different from the way it has been and is presently understood, and indeed it would have to be done along the lines that I have treated divine sorrow and grief.

49 M. Dodds insightfully notes that even within human compassion 'the essence of compassion is more truly embodied in the love from which compassion springs and in the will to alleviate the distress of the beloved than it is in the sadness which accompanies our loving response. . . . It is not the degree of suffering as such that we admire in the compassionate person, but rather the degree of love which that suffering manifests. When Jesus wept at the death of Lazarus, the crowd did not say, "See how he suffers," but "See how he loved him" (Jn 11:35–36).' *The Unchanging God of Love*, pp. 298–99.
      See also G. Hanratty, 'Divine Immutability and Impassibility Revisited,' pp 160–61, and Hill, 'Two Gods of Love: Aquinas and Whitehead,' p. 260.

Sorrow and grief are attributed to God not by way of predicating a passible emotional change within him, but rather by way of denoting that he is all-loving and good. Because he is perfectly loving and good, he finds sin and evil repugnant, and so he can be said to sorrow and grieve in the light of their presence. God does not grieve or sorrow because he himself experiences some injury or the loss of some good, nor that he has been affected, within his inner being, by some evil outside cause, but rather he grieves or sorrows only in the sense that he knows that human persons experience some injury or the loss of some good, and so embraces them in love. This sorrow and grief ascribed to God could contain the note of suffering only if we mean that, as all-loving, he is intensely concerned with the reality of sin and evil, and the suffering that ensues from them. To ascribe suffering to God is not to denote a positive passible emotional state as if such a state were distinct from a variety of other emotional states within God, but solely to specify the truth that God, as all-loving and good, is opposed to and finds abhorrent all that is not loving and good. To ascribe suffering to God does not then imply that God experiences inner emotional anguish or distress because he has experienced some injury or the loss of some good, nor that he has been adversely affected by some evil outside cause, but rather it accentuates the truth that God's perfectly actualized goodness is wholly adverse to all that is contrary to his goodness, and that in his perfectly actualized love he embraces those who suffer because of sin and evil. 'Suffering' would then be attributed to God metaphorically since it has been purged of the passible and emotional connotations found within human suffering, but it would retain and might intensify the authentic truth that God, in his goodness, abhors evil and so repudiates it, and in his love, embraces the sufferer. The innocent who suffer injustice know then that God, in his goodness, is adverse to the injustice suffered, and experience God's love as a love that is deeply concerned and consoling. As a way of expressing God's repudiation of evil and as a way of accentuating his loving care for the sufferer God could then be said 'to suffer in love,' but God could not be said 'to suffer in love' in the sense that he himself experiences some form of inner anguish or distress due to some personal injury or the loss of some good.[50]

---

50 It is in this manner that Pope John Paul II, in his Encyclical on the Holy Spirit, speaks of pain within God. He states that sin reveals *'pain,* unimaginable and inexpressible, which on account of sin the Book of Genesis in its anthropomorphic vision seems to glimpse in the "depths of God" and in a certain sense in the very heart of the Trinity. The Church, taking her inspiration from Revelation, believes and professes that *sin is an offence against God.'* He continues:

> The concept of God as the necessarily most perfect being certainly excludes from God any pain deriving from deficiencies or wounds; but in the 'depths of God' there is a Father's love that, faced with man's sin, in the language of the Bible reacts so deeply as to say: 'I am sorry that I have made him.' . . . But more often the Sacred Book speaks to us of a Father who feels compassion for man, as though sharing his pain. In a word, this inscrutable and indescribable *fatherly 'pain'* will *bring about* above all the wonderful economy of redemptive love in Jesus Christ. *Dominum et Vivificantem* (1986), 39.

However, having attempted to clarify in what sense God could be said to suffer, I believe that because suffering, both within the present cultural and theological milieu and within the very nature of human suffering itself, inevitably entails the notion of passible emotional states involving pain, distress and anguish, it would be better, for the sake of clarity and consistency, not to predicate suffering of God at all. To say that God suffers, even in my very restricted sense would, I fear, inevitably cause confusion and misunderstanding, for the experience and interpretation of 'suffering' is too enmeshed with the inner emotional state of discomfort caused by the presence of sin and evil. Whatever valid aspects of suffering can be applied to God are equally, and probably better, situated within the attributes of his compassion, grief and sorrow.

Conclusions

I have argued in this chapter that God as a trinity of persons cannot suffer, and that far from being a hindrance to his love, his inability to suffer actually enhances the nature of his fully actualized love in all of its various fully actualized facets. In so doing the mystery of God and his love remains incomprehensible, but I hope it remains with an enhanced clarity and realism and so with a more brilliant and awesome beauty.

There are two points now that I wish to make by way of conclusion which will direct us to the next chapter. First, while I have consistently throughout this chapter and in previous chapters spoken of God's all-consuming love for humankind and about humankind's ability to experience and know God's love, yet it is readily apparent that, because of sin, human persons are unable, without the aid of God, to experience fully and so fully know and thus fully appreciate the love that God has for them. Sin has so darkened the minds and hardened the hearts of human persons that they are incapable of laying hold of God's love for them or, at times, of even desiring it. Only if sin and its effects are removed, so as to establish a new and proper relationship with God can human beings once more experience the immense love of God.

The importance of this is seen with regard to human suffering. God loves those who suffer, for whatever the reason, with all of his perfect compassion and mercy, and yet because of the deadening and impairing effects of sin, those who suffer, for whatever reason, are incapable of fully experiencing it – even the innocent. They may partially experience and know the love of God's compassion, but only when these deadening and impairing effects are removed and the suffering person is once more in a proper relationship with God will that person experience God's full compassion.

The Papal International Theological Commission, while critical of much contemporary theology that attributes suffering to God (for reasons similar to my own), and while it gives a very cautious and nuanced assessment of the manner in which suffering may be said of God, nonetheless is also willing, in a similar manner to John Paul and myself, to speak of the suffering of God. See *Theology, Christology, Anthropology* (1983), II, B. For a brief but good commentary on this section of the document, see B. de Margerie, 'De la Souffrance de Dieu?', *Esprit et Vie* 93 (1983):110–12.

Second, redemption is the removal of sin and the healing of its effects so that humankind may once more be able to share fully in God's love, and thus be free to experience his compassion and mercy in the midst of suffering. This, Christians believe, was accomplished through the Incarnation of the eternal Son of God who as man took upon himself the whole of human sinfulness with all of its effects, including suffering, and brought reconciliation by offering on the cross his life in love to the Father. Having been reconciled to the Father, human beings, through faith in the risen Jesus as Lord and Saviour, partake of the life of the Trinity, as adopted sons and daughters, through the transforming power of the Holy Spirit dwelling within them.

Thus, only through the Incarnation and in Jesus' redemptive death and resurrection are the causes of suffering adequately and fully dealt with. Moreover, it is only from within this radically new relationship with God, now made available in Jesus' very person as the risen Savior and Lord, that human beings can be freed of the suffering caused by their own sin and so come to experience God's love fully, and equally come to experience God's love fully in the midst of suffering caused by the sin of others. To thoroughly appreciate the good news of Jesus Christ, in the light of sin and suffering, we must address all of these issues more fully, and so to that task we now turn.

8

The Incarnation –
The Impassible Suffers

Thus far in our study I have vigorously argued that the one God as a trinity of persons is impassible and so does not suffer, and I have done so to confirm and to intensify the consummate and ever-present love of the Trinity for creation. Nonetheless, sin and the suffering borne in its wake compelled the persons of the Trinity to immerse themselves more deeply in human suffering, not for their own sake, but for the sake of the creatures they loved. Humankind could not free itself from sin with all of its consequences, including death and damnation, and so could not free itself from suffering, most of all the suffering of everlasting separation from God, who is humankind's supreme good and perfect joy. Only the Trinity could free humankind from sin and its consequences and restore it to a life of peace and joy – ultimately a life within the Trinity itself.

Therefore, 'God so loved the world that he gave his only Son, so that everyone who believes in him may not perish but may have eternal life. Indeed, God did not send the Son into the world to condemn the world, but in order that the world might be saved through him' (Jn 3:16). This salvific 'giving' and 'sending' of the Son was into a world marred by sin and immersed in suffering, and so it was within this 'giving' and 'sending' that the Father manifested his absolute love (see 1 Jn 4:9). 'In this is love, not that we loved God but that he loved us and sent his Son to be the atoning sacrifice (ἱλασμὸν) for our sins' (1 Jn 4:11). It was through the Son's sacrificial death, with all the suffering that this entailed, that the Father not only freed humankind from sin, with all of its distressing effects, but equally obtained for humankind a new life, through the Holy Spirit, within the loving embrace of the Trinity. Suffering, then, is at the heart of redemption, and so it is within redemption that the mystery (and absurdity) of human suffering is transformed and granted a new and even rational significance.

It is here where much contemporary theology falls short. Many modern theologians are so consumed with championing a God who suffers in himself, that they fail to grasp the full significance of the Incarnation and the transforming effects of Christ's redemptive suffering.[1] The

---

1 While I focus, due to the topic at hand, on the suffering of Christ in these introductory remarks, the importance of the resurrection and the new life in the Holy Spirit will also become evident in the following chapters.

172

significance of Christ's suffering and death is no longer found in their historical truth and in the present and future efficacy that these actual events have upon human beings and their relationship to God, but rather, as is exemplified in the case of Moltmann, it is diminished to a mythological expression or symbol of what is happening transcendentally and ahistorically to and within God as God. Because contemporary theology has focused almost exclusively on God suffering within his divine nature, the true christological and soteriological import of Jesus' suffering is thus either misconceived or neglected, and so enfeebled.

Moreover, because much contemporary theology has failed to recognize the christological and soteriological significance of Christ's suffering, it has in turn failed to grasp the unique ecclesial significance of suffering, that is, that those who now suffer in Christ, as members of his body, suffer and experience suffering in a radically different manner than those who have not come to faith in him. The Father's response to sin and evil, and the suffering that flows from it, is Christ, and only those who fully live in Christ share fully in the Father's response. Thus the singular evangelistic import of Christ's suffering, within a tortured world which cries out in hopeless anguish, is completely lost.

In order to further elaborate and respond to these issues I wish, in this and the following two chapters, to do three things. First, in this chapter I will examine the nature of the Incarnation so as to demonstrate that the Son of God does indeed truly suffer as man. Second, in Chapter 9, I will establish the soteriological significance of the Son's suffering as man. Third, in Chapter 10, I will, in the light of Christ's redemptive work, interpret the significance of human suffering. As in what has gone before, all the various elements must be properly understood and correctly placed in relationship to one another. Only then will we accurately discern the whole salvific mystery.

The Incarnation and the Communication of Idioms

Since to argue from the New Testament evidence for the traditional understanding of the Incarnation would take us far afield from our present study, I adopt as my starting point, in accordance with the first four ecumenical councils and the inherited Christian tradition, three truths which must be simultaneously affirmed and upheld for a proper understanding of the Incarnation.[2] 1. It is *truly God* the Son who is man.

2 For some recent studies on New Testament christology as well as on the patristic christology which developed from it see, for example, Bauckham, *God Crucified: Monotheism and Christology in the New Testament*; R.E. Brown, *An Introduction to New Testament Christology* (New York: Paulist Press, 1994); J.D.G. Dunn, *Christology in the Making* (Philadelphia: Westminster Press, 1980); Galot, *Who Is Christ?*; Grillmeier, *Christ in Christian Tradition*, Vol. I; W. Kasper, *Jesus the Christ* (London: Burns & Oates, 1975); R.A. Kereszty, *Jesus Christ: Fundamentals of Christology* (New York: Alba House, 1991); I.H. Marshall, *Jesus the Saviour* (Downer Grove: InterVarsity Press, 1990); C.F.D. Moule, *The Origin of Christology* (Cambridge: Cambridge University Press, 1977); G. O'Collins, *Interpreting Jesus* (London: Geoffrey Chapman, 1983); G. O'Collins, *Christology* (Oxford: Oxford University Press, 1995); L. Sabourin, *Christology* (New York: Alba House, 1984); R. Schnackenburg, *Jesus in the Gospels* (Louisville: Westminster John Knox Press, 1995); W.M. Thompson, *The Jesus Debate* (New York: Paulist Press, 1985).

Here, the emphasis is focused upon the full divinity of the Son. 2. It is *truly man* that the Son of God is. Here the emphasis is focused upon the full and complete humanity. 3. The Son of God *truly is* man. Here the emphasis is focused upon the ontological union between the person of the Son and his humanity.[3] These three statements can be incorporated in the following declaration: Jesus is one ontological entity, and the one ontological entity that Jesus is is the one person of the divine Son of God existing as a complete and authentic man.[4]

Now what is fascinating and pivotal for our present study is that, historically, the practice within early Christian piety and theology, which gave rise to and was formative of this doctrinal development was the use of what has come to be termed the communication of idioms (*communicatio idiomatum*/ἀντίδοσις τῶν ἰδιωμάτων), that is, the predicating of divine and human attributes of one and the same person – the Son. Examples of the communication of idioms would be: 'The Son of God is born of Mary.' Or 'God suffered and died on the cross.' The use of such language is, in one sense, quite peculiar, and may appear to be even unintelligible. One could rhetorically ask, and historically such was done: 'How could God, who is self-existent and eternal, be born of a woman?' Or 'How could God, who is immutable and impassible, suffer and die?' The use and practice of the communication of idioms grew up and developed as a 'shorthand' way of accenting the reality and intensifying the implications of the Incarnation. God as God could not be born, but if he became man, he could truly be born. God as God could not suffer, but if he existed as man, he could actually suffer and die. Nonetheless, almost every christological heresy found the use of the communication of idioms to be a scandal to proper piety and an assault

---

3 See Aquinas, *ST*, III, 16, 1.
4 This traditional conciliar understanding of the Incarnation is, I believe, not merely in conformity with and inadverse to the New Testament, but one that is actually and positively intrinsic to its proclamation, and so, under the guidance of the Holy Spirit, necessarily developed from it.

    R. Bauckham is correct when he argues that the common distinction between the 'functional' christology of the New Testament and the 'ontic' christology of the Fathers is completely inadequate for explaining the christological development, and is not true to biblical revelation. He holds that the very first Christians believed that Jesus had a unique divine identity, and that the New Testament itself then placed Jesus within the unique identity of the one God of the Old Testament. Thus, belief in Jesus' divinity was not a gradual step by step process, but rather 'it was a step which, whenever it was taken, had to be taken simply for its own sake and *de novo*. . . . In my view, the New Testament evidence is best explained if this step was taken very early as the fundamental step on which all further christological development then rested.' *God Crucified*, p. 28. For Bauckham's arguments see pp. 25–42. Also see A.E. McGrath, *The Genesis of Doctrine: A Study in the Foundation of Doctrinal Criticism* (Grand Rapids: Eerdmans, 1997), pp. 58–65.

    This may also be the place to make what I find an interesting observation. Not every theologian who espouses a suffering God denies that Jesus is truly God in accordance with the conciliar tradition, but every theologian who denies that Jesus is truly God, and there are many today, espouses a suffering God. The reason for this is quite obvious. Having abandoned a traditional understanding of the Incarnation, which would uphold that God truly suffers as man, these theologians have no other recourse than to place the suffering within God himself.

upon philosophical and theological reason, and yet it was ultimately the undoing of every christological heresy.

For example, the Docetists denied the reality of Jesus' humanity precisely to protect the Son of God from encountering what seemed to them the unbecoming experiences of human weakness. In so doing they denied the second above stated truth. The Son of God could not be *truly* man and so truly hunger, thirst, suffer, and die. In contrast, one of the reasons Arius denied the full divinity of the Son was because, in taking on flesh and thus undergoing the weaknesses of the flesh, he could not possibly be *truly* God.[5] In so doing Arius denied the first above stated truth. Finally, Nestorius, while wishing to uphold the full divinity and the full humanity of Jesus, could not conceptually unite them in an ontological union for fear that such a union necessitated that the human experiences of the Son of God jeopardize the integrity of his divine status. In so doing he denied the third above stated truth that the Son of God *truly is* man.

Thus, the whole of orthodox patristic christology, including the conciliar affirmations, can be seen as an attempt to defend the practice and to clarify the use of the communication of idioms. Why is this so? Simply, embedded within the communication of idioms are the above three truths essential for an authentic understanding of the Incarnation, and it is only in the defense and clarification of the communication of idioms that these three truths became explicitly grasped and manifestly articulated. It is *truly* the Son of God who *truly* is man and so suffers *truly* as man. Historically, then, it was not an orthodox or a conciliar account of the Incarnation that gave rise to the communication of idioms, it was the communication of idioms that gave rise to the conciliar and orthodox account of the Incarnation. Moreover, the communication of idioms having given rise to the proper understanding of the Incarnation, this proper understanding of the Incarnation in turn clarified and validated its use. Therefore, the communication of idioms, today as in the past, continues to be the test of christological orthodoxy.

As we saw in the first chapter, many contemporary theologians, who espouse a God who suffers in himself, find the traditional understanding of the Incarnation, with its use of the communication of idioms, inadequate. For them it is not enough to say that the Son of God grieved, suffered, and died only as man, but remained unaffected as God. They wish to exploit the communication of idioms so as to establish the

---

5 The heart of Arius' difficulty was that he misconceived the Incarnation. Like the later Apollinarius he saw the Incarnation as the Son uniting himself to flesh/body alone, without a soul, in a substantial compositional union after the manner of the soul's union with the body within human beings. (This will be examined more fully later.) He did this to ensure a true ontological union. However, in conceiving the union in such a manner, the experiences of the flesh were placed within the very nature of the Son. Arius rightly perceived that this would entail that the Son of God changed his nature in becoming man and so was passible within his new fleshly existence. He thus concluded that, since God is immutable and impassible, the Son could not be God. Arius also denied the divinity of Son because he could not conceive how God could be one and the Son be God at one and the same time. See Grillmeier, *Christ in Christian Tradition*, Vol. 1, pp. 219–32; and Weinandy, *Does God Change?*, pp. 16–20.

premise that God, within the Incarnation, does indeed grieve and suffer as God. Even the death of Jesus affects his divinity. Because of this it is necessary to examine more closely the patristic and conciliar teaching and in so doing to clarify the exact nature of the Incarnation and the proper understanding of the communication of idioms.

The Council of Nicea with its champion, Athanasius, upheld the full divinity of the Son – the Son is God as the Father is God. The one being or reality of God is the Father begetting the Son and so the Son is *homoousion* (one in being) with the Father.[6] Thus, the first of our incarnational truths was defined. While Ignatius of Antioch (d. circa AD107) very early on defended, against the Docetists, the full humanity of Jesus through his use of the communication of idioms, it was only with the condemnation of Apollinarius, who denied the human soul of Jesus, that his full humanity was definitively defined, and so the second of our incarnational truths was made explicit.[7] The central incarnational issue subsequently arose within the Nestorian controversy. How could the Son

6 Athanasius' historic trinitarian insight is that the Father does not alone embody the Godhead, which as the early history of trinitarian thought confirms, tends toward tritheism and inevitably demands that the Son and the Spirit be subordinate to the Father, but that what the one God is is the Father begetting the Son. See Weinandy, *Does God Change?*, pp. 10–16. For a recent and excellent article on Athanasius' doctrine of the Trinity, see P. Widdicombe, 'Athanasius and the Making of the Doctrine of the Trinity,' *Pro Ecclesia* 6/4 (1997):456–78. As I have argued elsewhere, the Cappadocians in their trinitarian thought never fully grasped Athanasius' momentous insight. Their trinitarian theology still bears the vestiges of Platonic emanationism. See Weinandy, *The Father's Spirit of Sonship*, pp. 6–15.

7 While Ignatius does not systematically address the theological issues raised by the docetic denial of Jesus' real humanity, he is suprisingly clear, at this early date, that Jesus, while truly God (ὁ θεός) (see *Ephesians*, greeting, 18; *Romans*, greeting, and *Polycarp* 8), was indeed truly a man who actually was born, suckled, ate, suffered and died (see *Trallians*, 9–10 and *Smyrnaens*, 1–5). He is one of the first, if not the first, to accentuate these truths through his use of the communication of idioms. He does not hesitate to speak of 'divine blood' (*Ephesians* 1) and 'the passion of my God' (*Romans* 6). In poetic fashion he writes: 'There is only one Physician – Very flesh, yet Spirit too; Uncreated, and yet born; God-and-Man in One agreed, Very-Life-in-Death indeed, Fruit of God and Mary's seed; At once impassible and torn by pain and suffering here below: Jesus Christ, whom as our Lord we know.' *Ephesians* 7, see also *Polycarp* 3. E.T., *Early Christian Writings*, ed. M. Staniforth (London: Penguin, 1968). Ignatius would not have hesitated to give full assent to the decree of Chalcedon. Actually, if he had been of a more philosophical mind, he could have written it.

For a study that addresses the use of the communication of idioms in some of the earliest Fathers, see M. Slusser, *Theopaschite Expressions in Second-Century Christianity as Reflected in the Writings of Justin, Melito, Celsus and Irenaeus* (Oxford: D.Phil. Dissertation, 1975). Slusser, commenting on Justin and Irenaeus, writes: 'Belief in God's impassibility does not exclude theopaschite language; it only emphasizes its importance.' P. 125. See also his 'The Scope of Patripassianism,' *Studia Patristica*, Vol. 17/1, ed. E.A. Livingstone (Oxford: Pergamon Press, 1982), pp. 169–75.

It should also be noted that while patripassianism (early third century) was condemned, the real issue was not that the Modalists attributed suffering to the Father, but rather that they failed to distinguish adequately between the Father and the Son. Patripassianism was primarily a trinitarian and not a christological heresy. Because the Son was seen as merely a different temporary mode of expression of the Father, it could be said that the Father became man and so suffered. Patripassianism was therefore condemned not out of an excessive fear of ascribing suffering within the Incarnation, but out of a desire to assure that it was the Son, and not the Father, who became man and so suffered.

of God actually *become* man without jeopardizing the integrity of his full
divinity or his full humanity? It was the third of our incarnational truths
that now needed to be clarified and made explicit. Not surprisingly it
was the communication of idioms that sparked the controversy, but what
is not fully appreciated is that it was equally the communication of
idioms which was the hermeneutical key for unlocking the true ontological nature of the incarnational 'becoming' and the ensuing ontological
union between the divinity and humanity.

Nestorius and the Communication of Idioms

Nestorius rightly wished to uphold Christ's full divinity and the full
humanity. He realized that the Son of God must remain unchangeable
and immutable in becoming man not only for the sake of his divinity, but
also for the sake of the Incarnation itself. If the Son of God changed in
becoming man, it would no longer be the Son of God who is man.
Nestorius was fully aware that the Incarnation was not like the caterpillar changing into the butterfly where the caterpillar ceases to be in the
process. Moreover, Nestorius correctly desired to maintain the full and
complete integrity of the human nature. Thus the incarnational process
and ensuing union could not alter the human nature for then it would
not be truly human. Nestorius clearly grasped that the incarnational
process, the 'becoming,' could change neither the divine nature nor the
human nature for to do so would mean that Jesus be a *tertium quid* – a
hybrid – the confusion and mixture of divinity and humanity, thus being
neither fully God nor fully man. This, Nestorius believed, is what Cyril
had done.

> You [Cyril] do not confess that he is God in *ousia* in that you have
> changed him into the *ousia* of the flesh, and he is no more a man
> naturally in that you have made him the *ousia* of God; and he is not
> God truly or God by nature, nor yet man truly or man by nature.[8]

For Nestorius the use of the communication of idioms was sympto-
matic of such a notion of the Incarnation. To say that 'the Son of God was
born of Mary' (thus her title *Theotokos*), or that 'the Son of God suffered
and died' not only meant that the Son of God changed in becoming man,
through mixture and confusion, but that he, as divine, was also now
susceptible to human weaknesses – thirst, hunger, suffering and death.
His divinity had become mutable and passible, which Nestorius, rightly

---

The argument that ultimately defeated Apollinarius was primarily soteriological.
Gregory of Nazianzus stated it in its classic form: 'What is not assumed, is not healed'
(τὸ ἀπρόσληπτον, ἀθεράπευτον), (*Epistola*, 101).

8 *Liber Heraclidis*. E.T., *The Bazaar of Heracleides*, C.R. Driver and L. Hodgson, eds (Oxford:
Clarendon Press, 1925), p. 16. See also pp. 26–27. What we find in Nestorius is a
threefold argument for the immutability of God. 1. God, being all perfect, is immutable
in himself, and thus cannot change. 2. He must be immutable in relation to the
Incarnation, i.e., if God changes in becoming man he who is 'man' is no longer God but
that which he has changed into. 3. The Son must be immutable for the sake of the
human nature, i.e., a change in the Son in becoming man effects a change in the
humanity as well, rendering it no longer an authentic humanity.

it seems to me, held to be impossible. With his eye on Cyril, Nestorius writes against the Arians:

> They confuse his divine and his human [qualities], saying that the union with flesh resulted in one nature . . . even as the soul and the body are bound [together] in one nature in the body, suffering of necessity, whether he will or not, the sufferings of the nature which he took upon himself, as though he was not of the nature of the Father impassible and without needs. . . . He hungered and thirsted and grew weary and feared and fled and died; and in short they say that he naturally endured whatever appertained to the sensible nature which he assumed.[9]

Similarly, he accused Apollinarius that 'by granting that . . . he [the Son] accepted sufferings, you evacuate him of impassibility and of immortality, and of being consubstantial with the Father, because he acquired a change of nature, seeing that [the Son] accepts and [the Father] accepts not [these sufferings].'[10] Being clearly aware of what the Incarnation is not, the challenge that faced Nestorius (and all of the

---

9 *Liber Heraclidis*, pp. 8–9.
10 *Liber Heraclidis*, p. 39. See also pp. 91–95. Very perceptively R. Wilken argues that Arius is the real culprit behind the Nestorian controversy. Both the Antiochenes and the Alexandrians held that the Logos/Son was truly God as Nicea had declared, but they radically diverged within their respective biblical exegesis as to how best to defend such a belief. The Arians denied that the Son was truly divine precisely because the New Testament predicates human attributes of him. Thus he must be passible and so be a creature. In response to this charge, the Antiochenes interpreted such biblical passages as applying solely to the man Jesus and not to the divine Logos. The Alexandrians, on the other hand, argued that such passages referred to the Logos only in so far as he existed as man. Wilken argues that the Antiochenes, therefore, perceived the title *Theotokos* as a Trinitarian issue – How could the Son be truly divine if he was born? Whereas the Alexandrians perceived the title as a christological issue – If Mary was not *Theotokos*, how could one say that the Logos was truly man? See R. Wilken, 'Tradition, Exegesis, and the Christological Controversies,' *Church History*, 34 (1965):123–45. For excellent expositions of Cyril's scriptural exegesis also see Wilken, 'St Cyril of Alexandria: The Mystery of Christ in the Bible,' *Pro Ecclesia* 4 (1995):454–78 and 'St Cyril of Alexandria: Biblical Expositor,' *Coptic Church Review* 19/1–2 (1998):30–41.
    Nestorius' christology has grown in stature in recent years, principally because of his defense of the complete humanity of Christ. The irony, an irony that Nestorius would hardly appreciate, is that those theologians who most sing his praises are the same ones who most question the divinity of Jesus and/or the immutability and impassibility of God. But, as Wilken's article strongly suggests, it is these truths that lay at the heart of Nestorius' christology, and it is these that he was most eager to defend. J.J. O'Keefe is absolutely correct when he states: 'Nestorius worried far more about the impassibility of God than he did about the humanity of Jesus.' 'Impassible Suffering? Divine Passion and Fifth-Century Christology,' *Theological Studies* 58 (1997):52. See also pp. 40–41. See also his 'Kenosis or Impassibility: Cyril of Alexandria and Theodoret of Cyrus on the Problem of Divine Pathos,' *Studia Patristica*, ed. E.A. Livingston, (Leuven: Peeters, 1997), Vol. 32, pp. 358–65. Even such a staunch defender of Nestorius as M. Anastos acknowledges this point. See 'Nestorius was Orthodox,' *Dumbarton Oaks Papers* 16 (1962):140. See also H. Chadwick, 'Eucharist and Christology in the Nestorian Controversy,' *Journal of Theological Studies* 2 (1951):158; R.A. Greer, 'The Image of God and the Prosopic Union in Nestorius' *Bazaar of Heracleides*' in *Lux in Lumine*, ed. R.A. Norris (New York: Seabury Press, 1966), p. 46; Pelikan, *The Christian Tradition: A History of the Development of Doctrine 1*, p. 231.

Antiochenes) was how then does one properly conceive the relationship between the two natures so as to form a proper incarnational union?

For Nestorius the divine nature and the human nature were so closely joined together that they gave rise to what he termed a 'common prosopon of union.' So close was their relationship that they 'gave off' one common appearance. The distinctive empirical qualities of each of the natures, but not the natures themselves, intermingled or were woven together into one.[11] It is this common appearance that is called 'Christ.' However, this 'common prosopon,' unlike the divinity and the humanity, has no ontological depth. It was merely the phenomenological interplay between the divine and the human qualities due to the close relationship between the two natures. Nestorius' view of the Incarnation was similar to someone gazing up into the night sky and seeing 'one' very bright star only to be told by an astronomer that what one is really looking at is not one bright star, but actually two stars so closely aligned that they give off one very bright common appearance.[12] In the end, despite his best intentions and good faith, Nestorius was incapable of

---

11 For Nestorius each nature (φύσις) is comprised of an essence or substance (οὐσία) making it 'what' it is.‛Υπόστασις, which he employed less often, designates that complex of properties which individuates and distinguishes 'things' of the same nature. Thus each οὐσία possesses its own distinct ὑπόστασις. The term πρόσωπον refers to those external or empirical properties or attributes which outwardly manifest and so reveal a particular individual concrete nature or substance. Each nature (*physis*) in Christ is then composed of its own distinct *ousia* (substance) making it what it is; its own distinct hypostasis individuating the particular expression of its substance; and its own distinct prosopon which manifests empirically its distinct and individual *ousia* and hypostasis.

For discussions of Nestorius' and/or Cyril's terminology and concepts, see Anastos, 'Nestorius Was Orthodox,' pp. 123–27; Greer, 'The Image of God and the Prosopic Union in Nestorius,' pp. 47–48; Grillmeier, *Christ in Christian Tradition*, Vol. 1, pp. 457–63, 478–83, 501–7; Kelly, *Early Christian Doctrines*, pp. 313, 318; R.V. Sellers, *The Council of Chalcedon* (London: SPCK, 1961), pp. 138–39, fn. 7; J. McGuckin, *St Cyril of Alexandria: The Christological Controversy* (Leiden: E.J. Brill, 1994), pp. 138–45; H.E.W. Turner, 'Nestorius Reconsidered,' *Studia Patristica*, Vol. 13, ed. E.A. Livingstone (Berlin: Akademie Verlag, 1975), p. 313.

All scholars acknowledge that a major contributing factor to the untidiness of the Nestorian controversy lay in the use and meaning of terminology. Both sides were employing like terminology, such as *physis, ousia, hypostasis,* and *prosopon*, but employing them with different nuances. However, it would be erroneous, as Anastos does, simply to reduce the Nestorian controversy to a battle over the meaning and use of words, as if a clarification of the meaning of terms would have resulted in Nestorius and Cyril happily acknowledging that, in the end, they were really saying the same thing. (See Anastos, 'Nestorius was Orthodox,' p. 120.) The problem was not that Nestorius and Cyril were using different words for the same concepts, but rather they were using the same words for different concepts. What was at stake was not simply how one articulated the Incarnation, but also, and more so, how one conceived the Incarnation. While a helpful and necessary clarification of terminology did come, especially after the Council of Ephesus (AD431) with the Formula of Union (AD433), the deeper issue was that of first attaining conceptual clarity about the nature of the Incarnation. Only then could the terms assume and convey their rightful meaning.

12 Nestorius can even speak of the compenetration and perichoresis of the divine and the human *prosopa*, that is, that the qualities of the divine *ousia* and human *ousia* coalesce forming the one common *prosopon*. However, since only the term *ousia* denotes an onto-logical reality, the common *prosopon* is merely the phenomenological interplay between the two *ousiai*. While Anastos vigorously argues for Nestorius' orthodoxy in that Nestorius, as does the Council of Chalcedon, speaks of 'one person' and 'two natures,'

conceiving an ontological union between the divinity and the humanity so that one could actually uphold that the Son of God truly became and *is* man.[13] Consequently, while he was well aware that his christology could not support the traditional use of the communication of idioms, what he never perceived is that this was precisely because it did not allow for the Son of God to actually exist as man.[14] What was the cause of Nestorius' failure?

what he fails to grasp is that, within Nestorius' conception of the union, there is no ontological 'who' (subject) contained within the one *prosopon* of union. If one asks: 'Who is the *prosopon* of union?' Nestorius and Anastos would answer 'Christ.' But 'Christ,' as Nestorius and Anastos admit, is but the result of the close alignment of the natures so as to display the one common *appearance*. The term 'Christ' does not designate an ontological reality/subject, but merely a common *appearance*. See Anastos, 'Nestorius was Orthodox,' pp. 127–40. G.B. Bebis speaks of the *prosopon* of union as being *'a point of contact*, an external mark upon which the external characteristics or the properties and the qualities can meet or can concur.' '"The Apology" of Nestorius: A New Evaluation,' *Studia Patristica*, Vol. 11, ed. F.L. Cross (Berlin: Akademie Verlag, 1972), p. 109. K.P. Wesche states that 'The *Prosopon* in which is conjoined the divine and human *prosopa*, itself is not a person: it is not personal with its own personal center. It is merely an impersonal ontological framework within which two personalized natures come into conjunction.' 'The Union of God and Man in Jesus Christ in the Thought of Gregory of Nazianzus,' *St Vladimir's Theological Quarterly* 28/2 (1984):87. Similarly, Grillmeier, *Christ in Christian Tradition*, Vol. 1, p. 454. Nestorius could be termed a phenomenological Monophysite in that the qualities or appearances, but not the realities, of each nature are mixed or coalesce into one. See *The Bazaar of Heracleides*, pp. 141–50, 207–8, 218–19.

13 R.A. Greer maintains that Nestorius holds for a union of wills between the divinity and the humanity in Christ. 'It could hardly be more evident that the prosopic union is what might be called a voluntarist as opposed to a substantial union.' 'The Image of God and the Prosopic Union in Nestorius' *Bazaar of Heracleides*' in *Lux in Lumine*, p. 56. While H.E.W. Turner is sympathetic to Nestorius, he agrees that Nestorius only provides, despite his intentions, a voluntarist union. See 'Nestorius Reconsidered,' *Studia Patristica*, Vol. 13, pp. 308–9, 317, 321. R. Chestnut believes that Nestorius' christology is the way forward for contemporary theology, but does not hesitate to conclude that his christology proposes a unity of wills or activity between the divinity and the humanity. See 'The Two Prosopa in Nestorius' *Bazaar of Heracleides*,' *Journal of Theological Studes*, N.S. 29/2 (1978):393–409. For similar accounts see also A. Grillmeier, *Christ in Christian Tradition*, Vol. 1, pp. 446–63, 501–19; J.N.D. Kelly, *Early Christian Doctrines*, pp. 31–7; and J. McGuckin's excellent account in *The Christology of Cyril of Alexandria*, pp. 126–74.

J.J. O'Keefe believes that 'Antiochene Christology, far from being a low Christology, actually worried more about protecting the Son's divinity than it worried about the details of Jesus's human life. As a Christology, it was fairly "high." Indeed, it is striking how infrequently Jesus is mentioned; the term of preference is "Christ."' Thus he argues that Antiochene christology is similar to much contemporary christology which denies that Jesus is the divine Son of God, but is merely 'a man, with a profound sense of God, who points the way to the transcendent mystery beyond himself.' However, this means that, like the Antiochenes, God has no direct contact with the world and human suffering. 'Impassible Suffering? Divine Passion and Fifth-Century Christology', *Theological Studies*, 58 (1997):59–60. Similarly, R.A. Norris states that the Antiochenes have fixed an unbridgeable 'gulf' 'between non-generate and generate modes of being.' 'The Problem of Human Identity in Patristic Christological Speculation,' *Studia Patristica*, Vol. 17/1, ed. E.A. Livingstone (Oxford: Pergamon Press, 1982), p. 157.

14 The only legitimacy Nestorius could give to the communication of idioms was to interpret it as a christological linguistic device or word game in that it accented the close

Nestorius' conceptual starting point for conceiving the Incarnation was flawed. He knew that the humanity of Christ did not ontologically exist prior to its being joined to the divinity, nonetheless, he conceptually or mentally imagined both the divine nature and the human nature not only as distinct but also as separate prior to the union. Because of this mental imaging, he conceived the incarnational process, the 'becoming,' as the coming together or the joining of the two natures, but having mentally separated them prior to the joining, he could not possibly conceive them as becoming ontologically one without destroying them in the process. To make them ontologically one would demand that they be 'smashed' or 'squashed' together destroying them in the process, and so resulting in a *tertium quid*. Because of his initial misconception of the incarnational process, Nestorius (and all of the Antiochenes) could only conceive, in the end, a moral union between the divinity and the humanity.[15]

Nestorius was rightly aware of all the pitfalls one could encounter in conceiving the Incarnation. However, because he himself could not properly conceive of the Incarnation, he attributed to his opponents – principally Cyril of Alexandria – all the mistakes he was trying assiduously to avoid. He thought that Cyril too conceived the divinity and humanity as separate conceptual entities prior to the union, the difference being that Cyril ontologically 'smashed' them together forming one *ousia*, and in so doing destroyed both in the process. It was all too obvious to Nestorius that Cyril's demand that Christ be one nature (μία φύσις) and his use and defence of the communication of idioms were proof that his opponent had fallen into heresy.

---

relationship between the disparate natures. Since the *prosopon* of the divinity coalesced with the *prosopon* of the humanity giving rise to the common *prosopon*, one could attribute what belonged to the divine nature to the human nature and vice versa, but this attribution could only be at the level of the common *prosopon*, that is, on the phenomenological or empirical level, and not at the level of the natures. As M. Anastos, commenting on Nestorius' understanding of the communication of idioms, states: 'He does not mean of course that such an exchange [of attributes] was actually effected between the two natures, but rather between God the Logos and the human in Christ, through their prosopa.' 'Nestorius was Orthodox,' p. 136. What Nestorius and Anastos have failed to grasp is that, while the attributes of each nature cannot be predicated of the other nature, for such would demand the confusion of natures and so the demise of each nature, yet the attributes of each nature must be predicated of one and the same subject, for one and the same subject (the Logos) exists as God and man.

15 For a more detailed exposition and analysis of my understanding of Nestorius' christology, see Weinandy, *Does God Change?*, pp. 34–46. G.L. Prestige's words are very apt at this point:

A permanently valid doctrine of Christ could only be forthcoming from men who somehow made the unity of His person the ultimate ground for their thought about the duality of His natures, taking their start from what is single, not trying to reduce two incompatible concepts to identity. *Fathers and Heretics* (London: SPCK, 1968), p. 132.

This, as we will see shortly, is exactly what Cyril did.

Cyril of Alexandria and the Communication of Idioms

Cyril of Alexandria's christology, with his ardent defence of the communication of idioms, is crucial to the question of God's passibility and suffering, especially in the light of the subsequent christological tradition which licensed only that God suffers exclusively as man. Because both are frequently misunderstood and misinterpreted by many contemporary theologians, I want, in this section, to clearly present and correctly interpret his thought. This, as with all that has gone before, will take time and patience. Therefore, before we examine Cyril's christology, we must make a somewhat lengthy diversion, but one that, I believe, is essential for correctly understanding Cyril, for accurately conceiving the nature of the Incarnation, and for properly interpreting the communication of idioms.

The Soul–Body Model and the Incarnation

Once patristic theologians undertook a systematic enquiry into the relationship between the humanity and the divinity of Christ, they used the soul–body relationship as an apologetic and conceptual tool for understanding the Incarnation. They used it, implicitly or explicitly, in two ways. First, they employed the soul–body union to help affirm the ontological unity between the divinity and the humanity. As the soul and the body formed the one ontological reality of a human being so, similarly, the divinity and humanity formed the one ontological reality of Jesus. The soul–body union illustrated how two diverse and distinct 'things' (one spiritual and one material) could become and be one, and so it provided a persuasive philosophical apologetic for belief in the Incarnation. In this sense the soul–body relationship was used by way of analogy or comparison.

Second, it was also employed, inevitably and most often simultaneously, and probably unavoidably, as an exact model for conceiving the type of relationship and for formulating the manner of the union which existed between the divinity and the humanity. It was used then not only to illustrate that the divinity and the humanity were ontologically united in the one Christ, but also as the model for designing how this ontological oneness was achieved. As the soul relates to the body and so is united to it, so the divinity relates to the humanity and so is united to it.[16]

---

16 U. Lang has shown that Origen implicitly used the soul–body model within his christology. Moreover, at the Synod of Antioch (AD268/9) the Originist bishops used it in their argumentation against the adoptionism of Paul of Samosata. Paul refused to acknowledge that God could be united to a human nature as the soul is united to the body, and so denied that the Logos was truly God. See *Studies in the Christology of John Philoponus and its Place in the Controversies Over Chalcedon* (Oxford: D.Phil. Dissertation, 1999), Chapter 6. While the Synod rightly upheld the divinity of the Logos, yet Paul, as we will see shortly, rightly understood that the Logos could not be united to a human nature in the same manner as a soul is united to a body without jeopardizing his divinity. Here we have a case where the Synod had the right answer for the wrong reasons and 'the heretic' had the wrong answer for the right reasons.

In the West Tertullian may be the first to employ the soul–body model. While he does not explicitly state that he is using the soul–body union as a model for his chris-

Now the first use of soul–body union, as an illustrative analogy or comparison, can be legitimate. If one conceives the soul–body union as an ontological union giving rise to the one reality of a human being, then equally, the union between the divinity and the humanity is also an ontological union forming the one reality of Jesus. However, to model the relationship and the union between the divinity and the humanity after that of the soul and body is not just misleading, it is patently false. While the union between the divinity and the humanity, and the union between the soul and the body are both ontological bringing about either the one Jesus or the one human being, the relationship between the divinity and the humanity, which establishes their ontological union, differs in kind from the relationship between the soul and the body which establishes their ontological union, and so the manner or mode of their respective ontological unions differs in kind.[17] Nonetheless, within patristic christology, the soul–body relationship and union became, almost universally (Cyril being the exception, as we will see), the normative model for conceiving and articulating the Incarnation. This is the most lamentable, unfortunate, and misconceived intellectual stratagem in the entire history of christology. It not only caused all the christological misconceptions and heresies within the patristic period, but it also lies at the root of much consequent and contemporary christological error.[18] But why is the soul–body model for the Incarnation so erroneous?

---

tology, yet scholars have shown that his conception of the incarnational union is patterned after the Stoic *krasis* doctrine. For the Stoics there can be a union of distinct substances in which there is a total mutual compenetration of bodies, but without each losing their distinct properties. Tertullian saw the union of soul and body in such a manner (see *De Anima*, 52, 3). Similarly, Jesus is composed of two substances. Thus, he can speak of 'homo deo mixtus,' and that in Jesus there is a 'miscente [mingling] *in semetipso hominem et deum*' (*Apologia*, 21, 3). See also *Adversus Marcionem*, 2, 27 and *De Carne Christi*, 15, 6. Obviously, Tertullian is attempting to conceive a union between the divinity and the humanity whereby he can retain their integrity and simultaneously assert that Christ is one. The tensions within such a conception are evident. The problem, as we will see, is that by modeling the Incarnation on the soul–body union Tertullian has misconceived it at the onset. See Grillmeier, *Christ in Christian Tradition*, Vol. 1, pp. 129–31, and R. Cantalamessa, *La Cristologia di Tertulliano* (Paradosis 18), Fribourg, 1962.

17   While Aquinas agrees that the soul–body union can be used to illustrate the ontological oneness of Christ, he rightly perceives that there is no similarity ('*quantum ad hoc non attenditur similitudo*') between the ontological union of soul and body and that of the divinity and the humanity (*ST*, III, 2, 1, ad 2). See the whole of III, 2, 1 as well as *SCG*, IV, 35, 9 and 41, 2 and 4.

18   In a former article, while I distinguished the use of the soul–body union for illustrating how Christ is one from that of portraying the manner of the incarnational union, I referred to both as the soul–body analogy. I was wrong in so doing (see 'The Soul–Body Analogy and the Incarnation: Cyril of Alexandria,' *Coptic Church Review* 17 (1996):59–66). The first use of the soul–body union is more an analogical use – by way of illustration or comparison. As a human being is one composed of soul and body so similarly Christ is one 'composed' of divinity and humanity. The second is more strictly speaking an exact model for the Incarnation, for here the manner or mode of 'the composition' is seen as the same. Moreover, even to use the soul–body union as an analogy or a comparison for the manner or type of incarnational union would be misleading and wrong. There is no similarity between the way the soul is united to the body and the way the divinity is united to the humanity. I am indebted to P. Parvis for helping me distinguish between 'analogy' and 'model' in this instance.

If one conceives the soul–body relationship as forming an ontological union, this gives rise to a new and third reality called man. To apply this model to the Incarnation necessitates that the divine and the human natures are ontologically united so as to form a new composite nature – a *tertium quid* – neither fully God nor fully man. Jesus may be one, but he becomes a hybrid, for the divinity and the humanity, like the body and the soul, are seen as constitutive components whose ontological fusion gives rise to a new kind of being. Moreover, because the incarnational union is modelled after the soul–body, and so conceived as a compositional union of natures, then the divine and the human attributes necessarily are predicated directly to the different natures. Thus the Son would be passible and so suffer and die within his own nature, and the humanity itself would directly assume the attributes of the Son's nature. Thus, an unworkable and intolerable tension results. Either the divinity is diminished or the humanity is mutated. Both are unacceptable for a proper understanding of the Incarnation.

There are numerous historical examples of the above. Arius grasped, for legitimate soteriological reasons, that there must be an ontological union between the Logos and his flesh (though he denied a human soul). But in unconsciously modeling this union after the manner of the soul–body, he realized that the Logos would thus be changed in becoming flesh and subsequently that all possible fleshly changes would reside within the very nature of the Logos. This being so, Arius had further cause, along with wanting to maintain the oneness of God, for denying the divinity of the Logos.

Apollinarius, while upholding the full divinity of the Logos, nonetheless felt compelled to deny the human soul so as to allow for an ontological union and oneness between the Logos and his flesh. A complete divine being and a complete human being could not become one, but rather, as the soul and the body are parts from which a whole human being is composed, so the full divinity and the flesh alone are the component parts from which Christ is composed. 'A *physis* is made up of the two parts, as the Logos with his divine perfection contributes a partial energy to the whole. This is also the case with the ordinary man, who is made up of two incomplete parts which produce one *physis* and display it under one name.'[19] Christ is *mia physis* because, like the soul—body, the Logos and the flesh form one organic whole with the Logos being the vivifying and governing (ἡγεμονικόν) principle just as the soul is to the body. But having denied the human soul, and yet defending the full divinity, Apollinarius was logically forced either to hold that the Logos suffers in his divine nature or to underplay or deny, in order to protect the full divinity, the human passibility of Christ. He chose the latter. However, because of this dilemma, Pseudo-Athanasius argued that Apollinarius must 'call the economy of the passion and the death and resurrection a mere appearance; or like Arius and his followers, call the Godhead of the Word passible.'[20] (Arius is obviously the more logical of the two.)

19 *De Unione*, 5.
20 *Contra Apollinarem*, 2, 12.

Equally, while the Cappadocians defended the full divinity and the full humanity of Christ, they nonetheless conceived the union after the manner of the soul–body and so spoke, ambiguously (and in the end, in the light of Chalcedon, wrongly) of the Incarnation as a 'mixing' or 'mingling' (ἀνάκρασις) of the divine and the human natures. Here, as with Tertullian, they seem to be employing a Stoic understanding. Moreover, it is within a christological setting that Gregory of Nazianzus first employed within Christian theology the Neoplatonic term used to explain the relationship between the soul and the body – περιχώρησις.[21] This 'mixing' and 'coinherence' jeopardizes the integrity of the natures. Moreover, the attributes of each nature now 'coinhere' with one another. This results in a dubious conception the human nature's deification, one that boarders on Docetism. According to Gregory of Nyssa the humanity is like a drop of vinegar in the sea of the divinity.[22]

Moreover, having failed to interpret correctly, as we will shortly see, Cyril's use of the soul–body analogy, his later misguided Monophysite defenders again used it to defend the one *ousia* of Christ. Eutyches and some later Monophysites did what Nestorius wrongly believed Cyril did, that is, ontologically 'squashing' the two natures together so as to form one new nature. This tended to mean, despite the denials and best efforts of their finest theologians, such as Severus of Antioch, that the union between the divinity and the humanity formed one composite quiddity – a *tertium quid*.[23] Here again the communication of idioms becomes problematic for, while the Monophysites wish to maintain the integrity of the divinity, the human nature itself assumes divine qualities. By the very nature of the union, the divinity, being the stronger partner, seeps into the humanity transforming it into something less than authentically human.

Luther, likewise, sees the Incarnation as a union of natures modelled after the soul–body forming the one existential reality of the God-Man. In the light of this, Luther interpreted the communication of idioms, in a far more radical manner than did Calvin (see below), as the predicating of the divine and the human attributes directly of the other nature, thus creating an impossible tension, for it is now God as God who suffers and it is man as man who creates. It is this unresolved tension that gave birth to modern kenoticism.

This tension first erupted, not surprisingly, between the Lutheran theologians of Giessen and Tübingen in the years 1616-24. Both proposed

---

21 See *Epistola*, 101 and *Oratio*, 38, 13. See K.P. Wesche, 'The Union of God and Man in Jesus Christ in the Thought of Gregory of Nazianzus,' *St Vladimir's Theological Quarterly* 28/2 (1984):83–98.

22 See *Adversus Apollinarem*, 42.

23 For example, the extreme Monophysite bishop Julian of Halicarnassus in the sixth century held that Jesus' humanity was so purified of sin and shielded from its effects that it was incorruptible, impassible, and immortal from birth (*Aphthartodocetae*). Leontius of Byzantium and Severus of Antioch argued against him. See Leontius of Byzantium, *Contra Nestorianos et Eutychianos II*. See also U. Lang, *Studies in the Christology of John Philoponus*, Chapter 6; J. Meyendorff, *Christ in Eastern Christian Thought* (New York: St Vladimir's Press, 1975), pp. 88–89; and Meyendorff, *Byzantine Theology*, pp. 157–58.

their competing forms of kenotic christology. To the present kenotic christology continues, consciously or unconsciously, in the same erroneous manner. By conceiving the Incarnation as the union of natures, similar to that of the soul–body, Kenoticists, in contrast to the Monophysites, are forced to deprive Christ of his full divinity in order to preserve the full humanity, for in such a relationship, as the catalogue of patristic heresies confirms, a conflict between divine and human attributes is bound to arise. Because of their conception of the incarnational union, if the divine nature is not checked in some manner, the divine attributes will wash, as in Monophysitism, into the human nature making it omniscient and omnipotent, and thus not authentically human with limited knowledge and power.[24]

If one takes a more dualistic stance where the soul inhabits or is loosely related to the body, and so is not fully ontologically one with it, then within the Incarnation, while the divinity and the humanity are in some sense related to one another, they are not ontologically united, and so God *is not* man. Moreover, because the divinity and the humanity are not united ontologically, the communication of idioms becomes impossible. God cannot suffer because God *is not* man. Likewise, from this perspective, those who do advocate the communication of idioms will be accused of having united the two natures so as to form a *tertium quid*. There are equally historical examples of this use of the soul–body model.

The Antiochenes use the soul–body model of the Incarnation both to espouse their own position and to argue against Cyril. They primarily employ it, not to demonstrate how Christ is one, but rather to argue for the integrity of each nature even within the incarnational union. For Theodore of Mopsuestia the soul and body are two radically different natures, but they are joined together without being confounded or converted. The natures of the soul and the body persist intact, and the division between them remains even within their union though, because of this union, they are given one name – man.[25] In *De Incarnatione* Theodore makes similar comments about the distinction between the soul and body and their union, and concludes:

> In the same way we also say here [of Christ] that there is the divine nature and the human nature and that – understanding the natures in this way – the person of the union is one. If we try to distinguish the natures we say that the man is perfect in his hypostasis and the God perfect in his. But if we want to consider the union, we say that both the natures are a single person (and hypostasis) and acknowledge that because of its union with the Godhead the flesh receives honour beyond all creatures and the Godhead fulfils everything in him.[26]

Theodoret of Cyrus likewise argues that as the soul and body are not mixed and confused in the formation of a human person but retain their

---

24 For a fuller discussion of Luther's christology with its various schools and kenotic christology see especially Weinandy, *Does God Change?*, pp. 101–23; and also *In the Likeness of Sinful Flesh*, pp. 8–11.
25 See *Adversus Apollinarem*, 4.
26 *De Incarnatione*, VIII, 62. ET, Grillmeier, *Christ in Christian Tradition*, Vol. 1, p. 438.

distinct integrity, so neither are the divinity and the humanity in Christ mixed and confused, and therefore they cannot, as Cyril claims, form one composite nature.[27]

Nestorius, in his early writings, similar to Theodore and Theodoret, uses the soul–body relationship to demonstrate how the divinity and the humanity can be united while keeping their own distinct and separate properties.[28] However, in his later writings during the course of his controversy with Cyril, he rejects the use of the soul–body model. In a passage already quoted (see fn. 9), he reverses its use to criticize the Arians. The Arians claim that the union of the divinity and the humanity 'resulted in one nature . . . even as the soul and the body are bound (together) in one nature' and so the Son is deprived of his divine impassibility and must necessarily suffer, within his own nature, hunger, thirst, and death.[29]

In a similar fashion he criticizes Cyril. If the union between the divinity and the humanity is like that of the soul and the body, then the divinity must be passible and so suffer. 'As the soul naturally gives perception to the body, so by means of this perception it experiences the sufferings of the body, so that the perception of the sufferings of the body is given by the soul and to the soul; for it is possible.'[30]

There is no doubt that Calvin believed Jesus to be the Son of God existing as man. He upheld that the Son was fully God and that he assumed an authentic and full humanity in becoming man.[31] As long as he limited himself to interpreting the Incarnation from within a scriptural context he was in accord with the ancient Christian tradition. However, once he entered into the ontology of the Incarnation he became somewhat confused and ambiguous, and he did so precisely because he interpreted the act of incarnation as the union of natures modeled after the union of the soul and body. Calvin used the soul–body union not

---

27 See *Eranistes*, 2.

28 See *Nestoriana*, 197f. and 330–31.

29 See *The Bazaar of Heracleides*, pp. 8–9.

30 *The Bazaar of Heracleides*, p. 172. See M. Anastos, 'Nestorius was Orthodox,' 126–27; R. Chestnut, 'The Two Prosopa in Nestorius' *Bazaar of Heracleides*,' *Journal of Theological Studies*, NS 29/2 (1978):403–4; H.E.W. Turner, 'Nestorius Reconsidered,' *Studia Patristica*, Vol. 13, pp. 311–12.

P. Robinson, in an M.Phil. thesis (Oxford, 1997), argues that the basic problem with the Antiochenes did not lie within their christology, but within their anthropology. The union between the soul and body was no greater than that between the divinity and the humanity. So they were convinced that their understanding of the unity between the divinity and the humanity in Christ was completely adequate since a human being was one in exactly the same manner. But even if they did possess a better anthropology, their christology would still be inadequate since the divinity and the humanity are not united in a soul–body manner no matter how it is conceived.

I have purposely tried to avoid speaking in terms of a Stoic, Aristotelian, or Platonic understanding of the soul–body relationship. I have done so primarily because such a discussion would take us far afield of our present concerns and unduly lengthen an already extended digression. Moreover, many of the Fathers, Tertullian and the Cappadocians being exceptions, appear to be rather eclectic in their use of the soul–body model, that is, they employ it, not with philosophical rigor, but with an eye to what they wish to uphold with regard to the Incarnation.

31 See J. Calvin, *Institutes of the Christian Religion* (London: James Clarke Ltd, 1957), I, 13; II, 12 and 13.

only to show that the divinity and humanity are united so as to constitute the one reality of Christ as the soul–body constitute one man, but
also as a means for understanding the communication of idioms, and so
the relationship between the divinity and the humanity. While the
soul–body constitute one man, yet they retain their distinct properties.
Some human properties are proper solely to the soul and some are
proper solely to the body. Yet, some properties are applied to the whole
man. In this instance 'the properties of the soul are transferred to the
body, and the properties of the body to the soul.' 'Such modes of
expression intimate both that there is in man one person formed of two
compounds, and that these two different natures constitute one person.'
In like fashion, the hypostatic union for Calvin, is 'the union which of
two natures constitutes one person.' From the New Testament Calvin
realizes that this 'one person' is the Son, but here, because of his use of
the soul–body model, this 'one person' now appears no longer to be 'the
Son,' but rather, in a manner reminiscent of the Antiochenes, to be 'the
Christ' who comes to be out of the union of natures just as one human
person is constituted by the union of soul and body. Moreover, the scriptures 'sometimes attribute to him [Christ] qualities which should be
referred specially to his humanity, and sometimes qualities applicable
peculiarly to his divinity, and sometimes qualities which embrace both
natures, and do not apply specially to either. This combination of a
twofold nature in Christ they express so carefully, that they sometimes
communicate them with each other, a figure of speech which the ancients
termed ἰδιωμάτων κοινωνία (a communication of properties).' Because
Calvin interprets the incarnational act as the union of natures after the
manner of the soul–body union, he has lost the authentic use of the
communication of idioms, where all attributes, whether divine or
human, are applied to one and the same person of the Son. While Calvin
wants the properties of each nature truly, and so 'not causelessly,' to be
predicated of the other since Christ is one, yet he must simultaneously
speak of this transferral as done 'figuratively' or 'improperly' in order to
protect the integrity of each nature. The soul–body model has placed
Calvin in a christological bind. In the end, it would seem, what Calvin
terms 'a communication of properties' is merely a linguistic device used
to highlight the close union of natures, and so the oneness of Christ.[32]

---

32 All of the above quotations are taken from *Institutes*, II, 14. It is because of this that,
    despite Calvin's critique of Nestorius, he has been accused of Nestorian leanings. For a
    discussion of this charge see E.D. Willis, *Calvin's Catholic Christology* (Leiden: E.J. Brill,
    1966), pp. 3–5. I do not think Calvin is Nestorian, but he was forced to give a 'Nestorian'
    flavor to his interpretation of the communication of idioms so as, like Nestorius, to
    protect the integrity of the natures. For a further discussion of Calvin's christology see
    pp. 61–100. Willis concurs with J. Witte that Calvin has lost the Chalcedonian under-
    standing of the communication of idioms founded upon the unity of the person of the
    Son, and that 'he [Witte] is also probably correct in his judgment that Calvin has no
    clear concept of the ontological foundation of the Incarnation' (p. 66). See J. Witte, 'Die
    Christologie Calvins,' *Das Konzil von Chalkedon: Geschichte und Gegenwart* III, eds A.
    Grillmeier and H. Bacht (Würzburg, 1951), pp. 458–59.
       For a Protestant evangelical understanding of the Incarnation that is in keeping with
    the conciliar tradition see R.A. Muller, 'Incarnation, Immutability, and the Case for
    Classical Theism,' *Westminster Theological Journal* 45 (1983):22–40.

Two recent defences of the traditional understanding of the Incarnation labour under the same misconception as those above. Both T.V. Morris and R. Swinburne propose a 'two mind' or 'divided mind' model for the Incarnation. For both, while the divine mind or consciousness in Christ has access to the human mind or consciousness, the latter does not have access to the former, unless the former allows it. This obviates the problem of how the Son of God can be omniscient and all-good, and yet the historical man Jesus can possess limited human knowledge and free will, and so be tempted, etc. Thus, while the Son of God is associated with the human mind of Jesus and so knows what he is thinking and willing, and while the Son can influence the human mind of Jesus so that he will think and will what is proper, yet the Son allows the human mind to function normally. The human mind remains, for the most part, segregated, with its own distinct sphere of activity.

I have multiple concerns with both Morris and Swinburne, not the least of which is Swinburne's notion that God is 'a soul' and it is this 'divine soul' that acquires a human body with a human manner of thinking (human brain and senses) in the Incarnation, but I will limit myself to what I consider their fundamental error in conceiving the Incarnation. Both still conceive the incarnational act as a union of natures similar to that of the soul–body, and it is for this reason that the conflict between incompatible or mutually exclusive attributes arises. Their solution to this pseudo-problem is to offer a form of adoptionism, that is, the divine Son of God does not come to exist as a man and so is conscious of himself and thinks in a human manner, but rather the Son adopts or acquires the mind of the human Jesus. Within traditional christology the one person of the Son does have a human mind and a divine mind, but this is the result of the Son actually coming to exist as man. For Morris and Swinburne it is the union of minds in Christ that effects the 'Incarnation' – it is within the union of minds that 'the Incarnation' is actually established. While both wish to uphold the traditional understanding of the Incarnation, it is difficult to see how this union is an ontological union, that is, how this union of minds can establish the fact that the Son actually *exists* as man. Swinburne compounds the problem by giving his form of adoptionism an Apollinarian twist in that the divine soul replaces the human soul and merely adopts or acquires the use of a human body – human brain and senses. It would seem that the fundamental problem within his christology is his faulty anthropology where the normal human soul's relation to the body is no different from that of the divine soul's relation to its body. A human being is but a soul that has adopted a body.[33]

The verdict of this rather lengthy examination is clear. However one uses the soul–body as a model for the Incarnation it is completely inadequate, misleading, and even false, and equally then for properly interpreting the communication of idioms. The Incarnation establishes a

---

33 See T.V. Morris, *The Logic of God Incarnate* (Ithaca: Cornell University Press, 1986), and R. Swinburne, *The Christian God* (Oxford: Oxford University Press, 1994), pp. 192–238. For a more lengthy discussion and critique of Morris see my review of his book in *The Thomist* 51/2 (1987):367–72.

whole different kind of relationship and union, and, as a result, the communication of idioms must be conceived differently as well.

The Communication of Idioms and the Oneness of Christ

We now return to Cyril, and we do so to argue that he conceives the Incarnation and the communication of idioms in an entirely different manner than was just discussed above. However, it is only in contrast to the above that his christology, and most immediately his use of the soul–body relationship, becomes manifest.[34]

The hermeneutical key for unlocking Cyril's christology is the communication of idioms for it is the very same key he himself employed to unlock the mystery of the Incarnation. It was, in accordance with my earlier stated principle, the inner christological logic imbedded within the communication of idioms which permitted, and even propelled, Cyril to grasp, conceptualize, and articulate the three incarnational truths which must be maintained for a proper understanding of the Incarnation. Through faith Cyril knew that the communication of idioms demanded that it be truly the full divine Son of God who is man, that it be truly a complete man that the Son of God is, and thus that the Son of God actually does exist as man.[35] Moreover, in the process of clarifying the mystery of the Incarnation through his defense of communication of idioms, the proper use and rendering of the communication of idioms was itself corroborated and so sanctioned. Cyril's christology befittingly depicts a man of faith passionately seeking understanding.[36]

---

34 Having inherited his foundational principles and convictions from within the Alexandrian tradition, especially from Athanasius, and having given considerable thought to christological concerns in his previous scriptural commentaries, Cyril's polemical and doctrinal writing, from the onset of the Nestorian controversy, abundantly (even repetitiously) testifies to his established christological stance. However, because he was always attempting to clarify and deepen his understanding, there is a sense of an ever-advancing movement within his continually recurrent themes and concerns. This gives fluidity, but not contradiction to Cyril's thought. Thus each word and phrase must be interpreted within the shifting context of the various points he is making at any given time. McGuckin aptly describes Cyril's writing as a theological 'narrative' which is 'flexible' and 'discursive.' See *St Cyril of Alexandria: The Christological Controversy*, pp. 175–76.

    For general studies of Cyril's christological thought, see Grillmeier, *Christ in Christian Tradition*, Vol. 1, pp. 473–83; Kelly, *Early Christian Doctrines*, pp. 317–23; and F. Young, *From Nicaea to Chalcedon* (London: SCM, 1983), pp. 213–29, 240–65. For a more detailed account of Cyril's christology, see McGuckin, *St Cyril of Alexandria*, pp. 175–226 and B. Meunier, *Le Christ de Cyrille D'Alexandrie: L'Humanité, Le Salut et La Question Monophysite* (Paris: Beauchesne, 1997).

35 Because Cyril is an Alexandrian, some scholars still wish to designate his christology as an example of *logos–sarx* christology. This is a misleading and even false designation. While Cyril may not have fully developed, theologically, the christological significance of Jesus' human soul, he did hold for such a human soul and did give some critical importance to it. See L. Welch, 'Logos–Sarx? Sarx and the Soul of Christ in the Early Thought of Cyril of Alexandria,' *St Vladimir's Theological Quarterly* 38 (1994):271–92.

36 It was through the Creed of Nicea that Cyril discerned, in faith, the full incarnational significance of the communication of idioms. The Son who was *homoousios* with the Father was the same Son who 'suffered and rose again on the third day.'

    The holy and great Council stated that 'the only-begotten Son', 'begotten' by nature 'of the Father', 'true God from true God', 'light from light', 'through whom'

For Cyril then, the communication of idioms demanded that Christ be one in two ways. First, it demanded that Jesus be one existing reality or being – one entity – for if he were not one, then one could not authentically predicate of him divine and human attributes. Second, the one existential reality of Jesus must be, moreover, the one and same divine Son of God existing as incarnate – as man – for if it were not the one Son existing as man then it would not be the one and same Son who was *homoousios* with the Father and who was born, suffered, died, and rose as man. It is simply this double conception of Jesus' oneness – that he is one entity and that the one entity that Jesus is, is the one Son existing as man – which Cyril found implanted within the very heart of the communication of idioms and which he continually attempted to conceptualize and articulate.[37]

---

the Father made all things did himself 'come down, was incarnate, made man, suffered, rose again the third day, and ascended into heaven'. These declarations and these doctrines we too must follow, taking note of the Word of God's 'becoming incarnate' and 'being made man'. We do not mean that the nature of the Word was changed and made flesh or, on the other hand, that he was transformed into a complete man consisting of soul and body, but instead we affirm this: that the Word personally (καθ᾽ ὑπόστασιν) united to himself flesh, endowed with life and reason. *Ad Nestorium*, 2, 3. E.T. from *Cyril of Alexandria: Selected Letters*, ed. L.R. Wickham (Oxford: Clarendon Press, 1983), but slightly altered. See also *Ad Nestorium*, 3, 3.

J.J. O'Keefe argues that Cyril was not only more faithful to Nicea than were the Antiochenes, but that he was also more faithful to the New Testament proclamation. Unlike the Antiochenes, he fashioned his philosophical concepts to be in conformity with the biblical narrative. 'The Antiochene position interprets the text in the light of philosophy, the Alexandrian position interprets the philosophy in the light of the text.' 'Kenosis or Impassibility: Cyril of Alexandria and Theodoret of Cyrus on the Problem of Divine Pathos,' *Studia Patristica*, Vol. 32, p. 365. In the end Cyril was not only the better theologian, but, contrary to common scholarly opinion, he was equally the better exegete. See also O'Keefe, 'Impassible Suffering? Divine Passion and Fifth-Century Christology,' *Theological Studies* 58 (1997):41–45, 55–58.

37 R.A. Norris argues that Cyril has two christological models ('Christological Models in Cyril of Alexandria,' *Studia Patristica*, Vol. 13, ed. E.A. Livingstone (Berlin: Akademie Verlag, 1975), pp. 255–68). The first, which Norris believes is Cyril's primary model, is what he calls 'a subject-attribute model.' Within this model Cyril can attribute divine and human predicates of one and the same subject – the Son. However, Norris also sees within Cyril's christology 'a compositional model.' Here the Incarnation is seen as the act of 'putting together' two different realities (divinity and humanity), similar to the union of soul and body. Thus Christ is one composite entity. Norris believes that it is Cyril's use of this second model that causes 'such a remarkable conceptual chaos' within his christology (p. 265). Norris is correct in that Cyril does speak of the Incarnation in two different manners, but as my following argument will show, he does not have two different christological models. What Norris fails to grasp is that Cyril uses two different sets of language or concepts not to articulate two different conceptions of the Incarnation but to state two different truths about his one conception of the Incarnation. As we will see, he uses the soul–body language to confirm the truth that Christ is one ontological being or entity (Norris' compositional model), and he will use the subject-attribute 'model' in order to designate who and what the one Christ is – the one person of the Son existing as man. While Cyril is aware that he is attempting to articulate these two truths, I would agree with Norris that he seems unaware at times that he is not distinguishing them in a manner that is unambiguous.

The Mia Physis *Formula*

This is readily apparent at the very onset of the controversy in Cyril's championing the *mia physis* formula, that is, that Jesus is 'the one nature of the Word incarnate' (μία φύσις τοῦ λόγου σεσαρκωμένη), for it contains his dual concern about the oneness of Christ. That is why Cyril clung to it with such tenacity. The first question, one that bears directly on Christ being one entity and on our previous examination of the soul–body relationship, is: What does Cyril mean by *mia physis*? I have argued extensively elsewhere, and will develop more fully here, that by *mia physis* Cyril is not saying that Christ is one nature or essence (*physis*), in the sense of quiddity, as if the divine nature and the human nature were ontologically united, through mixture and confusion, so as to form a common third nature (quiddity) which would be neither fully divine nor fully human. This is how Nestorius and the Antiochenes interpreted the formula, and how the later Monophysites, having misunderstood Cyril, would interpret it. Rather, Cyril primarily used *mia physis* to emphasize that Christ is one being or reality – one entity.

The clue to this interpretation is in the comparison Cyril made between the soul–body union and that found within the Incarnation. He primarily and almost exclusively used the soul–body union, which normally appears immediately either before or after the *mia physis* formula, to illustrate that as the soul and the body of a human being are ontologically united to form one reality or entity – the human being – so the Son of God is ontologically united to the humanity to form the one reality of Jesus. For the sake of clarity and demonstration, Cyril must be quoted at some length.

> As for our Saviour's statements in the Gospels, we do not divide them out to two subjects (ὑποστάσεσι) or persons (προσώποις). The one, unique Christ has no duality though he is seen as compounded in inseparable unity out of two (ἐκ δύο) differing elements in the way that a human being, for example, is seen to have no duality but to be one (εἷς) consisting of the pair of elements, body and soul.[38]

Because Cyril spoke of Christ being one nature (*mia physis*) formed out of two (*ek duo*), the Antiochenes held that he could only mean that the divinity and humanity were united so as to form a *tertium quid*. While the 'out of two' is ambiguous and will be clarified by Chalcedon, it is nonetheless evident that Cyril did not mean what the Antiochenes thought he meant. First, as the Gospels bear witness, there is one subject or person in Christ. Second, the reason there is one subject or person is that the divinity and the humanity are united in the one person so as to form the one nature of Jesus in the sense of one entity (not quiddity), similar to the way the soul and body form the one entity of a human being. The comparison is used only to denote the oneness and not the manner of the oneness. As Cyril states:

> The nature (φύσις) of the Incarnate Word himself (ἡ αὐτοῦ τοῦ λόγου σεσαρκωμένου) is after the union now conceived as one (μία) just as

38 *Ad Nestorium*, 3, 8.

will reasonably be conceived in regard to ourselves too, for man is one, compounded of unlike things, soul I mean and body.[39]

Or again, in defending his use of the *mia physis* formula, Cyril writes:

May we illustrate the case from the composition which renders us human beings? We are composed out of (ἐκ) soul and body and observe two different natures (δύο φύσεις), body's and soul's; yet the pair yields a single united human being, and composition out of two natures does not turn the one man into two men but, as I said, produces a single man, a composite of soul and body.[40]

Or again:

Take the normal human being. We perceive in him two natures (δύο φύσεις): one that of the soul, a second that of the body. We divide them, though, merely in thought accepting the difference as simply residing in fine-drawn insight or mental intuition; we do not separate the natures out or attribute a capacity for radical severance to them, but see that they belong to one man so that the two are two no more and the single living being is constituted complete by the pair of them. So though one attributes the nature of manhood and of Godhead to Emmanuel, the manhood has become the Word's own and together with it is seen as one Son.[41]

The sole point Cyril wishes to make within the above quotations is that as a human being is one entity so Christ is one entity. In no way does he use the manner of the relationship between the soul and body or the mode of union established between the soul and the body as a model for the manner of the relationship between the divinity and the humanity or for the mode of the union established between the divinity and the humanity. He is merely making a comparison in order to draw a conclusion – Christ is one.[42] Thus, to insist that Christ is *mia*

39 *Adversus Nestorii Blasphemias, 2: proema.* E.T. (slightly altered): *Cyril of Alexandria: On the Incarnation Against Nestorius*, Library of the Fathers (Oxford: James Parker & Co., 1881).
40 *Ad Succensum*, 1, 7. E.T., Wickham.
41 *Ad Succensum*, 2, 5. E.T., Wickham.
    Similar citations, demonstrating the same point, can be found in *Ad Nestorium*, 3, 4; *Ad Succensum*, 2, 2 and 3; *Ad Eulogium*; *Ad Monachos*, 12; *Scholia de Incarnatione Unigeniti*, 27 (In McGuckin's translation, 26); *Contra Diodorum et Theodorum*, 1, 9 and 22, 2, 4; *Quod Unus Sit Christus*.
42 B. Meunier equally argues that Cyril used the soul–body union as a 'simple illustration pédagogique' and not as an exact model for the incarnational union (*Le Christ de Cyrille D'Alexandrie*, p. 235).
    Pour Cyrille, il n'y a pas de correspondance terme à terme dans la comparaison: on ne saurait dire qu'à la chair du Verbe correspond le corps humain, et au Verbe, l'âme; l'argumentation vise surtout à montrer qu'il y a unité de sujet, et que derrière la chair, c'est le Verbe lui-même qui est impliqué. Le parallèle n'est pas le poussé jusqu'au bout: du côté christologique, ce n'est pas le 'tout', c'est-à-dire le Christ comme composé Verbe-chair, qui est le sujet unique (le Verbe ne représenterait qu'une 'partie' dans la comparaison, ce que Cyrille n'accepterait pas de dire); à l'inverse, le modèle anthropologique n'est pas adapté à son usage christologique, sinon, il faudrait dire que l'âme dans l'homme est le sujet véritable, ce qui suppose qu'elle vient assumer le corps et donc, d'une certaine façon, lui préexiste, ce que Cyrille se refuse également à dire. On voit donc qu'il ne faut pas

physis simply affirms that he is one entity and not that he is one quiddity.[43]

---

vouloir trop déduire de la comparaison, sous peine d'en trahir l'intention (pp. 241–42).

From the above we see that Meunier interprets Cyril's use of the soul–body union to illustrate that the Word is the one subject. I agree that this is a conclusion that Cyril drew from its use, but Cyril's actual use of the soul–body union, I would argue, is primarily to illustrate that Christ is one being, and then only did he conclude that the one being that Christ is, is the one subject of the Son of God existing as man.

Given the whole patristic christological tradition, the Holy Spirit must have worked overtime to assure that while The Athanasian Creed ('*Quicumque* Creed') employs the soul–body analogy, it does so only to illustrate that Christ is one being. 'As a rational soul and flesh are one man, so God and man are one Christ' ('*Nam sicut anima rationalis et caro unus est homo, ita Deus et homo unus est Christus*'), Denz.-Schön., 76. Aquinas caught the limited and legitimate use of the analogy within the Creed. See *ST*, III, 2, 1, obj. 2 and ad 2.

43 For the sake of completeness and honesty, it must be noted that on one occasion Cyril did use the manner of the relationship between the soul and body to compare the manner of the relationship between the divine and the human natures, and not just to illustrate that Christ is one entity, but to portray the workings of the communication of idioms. Cyril speaks of the relationship between the two natures as ineffable, and adds that even the relationship between the soul and body is beyond our comprehension. He then states:

I should say (although the description altogether falls short of the truth) that it is fitting to understand the union of Emmanuel to be such as the soul of a man might be thought to have with its own body. For the soul appropriates the things of the body even though in its proper nature it is apart from the body's natural passions, as well as those which impinge on it from without. For the body is moved to physical desires, and the soul which is within it feels these things too, because of the union, but in no way does it participate in these things, except in so far as it takes the fulfilment of desire as its own gratification. If the body was struck by a sword, or tortured on an iron grid, the soul would share in its grief, because it is its own body which is suffering. But in its own nature the soul does not suffer anything of these things.

This indeed is how we attribute the union to Emmanuel. For it was necessary that the soul united to it should share in the grief of its own body, so that rising above these sufferings it could submit itself as obedient to God. But it is foolish to say that God the Word shared in feeling the sufferings. For the Godhead is impassible and is not in our condition. Yet [the Word] was united to the flesh endowed with a rational soul, and when the flesh suffered, even though he was impassible, he was aware of what was happening within it, and thus as God, even though he did away with the weaknesses of the flesh, still he appropriated those weaknesses of his own body. This is how he is said to have hungered, and to have been tired, and to have suffered for our sake. *Scholia de Incarnatione Unigeniti*, 8. E.T., McGuckin, *St Cyril of Alexandria*, pp. 300–1.

I have quoted Cyril at length so as to leave no doubt that, while he employs the soul–body relationship, he does so not as a model for the Incarnation, but solely as an illustrative comparison for understanding the communication of idioms. As the soul can appropriate the sufferings of the body and make them its own, so the Word, in becoming man, can make the weaknesses of his humanity his own. While I am not particularly pleased with the illustration for reasons that are now apparent, the reason Cyril could make such a comparison is precisely because Christ, like a human being, is one and the one that he is, is the person of the Son of God existing as man. 'Accordingly, the union of the Word with humanity can reasonably be compared with our condition. Just as the body is of a different nature to the soul, still from both we say that one man results, so too from the perfect hypostasis of God the Word and from a humanity perfect in his own right there is one Christ, and the selfsame is at once God and man.' *Scholia*, 8.

Likewise when Cyril speaks of the union being 'natural' (ἕνωσις φυσική) or 'according to nature' (κατά φύσιν), he is making the same point. The union is 'natural' or 'according to nature' not in the sense that the divine and the human natures are compositionally united so as to form a third nature in the sense of quiddity, but in the sense that it brings about the one ontological entity of Christ. Just as the union of soul and body is 'natural' forming the one entity of man so the union of the divinity and the humanity is natural bringing about the one Christ.[44]

While these quotations confirm that Cyril employed *mia physis* to declare Christ to be one entity and not one quiddity, it is equally clear that he used the term *physis* in two different senses. For he also simultaneously speaks of the soul and body, and the divinity and the humanity as each being a *physis* in the sense of nature or quiddity. This equivocal, and so ambiguous, use of the term *physis* obviously caused, and still causes, confusion and misunderstanding.

Assuming then that *mia physis*, for Cyril, designates that Jesus is one entity, and that he affirms this in order to confirm the communication of idioms, for only if the Son of God *truly is* man, and so one with his humanity, can the attributes of each nature be predicated of him, what then does the remainder of the formula tell us? The answer to this question bears upon Cyril's second concern about Christ's oneness and the manner of that oneness. The remainder of the formula designates

---

While McGuckin provides a good explanation of Cyril's use of the soul–body relationship, and rightly sees it as central to his thought, he does not appreciate Cyril's singular and proper use of it. He assumes that the above use is Cyril's primary and sole understanding. See *St Cyril of Alexandria*, pp. 198–207, and his Introduction to Cyril's *On the Unity of Christ* (Crestwood: St Vladimir's Press, 1995), pp. 38, 40. For a similar understanding of the above passage see H. Chadwick, 'Eucharist and Christology in the Nestorian Controversy,' *Journal of Theological Studies*, NS 2 (1951):159–62. B. Meunier interprets the above passages in a manner similar to my own. See *Le Christ de Cyrille D'Alexandrie*, pp. 243–53. F. Young not only has an equal understanding of the above passages, but she also grasps that Cyril's primary use of the soul–body analogy is to illustrate that Christ is one being, and therefore should 'not be taken as an analysis of the relationship' between the divinity and the humanity. 'A Reconsideration of Alexandrian Christology,' *Journal of Ecclesiastical History* 22/2 (1971):106. See also pp. 105 and 112, and her *From Nicaea to Chalcedon*, pp. 260–63. G. Gould has also given a clear account of Cyril on this point. See 'Cyril of Alexandria and the Formula of Reunion,' *Downside Review* 106 (1988):238–43. While R.A. Norris believes that Cyril's primary christological model is that of the subject-attribute model, he nonetheless interprets, wrongly I believe, Cyril's use of the soul–body union as a way for him to espouse, in a confused and contradictory manner, a compositional model of the Incarnation whereby the divinity and humanity form one nature (see 'Christological Models in Cyril of Alexandria,' *Studia Patristica*, Vol. 13, pp. 261–67. See also R.A. Norris, 'Toward a Contemporary Interpretation of the Chalcedonian *Definition*' in *Lux in Lumine*, p. 68.

44 For examples of Cyril speaking of the union of the divinity and the humanity as 'natural' (ἕνωσις φυσική) or 'according to nature' (κατά φύσιν), see *Adversus Nestorii Blasphemias*, 2, 1 and 13; *Ad Nestorium*, 3, 4, 5, and Anathema 3.
    Here I disagree with Wickham's translation and interpretation. He makes an equivalence between Cyril's saying that the union is 'natural' and that the union is καθ' ὑπόστασιν giving the meaning 'substantial union' to both. While both do designate a substantial union, Cyril uses 'natural' to emphasize that the union establishes Christ as one entity, and he uses, as will be seen shortly, καθ'ὑπόστασιν ('according to person' or 'personally') to designate the distinctive and singular type of substantial union it is. See Wickham, *Cyril of Alexandria: Selected Letters*, p. 4, fn. 6.

who/what the one reality of Jesus is. The one reality or entity (μία φύσις) is that of the Word incarnate (τοῦ λόγου σεσαρκωμένη). Contained within the *mia physis* formula then, something Cyril instinctively realized and appreciated, but which others found too subtle to grasp, was the notion of one subject or person and the manner of the one subject's existence. The subject (the who) of the *mia physis* (of the one entity) is the Word. The manner or mode of the Word's existence as *mia physis* (as one entity) is as man. This is why Cyril could write: 'Accordingly all the sayings contained in the Gospels must be referred to a single person (ἑνὶ προσώπῳ), to the one incarnate subject of the Word (ὑποστάσει μιᾷ τῇ τοῦ λόγου σεσαρκωμένη).'[45] Here the prevalent term *physis* has been substituted by the terms *prosopon* and *hypostasis* which acquire the more Chalcedonian sense of 'person' or 'subject'. The reason Cyril can make such a substitution is that, for him, the one entity of Christ (*physis*) is none other than the one divine person/subject (*prosopon/hypostasis*) of the Son existing as incarnate.[46] The *mia physis* formula, for Cyril, embodied all three truths needed for a proper understanding of the Incarnation, and this is why he loved it. It said it all. However, as the above exposition probably demonstrates, it may try to do too much. It requires a 'Cyrilian insight.' Something his detractors, past and present, lack.

---

45 *Ad Nestorium*, 3, 8. E.T., Wickam.
46 Bearing on this point, Cyril actually has two readings of the *mia physis* formula. The more prevalent one is: μία φύσις τοῦ λόγου σεσαρκωμένη. The other, less common rendering, ends in σεσαρκωμένου. I have waffled over the years on whether or not the two are significantly different in meaning. I presently hold that both, in the light of the soul–body comparison, which accompanies both, denote that *mia physis* be understood as denoting one entity. However, this is most clearly seen within the σεσαρκωμένου rendering where it modifies the τοῦ λόγου. The translation would be: 'The one nature (entity) of the incarnate Word.' The one entity of Jesus is the Word existing as man. Where the σεσαρκωμένη modifies the μία φύσις the formula is translated: 'The one incarnate nature of the Word.' This too specifies that Christ is one entity – one incarnate entity – but now the one incarnate *physis* is that of the Word, and so hidden within the use of the term *physis* is the notion of one subject or person as well. Thus this rendering of the formula could be translated: 'The one incarnate nature/person of the Word.' This translation, it seems to me, best articulates Cyril's meaning and is one that is closest to Chalcedon's understanding. The whole problem could have been solved if Cyril had consistently used πρόσωπον or ὑπόστασις instead of φύσις.
   McGuckin interprets Cyril's use of the formula in a similar manner. 'For Cyril, if the christological union means anything it means that there is only one reality to be affirmed henceforth. This concrete reality (physis) is what stands before the Christian observer; it is a single concrete enfleshed reality before us: Mia Physis Sesarkomene. What is more, the concrete, fleshed-out reality, is that of the Word of God, none other. In short, by using the phrase Cyril is attributing the person of the Word as the single subject of the Incarnation event.' *St Cyril of Alexandria*, p. 208. However, 'Cyril himself, in the negotiations with the Antiochenes after the council of Ephesus, began to realise for clarity's sake the use of physis as a subject-referent could no longer be sustained.' P. 140. See also pp. 148 and 210. For an historical assessment of the *mia physis* formula in the context of the Council of Ephesus, the Formula of Union, and the Council of Chalcedon, see J. Romanides, 'St Cyril's "One *Physis* or *Hypostasis* of God the Logos Incarnate" and Chalcedon' in *Christ in East and West*, eds P. Fries and T. Nersoyan (Macon: Mercer Press, 1987), pp. 15–34.

'Becoming' as Personal/Existential

Moreover, in the course of expounding the meaning of the formula, Cyril was able to clarify the true nature of the incarnational 'becoming' and the subsequent union between the Son/Word of God and his humanity, and this is why he is willing, in the end, to lay it aside. This he did by designating that the union of the natures takes place within the person of the Word. The incarnational 'becoming' and ensuing union is 'according to the person' (καθ᾽ ὑπόστασιν). 'We affirm this: that the Word personally [according to the person] united to himself flesh (σάρκα ... ἐνώσας ὁ λόγος ἑαυτῷ καθ᾽ ὑπόστασιν).[47] This was the heart of his beloved formula, but now stated more precisely, more explicitly, and possibly, more accurately. Here we witness a true christological breakthrough, one that springs from the communication of idioms and, simultaneously, precisely defines it.

In designating the incarnational 'becoming' as *kath hypostasin* Cyril has clarified and established three points concurrently. First, he has distinguished between the person (the who) and the person's nature (the manner of the who's existence). It is one and the same person, who existed eternally as God, who now exists as man. Second, he has clarified the exact nature of the incarnational 'becoming'. The Incarnation does not involve the changing, mixing, or confusing of natures (as in the soul–body model), but rather the person of the Word taking on a new mode or manner of existence, that is, as man. There is a change or newness in the mode of the existence of the Son, though not a change or newness within the natures. The Son now newly exists as man. Third, by correctly conceiving and articulating that it is the person of the Son who exists as man, Cyril, as we will fully examine momentarily, equally has validated the communication of idioms. Cyril's understanding of the Incarnation is what I have come to refer to as a personal/existential conception. Jesus is the *person* of the Son *existing* as a man.[48] While the Incarnation remains a mystery, Cyril, in accordance with authentic doctrinal development, has clarified more exactly what the mystery is – it is truly the person of the divine Son who truly exists as a true man.

In the light of Antiochene concerns and Leo's *Tome* and in response to Eutyches' monophysitism, the Council of Chalcedon (AD451) stated that the Son was 'made known in two natures' (ἐν δύο φύσεσιν) as opposed to stating that the Son was composed 'out of' (ἐκ δύο) two natures, thus clarifying the remaining ambiguities within Cyril's christology.

47 *Ad Nestorium*, 2, 3: see also 2, 4 and 3, 11. As noted above, I disagree with Wickham's translation. He translates καθ᾽ ὑπόστασιν as 'substantially.' While it does designate a substantial union, Cyril saw it as a substantial union of a special and singular type. The incarnational act does not bring about a union of natures, but rather it is the act by which the humanity is united substantially to the person (ὑπόστασις) of the Word. Likewise, Wickham interprets μία φύσις as equivalent to ὑποστάσει μιᾷ. While the ὑποστάσει μιᾷ is contained within the μία φύσις, the nuance is quite significant. The *mia physis* is emphasizing the one entity of Christ. The *hypostasis mia* is highlighting who the subject is within the one entity of Christ – the one Word/Son.
48 On the personal/existential understanding of the Incarnation, see Weinandy, *Does God Change?*, pp. 53–55. R.A. Norris appears to interpret Cyril's christology in a similar manner. See 'Toward a Contemporary Interpretation of the Chalcedonian *Definition*' in *Lux in Lumine*, pp. 69–73.

Nonetheless, Cyril's stamp on the Council's Creed is unmistakable, and it is his understanding of the Incarnation that bears its *imprimatur*. To read the Chalcedonian Creed except through the eyes of Cyril is to misread it.

Three times the Council employs the Cyrilian phrase 'one and the same' (ἕνα καὶ τὸν αὐτὸν) and five times speaks of 'the same' (τὸν αὐτὸν). Who it is who is 'one and the same' and 'the same' is none other than the person of the Son. It is one and the same Son who is 'perfect in Godhead' and 'perfect in manhood, truly God and truly man . . . consubstantial (ὁμοούσιον) with the Father in Godhead, and the same consubstantial (ὁμοούσιον) with us in manhood.' It is the same Son, who existed eternally with the Father, who came to exist as man. In so speaking the Council thoroughly endorsed Cyril's personal/existential understanding of the Incarnation.

Moreover, the Council declared that the two natures were united 'without confusion, without change, without division, without separation' (ἀσυγχύτως, ἀτρέπτως, ἀδιαιρέτως, ἀχωρίστως). Why are the natures not confused and changed? Why are they undivided and unseparated? Is not this an arbitrary jumble of words? How is it possible to hold both sets of seemingly contradictory concepts together in an intelligible manner? Is the Council here merely making negative statements in order to ward off various heresies, or did it also have a positive theologically informed conception of the Incarnation which authorized it to do so? I believe it is the latter. The Council grasped, in agreement with Cyril, that the natures are not confused and changed because the incarnational act, the 'becoming,' is not the compositional union of natures which would demand change and confusion. Rather, the incarnational act, the 'becoming,' equally in agreement with Cyril, is the person of the Son uniting to himself a human nature so as to exist personally as man. Thus the natures are not divided or separated, but find their unity in the one person of the Son. As the Council states: 'the difference of the natures being by no means removed because of the union [the reason being that the union is not a union of natures], but the property of each nature being preserved and harmonized (συντρεχούσης) in one *prosopon* and one *hypostasis*.' This too testifies to the Council's personal/existential understanding of the Incarnation.

It is this understanding of the Incarnation which provided, at last, the christological justification for and a proper reading of the communication of idioms. However, as I have argued, it was not a proper understanding of the Incarnation which gave rise to the communication of idioms, for it was used long before a proper understanding was fully articulated, but rather it was the communication of idioms which gave rise to a proper understanding of the Incarnation.[49]

---

49 For a more complete exposition of my interpretation of Chalcedon, see Weinandy, *Does God Change?*, pp. 63–66.

For two recent misreadings of Chalcedon, see A. Baxter, 'Chalcedon, and the Subject of Christ,' *Downside Review* 107 (1989):1–21 and T.W. Bartel, 'Why the Philosophical Problems of Chalcedonian Christology Have Not Gone Away,' *Heythrop Journal* 36 (1995):153–72. The problems they perceive within Chalcedon are due to their own

Here we perceive that the Incarnation is the culmination and summit of biblical revelation. Throughout this study I have emphasized that the foundational mystery of all biblical revelation is that God is present to the world and active within history, in all his wholly otherness, without losing his wholly otherness in so doing. In the Incarnation the wholly other divine Son of God truly becomes an authentic man without losing his wholly otherness as God. It is precisely his wholly otherness as God which gives significance to the Son's incarnate existence. If it were not truly the Son, *homoousios* with the Father, who became man, then the whole import of his being man, *homoousios* with all men, would be forfeited.[50] It is precisely the communication of idioms that accentuates and intensifies these truths. He who is truly God actually lives an authentic human life without ceasing to be truly God.[51]

The Communication of Idioms and the Suffering of God
The long patristic tradition, sanctioned, as Cyril grasped, by the Creed of

---

misconceptions. They read Chalcedon as espousing a union of natures after the model of the soul–body union.

Some recent forms of 'Spirit Christology' have also misinterpreted not only Chalcedon but Nicea as well. For example see R. Haight, 'The Case for Spirit Christology,' *Theological Studies* 53 (1992):257–87; G.W.H. Lampe, 'The Holy Spirit and the Person of Christ' in *Christ, Faith and History*, eds S.W. Sykes and J.P. Clayton (Cambridge: Cambridge University Press, 1972), pp. 111–30, and *God as Spirit* (Oxford: Clarendon Press, 1977). For critiques of these positions, see T. Weinandy, 'The Case for Spirit Christology: Some Reflections,' *The Thomist* 59/2 (1995):173–88, and J. Wright, 'Roger Haight's Spirit Christology,' *Theological Studies* 53 (1992):729–35.

For an excellent discussion of the ecumenical significance of and obstacles within the Chalcedonian definition in the light of recent various inter-church dialogues, particularly among and with the 'Nestorian' and 'Monophysite' churches, see D. Wendebourg, 'Chalcedon in Ecumenical Discourse,' *Pro Ecclesia* 7/3 (1998):307–32.

50 Many contemporary theologians, in their attempt to assure the full humanity of Jesus, deny his full divinity. However, in so doing they depreciate the significance of the very thing they want to enhance – the humanity. One never enhances the import of Jesus' full humanity, in all its authentic historicity, by denying that it is truly the divine Son who is man. The awesome significance of the humanity lies precisely in the fact that who this man is, is none other than the eternal Son of God.

For one recent example of this totally misconceived approach to the humanity of Christ, and so a thorough misrepresentation of Cyril and the christological tradition, see J. Macquarrie, *Christology Revisited* (London: SCM, 1998), pp. 43–60. Also see his *Jesus Christ in Modern Thought* (London: SCM, 1990). For a critique of Macquarrie see C.C. Hefling, 'Reviving Adamic Adoptionism: The Example of John Macquarrie,' *Theological Studies* 52 (1991):476–94.

51 In its desire to clarify false understandings, past and present, of the Incarnation, the Papal International Theological Commission has stated that the Council of Chalcedon demands that one uphold within the Incarnation both God's transcendence and his immanence.

Both these aspects must be asserted unrestrictedly, while excluding anything that would smack of juxtaposition or admixture. In Christ, then, transcendence and immanence are perfectly conjoined. . . . [T]he definition of Chalcedon radically transcends Greek thought, for it lets coexist two viewpoints which Greek philosophy had always regarded as irreconcilable: divine transcendence, the very soul of the Platonic system, and divine immanence, which is the spirit of the Stoic theory. *Select Questions on Christology* (1981), II, B, 6. See the whole of section II, B.

Nicea, employed the communication of idioms. What the tradition had never clearly achieved, as witnessed in the Antiochene rejection, was a proper theological rationale for its use, and thus a precise understanding of the manner in which these attributes where predicated of the Son. Cyril in providing the christological basis for its use equally clarified the manner in which it was used and he did so in two ways. Negatively, he recognized that the human attributes were not predicated of the divine nature, nor in turn, were the divine attributes predicated of the human nature. Such an understanding of the communication of idioms would mean that, in some manner, the natures where confused and mixed and so changed within the incarnational process. This is how Nestorius interpreted its use, and if it had been the correct interpretation, he would have been justified in rejecting it. Positively, Cyril grasped and explicitly stated, for the first time, that the attributes were predicated not of the natures, but of the person, for the Incarnation is not the compositional union of natures but the person of the Son taking on a new manner or mode of existence.[52] Because the incarnational 'becoming' is *kath hypostasin*, according to the person, it can actually be said then that the person of the Son of God is truly born, grieves, suffers and dies, not as God, but as man for that is now the new manner in which the Son of God actually exists.[53]

---

52 In fairness it should be noted that Athanasius grasped that the divine and human attributes were predicated of one and the same Son. However, what Athanasius failed to achieve, although his understanding of the communication of idioms placed him on the brink, was the precise and comprehensive conceptual understanding of the Incarnation which could properly justify such predication. See Weinandy, *Does God Change?*, pp. 20–25.

53 R.A. Norris rightly argues that Cyril's and Chalcedon's primary christological model is that of the subject-attribute model (though I disagree with the term 'model'). 'The Fathers of Chalcedon agreed with Cyril of Alexandria and with the long tradition preceding him that the subject of statements about Christ was simply the divine Word.' 'Toward a Contemporary Interpretation of the Chalcedonian *Definition*' in *Lux in Lumine*, p. 79. See also pp. 74–75, 77–79. Yet Norris interprets such an understanding not as a metaphysical statement about the ontological constitution of Christ, but merely as a linguistic or grammatical tool to govern Christological language. Commenting on the Chalcedonian definition, he states:

> What our historical analysis suggests is that the *Definition*'s terminology can best be treated as *second-order language*. Functionally considered, the nature-substance terminology reflects not a metaphysic but something more elementary: a view of the logical structure of the normal sentence. Hence it becomes intelligible in its Christological use when it is understood not as a direct account of the constitution of the Person of Christ, but as a definition of the normative form of any statement about Christ, without consideration of the metaphysical framework which such a direct statement must inevitably presuppose. Pp. 76–77. See also pp. 71–75.

> What Norris fails to appreciate is that Cyril's and Chalcedon's insistence that the divine and human attributes be predicated of the one and same subject of the Son is founded upon their metaphysical understanding of how Christ is ontologically constituted. The communication of idioms was the catalyst that gave rise to such an understanding (that Christ is the one person/subject of the Son *existing* as God and man), but such an understanding in turn provided the metaphysical warrant for the use of such language (that divine and human attributes must therefore be predicated of the one Son). Christological grammar and logic are dependent upon christological ontology. Getting the christological ontology right was at the heart of the Nestorian and Monophysite controversies and Chalcedon's response to them.

To call Mary *Theotokos* does not mean that she gave birth to God as God, 'no, it means that he [the Son] had fleshly birth because he issued from woman for us and for our salvation having united humanity to himself personally (ἐνώσας ἑαυτῷ καθ' ὑπόστασιν τὸ ἀνθπώπινον).' Equally, when it is said that the Son of God suffered and died, it is not meant 'that God the Word suffered blows, nail-piercings or other wounds in his own nature (the divine is impassible because it is incorporeal) but what is said is that since his own created body suffered these things he himself "suffered" for our sake, the point being that within the suffering body was the Impassible (ὁ ἀπαθὴς ἐν τῷ πάσχοντι σώματι). We interpret his dying along exactly comparable lines'.[54] In the twelfth of his infamous anathemas Cyril provocatively declared:

> Whoever does not acknowledge God's Word as having suffered in flesh, being crucified in flesh, tasted death in flesh and been made first-born from the dead because as God he is Life and life-giving shall be anathema.[55]

Here, at last, having put all the christological pieces in their proper place, we can discern the full import of the communication of idioms for the question of God suffering. First, who is it who truly experiences the authentic, genuine, and undiminished reality of human suffering? None other than the divine Son of God! He who is one in being (*homoousion*) with the Father. What is the manner in which he experiences the whole reality of human suffering? As man! It is actually the Son of God who lives a comprehensive human life, and so it is the Son who, as man, experiences all facets of this human life, including suffering and death.[56]

The Son is the exclusive active subject in what he experiences and in

---

R. Siddals agrees with Norris' interpretation of Cyril, but argues that underlying Cyril's use of the communication of idioms is a subject-accident christological model, that is, the Son being God actually possesses the divine attributes as part of his being, but acquires, within the Incarnation, the human attributes as 'virtual accidents'. Cyril 'treats humanity etc. as mysteriously inhering within the Word as an *accident* inheres within a subject.' 'Logic and Christology in Cyril of Alexandria', *Journal of Theological Studies* NS 38/2 (1987):351 and 356. However, for Cyril, the Son does not acquire the humanity as an 'accident', as if it were something that he substantially and existentially was not, but only a new characteristic attached to his divine nature. For Cyril the Son *is* God, and in the Incarnation, he actually *comes to be* man, and so equally *is* man. Being a man is what the Son of God *is*, and so the humanity is not a mere 'accident' added to his more substantial divine being. Thus the use of the communication of idioms is not a mere espousal of accidental predicates to the Son, but statements about his actual mode of being or manner of existing. See Siddals' entire argument, pp. 242–67, and her 'Oneness and Difference in the Christology of Cyril of Alexandria,' *Studia Patristica*, Vol. 18/1, ed. E.A. Livingstone (Kalamazoo: Cistercian Publications, 1985), pp. 207–11. For a similar criticism of Siddals, see B. Meunier, *Le Christ de Cyrille D'Alexandrie*, pp. 276–79.

54 *Ad Nestorium*, 2, 3 and 4. For Cyril 'all the sayings contained in the Gospels must be referred to single person (ἑνὶ προσώπῳ), to the one incarnate subject of the Word (ὑποστάσει μιᾷ τῇ τοῦ λόγου σεσαρκωμένη). *Ad Nestorium*, 3, 8. See *Ad Nestorium*, 3, 9–11.

55 *Ad Nestorium*, 3, Anathema 12.

56 Pope John Paul II stresses that the Son who is consubstantial with the Father is the same Son who truly suffers as man. See *Salvifici Doloris*, n. 17.

what he does, and the manner or mode under which he experiences and acts is as man.

But it is here that the critics will immediately protest that, after all is said and done, this is precisely the problem with Cyril and the subsequent christological tradition. It does not allow the human suffering to be experienced by the Son of God in his divinity, and so falls short of allowing God truly to suffer. Did not Cyril himself adamantly refuse to allow suffering to touch the divinity of the Son?

> He [the Son] suffered without suffering.... If we should say that through conversion or mutation of his own nature into flesh, it would be in all ways necessary for us even against our will to confess that the hidden and divine nature was passible. But if he has remained unchanged albeit he has been made man as we, and it be a property of the heavenly nature that it cannot suffer, and the passible body has become his own through the union: He suffers when the body suffers, in that it is said to be his own body, he remains impassible in that it is truly his property to be unable to suffer.[57]

Provoked as it is by the fundamentally erroneous conviction that God as God suffers, this criticism is postulated upon the false premise that the Son of God must suffer within his divine nature in order for the suffering to be theologically and soteriologically significant. However, because of these mistaken assumptions, this criticism actually ignores the inner christological and soteriological logic contained within the communication of idioms, and so neglects its true import.

The communication of idioms, as understood by Cyril and the authentic tradition, does wish to uphold that the fully divine Son of God did indeed suffer and die. This is precisely what Nestorius wanted to deny and Cyril wanted to vindicate. This is exactly why Cyril asserts that he who is impassible as God actually is passible as man. The Impasssible suffered.[58] To say, in accordance with Cyril and the Christian tradition,

---

57 *Scholia de Incarnatione Unigeniti*, 37. Cyril earlier states: 'He suffers humanly in the flesh as man, he remains impassible divinely as God.' *Ibid.*, 36. See also 33–35. In *Quod Unus Sit Christus*, he writes: 'So, even if he [the Son] is said to suffer in the flesh, even so he retains his impassibility insofar as he is understood as God.' (E.T., J. McGuckin, *On the Unity of Christ*, p. 117.

   References to Cyril speaking of the Son being impassible as God and passible as man could be multiplied, but especially see *Ad Succensum*, 2, 2 and his three defences of the twelve anathamas: *Explicatio pro Duodecim Capitibus Adversus Orientales Episcopos; Epistola ad Euoptium;* and *Explicatio Duodecim Capitum Ephesi Pronuniata.*

   The Papal International Theological Commission in its document *Theology, Christology, Anthropology* (1983) states:

   > According to the Council of Ephesus (cf. The letter of St. Cyril to Nestorius: *COD*, 3, 42), the Son made his own the sufferings to be inflicted on his human nature (*oikeiosis*). Attempts to reduce this proposition (and others like it in the tradition) to a simple *manner of speaking* do not sufficiently recognize its profound meaning. But the Christology of the Church does not allow us to affirm formally that Jesus Christ could suffer according to his divine nature (cf. *DS* 16, 166, 196 s., 284, 293 s., 300, 318, 358, 504, 635, 801, 852). II, B, 3.

58 I concur with J. Hallman that, as far as I can also ascertain, this exact phrase (ἀπαθός ἔπαθεν) is not found in Cyril's Greek. See 'The Seed of Fire: Suffering in the

that 'the Impassible suffers' is not, then, to be incoherent, but to state the very heart of the incarnational mystery. First, the term 'the Impassible' guarantees that it is actually God, in all his wholly transcendent otherness as God, who suffers, and not 'God' in some mitigated or semi-divine state. The fact that God does not lose his wholly transcendent impassible otherness in so suffering enhances to the extreme the import of the suffering, for it means that the Son who is incapable of suffering as the wholly other God is precisely the same one who is actually suffering as man. But it is at this juncture that those who advocate a suffering God miss the logic and so the heart of the communication of idioms. The communication of idioms, secondly, equally ensures that it is truly human suffering that the Son of God experiences and endures.[59]

Christology of Cyril of Alexandria and Nestorius of Constantinople,' *Journal of Early Christian Studies* 5:3 (1997):383, fn. 57. Nonetheless, it is Cyrilian in tone and meaning. Cyril did state 'that within the suffering body was the Impassible' (ἦwv γὰρ ὁ ἀπαθὴς ἐν τῷ πάσχοντι σώματι) (*Ad Nestorium*, 2, 5), and that 'he [*the Son*] was in the crucified body claiming the sufferings of his flesh as his own impassibly' (ἦν ἐν τῷ σταυρωθέντι σώματι, τὰ τῆς ἰδίας σαρκὸς ἀπαθῶς οἰκειούμενος πάθη). *Ad Nestorium*, 3, 6. He also stated that the Son 'suffered, as it were, impassibly' (πάθοι ἄν ἀπαθῶς), *De Recto Fide*, 27.

59 Many scholars miss the logic of Cyril's christology. They argue that Cyril, unlike Nestorius and the Antiochenes, showed little interest in the humanity of Jesus. Actually, the precise opposite is the case. Cyril was concerned with the divinity of the Son but primarily for incarnational reasons. He wished to assure that it was actually the divine Son who lived a full human life. This is why he adamantly defended the communication of idioms. Because Cyril gloried in the biblical drama of the Incarnation, that is, that it truly was the impassible Son of God who did actually suffer as man, he was not afraid to use language that appeared to be incoherent, yet was logically coherent in the light of christological ontology. See J.J. O'Keefe, 'Impassible Suffering? Divine Passion and Fifth-Century Christology,' *Theological Studies* 58 (1997):46–51, and B. Meunier, *Le Christ de Cyrille D'Alexandrie*, pp. 243–75.

A case in point is J. Hallman. Because Cyril insisted that the Son of God remains impassible as God and yet truly suffers as man, Hallman, similar to his criticisms of the Fathers that we noted in Chapter 5, accuses him of being illogical. See 'The Seed of Fire: Divine Suffering in the Christology of Cyril of Alexandria and Nestorius of Constantinople,' *Journal of Early Christian Studies* 5/3 (1997):384 and 391. I previously noted that Hallman consistently mistakes the logic of the Fathers, and here again he completely misses Cyril's logic. So captivated is he by the idea of God suffering as God, that he is incapable of grasping that what is truly at issue is God suffering as man in a human manner. Moreover, behind Hallman's accusation that Cyril is illogical lies the erroneous premise that the incarnational process is a compositional union of natures modeled after the soul–body union. This is how Hallman ultimately wants to conceive the incarnational union for it then would allow God to suffer as God. If Cyril did conceive the Incarnation in such a manner, then he would be illogical. However, since Cyril's understanding of the Incarnation is radically different – being a personal/existential understanding – he is not illogical at all. The person of the Son, within his existence as God, is impassible. Within his existence as man, the Son is passible. While not fully comprehensible, this is the rational, intelligible, and coherent logic that the mystery of the Incarnation demands.

In the course of the Monophysite controversy, Leontius of Jerusalem defended Cyril's and Chalcedon's understanding of the Incarnation and the communication of idioms. See K.P. Wesche, 'The Christology of Leontius of Jerusalem: Monophysite or Chalcedonian?', *St Vladimir's Theological Quarterly*, 31/1 (1987):65–95. Equally, as a result of the Theopaschite controversy, the Second Council of Constantinople (AD553) upheld Cyril's and Chalcedon's understanding of the communications of idioms by condemning those who denied that 'one of the Trinity suffered in the flesh.'

Even if one did allow the Son of God to suffer in his divine nature, this would negate the very thing one wanted to preserve and cultivate. For if the Son of God experienced suffering in his divine nature, he would no longer be experiencing human suffering in an authentic and genuine human manner, but instead he would be experiencing 'human suffering' in a divine manner which would then be neither genuinely nor authentically human. If the Son of God experienced suffering in his divine nature, then it would be God suffering as God *in a man*. But the Incarnation, which demands that the Son of God actually exists as a man and not just dwells in a man, equally demands that the Son of God suffers *as a man* and not just suffers divinely in a man. If one wishes to say in truth that the Son of God actually experienced and knew what it was like to be born, eat, sleep, cry, fear, grieve, groan, rejoice, suffer, die, and most of all, love *as a man*, and it seems this is precisely what one does want to say, then the experience and knowledge of being born, eating, sleeping, crying, fearing, grieving, groaning, rejoicing, suffering, dying, and again most of all, loving must be predicated of the Son of God solely and exclusively *as a man*.[60] Thus, to replace the phrase 'the Impassible suffers'

---

60 M. Dodds concurs when he states: 'Even if we were to suppose the impossible situation that in Christ God suffers as God in his divine nature, his suffering would then have little to do with us, for we do not suffer *as God*, but *as humans*.' He quotes then Aquinas:

> Compassion (*miseratio*) is said as a heart is sorrowful (*miserum*) at the miseries (*miseria*) of another. This may happen in two ways. One way is through understanding alone. And thus God, without any passion, understands our misery. For he knows our frame as it is said in *Ps.* 102:14. Another way is through experience. And thus Christ has experienced our misery, especially in [his] Passion. *Super ad Heb.* II, lect. 4 [§153].

And he then concludes: 'In order to affirm that Christ experienced *our* miseries and suffered as we do, we must maintain not that Christ suffered in his divinity, but that he, like us, suffered in his humanity.' *The Unchanging God of Love*, pp. 306–7. See also pp. 305–9. Similarly, see M. Gervais, 'Incarnation et Immuabilité Divine,' *Revue des Sciences Religieuses* 50 (1976):234–37; W. Hill, 'Does Divine Love Entail Suffering in God?' in *God and Temporality*, pp. 64–66; and Sebastian Moore, 'God Suffered,' *Downside Review* 27 (1959):122–40. On maintaining the distinction between what is divine and what is created within the Incarnation, see D. Burrell, 'Incarnation and Creation: The Hidden Dimension,' *Modern Theology* 12/2 (1996): 211–20.
     It is well known that Pope Leo in his famous *Tome* to Flavian, which was sanctioned by the Council of Chalcedon and held in high esteem by the Antiochenes, stated that some things Jesus did he did as God and some things Jesus did he did as man. This appears at first sight to negate what I have just espoused. Leo wished, in so saying, to uphold the two natures of Christ in opposition to Eutyches. While this is not the most apt form of expression (Leo may be great, but this, hopefully, was not the apex of his greatness), it must be remembered that he said this within in the context of noting how Jesus revealed himself. Some actions revealed that he is man – eating, grieving, suffering, etc. Some actions revealed that he was God – working miracles. This is true. What Leo failed to note is that the actions which revealed that Jesus was God were done as a man. If they were not done as a man, he would not have revealed that it is indeed the Son of God who is a man. While the bishops at Chalcedon may have proclaimed that 'Peter speaks through Leo!', it is only because Peter first spoke more clearly through Cyril and Leo was found, after much debate, to be in agreement with him, that Leo's *Tome* was found acceptable. On such a central dogmatic issue of the faith, that Leo's *Tome* was found acceptable is hardly surprising for, if what Cyril said was true, Leo, being the Pope, would never have held an opposing view, even if his concerns were somewhat different and his form of expression was not the most apt.

with 'the Passible suffers' immediately purges the suffering of all incarnational significance. The very reading of the phrase rings hollow.

It may be helpful to illustrate this understanding of the communication of idioms with an example. Allow me to use an example that I pose to my students, which has come to be known in some circles as 'Dr Weinandy's carrot example.'

Jesus goes to Martha's, Mary's, and Lazarus' home for dinner. Martha serves as a starter (to use the English term) raw carrots with garlic dip (a yet to be discovered American culinary invention). Jesus ate the carrots. Who was it who ate the carrots? Who was the acting subject? It was the Son of God who ate the carrots. Was he eating the carrots as God or as man? Obviously, he was eating the carrots as man. God as God cannot eat carrots for he does not have teeth, a mouth, a stomach, etc. Lazarus also ate the carrots, but unfortunately he ate a rotten carrot and died of food poisoning. Four days later Jesus returned and raised Lazarus from the dead. Who was it who raised Lazarus from the dead? It was the Son of God who raised Lazarus from the dead. But did he raise Lazarus from the dead as God or as man? At this juncture there is silence among the students. Inevitably the more pious students first break the silence by saying that Jesus raised Lazarus from the dead 'as God.' I remain silent. Then some brave soul, usually a girl, will hesitantly whisper, almost inaudibly, 'as man.' That is precisely the correct answer. Within the Incarnation the Son of God never does anything as God. If he did, he would be acting as God *in a man*. This the Incarnation will never permit. All that Jesus did as the Son of God was done *as a man* – whether it was eating carrots or raising someone from the dead. He may have raised Lazarus from the dead by his divine power or, better, by the power of the Holy Spirit, but it was, nonetheless, as man that he did so. Similarly, the Son of God did not suffer as God in a man, for to do so would mean that he was not a man. The Son of God suffered as a man.

Nonetheless, if the Son of God suffers as man, why does this suffering not affect his divinity given that the Son of God is equally God? Here we enter the heart of the mystery. While the mystery of the Incarnation, by its very nature, remains, the answer lies in the fact that as God the Son is not deprived of any good which would cause him to suffer as God. If the Son of God, as God, were deprived of some good which would cause him to suffer as God, it would mean, as I argued in previous chapters, that he is actually no longer God. Strange as it may seem, but not paradoxically, one must maintain the unchangeable impassibility of the Son of God as God in order to guarantee that it is actually the divine Son of God, one in being with the Father, who truly suffers as man. As man the divine Son of God was deprived, as are we, of human goods which did cause him, like us, to suffer.

McGuckin provides an excellent analysis of Cyril's thought and Leo's *Tome* in relationship to the Creed of Chalcedon. See *St Cyril of Alexandria*, pp. 233–40. For a similar comparison between Cyril's christology and that of the Formula of Reunion, see G. Gould, 'Cyril of Alexandria and the Formula of Reunion,' *Downside Review* 106 (1988):235–52.

This is the marvellous truth of the Incarnation. God from all eternity may have known, within his divine knowledge, what it is like for human beings to suffer and die, and he may have known this perfectly and comprehensively. But until the Son of God actually became man and existed as a man, God, who is impassible in himself, never experienced and knew suffering and death as man *in a human manner*. In an unqualified manner one can say that, as man, the Son of God had experiences he never had before because he never existed as man before – not the least of which are suffering and death. This is what humankind is crying out to hear, not that God experiences, in a divine manner, our anguish and suffering in the midst of a sinful and depraved world, but that he actually experienced and knew first hand, as one of us – as a man – human anguish and suffering within a sinful and depraved world.

This is what a proper understanding of the Incarnation requires and affirms, and this is what the communication of idioms so remarkably, clearly, and even scandalously safeguards, advocates, and confesses. The eternal, almighty, all-perfect, unchangeable, and impassible divine Son, he who is equal to the Father in all ways, actually experienced, as a weak human being, the full reality of human suffering and death. What was an infamy to the Docetists, to Arius, and to Nestorius was for Cyril and the subsequent Christian tradition the glory and grandeur of the gospel. Even among those who advocate a suffering God, the Incarnation is still a scandal, for, while with the best of intentions, having locked suffering within God's divine nature, they have, in so doing, locked God out of human suffering.

I hope that this rather lengthy exposition of the Incarnation and the communication of idioms has clarified, but not dissolved, the mystery of each, and in so doing intensified their significance with regard to the question of God's suffering. However, I have not finished. I still want to enhance, in a threefold manner, the suffering of the Son of God as man.

The Son's *Esse Personale*

The first way that I wish to enhance the communication of idioms, and so its significance, is to specify the philosophical nature of the relationship between the Son of God and his humanity. We have seen thus far that Cyril grasped and Chalcedon sanctioned a personal/existential understanding of the Incarnation. The incarnational 'becoming' is not the compositional union of natures which would demand change and mutation within both the divinity and the humanity, but rather the person of the Son taking on a new mode of existence as man. Such an understanding allows the Son to remain immutable as God in becoming man so as to ensure that it is truly God, in the fullness of his divinity, who is man, and equally ensures that the humanity is not changed, thus safeguarding that it is truly man that the Son of God is. This personal/existential conception provides the christological warrant for the communication of idioms. All the divine and human attributes can properly be predicated of one and same person, the Son, for he exists personally as God and as man. This personal/existential conception contains within it a singular kind of relationship (for the Incarnation is a singular event) between the person of the Son and his humanity, and though Cyril and Chalcedon did not explicitly treat this philosophical issue, Aquinas did.

When examining Aquinas' understanding of the trinity of persons as subsistent relations in act and their one nature as *ipsum esse*, I stressed that both concepts connote pure actuality – *actus purus*. I also argued that because the trinity of persons are subsistent relations fully in act, in harmony with their one nature being fully in act, they require no mediating actions in order to relate something to themselves, but have the singular ability to relate something to themselves as they are in themselves in an immediate, dynamic, intimate, and enduring manner. Being subsistent relations fully in act, the persons of the Trinity need not surmount or actualize any relational potential within themselves in order to form relations. They are utterly relational for they simply are relations.

The act of creation, we saw, exemplifies this. The persons of the Trinity, in the act of creation, immediately, dynamically, intimately, and enduringly relate creation to themselves and in so doing creation comes to be and continues to exist. This type of relationship is referred to as a mixed relationship for it specifies a relationship between two different ontological orders whereby the logical term is actually related to the real term because the real term is related to the logical term as it actually is. In the act of creation the trinity of persons (the logical term) are actually related to creatures (the real term) for the creatures only come to be and continue to exist by being related to the persons of the trinity as they are.

For Aquinas, the Incarnation also establishes a mixed relation.[61] In the act of 'becoming man' the humanity is not related to the Son by some mediating action on the part of the Son, that is, the Son performs no specific action, different from the act that he is as Son, which would relate the humanity to himself. If the act of 'becoming man' were through some mediating act on the part of the Son, that very act would not only entail a change in the Son in becoming man, but also, and more importantly here, would diminish the relationship between the person of the Son and his humanity. The very mediatory character of the action, while entailing a relationship, keeps the humanity from actually being related to the Son as the Son actually exists.[62] In contrast, Aquinas argued that the incarnational act is precisely the Son relating the humanity to his very person as Son, 'to the personal being (*ad esse personale*) of the

---

61 In the following I will be both summarizing and developing what I wrote in *Does God Change?*, pp. 82–100, 184–86.

62 Human beings relate to one another through mediating acts – words, hugs, kisses. While these actions bring about actual relations, the very fact that they are mediating acts means that human beings are never fully in communion with one another as they are in themselves. For example, if two people intensely love one another, their words and acts of love never fully express the whole of their love for the acts, being mediatory, do not fully embody or express the entirety of the love.

Logos'.[63] Because the Son subsists, in his *esse personale*, as a relation fully in act, he is able to relate the humanity to himself as he is. Here there is no mediatory action involved which would hinder and diminish the relationship. Rather, in so conceiving the incarnational relationship, Aquinas first guarantees that it is truly the Son of God who is man for the Son is not changed in becoming man, and can actually only establish such a relationship because he is immutably a subsistent relation fully in act. This is why Aquinas refers to the Son as the logical term of the relationship. But second, since the Son, as the logical term, is not changed in the relationship, such a relational conception specifies the closeness and depth of the humanity's relation to the Son. The humanity, as the real term of the incarnational relationship, is so closely related to the Son as the Son is in his very *esse personale* that the Son actually comes to exist as a man. The relationship does not then denote even a change in the humanity which might render it less than fully human, but rather specifies that the humanity comes into existence and is united to the person of the Son in the most immediate and utterly intimate manner, so immediate and intimate that it as man that the Son now exists.

In conceiving the incarnational relationship in such a manner, Aquinas not only gives greater philosophical precision to the personal/ existential understanding of the Incarnation, he equally provides, although he does not elucidate this, a more intense perception to the communication of idioms. Because the humanity is united to the very person of the Son, as the Son exists as God in his *esse personale*, we see that it is truly the divine Son, in the very *esse personale* which defines him as the Son, who actually experiences the full reality of being human. There is no mediatory action between the Son and his humanity which would diminish or abridge the Son's experience as man. The Son, precisely as he exists divinely as Son, is the exclusive experiencing and active subject within his humanity. Thus, because the humanity is united to the very *esse personale* of the Son so as to allow the Son to exist as an authentic man, it can be said in truth that the Son, at the very heart of what defines him as Son – his own distinctive divine *esse personale* – was born, rejoiced, grieved, suffered, and died.[64]

---

63 *ST*, III, 8, 5, ad 3. Aquinas also states: 'The grace of union [that is, the created relational effect within the humanity] is the personal being itself (*ipsum esse personale*) that is given gratis from above to the human nature in the person of the Son.' *ST*, III, 6, 6.

  While I would disagree with some of his conclusions, R. Cross does demonstrate that Aquinas did not conceive the Incarnation as a union of natures, but as the humanity being united to 'the person' of the Son. See 'Aquinas on Nature, Hypostasis, and the Metaphysics of the Incarnation,' *The Thomist* 60/2 (1996):171–202.

64 Aquinas states:

  Every change or passion, furthermore, proper to one's body can be ascribed to him whose body it is. . . . So, if the body of Peter is wounded, scourged, or dies, it can be said that Peter is wounded, scourged, or dies. But the body of that man is the body of the Word of God. Therefore, every suffering that took place in the body of that man can be ascribed to the Word of God. So it is right to say that the Word of God – and God – suffered, was crucified, died, and was buried. *SCG*, IV, 34, 11.

  See also *SCG*, IV, 34, 29; 39, 2, and *ST*, III, 14–15; 16, 4–5.

  While it is completely contrary to the perceived theological wisdom of the age, what we must conclude from the above is that the Son of God is only truly possible as man

The Human 'I' of Jesus

Because the humanity is ontologically related to the very *esse personale* of the Son so as to allow the Son actually to exist as man, the second way that I wish to enhance the communication of idioms is by proposing that such a union entitles the Son, as man, to possess an authentic human 'I'. While such a proposal may sound Nestorian, I believe it is firmly founded within Cyril's, Chalcedon's, and Aquinas' personal/existential understanding of the Incarnation.[65]

On the 'personal' side of this equation, traditional Thomistic christology, in accordance with Cyril's and Chalcedon's insistence that Christ is one person (*prosopon* or *hypostasis*), has maintained that there is only one 'I' corresponding to the one divine person of the Son. It correctly perceived that if the 'I' is not identified as the person of the Son, there would be no true incarnation. Jesus would just be another man. However, what the tradition has not clearly distinguished is the identity (the *prosopon* or *hypostasis* – the 'who') of the one 'I' and the existential mode under which the one 'I' exists.

Cyril argued and Chalcedon demanded that the identity of Jesus be that of the divine Son. They employed the terms *prosopon* and *hypostasis* to designate Jesus' ontological identity, who he is. To the question: *Who is the man Jesus?* The answer must be that *he is the Son of God*. The Son is the subject, as the communication of idioms illustrates and requires. Thus, on the 'personal' side of the personal/existential equation, the Son is identified as the person or subject (the *prosopon* or *hypostasis*).

Now the whole point in asserting that Jesus' identity (who he is) is that of the Son is to guarantee that it is as man that the Son is so identified. If one asked: Under what manner or mode of existence is Jesus identified as the Son? The answer must be: as man. In this sense, from the 'existential' side of the equation, the Son has assumed a human identity. It is within his existence as man that the Son comes to be identified as the divine Son. If the Son is man and has identified himself as a man, then, it seems to me, that he exists, as incarnate, totally within the parameters or boundaries of all that is human. Thus the Son of God not only has a human body, soul, intellect, will, and emotions, etc., but equally he also has an integral human 'I,' a psychological centre within which all of these are expressed and experienced. The human 'I' of Jesus is the human psychological self-consciousness of the divine Son. He thought, spoke, and acted as well as underwent all his experiences from within the limits of his human 'I.' When Jesus said 'I,' it was truly the Son of God saying 'I' in a fully authentic

---

because he is immutable as God. The immutability of God, far from being a stumbling block to the Incarnation, is actually its prolegomenon. It is only because the Son is able to remain immutably himself, as a subsistent relation fully in act, that he is able to come to exist as man, and thus be truly passible as man. For a fuller discussion of this point, see Weinandy, *Does God Change?*, pp. 96–100, 184–90.

65 I will be summarizing and developing here what I wrote in *In the Likeness of Sinful Flesh*, pp. 12–13; *The Father's Spirit of Sonship*, pp. 120–2, and more extensively in 'The Human "I" of Jesus,' *The Irish Theological Quarterly* 62/4 (1996/97):259–68.
   This last article gives a rather full bibliography with some critique of recent, primarily Catholic, authors on this topic.

human manner. What the Incarnation demands is that the identity (the who
– the *prosopon* or *hypostasis*) of this human 'I' be truly that of the divine Son,
but it is, nonetheless, within that human 'I' that the Son is so identified.[66]

In contrast then to the later tradition, but nonetheless in keeping with
Cyril, Chalcedon, and Aquinas, I would argue that Jesus does have one
'I', but it is the human 'I' of the Son. The identity of the Son and of the
human 'I' are, as Chalcedon insists, one and the same.[67]

---

66 The similarity and difference between Jesus and other human beings can be illustrated
in that when, for example, a human being says 'I am John Smith' that human 'I' is identifying a human person who is John Smith – that is *who* this human person is. Jesus too
speaks with a human 'I', but the identity of this human 'I' is not that of a human person
(a human 'who'), but that of the Son of God (a divine 'who').

A couple of scriptural illustrations may be helpful as well. Jesus said: 'I have come
not to abolish the Law and the prophets, but to fulfil them' (Mt 5:17). Who is it who is
saying this? The Son. The Son is the subject of the 'I'. But, while the subject or identity
of the 'I' is divine, the 'I' itself is human for the Son is saying 'I' as a man. If the Son were
saying 'I' in a divine manner, then it would be the Son, as God, speaking *in a man* and
not *as a man*. In this particular verse it would then mean that the Son came to fulfil the
Law and the prophets *as God* in a man rather than fulfilling them *as a man*.

Even those passages within the Gospel of John, which stress the divine identity of
Jesus, illustrate this. For example, Jesus said: 'Truly, truly, I say to you, before Abraham
was, I am' (Jn 8:58). While the 'I am' reveals Jesus' divine identity, that 'I am' was
conceived within a human mind and formed with human words and so was spoken
from within a human self-consciousness, within the parameters of a human 'I.' Jesus is
revealing the identity of his human 'I.' The 'I' of the 'I am' is a human 'I,' but in saying
'I am' Jesus is identifying his human 'I' as that of the eternal 'I am' of Son of God. As
Jesus, the Son of God becomes conscious of himself as the divine Son within his human
'I.' It is as a man that the Son becomes self-consciously aware of his divine identity, and
so can say – with(in) a human 'I' as a man – 'I am the Son of God.'

67 The distinctiveness of my position might be seen in comparison with J. Galot's. I
reproduce here a partial footnote from 'The Human "I" of Jesus' (fn. 15, pp. 267–8).

While J. Galot proposed a position that is very similar to the present thesis, yet he
would deny that Jesus possesses a human 'I'. He writes in *Who is Christ?*:

> Does Jesus possess a human 'I'? There can be no doubt that Jesus possesses an 'I'
> perceived in a human way by his human consciousness. But must this 'I' necess-
> arily be a human 'I'? Are we obliged to admit that there are two 'I's' in Christ, one
> divine and the other human, or must we say, on the contrary, that there is in him
> only the one identical 'I' of the Son of God? P. 320.

From his examination of scripture, he concludes:

> Obviously, we are not speaking of a divine 'I' that manifests itself as such in its
> pure state, but of a divine 'I' in a human context, of an 'I' that asserts itself within
> a human consciousness and in human language. It is the divine 'I' of a man who
> is living a genuinely human life. P. 321–22.

Or again:

> The autonomy of Jesus' human psychology likewise accounts for the fact that his
> divine 'I' manifests itself only in an integrally human consciousness. We have
> already noted that this 'I' did not reveal itself in its pure state. It always appeared
> within a human consciousness, and its expression was entirely human. The reason
> certain scholars have tended to speak of a human 'I' in Christ may stem from their
> desire to emphasise this fact. However, while the 'I' of Christ asserted itself with
> a profoundly human psychology, it remained the divine 'I' of the Son. P. 334.

The obvious reason Galot wishes to maintain that the 'I' of Jesus is divine is to
guarantee the same identity of the 'I' and of the person of the Son. Jesus cannot possess
two 'I's.' This identity I too wish to maintain. I agree that Jesus cannot possess two 'I's'.
However, it is precisely because it is the divine 'I' not in its 'pure state', but under

Now the significance of all this, for our present discussion, is that, while it is truly the Son who is the active subject of all experiences and actions, he is the active subject within or, better, as a genuine and authentic human 'I.' Thus, when the Son of God rejoices, grieves, suffers, and dies, he does so from within his human self-conscious 'I.' When Jesus groans within himself, it is the Son of God groaning within an authentic human self-consciousness. As a genuine human 'I' the Son of God can say: 'I am groaning.' When Jesus cries in anguish: 'I thirst,' it is the Son of God who thirsts, but he is truly experiencing that anguish of thirst within his own human 'I.' Most of all when Jesus cries out: 'My God, my God, why have you forsaken me!' It is within his human self-consciousness, within the anguish of his own human 'I,' that the Son of God experiences the total abandonment of his loving Father. The human 'I,' in that it is identified as the human 'I' of the divine Son, ensures both the total authenticity of the human experiences and that it is truly the Son who experiences them. Moreover, when we attribute all human experiences, especially suffering and death, to the Son, in accordance with the communication of idioms, we are predicating them of the one Son, but we are doing so as he experienced them within his own authentic human 'I,' and so enhancing the depth and reality of such predication.

In the Likeness of Sinful Flesh

The third way I wish to enhance the communication of idioms is to state that in the Incarnation the Son of God did not assume some generic humanity, but our own sinful humanity.[68] 'The Word became flesh

---

'human conditions' that I argue that it is therefore more correct to state that it is the human 'I' of a divine person, of the Son. I wish to make a distinction between the subject (the who) of the 'I' and the manner of the 'I's' (the who's) expression. The identity of the 'I' (the who) is the same, that of the Son, but the manner of the subject's identity is as man, and therefore the 'I' is the human 'I' of a divine subject or person.

See also Galot's *La Conscience de Jésus* (Paris: Duculot-Lethielleux, 1971).

R. Williams may be suggesting something similar to what I propose here. See '"Person" and "Personality" in Christology,' *Downside Review* 94 (1976):253–60.

68 My whole book *In the Likeness of Sinful Flesh* is devoted to defending and explicating the christological and soteriological significance of this thesis. I argue for this position firstly from an historical (patristic, medieval, and contemporary authors) and theological basis, and secondly, and primarily, from scripture. My guiding principle throughout was the patristic dictum that 'what is not assumed is not saved,' and thus only if the Son assumes our fallen nature, does he save it.

T.F. Torrance argues in a similar fashion:

The Incarnation is to be understood as the coming of God to take upon himself our fallen human nature, our actual human existence laden with sin and guilt, our humanity diseased in mind and soul in its estrangement or alienation from the Creator. This is the doctrine found everywhere in the early Church in the first five centuries, expressed again and again in the terms that the whole man had to be assumed by Christ if the whole man was to be saved, that the unassumed is unhealed, or that what God has not taken up in Christ is not saved. *The Mediation of Christ* (Edinburgh: T & T Clark, 1992), p. 39. See also pp. 40–42.

In The Fourth Constantinople Lecture, *The Humanity of Christ* (London: Anglican and

(σάρξ)' (Jn 1:14), and thus shared in all of our human weakness. The
Father sent 'his own Son in the likeness of sinful flesh' (Rom. 8:3), and he
even 'made him to be sin who knew no sin' (1 Cor. 5:21).[69] While he never
sinned personally (see Heb. 4:15, 1 Pet. 2:22, Jn 8:46, 1 Jn 3:5), and while
he did not have an inner propensity to sin (concupiscence), yet his
humanity was of the race of fallen Adam. Being of Adam's fallen race,
Tertullian aptly stated that he bore 'the birthmark of sin,' and thus, by
necessity, he experienced the effects of having assumed such a
humanity.[70] Like all human beings living within the fallen human
condition, the Son of God, as man, truly experienced hunger and thirst,
sickness and sorrow, temptation and harassment by Satan; being hated
and despised, he experienced fear and loneliness; on the cross he even
underwent death and separation from God.

While this notion lay dormant within the church's theological
tradition, it is, I believe, absolutely essential for a complete understanding of the Incarnation and for founding, as we will see shortly, an
adequate and comprehensive soteriology. Here I only want to emphasize
that by assuming an Adamic 'sinful humanity,' the Son did not quarantine himself from our sinful and suffering plight, but instead immersed
himself within it. This again intensifies the significance of the communication of idioms, for the human experiences of the Son were neither
anaesthetized by his divinity nor desensitized by some generic or
pedigreed humanity which differed from our own. Rather, this fallen
humanity was united immediately and intimately to the Son as he exists
personally as God, in his *esse personale*. Moreover then, his human 'I' was
the human 'I' of a humanity contaminated by our sinful condition. The
Son of God, within the unmediated immediacy of his own human 'I,'

Eastern Churches Association, 1985), Bishop K. Ware, arguing from the same premise
that what is not assumed is not saved, also maintains:

> Surely the Saviour's solidarity with the human race will be fatally incomplete if he
> is not identified with us in our present fallen situation. What is required is not
> merely an exterior, juridical imputation of our guilt to Christ, but something far
> deeper and more costly: an inner, organic sharing on his part in all our brokenness.
> P. 4.

For other contemporary authors who argue for a similar position, see K. Barth,
Church Dogmatics, I/2, pp. 151–58; J.D.G. Dunn, 'Paul's Understanding of the Death of
Jesus as Sacrifice' in *Sacrifice and Redemption: Durham Essays in Theology*, ed. S.W. Sykes
(Cambridge: Cambridge University Press, 1991), pp. 35–40; H.U. von Balthasar,
Mysterium Paschale (Edinburgh: T & T Clark, 1990), pp. 11–48, and *Theo-Drama IV: The
Action*, pp. 247–54, 267–73.

69 I argue in my book *In the Likeness of Sinful Flesh* that Paul used the term 'likeness'
(ὁμοιώματι) not to emphasize the dissimilarity of the Son from us, as if he merely took
on the appearance or guise of sinful flesh, but rather to emphasize his similarity to us.
The Son assumed the reality of sinful flesh and so actually and visibly bore our likeness.
I similarly argue that 'made to be sin' means that the Son assumed both our sinful
condition in the Incarnation and, in his death, the full weight of our sin and condemnation. See pp. 78–82.

70 *De Carne Christi*, 16, 25. See the whole of 16 where Tertullian argues that the Son
assumed a real and not a phantasmal humanity; that he assumed a humanity which
truly bore the likeness to sinful flesh; and yet within this 'sinful humanity' he did not
sin.

experienced the totality of suffering entailed in being affiliated with the fallen race of Adam.

Conclusion

Throughout this study I have attempted to be faithful to the biblical notion of God and of his relation to the created order. To do so I have argued that God is the Wholly Other who relates to and acts within the created order as the Wholly Other without losing his total otherness in so doing. For God to lose his complete otherness in relating to and acting within the created order would mean that it is no longer the Wholly Other who is so relating and acting, but some mitigated form of his divine being.

In this chapter we have discerned that this biblical notion of God and of his relation to the created order finds its foremost expression in the Incarnation. The Son of God, in the fulness of his divinity, has actually come to exist as an authentic man without losing the fulness of his divinity in so doing. He who is unconditionally transcendent as God is the very same one who, in his unconditional transcendence, is unconditionally immanent as man.

Moreover, this in turn guarantees that the Son, in all his transcendent otherness, is the sole acting and experiencing subject as man. Within the immanent created order of time and history, the Son of God lives a fully and unqualifiedly human life, and he does so as he exists as God. If the Son of God, even in the slightest manner, 'lost' some of his divinity in so living a full human life, then it would no longer be the divine Son who lived a full human life. Nor must the Son of God, in even the slightest manner, 'lose' the fulness of human life, for then it would no longer be an authentic human life that the Son of God lived. In accordance with our three incarnational truths: He who is truly God truly is truly man. This is what the Incarnation demands and what the communication of idioms so candidly and scandalously expresses – the Impassible suffers!

9

The Redemptive Suffering
of Christ

In the previous chapter I argued that a proper conception of the Incarnation mandates that the divine Son of God truly suffers as man. I equally stressed that confining the suffering to his human state, far from limiting the significance of the Son's suffering, actually enhances it. He truly experienced the full brunt of human suffering in an authentic human manner and not in some mitigated divine manner. However, it is far from sufficient merely to demonstrate that the Son of God lived as man and so suffered.

Many contemporary theologians, who posit suffering within God's divine nature, give the impression that once they have demonstrated this, they have done all that is required and significant. The soteriological import of divine suffering remains barren. It does not achieve any end other than to register that God does indeed suffer in solidarity with humankind, and so comfort can be taken from this. Why we should be comforted by a suffering God remains unclear, especially if he, like us, can now do little to alleviate it and is rendered helpless in vanquishing its actual causes.

Because I believe that Jesus and his redemptive work is the Father's full and decisive response to human suffering and its causes, this chapter has three inter-related ends: 1) While this is not the setting to articulate a full systematic soteriology, yet I want in this chapter to present what I consider to be some important and essential elements of Jesus' redemptive work. In so doing I wish to be faithful to the biblical proclamation, and not arbitrarily construct a soteriology of my own philosophical making. Therefore, what is said here will be set out, primarily, but not exclusively, in scriptural terms and concepts.[1] It is only in the light of this

---

1 In primarily employing biblical terms and concepts, I am attempting to avoid presenting some specific 'model' or 'theory' of salvation. While there are various aspects or elements to Christ's redemptive work, no one salvific model or theory can adequately express the whole of this work. Only the unity of the various biblical aspects can account for an adequate understanding of Jesus' saving work. I do not wish then that what I propose here be seen as some theory or model. Equally, I am trying to avoid the classifications that are normally attached to such theories or models, such as; 'The Satisfaction Theory,' 'The Ransom Model,' 'The *Christus Victor* Model,' 'The Exemplar Model,' or 'The Penal Substitution Theory.' While such classifications have some legitimacy and value, because of the history and controversy surrounding them, I believe

biblical soteriology that the Christian view of suffering can be properly discerned and appreciated. **2)** I see Jesus' passion, death, and resurrection as one salvific event that gave rise to Pentecost. Thus, I especially wish to discern the causal soteriological connections between these various salvific aspects, and why they together allow for the outpouring of the Holy Spirit.[2] I also want to articulate the effects that this outpouring has upon those who become Christians, for it is these effects that fashion the Christian perspective on human suffering. **3)** In the light of the above, I am simply attempting to demonstrate that the outpouring of the Spirit established a new salvific order, one that was not previously present or available. While God's action within the Old Testament era provided the

---

they would only confuse what I am attempting to do here. Thus, I will not attempt any full critique of the various theories or models, but limit myself to quoting authors who, on the whole, support a specific point I wish to make. Here I merely wish to give authentic weight to various elements that make up the biblical account of salvation.

For modern studies of the various soteriological theories and models that have been proposed within Christian theology, see G. Aulén, *Christus Victor* (London: SPCK, 1931); R. Cessario, *The Godly Image: Christ and Salvation in Catholic Thought from Anselm to Aquinas* (Petersham: St Bede's Publications, 1990); R. Culpepper, *Interpreting the Atonement* (Grand Rapids: Eerdmans, 1966); F.W. Dillistone, *The Christian Understanding of the Atonement* (London: James Nisbet, 1968); P. Fiddes, *Past Event and Present Salvation: The Christian Idea of Atonement* (London: Darton, Longman & Todd, 1989); J. McIntyre, *The Shape of Soteriology* (Edinburgh: T & T Clark, 1992); L. Richard, *The Mystery of Redemption* (Baltimore: Helicon, 1965); J. Rivière, *The Doctrine of the Atonement: A Historical Essay* (London: Kegan Paul, 1909); H.E.W. Turner, *The Patristic Doctrine of Redemption* (London: Mowbray, 1952).

While I wish to employ scriptural terms and concepts with clarity and with some precision, for the most part I am not able, in this study, to give a detailed exegesis of the various passages noting the diverse interpretations and the exegetical problems associated with them. Likewise, I cannot give detailed accounts of the biblical and extra-biblical use of such concepts as: ransom, sacrifice, expiation, and propitiation. Nonetheless, I hope that what I have to say will be in accord with genuine scholarship.

Besides the standard biblical dictionaries, for a good exposition of the biblical terms and concepts related to salvation, see S. Lyonnet and L. Sabourin, *Sin, Redemption, and Sacrifice: A Biblical and Patristic Study* (Rome: Biblical Institute Press, 1970). See also S.B. Clark, *Redeemer* (Ann Arbor: Servant Publications, 1992); M. Hengel, *The Atonement: A Study of the Origin of the Doctrine in the New Testament* (London: SCM, 1981), *The Cross of the Son* (London: SCM, 1986); D.R. Jones, 'Sacrifice and Holiness' in *Sacrifice and Redemption*, pp. 9–21; V. Taylor, *Forgiveness and Reconciliation: A Study in New Testament Theology* (London: Macmillan, 1946), *The Atonement in New Testament Teaching* (London: Epworth, 1958), *Jesus and His Sacrifice* (London: Macmillan, 1959); F. Young, *Sacrifice and the Death of Christ* (London: SCM, 1983).

2 The term 'because,' in the sense of 'being the cause of' or 'bringing about an effect' will be an important concept in this chapter.

M. Winter comments that many modern theologians, such as K. Barth, J.P. Galvin, H.E.W. Turner, D.M. Baillie, F.W. Dillistone, C. Gunton, and M. Hengel, are in agreement that the New Testament 'does not tell us how the atonement was effected, yet they offer no explanation of it themselves to compensate for that omission. Ironically, it is precisely this explanation which is so badly needed by the modern reader, who finds the violent death of Jesus so repugnant.' *The Atonement* (London: Geoffrey Chapman, 1995), p. 30. See pp. 30–37.

I hope to show that the New Testament does offer an account of the causal workings and connections of Jesus' passion, death, and resurrection. Winter himself limits the efficacy of Jesus' death to his role as an intercessor, obtaining our forgiveness and new life with God. While this may be true, it is hardly a full and adequate expression of the rich biblical proclamation.

historical and theological foundation for Jesus' redemptive work, and even anticipated what he himself would accomplish, yet Jesus and his redemptive work radically altered, in the outpouring of the Spirit, humankind's salvific standing. Thus, human suffering can only be properly interpreted and understood from within this new salvific context. Thus, the ultimate goal of this chapter is to provide the soteriological prolegomenon for examining the Christian view of human suffering. This I will do in the following chapter.

The Work of the Cross

We saw in the previous chapter that for the Son of God to become man means that it was actually the person of the Son (in his *esse personale*) who was truly the experiencing and acting subject within his human existence as man. The subjective identity of the man Jesus, *who* this man was, was God the Son. Moreover, the Son, as the sole subject, actually experienced the whole of human life and acted in a fully human manner from within the confines of his own human 'I.' This assures the authenticity of his human experience and action. Last, I argued that the Son did not assume some generic, antiseptic, or immunized humanity, which would quarantine him from our sinful human history and condition, but rather he assumed a humanity which bore the birthmark of sinful Adam, and so entered into our human history as one like ourselves.

All of the above must now be taken to the event of the cross so as to discern the soteriological significance of Jesus' death. I now want to argue that on the cross the Son of God as man simultaneously performed three actions: 1) He assumed our condemnation. 2) He offered himself as an atoning sacrifice to the Father on our behalf. 3) He put to death our sinful humanity.[3]

Assuming Our Condemnation
Sin, it must be remembered, is contrary and hostile to all that is good, holy, and loving, and so is an affront to the perfectly good, holy, and loving God. As such the unredeemed (or unrepentant) sinner reaps sin's intrinsic and inevitable consequence – separation from God. God and sin cannot abide with one another. Biblically, physical death gives expression to the deeper death of having been separated from the God of life.

However, while sin had made humankind God's enemies, the Father's response to sin was not that of allowing humankind to suffer its just fate. Rather, the Father's salvific goal reconfirms his plan first inaugurated at the dawn of creation. He desires that we share fully in the eternal life of the Trinity (see Eph. 1:3–14). Being conformed into the likeness of his Son through the Holy Spirit, the Father becomes our Father. The Trinity then is the source and goal both of creation and redemption. Thus, in love, the

---

3 Jesus may have performed more than three actions through his death on the cross, nonetheless, here I will be limiting my discussion to these three. While most of what I will be saying here is new, it should be noted that I am developing some of the ideas that I discussed in my book, *In the Likeness of Sinful Flesh*.

Father sent his Son into the world so that we might not perish in our condemnation, but have eternal life with him (see Jn 3:16; 1 Jn 4:9).[4] This is the point of our soteriological departure.

First then, in this 'sending' the Son assumed not only our sin-marred humanity, but also, in his death, the full weight of its condemnation. The Father sent 'his own Son in the likeness of sinful flesh, and to deal with sin, he condemned sin in the flesh' (Rom. 8:3). The cross actualized the Father's condemnation of our sinful flesh, for sin itself, 'when it is fully grown, gives birth to death' (James 1:15). 'The wages of sin is death' (Rom. 6:23; see Gen. 2:17). Even though Jesus never personally sinned (see Heb. 4:15, 1 Pet. 2:22, Jn 8:46, 1 Jn 3:5), yet the Father, for our sake, 'made him to be sin who knew no sin' (2 Cor. 5:21). This he did both in sending the Son in the likeness of sinful flesh and in having him mount the cross upon which sin was condemned. Thus the Incarnation leads directly to the cross, for the cross expresses the Son's complete solidarity with our sinful condition and its condemnation.[5] The Son of God was truly born under the law, and thus under its curse (see Gal. 4:4).

This condemnation, due to sin, is nothing less than being separated from God. In the garden of Gethsemane, it was this cup of condemnation that the Son, in agony, saw set before him in its full horror, and ardently implored the Father to remove (see Mt 26:36–46; Mk 14:32–42; Lk 22:39–46; Jn 12:27; Heb. 5:7–9). Thus, the Son's human cry from the cross – 'My God, my God, why have you abandoned me?' (Mt 27:46) – was no mere charade, but the authentic lamentation of one who was suffering the wages of humankind's sin. The Son of God truly tasted death for us, not just the suffering of physical death, but the deeper 'second death' of being separated from God (see Heb. 2:8–9).[6] Having been 'made sin', the Son of God, as man, literally suffered the pains of hell, for hell is simply the experience of the absolute loss of God's loving presence.

Moreover, the loss of God's loving presence is experienced not as a mere absence. This would indeed be horrendous in itself. But, more positively and abhorrently, the divine Son actually experienced, as man, the very wrath of God. While this must be properly nuanced, yet it must not

4 Pope John Paul II states that love is 'the fullest source of the answer to the question of the meaning of suffering. This answer has been given by God to man in the cross of Jesus Christ.' *Salvifici Doloris*, n. 13.

5 Hans Urs von Balthasar states that Jesus' sinful humanity provided the vital bond between the Incarnation and the cross. 'He who says Incarnation, also says Cross' (*Mysterium Paschale*, p. 22). Thus, 'to "take on manhood" means in fact to assume its concrete destiny with all that entails – suffering death, hell – in solidarity with every human being' (p. 20). For von Balthasar's complete argument see pp. 11–48. See also *The Von Balthasar Reader*, eds M. Kehl and W. Loser (New York: Crossroad, 1982), pp. 144–50. Von Balthasar also discusses Jesus taking on our condemnation in the light of the teaching of the Fathers. See *Theo-Drama IV: The Action*, p. 349–54. See also Pope John Paul II, *Salvifici Doloris*, n. 14.

6 This passage from the Letter to the Hebrews is normally translated: 'We see Jesus, who for a little while was made lower than the angels, crowned with glory and honour because of the suffering of death, so that by the grace of God (χάριτι θεοῦ) he might taste death for everyone.' Some ancient manuscripts have an alternative rendering: 'so that apart from God (χωρὶς θεοῦ) he might taste death for us.' This alternative, it seems to me, better states in what manner Jesus tasted death. He could taste the full reality of death only if he experienced being 'apart from God.'

be mitigated, for here we discover the depths to which the Son was willing to descend so as to seize the extreme limit of human suffering.

As stated above, sin is an act contrary to all that is good and holy, and thus an affront to the all-loving God. Thus sin is a free act of separation – the separating of oneself from God. It is this sinful act of separating oneself from God which literally creates hell, for that is what hell is – being separated from God. If this separation is not healed, the sinner experiences this separation not merely as the absence of God, but more emphatically as his actual abandonment. 'To be abandoned by God' adds to the conception of 'separation' the positive notion of God's wrath, for such an abandonment testifies to God's righteous judgment upon the sinner. There is no other manner in which the sinner can now experience the absence of God, not because God has changed from being a loving God to being a wrathful God, but because the sinner now literally embodies all that is ungodly. To experience the wrathful abandonment of God is but the self-verification of what one has indeed become – ungodly. Obviously then, to experience the wrath of God is not an experience of God avenging himself in rage or capriciously punishing in anger. God does not hate the damned. God remains the God of love, but within and because of his love, he hates and despises what the sinner has become. God is experienced as being wrathful, for God judges or sanctions that such a separation is the proper and only just consequence (and so punishment) of sin, not because he has so said, but because sin itself has so said. The wrath of God is simply God's approval of what sin itself rightfully demands.[7]

It is the wrath of God in this sense, as the ultimate necessary consequence of the playing out of sin in the presence of the good and holy God, which the Son of God experienced. Having assumed our condemnation, he experienced the wrathful abandonment of God.[8] He plunged

---

7   It is frequently argued that if God is all loving and good, then the obstinant sinner could still experience the mercy and compassion of God, and even obtain heaven. A loving God would never permit, sanction or tolerate hell. This is the thesis of those who espouse a universalist notion of salvation – all will ultimately be saved. Such a view, rather than upholding a loving and good God actually repudiates a loving and good God. A loving and good God could never permit, sanction, or tolerate unrepentant sin and all of the ungodliness that it entails. If he did so, he would become evil, for to sanction or even tolerate evil is to be evil. Such a view would demand that all the horrendous evil perpetrated throughout history, including the Holocaust, is of no real concern or consequence to God. In the end, he could not care less. However, the whole of biblical revelation manifests that Yahweh, unlike the pagan gods, is absolutely holy, good and loving, and thus he demands such virtues of those created in his likeness. The goodness and love of God demand then the actual possibility of eternal damnation. The real possibility of hell testifies to the intrinsic value and worth of human beings, a value and worth so great that these cannot be violated without eternal consequences. Equally, hell upholds the dignity of human freedom even in relationship to God. God so respects the dignity of human freedom that he will not transgress it even if one uses it to become ungodly. Hell, with its experience of the wrath of God, is then but a necessary expression of his perfect goodness and love. Christians must hope that all are saved, but they cannot hope that hell does not exist.

8   Jesus' experience of the wrath of God should not then be interpreted in what is commonly, though unfairly, understood as the classic Reformation (Lutheran) view, that is, that God took out his wrath on Jesus rather than on us. It is because of sin, and not because of God, that one experiences God as wrathful, and one does so precisely

to these depths of suffering in a manner that was genuinely human, and not in some abridged, and so humanly inauthentic, divine manner. He stood in our stead, and he did so out of love for us, that we might never encounter such a tragic end. In conformity with the ancient patristic principle, he assumed our condemnation that we might be saved from it.[9]

It is difficult to overstate this point, and it is equally difficult to appreciate its full significance. Because of our present sinful condition and, more so, because of our own personal sin, we, as human beings, are incapable of experiencing full communion with the loving Father. However, the Son of God, while he assumed a humanity marred by sin, nonetheless lived in perfect obedience to the Father, and so humanly experienced, as far as is humanly possible in this life, the consummate

---

because God is good and loving and the sinner is not. Thus Jesus, in assuming our sinful flesh and with it our condemnation, experienced the wrath of God as a consequence of so doing, and not because God purposefully avenged or sated his wrath upon him. I am thus not comfortable when von Balthasar states that 'God unloaded his wrath upon the Man' (*Theo-Drama IV: The Action*, p. 345). Nonetheless, I would agree with von Balthasar when he argues for Jesus' 'Holy Saturday' experience, which forms a major theme within his own christology. 'Jesus does not only accept the (to be sure, accursed) mortal destiny of Adam. He also, quite expressly, carries the sin of the human race and, with those sins, the "second death" of God-abandonment.' *Mysterium Paschale*, p. 90. See also pp. 148–88. Von Balthasar concurs with K. Barth that the Son of God actually suffered 'the wrath of God that we merited' (*Theo-Drama IV: The Action*, p. 346). See also pp. 339–51. For Barth see *Church Dogmatics*, II/1, p. 396.

Pope John Paul II states:

Together with this horrible weight, *encompassing* the 'entire' evil *of the turning away from God* which is contained in sin, Christ, through the divine depth of his filial union with the Father, perceives in a humanly inexpressible way *this suffering which is the separation*, the rejection *by the Father*, the estrangement from God. *Salvifici Doloris*, n. 18.

It should be noted that while the Son, as man, experienced the full weight of our condemnation, he did not have the mind of a condemned sinner. The damned find God to be utterly loathsome and detestable, for he embodies all that is abhorrent to the condemned sinner – goodness, holiness and love. Jesus, in the midst of his abandonment, maintained a firm love of his Father and trusted that his Father would restore his loving presence. While Jesus, through Psalm 22, gave voice to this abandonment, yet this same psalm expressed his trust and confidence in God's merciful power to rescue him. Though his experience was that of one of being abandoned, yet, in faith and trust, he was assured, despite all appearances, of his Father's unimpaired love. His *'Abba'* prayer in Gethsemane (the only place in the Gospels where such an intimate prayer is explicitly expressed) also manifested this trust in his loving Father (*Abba*), despite the seeming evidence and real emotions to the contrary. This too is the same point made in the Letter to the Hebrews. 'In the days of his [the Son's] flesh, he offered up prayers and supplications, with loud cries and tears, to the one who was able to save him from death, and he was heard because of his reverent submission' (5:7).

9   Aquinas expresses this same thought with regards to Jesus' descent into hell. 'Since it was fitting for Christ to die in order to deliver us from death, so it was fitting for him to descend into hell in order to deliver us also from going down into hell' (*ST*, III, 52, 1). However, this bold statement appears to be mitigated, or even contradicted, in the next article.

T.F. Torrance also states that Christ must take upon himself our sin and guilt, if he is to save us from it. See *The Mediation of Christ*, p. 39.

See also von Balthasar's discussion of 'vicarious punishment' within the Fathers and modern authors (*Theo-Drama IV: The Action*, pp. 290–98).

love of his Father. Only when one has experienced the fulness of the Father's love, can one fully know the utterly depressing agony and despair of being abandoned. But how, in taking on and experiencing our condemnation, did the Son of God save us from it? Again, it is not enough for him just to have experienced the ultimate in human suffering.

Offering an Atoning Sacrifice

Jesus in his death did not just experience our condemnation. Rather, his death also achieved humankind's reconciliation to the Father. One of the common refrains throughout the New Testament is that Christ 'died for us' (see Rom. 5:6 and 8, 14:9 and 15; 1 Cor. 8:11, 15:3; 2 Cor. 5:14–15; Gal. 2:20–21; 1 Thess. 5:10; 1 Pet. 3:18) or that 'he gave himself up for us' or that 'he was given up for us' (see Mt 20:28; Mk 10:45; Jn 3:16; Rom. 4:25, 8:32; Gal. 1:4, 2:20; Eph. 5:2 and 25; Titus 2:14). Humankind, not God, is the beneficiary of Jesus' death. Through Jesus' death God is not reconciled to us, but we are reconciled to God. But how does Jesus' death alter our relationship to God and in so doing change us? Here we must examine the sacrificial nature of Jesus' death.

The biblical understanding of sacrifice can only be understood within the equally biblical context of God's relationship to his people and the sin that violates that relationship. While sin initially broke humankind's relationship with its Creator, God established a covenant with Israel. This covenant was ratified by a sacrifice. Moses, in the sprinkling of the blood (the symbol of life) upon the altar and the people, manifested that through this covenant God and Israel would share a common life (see Exod. 24). Yahweh would be the God of Israel and Israel would be his holy people (see Deut. 7:6, 14:2 and 21, 28:9). The commandments embodied the holy life that Israel was to live. It is sin that repudiates this holy life and so transgresses the covenant. Sin itself, if not fully the sinner, embodies all that is ungodly. In itself it knows no goodness, justice, truth, love or holiness. The sinful act not only repudiates them, but also positively wars against them in order to achieve, at whatever the cost to them, its own selfish ends. This is the arrogance of sin. It warrants neither God nor others but itself alone.

In contrast, sacrifice, as a means of atoning for sin, is always seen within the Old Testament liturgical rites as the act whereby human beings lovingly offer something to God, for example a lamb, that is pure and unblemished, and so precious. The act of sacrifice outwardly represents and expresses, and so embodies, the interior desire to atone or make reparation for the sinful actions committed so as to be cleansed of ungodliness with its condemnation, and so assume once more a godly state within the covenantal relationship. The sacrifice, by its very nature, entails suffering, for one suffers the loss of something precious, but here the suffering is experienced as something good and right, for one has lovingly offered it to God, instead of claiming it for oneself. It is the repentant or atoning love with which the sacrifice is offered that makes it meritorious, and it is the suffering (not of the animal but of the one making the offering) contained within the sacrifice which manifests the depth of the love. Only within this Old Testament understanding of sacrifice can we discern the sacrificial nature of Jesus' death.

Jesus stated that 'the Son of Man came not to be served but to serve, and to give his life as ransom (λύτρον) for many' (Mt 20:28; Mk 10:45). Jesus ransomed us in the sense that he freed us from our condemnation – the slavery of sin, the dominion of Satan, and the fulness of death. He did so by offering, in our stead and on our behalf, his life to the Father. But why did Jesus have to become a sacrificial offering on our behalf in order to ransom us?

It was not the Father who, in righteous anger, vindictively imposed such a sacrifice, but rather, as prefigured in the Old Testament, sin itself demanded such a sacrifice. Only a pure, holy and loving sacrifice of atonement could ultimately free us from sin's condemnation, and so reconcile us to the Father. It was actually the Father who provided, in the person of his incarnate Son, the means of our reconciliation. 'All of this is from God, who reconciled us to himself through Christ' (2 Cor. 5:18–19; see Rom. 5:10–11; Col. 1:19–20). It is God himself who 'has rescued us from the power of darkness and transferred us into the kingdom of his beloved Son, in whom we have redemption (ἀπολύτρωσιν) the forgiveness of sin' (Col. 1:14). God himself obtained the Church 'with the blood of his own Son' (Acts 20:28; see Titus 2:14).[10]

Jesus assumed the debt of sin in assuming our condemnation, and he paid the debt of sin in offering his life in love to the Father on our behalf (see 1 Cor. 6:20, 7:23). He freed us from the debt that sin imposed. While Jesus offered himself in sacrifice to the Father, such a sacrifice was offered not for the Father's benefit, but for ours. We, not the Father, are the beneficiaries of such a sacrifice. 'You [Jesus] were slaughtered and by your blood you ransomed/purchased (ἠγόρασας) for God saints from every tribe and language and people and nation' (Rev. 5:9). On the cross Jesus not only became 'a curse for us' in assuming our condemnation, but he simultaneously redeemed us 'from the curse of the law' through his sacrificial death (Gal. 3:13). Jesus set aside our condemnation by 'nailing it to the cross' (Col. 2:14).

Thus, Jesus is the lamb of God (see Jn 1:36; Rev. 5:6, 12), who takes upon himself all sin with its punishment (see Isa. 53; Acts 8:31–5), and offers his life blood in expiation (see Lev. 17:11, 14). Jesus 'loves us and freed us from our sins by his blood' (Rev. 1:5). Equally, he is the Passover lamb of our redemption (see Exod. 12:46; Jn 19:36; 1 Cor. 5:7). 'You know that you were ransomed (ἐλυτρώθητε) from the futile ways inherited from your ancestors, not with perishable things like silver or gold, but with the precious blood of Christ, like that of a lamb without defect or blemish' (1 Pet. 1:18–19). Because Jesus, as the lamb of God, offered his

---

10 It is well known that some of the Fathers construed the ransom as being paid to the devil so that he would release humankind. See Origen, *Commentariorum in Matthaeum*, 16, 8; Gregory of Nyssa, *Oratio Catechetica*, 21–24; and Augustine, *De Trinitate*, 13, 15–22. However, this is to misconstrue the analogy. Jesus ransomed humankind from the bondage of sin and death, not by 'buying off' Satan, but by reconciling us to God. Such a reconciling action set humankind free from the condemnation of sin and death. See Gregory of Nazianzus' refutation of Nyssa's interpretation, *Oratio*, 45, 22. For a study of the biblical notion of 'ransom' and 'redemption' see S. Lyonnet, *Sin, Redemption, and Sacrifice*, pp. 79–103.

life (blood) to the Father to free us completely and forever from the bondage of sin, so his blood is equally the blood of the new and ever-lasting covenant with the Father (see Mt 26:26–28; Mk 14:22–24; Lk 22:19–20; 1 Cor. 11:23–25).

Furthermore, within the Pauline corpus, 'Christ died for the ungodly,' for it was 'while we still were sinners [that] Christ died for us' (Rom. 5:6, 8). Thus, 'we have been justified by his blood,' and 'saved through him from the wrath of God,' for 'while we were enemies, we were reconciled to God through the death of his Son' (Rom. 5:9–10). The logic is straight-forward: Sin made us ungodly enemies of the Father and so subject to his wrath. Jesus justified us through his sacrificial death on the cross, thus reconciling us to the Father. Again, it is humankind, and not the Father, who reaps the benefits of Jesus' sacrifice. His atoning sacrifice allows us to be once more at one with God. In fact 'God was pleased to reconcile to himself all things, whether on earth or in heaven, by making peace through the blood of his cross' (Col. 1:20). Thus, 'in him we have redemp-tion (ἀπολύτρωσιν) through his blood, the forgiveness of our trespasses' (Eph. 1:7). Humankind is reconciled to the Father and made holy 'through the redemption (ἀπολυτρώσεως) that is in Christ Jesus, whom God put forward as an expiation (ἱλαστήριον) by his blood' (Rom. 3:24–5). While living within our sinful condition, Jesus reversed or coun-teracted the sinful disobedience of humankind, by living under obedience to the Father even unto death. His one righteous act of obedience brought 'acquittal and life for all' and so 'many will be made righteous' (Rom. 5:18–19).[11]

The Letter to the Hebrews confirms that, while the Son of God was of our same sinful stock (see Heb. 2:11, 14–15), and so was tempted in every way, yet he nonetheless lived, unlike us, in complete obedience to the Father and so never sinned (see Heb. 2:17–18, 4:15). The Father prepared a body for his Son, and it was within that body that the Son declared: 'Lo, I have come to do your will, O God,' and 'it is through that will that we have been sanctified though the offering of the body of Jesus Christ once for all' (Heb. 10:5–10). It was through the Son's human will, through his human 'yes' to the Father, that we have been sanctified. Jesus himself is the High Priest and victim for he offers himself for our cleansing from sin. 'He entered the Holy Place, not with the blood of goats and calves, but with his own blood, thus obtaining eternal redemption (λύτρωσιν)' (Heb. 9:12; see 9:22). It is only because the Son offered his human life through the Holy Spirit that such an offering is holy and so efficacious. If the blood of animals was able, in the past, to purify the flesh, 'how much more will the blood of Christ, who through the eternal Spirit offered himself without blemish to God, purify our conscience from dead works to worship the living God?' (Heb. 9:14).[12]

From this brief exposition of the sacrificial nature of Jesus' death, a number of points must be highlighted. I especially want to note the

11 See J.D.G. Dunn, 'Paul's Understanding of the Death of Jesus as Sacrifice' in *Sacrifice and Redemption*, pp. 35–56.
12 For a more complete study of the biblical notion of 'expiation' and the sacrificial nature of Jesus' death, see S. Lyonnet, *Sin, Redemption, and Sacrifice*, pp. 120–84.

various causal connections, that is, the efficacious nature of Jesus' passion and death.

First, Jesus' sacrifice of himself was a twofold act of love. It was an act of sacrificial love offered to the Father, for in love the Son offered his own life to the Father to atone for and so offset or, literally, counteract all humankind's ungodly sinful acts. This act of love was done out of complete obedience to the Father for it was ultimately the Father who was reconciling the world to himself through his Son. Moreover, it was an act of sacrificial love performed out of love for humankind, for the incarnate Son did, out of love for humankind, what it could not do on its own behalf. It was this twofold perfect act of love which made Jesus' sacrifice meritorious. Moreover, it was the suffering of death contained within this sacrifice, the very handing over of his holy and precious life on our behalf to the Father, which embodied and manifested the consummate depth of his love, so making it supremely efficacious.[13]

From the above we must, second, grasp the causal connection between the atoning nature of Jesus' sacrificial death and its reconciling effect. In offering himself out of love for us, the incarnate Son offered a sinless, perfect, and holy sacrifice to the Father, one that would fully and adequately express humankind's reparational or atoning love in the face of sin. Thus, this sacrifice atoned for all the sin of humankind, but in so doing it effected a reconciliation with God. This is why Jesus' blood is the blood of an everlasting and unbreakable covenant. Jesus' pure and holy sacrifice so abundantly atoned for sin that there is no longer any sin that has not been dealt with. Every human being can reap the benefit of Jesus' atoning sacrifice and so be reconciled to God within the new covenant established in his blood.

Third, it must be equally clearly perceived that, while it was truly the person of the Son who offered the sacrifice, he did so, in accordance with the truth of the Incarnation, as man. The merit of the sacrifice, which expiated our guilt and condemnation thus reconciling us to the Father, was precisely located in the Son's human love for the Father and for us. The Son of God then did not offer his divine life to the Father *in a man*. If this were the case, it would demand that his human life, with his human love, and the suffering that that love entailed, were of no salvific value. They would become mere symbols attesting to what the Son was doing as God. It must be the Son of God *as man* who lovingly assumed our condemnation and, as one of us on our behalf, who offered his human

---

13 Aquinas stresses that it is love that makes Jesus' sacrifice supremely efficacious. See *ST*, III, 48, 2–3.

It can rightly be said that during his human life Jesus grew in his love for humankind. Love is not merely expressed in loving deeds, but it is equally in the very doing of these loving deeds that love matures. Thus, the cross is not merely the consummate expression of Jesus' love for us, but it is equally on the cross that he enacted, and so attained, the full maturity of his love for us. 'Greater love has no man than this, that a man lay down his life for his friends' (Jn 15:13). The cross did manifest Jesus' 'greater love,' but he manifested it only because on the cross he achieved it. If he had not laid down his life for us, Jesus would not have possessed nor would he have attained this 'greater love.'

life in love to the Father.[14] The merit of this love is actualized and expressed in the extent of the human suffering he willingly endured. In his suffering, the very Son of God actually experienced, as an authentic man, the depth of humankind's sinful plight, and he equally experienced as man the price that needed to be paid in order to rescue us from it – the atoning sacrifice of his own human life. The humanity of the Son, the humanity that was offered to the Father, was the efficacious means through which redemption and reconciliation was obtained.[15]

Fourth, Jesus triumphed over or vanquished the suffering of our condemnation by or through the sacrificial suffering of offering his life to the Father on the cross. This causal connection, to my knowledge, has never been adequately discerned. Jesus suffered our condemnation on the cross and, in the very same act of assuming our condemnation, he simultaneously and equally offered, in love, his life to the Father as an atoning sacrifice on our behalf for that condemnation. Jesus' sacrificial offering of his life to the Father on our behalf transformed the suffering of our condemnation into an act of freeing us from such condemnation. This was due to the perfect love simultaneously contained and expressed within both aspects of this one act of suffering death on the cross. In death Jesus assumed and so suffered, out of love for us, our condemnation, and, in the same suffering of death, Jesus lovingly offered his life to the Father out of love for us. The love contained and expressed within the sacrificial suffering vanquished the suffering of our condemnation, so freeing us from it.[16]

Fifth, as I have emphasized above, Jesus' sacrifice must not be seen as placating an angry God, as if he were an offended person, who

---

14 Torrance writes:

> Both Liberals and Fundamentalists, however, react with a kind of shock when the humanity of Jesus and substitution are linked together for they have not a little difficulty with the idea that it is *as man* that Jesus Christ takes our place, acts on our behalf and in our stead, and that it is precisely as man that God himself comes to us in the Incarnation. *The Mediation of Christ*, p. 81.

15 Again Aquinas emphasizes that it is only because of the Son's solidarity with us as man, and therefore as the Head of the Church, that salvation comes to those united to him. 'Christ's passion causes forgiveness of sins by way of redemption. For since he is our head, then, by the passion which he endured from love and obedience, he delivered us as his members from our sins, as by the price of his passion.' *ST*, III, 49, 1. See also *ST*, III, 48, 1; 48, 2, ad 1; 49, 3, ad 3.

16 Commenting on Isaiah 53, Pope John Paul II writes:

> Even more than this description of the passion, what strikes us in the words of the prophet is *the depth of Christ's sacrifice*. Behold, he, though innocent, takes upon himself the sins of all. 'The Lord has laid on him the iniquity of us all': *all* human sin in its breadth and depth becomes the true cause of the Redeemer's suffering. If the suffering 'is measured' by the evil suffered, then the words of the prophet enable us to understand *the extent of this evil* and suffering with which Christ burdened himself. It can be said that this is 'substitutive' suffering; but above all it is 'redemptive.' The Man of Sorrows of that prophecy is truly that 'Lamb of God who takes away the sin of the world.' In his suffering, sins are cancelled out precisely because he alone as the only-begotten Son could take them upon himself, accept them *with that love for the Father which overcomes* the evil of every sin; in a certain sense he annihilates this evil in the spiritual space of the relationship between God and humanity, and fills this space with good. *Salvifici Doloris*, n. 17.

demanded in justice, to be propitiated and appeased. It is sin itself, in conformity with the justice of God, that has justly imposed upon humankind a debt, and it is this debt that is expiated through the death of Jesus. Jesus rightly offered his life as a sacrifice of atonement to the Father for our benefit and not his. Through his sacrificial death he made reparation for us. Such a sacrifice vanquished our sin and our condemnation, and in so doing enabled us to be reconciled to the Father.

Putting to Death Our Sinful Humanity

Simultaneously with the experience of complete abandonment and the offering of his human life in sacrifice to the Father for the forgiveness of sin, the Son also put to death our old sinful humanity, the same sin-marred humanity that he himself had assumed. 'We know that our old self (παλαιὸς ἡμῶν ἄνθρωπος) was crucified with him so that the body of sin (τὸ σῶμα τῆς ἁμαρτίας) might be destroyed, and we might no longer be enslaved to sin' (Rom. 6:6). On the cross our sinful flesh died, for that is the flesh that the Son assumed.

Paul also states that 'in him also you were circumcised with a spiritual circumcision, by putting off the body of the flesh (τοῦ σώματος τῆς σαρκός) in the circumcision of Christ (Col. 2:11, see 2 Tim. 2:11). 'Flesh' (σάρξ) for Paul, similar to 'the body of sin,' connotes the whole person mastered by the disposition of sin with its passions and desires. Jesus' death on the cross was the true and authentic circumcision for it was there that he was freed of our sin-marred humanity.

Now the reason that our sinful flesh died on the cross is twofold. It died for in Jesus it had experienced its just condemnation – not only physical death but also the absence of God's presence. Simultaneously, it was offered lovingly to the Father in reparation for sin. 'One has died for all; therefore all have died' (2 Cor. 5:14). Because the Son of God lived a pure and holy life of obedience to the Father as a member of the sinful race of Adam, with his own sin-marred humanity, the loving offering of that humanity on the cross brought about its demise. Our sinful human nature was put to death for the Son of God transformed it into a pure, holy, and loving sacrifice to the Father.

From our examination of these three soteriological truths we have seen that Jesus not only suffered, but that in so doing he also confronted the very source of all suffering – sin. This is what makes Jesus and the suffering he endured unique. All human beings suffer because of sin. The incarnate Son also suffered because of sin, though not his own. But in suffering Jesus freed himself and the whole of humankind from suffering's cause – sin. He did this by enduring the full consequence of sin – our sinful condemnation.[17] More positively, he suffered in love, for he offered his own life as a sacrifice to the Father on our behalf. Together these resulted both in the death of our sinful nature and in our being reconciled to the Father. On the cross then, Jesus thoroughly dealt with

17 Pope John Paul II emphasizes that damnation, due to sin, is 'the definitive suffering.' Thus Christ's death on the cross 'strikes evil right at its transcendental roots,' that is, sin and death, 'for they are at the basis of the loss of eternal life.' *Salvifici Doloris*, n. 14. Also see n. 15.

sin.[18] However, this was not the only result of the Son's death on the cross. Because his sacrifice was the loving offering of his holy life by which we were reconciled to the Father and so set free from sin with its condemnation, Jesus won for us the new resurrected life of the Holy Spirit.[19]

The Resurrection: The Father's Love for the Son

Jesus' suffering on the cross then forms a part of the whole redemptive mystery, for it only finds its salvific significance in the light of the resurrection and the consequent sending forth of the Holy Spirit. If the Father had not raised Jesus from the dead, it would not merely mean that we would never have known that on the cross our condemnation had been annulled, nor that we had been reconciled to the Father, nor that our sinful humanity had been put to death. More profoundly, the absence of Jesus' resurrection would simply, but frankly, attest that none of these had actually been accomplished. Jesus would rightly stand discredited and condemned as a blasphemous fraud. It is here that we must discuss the Father's attitude toward Jesus' suffering and death.

Much recent theology, as we saw, has stressed not only that the Son suffered on the cross, but that the Father also actually suffered in union with the Son. Moltmann, for example, argues that as the Son experienced being abandoned by his Father, so the Father himself equally suffered the loss of his Son.[20] For Moltmann and others, if the Father did not suffer in solidarity with his Son, it would mean that the Father was detached from and indifferent to Jesus' plight. What is to be made then of such claims that the Father suffered?

I have argued extensively that, because the persons of the Trinity perfectly possess all goods as fully actualized, they are incapable of suffering within their divine nature for they never suffer, unlike human beings, the loss of some good. Since the persons of the Trinity can never be deprived of their divine perfection, they never experience any inner *angst* over their own state of being which would cause them to suffer. Moreover, they cannot undergo successive changes of emotional states. What must be remembered is that this lack of suffering within the Trinity actually purifies their love of all selfish concerns, and so allows it to be

---

18 Aquinas succinctly summarizes many of the causal connections within Christ's passion and death.

> Christ's passion, according as it is compared with his Godhead, operates in an efficient manner: but in so far as it is compared with the will of Christ's soul it acts in a meritorious manner: considered as being within Christ's very flesh, it acts by way of satisfaction, inasmuch as we are liberated by it from the debt of punishment; while inasmuch as we are freed from the servitude of guilt, it acts by way of redemption: but in so far as we are reconciled with God it acts by way of sacrifice. *ST*, III, 48, 6, ad 3.

19 Aquinas states: 'Christ's passion wrought our salvation, properly speaking, by removing evils; but the resurrection did so as the beginning and exemplar of all good things.' *ST.*, III, 53, 1, ad 3. See also the entire article.

20 See Chapter 1.

thoroughly altruistic. The Trinity loves freely and never in a manner that would benefit themselves – such as to relieve their own suffering. Likewise, I have emphasized that this absence of suffering within the Trinity does not make the persons of the Trinity less compassionate and merciful. Rather, these attributes are intensified, for the absence of suffering allows their love to be perfect, that is, fully actualized. Thus all facets of love are fully in act – goodness, commitment, affection, joy, kindness, as well as mercy, compassion, grief, and sorrow. The Trinity then does not need to actualize sequentially various aspects or expressions of love depending upon changing circumstances and situations. They are all subsumed within their perfect actualized love. In addressing then the issue of whether or not the Father suffers, the guiding principle must be his absolute, perfect, and unchanging love for the Son.

First, from within the Trinity itself the Father did not suffer the loss of his Son nor was he deprived of his presence. The Father, the Son, and the Holy Spirit are eternally united within their trinitarian life as the one God. The death of the Son as man cannot then be conceived as the 'break-up' of the Trinity. This would reduce the passion and death of Jesus to a myth whereby what would be taking place in history is but the mythical expression of what is actually taking place on a divine transcendent level. Likewise, the resurrection would then be seen not as the glorious reconstitution of the incarnate Son, but as the constitution or reconstitution of the Trinity. This would equally demand that the Father raised his Son from the dead not solely for the well-being of his Son and for the well-being of humankind, but more so for the well-being of himself. The entire altruistic nature of the Father's love would thus be lost. The Father, having suffered the loss of his Son, would then alleviate his own suffering by raising his Son from the dead. This again would also undermine the historical and salvific significance of the resurrection, for it now would become a mere mythical symbol of what would be more importantly taking place ahistorically and transcendently within God. The vanquishing of human suffering with its causes would be cast off the stage of human history, and would be replaced by the more important issue of vanquishing, ahistorically, the suffering of God.[21]

Second, it must also be maintained, from within the historical and incarnational setting of Jesus' passion and death, that the Father did not suffer, for he himself suffered no loss of any good. Nonetheless, from within the event of the cross, with all the suffering that this event entails, the Father's love was present. The Incarnation of the Son with his subsequent passion and death demanded that the Father not merely loved the Son as he exists eternally as Son, but that the Father also loved the Son as he existed as man. The Incarnation thrust the Father's love upon the stage of human history, and it was upon the historical event of the cross that the Father's love was focused. The Father's love was not focused on his own divine well-being, nor even on the divine well-being of his Son. Rather, he was fully attentive to the well-being of his Son as he existed as

---

21 H.U. von Balthasar also sees Moltmann's notion of a suffering God as mythological. See *Theo-Drama IV: The Action*, p. 333 and *Theo-Drama V: The Last Act*, pp. 231–33.

man and, from within that well-being, he was equally, and maybe even more so, vigilant of the well-being of all humankind.[22]

Third, from within his fully actualized love it is possible to attribute grief and sorrow to the Father. While grief and sorrow are predicated of the Father metaphorically, in that such emotions do not imply that the Father underwent emotional changes of state or that he suffered some form of divine mental and emotional distress comparable to human beings, yet what is expressed within these metaphors is nonetheless absolutely true. The Father did grieve over what his incarnate Son had lost – his human well-being and life. He grieved, in love, over all that his Son suffered, physically and mentally, as man. In compassion his love went out to his Son as he humanly experienced being abandoned in hell. One might say that the Father was even angered, in the sense that he recognized that so grave an injustice had been committed against his holy and innocent Son (see Mt 21:33–46 and parallels). His deep sorrow and grief did not spring from or manifest suffering and loss within himself, but rather they sprang from, manifested, and expressed his completely beneficent, all-consuming, and perfect love for his Son.

Fourth, what is often lost sight of when discussing the grief, sorrow and compassion of the Father over the passion and death of his Son is that the Father, equally and simultaneously, was pleased with his Son and rejoiced over what his Son was doing or had done. Actually, despite what may be its theological validity, there is little or no New Testament warrant for asserting that the Father grieved over the death of his Son.[23] In contrast there is scriptural evidence that the Father was well pleased with his Son for, out of love for him and for his people, he willingly suffered and died (see Mt 20:28; Jn 15:13; Eph. 5:2; 1 Jn 3:16). The theology of Jesus' baptism manifests that the Father was pleased with his Son

---

22 Again it must be remembered that it was solely out of love for humankind that the Father sent his Son into the world (see Jn 3:16). The Father proved his love for us through the death of his Son (see Rom. 5:10; 1 Jn 4:10). In this the Father manifested the richness of his mercy (see Eph. 2:4). It is precisely the Father who 'did not withhold his own Son, but gave him up for all of us' (Rom. 8:32). The whole work of reconciliation was initiated and accomplished according to the loving will of the Father (see Eph. 1:3–14). 'All of this is from God, who through Christ reconciled us to himself. . . . God was in Christ reconciling the world to himself' (2 Cor. 5:18–19). The Father then is not concerned with mythologies about divine suffering, but with actual human history, for it is within the lives of historical human beings, including the historical human life of his own Son, that real suffering is endured. Denying that the Father suffered ensures that his love was not egotistically focused upon himself. Moreover, far from under-mining the Father's love, such a denial equally preserves and confirms that his love was thoroughly and solely focused upon human suffering – that of his Son and of humankind.

23 One may be able to appeal to the parable of the Prodigal Son, but even here the father grieves solely over what his son has lost (see Lk 15:11–32). The father's love is completely altruistic, and thus his grief is in no way selfishly focused upon himself and his suffering. Similarly, the Father may have grieved over the incarnate Son who assumed our prodigality, yet his concern bore no trace of self-interest. Likewise, it could be argued that, since to see the Son is to see the Father (see Jn 14:9), Jesus' suffering reflects the suffering of the Father. Yet, what is reflected in Jesus is not so much the suffering as the love expressed within the suffering. To behold the suffering of Jesus is not to behold the suffering of the Father, but rather the immense love of the Father reflected in his suffering Son.

precisely because, as the anointed Messiah, he would be obedient even unto death.[24] Moreover, Jesus proclaimed that 'The Father loves me, because I lay down my life in order to take it up again' (Jn 10:17; see also Jn 3:35, 5:20, 8:29). The whole Johannine theology of the Father glorifying the Son portrays the cross not as an event in which the Father suffers, but as the moment in which the Father actually glories in what his Son is doing, and so it is the historical moment when the Father glorifies him. Through the cross, the Father manifested, and continues to manifest, to the sinful world the glory of his Son. While, within his fully actualized love for his incarnate Son, the Father may have grieved over his Son's suffering and death, yet his pleasure and even joy over what the Son had accomplished completely relativizes and even overshadows his grief or sorrow.

Fifth, as I noted in an earlier discussion, God's compassion and mercy is seen most fully in its effects and not simply in some divine 'emotional' self-expression.[25] It is in the dispelling of evil, and so of the suffering caused by it, that God properly manifests his grief, sorrow, compassion, and mercy. Thus God's compassion and mercy, which contain no suffering, are of far greater significance than human compassion and mercy, which do contain suffering. Unlike human beings, who are often incapable of relieving the evil which is causing the suffering, God is capable of vanquishing the evil and the suffering that accrues to it. More positively, God can restore to someone the good that was lost through the evil suffered. This is precisely what the Father did, in the most unprecedented manner, when he raised Jesus gloriously from the dead. The resurrection manifests the Father's all-consuming love for his incarnate Son and testifies to his profound mercy and compassion for what his Son had endured. If one wishes to know the inner mind of the Father in the face of his Son's passion, death, and descent into hell, one only needs to look at the resurrection. The resurrection is the Father's conclusive answer to the suffering of his Son, and with it his consummate answer to all human suffering.

The Resurrection: The Father's Vindication of His Son

The Father validated and manifested the efficacy of his Son's suffering in raising him gloriously from the dead. Actually, the Father's raising Jesus from the dead was the direct fruit of the cross, and the Father ensured that Jesus himself was the first to have experienced it.[26] It is to this intrinsic connection between Jesus' suffering on the cross and his resurrection with the resultant gift of the Spirit that we will now turn.

---

24 The baptism initiated Jesus' ministry as the Messiah. The Father's proclamation at Jesus' baptism comes from Psalm 2:7 ('You are my beloved son') and from Isaiah 42:1 ('Behold my servant, in whom I well pleased'). The Father is pleased with his Son for he will be the suffering servant who, in filial obedience, will lay down his life. This is what it means for Jesus to be the Messiah.
25 See pp. 165 and 167–68 above.
26 Aquinas states that Christ, through his passion and death, merited his own resurrection and exultation. See *ST*, III, 49, 6. Moreover, 'Christ by his passion merited salvation, not only for himself, but likewise for his members.' *ST*, III, 48, 1.

According to Acts, Peter proclaimed at Pentecost that the very one whom the Jewish and Roman authorities thought worthy of crucifixion is the very same one whom God considered worthy of raising up, 'having freed him from death because it was impossible for him to be held in its power' (Acts 2:24).[27] 'God has made both Lord and Messiah, this Jesus whom you crucified' (Acts 2:36). But why could death not hold Jesus in its power; the presupposition being that death, in the full theological sense of physical death accompanied with its condemnation, did hold him for a time in its power? Moreover, why did the Father make him both Lord and Christ?

The Father would not abandon his Holy One in Hades nor allow him to experience corruption (see Acts 2:25–32; Ps. 16:8–11). Jesus was freed from Hades (from condemnation) and raised up incorruptibly because, as the Holy One, he offered his holy life to the Father in loving obedience. Being innocent and holy the Father could not leave him abandoned. In the resurrection the Father established and authenticated Jesus' holiness and the work he had accomplished on the cross. Moreover, the resurrection expressed the Father's abundant delight in his Son and in what his Son had achieved.

Likewise, 'being exalted at the right hand of God, and having received from the Father the promise of the Holy Spirit, he has poured out this that you both see and hear' (Acts 2:33, see 1:4–5). Having defeated all of humankind's enemies – sin, death, and condemnation, and having reconciled sinful humankind to the Father through his death on the cross, Jesus, now as the risen Lord, was empowered to pour out upon humankind the benefit of that reconciliation – the Holy Spirit. The sending forth of the Holy Spirit, with all that this sending forth entails, equally establishes then the efficacy of the cross and confirms the present exalted reality of Jesus as Lord. Moreover, it is precisely the present availability of the promised Holy Spirit, as the concomitant consummation of Jesus' death and resurrection, which contains the potential, as we will see, for radically altering the context, experience, and meaning of human suffering.

The Pauline corpus accents that it is the Father who raised Jesus from the dead so making him Lord (see Rom. 6:4, 8:11, 10:9; 1 Cor. 6:14, 15:15; 2 Cor. 4:14; Gal. 1:1; Eph. 1:20; Col. 2:12; 1 Thess. 1:10; see also 1 Pet. 1:21). The risen salvific lordship of Jesus is predicated upon his crucifixion. Having put to death the sinful flesh he had inherited from Adam through suffering our condemnation, and having offered his life as an atoning sacrifice to the Father on our behalf, Jesus, in being raised bodily from the dead, is the first to experience the efficacy of the cross. In the resurrection Christ himself bears the first-fruit of his own redemptive death (see 1 Cor. 15:20). He is 'the *firstborn* from the dead' (Col. 1:18). Through his righteous obedience Jesus, on the cross, reversed the disobedience of Adam and his progeny. Having overcome the congenital sin and death

---

27 See M. Hooker, *Not Ashamed of the Gospel* (Carlisle: The Paternoster Press, 1994), pp. 7–19 on the scandalous nature of the cross within Roman culture and Old Testament thought, and how the New Testament writers coped with the scandal of Jesus' crucifixion.

of Adam's race, he has become, through his resurrection, the new man – the new Adam (see Rom. 5:12–21; 1 Cor. 15:22–23, 45; Eph. 2:15). Being the new Adam, Jesus, as the risen Lord, has become the father of a recreated human race.

This divine wisdom of a crucified Lord is foolishness to the Jews and Greeks alike, nonetheless he who was crucified is humankind's 'righteousness and sanctification and redemption' and so is 'the Lord of glory' (1 Cor. 1:30 and 2:8; see also 1:18—2:7). While it was the Father who handed him over to death for our sins, he nonetheless made him Lord by raising him from the dead (see Rom. 4:24–25). On the cross Jesus 'died to sin once for all,' and *therefore* 'death no longer had dominion over him.' As risen, 'the life he lives, he lives to God' (Rom. 6:9–10). Moreover, it is only because Jesus is the risen Lord that we have the assurance that through his blood we are now reconciled to God (see Rom. 5:9). 'For if while we were enemies, we were reconciled to God through the death of his Son, much more surely, having been reconciled, will we be saved by his life' (Rom. 5:10).

It was precisely because the Son humbled himself not only in becoming man, but also in accepting death even on the cross, that God 'highly exalted him and gave him the name that is above every name' (Phil. 2:6–11). It is the depth of Jesus' humility, his dying for sin, that is the cause of his supreme exaltation as the risen Lord. For Paul the gospel itself concerns the Son who, having descended from David's flesh, has now been 'declared to be Son of God with power according to the Spirit of holiness by resurrection from the dead, Jesus Christ our Lord' (Rom. 1:3–4).

Similar to Acts, the resurrection as the charter of Jesus' lordship testifies, within the Pauline corpus, to the salvific efficacy of his suffering and death. Moreover, this efficacy is not only seen within the resurrected Jesus himself, but also in the new life of the Holy Spirit given to those who now live in Christ. 'If the Spirit of him who raised Jesus from the dead dwells in you, he who raised Christ from the dead will give life to your mortal bodies also through his Spirit that dwells in you' (Rom. 8:11).

Within the Gospel of John the efficacy of Jesus' death on the cross is richly portrayed in a more symbolic, but nonetheless real, manner. Jesus' obedience manifests that he is truly the Son of the Father (see Jn 4:34, 10:36–38). This is most fully witnessed in his being lifted up (see Jn 8:28). The 'lifting up' for John refers not only to the cross, but also to his resurrection and ascension. The hour of Jesus' death is equally the hour of his glory, for in his death he will bring forth new life. 'The hour has come for the Son of Man to be glorified. Very truly, I tell you, unless a grain of wheat falls into the earth and dies, it remains just a single grain; but if it dies, it bears much fruit' (Jn 12:23–24; see also vv. 20–27). The implication is that the resurrection, and the abundance of life that it brings, is the direct result of the cross.

Throughout John's passion narrative Jesus is not seen as passively undergoing his passion and death. Rather, he is the primary actor and the one exercising ultimate authority. He 'came forward' to meet those who came to arrest him, and he initiated the questioning (see Jn 18:4). While he is handed over to be crucified, nonetheless he took the cross, he carried it himself, and he went, and was not led, to Golgotha (see Jn 19:16–17). Not surprisingly Jesus himself brought the salvific drama to a close. The Gospel of John reports that Jesus' last words were 'It is finished,' that is, the saving work entrusted to him by the Father. Death did not come upon him and rob him of his life. He was not put to death. Rather, 'he bowed his head and gave up his spirit' (Jn 19:30).

The active completion of his work and the active giving of his life to the Father is equally the cause of his active breathing forth of his spirit. The phrase 'gave up his spirit' (παρέδωκεν τὸ πνεῦμα) is unique to the Gospel of John and is found nowhere else in antiquity as a description of death. The same breath in which Jesus put to death our sinful flesh (σάρξ), and, as the Lamb of God handed over his life to the Father in reparation for sin, is the same breath by which the Holy Spirit was poured out upon the world. For John, the last agonizing breath of Jesus, a life given in suffering love to the Father, was the first breath of new and eternal life for humanity. The 'giving up his spirit' then proceeds in two directions. It is given up to the Father, and simultaneously it is given up to the world. There is simultaneous causality here. The efficacy of Jesus' death (the breathing forth of his spirit to the Father) is witnessed in his simultaneously breathing forth the Spirit upon the world. Jesus could not breathe forth his Spirit upon the world if his breathing forth of his spirit to the Father had not achieved humankind's reconciliation. In the breathing forth of his life to the Father, Jesus procured for humankind the new breath of the Holy Spirit. The moment of Jesus' death is then the moment of new life for it is his death that simultaneously gives rise to the new life. Again, we see that the Spirit could only come forth, and did only come forth, when Jesus was glorified (see Jn 7:39).

Jesus died at the hour when the paschal lambs were being sacrificed in the temple, and not having his legs broken, since he was already dead, confirmed that he truly was the suffering sacrificial lamb of God who takes away the sin of the world (see Jn 19:32–35; Exod. 12:46, Jn 1:36). Moreover, the coming forth of blood and water from his pierced side also symbolized the efficacy of his sacrificial death. Having cleansed us in the outpouring of his blood (see 1 Jn 1:7; Lev. 17:11, 14) and so reconciling us to the Father, Jesus enabled us to share in the living water of his Spirit. The life-giving water of the Holy Spirit testified that his blood (the offering of his life) had atoned for humankind's sins. The Father manifested the efficacy of this sacrifice in allowing the outpouring of the Holy Spirit.

Likewise in the Gospel of John, Jesus appeared to his disciples on the first Easter evening. This is a resurrection account of what happened on the cross. Jesus, displaying the marks of suffering in his hands and side, twice greeted them with 'Peace be with you' (Jn 20:19, 21; also see 26). Peace is the immediate effect of Jesus' death. He has reconciled humankind to the Father (see 1 Jn 2:2, 4:10), and so his Father has now become our Father (Jn 20:17). Moreover, similar to his action on the cross, Jesus, breathing upon the disciples, conferred upon them the Holy Spirit (Jn 20:22). This is the Johannine Pentecost, and it is reminiscent of the second creation story where God breathed his own very spirit into the first man (see Gen. 2:7). This spirit was lost through sin, but now Jesus, having atoned for that sin, once more recreates humankind as its risen glorified Lord through the breathing forth of the Holy Spirit (see Jn 7:39). Once more humankind can be born of the Spirit (see Jn 3:1–6). As John the Baptist had prophesied at the onset of the Gospel, it is the paschal Lamb of God who would baptize with the Holy Spirit (see Jn 1:29–34). This too testifies to the previous pattern. The cross necessarily gave rise to the resurrection which, in turn, necessarily entailed the sending forth of the new life of the Holy Spirit.[28]

Moreover, the Letter to the Hebrews specifies that the sacrificial nature of Jesus' death accounts for his exalted risen status. 'When he had made purification for sin, he sat down at the right hand of the Majesty on high, having become as much superior to angels as the name he has inherited is more excellent than theirs' (Heb. 1:3–4). Though the Son was made for a while a little lower than the angels, he is now 'crowned with glory and honour because of the suffering of death' (Heb. 2:9). Jesus was made perfect through his suffering (see Heb. 2:10). Because the Son participated in our own sinful flesh, the offering of his own blood sanctified him (see Heb. 10:29). Through the offering of his life to the Father, he has become a priest 'through the power of an indestructible life' (Heb. 7:16). As high priest Jesus does not need to repeat his sacrifice, 'this he did once for all when he offered himself.' Thus, in raising him from the dead, the Father appointed him to be the eternal high priest, 'a Son who has been made perfect forever' (Heb. 7:27–28). Because of the joy held out

---

28 The synoptic tradition is not as explicit in making a theological or salvific connection between Jesus' death and resurrection. When asked for a sign to prove that he was the Messiah, Jesus responded that no sign would be given except the sign of Jonah. 'For three days and three nights the Son of Man will be in the heart of the earth' (Mt 12:40; see also 12:38–42, Lk 11:29–32). That Jesus is truly the anointed Savior of God would be seen in his death and resurrection. Peter proclaimed Jesus to be the Messiah, the Son of God, but it was Jesus who clarified its true meaning by stating on three occasions that he, therefore, must go to Jerusalem to suffer and die, and on the third day rise from the dead (see Mt 16:13–23, 17:22–23, 20:17–19 and parallels). Here there is an obvious connection between Jesus suffering and his rising, but the salvific significance remains implicit. The Transfiguration, which is closely associated with Jesus being the suffering Messiah, is seen, especially in Luke, as prefiguring the salvific 'passing over' or 'exodus' of Jesus from death to glory (see Lk 9:28–36). Luke also has Jesus speak of his coming death and resurrection as a baptism he must undergo, but again the salvific connection remains hidden (see Lk 12:49–50). Quoting Psalm 118:22–23, Jesus asserted that he is the stone rejected by the builders, but that God will nonetheless make him the cornerstone (see Mt 21:42 and parallels). The implication is that the crucifixion will be seen as the world's rejection and the resurrection will be seen as God's vindication. Because of his death and resurrection he will become the cornerstone of salvation (see Eph. 2:20, 1 Pet. 2:4–8). Within the Synoptics the most obvious connection between Jesus' death and resurrection is the actual historical events themselves. Jesus dies and three days later he rises in glory, but the theological significance of the connection is, for the most part, not explicated. Only Luke tells of Jesus' impatience at the disciples' lack of faith in what the prophets had foretold. 'Was it not necessary that the Messiah should suffer these things and then enter into his glory' (Lk 24:25). Yes, but why? Only at the very end of the Gospel did Jesus say that he had fulfilled what was written in the Law, the prophets and the psalms. 'Thus it is written, that the Messiah is to suffer and rise from the dead on the third day, and that repentance and forgiveness of sins is to be proclaimed in his name to the nations' (Lk 24:46–47). Here we clearly see that the forgiveness of sins is predicated upon Jesus' salvific suffering and his subsequent resurrection.

to him, Jesus 'endured the cross, disregarding its shame, and has taken his seat at the right hand of the throne of God' (Heb. 12:2).

Equally, the Book of Revelation proclaims clearly that Jesus is glorified as the risen Lord only because of his sacrificial death. It is the slain sacrificial Lamb who ransomed men for God, and who is therefore worthy to receive 'power and wealth and wisdom and might and honour and glory and blessing' (Rev. 5:6, 9–10, 12–13). The heavenly court worship the glorious and risen Jesus only because he merited such honor as the slain lamb. He who is Lord of lords and the King of kings, the Alpha and the Omega, the First and the Last is the one who is 'clothed in a robe dipped in blood, and his name is called The Word of God' (Rev. 19:13). It is the glory of the cross, the lamp of the risen Lamb, which illuminates the heavenly city (Rev. 21:22–23).

In the above discussion it has become abundantly clear that the cross directly led to the resurrection which resulted in the outpouring of the Holy Spirit. Because Jesus suffered our condemnation, having put to death our sinful nature, and because he equally offered his holy life as a loving sacrifice to the Father, the Father has raised him gloriously from the dead. Being the risen Lord, he is now empowered to send forth the new life of the Holy Spirit. In the person of the resurrected Jesus himself the *eschaton* is now fully present and actualized, and so, in him, the end is beginning to be made available to all. It is here in the resurrected Jesus that the new eschatological life of the Spirit, a life that will be entirely free from suffering, because it is entirely free from sin, finds its beginning and its end. Moreover, we clearly and fully discern here, for the first time, what I noted at the onset of this chapter. Through his death and resurrection Jesus established a whole new salvific order. This new salvific order, while it arises from his redemptive work, is founded upon and discovered within the eschatological presence of the Holy Spirit.

The Son of God Risen as a Complete Man

I have now argued, at some length, that the Father manifested his love for his incarnate Son and vindicated him by raising him from the dead. The Father raising Jesus from the dead was the direct result of the efficacy of the cross. Likewise, the eschatological outpouring of the Holy Spirit equally manifested the efficacy of Jesus' death and confirmed his resurrection lordship. I want now to make one further important point which all the above has presupposed. Yet, while the above was founded upon this presupposition, it is only at this juncture that, I believe, it can truly be appreciated. I have presupposed throughout, and it was likely evident to the reader, that Jesus, in accordance with the New Testament, the Creeds, and the Christian tradition, was gloriously raised from the dead as a complete and entire man – body and soul. The Son of God is still incarnate, though now incarnate as a risen and glorious man. I do not want here to argue for the truth of this position, but simply to note its significance for our present study.

First, it was as man that the Son of God suffered and died and so, if the Father was to manifest his love for his incarnate Son, he must do so by raising his Son from the dead as a complete man – body and soul. Jesus' suffering involved real physical pain and authentic emotional trauma, and if the Father did not raise him from the dead as a man, it would mean that this genuine human suffering was of no interest to him. However, it is precisely in physically raising his Son from the dead as a complete man that the Father absolutely confirmed his love for and pleasure in his Son as incarnate. Simply put, the Father demonstrated his love for the human historical Jesus, for who he is as his incarnate Son and for all that he had done as man, by raising the human historical Jesus – the man Jesus – gloriously from the dead.

Second, the Father vindicated his incarnate Son and revealed the efficacy of his suffering and death by gloriously raising him from the dead as man. In the resurrection the Father verified that it was truly the genuineness of his Son's human suffering and death which conquered sin and death and so secured the new life of the Holy Spirit. The Father, in raising Jesus from the dead as a complete man – body and soul – so that he now exists as an authentic glorious man, confirmed that what he genuinely suffered – physically and emotionally – as an authentic man was indeed of salvific significance. The bodily resurrection testifies that what the Son of God did and experienced as a man, especially within his suffering and death, was the means by which the whole of human life, including suffering and death, was redeemed and so transformed. If the Son of God is not a risen glorious man, then we who are humans are not saved in accordance with who we are – bodily creatures.

Third then, without Jesus' bodily resurrection, salvation would consist of a Platonic flight, a breaking free, from this material world of bodily and emotional suffering and physical death to a better and more authentic spiritual and disembodied realm of existence.[29] If, after his human death, the Son of God merely continued to exist as God, or if the resurrection merely consisted of some sort of spiritual, in the sense of immaterial, existence, or if the resurrection merely consisted of the subjective experience or event within the hearts and minds of his disciples and not actually an experience or event which happened to Jesus himself, then it would mean that his human suffering and death were ultimately unimportant and salvifically insignificant. They would merely be the sad but necessary path of escape. Human life, with its suffering and its finality of death, is not then something that can be redeemed but only something that must be endured and finally relinquished and abandoned. Without the resurrection of Jesus as a full and glorious man the absurdity and meaninglessness of human suffering would still prevail.

Fourth, as we saw above and as will become even more evident in what follows, the glorious resurrection of the Son of God as a complete man is the means by which not only his human life was transformed and made new, but also the means by which the lives of all human beings can

---

29 It must be noted that while Paul states that at the resurrection we will possess a spiritual body (πνευματικόν), yet it is nonetheless a real body that we will possess (see 1 Cor. 15:42ff). The absence of a bodily resurrection has profound effects not only on how we view and conceive human life, but also on how we view and conceive the whole material order.

be transformed and made new. The resurrection of Jesus as a complete man – body and soul – affirms, as we will see in the next chapter, not only that Jesus' suffering and death was significant, but also that the suffering and death of every human person is of eternal value and worth. Thus we grasp that the traditional doctrine of Jesus' resurrection as a glorious man is not tangential to our concerns here, but central, for the bodily resurrection of Jesus ensures that the whole of human life, even suffering and death, is of value and ultimately redeemable.

Fifth, since it was the Son of God as man who suffered and died in order to obtain salvation, it must now be the Son of God as the risen and glorious man who pours out the Holy Spirit. If it is not the Son of God as the risen man who makes present the eschatological Spirit, then it would mean that it was not as man that he obtained our salvation. If the Son of God, as the risen man, does not send forth the Spirit, then what he did as man, in his suffering and death, was not the means by which he obtained his risen lordship so as to be empowered and authorized to send forth the Spirit. As it was as man that the Son died on our behalf reconciling us to the Father, so it is now as the risen man that the Son makes available the fruit of his human suffering and death in the new life of the Holy Spirit.

What difference, then, does the new eschatological life of the Spirit make to those who believe? What happens to the person who appropriates in faith Jesus' salvation? What transpires within the person who possesses the Holy Spirit? What is it like to live within this new salvific order? Most importantly for our present study, how does the Christian believer now experience and interpret suffering? Before we can address the last question, we must first examine the transforming effects of the new life of the Holy Spirit within the life of the Christian.

Being a New Creation in Christ

To enter into the new salvific order is primarily to become a new creation in Christ through the indwelling Spirit.

We have seen that Jesus, through his death and resurrection, underwent a marvelous transformation. Now the good news is that those who come to faith in Jesus and are baptized undergo this same transformation.

> How can we who died to sin go on living in it? Do you not know that all of us who have been baptized into Christ Jesus were baptized into his death? Therefore we have been buried with him by baptism into death, so that, just as Christ was raised from the dead by the glory of the Father, so we too might walk in newness of life. For if we have been united with him in a death like his, we will certainly be united with him in a resurrection like his. We know that our old self was crucified with him so that the body of sin might be destroyed, and we might no longer be enslaved to sin. For whoever has died is freed from sin. But if we have died with Christ, we believe that we will also live with him. We know that Christ, being raised from the dead, will never die again; death no longer has dominion over him. The death

he died, he died to sin, once for all; but the life he lives, he lives to God. So you also must consider yourselves dead to sin and alive to God in Christ Jesus (Rom. 6:2–11).

Paul's logic here is straightforward. The Son of God, having assumed our fallen humanity, put our 'old self' to death on the cross. In rising from the dead he was freed from that fallen humanity with its dominion of death, and now lives gloriously as a new man unto God. Through baptism Christians participate in this same transformation. We are 'baptized into his death' not just figuratively or symbolically, but rather we are actually inserted into his very act of dying. We are truly 'buried with him,' literally – 'co-buried' (συνετάφημεν) with him, and so share the same grave. If 'one has died for all, therefore all have died' (2 Cor. 5:14). Therefore, our own sinful nature is put to death, and we too are then freed from sin with its condemnation. Equally through baptism, we share in his resurrection, and so can 'walk in newness of life.' We are not then saved by any works of righteousness, 'but according to his mercy, through the water of rebirth and renewal by the Holy Spirit' (Titus 3:5; see Heb. 10:22). Thus, Christians must consider themselves 'dead to sin and alive to God in Christ Jesus.'

This same pattern of thought appears in the Letter to the Colossians.

> In him also you were circumcised with a spiritual circumcision, by putting off the body of the flesh in the circumcision of Christ; when you were buried with him in baptism, you were also raised with him through faith in the power of God, who raised him from the dead. And when you were dead in trespasses and the uncircumcision of your flesh, God made you alive together with him, when he forgave us all our trespasses, erasing the record that stood against us with its legal demands. He set this aside, nailing it to the cross. He disarmed the rulers and authorities and made a public example of them, triumphing over them in it. Col. 2:11–15.

Circumcision in the Old Testament was understood as the external sign of the covenant (see Gen. 17:9–14). To be circumcised was to be cut free from sin and all unholiness, and to be set apart for God (see Lev. 26:41; Deut. 10:16; Jer. 4:4). The Christian, through baptism, experiences the true spiritual circumcision. As Christ was circumcised of his sinful flesh, having nailed it to the cross, and as he rose in the holiness of his resurrected humanity, so Christians now in baptism also put off the body of sinful flesh and are raised to live a new life with God in Christ. 'If we have died with him, we will also live with him' (2 Tim. 2:11).

Johannine theology is similar to the Pauline corpus. Jesus assured Nicodemus: 'Very truly, I tell you, no one can see the Kingdom of God without being born from above' (Jn 3:3). To be born from above demands that one be born of water and Spirit. 'What is born of the flesh is flesh and what is born of the Spirit is spirit' (Jn 3:7). Within Johannine theology one is born naturally of sinful flesh and must be reborn of the Spirit in order to enter into the eternal life of God's kingdom. The implication being then that in so being born again one puts off the flesh and becomes a new creation in the Spirit.

What must be grasped clearly here is that the Son of God, having assumed our sinful flesh and having put it to death on the cross, rose as a new and glorious man now set free from sin and all its effects. Through his resurrection then the Son of God incarnate presently lives as an entirely new man. The Son of God is still a man but now he is a new kind of man – a risen and glorious man. When Christians appropriate Jesus' salvation through baptism, this very same event takes place within them. Through the indwelling Spirit, they abide in the risen Christ and so share in his risen humanity. 'If anyone is in Christ, there is a new creation: everything old has passed away; see, everything has become new! . . . For our sake he [God] made him to be sin who knew no sin, so that in him we might become the righteousness of God' (2 Cor. 5:11, 21; see Gal. 6:15). Because of Jesus' single offering 'he has perfected for all time those who are sanctified' (Heb. 10:14).

Christians prior to conversion may have been fornicators, idolaters, and drunkards, but now 'you were washed, you were sanctified, you were justified in the name of the Lord Jesus Christ and in the Spirit of our God' (1 Cor. 6:11; see Eph. 5:26). Christians are still men and women, but now they have been radically transformed. They differ from those who are not Christian not simply in degree but in kind, for unlike those who are not Christian, their sinful nature has died, and they have become, through the Holy Spirit, new men and women in Christ. 'You are not in the flesh, you are in the Spirit, since the Spirit of God dwells in you' (Rom. 8:9; see 8:11). Being a new creation in Christ, and so living within the new salvific order, has other profound ramifications for the kind of life Christians live.

Living in Christ

First, Christians are forgiven their sins and freed from sin's condemnation (see Col. 1:14): 'There is therefore now no condemnation for those who are in Christ Jesus' (Rom. 8:1). While Christians may continue to sin, their sin need no longer fashion them into enemies of God. Jesus, the risen High Priest, continually makes intercession for those who approach God (see Heb. 7:25). They are liberated from the bondage of sin and have become slaves of righteousness (see Rom. 6:18, 20–22). Through the Spirit they have been set free 'from the law of sin and death' (Rom. 8:2).

Second and more positively, Christians are, through faith and baptism, and not through works, justified, made righteous and holy before God (see Rom. 1:17, 3:28, 4:5; Gal. 2:16, 3:8; Phil. 3:9). Thus they possess the ability both to abandon sin and to live in the freedom of the Spirit. 'For freedom Christ has set us free' (Gal. 5:1). This new freedom, first of all, empowers Christians to have new minds and to think in a new kind of way. In the Spirit, they have taken on the very mind of Christ (see 1 Cor. 2). Because Christians have already been raised with Christ at the Father's right hand, they are able to set their minds not on things of this world but on things above (see Col. 3:1–2). Their minds are renewed so that they can do the will of God – 'what is good and acceptable and perfect' (Rom. 12:2). Moreover then, because of their renewed minds, Christians are able to live lives of virtue. They are God's workmanship, created in Christ 'for good works' (Eph. 2:10). 'You were taught to put away your former way of life, your old self (τὸν παλαιὸν ἄνθρωπον), corrupt and deluded by its lusts, and to be renewed in the spirit of your minds, and to clothe yourselves with the new self (τὸν καινὸν ἄνθρωπον), created according to the likeness of God in true righteousness and holiness' (Eph. 4:22–24). Christians no longer do the deeds of the flesh, but rather they do the deeds of the Spirit (see Rom. 8:5–6), and they do so for they are no longer 'in the flesh,' but 'in the Spirit' for the Spirit of God dwells in them (Rom. 8:9). Their daily lives consist in putting to death the deeds of the flesh and living by the Spirit (see Rom. 8:13). In so doing Christians bear the fruit of the Spirit – love, joy, peace, patience, etc. (see Gal. 5:19–23).

Third, as his brothers and sisters, Christians share the same intimacy with the Father as Jesus the Son. Because Christians have died and risen with Christ, and so live in him through the indwelling of the Holy Spirit, their relationship with the Father has not just improved by degree, but has changed in kind. Not only are they reconciled to God and so are at peace with him, but being new creations in Christ, they also have been transformed by the indwelling Spirit of sonship into sons of the Father. They are able to call out, in union with the Son, '*Abba*, Father' (Gal. 4:6; Rom. 8:15). The prayer that Jesus taught his disciples bears witness to this singular privilege. They are entitled to call God 'Our Father' (see Mt 6:9; Lk 11:2; Jn 20:17). Moreover, the same Spirit which conforms Christians into his children, equally pours out the paternal love of the Father into their hearts (see Rom. 5:5). According to the Gospel of John, Jesus prayed that, since he has made his Father known to his disciples, the very love of the Father, with which he himself is loved, would be in them (see Jn 17:26). The marvelous truth is that Christians are incorporated into the life of the Trinity itself, and so share in the divine relationships by which the Father, the Son and the Holy Spirit are the one God. In Christ the Son, Christians possess, as his brothers and sisters through the Spirit of sonship, the same Father.

Christians are then no longer strangers or aliens, 'but members of the household of God' (Eph. 2:20). They have become God's holy people set apart as his own possession (see Eph. 1:14; Col. 1:12; 1 Pet. 2:9–10). The very curtain of the temple dividing the holy God from his unholy people has been rent in two (see Mt 27:51; Exod. 26:31–33). Having been purified by the blood of Jesus and cleansed in the waters of baptism, they confidently enter into the very heavenly sanctuary of God (see Heb. 10:19–23). They become the very temple of God (ναος τοῦ θεοῦ) where the Holy Spirit resides (see 1 Cor. 3:16–17, 6:19). Within this living temple they, with Christ, offer spiritual worship to the Father (see 1 Pet. 2:4–10; Eph. 2:22; Jn 4:20–24).

Fourth, the relationship among Christians radically differs from their relationship with those who are not Christian. To live together in Christ as children of the Father in and through the Holy Spirit is a new and singular kind of relationship. Christians, whether Jews or Greeks, have become one new man in Christ (see Eph. 2:15). Therefore, together in Christ, 'both of us have access in one Spirit to the Father' (Eph. 2:18). In Christ all Christians, through the Spirit of sonship, have one common

Father. So radical is this union that there is no longer Jew or Greek, slave or free, male or female for all are 'one in Christ Jesus' (Gal. 3:28; see Rom. 10:12; 1 Cor. 12:13; Col. 3:11). The whole social order – husbands/wives, parents/children, masters/slaves – must be reconceived in the light of sharing a common life in Christ (see Eph. 5:21—6:9; Col. 3:18—4:1, Philemon).

This whole realignment of the divine and social orders – the Christian's relationship with God and with one's fellow Christians – is predicated upon the fact that Christians, together with Christ their head, form one body in and through the one Spirit (see Rom. 12:4–5; 1 Cor. 12:12–13). While it is through faith and baptism that this relationship is established, it is most fully expressed and nurtured within the Eucharist (see 1 Cor. 10:15–17, 11:27–32).

Fifth, in the light of becoming a new creation in Christ through the indwelling Spirit, Christians live in anticipation both of Jesus' return in glory and of their own resurrection. The Son of Man will come with great glory and power to gather his elect (see Mt 24:30–31) and to judge the living and the dead (see 2 Tim. 4:1; 1 Pet. 4:5). Now the whole of creation is groaning waiting to share in the glorious freedom of the children of God (see Rom. 8:19–22). Christians themselves, 'who have the first fruits of the Spirit,' presently groan as they 'await for adoption, the redemption of our bodies' (Rom. 8:23). When Jesus comes at the end of time, he will complete the good work that has already begun in those who believe (see Phil. 1:6). 'Christ, having been offered once to bear the sins of many, will appear a second time, not to deal with sin, but to save those who are eagerly waiting for him' (Heb. 9:28). Through his own resurrection Christ is the first fruit of redemption, 'then at his coming those who belong to him' (1 Cor. 15:23; see 1 Thess. 4:16). Already Christians are citizens of heaven, and it is from there that they await their Savior, the Lord Jesus. 'He will transform the body of our humiliation that it may be conformed to the body of his glory, by the power that also enables him to make all things subject to himself' (Phil. 3:20–21). The indwelling of the Holy Spirit, the same Spirit through whom the Father raised Jesus from the dead, is 'the guarantee' and the 'first instalment' of the Christian's future resurrected inheritance (Eph. 1:14; 2 Cor. 1:22; see Rom. 8:11). What has been sown in perishability, dishonour, and weakness will be raised imperishable, in glory and in the fulness of power (see 1 Cor. 15:42–44, 53–54). 'Just as we have born the image of the man of dust, we will also bear the image of the man of heaven' (1 Cor. 15:49). Because Christians have already died with Christ, and their present life is now hidden with Christ, when he appears, then they will also appear with him in glory (see Col. 1:2–3).[30] With the coming of Jesus in glory and power all of his enemies, including death itself, will be vanquished and he will hand over the kingdom to his Father (see 1 Cor. 15:24–28; Eph. 1:20–23; Heb. 1:13—2:9).

---

30 Within the Gospel of John, since Christians already partake of the risen body and blood of Jesus, they are assured of being raised up on the last day. Just as Jesus lives because of the Father so Christians, who abide in him through the Eucharist, will live for ever (see Jn 6:53–59).

The final coming of Jesus in glory with our concomitant resurrection is of the utmost importance for this study. Eternal life within the Trinity is the ultimate consequence of Jesus' suffering, for through his suffering he obtained both his and our resurrection. Thus, when Jesus returns in glory, he will bring to a just and glorious close all human suffering. Sin, the cause of all suffering and death, will completely end. 'The sting of death is sin, and the power of sin is the law. But thanks be to God, who gives us the victory through our Lord Jesus Christ' (1 Cor. 15:56–57). The Lamb, who had himself sacrificed his life, will be the one who will wipe away every tear (see Rev. 7:17). 'Death will be no more; mourning and crying and pain will be no more, for the first things have passed away' (Rev. 21:4). There will be a new heaven and a new earth (see 2 Pet. 3:13; Rev. 21:1). This is why the Christian church, the bride of Christ, in the midst of its and the world's present suffering, cries out in the Spirit: 'Come, Lord Jesus!' (Rev. 22:17–20).[31]

One final point must be made before we conclude this chapter. I have stressed that the new life in the Spirit brings about changes in kind and not simply in degree. It is these changes in kind which make up the new salvific order.[32] Christians, through the indwelling Spirit, have become new creations in Christ, and thus they possess a new kind of relationship

31 Process theology makes much of God being a 'fellow sufferer.' The despair of such a notion is witnessed in the fact that, if process thought is correct, there is no personal immortality nor any notion of Jesus' return in glory when all evil and suffering will be vanquished. Nonetheless, D. Griffin is rather nonchalant and indifferent to this issue. He holds that while 'life beyond bodily death' may give 'one's faith additional dimensions of both vitality and peace, and that this belief also generally deepens one's sense of the importance of other human life and thereby one's concern for others, including the concern for human justice,' it is nonetheless 'not central to the present process theodicy.' *God, Power, and Evil*, pp. 312 and 311. In actual fact, the metaphysical principles contained within process thought do not hold out any hope for personal life after bodily death even for those who desire such. (Of course, any prospect of a bodily resurrection is absolutely impossible and the anticipation of such would be absurd.) Human beings, with their experiences, are but the ontological components out of which God constructs his everlasting existence. In response to this Goetz writes: 'If the purpose of our life and death is finally that we contribute to "the self-creation of God," how, an outraged critic of God might demand, does God's love differ from the love of a famished diner for his meat course?' 'The Suffering God: The Rise of a New Orthodoxy,' *The Christian Century* 103/13 (1986):388.

Nonetheless, Griffin holds that even if one did allow 'a situation where our souls would no longer be influenced by our bodies, there would still be a multiplicity of influences upon each individual, and each individual would still have its capacity for self-determination, even *vis-à-vis* God. The same metaphysical principles which make evil possible now would still obtain then' (p. 312). See also D. Griffin, 'The Possibility of Subjective Immortality in Whitehead's Philosophy,' *The Modern Schoolman* 53 (1975):39–57. So, even if one allowed for 'the hope' of life after bodily death, it would hardly be heaven, but rather an everlasting hell. But it is to this hellish existence that process theology has condemned God, for he is forever doomed to participate in a metaphysical process that is ontologically enmeshed in evil with no hope of perfection. In process thought it is ultimately better to be human and die (cease to exist), than to be God and live for ever. See Goetz, 'The Suffering God,' pp. 388–89.

32 I believe that much contemporary soteriology is gnostic precisely because it refuses to allow Jesus' redemptive work to bring about 'changes in kind,' but only permits 'changes in degree.' See my 'Gnosticism and Contemporary Soteriology: Some Reflections,' *New Blackfriars* 76 (1995):546–54.

with the Father and among themselves. However, the heavenly resurrected life will only differ in degree from the life Christians presently possess and experience. The heavenly life is but the glorious fulfilment of the life already begun here on earth within the present salvific order. There Christians will become fully recreated in Christ and so, in the Spirit, obtain full communion with the Father and with one another.

Conclusion

I trust that I have presented an accurate, if not complete, account of the great drama of salvation. I have done so at some length in order to manifest all its various aspects, and equally to demonstrate how these aspects form the one grand salvific event. I have likewise presented, in some detail, the fruit of this redemptive work in the lives of those who believe and are baptized. In so doing I hope that, at least in some small way, the brilliance and magnificence of this redemptive work, with its abounding efficacy, shines forth in all its splendor.

This was my desire, for Jesus is the Father's decisive and ultimate response to human suffering. In the light of Jesus as the risen Lord, human suffering is newly conceived and radically transformed through the Holy Spirit. This is especially so for those who now live in Christ. It is to this soteriological theme that we now turn.

10

Suffering in the Light of Christ

The mystery of Jesus, as the incarnate Son of God who died for our sins and rose that we might have eternal life, is the Father's response to the mystery of human suffering. Therefore, the experience of suffering can only be fully understood and adequately interpreted in the light of Jesus.[1] As Pope John Paul II states:

> One can say that with the passion of Christ all human suffering has found itself in a new situation. And it is as though Job had foreseen this when he said: 'I know that my Redeemer lives . . .,' and as though he had directed towards it his own suffering, which without the Redemption could not have revealed to him the fullness of its meaning. In the cross of Christ not only is the Redemption accomplished through suffering, but also human suffering itself has been redeemed. Christ – without any fault of his own – took on himself 'the total evil of sin' . . . . The eloquence of the cross and death is, however, completed by the eloquence of the resurrection. Man finds in the resurrection a completely new light, which helps him to go forward through the thick darkness of humiliations, doubts, hopelessness and persecution.[2]

In the previous chapter we examined what the Son of God as man accomplished through his suffering and death on the cross. This redemptive suffering and death not only led to his own resurrection, but it also commenced the eschatological outpouring of the Holy Spirit with all of the effects that flow from it. Through faith and baptism Christians come to share a new life with the Father in Christ through the indwelling of the Holy Spirit. As Pope John Paul II stated above, it is in the light of this gospel of Jesus Christ that human suffering assumes a whole new meaning, and for Christians, through sharing in this gospel life, suffering is experienced and interpreted in an entirely new manner. In this chapter I wish to examine the meaning of all human suffering in the light of the

1 There are obviously other attempts at a philosophical or religious answer to the mystery of suffering, but whatever solution is offered it can only be partially true at best and erroneous at worst.
2 *Salvifici Doloris*, nn. 19 and 20. This is the first official Roman Catholic document that specifically treats the subject of suffering. The Pope's reference to Job's foreseeing the resurrection may have been taken from St Gregory the Great, who makes the same point in his *Expositio in Librum Iob*, 14, 67.

gospel, and more specifically the Christian experience and interpretation of human suffering from within the context of sharing in Jesus' death and resurrection.

It must be remembered that those who espouse a passible and so suffering God have done so in order to give meaning and significance to human suffering. However, as I have extensively argued throughout this study, in making God a passible suffering God, they have not only undermined a true understanding of God, but they have also, in the end, distorted the Christian gospel. In so doing, I believe, they have equally disfigured the Christian experience, interpretation and meaning of human suffering. This chapter wishes to provide a framework for a Christian understanding of human suffering. Thus, while the issue of God's impassibility may seem to have faded into the shadows, this chapter is actually the culmination and completion of all that has gone before.[3]

This will be a rather lengthy chapter. The reason for this is twofold. First, I want to address, as far as possible, the various particular causes of suffering and, in the light of these multiple causes, evaluate the distinct Christian interpretations of and responses to the suffering that these causes have occasioned. Second, because I want to address the actual lived experiences of people, I will try to make this chapter as practical and concrete as possible.[4]

Suffering and the Body of Christ

The keystone of this chapter is the ecclesial reality of the body of Christ. We saw in the last chapter that all those who come to believe in Jesus as their Lord and Savior and are baptized come to live in Christ. 'For as many of you as were baptized into Christ have put on Christ. There is neither Jew nor Greek ... for you are all one in Christ Jesus' (Gal. 3:27–28). Christians constitute one living body (see Rom. 12:4–5; 1 Cor. 6:15; Eph. 3:6; Col. 3:15) with him as the head (see Eph. 1:22–23). The great mystery revealed by the Father is that all would be united in Christ (see Eph. 1:10). 'He is the head of the body, the church' (Col. 1:18). This incorporation into Christ's body is the work of the Holy Spirit, who is its principle of life (see Eph. 4:4).

> For just as the body is one and has many members, and all the members of the body, though many, are one body, so it is with Christ. For in the one Spirit we were all baptized into one body –

---

3 As with the previous chapter, my discussion of human suffering and its meaning will be primarily from a scriptural perspective. Other authors will be cited only to illustrate this scriptural understanding. For extracts from, as well as the teaching of the Fathers on suffering, see J. Walsh and R.G. Walsh, *Divine Providence and Human Suffering* (Wilmington: Michael Glazier, 1985).

4 It must be remembered that, while I wish to be as practical and concrete as possible, what I say about the Christian experience, interpretation and response to evil and to the suffering that it causes does not in any way imply that all Christians actually, within their own hearts and minds, experience, interpret and respond to such suffering in this manner. How to experience, interpret and respond to evil and to the suffering that it causes in a Christian manner can itself be a life-long, and often unfinished, process.

Jews or Greeks, slaves or free – and we were all made to drink of the one Spirit (1 Cor. 12:12–13).

Christ and the members of his body actually form one new man (Eph. 2:15–16). As the one new man in Christ Christians live within and so share the very life of the Trinity.

Because a proper understanding of the body of Christ is central to our present discussion, we must clearly discern the similarities and the differences between the human body and the body of Christ. First, this Pauline conception of the body of Christ is more than a mere metaphor in that the body of Christ is not merely a moral body or association, but is an actual and true living reality just as the human body is one living reality. There is a genuine correspondence between the relationship of Christ and Christians and the relationship of the members or parts of the living human body. Second, this correspondence lies precisely in that both share, in a similar fashion, one common life by which they are one living reality. The human body is one for all the members or parts of the body are constituted as one living reality or being through the soul. Similarly, the body of Christ is one living reality, and it is the Holy Spirit who forms it into one living reality. As the human soul gives life and so unites the members of a human body, so it is the Spirit that causes Christ and his members to be one living body. Third, the important difference between the body of Christ and the human body is that the body of Christ is composed of distinct persons while the members of the human body form one person. While the Holy Spirit establishes that Christ and the members of his body are one, this living unity does not diminish or undermine the distinct individuality of its members, rather the personal integrity of each Christian member is enhanced.[5]

---

5 It is because of this likeness and difference between the human body and the body of Christ that the Christian tradition, especially within Catholic Church, has termed this reality 'the Mystical Body of Christ.' The term 'Mystical Body,' first, wishes to assert that the body of Christ is more than a moral entity, but, like the human body, is indeed one living reality. Pope Pius XII stated in his encyclical *Mystici Corporis*:

> In the body which is called moral, there is no other principle of unity than the common end and the common pursuit by all of the same end by means of a social authority. But in the Mystical Body of which we are speaking, another internal principle of unity is added to this common pursuit, which, existing truly in the entire organism as well as in each one of its parts, and active there, is of such excellence that by itself it immeasurably surpasses every other body of unity which supplies the cohesive force for any body, whether physical or moral.

> Moreover, the term 'Mystical Body' specifies that Christ's body, unlike the human body, is composed of distinct human persons who do not lose their distinctiveness in becoming members of his body. As Pius XII stated:

> For while in the natural body the principle of unity joins all the parts in such a way that each one lacks in an absolute manner what is called proper subsistence, on the contrary in the Mystical Body the force of the mutual union, although intimate, joins all the members among themselves in such a way that each one of them has full enjoyment of his proper personality.

> And third, Christ's body is mystical in that it is formed into one reality not by some natural principle of life as is the human body, but by the supernatural life of the Holy Spirit, who is the soul or life principle of the body of Christ. Again Pius XII asserted:

I want to contend that this ecclesial reality – the body of Christ – is the pre-eminent locus from which to understand fully and in which to interpret properly all human suffering, both the suffering of Christians and non-Christians alike. This one ecclesial reality of the body of Christ is now the new existential context either in which or around which all sin and evil is enacted and all human suffering is experienced. Everything that now occurs within time and human history, including every sin and evil, and every form of suffering that accrues to every sin and evil, is subsumed, in some manner, within the one reality of Christ and his body. Thus all evil and the suffering due to it must be interpreted from within this ecclesial context. From within this context I want initially to discuss two essential truths that pertain to human suffering as a whole or in general. I will then proceed to discuss the various causes of suffering with their related interpretations and responses.

Human Suffering: Sharing in the Resurrection of Christ

The first essential truth is that Christians, as members of Christ's body, are united to *the risen Christ* as to their head. Being incorporated into the body of Christ, Christians become a new creation in Christ, sharing in the resurrected life of his Spirit (see 2 Cor. 5:17). Moreover, as I will argue shortly, all of humankind, through his body the church, is adjoined to *the risen Christ*. Thus all human suffering must be interpreted from within the context that all who suffer are united, to a greater or lesser extent, to *the risen Christ*. For the sake of clarity and order, I will first examine the suffering of Christians, and then the suffering of those who are not.

In the Gospel of John Jesus exhorted his disciples to be at peace. 'In the world you have tribulation; but be of good cheer, I have overcome the world' (Jn 16:33). Their hearts should not be troubled because there are many rooms in his Father's house, and he is going to prepare a place for them. 'I will come again and will take you to myself that where I am you may be also' (Jn 14:1–3). In the midst of tribulation and suffering, Christians cannot only be untroubled, but they can even be cheerful because of the hope of the resurrection held out to them through the victory of Jesus.

Christians can possess such an attitude in the midst of their present suffering because, as members of Christ's body, they are already united

---

It is to this Spirit of Christ as to an invisible principle that is to be attributed the fact that all the parts are united among themselves as well as with their sublime Head, since he is entire in the Head, entire in the Body, entire in each of the members.... [as] Leo XIII expressed in succinct and energetic fashion in his Encyclical Letter *Divinum Illud*: 'It is sufficient to affirm that if Christ is the Head of the Church, the Holy Spirit is its soul.'

In *Lumen Gentium* n. 7, the Second Vatican Council reaffirmed Pope Pius XII's understanding of the Mystical Body of Christ including the notion that the Holy Spirit can be seen as its soul. The Council not only footnotes previous magisterial statements, but also patristic and medieval authors, such as Augustine, John Chrysostom, Didymus of Alexandria, and Thomas Aquinas.

to their risen Lord, and therefore, already share in his victory. God the Father 'made us alive together with Christ (by grace you have been saved), and raised us up with him, and made us sit with him in the heavenly places in Christ Jesus' (Eph. 2:5–6). Christians are presently 'alive together with' Christ (Col. 2:13). It must be remembered that Jesus is risen as a glorious man, and Christian men and women, as members of his body through the Holy Spirit, live in him, and so they are already in communion with and share in his risen humanity.[6] Because Christian men and women are united to the risen man Jesus, their physical and emotional sufferings are experienced from within his resurrected humanity. In this life Christians presently suffer and die in Christ, and so they suffer and die as partakers of his resurrection. Christians, as members of his body, belong to the risen Lord (see Rom. 14:8), and thus, the grandeur of God's great mystery is 'Christ in you, the hope of glory' (Col. 1:27).

Because Christians already share in Christ's resurrection as living members of his body, they are enjoined to set their minds not on the tribulations of this present world, but on the realities of their future glory. 'For you have died, and your life is hid with Christ in God. When Christ who is our life appears, then you also will appear with him in glory' (Col. 3:1–4). Having shared in Christ's death through baptism, 'we shall certainly be united with him in a resurrection like his' (Rom. 6:5). Because Christians are children of the Father, they are fellow heirs with Christ, provided they willingly suffer with him in order that they 'may also be glorified with him' (Rom. 8:17). Christians have conquered death and all of the evils that it embodies, for 'thanks be to God, who gives us the victory through our Lord Jesus Christ' (1 Cor. 15:57). Paul could declare that 'I consider that the sufferings of this present time are not worth comparing with the glory that is to be revealed to us' (Rom. 8:18). Therefore, Christians not only rejoice in their 'hope of sharing the glory of God,' but as Paul further stated:

> More than that, we rejoice in our sufferings, knowing that suffering produces endurance, and endurance produces character, and character produces hope, and hope does not disappoint us, because God's love has been poured into our hearts through the Holy Spirit which has been given to us. Rom. 5:2–5.

No evil – tribulation, distress, persecution, famine, nakedness, peril, or the sword – can separate Christians from the love of God in Christ. 'No, in all these things we are more than conquerors through him who loved us' (Rom. 8:35–39). Just as Christians, in their suffering, have borne the image of the man of dust, so shall they 'bear the image of the man of heaven' (1 Cor. 15:49). Christians are not to lose heart.

> Though our outer nature is wasting away, our inner nature is being renewed every day. For this slight momentary affliction is preparing

---

6 It is by partaking of the Eucharist that Christians come to share most fully in the risen life of Jesus for they eat his risen body and drink his risen blood (see John 6). The Eucharist will be discussed more fully later.

for us an eternal weight of glory beyond all comparison, because we look not to the things that are seen but to the things that are unseen; for the things that are seen are transient, but the things that are unseen are eternal. 2 Cor. 4:16–18.

For the sake of Christ Paul willingly suffered the loss of everything. He depended entirely on the righteousness of God that he might know the power of Christ's resurrection, and 'may share his suffering becoming like him in his death, that if possible I may attain the resurrection from the dead' (Phil. 3:8–11).

James exhorts his readers: 'Blessed is the man who endures trial, for when he has stood the test he will receive the crown of life which God has promised to those who love him' (James 1:12). The First Letter of Peter similarly states:

Beloved, do not be surprised at the fiery ordeal which comes upon you to prove you, as though something strange were happening to you. But rejoice in so far as you share Christ's suffering, that you may also rejoice and be glad when his glory is revealed. 1 Pet. 4:12–13.

The final scene of heavenly glory is depicted in the Book of Revelation:

Behold, the dwelling of God is with men. He will dwell with them, and they shall be his people, and God himself will be with them, he will wipe away every tear from their eyes, and death shall be no more, neither shall there be mourning nor crying nor pain any more, for the former things have passed away. . . . Behold, I make all things new. Rev. 21:3–5.

Thus, being members of his body, and so living in communion with the risen Christ, is the supreme consolation experienced by Christians in the midst of their suffering and death. There is none greater, and its importance cannot be overestimated. Paul reminded the Corinthians that 'as we share abundantly in Christ's suffering, so through Christ we share abundantly in comfort too' (2 Cor. 1:5). As the above demonstrates this consolation is multifaceted.

First, Christians are confident in faith that, in Christ, they have been freed from the final and greatest evil with its everlasting and unimaginable suffering – the damnation of hell – for there is 'no condemnation for those who are in Christ Jesus' (Rom. 8:1). This is a source of great hope and consolation for Christians, one that should not be ignored or ridiculed.[7]

Second, Christians know that whatever evil befalls them or whatever suffering they endure they are inseparably united, in the here and now, to Jesus their risen Lord. Being united to their risen Lord, Christians can experience, through the Holy Spirit, the love, consolation, mercy, and

---

7 While many today either deny the reality of hell or believe that no one will actually experience it, they hold such errors at their own and others' peril. Scripture and the Christian tradition both speak of hell as a reality, and while Christians may hope that all are saved, they must perceive it as a reality from which they have been saved and as a reality that they and others, because of unrepented 'mortal' sin, could actually experience. See *Catechism of the Catholic Church*, nn. 1033–37.

compassion of their heavenly Father (see Rom. 5:5). To abide within the body of Christ is to abide within the very life of the Trinity, and thus to experience and know, even in the midst of suffering, this abounding and consummate communion of love and life.

Third, being so presently united to Christ, Christians have the guarantee and the assurance that the fulness of joy and the blessedness of eternal life will ultimately be theirs no matter what their present circumstances may be.

The above is equally the consolation that Christ, through his church, offers to all of God's people. The church, as Christ's body, is commissioned to proclaim to all peoples the good news of redemption in Christ Jesus (see Mt 28:18–20). The good news is that, in the midst of the world's horrendous evil and suffering, all men and women, of every nation and race, can come to experience and know the consolation and the hope of the risen Jesus in this life, and come to obtain the full reality of his resurrected glory in heaven. Christians offer not their own but the Father's definitive answer to a suffering and sin-bound world. The consolation and hope experienced by Christians, as members of Christ's body, should compel them, in love and compassion, to bear witness both to Jesus' victory over sin and condemnation and so over all suffering, and to the new freedom and life of the Holy Spirit. In the face of the world's suffering, to deprive humankind of the gospel is to deprive men and women of hope, and so enslave them in despair. In the midst of their own suffering Christians are exhorted to 'always be prepared to make a defence to any one who calls you to account for the hope that is in you, yet do it with gentleness and reverence' (1 Pet. 3:15).[8]

While love demands, in the face of sin and death, that the church's first and highest priority is to proclaim the gospel so as to bring others into full communion within the body of Christ, it is not the church's sole obli-

---

8 This is not the place to articulate a whole theology of evangelization, but its importance should not be neglected. If the Father, the supreme evangelizer, in that, he is the eternal author of his Word, thought it necessary to send his Son into the world in order that humankind might be saved, then the church ought to possess the same mind of the Father with all its urgency. The church, in conformity with the Father's mind, recognizes that the eternal destiny of his people is at stake.

While it must be affirmed that those who are not Christian can be saved and that other religions do contain 'seeds' of truth, yet the reality is that those who have not come to faith in Christ cannot possess the same quality of assurance that the Christian gospel offers.

For Roman Catholic statements on the importance of evangelization see the Second Vatican Council's *Lumen Gentium*, nn. 13–17 and *Ad Gentes Divinitus*; Pope Paul VI's classic *Evangelii Nuntiandi*; Pope John Paul II's *Redemptoris Missio*; and *Catechism of the Catholic Church*, nn. 836–59.

Moreover, it should be noted that inherent within a theology of a suffering God is a feeble theology of evangelization. Those who propose that God suffers in himself speak as if this gives consolation to those who suffer. This has been shown to be a deceptive consolation. Moreover, they speak as if everyone, regardless of whether one is a Christian or not, is equally consoled by a suffering God. Thus, there is no urgent need to preach the gospel. But this too is false to the gospel. The Father does wish to console everyone, and that is precisely why he sent his Son into the world. However, the Father can only fully console those who are in union with Christ for Christ is the Father's consolation. In is only in Christ Jesus that one can come to experience fully the riches of the Father's mercy (see Eph. 1:3, 2:4–7).

gation. It must not be forgotten that through the Incarnation, the Son of God, as the Second Vatican Council stated, 'has in a certain way united himself with each man.'[9] Therefore, the risen Christ, who suffered and died for all, now reaches out to all that suffer. But it is not Christ, as if in isolation from his body, who compassionately embraces all who suffer, but he does so only in union with his body the church.

Through the outpouring of the Holy Spirit Christ established his body, the church, 'as the universal sacrament of salvation.'[10] As the universal sacrament, the church is 'sign and instrument, that is, of communion with God and of unity among all men.'[11] The church makes Christ's salvific work present to the whole world, and in so doing joins all men and women to Christ.

All men are called to this catholic unity which prefigures and promotes universal peace. And in different ways to it belong, or are related: the Catholic faithful, others who believe in Christ, and finally all mankind, called by God's grace to salvation.[12]

Because the church, as the universal sacrament of salvation, is so united to all, Pope John Paul II has resolved that the church must embrace 'the hopes and sufferings' of all. 'Indeed, precisely because Christ united himself with her in his mystery of Redemption, the Church must be strongly united with each man.'[13] The church unites itself to all men and women who suffer in at least two ways.

First, the efficacy of the church's prayer must be noted. In union with Christ its head, the church continually and steadfastly intercedes for all of God's people – Christian and non-Christian alike. Because Christ now acts in union with his body, the prayer of the church, including that of the church of glory (Mary and the communion of saints), is the spring from which Christ's grace and consolation flows to all who suffer. Through its prayer, whether in and through its eucharistic liturgy or in and through the personal prayer of individual Christians, the church gathers all human beings who suffer evil and injustice close to Christ who suffered and died for all.[14] Through its prayer Christ's body embraces all of humankind, and so allows all men and women, even if

---

9 *Gaudium et Spes*, n. 22.
10 *Lumen Gentium*, n. 48.
11 *Lumen Gentium*, n. 1.
12 *Lumen Gentium*, n. 13. See also *Gaudium et Spes*, n. 43; *Ad Gentes*, nn. 7, 21; and Pope John Paul II, *Dominum et Vivificantem*, nn. 61–64 and *Redemptoris Missio*, n. 9.2.
13 *Redemptor Hominis*, n. 18.1.
14 The third eucharistic prayer of the Catholic church states: 'Lord, may this sacrifice, which has made our peace with you, advance the peace and salvation of all the world. . . . In mercy and love unite all your children wherever they may be.' The fourth eucharistic prayer prays that the Father would 'Remember those who take part in this offering, those here present and all your people, and all who seek you with a sincere heart.'
   It should be noted as well that contemplative religious orders of men and women embody in their vocation the truth of this reality. These men and women live within the confines of their monasteries, and so, normally, do not have a great deal of personal contact with those who suffer outside their walls. Nonetheless, through their prayer, as members of Christ's body, they are a fount from which Christ pours out great consolation and compassion upon those who suffer.

they are not consciously aware of its source, to share in, to some degree, the grace and the consolation of Jesus and the hope that only the Spirit of life can give.

Second, the church, through its various associations – parishes, local churches, religious orders, national and international charitable and social institutions, etc., as well as through the good works of its individual members, reaches out to those who suffer. Other secular social and charitable institutions as well as men and women of good will may equally care for those who suffer from poverty, famine, natural disasters, and war. However, Christians, while performing similar work, do so knowing that Christ, through his Incarnation, has united himself to all of God's people and so they too, as members of his body, are united to all.[15]

Thus Christians, through their charitable work, embrace those who suffer not solely from a humanitarian viewpoint, but from within the truth that all men and women are their brothers and sisters in Christ. Jesus distinctly told his disciples that when they feed the hungry, give drink to the thirsty, welcome the stranger, clothe the naked, visit the imprisoned, they do so to him. So much is this the case that they will be judged on the fulfilment of this truth (see Mt 25:31–46). In actual fact Christians, as followers of Christ, must be known by their love for others, and so in loving others manifest and make present the love of Jesus (see Jn 13:35).[16]

In their efforts, then, to alleviate the evils of social, economic and political injustice, or in their fight to protect the rights of the unborn, the mentally impaired and the terminally ill, or in their care for the poor, the sick, and the dying, Christians bear witness and make real the love and consolation of Jesus. In so doing they make Jesus himself present. The charitable work of Christians gathers all men and women within the domain of Jesus and his church. In this way those who suffer are not only physically, materially and emotionally sustained in the midst of their suffering, but they equally come to share in a hope and reality that transcends their present condition. They come to experience the love of the Father who cares for the weak and oppressed, and who desires that they share in his eternal glory through Christ his Son. The good deeds of Christians also bear witness that evil, with all its suffering, will ultimately not have the final word. Through their acts of charity, Christians make present, even to those who do not believe, the hope and assurance that good will ultimately triumph over evil, an assurance founded upon

---

15 Pope John Paul II has stated that the church, 'as the sacrament of salvation for all mankind ... is the sign and promoter of Gospel values.' Thus the church contributes to 'mankind's pilgrimage of conversion to God's plan through her witness and through such activities as dialogue, human promotion, commitment to justice and peace, education and the care for the sick, and aid to the poor and to children. In carrying on these activities, however, she never loses sight of the priority of the transcendent and spiritual realities which are premises of eschatological salvation.' *Redemptoris Missio*, n. 20.4.

16 Scholars debate whether or not the above two passages refer solely to the care and love of Christians for one another or to the Christians' care and love of all. The common traditional interpretation is that Jesus' words include not just Christians but everyone.

the mystery of Christ's death and resurrection. This hope, and so the consolation of such hope, thus penetrates the hearts of those who suffer.[17]

The Risen Christ: Sharing in Human Suffering

In the above discussion I have argued that Christians, as members of Christ's body, share in his resurrected life, and so the suffering that they presently endure is experienced in communion with the victorious risen Jesus. As I will discuss later, there is a difference between the suffering caused by one's own personal sin and the suffering due to one's faithfulness to the gospel, yet both forms of suffering are experienced in communion with the resurrected Jesus. I have also discussed how those who are not Christians, through evangelization, and through the prayer and the charitable work of Christians, also participate in the consolation and the hope that comes from the risen Christ. I want now to discuss the second general truth concerning human suffering within the context of the body of Christ. It is complementary or reciprocal to the above first truth.

If, by becoming members of Christ's body, Christians come to live, in the midst of their suffering, in communion with the risen Christ, equally the risen Christ, as the head of his body, comes to share in their sufferings, regardless of whether their suffering is due to their own personal sin or to their faithfulness to the gospel. While Jesus is gloriously risen, and thus beyond sin and death and so evil, yet as head of his body, which is still suffering under the constraints of sin, evil, and death, he too, as the head, is still, in some real sense, suffering.[18] As head of his body he cannot be immune from the lived experiences of his body, whether they be good or evil, for both head and members embody one life through the

---

17 The most notable and obvious, but by no means exclusive, recent example of this is Mother Theresa of Calcutta's work with the poor and the dying.

18 I must admit that this is a mystery that I am not sure I fully understand, not in the sense of comprehending it, for no Christian mystery can be fully comprehended, but in the sense that I do not even know fully what the mystery is. Nonetheless, I will attempt to articulate as much of this mystery as I presently grasp.

When I say that the risen Christ 'suffers,' I do not mean that he physically and emotionally suffers as we do who are not risen. As a risen and glorious man, the Son of God can no longer suffer physically and emotionally in the same sense as we do. However, as risen and glorious, Christ is still a man, and thus still possesses human emotional states, though now in a risen manner. He still possesses the human emotions of joy, compassion and love. He continues to find sin and evil, and the suffering they cause, repugnant. Being in communion with the members of his body, who are not risen, their experiences are his experiences. The manner in which he, as risen, experiences these 'un-risen' experiences of his earthly body, I do not know. Thus, I am stating something that I believe has to be the case, but I do not understand the manner or the mode in which it is the case.

It might also be worth noting that it is easier for Christians to know what it means to share in the resurrected life of Christ as being members of his body. The reason being that, through faith and the working of the Holy Spirit, it is *their experience*. However, it is much more difficult, if not impossible, to grasp fully the risen Christ's experience of our suffering for that is *his experience*. My spiritual instinct tells me that the more Christians grow in holiness, and so are able to unite themselves more fully to the sufferings of others, both of Christians and non-Christians alike, the more they will understand how the risen Christ himself suffers. But I am not yet 'there.'

Holy Spirit. Moreover, if the body of Christ reaches out and embraces all who suffer so as to gather them within the consolation that comes from the risen Christ, so the risen Christ, in union with his body who embraces all peoples, comes to share in their suffering as well. Pope John Paul II has stated that Christ 'himself in his redemptive suffering has become, in a certain sense, a sharer in all human suffering.'[19] Thus the consolation of all who suffer, Christians and non-Christians alike, resides not only in their sharing in Christ's risen life, but also in his sharing in their present tribulation. There is scriptural warrant for maintaining such a position, and it is this truth that I now wish to develop.

When Jesus, in the glorious light and splendor of his risen state, appeared to Paul on the road to Damascus, he did not tell Paul that he was persecuting 'his followers' or 'his disciples' or even 'his body.' Rather, Jesus was emphatic: 'Saul, Saul, why do you persecute me?' When Paul asked who he was, seemingly in defense since he thought he was only persecuting earthly Christians and not some heavenly being, Jesus answered: 'I am Jesus, whom you are persecuting' (Acts 9:4–5). I believe that it is from this conversion experience that Paul first perceived and later developed his understanding of the body of Christ, but, more importantly for our present purposes, Paul realized that in persecuting Christians, and so making them suffer, he was actually persecuting Jesus and so making him suffer. As Paul would later declare: 'If one member suffers, all suffer together' (1 Cor. 12:26). It is not just Christians who suffer together as Christ's body. As its head Jesus too is a member of his body, and so is not exempt from the sufferings of his body, whether these be through persecution, the sins of its members, or any other evil.[20]

It is in the light of this truth that we must interpret, I believe, those passages within the New Testament which speak of Christians sharing in the sufferings of Christ. For example, in a passages already quoted, Paul told the Corinthians: 'For as we share abundantly in Christ's sufferings (ὅτι καθὼς περισσεύει τὰ παθήματα τοῦ Χριστοῦ εἰς ἡμᾶς), so thorough Christ we share abundantly in comfort too' (2 Cor. 1:5). Equally, Paul spoke of his desire 'to share his [Christ's]sufferings (κοινωνίαν παθημάτων αὐτοῦ), becoming like him in his death' so that he might also share in his resurrection (Phil. 3:10). Paul also assured the Romans that they are heirs of Christ, 'provided we suffer with him (συμπάσχομεν) in order that we may also be glorified with him' (Rom. 8:17). Moreover, the First Letter of Peter exhorts its readers: 'Rejoice in so far as you share Christ's sufferings (Καθὸ κοινωνεῖτε τοῖς τοῦ Χριστοῦ παθήμασιν χαίρετε), that you may also rejoice and be glad when his glory is revealed' (1 Pet. 4:12). The author stated that he is himself 'a witness of the sufferings of Christ

---

19 *Salvifici Doloris*, n. 20.
20 With reference to this passage Augustine stated:

> Christ is now raised above the heavens; but he still experiences on earth whatever sufferings we his members feel. He showed that this is true when he called out from heaven: 'Saul, Saul, why do you persecute me?' And: 'I was thirsty and you gave me drink.' *Sermon on the Ascension* taken from *The Liturgy of the Hours According to the Roman Rite*, Solemnity of the Ascension.

(μάρτυς τῶν τοῦ Χριστοῦ παθημάτων) as well as a partaker in the glory that is to be revealed' (1 Pet. 5:1).[21]

The experience of suffering articulated in these passages is multifaceted. To grasp their full significance each facet of the experience must be clearly perceived as well as the total unity of the experience. First, it is obviously Christians who are presently suffering – Paul, the Corinthians, the Romans, the readers of First Peter and the author himself. It is the present suffering of Christians that is the cause for comment.

Second, it is the present suffering of Christians that constitutes, as the Greek present tense attests, the present suffering of Christ. The passages are not referring merely to the past suffering of Christ, although this is implied. Nor are Christians merely imitating the past suffering of Christ by way of following his example. Rather, Christians, in their present suffering, are sharing in the present suffering of Christ.[22]

Third, as the last point intimates, what is most striking about these passages is that the suffering of Christians is primarily predicated not of themselves but of Christ. It is not simply that Christ is united to their suffering, but that they, in their suffering, are united to his suffering. These passages, then, are in conformity with and testify to the truth of Paul's conversion experience. It is primarily Christ who continues to suffer in communion with his body.

This may at first appear an odd turn about, but it actually expresses the great mystery of Christ and his body. It is Christ who is the head of his body, and therefore, what accrues to his body primarily accrues to him as its head. Christ is the primary subject of all the acts and the experiences of Christians, that is, those who are members of his body (see Phil. 1:21). Thus, as members of his body, the suffering of Christians is predicated not of the body itself, that is, of themselves, but of him who is the head of the body – Christ himself – for as the head of his body Christ has made the suffering of his body truly his own. As its Savior, Christ first suffered on behalf of his body, and now, as its Lord and head, he continues to suffer in union with it.[23]

While we will have reason to discuss the following passage again later, it is here that the meaning of Colossians 1:24 might be properly interpreted. Paul (or another author) wrote: 'Now I rejoice in my sufferings for your sake, and in my flesh I complete what is lacking in Christ's afflictions (ἀνταναπληρῶ τὰ ὑστερήματα τῶν θλίψεων τοῦ Χριστοῦ ἐν τῇ

21 For an excellent article on these and related passages see M. Hooker, 'Interchange and Suffering' in *Suffering and Martyrdom in the New Testament*, eds W. Horbury and B. McNeil (Cambridge: Cambridge University Press, 1981), pp. 70–83. See also her *Not Ashamed of the Gospel*.

22 See L. Dupré, 'Jesus Still in Agony?: Meditation on a Negro Spiritual,' *Word and Spirit: A Monastic Review* 1 (1979):191–95.

23 This is in keeping with the human body analogy. When my stomach is upset, I can say that such is the case, but I also say: 'I am sick.' I normally do not say: 'My stomach is sick.' It is the human person who is sick and so suffers when one of his or her members is infected or diseased. Similarly, it is Christ himself who suffers when one of his members suffers. He does not say: 'My body is suffering.' He says: 'I am suffering.' The difference being that in the body of Christ both Christ and his members are persons in themselves, and so both are personally conscious and so suffer as distinct persons in communion with one another.

σαρκί μου) for the sake of his body, that is the church.' Yes, Christ has completed the work of salvation through his suffering on the cross. There is nothing more for him to do in order to conquer sin and death. Therefore, Paul's suffering should not be interpreted as if he, in his suffering, was accomplishing something that Christ left incomplete. Rather, Paul realized that his own sufferings in the flesh are the afflictions of Christ who is the head of the body, and thus his sufferings were the completion of or the filling up of Christ's present suffering. It is the present afflictions of Christ and not the past sufferings that Paul was completing. Paul was suffering, in union with Christ the head, on behalf of the body, the church. Paul's present suffering was truly Christ's present affliction, and its purpose was the same as that of Christ's, that is, for the up-building and growth of the body so that it might reach full maturity with Christ its head.[24] That is why Paul could rejoice in his sufferings. He knew that they were contributing to the growth of Christ's body, the church.[25]

24 I noted in the previous chapter that Jesus, during his earthly life, grew in his love for us, the cross being the attainment of its perfection. I wonder though, in the light of his present suffering in union with his body, if, as a risen man, Christ's love is not continuing to grow since, as a risen man, he continues to enact deeds of love on our behalf. Heaven may be the experience of the everlasting maturing of Christ's love for his body and the everlasting maturing of his body's love for him and one another for all are striving to achieve the perfection of divine love, the depth of which can never be attained.

25 Pope John Paul II interprets this passage in a similar fashion.

Thus, with this openness to every human suffering, Christ has accomplished the world's Redemption through his own suffering. For, at the same time, this Redemption, even though it was completely achieved by Christ's suffering, lives on and in its own special way develops in the history of man. It lives and develops as the Body of Christ, the Church, and in this dimension every human suffering, by reason of the loving union with Christ, completes the suffering of Christ. It completes that suffering *just as the Church completes the redemptive work of Christ.* The mystery of the Church – that body which completes in itself also Christ's crucified and risen body – indicates at the same time the space and context in which human sufferings complete the suffering of Christ. Only within this radius and dimension of the Church as the Body of Christ, which continually develops in space and time, can one think and speak of 'what is lacking' in the sufferings of Christ. The Apostle, in fact, makes this clear when he writes of 'completing what is lacking in Christ's afflictions for the sake of his body, that is, the Church.' *Salvifici Doloris,* n. 24.

A.E. Harvey, in his insightful study *Renewal Through Suffering: A Study of 2 Corinthians* (Edinburgh: T & T Clark, 1996), argues that Paul's experience of nearly dying at Ephesus, just prior to his writing 2 Corinthians, radically altered his perception of what it means to suffer in Christ. Moreover, from this experience Paul clearly grasped the spiritual and apostolic benefits that flowed from such suffering. Harvey believes that 2 Corinthians and Paul's subsequent letters testify to this deeper understanding of Christian suffering.

His [Paul's] experience of suffering bringing the suffer closer to Christ, causing an inward renewal and spilling over into benefits for others, caused him to write of it as something of positive value in itself; and this, it seems, is without precedent in any Jewish or pagan sources known to us, and is hard to parallel in the revered writing of any other major religion. P. 129.

A.T. Hanson concludes his study on Paul's notion of suffering by stating: 'We cannot avoid the conclusion that Paul regarded the sufferings and possible death of the

Fourth, in being united to the sufferings of Christ their head, Christians are not just imitating the past suffering of their Savior, they are presently being conformed into, by sharing in, his crucified likeness. In their suffering Christians bear the marks of Jesus in their own flesh (see Gal. 6:17). As Paul stated: 'I have been crucified with Christ; it is no longer I who live, but Christ who lives in me; and the life I now live in the flesh I live by faith in the Son of God, who loved me and gave himself for me' (Gal. 2:20).

Fifth, by being conformed, through their suffering, into the likeness of their crucified Savior, Christians are comforted in knowing that they are presently, as the above passages attest, equally sharing in Christ's resurrection, and so being conformed into the likeness of their glorified head. It must be remembered that it is the risen and victorious Christ who is suffering, and so it is the Christ who has already conquered sin, death and all evil. Thus Christians who share in Christ's present suffering, as members of his body, do so as sharers in Christ's victory. Christians, through their present suffering, are sharing Christ's present suffering so that, in being conformed into the likeness of his death, they might, in the future, come to share fully in the likeness of his present risen glory (see Rom. 6:5).

These truths, I believe, are again a source of great comfort to Christians in the midst of their suffering. They know, in faith, that the suffering they experience is not merely experienced by Christ their head, but more deeply that the suffering they experience is primarily the suffering of Christ their head. They are simply, yet significantly and profoundly, suffering in communion with him for the sake of their brothers and sisters and for the salvation of the world. But they equally know, in faith, that Christ their head is not only their suffering head but also their risen head, and thus they are assured that he and they, in communion with him, have conquered all suffering. Their suffering, as was Christ's, is their path to eternal glory.[26]

---

apostles as possessing an atoning, reconciling, salvific value.' The reason for such a conclusion resides in the truth that 'all that Paul and his companions did and suffered they did and suffered *in Christ.' The Paradox of the Cross in the Thought of St Paul* (Sheffield: JSOT Press, 1987), p. 36. See also pp. 25–37. Similarly, Hanson sees that, within the Pauline theology of the cross, Christians, as the *Militia Christi*, are waging the same battle as did Christ, and so participate in his same sufferings (see pp. 100–28). (I am grateful to A. Moore for alerting me to the above two studies.)

    W.F. Flemington interprets Colossians 1:24 as part of the Pauline theology of being 'in Christ.' This is true, but it fails to recognize that to be 'in Christ' is to share not merely in Christ's past sufferings but in his present sufferings. See 'On the Interpretation of Colossians 1:24' in *Suffering and Martyrdom in the New Testament*, pp. 84–90.

26 The notion of the Communion of Saints is also significant here. The saints are still living members of the body of Christ. Thus, they are living testimonies of hope for their brothers and sisters who still reside within this world – a world of suffering and tears. Moreover, they are still working members within the body of Christ. Thus, they equally intercede and act on behalf of their 'earthly' brothers and sisters. In solidarity with the 'earthly' body, they indeed continue to suffer in union with Christ their head. This is why Catholics 'pray' to the saints. They realize that the saints are their brothers and sisters, and that they are as much a part of their lives, if not more so, as those on earth. Thus the Saints in heaven are a source of great consolation for the saints on earth.

To re-enforce our scriptural examination of Christ's present suffering, it is also worth noting the Christian tradition on this crucial point. H. de Lubac provides patristic and medieval selections which speak of Christ continuing to suffer with his body. Origen, for example, commenting on Jesus' words 'I tell you, I will never again drink of this fruit of the vine until that day when I drink it new with you in my Father's kingdom' (Mt 26:29), argued that, since this is held out to the apostles as a future joy and one that he himself will not enjoy until they enter the Father's kingdom, he himself continues to grieve and suffer until all are united with him in the heavenly kingdom.

> It is inconceivable that Paul should grieve over sinners and weep over those who fall away, while my own Lord Jesus should be dry-eyed as he approaches his Father, when he stands by the altar and offers propitiation for us. 'He who approaches the altar does not drink the wine of gladness,' that is to say he still tastes the bitterness of our sins. He has no heart to drink that wine alone in the Kingdom of God – he is waiting for us; for did he not say, 'until I drink with you'? It is we then who by the negligence of our lives delay his happiness.

> Surely, too, if you who are a member have not perfect joy as long as a member is missing, how much more will he, our Lord and Savior, consider his joy incomplete while any member of his body is missing. ... He is loath to receive his perfect happiness without you, that is, without his people who constitute his body and his members.[27]

Julian of Norwich can speak of the continual thirst of Christ until the end of time.

> For this is the ghostly thirst of Christ: the love-longing that lasteth and ever shall, till we see that sight [the oneing of all mankind that shall be saved unto the Blessed Trinity] at Doomsday. For we shall be saved and shall be Christ's joy and his bliss, some be yet here and some be to come, and so shall some be, unto that day. Therefore this is his thirst and love-longing, to have us all together whole in him, to his bliss .... Anent that Christ is our Head, he is glorified and impassible; and anent his Body in which all his members be knit, he is not yet fully glorified, nor all impassible. Therefore the same desire and thirst that he had upon the Cross (which desire, longing and thirst, as to my sight, was in him from without beginning) the same hath he yet, and shall, unto the time that the last soul that shall be saved is come up to his bliss.... The ghostly thirst is lasting in him as long as we be in need, drawing us up to his bliss.[28]

Adelman of Brescia, commenting on Colossians 1:24 where the author speaks of completing what is lacking in the sufferings of Christ, states that Paul equates his own sufferings with those of Christ's present sufferings. 'Therefore Christ suffered in Paul and was crucified in Peter, both

<hr>

27 *Hom. in Leviticum*, 7. This and the following two passages are taken from H. de Lubac, *Catholicism* (San Francisco: Ignatius Press, 1988), pp. 397–407. I am grateful to N. Healy for pointing out these passages.

28 *Revelation of Divine Love*, Chap. 31.

Peter and Paul being in Christ citizens of heaven.' Even though Paul, in one sense was already with Christ in heaven, yet, since Paul was 'still being buffeted on earth by an angel of Satan' so too was Christ. The reason being that when one member of the body suffers so too do all members suffer including Christ. This suffering will not come to an end until 'the whole Body will be clothed with the glorious state of immortality, and all the members will be conformed to the Head.'[29]

Augustine also clearly stated that Christ suffers with his earthly body.

> Since we now identify head and body (him as head, us as body), when we hear his voice we must hear it as coming from both head and body. For whatever he has suffered we too have suffered with him, and what we suffer he too suffers with us. If the head suffers in any way, how can the hand assert that it does not suffer? If the hand suffers, how can the head say that it does not suffer? If the foot feels something, how can the head say that it does not feel it too? When one part of our body is in any pain, all the rest rush together to help the suffering member.

> It follows then that if he has suffered and we have suffered with him, and he is now ascended into heaven and is seated at the right hand of the Father, whatever his Church suffers by way of this life's tribulations, temptations, constrictions and deprivations (for she must be schooled to be purified like gold in the fire), this he also suffers.[30]

In the above I have emphasized that it is Christians who share in the sufferings of Christ, and so share in his consolations. Those who are not Christians do not know and cannot fully experience the consolation of sharing in the sufferings of Christ so as to encounter the hope of his risen glory. Again, this urgently bids Christians to proclaim, in love, the good news. Nonetheless, as we discussed above, the church, as the universal sacrament of salvation, reaches out to all that suffer so as to embrace them within the consolation of the risen Christ, so the church equally, embraces their sufferings so as to subsume them within the sufferings of Christ. Pope John Paul II states that through his body 'Christ wishes to be united with every individual, and in a special way he is united with those who suffer.'[31]

Again, through its prayer, liturgical and personal, and through its charitable deeds the church lovingly unites all who suffer to the suffering Christ. Through the church, the body of Christ, Christ himself embraces the suffering of all who suffer through sin, sickness, natural disasters, poverty, injustice, prejudice, war, and death, and he makes their suffering his own. Non-Christians may not be aware that Christ is suffering in union with them and that they are suffering in union with him, but whatever consolation they experience in the midst of their suffering is ultimately due to their being embraced, through his body, by him.

---

29 *Ademanni ex scholastico Leodiensi episcopi Brixiensis, de Eucharistae sacramento ad Beregarium epistola.*
30 *Enarrationes in Psalmos*, 62, 2. Translation taken from J. Walsh and P.G. Walsh, *Divine Providence and Human Suffering*, p. 175.
31 *Salvifici Doloris*, n. 24.

Moreover, Pope John Paul II advances this line of argument one significant step further. He states that not only are suffering non-Christians united to Christ, but their suffering is equally able to contribute to the world's redemption. '[I]n the mystery of the Church as his Body, Christ has in a sense opened his own redemptive suffering to all human suffering. Insofar as man becomes a sharer in Christ's sufferings – in any part of the world and at any time in history – to that extent *he in his own way completes* the suffering through which Christ accomplished the Redemption of the world.'[32]

The Eucharist: Suffering in the Risen Christ

The place where the ecclesial reality of the body of Christ is most fully enacted, and so where it is most fully experienced, is within the eucharistic liturgy. It is 'the source and summit of the Christian life.'[33] Within the eucharistic liturgy, Christ, the risen head, unites himself most fully with his body here on earth in anticipation of the heavenly consummation. Thus, it is here in the eucharistic liturgy that all that we have discussed above finds its foremost expression.[34]

First, within the eucharistic liturgy Christians do not simply remember and recall the past event of Christ's sacrificial offering of himself to the Father, rather they are actually united to it. Christ, within the very action of the liturgy itself, unites his body to his once for all sacrifice.[35] Thus, Christians participate in and so reap the benefits of Christ's sacrificial death. From within the eucharistic action itself, they experience and know Christ's victory over sin – the root of all evil and suffering.

Second, in being united to the one sacrifice of Christ, Christians place their own present suffering, whatever its cause, upon Christ's cross, and Christ accepts it. Thus Christians not only know that, in Christ, their suffering is redeemed and conquered, but equally that Christ has assumed their present suffering to himself. It is within the eucharistic liturgy that the present suffering of Christians becomes most fully the present suffering of Christ.

Third, not only does Christ take to himself the present suffering of Christians, but they, in turn, participate in his suffering as their head. Christians, in communion with Christ their head, unite themselves to the sufferings of all their brothers and sisters, Christians and non-Christians alike, and in union with Christ their head make intercession for them. It is within the liturgy that Christ, in union with his body, embraces the suffering of all, and thus it is within the liturgy that Christians most fully share in the sufferings of Christ. Within the eucharistic liturgy Christians participate in the suffering of Christ, and so complete what is still lacking for the sake of his whole body and for the salvation of the world.

---

32 *Salvifici Doloris*, n. 24.
33 *Lumen Gentium*, n. 11.
34 I am not attempting here to present a complete eucharistic theology. I merely want to highlight some aspects of the Eucharist that pertain to what we have already discussed.
35 See *Catechism of the Catholic Church*, nn. 1362–72.

Fourth, it is in partaking of the risen and glorious body and blood of Jesus, the body that was once crucified and the blood that was once shed, that Christians commune most fully with their risen Lord. In partaking of the risen humanity of Jesus, the eating of his risen body and the drinking of his risen blood, Christians become most fully one with one another and with Christ their head. In the eucharistic communion Christ's body becomes fully what it is.[36] 'The cup of blessing which we bless, is it not participation in the blood of Christ? The bread which we break, is it not a participation in the body of Christ? Because there is one bread, we who are many are one body, for we all partake of one loaf' (1 Cor. 10:16–17). Here, in the eucharistic communion, Christ embraces most fully the sufferings of his body and equally shares with his body the risen life of his Spirit. Moreover, Christians, especially those who together have partaken of Christ's body and blood within the present liturgy, are united to one another as brothers and sisters in Christ. Together they too share in each other's suffering and make common intercession for one another in union with Christ. Equally, together as Christ's body, they experience the consolation of knowing that nothing can separate them from their risen Lord, and so nothing can separate them from his victory.[37] They expectantly look to his coming in glory and to their own participation in the fulness of eternal life. In faith, Christians lay hold of the truth of Jesus' words.

> He who eats my flesh and drinks my blood has eternal life, and I will raise him up at the last day. For my flesh is food indeed, and my blood is drink indeed. He who eats my flesh and drinks my blood abides in me, and I in him. As the living Father sent me, and I live because of the Father, so he who eats me will live because of me. Jn 6: 54–57.

Likewise, as Christians make intercession for the whole world, Christ, in communion with his body, joins all suffering people to the Father of mercy and the God of all consolations.[38]

---

36 See *Catechism of the Catholic Church*, n. 1396.
37 See *Catechism of the Catholic Church*, nn. 1402–5.
38 I have unmistakably and purposefully put forward a Roman Catholic understanding of the eucharistic liturgy. I have done so because I believe that only a Catholic understanding, one that the Eastern Orthodox would equally share, can adequately account for the truths that I wished to espouse. Only if Christians are actually united to the one sacrifice of Christ within the liturgy, can Christians give and he embrace their sufferings within his redemptive death. Moreover, only if the bread and wine are genuinely transformed into the risen Christ, so as to allow him to be truly present as he now actually exists in his risen state, can Christians come into full communion with him. Only within the reality of this eucharistic communion can he assume, in the fullest manner possible within this life, the suffering of his body, and his body assume, in the fullest manner possible in this life, the risen life of his glorious body. If Christ is merely symbolically present in the Eucharist, then all of these truths are merely symbolically enacted. The existential consolation and the certain hope contained within the eucharistic liturgy must be founded upon the actual efficacy, and so reality, of the liturgical action.

A Radical Departure

In the above presentation, by locating human suffering within the ecclesial reality of the body of Christ, I have radically departed from those who espouse a passible and so suffering God. Many, if not most, of these theologians interpret the meaning and experience of suffering primarily and solely in the light of the suffering of God as God. In so doing they have, in their turn, radically departed from the Christian experience and understanding of human suffering.[39]

First, many have ultimately divorced suffering from the historical reality of Jesus' redemptive suffering. Jesus' redemptive death and resurrection do not place human suffering within an entirely new context, that is, within the salvific and ecclesial reality of Christ's body. Jesus' death becomes merely the revelatory sign or clue that God is always, ahistorically, suffering as God.

Second, Jesus' death and resurrection do not radically alter the context within which suffering is experienced, that is, within the context of being a member of Christ's body. Thus, those who espouse a suffering God presume, as noted above, that everyone, regardless of whether or not one is a Christian, experiences equally whatever consolation can be obtained from a suffering God. The full riches of the Father's mercy and compassion are no longer found in Jesus, his Son, and his mercy and compassion are no longer experienced from within his Son's church. Nor, then, is the Father's compassion and consolation mediated to all, even to those who are not Christians, through Christ and his church.

Third, therefore, those who espouse solely a suffering God can hardly avoid divorcing the sufferer from the present historical communal and ecclesial dimension of Christ's living body, the church. Instead they isolate the sufferer in his or her suffering. This is humanly and emotionally devastating. The sufferer stands alone in his or her suffering before a suffering God, who is himself a helpless and impotent victim. No longer is the sufferer united to and so embraced, in love and compassion, by the risen Christ and by his or her brothers and sisters within Christ's body. The Holy Spirit is no longer the bond of unity and life among God's people, but is often now replaced by some political, national, ethnic, or humanistic fellowship. In themselves, these may be good, but they cannot adequately address the evil of suffering, nor can they provide the consolation of Christ and his body.

Ultimately, many of those who espouse a God who suffers in himself attempt to solve the mystery of suffering though some philosophical cosmology. However, evil, in all its forms and with all its suffering, cannot be conquered by some ahistorical philosophical cosmology of a suffering God. It can merely, at best, be an attempt to explain it. Only the Christian gospel proclaims that sin, the source of all evil and suffering, has been conquered. The Father has defeated sin and death through the

---

39 Similar to the comment I made that the denial of Christ's divinity necessarily leads to the embracing of a suffering God, equally, while not every theologian who espouses a suffering God possesses a deficient ecclesiology, many theologians who possess a deficient ecclesiology espouse a suffering God.

historical death and resurrection of his incarnate Son. All of humankind can only share fully in this victory, in the midst of their historical suffering, by being united through the Holy Spirit to his historical and earthly body, the church, and so be united to the living and glorious Christ.

Causes of and Responses to Human Suffering

Having discussed two cardinal truths that bear upon suffering in general or as a whole, I now wish to address some specific types of suffering and the various Christian responses to them. Pope John Paul II states that what makes suffering uniquely human is that it gives rise to the question: Why? It is this very question that makes human suffering so emotionally painful.

> Only the suffering human being knows that he is suffering and wonders why; and he suffers in a humanly speaking still deeper way if he does not find a satisfactory answer. This *is a difficult question.*[40]

Christian revelation, as recorded in the Bible, provides a rich account of the causes of and the reasons for suffering. The Bible is a very realistic book, and thus it grasps that, while suffering is ultimately due to the evil of sin, there are many varieties of suffering which originate from different sinful and evil sources. Equally, it perceives that suffering serves many, and often inter-related, purposes which necessitate diverse responses.

One of the weaknesses of those who advocate a passible and suffering God is their often somewhat simplistic view of the causes and types of human suffering. They are rightly aware that suffering is perpetrated against the innocent, the oppressed, and the marginalized. Remember that Auschwitz is the contemporary icon of human suffering. Suffering, within their theology, is most often placed therefore within an unjust and repressive political, cultural, and economic milieu. The history of the world since Auschwitz only adds to this overwhelming truth. However, suffering cannot be placed exclusively within such a context. Suffering, with its various causes, is much more complex, and equally how it is experienced and interpreted is more complex. While the following account of the varieties and purposes of suffering will not be exhaustive, it is hoped that it will provide a much fuller account, and therefore a more adequate and realistic description and explanation than that provided by many who espouse a passible God.

Suffering Due to Personal Sin

What is often overlooked or forgotten within contemporary theology is that one of the greatest causes, if not the greatest cause, of suffering within the lives of all human persons is their own personal acts of sin. Suffering is the offspring born of sin. From within the biblical perspective

---

40 *Salvifici Doloris*, n. 9.

sin contains its own punishment – suffering – even to the extent of suffering damnation. Adam and Eve suffered the consequences of their sin – separation from God, friction and division among themselves, and death (see Gen. 3). The Israelites were carried off to Assyria. 'This occurred because the people of Israel had sinned against the LORD their God' (2 Kgs 17:6–7). Because the Israelites rebelled against God and killed the prophets, 'therefore you [God] gave them into the hands of their enemies, who made them suffer' (Neh. 9:26–27). The Book of Psalms portrays the evil-doer as suffering the results of his own folly.

> They made a pit, digging it out, and fall into the hole that they have made. Their mischief returns upon their own heads, and on their own heads their violence descends. Ps. 7:15–16; see also Pss 37:1–3, 38:3, 52:1–5, 73:12–20, 92:7.

Ultimately, God holds each person accountable for his or her own actions, and thus each person suffers the inevitable punishment due to sin (see Ezek. 18).

The works of the sinful flesh – immorality, impurity, licentiousness, idolatry, sorcery, enmity, strife, jealousy, anger, selfishness, dissension, party spirit, envy, murder, drunkenness, carousing, and the like – do not just cause others to suffer, they equally bring suffering upon the perpetrator of such actions (see Gal. 5:19–21; Rom. 1:29–30). This is easily witnessed in the drunkard and the drug addict, but it is also true of the person who commits any sin. One has only to examine one's own life to perceive how much of one's suffering – anxiousness, distress, fear and guilt – is due to one's own sinful attitudes and actions.

Pride breeds selfish ambition and the craving for recognition, and so gives rise to worry and dread. Arrogance, while displaying the veneer of bravado, actually hides the suffering due to low self-esteem and the lack of inner confidence. But this in turn gives rise to the dread of being exposed, which causes nervousness, disquietude, and the fear of failure. Greed drives one not only to work beyond what is physically healthy, but also causes great emotional stress. Bitterness, resentment, envy and hatred engender immense emotional agitation, and ultimately distort one's whole personality. Unbridled lust, whether in thought or deed, undermines not only the dignity of others, but also one's own self-respect. Lying and deception demand that one be manipulative and controlling, but one then suffers from the lack of open, honest and forthright relationships. One becomes isolated and even paranoid in the pursuit of one's selfish ends.

It is unnecessary to compile a longer list of various sins with their accompanying forms of suffering. The end result is the same. Sin ultimately causes human beings to loathe themselves with deep inner groans of suffering. If they steel and repress their conscience in an attempt to suppress the suffering, they either become mentally and emotionally impaired, or they become human beings with little moral integrity whatsoever, which is its own form of mental affliction. While it may be impossible to scientifically demonstrate to what extent psychosomatic illness is due to sin, there is little doubt that it can be a contributing factor.

Paul recognized the suffering due to sin's enslavement. Obedience to sin 'leads to death' (Rom. 6:16). 'For the wages of sin is death' (Rom. 6:23). Prior to coming to faith in Christ, Christians were 'living in the flesh.' Their sinful passions were aroused and they bore 'the fruit for death' (Rom. 7:5–6). 'To set one's mind on the flesh is death' (Rom. 8:6). The Letter of James also testifies that 'desire when it has conceived gives birth to sin; and sin when it is full-grown brings forth death' (James 1:16). These passages are speaking not only of the death of damnation of which physical death is its symbol, but also of the suffering within this life due to sin. To live a life of sin is to live a life of death with all its suffering.

Now it is precisely from this type of suffering that God wishes to free humankind. God never wants any human person to suffer because of his or her own personal sin. In itself it serves no purpose for the individual sinner other than for one's own condemnation. However, even such suffering can lead to good. The positive result borne of the suffering of personal sin is that the suffering leads the sinner to repentance. The sinner, because of guilt, shame and embarrassment, becomes so demoralized by his or her suffering, that he or she turns to God in humble repentance.[41] Paul reminded his Corinthian readers that he rejoiced not simply because they grieved, 'but because you were grieved into repenting; for you felt a godly grief, so that you suffered no loss through us. For godly grief produces a repentance that leads to salvation and brings no regret, but worldly grief produces death' (2 Cor. 7:9–10). Worldly grief, that is, merely the shame and guilt of doing wrong with no intention of repentance and a change of heart, leads to further suffering and spiritual death. Godly grief, as true repentance accompanied by a firm purpose of amendment, leads to salvation and life. Thus the grief and suffering that necessarily accompanies sin becomes medicinal and remedial. As the author of Second Maccabees noted:

> Now I urge those who read this book not to be depressed by such calamities, but to recognize that these punishments were designed not to destroy but to discipline our people. In fact, it is a sign of great kindness not to let the impious alone for long, but to punish them immediately.... Therefore he [God] never withdrew his mercy from us. Although he disciplined us with calamities, he does not forsake his own people. For we are suffering because of our own sins. And if our living Lord is angry for a little while, to rebuke and discipline us,

---

41 It is fashionable in some quarters today to see guilt as psychologically harmful. It represses one's freedom and self-expression. It is perceived as a remnant of an unenlightened culture or society, or the vestige of a superstitious and oppressive religious formation. Obviously, if a person experiences guilt for no rational reason, it is detrimental to his or her psychological well-being. However, the experience of guilt over sin, within a properly informed conscience, is actually psychologically healthy for it moves one to repentance and to the amending of one's life. This advances psychological and spiritual maturity. Not to experience guilt over one's sins is an extremely dangerous state in which to be. It is hazardous not only for oneself, since one does not then realize the moral and psychological damage that one is inflicting upon oneself, but also for others, for it means that one is morally indifferent to the injurious effects that one's sinful actions have upon others. The person with no moral conscience, who never experiences guilt, is a grave liability to himself and to others.

he will again be reconciled with his own servants. 2 Macc. 6:12–13, 16; 7:32–33.[42]

Pope John Paul II states that this is 'an extremely important aspect of suffering.' '*Suffering must serve for conversion, that is, for the rebuilding of goodness* in the subject, who can recognize the divine mercy in this call to repentance.'[43]

This is what redemption in Christ is all about. Christ sets the sinner free from personal sin with its suffering so that he or she might be free to live a holy and righteous life of joy and peace. 'For freedom Christ has set us free' (Gal. 5:1). Thus, as a person grows in Christian holiness through repentance, prayer, participation in the sacraments, and the striving to live by God's commandments, the suffering caused by personal sin decreases. This is one of the great and marvelous benefits due to the ongoing work of the Holy Spirit within the lives of Christians who are members of Christ's body.[44]

In concluding this section, it should be noted that Christ, as the head of his body, suffers and grieves due to the sinful actions of his members, for their sin not only enfeebles their own spiritual life, but it equally then impairs the life of the Spirit within his whole body. He equally suffers because of the sinful actions of those who are not members of his body for he loves them and desires their salvation. However, Christ, as the risen Lord and head of his body, responds to such suffering by interceding for all sinners, and by ever sending forth his Spirit to bring about a deeper conversion within his body or to bring others to initial conversion and faith in him. Pope John Paul II stated an obvious historical truth when he wrote:

> Down through the centuries and generations it has been seen that *in suffering there is concealed* a particular power that *draws a person interiorly close to Christ*, a special grace. To this grace many saints,

---

42 The suffering of the Israelites due to their sin often led them to repentance. For example, see Neh. 9:27, 32–37, Ezra 9:6–15, and Dan. 3:26–45. See also Ps. 51 for David's prayer of repentance. Paul also saw the punishment of excluding the scandalous sinner from the Christian community as a means of leading the person to repentance. See 1 Cor. 5:5, 9–13; 2 Cor. 2:5–11; and 2 Thess. 3:6–15.

43 *Salvifici Doloris*, n. 12.

44 It should be noted that it is in this context that the notion of *apatheia* within the spiritual writings of the Fathers can be properly understood. *Apatheia* does not pertain to the complete suppression or denial of emotion within the growth to full Christian holiness. Rather *apatheia* has to do with overcoming the sinful passions and desires. As these are overcome, as the person becomes 'apathetic' to sinful passions, the person truly comes alive, with all of one's heart and mind, to the love of God and neighbour. See L. Bouyer, *The Spirituality of the New Testament and the Fathers* (New York: The Seabury Press, 1963), pp. 273–75, 297–98, 384–87, 503–6; and *From Glory to Glory: Texts from Gregory of Nyssa's Mystical Writings*, ed. and trans. by H. Musurillo, with an Introduction by J. Daniélou (Crestwood: St Vladimir's Press, 1979), pp. 46–56.

It should also be noted that the possibility of being set free from the suffering of personal sin is another important reason for evangelizing non-Christians. They do not realize that much of their suffering is unnecessary and that, in Christ, as members of his body through the Spirit, they can be released from such suffering.

such as St Francis of Assisi, St Ignatius of Loyola and others, owe
their profound conversion.[45]

The Good Groaning of Christians

Christians also suffer because they are groaning. However, this groaning
is good groaning for it is the groaning that accompanies the taking on of
the new life of the Spirit.

First, 'we have this treasure [of Christ's glory] in earthen vessels' (2
Cor. 4:7), and thus we 'are always being given up to death for Jesus' sake'
(2 Cor. 4:11). Presently, the 'earthly tent' of our sinful mortality is being
destroyed, and 'so indeed we groan, and long to put on our heavenly
dwelling.' Thus, 'we sigh with anxiety; not that we would be unclothed,
but that we would be further clothed so that what is mortal may be
swallowed up by life' (2 Cor. 5:1–4).

Second, growth in holiness is a life-long process, and one that culmi-
nates in the eternal life of our heavenly dwelling where we are clothed in
the glory of our risen humanity. This growth in holiness involves
struggles and groaning as well. Someone (Paul) exhorted Timothy to
'fight the good fight of faith' (1 Tim. 6:12). The front line of the Christian
battle is within oneself. Paul expressed the conflict well. 'I do not understand my own actions. For I do not do what I want, but I do the very
thing I hate.... Wretched man that I am! Who will deliver me from this
body of death?' (Rom. 7:15, 24; see the whole of vv. 15–24). Paul gave
thanks in the knowledge that through Christ he could be delivered (see
Rom. 7:25), but he equally realized that there was the constant battle to
put to death the sinful attitudes and passions that give rise to sinful
deeds. Each day brings its own set of temptations that must be repulsed
in the Spirit.

This battle for Christian holiness obviously causes suffering within the
Christian. The sin within us does not want to die, and we are loath to
crucify it. Jesus told his disciples that 'if any man would come after me,
let him deny himself and take up his cross daily and follow me. For
whoever would save his life will lose it; and whoever loses his life for my
sake, he will save it' (Lk 9:23–24; see also Mt 10:38–39, Mk 8:34–38. Luke
stresses the daily nature of taking up one's cross.) It is the denial of one's
sinful drives and passions, the refusal to obey them, which is at the heart
of the Christian's experience of the cross. The Christian loses, gives up,
or puts to death his or her sinful life, the life, in Pauline terminology, of
the flesh, so as to save his or her true life, the new life in Christ through
the Holy Spirit (see Rom. 6).

Jesus strikingly illustrated the violent nature, and so suffering, of this
exercise.

> If your right eye causes you to sin, pluck it out and throw it away; it
> is better that you lose one of your members than that your whole
> body be thrown into hell. And if your right hand causes you to sin,
> cut it off and throw it away; it is better that you lose one of your

---

45 *Salvifici Doloris*, n. 26.

members than that your whole body go into hell. Mt 5:29–30; see Mt 18:8–9.

Why did Jesus use such violent language? Are his words mere hyperbole, used for effect? Why not just 'close one's eye' in the face of lustful temptations? Obviously, Jesus did not wish his words to be taken literally, yet he was articulating a Christian truth. If one wishes to live the Christian life, one must do violence to one's fallen nature. It takes an ardent act of the will, a violent act of the will, to oppose the sin that lies deep within one's heart so as to put it to death – to crucify it in Christ. Concerning himself Paul stated that 'I do not box as one beating the air; but I pommel my body and subdue it, lest after preaching to others I myself should be disqualified' (1 Cor. 9:26–27).[46]

This violence obviously causes within the Christian inner groaning for one is striving to free oneself from sin so as to live a righteous and holy life. Again, Paul is also well aware of this type of groaning.

We know that the whole creation has been groaning in travail together until now; and not only the creation, but we ourselves, who have the first fruits of the Spirit, groan inwardly as we wait for adoption as sons, the redemption of our bodies. For in this hope we were saved. Rom. 8:22–24.

Christians possess the new life of the Holy Spirit, and so the first fruit of Christ's resurrection, but they do not yet possess the Spirit's fulness. They are still groaning in their sin, struggling to be set free in the Spirit, so as to obtain their full adoption as children of the Father. While this is a necessary and painful groaning, a groaning due to the sin from which they must yet be freed, nonetheless it is the groaning of spiritual growth. It is a suffering and groaning in the hope that is held out to them as they await the resurrection of their bodies.[47]

---

46 Paul's use of athletic imagery follows this same line of thought. The athlete trains and disciplines his body so as to master himself, and thus to be assured of winning the race. See 1 Cor. 9:24–26, Phil. 3:12–14, 1 Tim. 4:7. Paul would give his ardent approval of the jargon among contemporary body-builders: 'No pain, no gain.' The Letter to the Hebrews equally exhorts its readers to 'lay aside every weight, and sin which clings so closely, and let us run with perseverance the race that is set before us.' Heb. 12:1.

47 I do not know whether Michelangelo had Romans 8:22–24 in mind when he carved his 'unfinished' statue of 'The Bound Slave,' but it is an excellent depiction in stone of this theological truth. Not only is the slave portrayed as struggling to be set free from his bonds, but the slave himself is still partially encased in the marble, and so is equally struggling and groaning to be set free of the marble that still restrains him. Similarly, Christians were slaves to sin and, while set free in Christ, are still groaning to be set free from the sin that still restrains them from obtaining the fulness of their freedom – the glorious image of the new man Christ.

It is interesting to note as well that, as the whole of creation has been affected by humankind's sin (see Gen. 3:17–18, Rom. 8:20), so Paul saw the whole of creation continuing to groan as it awaits the full redemption of humankind. It too will participate in 'the glorious liberty of the children of God' (Rom. 8:21). The 'natural disasters' that still afflict humankind, and cause such suffering and devastation, may be theologically interpreted in this context. These are but the whole of creation continuing to groan under the weight of human sin. They will cease when there is a new heaven and new earth. Creation will then be a source of life and abundance, and not a cause of suffering and death (see Hos. 2:23–24, Amos 9:13–15, Is. 65:17, Ezek. 47:6–12, Rev. 21:1, 22:2).

Thus, Christians should not lose heart in the midst of this good groaning. As Paul stated, Christians are fighting the good fight of faith. Yes, it is a fight and with this fight comes suffering. But it is a good fight for it is fought in the sure knowledge of faith that the victory has already been won in Christ. As members of his body, they already share in his victory. 'Fight the good fight of faith; take hold of the eternal life to which you were called when you made the good confession in the presence of many witnesses' (1 Tim. 6:12).

This groaning is not merely the groaning of individual Christians. It is the groaning of the whole body of Christ, and so it is the groaning of Christ himself. Christ groans in union with his whole body as it strives to appropriate the new life of the Spirit which, as the risen head, he nurtures within his body. Moreover, knowing that Christ groans in communion with his body, all its members, as individuals and as the one church, possess the consolation that their groaning will not be in vain, for it is the risen Christ who groans with and in them, and thus victory is secured.

One final point. The suffering due to personal sin and the groaning to overcome sin are often inter-connected. One may suffer the consequences of one's sins and simultaneously struggle to be freed from them. Yet, these two types of suffering should not be confused. It is in confusing these two types of suffering that Christianity is often thought to be an onerous and burdensome way of life. However, it is in living the gospel that one is freed from the real oppression of sin, and ultimately from its eternal condemnation, so as to strive, in the freedom of the Spirit, to live in holiness. While humankind labors and is heavy-burdened under the yoke of the slavery of sin, yet Christians learn that in Christ they can find rest. 'For my yoke is easy, and my burden is light' (Mt 11:28–30). To be yoked to Christ and so strive to live a virtuous life in the Spirit is far different from being yoked to Satan and so be harnessed to sin.

The Father Disciplines and Educates His Children

Within the context of the above two types of suffering there is closely aligned a third. Those whom he loves, God disciplines in order to free them from sin, and so educates them in the paths of holiness. This discipline and education takes the form of trials and tests that involve suffering.

Quoting Proverbs 3:11–12, the author of the Letter to the Hebrews reminded his readers of what they should expect from the Father if they are truly his sons.

'My son, do not regard lightly the discipline of the Lord, nor lose courage when you are punished by him. For the Lord disciplines him whom he loves, and chastises every son whom he receives.' It is for discipline that you have to endure. God is treating you as sons; for what son is there whom his father does not discipline? If you are left without discipline in which all have participated, then you are illegitimate children and not sons. Besides this, we have had earthly fathers to discipline us and we respected them. Shall we not much more be subject to the Father of spirits and live? For they disciplined us for a short time at their pleasure, but he disciplines us for our good, that we may share his holiness. For the moment all discipline seems painful rather than pleasant; later it yields the peaceful fruit of righteousness to those who have been trained by it. Heb. 12:3–11.

While pain and suffering accompany discipline, yet there is a twofold goal of such discipline – freedom from sin and the resulting freedom to live in righteousness and holiness. It is because of this twofold goal that such discipline is an act of fatherly love on the part of God. Because of his mercy, God disciplines his children (see Wis. 11:9–10).

First then, God disciplines those he loves because he does not want them to be condemned in their sin. As Paul told the Corinthians: 'But when we are judged by the Lord, we are chastened so that we may not be condemned along with the world' (1 Cor. 11:32). Because one of the goals of discipline is to free the person of sin, it is often depicted within the Bible as refining and purifying. The prophet Malachi told the Israelites that God would send a messenger who will be 'like a refiner's fire and like fullers' soap' who will purify God's people and refine them like gold and silver so that they will become his holy people (Mal. 3:3). As Judith, in the face of persecution, reminded her fellow Jews:

> Remember what he [God] did with Abraham, and how he tested Isaac, and what happened to Jacob.... For he has not tried us with fire, as he did them, to search their hearts, nor has he taken vengeance on us; but the Lord scourges those who are close to him in order to admonish them. Jud. 8:26–27.

Actually, this testing and purification through discipline advances the second goal – the living of a holy life. Within the discipline and accompanying suffering the person advances in holiness, and so simultaneously manifests that one is worthy of God. In the Book of Sirach, Wisdom disciplines her children until she can trust them (see Sir. 4:17). Moreover, those who come to serve the Lord must prepare themselves for testing as gold is tested in fire. It is in such testing that God finds his servants acceptable (see Sir. 2:1–6).

The above is admirably exemplified in the lives of parents. They suffer the trials and tribulations of rearing their children. However, it is this daily responsibility of caring for their children that provides parents with the opportunity to break free of their own selfishness, and simultaneously to go out in love to their children. Married couples in their care for one another and for their children, in the midst of life's vicissitudes, grow in virtue – patience, fortitude, kindness, compassion, mercy, forgiveness, and love. After the example of Christ, love is in the doing of loving deeds, and it is these loving deeds which foster the growth of love. The suffering of life's daily hassles, problems, and difficulties can then be the catalyst, if approached in the Spirit, for spiritual growth within the lives of all men and women. Such tribulations are never pleasant and may even cause immense grief and sorrow, yet, in the eyes of God and even in the eyes of the sufferer, they can be the means to heroic sanctity.

Thus, this discipline is not merely a means to spiritual growth, it also allows one to display one's true metal. Job is the supreme example of this within the Old Testament. Job, in the midst of his trials, remained faithful to God and so his true stature was revealed, a stature that would have otherwise remained hidden.[48] Even Jesus learned what it meant for him to be a loyal Son of the Father through his suffering. 'Although he was a Son, he learned obedience through what he suffered; and being made perfect he became the source of eternal salvation to all who obey him' (Heb. 5:8–9). The truth that Jesus is the Son of God is revealed precisely in his suffering and death on the cross (see Mk 15:39). 'When you have lifted up the Son of man, then you will know that I am he' (Jn 8:28). Within the Gospel of John it is the cross that is then the revelation of his glory (see Jn 17:1–5).

Thus, through discipline God provides everyone an opportunity to grow in perfection and to manifest one's holiness, and so be glorified in the midst of one's suffering. For example, those people who are most admired and respected, no matter what their vocation in life may be, even children and young adults, are not those who never seem to suffer any affliction or hardship, but those who suffer such affliction and hardship with courage, patience, fortitude and love. It is their virtue in the midst of evil that makes them lights to the world around them.

> Having been disciplined a little, they will receive great good, because God tested them and found them worthy of himself; like gold in the furnace he tried them, and like a sacrificial burnt offering he accepted them. In the time of visitation they will shine forth, and will run like sparks through the stubble. Wis. 3:5–6.

Christians then should actually rejoice in their tribulations for, in being steadfast in the midst of such, they are contributing to their own glory.

> In this you rejoice, though now for a little while you may have to suffer various trials, so that the genuineness of your faith, more precious than gold which though perishable is tested by fire, may redound to praise and glory and honour at the revelation of Jesus Christ. 1 Pet. 1:6–7.

Christians rejoice in the their hope.

> More than that, we rejoice in our sufferings, knowing that suffering produces endurance, and endurance produces character, and character produces hope, and hope does not disappoint us, because God's love has been poured into our hearts through the Holy Spirit which has been given to us. Rom. 5:2–5.

What must always be kept in mind, when suffering the discipline of the Father, is that the goal is one's perfection.

> Count it all joy, my brethren, when you meet various trials, for you know that the testing of your faith produces steadfastness. And let

---

48 Job is frequently cited by the Fathers to illustrate how Christians are to experience and interpret suffering. See the references to Job listed in the index of J. Walsh and P.G. Walsh, *Divine Providence and Human Suffering*.

steadfastness have its full effect, that you may be perfect and complete, lacking in nothing. James 1:2–4.

Love – love of God and love of others – given in suffering reaps love's reward – eternal life. 'Blessed is the man who endures trial, for when he has stood the test he will receive the crown of life which God has promised to those who love him' (James 1:12). Thus Christians need not fear the suffering of trials. They need only to stand firm in their faith and trust. 'Be faithful unto death, and I will give you the crown of life' (Rev. 2:10).[49]

Again, in concluding this section, what has been stated above applies to Christ's body as a whole. The Father, in mercy and love, can discipline the church in order that it might grow in holiness and manifest its true glory. Throughout its history the church has suffered trials and tribulations, and these, while not always with complete success, have contributed to its upbuilding.[50] (More will be said about this below when we discuss the suffering caused by persecution.)

Suffering Caused by the Sins of Others

In the light of the above, one particular form of trial must be discussed at some length, that is, the suffering caused by the sins of others. Everyone is sinned against. No one is immune from suffering at the hands of

---

49 It is in the context of God's discipline that the suffering caused by 'natural disasters' might be placed. Losing one's possessions in a flood or tornado compels one to consider what is of true value. Even the loss of a loved one through a natural disaster necessitates that one consider the precariousness of this life in contrast to the security of eternal life. Natural disasters also bring forth solidarity and generosity in the midst of shared suffering.

Equally, sickness can often be interpreted as part of God's discipline. Sickness not only alerts us to our own mortality, but also provides the occasion for us to take stock of our lives. It not only provides 'a pause' from our often frantic and ill-considered lives in which we can consider the course and meaning of our lives, but it also provides God 'a pause' in which he can speak to us about our lives. Sickness and hardship have been the catalyst for deeper conversion in the lives of many saints, for example St Francis of Assisi, St Ignatius of Loyola, and St Teresa of Avila.

50 C.H. Talbert, in his excellent little book *Learning through Suffering: The Educational Value of Suffering in the New Testament and in its Milieu* (Collegeville: The Liturgical Press, 1991), summarizes the meaning of suffering as God's discipline.

Suffering is the arena in which the Christian can be (1) disciplined, in the sense of training that develops strength; (2) refined, in the sense of the smelting processes' use of fire to purify precious metal; and (3) educated, in the sense of learning the right way to live. Looked at in this way, suffering and adversity as divine education are not only compatible with God's loving nature but also inherent in Christian existence in the world. p. 92.

Peter of Blois, in the twelfth century, was the first to write an extended treatise on suffering: *The Twelve Advantages to Tribulation*. They are: 1. Growth in virtue, 2. Shuts the devil's mouth, 3. Purges sin, 4. Engenders self-knowledge, 5. Hastens one's journey to God, 6. Helps pay the debt of sin, 7. Enlarges the heart, 8. Compels one to seek heavenly consolation, 9. Compels God to remember you, 10. Causes prayers to be heard, 11. Guards and nourishes the heart, 12. Evidence of God's love. For a translation of this treatise see J. Walsh and P.G. Walsh, *Divine Providence and Human Suffering*, pp. 141–62.

others. It is morally wrong to cause such suffering for the evil done and the suffering that ensues violates the inherent dignity of human persons depriving them of their endowed rights and goods as created in the image and likeness of God. Sins against others always infringe or repudiate their personal well-being.[51] Such sin and suffering is encountered within personal relations – within families and among friends. These wrongs include gossip, slander, theft, physical and sexual abuse, rape, prejudice, hatred, and even murder. On a larger scale suffering is caused by the evils of social, political, and economic injustice that is perpetrated upon whole classes of people because of their race, nationality, social class, economic status, gender, or religion.[52] It is within this context that the suffering of the innocent – the unborn, the poor, the weak, the marginalized, the sick, the physically and mentally handicapped, the elderly and the dying – is most acutely apparent. Moreover, it is within this context that Christians suffer persecution for the sake of the gospel.

It is impossible to discuss all the various scenarios in which all of us suffer at the hands of one another. Nonetheless, a number of important and inter-related questions arise. How are Christians to interpret such suffering? What meaning or value does such suffering contain? Does such suffering possess any gospel significance either for the church as a whole or for individual Christians within it? Moreover, how are those who personally experience this suffering caused by the sins of others and/or who witness such suffering caused by the sins of others to respond? From within a Christian, primarily scriptural, perspective I will now address, under various headings, these and similar questions.

Obtaining the Father's Approval
While God does not wish people to suffer because of the sinful deeds of others, yet, because sin and evil are inevitable within this life, he uses it

---

51 Without lightly dismissing the evil and suffering caused by the sins of others, it is a form of pride to think that, in the present sinful world, one should be immune from such suffering. While objectively one's personal integrity should never be violated and while it is morally wrong to have it violated, yet to imagine or assume that one must, therefore, be exempt from experiencing the sins of others or that one should 'get through life' unscathed by the sins of others is a display of arrogance. God does not even make himself an exception, nor did Jesus. Self-righteous indignation and pretentious outrage over being offended exemplify such inflated self-importance.

52 In his 1984 Post-Synodal Apostolic Exhortation, *Reconciliatio et Paenitentia*, Pope John Paul II stated that 'social sin is every sin against the rights of the human person ... against other's freedom ... against the dignity and honour of one's neighbour ... against the common good.' He stated that such sins can be between 'various human communities' – economic and cultural groups, or nations and peoples. However, the Pope warns that 'social sin' should not be interpreted 'in the sense that blame for it is to be placed not so much on the moral conscience of an individual, but rather on some vague entity or anonymous collectivity, such as the situation, the system, society, structure, or institution.' There are situations that are sinful, such as racial discrimination, and structures that are evil, such as slavery; but these are due not to any impersonal entity, but are 'the accumulation and concentration of many personal sins.' The impersonal structures or institutions are not responsible even though it may be through them that sin is perpetuated. 'At the heart of every situation of sin are always to be found sinful people' (n. 16).

for his own good purpose (see Rom. 8:28). Without minimizing the evil and the suffering that it causes, to be sinned against provides the victim an opportunity to respond to such evil in a godly manner, and so to grow in holiness. While one may be a victim of sin and evil, one need not be a passive victim. To be sinned against and to be suffering because of this sin, always calls forth, from within a Christian perspective, a proactive virtuous response.

The First Letter of Peter exhorts its readers to follow the example of Christ who, though he committed no sin, 'was reviled,' but 'he did not revile in return.' 'When he suffered, he did not threaten, but he trusted to him who judges justly.' Christians who suffer for doing wrong receive no credit. However, 'one is approved if, mindful of God, he endures pain while suffering unjustly. . . . If when you do right and suffer for it you take it patiently, you have God's approval' (1 Pet. 2:18–23). The letter also commands: 'Do not return evil for evil or reviling for reviling; but on the contrary bless, for to this you have been called' (1 Pet. 3:9). Even if one is unjustly harmed by others, and so suffers for 'righteousness sake, you will be blessed.'

> Have no fear of them, nor be troubled, but in your hearts reverence Christ as Lord ... keep your conscience clear, so that, when you are abused, those who revile your good behaviour in Christ may be put to shame. For it is better to suffer for doing right, if that should be God's will, than for doing wrong. For Christ also died for sin once for all, the righteous for the unrighteous, that he might bring us to God. 1 Pet. 3:14–18.

This kind of exhortation chafes our fallen nature. Our instinctive response is to answer in kind, but to do so means that we create a situation where one sin is answered by another – our own. Thus, instead of exploiting the sins committed against us as an opportunity for growth in virtue, we aggravate the sinful situation by adding our own sin. While one may be justly angry at the evil done, one must not 'let the sun go down on your anger, and give no opportunity to the devil' (Eph. 4:26–27). The devil loves nothing more than for sinful and evil situations to spiral out of control by mutual recrimination, and he will do all in his power to ensure that such does happen. Satan glories in the suffering and anguish caused by the reciprocating salvoes of sin.[53]

While it is very difficult to do, and can only be done by the power of the Holy Spirit, Christians are called to respond to the sins of others after the manner of Christ. While forthrightly confronting the evil with truth and justice, yet one must do so with endurance, patience, forgiveness, and love.

---

53 A major practical problem is that in real-life situations, especially on the personal level, we like to paint situations black and white. One side stands for good, righteousness, and truth (our side), and the other side stands for all that is diabolical. In reality, both sides may have legitimate, though different, concerns. The dilemma is that both sides may be pursuing their cause for truth in a sinful manner. In such situations self-righteousness abounds causing an abundance of suffering on all sides.

Forgiving One's Enemies

While one rightly acknowledges that evil has been done and ardently
strives for its removal, yet equally the Christian is called to forgive the
evil-doer and to strive to love the sinner.

> You have heard that it was said, 'You shall love your neighbour and
> hate your enemy.' But I say to you, Love your enemies and pray for
> those who persecute you, so that you may be sons of your Father in
> heaven; for he makes his sun rise on the evil and on the good, and
> sends rain on the just and on the unjust. For if you love those who
> love you, what reward have you? Do not even the tax collectors do
> the same? And if you salute only your brethren, what more are you
> doing than others? Do not even the Gentiles do the same? You,
> therefore, must be perfect as your heavenly Father is perfect. Mt
> 5:43–58, see also 39–42; Lk 6:27–36.[54]

To forgive and even to love those who sin against us is undoubtedly
the most difficult of Jesus' commands. Again, it is contrary to everything
our fallen nature embodies. Our dignity and rights have been unjustly
violated. Right is on our side. And rightly, we can wish, and even
demand, that no such evil perpetrated against us be repeated. Yet
Christian perfection, in imitation of the Father, resides primarily in being
merciful for his own perfect goodness is displayed in his mercy (see Lk
6:36). In forgiveness Christians prove that they are truly sons of God for
they make their own the words of Jesus, the Son: 'Father, forgive them;
for they know not what they do' (Lk 23:34).

What is often forgotten in our frequent self-righteous struggle to
forgive is that we too have often sinned against others causing them to
suffer. We forget that we too are in need of mercy and forgiveness.

> Let all bitterness and wrath and anger and clamour and slander be
> put away from you, with all malice, and be kind to one another,
> tenderhearted, forgiving one another, as God in Christ Jesus forgave
> you. Eph. 4:31–32; see Col. 3:13.

Jesus not only told Peter that we must forgive 'seventy times seven,'
but also that his heavenly Father will withhold his mercy and forgiveness
to those who refuse mercy and forgiveness (see Mt 18:23–35). In the 'Our
Father' Jesus specifically taught us to pray that the Father would forgive
us as we have forgiven others (see Mt 6:12). To refuse to forgive and to
pray such a prayer is to call down judgment upon oneself. Judgment will
be without mercy upon those who have shown no mercy; yet 'mercy

---

54 Jesus also made the astounding exhortation:

> You have heard that it is said, 'An eye for an eye and a tooth for a tooth.' But I say
> to you, Do not resist one who is evil. But if any one strikes you on the right cheek,
> turn to him the other also; and if any one would sue you and take your coat, let him
> have your cloak as well. Mt 5:39–40; see Lk 6:39.

> Jesus is not suggesting that Christians should allow evil-doers to 'walk over' them,
> nor is he advocating a social policy that allows criminals to go unchecked and unpun-
> ished, but he is stating very dramatically that revenge and mutual recrimination is
> contrary to the gospel.

triumphs over judgment' (James 2:13). Moreover, as Paul reminded the Romans, they are to 'bless those who persecute you; bless and do not curse them' (Rom. 12:14). They are to leave judgment, and even wrath and vengeance, in the hands of God. 'Do not be overcome by evil, but overcome evil with good' (Rom. 12:19–21).

This gospel teaching on mercy and forgiveness in the midst of sin and evil is difficult to implement, and again without the Holy Spirit it is impossible. Many consider such acts of mercy and forgiveness degrading and impractical. Yet, it resides at the very heart of who God is in his perfect and unchanging love. Moreover, it is equally at the heart of Jesus' work of redemption, for he is the only completely innocent person who suffered unjustly even unto death, and in so doing won mercy and forgiveness for all of humankind. If one examines the wars and conflicts (even among individuals) today, in which many innocent people suffer immense injustice, most, if not all, of them are due to the absence of mercy and forgiveness. Hatred, bitterness, and resentment nurtured on past, and sometimes long past, injuries have so marred and distorted the psyche of whole peoples and nations that, in vengeance, they perpetrate the same evils upon others that have been perpetrated upon them. And so the cycle of evil, due to a lack of mercy and forgiveness, continues unabated and ever increases. Jesus has provided a practical solution to a very practical problem – how to respond to the suffering caused by the sins of others – and the answer is the one that he himself made possible – mercy and forgiveness.[55]

---

55 It should also be noted in concluding this section that 'forgiveness' is not the same as 'excusing.' I excuse someone who accidentally injuries me because the person did not intentionally do so. I forgive someone who injures me and does so knowingly and intentionally. In 'forgiveness' I acknowledge the wilful intent of the evil done and strive to ensure that it is not repeated, but I, nonetheless, grant pardon to the offender and strive to hold no bitterness or resentment against him or her.

Moreover, forgiveness is not predicated upon the offender acknowledging his or her guilt and asking forgiveness. Such repentance may make it easier for the person who has been sinned against to forgive, but forgiveness itself is required regardless of whether or not the offender seeks reconciliation.

For an example of my own struggle with forgiveness, see T. Weinandy, 'Toward Overcoming the Spirit of Resentment in a Polarized Church,' *New Oxford Review* 57/9 (1990):14–17. This article has subsequently been republished in eight other periodicals.

Recently psychotherapy has shown interest in forgiveness as a practical means to emotional healing. See R.P. Fitzgibbons, 'The Cognitive and Emotive Uses of Forgiveness in the Treatment of Anger,' *Psychotherapy* 23/4 (1986):629–33. See also R. Enright and R.P. Fitzgibbons, *Forgiveness in Psychotherapy: The Path to Resolving Excessive Anger* (New York: APA Press, 1999), and the website of the International Forgiveness Institute: www.forgiveness-institute.org.

See also S. Wiesenthal, *The Sunflower: On the Possibilities and Limits of Forgiveness*, revised edition (New York: Schocken Books, 1997). Here Wiesenthal presents an account of his personal confrontation with the question of forgiveness. While imprisoned in a Nazi concentration camp, Wiesenthal was taken to the bedside of a dying member of the SS. The young soldier, overwhelmed by the guilt of his crimes, graphically confesses to Wiesenthal what he has done and asks him, as a Jew, for forgiveness. After listening to and anguishing over what he had heard, Wiesenthal simply departs in silence. At the time and subsequently Wiesenthal questions whether he did what was right. Should he have forgiven the SS soldier? Was it possible for him to forgive? The book contains responses from many leading Jews and Christians to Wiesenthal's

The Vanquishing of Evil

While forgiveness is a virtuous act, so too is the fight against evil. Whether one is a Christian or not, all must strive to ensure, within one's capability and within moral bounds, that those who perpetrate evil cease to do so. Obviously, one may not be successful, nonetheless all are called to combat evil and alleviate the suffering it causes. From within a Christian perspective this fosters the kingdom of God and cultivates peace and justice within this world. It is a fundamental task of the body of Christ, a task that actually nurtures and strengthens the life of the Spirit within the body, for it is in accord with Christ's own will and action. This endeavor to vanquish evil and to assuage the suffering left in its wake, in tandem with the furtherance of truth, justice and harmony sanctifies individuals and the body of Christ as a whole. However, it contains a twofold paradox.

First, one is more likely to assail evil and to embrace suffering on behalf of others the more one is freed from the suffering due to one's own personal sin. The more one is engrossed in pursuing one's own selfish ends, and so is paralyzed by the suffering that such self-centeredness causes, the less one will be compassionately concerned about the well-being of others. The Christian paradox is that Christ redeems us from the suffering due to our own sin so that we might be free to confront evil and embrace those, in love, who suffer from such evil, making their suffering our own. In actual lived experience, the suffering caused by the sin of others, whether the evil is enacted against us personally or to others, often impels us to rise above our selfish inclinations and so take up the cause of truth and justice.[56] In so doing Jesus empowers us in the Spirit, after the example of his own life, to bear witness to the truth, embrace the suffering involved, and promote the good.

Second, in confronting evil with its concomitant suffering, one, by necessity, embraces suffering. One, in love and compassion, not only suffers in solidarity with those who suffer, but one also makes oneself vulnerable to those who are perpetrating the evil.[57] For example, in today's pro-abortion climate, a young medical student who refuses to perform abortions is not only defending the lives of the unborn, but can equally be putting his or her medical career in jeopardy. Or, to contest

---

dilemma, many of which are, to my mind, rather superficial. Wiesenthal's experience tore at the very heart of his being – a Jew, who had suffered despicable humiliations and torments, along with countless fellow Jews, at the hands of the Nazis. Yet, the confession of the soldier equally invoked, deep within him, the question of mercy and forgiveness. I believe Wiesenthal's silence speaks to both issues. It acknowledges the evil, but it does not say 'No' to mercy.

56 This could also be the case with 'natural disasters' and sickness. Such suffering can release us from our selfish concerns and compel us to respond in generosity and compassion. In the midst of their 'severe test' and 'extreme poverty' the churches in Macedonia joyfully and liberally contributed to Paul's collection for the poor in Jerusalem (2 Cor. 8:1–5).

57 A. McGill perceptively wrote: 'The instant a person renounces his self-enclosed identity and repudiates the power of domination as his lord, he provokes the world against him. He stands as an offence to the world, as a fanatic or a fool.' *Suffering: A Test of Theological Method*, p. 114.

economic, political and social injustice may easily lead to violence being perpetrated against oneself. 'Indeed all who desire to live a godly life in Christ Jesus will be persecuted, while evil men and impostors will go on from bad to worse, deceivers and deceived' (2 Tim. 3:12). History abounds with examples of such heroic godly men and women who gave their lives for the cause of truth and in the defense of others.[58] Jesus' promise must be remembered: 'Blessed are those who are persecuted for righteousness' sake, for theirs is the kingdom of heaven' (Mt 5:10).

Sharing in the Sufferings of Christ

It is here then that we, from a Christian perspective, must once more take up the topic of sharing in the sufferings of Christ. By actively confronting sin and evil and by bearing witness to truth, goodness, and justice, Christians participate in the redemptive work of Christ. Christians 'complete what is lacking in Christ's afflictions for the sake of his body, that is, the church' (Col. 1:24). In uniting themselves to the cross of Christ, Christians embrace the suffering due to sin, and offer their lives, in union with Christ, for the redemption of all – even for those who are perpetrating the evil. While Christ's work of redemption has been accomplished once for all, yet Pope John Paul II has stated:

> In the mystery of the Church as his Body, Christ has in a sense opened his own redemptive suffering to all human suffering. Insofar as man becomes a sharer in Christ's suffering – in any part of the world and at any time in history – in that extent *he in his own way completes* the suffering through which Christ accomplished the Redemption of the world.

Christ's redemption, 'through satisfactory love, *remains always open to all love* expressed *in human suffering.*' Thus Christ's redemptive suffering lives on and develops.

> It lives and develops as the Body of Christ, the Church, and in this dimension every human suffering, by reason of the loving union with Christ, completes the suffering of Christ. It completes that suffering *just as the Church completes the redemptive work of Christ.*[59]

Jesus did not give Christians a philosophical answer to the meaning of suffering. Rather, as Pope John Paul has again stated, he exhorted his disciples:

> 'Follow me!' Come! Take part through your suffering in this work of saving the world, a salvation achieved through my suffering!

---

58 As noted earlier, J.-B. Metz denies that there is suffering 'in God.' He argues that it is more correct to speak of 'suffering unto God.' By this he means the biblical notion, found in such books as the Psalms, Job, and Lamentations, where men and women offer their suffering unto the God of love and righteousness. He refers to this as 'the mysticism of suffering unto God.' See 'Suffering Unto God,' *Critical Inquiry*, 20 (1994):611–22 and *A Passion for God: The Mystical-Political Dimension of Christianity*, pp. 42, 69–71, 116–20.

59 All the above passages are from *Salvifici Doloris*, n. 24.

Through my cross! Gradually, *as the individual takes up his cross,* spiritually uniting himself to the cross of Christ, the salvific meaning of suffering is revealed before him. He does not discover this meaning at his own human level, but at the level of the suffering of Christ.[60]

Christians, in their own suffering, and in solidarity with and on behalf of others, offer their lives, in union with Christ, as a sacrifice, even unto death, not only to achieve peace and justice within the world, but also for the eternal salvation of all. The Father comforts Christians so that they may be able to 'comfort those who are in any affliction, with the same comfort with which we ourselves are comforted by God. For as we share abundantly in Christ's sufferings, so through Christ we share abundantly in comfort too' (1 Cor. 1:3–5). By suffering in loving union with others and comforting them with the Father's love and the hope of Jesus' resurrection, Christians willingly and even, because of the Father's love and Jesus' resurrection, joyfully fulfil, in a supreme manner, Christ's new commandment.[61] 'This is my commandment, that you love one another as I have loved you. Greater love has no man than this, that a man lay down his life for his friends' (Jn 15:12–13).

It is not merely Christians who suffer on behalf of others and lay down their lives. As already quoted above, Pope John Paul II sees such suffering as participating in the sufferings of Christ, not only for those who are Christians, but 'in many others also who, at times, even without belief in Christ, suffer and give their lives for the truth and for a just cause. In the sufferings of all of these people the great dignity of man is strikingly confirmed.'[62]

Suffering for the Sake of the Gospel
While the above discussion did not exclude the suffering caused by religious persecution and often implied it, it purposely did not address this issue directly. The reason being that, while much of what has been said above is relevant, the New Testament has quite specific instructions for Christians who endure persecution.[63]

First, Christians are to expect persecution. This expectation is squarely founded upon the persecution of Jesus himself. If he suffered death for doing the work of the Father, then his followers must anticipate the same fate. According to the Gospel of John, because his disciples are not of this world as he is not of this world, Jesus assured them that, as the world hated him, so it will equally hate them. 'Remember the word that I said to you, "A servant is not greater than his master." If they persecuted me,

---

60 *Salvifici Doloris,* n. 26.
61 A. McGill has stated that 'the Christian can know joy in connection with sorrow, but only because he knows the power of God overcoming the power of evil. . . . The joy of life in Christ is a consolation for our sorrow as human beings; it does not remove that sorrow.' *Suffering: A Test of Theological Method,* pp. 117 and 118.
62 *Salvifici Doloris,* n. 22.
63 Obviously, the Old Testament also contains stories and teaching on persecution and martyrdom. See for example Judith, Esther, Daniel 3 and 6, 1 and 2 Maccabees and Jeremiah 11:18–23, 18:18–23, 20:7–18, 26, 36–40.

they will persecute you' (Jn 15:18, 20; see 1 Jn 3:13, Mt 10:24–25). He fore-
warned them that they would be handed over to sanhedrins and
governors, where they would be beaten and scourged. Jesus bluntly
stated that he did not come to bring peace, rather his gospel would bring
division even within families (see Lk 12:51–53). 'Brother will deliver up
brother to death, and the father his child . . . , and you will be hated by all
for my name's sake' (Mt 10:21–22; see Mt 10:17–23, Mk 13: 9–13, Lk
21:12–19).[64]

Historically the apostolic church forthwith became aware that Jesus'
warnings were indeed accurate. The Acts of the Apostles is a narration of
the persecutions, and even death, of the first Christians who coura-
geously proclaimed the gospel (see Acts 4:1–31, 5:17–42, 7:1–60, 9:1–2,
12:1–19, 16:16–24, 18:1–11, 19:21—26:32). Paul was well aware that this
was an evil age in which those who followed Christ would suffer many
trials (see Gal. 1:4; Eph. 5:16; 2 Thess. 3:2–3). He detailed what he himself,
as a prisoner in the Lord, suffered for the sake of the gospel (see 2 Cor.
6:1–10, 11:22–33, 12:7–10; Eph. 4:1; Phil. 1:13, 4:12–13; 1 Thess. 2:2, 2 Tim.
1:8, 3:10–11). The apostles are 'sentenced to death,' 'a spectacle to the
world,' 'fools for Christ's sake,' 'the refuse of the world, the offscouring
of all things' (1 Cor. 4:9–13). The epistles abound with warnings of
impending persecutions or references to the sufferings their readers were
presently enduring, many of which make reference to imitating the
sufferings of Christ (see Phil. 1:28–29; 1 Thess. 1:6, 2:14, 3:3–5; 2 Tim. 4:5;
Heb. 10:32–39, 13:3 and 13, 1 Pet. 2:21–25, 3:13–17, 4:1–6 and 12–19). The
Book of Revelation envisions persecution in an apocalyptic manner.
Babylon the Great, the mother of all prostitutes will become 'drunk with
the blood of the saints and martyrs of Jesus' (Rev. 17:5–6; see 18:24).

Second, in the midst of certain persecution Christians are not to cower
in fear. Despite Jesus' grim vision for his future followers, their response
was not to be one of distress and dread. In the face of accusations and
charges they should not be anxious about what they are to say. 'Say
whatever is given you in that hour, for it is not you who speak, but the
Holy Spirit' (Mk 13:11–12). Not only is the Spirit with them, but they are,
even in the midst of persecution, embraced by the providential care of
God. While they will be hated because of Jesus' name, not a hair of their
head will perish. 'By your endurance you will gain your lives' (Lk
21:18–19).

Third, Christians are not to be ashamed of bearing witness to the
crucified Jesus as Lord, but 'as good soldiers' they must be willing to take
their 'share of suffering for the gospel in the power of God' (2 Tim. 1:8
and 2:3). Courage is the virtue of the Christian apostle (see 1 Cor. 16:13).
'The following night the Lord stood by him [Paul] and said, "Take
courage, for as you have testified about me at Jerusalem, so you must
bear witness also in Rome"' (Acts 23:11). Christians must possess steadfastness, perseverance and faith in the midst of every trial and tribulation
rejoicing in the knowledge that they do not labour in vain (see 1 Cor.

---

64 For studies on the New Testament teaching concerning persecution and martyrdom,
see the relevant essays in *Suffering and Martyrdom in the New Testament*, especially
G.W.H. Lampe, 'Martyrdom and Inspiration,' pp. 118–35.

15:58; Phil. 4:4–6; Col. 1:11, 23; 2 Tim. 2:12; Heb. 10:35; James 1:12, 5:10–11; Rev. 13:10). 'Therefore we ourselves boast of you in the churches of God for your steadfastness and faith in all your persecutions and in the afflictions which you are enduring' (1 Thess. 1:4). Notwithstanding persecution and death, Christians must above all 'contend for the faith' (Jude 3).[65]

Fourth, persecution must be interpreted in the light of Jesus' resurrection. This is the ultimate assurance of hope that, even in the face of death itself, they will obtain life. Christians know that they will come to eat and drink in Jesus' kingdom (see Lk 22:28–30). This very suffering for the sake of the gospel is what makes them worthy of such a reward.

> This is evidence of the righteous judgement of God, that you may be made worthy of the kingdom of God, for which you are suffering – since indeed God deems it just to repay with affliction those who afflict you, and to grant rest with us to you who are afflicted, when the Lord Jesus is revealed from heaven with his mighty angels in flaming fire. 2 Thess. 1:5–7.

Paul knew well that 'The Lord will rescue me from every evil and save me for his heavenly kingdom' (2 Tim. 4:18). Christians must remember that 'this slight momentary affliction is preparing for us an eternal weight of glory beyond all comparison' (2 Cor. 4:17). Because they look to what is unseen, Christians can rejoice in such persecution.

> Beloved, do not be surprised at the fiery ordeal which comes upon you to prove you, as though something strange were happening to you. But rejoice in so far as you share Christ's sufferings, that you may also rejoice and be glad when his glory is revealed. If you are reproached for the name of Christ, you are blessed, because the spirit of glory and of God rests upon you. 1 Pet. 4:12–14.

Lastly, glory – to give glory to Jesus through the preaching of the gospel - is the glory of the Christian. While one should not seek martyrdom, yet to suffer for the sake of the gospel and even to die for the name of Jesus is a Christian's supreme honor. It is the Christian's consummate boast.[66] The world may presently rejoice while Christians weep, but upon seeing the glorious Jesus their 'hearts will rejoice,' and no one will take that joy from them (Jn 16:20–22; see Rev. 11:11–12). Jesus assured those who suffer on his account that they are indeed blessed, and so should rejoice. 'Blessed are you when men revile you and persecute you and utter all kinds of evil against you falsely on my account. Rejoice and be glad, for your reward is great in heaven' (Mt 5:11). The martyrs are the ones 'who have come out of the great tribulation; they have

65 In the light of today's moral relativism, Pope John Paul II has eloquently spoken of the need for Christian martyrs who would defend moral truth. 'Martyrdom, accepted as an affirmation of the inviolability of the moral order, bears splendid witness both to the holiness of God's law and to the inviolability of the personal dignity of man, created in God's image and likeness.' *Veritatis Splendor*, n. 92.1. See also nn. 90–94.
66 In the early church this is exemplified most fully in Ignatius of Antioch. See his *Letter to the Romans*. For other patristic references see J. Walsh and P.G. Walsh, *Divine Providence and Human Suffering*, pp. 126–31.

washed their robes and made them white in the blood of the Lamb.' Therefore, they will find rest and comfort 'before the throne of God' (Rev. 7:14–15). They have conquered Satan 'by the blood of the Lamb and by the word of their testimony, for they loved not their lives even unto death. Rejoice then, O heaven and you that dwell therein!' Rev. 12:11–12.

The Cross: The Glory of Man

In this chapter we have seen that the Christian experience of human suffering is rich in significance. Human beings may suffer because of their own personal sinfulness, or for the sake of God's discipline, or because of the sins of others. However, all suffering, whatever its cause, is to redound to the glory of those who suffer. In the light of the cross of Christ, while suffering may be due to evil, it can be transfigured through the Holy Spirit into a means of obtaining and manifesting heroic virtue.[67]

I have written at length about the Christian experience and interpretation of human suffering not only because it is crucial for understanding the gospel, but also because it is central to this study. Those who espouse a suffering God often fail to perceive the richness of the Christian experience of human suffering, nor do they appreciate the depth of the Christian response to human suffering. Moreover, they do not fully grasp the glory embodied and the virtue expressed within the Christian account of suffering. They rightfully comprehend the immense suffering which evil causes. However, they frequently limit the meaning of suffering to that of merely being the suffering of a passive victim of grave injustice and evil. Having limited the meaning of such suffering to that of a passive victim, they attempt to compensate for its now seeming 'meaninglessness' by espousing a God who suffers in solidarity with the victim. This co-suffering of God with the suffering victim is intended to engender hope and consolation. At times one feels that what they wish is a God who feels sorry for them because of their plight – a God who authenticates and justifies their self-pity. Actually, such a view, as the above demonstrates, radically diminishes the salvific significance of Christ's redemptive suffering and so the import of his body, as the whole church and as individual members within it, which actively co-suffers with him for its own sanctification and for humankind's well-being and salvation.

While the cross reveals the great love of the Father, in that he was willing to send his Son into the world, and while the cross reveals the glory of the Son, in that he was willing to assume authentic human suffering for humankind's salvation, yet this is not the sole meaning of the cross. The cross now also reveals the glory of all those men and

---

67 Pope John Paul II has stated that 'suffering is, in itself, an experience of evil. But Christ has made suffering the firmest basis of the definitive good, namely the good of eternal salvation.' *Salvifici Doloris*, n. 26.

  The Second Vatican Council declared that all our virtuous deeds – the promotion of 'the goods of human dignity, familial communion, and freedom, that is to say, all the good fruits of our nature and effort' – will be found in heaven, 'but cleaned of all dirt, lit up, and transformed, when Christ gives back to the Father an eternal and universal kingdom.' *Gaudium et Spes*, 39.

women who equally suffer, in accordance with the Father's will and in union with Christ, for the sake of their own sanctification and that of their brothers and sisters. From within a Christian perspective the meaning and value of redemptive suffering is always placed within history and the concrete lives of human beings for it is here that men and women of flesh and blood encounter evil and endure suffering. It is equally within time and history that the body of Christ, by actively embracing the cross, advances in holiness and co-operates in the labour of salvation. The meaning and value of suffering must never be relegated to some divine mythical ahistorical sphere. For the Father, the cross of suffering is ultimately for the glory of his Son and for the glory of those who suffer in union with him, and not for his own self-aggrandizement.

It must be remembered that while the Father detests all evil and grieves over all who suffer, yet his response is not that of being over-wrought or alarmed. Rather he, as with his Son, is well-pleased with those who are willing to suffer for the sake of righteousness. He rejoices and glories in their courage, their nobility, their faith, their hope, and in their love. He comprehends, more even than those who suffer, their glory and the glory to which they are attaining – that of eternal blessedness.

Allow me to close with one remarkable example of a person who beautifully illustrates, in her own life, most of what has been discussed in this chapter.

Edith Stein: Completing the Afflictions of Christ

Saint Edith Stein (Sister Teresa Benedicta of the Cross, OCD) is an especially appropriate example, in the context of this present study, of a person who groaned because of her own sinfulness and suffered the purifying discipline of God. Moreover, and more so, she exemplifies a person who made her own suffering and death a sharing in the sufferings of Christ for the salvation of her own Jewish people and for the redemption of her German nation.[68]

68 The following brief sketch of Edith Stein's life is based exclusively upon F.M. Oben's excellent book, *Edith Stein: Scholar, Feminist, Saint* (New York: Alba House, 1988). For other biographies and studies of Stein, see H. Graef, *The Scholar and the Cross* (Westminster, MD: The Newman Press, 1955); W. Herbstrith, *Edith Stein: A Biography* (San Francisco: Ignatius Press, 1992); the small booklet *Blessed by the Cross: Five Portraits of Edith Stein*, ed. J. Sullivan (New Rochelle: Catholics United for the Faith, 1990); and the short biography that appeared in *L'Osservatore Romano* at the time of her canonization (No. 41(1562), 14 October 1998).

While all Christian saints and heroes have recognized that they are called to suffer in union with Christ, and have indeed done so, Edith Stein's death at Auschwitz is particularly relevant here, for, as noted at the outset of this study, the Holocaust has become the experience of this century which has furthered the cause for a passible and so suffering God. One needs only to recall E. Wiesel's story and Moltmann's book *The Crucified God* to perceive the impact that the Holocaust has had upon this issue.

In focusing upon Edith Stein, I do not wish in any way to underestimate or discount the heroism of other Christians. This present century has produced more Christian martyrs than all previous 'Christian' centuries combined. This persecution presently continues, and is often ignored. See N. Shea, 'Atrocities Not Fit to Print,' *First Things* 77 (1997):32–35. Nor, indeed, do I want to cheapen the heroic suffering or undervalue the holy lives of the millions of Jews, who were systematically humiliated and brutally

Edith was born on *Yom Kippur* (The Day of Atonement), 12 October 1891. While she was raised within a devout Jewish family, at the age of fifteen Edith gave up the practise of her faith, and said that she could no longer believe in a personal God. Nonetheless, Edith maintained throughout this period of unbelief her special gift to empathize with others. Later, her doctoral thesis would be entitled *On the Problem of Empathy*.[69] During her years at the University of Göttingen she studied philosophy, and came under the influence of its renowned philosophers, many of whom had become Christians, either Lutheran or Catholic – Adolf Reinach, Theodor Conrad, Hedwig Martius, Dietrich von Hildebrand, Max Scheler, and Edmund Husserl. This circle of philosophical colleagues and friends provided her with the intellectual and spiritual environment in which she could reconsider her own religious stance.[70] She slowly, but steadily, was drawn to Christianity. After an all-night reading of St Teresa of Avila's autobiography, she exclaimed: 'This is the truth.' Even though it caused anguish among her Jewish relatives, especially for her mother, Edith decided to become a Catholic, and on 1 January 1922 she was baptized. Her natural intelligence coupled with her work in phenomenology and her study and translation of Aquinas and John Henry Cardinal Newman made her a rising luminary among the Catholic intellectuals of Europe.[71] Moreover, her concern for women motivated her to lecture and write extensively on the education of women and on their importance and status within the family and society.[72] While she had obtained a teaching post in Münster, she was forced to abandon it because of Hitler's anti-Jewish legislation. Clearly perceiving what was happening to her and around her, she foresaw that danger was at hand for Jews and Christians alike. She wrote at this time: 'Now on a sudden it was luminously clear to me that once again God's hand lay heavy on his people, and that the destiny of this people was my

---

killed in the Holocaust. Nor must it be forgotten that there are countless innocent men and women, of every race, nation and religion, who have suffered and died because of hate and injustice.

I have chosen Edith for the obvious reason that she was a Jew by birth and one who remained so as a Christian by faith, and she attempted to respond to the Holocaust in a manner whereby she could be supremely faithful to both. In his homily at her canonization Pope John Paul II called Edith 'this *eminent daughter of Israel and faithful daughter of the Church*' (*L'Osservatore Romano*, No. 41(1562), 14 October 1998). If the Holocaust is the contemporary icon of suffering, Edith's life and death may well be the contemporary hermeneutical icon of its interpretation. It is often the lives of saints who best interpret the significance of events, and not the scholarly jottings of historians, philosophers, and theologians.

69 See *On the Problem of Empathy*, trans. W. Stein (The Hague: Martinus Nijhoff, 1964).
70 She tells of her experiences as a student in Göttingen in her autobiography, *Life in a Jewish Family*, trans. J. Koeppel (Washington, DC: ICS Press, 1986), Ch. 7.
71 During this time she wrote *Finite and Eternal Being, Potency and Act*, and contributed an article to the *Festschrift* honouring E. Husserl entitled: 'Husserl's Phenomenology and the Philosophy of St Thomas Aquinas.' She also translated into German Newman's *Letters and Journals* (1801–45), and Aquinas' *De Veritate*. See *Edith Steins Werke*, eds. L. Gelber and R. Leuven (Louvain: E. Nauwelaerts; Freiburg: Herder).
72 See her remarkably perceptive essays in *Essays on Woman*, trans. F.M. Oben (Washington, DC: ICS Press, 1987).

own.'[73] Edith, in her desire to embrace the suffering of her people and to combat the evil which she saw swelling around her, became convinced that her long-cherished yearning to be a Carmelite Nun was indeed God's will. She desired this vocation not only because of her initial love of St Teresa of Avila, but more so because she discerned that the specific Carmelite charism was that of embracing the cross of Christ for the salvation of the world. As Edith later wrote:

> Everyone who, in the course of time, has borne an onerous destiny in remembrance of the suffering Saviour or who has freely taken up works of expiation has by doing so cancelled some of the mighty load of human sin and has helped the Lord carry his burden. Or rather, Christ the head effects expiation in these members of his Mystical Body who put themselves, body and soul, at his disposal for carrying out his work of salvation.[74]

On 14 October 1933 Edith entered the Mary Queen of Peace Carmel in Cologne. In the wake of *Kristallnacht* (9 November 1938) she was persuaded to flee to the Carmel in Echt, Holland on 31 December. On Passion Sunday (26 March 1939), the day after Hitler declared that Poland must be totally subjected, Edith wrote a note to her prioress.

> Dear Mother, I beg your Reverence's permission to offer myself to the Heart of Jesus as a sacrificial expiation for the sake of true peace: that the Antichrist's sway may be broken, if possible without another world-war, and that a new order may be established. I am asking this today because it is already the twelfth hour. I know that I am nothing, but Jesus wills it, and he will call many more to the same sacrifice in these days.[75]

In 1941 Edith's sister, Rosa, having also become a Catholic, joined her at Echt as a third-order Carmelite. Hitler invaded Holland in May, and on 1 September both sisters were required to wear the Yellow Star of David inscribed with the word 'Jew.' On 26 July 1942 the Dutch bishops published a pastoral letter condemning the Nazis' treatment and deportation of Jews. In reprisal the Nazi authorities decreed that all Catholics of Jewish ancestry be arrested. Edith and Rosa were taken from their convent that same evening. As they were escorted away under armed guard, Edith's words to her sister were: 'Come, let us go for our people.'[76] During the ensuing week they were taken first to two Dutch concentration camps, and finally to Auschwitz. When she was arrested she was in the process of attempting to finish her study on the writings of St John of the Cross. While this book was never completed, during her final days,

73 Oben quotes Teresia de Spiritu Sancto Posselt, *Edith Stein* (New York: Sheed and Ward, 1952), p. 117.
74 *The Hidden Life: Essays, Meditations, Spiritual Texts*, trans. W. Stein (Washington, DC: ICS Publications, 1992), p. 92.
75 Oben quotes Posselt, *Edith Stein*, p. 212.
76 Oben quotes E. Stein, *Briefauslese 1917–42* (Freiburg: Herder, 1967), p. 136.

Edith's own life became its completion, its final chapter, for she lived out to the very end *The Science of the Cross.*[77]

Later, witnesses who survived the deportations spoke of Edith's love of and care for her fellow sufferers. Even one of her captors would testify that when he met her at the Dutch camp at Westerbork that he knew she was a holy woman.

> She was in the hell of Westerbork only a few days, walking among the prisoners, talking and praying like a saint. Yes, that's what she was. That's the impression which this elderly woman gave, though, on the other hand, she seemed quite young. She spoke in such a clear and humble way that anybody who listened to her was seized. A talk with her was like a visit to another world.[78]

According to the Dutch Red Cross, Edith and Rosa arrived at Auschwitz in the early morning of 9 August 1942 where they were exterminated that same day.

Some months previously Edith had written:

> I am quite content in any case. One can only learn a 'Science of the Cross' if one feels the cross in one's own person. I was convinced of this from the very first and have said with all my heart 'Hail Cross, our only hope.'[79]

Edith Stein was not the only person, Jew or Gentile, who gave their lives in loving sacrifice within Hitler's barbarous and inhuman death camps.[80] Yet, as a Jewish Christian, she, in a unique manner, through her life and especially in her death, spoke her own answer to the Holocaust and to all similar examples of man's barbarity perpetrated against his fellow human beings. She must suffer *on behalf of*, 'for our people.' This was the very answer, she believed, which had been provided by her heavenly

77 See *The Science of the Cross: A Study of St John of the Cross*, trans. H. Graef (Chicago: Henry Regnery, 1960). This work consolidates the spiritual wisdom of Edith, a wisdom that she herself embodied. See also *The Hidden Life*.
78 Oben quotes from Posselt, ch. 7 where she treats Edith's arrest, imprisonment and death.
79 Oben quotes E. Stein, *Briefauslese*, p. 127.
80 Of those whose biographies or works I have read, other known Christians who suffered and died for the faith during this time are the following. Because of his opposition to Nazism, Dietrich Bonhoeffer was imprisoned at Buchenwald and hanged by the Gestapo at Fossenbürg in 1945. See the bibliography in *The Oxford Dictionary of the Christian Church*, p. 223. In 1940 Titus Brandsma, OC was appointed by the Dutch bishops to act as a Catholic spokesman against the treatment and deportation of the Jews. He was arrested by the Nazis on 19 January 1942 and killed at Dachau in April. See B. Hanley, *Through a Dark Tunnel: The Story of Titus Brandsma* (Athlone: Veritas Publications, 1987). Because of his anti-Nazi sympathies Alfred Delp, SJ was tried for treason and executed in the Plotzensee prison in 1945. See *The Prison Meditations of Father Delp* (New York: Macmillan, 1963). Franz Jägerstätter was a young Catholic married layman who refused active military service within Hitler's army. He was tried for sedition and treason, and executed in 1943. See E. Putz, *Against the Stream: Franz Jägerstätter* (London: Pax Christi, 1996). Maximilian Kolbe, OFM, Conv. was arrested and sent to Auschwitz because of his Christian publications. He volunteered to take the place of a young man who was to die by starvation because of an attempted escape. He was killed by lethal injection in 1941. See D.H. Farmer, *The Oxford Dictionary of Saints* (Oxford: Oxford University Press, 1992).

Father and which had been obediently carried out by his Son in the love of the Spirit. So, in communion with Christ, one was called to offer one's own life as an atonement for sin for the salvation of all.[81] Edith did not simply perceive the intellectual meaning of Paul's words, rather she actually embodied their truth in her own life, and in so doing bore witness to their truth. 'Now I rejoice in my suffering for your sake, and in my flesh I complete what is lacking in Christ's afflictions for the sake of his body, that is, the church' (Col 1:24).[82]

81 While, as a Christian, I am particularly drawn to Edith Stein's response to the Holocaust, there have been numerous, and often conflicting, Jewish and Christian attempts at providing a religious and/or rational interpretation and response to it. The following is the small portion of the existing literature that I have consulted.

For various Jewish responses see: D. Cohn-Sherbok, *God and the Holocaust* (Leominster: Gracewing, 1996); O. Leaman, *Evil and Suffering in Jewish Philosophy* (Cambridge: Cambridge University Press, 1995, pp. 185–219; R.L. Rubenstein, *After Auschwitz: History, Theology, and Contemporary Judaism*, second edition (Baltimore: The Johns Hopkins University Press, 1992), pp. 83–209; N. Solomon, *Judaism and World Religion* (London: Macmillan, 1991), pp. 173–200.

See also D.B. Batstone, 'The Transformation of the Messianic Idea in Judaism and Christianity in Light of the Holocaust: Reflection on the Writings of Elie Wiesel,' *Journal of Ecumenical Studies* 23/4 (1986):587–600; G. Baum, 'Theology After Auschwitz' in *The Social Imperative* (New York: Paulist Press, 1979), pp. 39–69; D.R. Blumenthal, *Facing the Abusing God: A Theology of Protest* (Louisville: Westminster/John Knox Press, 1993; A. Cohen, 'In Our Terrible Age: The *Tremendum* of the Jews' in *Concilium*, vol. 175, *The Holocaust as Interpretation*, eds D. Tracy and E. Schlüsser Fiorenza, 5 (1984):11–16; S.R. Haynes, 'Christian Holocaust Theology: A Critical Reassessment', *Journal of American Academy of Religion*, 62/2 (1994):553–83; H. Jonas, 'The Concept of God after Auschwitz: A Jewish Voice,' *The Journal of Religion* 67 (1987):1–13; R. Martin, *The Suffering of Love* (Petersham: St Bede's Publications, 1995); J.-B. Metz, 'Christians and Jews after Auschwitz' in *The Emergent Church: The Future of Christianity in a Postbourgeois World* (New York: Crossroad, 1981); J.-B. Metz, 'Facing the Jews, Christian Theology after Auschwitz' in *Concilium*, vol. 175/5 (1984):26–33; J.-B. Metz, *A Passion for God: The Mystical-Political Dimension of Christianity*, especially pp. 121–32; J.F. Moore, 'A Spectrum of Views: Traditional Christian Responses to the Holocaust,' *Journal of Ecumenical Studies* 25/2 (1988):212–24; J. Pawlikowski, 'The Holocaust and Contemporary Christology,' in *Concilium*, vol. 175/5 (1984):43–9.

82 At Edith's beatification in Cologne on 1 May 1987, Pope John Paul II stated:

After she began seeing the destiny of Israel from the standpoint of the Cross, our newly beatified sister let Christ lead her more and more deeply into the mystery of his salvation to be able to bear the multiple pains of humankind in spiritual union with Him and to help atone for the outrageous injustices in the world. As *Benedicta a Cruce* – Blessed by the Cross – she wanted to bear the cross with Christ for the salvation of her people, her Church and the world as a whole. She offered herself to God as a 'sacrifice for genuine peace' and above all for her threatened and humiliated Jewish people. After she recognized that God had once again laid a heavy hand on his people, she was convinced 'that the destiny of this people was also my destiny.' Trans. from *Blessed by the Cross*, p. 34.

Conclusion

I believe that little needs to be said by way of concluding this book. I have, as best as I was able, put forth my arguments as clearly and as cogently as possible. In executing this endeavor I have attempted to be faithful to Christian doctrine and to the inherited theological tradition. I did not wish to be enslaved to some past fossilized canon, but rather I wanted to confirm that the authentic Christian tradition not only is alive, but that it could also be applied and actually be employed in an ever-creative and, indeed, ever-new and life-giving manner. It is ultimately the Christian doctrines of the Trinity, of creation, of the Incarnation, of redemption, of the Holy Spirit, and of the church that bear upon the question of human suffering. It is in the proper interpretation and in the accurate understanding of these doctrines that I have sought to bring clarity and understanding to the question of God and human suffering.

Moreover, as I have often reminded the reader, I was not attempting, in taking up the question of God and suffering, to solve a philosophical problem, nor was I attempting to make fully comprehensible a theological mystery. To attempt the first would be to misconceive the task at hand. To attempt the second would be utter folly. Rather, I was merely attempting to articulate more precisely the mystery of God's relationship to human suffering by clarifying the various Christian mysteries associated with it. In so doing my aim was to allow the glory of these mysteries to shine forth ever more radiantly, and with them then the pure radiance of God's love for all who suffer. Whether or not I have been successful in all my efforts must now be left to the judgment of each reader.

In conclusion, I merely want to state again that Jesus, as the incarnate Son, who through his death overcame our sin and in his resurrection obtained for us the Spirit of truth and life, is the Father's merciful and loving response to human suffering. There neither was, nor is there now, nor will there ever be, another. I, as a member of the world's history of untold human suffering and in communion with all of God's people, eagerly await that day when Jesus will return in glory to wipe away every tear.

Bibliography

For edited works only the editor(s) and title are listed. For specific authors and articles within these works consult the footnotes.

Anastos, M., 'Nestorius was Orthodox,' *Dumbarton Oaks Papers* 16 (1962):117–40.

Anderson, J.F., 'Creation as a Relation,' *The New Scholasticism* 24 (1950):263–83.

Andresen, C., 'Justine und die mittlere Platonismus,' *Zeitschrift für die neuerstamentliche Wissenschaft* 44 (1952–53):157–95.

Aquinas, T., *Summa Theologica*, trans. English Dominican Province. New York: Benziger Brothers, 1947.

—, *Summa Contra Gentiles* (*On the Truth of the Catholic Faith*, trans. A. Pegis, V.J. Bourke, J. O'Neil). Garden City: Image Books, 1955–57.

—, *De Ente et Essentia* (*On Being and Essence*, trans. A. Maurer). Toronto: Pontifical Institute of Mediaeval Studies, 1968.

Armstrong, A.H. (ed.), *The Cambridge History of Greek and Early Medieval Philosophy*. Cambridge: Cambridge University Press, 1970.

Attfield, D.G., 'Can God Be Crucified? A Discussion of J. Moltmann,' *Scottish Journal of Theology* 30 (1977):47–56.

Aulén, G., *Christus Victor*. London: SPCK, 1931.

Barnard, L.W., *Justin Martyr: His Life and Thought*. Cambridge: Cambridge University Press, 1967.

Bartel, T.W., 'Why the Philosophical Problems of Chalcedonian Christology Have Not Gone Away,' *Heythrop Journal* 36 (1995):153–72.

Barth, K., *Church Dogmatics* I/2 and II/I. Edinburgh: T & T Clark, 1957.

Batstone, D.B., 'The Transformation of the Messianic Idea in Judaism and Christianity in the Light of the Holocaust: Reflection on the Writings of Elie Wiesel,' *Journal of Ecumenical Studies* 23/4 (1986):587–600.

Bauckham, R., '"Only the Suffering God Can Help": Divine Passibility in Modern Theology,' *Themelios* 9 (1984:3):6–12.

—, *The Theology of Jürgen Moltmann*. Edinburgh: T & T Clark, 1995.

—, *God Crucified: Monotheism and Christology in the New Testament*. Carlisle: Paternoster Press, 1998.

Baum, G., *The Social Imperative*. New York: Paulist Press, 1979.

Baxter, A., 'Chalcedon and the Subject of Christ,' *Downside Review* 107 (1989):1–21.

Bebis, G.B., '"The Apology" of Nestorius: A New Evaluation,' *Studia Patristica* 11 (1972):107–12.

Bettenson, H., *The Early Christian Fathers*. Oxford: Oxford University Press, 1956.

Birch, C. (ed.), *Liberating Life: Contemporary Approaches to Ecological Theology*. Maryknoll: Orbis, 1990.

Blumenthal, D.R., *Facing the Abusing God: A Theology of Protest*. Louisville: Westminster/John Knox Press, 1993.

Boff, L., *Passion of Christ, Passion of the World*. Maryknoll: Orbis, 1987.

—, *Trinity and Society*. Maryknoll: Orbis, 1988.

Bonhoeffer, D., *Letters and Papers from Prison*. London: SCM, 1967.

Botterwick, G.J. and H. Ringgren (eds), *The Theological Dictionary of the Old Testament*. Grand Rapids: Eerdmans, 1986.

Bouyer, L., *The Spirituality of the New Testament and the Fathers*. New York: Seabury Press, 1963.

Bracken, J.A., and M.H. Suchocki (eds), *Trinity in Process: A Relational Theology of God*. New York: Continuum, 1997.

Bradshaw, D. '"All Existing is the Action of God": The Philosophical Theology of David Braine,' *The Thomist* 60/3 (1996): 379–416.

Braine, D., *The Reality of Time and the Existence of God*. Oxford: Clarendon Press, 1988.

Brasnett, B.R., *The Suffering of the Impassible God*. London: SPCK, 1928.

Brigg, C., *The Christian Platonists of Alexandria*. Oxford: Clarendon Press, 1913.

Brinkmann, B.R., *To the Lengths of God*. London: Sheed & Ward, 1988.

Brown, R.E., *An Introduction to New Testament Christology*. New York: Paulist Press, 1994.

Bulgakov, S., *Agniec Bozij*. Paris: YMCA Press, 1933. French edition: *Du Verbe Incarné*. Paris: Aubier, 1943.

Burnley, E., 'The Impassibility of God,' *The Expository Times* 67 (1955–56):90–1.

Burrell, D., *Aquinas: God and Action*. London: Routledge & Kegan Paul, 1979.

—, 'Does Process Theology Rest on a Mistake?' *Theological Studies* 43 (1982):125–35.

—, *Knowing the Unknowable God*. Notre Dame: University Press of Notre Dame, 1986.

—, *Freedom and Creation in Three Traditions*. Notre Dame: University of Notre Dame Press, 1993.

—, 'Incarnation and Creation: The Hidden Dimension,' *Modern Theology* 12/2 (1996):211–20.

Burrell, D. and B. McGinn (eds), *God and Creation: An Ecumenical Symposium*. Notre Dame: University of Notre Dame Press, 1990.

Cain, C., 'A Passionate God,' *St Luke's Journal of Theology* 25 (1981):52–57.

Calvin, J., *Institutes of the Christian Religion*. London: James Clarke Ltd, 1957.

Cantalamessa, R., *La Cristologia di Tertulliano* (Paradosis 18). Fribourg, 1962.

—, *The Power of the Cross*. London: Darton, Longman & Todd, 1996.

Cargas, H.J. and B. Lee (eds), *Religious Experience and Process Theology*. New York: Paulist Press, 1976.

Catechism of the Catholic Church. New York: Catholic Book Publishing Co., 1994.

Cessario, R., *The Godly Image: Christ and Salvation in Catholic Thought from Anselm to Aquinas*. Petersham: St Bede's Publications, 1990.

Chadwick, H., 'Eucharist and Christology in the Nestorian Controversy,' *Journal of Theological Studies* 2 (1951):145–64.

Chestnut, R., 'The Two Prosopa in Nestorius' *Bazaar of Heracleides*,' *Journal of Theological Studies* NS 29/2 (1978):393–409.

Childs, B.S., *Old Testament Theology in a Canonical Context*. London: SCM, 1985.

Clark, K.J. (ed.) *Our Knowledge of God*. Dordrecht: Klwer Academic Press, 1992.

Clark, S.B., *Redeemer*. Ann Arbor: Servant Publications, 1992.

Clarke, B.L. and E.T. Long (eds), *God and Temporality*. New York: Paragon House, 1984.

Clarke, W.N., *The Philosophical Approach to God: A Neo-Thomistic Perspective*. Winston-Salem: Wake Forest University Press, 1979.

Clément, O., *The Roots of Christian Mysticism*. London: New City, 1993.

Cobb, J.B., *A Christian Natural Theology*. London: Lutterworth Press, 1966.

Cobb, J.B. and D. Griffin (eds), *Process Thought: An Introductory Exposition*. Philadelphia: Westminster Press, 1976.

Cohn-Sherbok, D., *God and the Holocaust*. Leominster: Gracewing, 1996.

Cone, J., *God of the Oppressed*. London: SPCK, 1977.

Congar, Y., *The Word and the Spirit*. London: Geoffrey Chapman, 1986.

Copleston, F., *The History of Philosophy*, Vol. 1. New York: Doubleday, 1962.

Cousins, E.H. (ed.), *Process Theology*. New York: Paulist Press, 1971.

Creel, R., *Divine Impassibility*. Cambridge: Cambridge University Press, 1986.

Cross, R., 'Aquinas on Nature, Hypostasis, and the Metaphysics of the Incarnation,' *The Thomist* 60/2 (1996):171–202.

Crouzel, H., 'La Passion de L'Impassible: Un essai apologétique et polémique du III siècle,' *L'Homme Devant Dieu: Mèlanges Offerts au Père Henri de Lubac*. Paris: Aubier, 1963.

—, *Origen*. Edinburgh: T & T Clark, 1989.

Culpepper, R., *Interpreting the Atonement*. Grand Rapids: Eerdmans, 1966.

Cyril of Alexandria, *On the Incarnation Against Nestorius*. Oxford: James Parker & Co., 1881.

—, *Selected Letters* (ed. and trans. L.R. Wickham). Oxford: Clarendon Press, 1983.

—, *On the Unity of Christ* (trans. J. McGuckin). Crestwood: St Vladimir's Press, 1995.

Daniélou, J., *Gospel Message and Hellenistic Culture*, Vol. 2. London: Darton, Longman & Todd, 1973.

—, *Origen*. London: Sheed & Ward, 1995.

Davies, B., *Thinking About God*. London: Geoffrey Chapman, 1985.

—, *The Thought of Thomas Aquinas*. Oxford: Clarendon Press, 1992.

de Lubac, H., *Catholicism*. San Francisco: Ignatius Press, 1988.

de Margerie, B., *The Christian Trinity in History*. Petersham: St Bede's Publications, 1981.

—, 'De la Souffrance de Dieu?' *Esprit et Vie* 93 (1983):110–12.

Denzinger, H. and A. Schönmetzer (eds), *Enchiridion Symbolorum*, 36th edition. Fribourg: Herder, 1976.

de S. Cameron, N.M. (ed.), *The Power and the Weakness of God*. Edinburgh: Rutherford House Books, 1990.

di Berardino, A. (ed.), *Encyclopedia of the Early Church*. Cambridge: James Clarke & Co., 1992.

Dillistone, F.W., *The Christian Understanding of the Atonement*. London: James Nisbet, 1968.

Dillon, J., *The Middle Platonists: A Study of Platonism 80 BC–AD 220*. London: Duckworth, 1977.

Dodds, M., *The Unchanging God of Love*. Fribourg: Editions Universitaires Fribourg Suisse, 1985.

—, 'St Thomas Aquinas and the Motion of the Motionless God,' *New Blackfriars* 86 (1987):233–42.

—, 'Thomas Aquinas, Human Suffering, and the Unchanging God of Love,' *Theological Studies* 52 (1991):330–44.

Dorner, I.A., *Divine Immutability: A Critical Reconsideration*. Minneapolis: Fortress Press, 1994.

Dunn, J.D.G., *Christology in the Making*. Philadelphia: Westminster Press, 1980.

Dupré, L., 'Jesus Still in Agony?: Meditation on a Negro Spiritual,' *Word and Spirit: A Monastic Review* 1 (1979):191–95.

Edwards, M., 'On the Platonic Schooling of Justin Martyr,' *Journal of Theological Studies* 42 (1991):17–34.

—, 'Justin's Logos and the Word of God,' *Journal of Early Christian Studies* 3/3 (1995):261–80.

Edwards, R.M., 'The Pagan Dogma of the Absolute Unchangeableness of God,' *Religious Studies* 14 (1978):305–13.

Enright, R. and R.P. Fitzgibbons, *Forgiveness in Psychotherapy: The Path to Resolving Excessive Anger*. New York: APA Press, 1999.

Evans, E. (ed. and trans.), *Tertullian's Treatise on the Incarnation*. London: SPCK, 1956.

Fairbairn, A.M., *The Place of Christ in Modern Theology*. New York: Charles Scribner's Sons, 1893.

Farrow, D.B., 'Review Essay: In the End Is the Beginning: A Review of Jürgen Moltmann's Systematic Contributions,' *Modern Theology* 14/3 (1998):425–47.

Ferguson, E. (ed.), *Encyclopedia of Early Christianity*. London: Garland Publishing, 1990.

Fiddes, P., *Past Event, Present Salvation: The Christian Idea of Atonement*. London: Darton, Longman & Todd, 1989.

—, *The Creative Suffering of God*. Oxford: Clarendon Press, 1990.

Fitzgibbons, R.P., 'The Cognitive and Emotive Uses of Forgiveness in the Treatment of Anger,' *Psychotherapy* 23/4 (1986):629–33.

Frankenberry, N., 'Some Problems in Process Theodicy,' *Religious Studies* 17 (1981):179–97.

Fretheim, T.E., *The Suffering of God: An Old Testament Perspective.* Philadelphia: Fortress Press, 1984.

—, 'Divine Foreknowledge, Divine Constancy and the Rejection of Saul's Kingship,' *Catholic Biblical Quarterly* 47 (1985):595–602.

—, 'The Repentance of God: A Study of Jeremiah 18:7–10,' *Hebrew Annual Review* 11 (1987):81–92.

—, 'The Repentance of God: A Key to Evaluating Old Testament God-Talk,' *Horizons in Biblical Theology* 10 (1988):47–70.

—, 'Suffering God and Sovereign God in Exodus,' *Horizons in Biblical Theology* 11 (1989):31–56.

Friedman, D.N. (ed.), *The Anchor Bible Dictionary.* New York: Doubleday, 1992.

Fries P. and T. Nersoyan (eds), *Christ in East and West.* Macon: Mercer Press, 1987.

Galot, J., *La Conscience de Jésus.* Paris: Duculot-Lethielleux, 1971.

—, *Vers une Nouvelle Christologie.* Paris: Ducolot-Lethielleux, 1971.

—, *Dieu Souffre-t-il?* Paris: Editions P. Lethielleux, 1976.

—, 'La Réalité de la Souffrance de Dieu,' *Nouvelle Revue Theologique* 101 (1979):224–45.

—, 'La Révélation de la Souffrance de Dieu,' *Science et Esprit* 31 (1979):159–71.

—, *Who is Christ?* Chicago: Franciscan Herald Press, 1981.

—, 'Le Dieu Trinitaire et la Passion du Christ,' *Nouvelle Revue Theologique* 104 (1982):70–87.

—, *The Person of Christ.* Chicago: Franciscan Herald Press, 1983.

—, 'Le Mystère de la Souffrance de Dieu,' *Esprit et Vie* 100 (1990):261–68.

—, *Abba, Father.* New York: Alba House, 1992.

—, *Père, qui es-Tu?* Versailles: Éditions Saint-Paul, 1996.

—, *Notre Père qui est Amour.* Saint-Maur: Parole et Silence, 1998.

Geach, P.T., 'God's Relation to the World,' *Sophia* 8/2 (1969):1–4.

Gervais, M., 'Incarnation et Immutabilité Divine,' *Revue des Sciences Religieuses* 50 (1976):215–43.

Gestrich, C., *The Return of Splendor in the World: The Christian Doctrine of Sin and Forgiveness.* Grand Rapids: Eerdmans, 1997.

Gillet, L., 'Le Dieu Souffrant,' *Contacts* 17 (1965):239–54.

Gillon, L.B., 'Dieu Immobile et Dieu en Mouvement,' *Doctor Communis* 29 (1976):135–45.

Gilson, E., *The Spirit of Mediaeval Philosophy.* London: Sheed & Ward, 1936.

—, *God and Philosophy.* New Haven: Yale University Press, 1941.

—, *The Christian Philosophy of St Thomas Aquinas.* London: Gollancz, 1957.

Goetz, R., 'The Suffering God: The Rise of a New Orthodoxy,' *The Christian Century* 103/13 (1986):385–89.

Goitein, S.D., 'YHWH The Passionate: The Monotheistic Meaning and Origin of the Name YHWH,' *Vetus Testamentum* 6 (1956):1–9.

Goodenough, E.R., *An Introduction to Philo Judaeus.* Oxford: Basil Blackwell, 1962.

—, *The Theology of Justin Martyr.* Amsterdam: Philo Press, 1968.

Gould, G., 'Cyril of Alexandria and the Formula of Reunion,' *Downside Review* 106 (1988):238–43.

Graef, H., *The Scholar and the Cross*. Westminster: The Newman Press, 1955.

Grant, C., 'Possibilities for Divine Passibility,' *Toronto Journal of Theology* 4/1 (1988):8–14.

Grant, R., *The Early Christian Doctrine of God*. Charlottesville: University Press of Virginia, 1966.

—, *Greek Apologists of the Second Century*. Philadelphia: Westminster Press, 1988.

Griffin, D., *A Process Christology*. Philadelphia; Westminster Press, 1973.

—, 'The Possibility of Subjective Immortality in Whitehead's Philosophy,' *The Modern Schoolman* 53 (1975):39–57.

—, *God, Power, and Evil*. Lanham: University of America Press, 1991.

Grillmeier, A., *Christ in Christian Tradition*, Vol. 1. London: Mowbrays, 1975.

Grisez, G., *Beyond the New Theism*. Notre Dame: University Press of Notre Dame, 1975.

Groves, P., *Ineffability and Divine Impassibility*. Oxford: D.Phil. dissertation, 1995.

Gunton, C., 'Process Theology's Concept of God,' *The Expository Times* 84 (1972–73):294–96.

—, *The One, the Three and the Many*. Cambridge: Cambridge University Press, 1993.

Gunton, C. (ed.), *The Cambridge Companion to Christian Doctrine*. Cambridge: Cambridge University Press, 1997.

Guroian, V., 'The Suffering God of Armenian Christology: Towards an Ecumenical Theology of the Cross,' *Dialog* 32/2 (1993):97–101.

Gutiérrez, G., *On Job, God-Talk and the Suffering of the Innocent*. Maryknoll: Orbis, 1987.

Haight, R., 'The Case for Spirit Christology,' *Theological Studies* 53 (1992):257–87.

Hall, D.J., *God and Human Suffering: An Exercise in the Theology of the Cross*. Minneapolis: Augsburg, 1986.

Hall, S.G., *Doctrine and Practice in the Early Church*. London: SPCK, 1991.

Hallman, J., 'The Mutability of God: Tertullian to Lactantius,' *Theological Studies* 42 (1981):373–93.

—, 'Divine Suffering and Change in Origen and *Ad Theopompum*,' *The Second Century* 7 (1989–90):85–98.

—, *The Descent of God: Divine Suffering in History and Theology*. Minneapolis: Fortress Press, 1991.

—, 'The Seed of Fire: Suffering in the Christology of Cyril of Alexandria and Nestorius of Constantinople,' *Early Christian Studies* 5/3 (1997):369–91.

Hanson, A.T., *The Paradox of the Cross in the Thought of St Paul*. Sheffield: JSOT Press, 1987.

Hart, T. and D. Thimell (eds), *Christ in Our Place*. Exeter: Paternoster Press, 1987.

Hartshorne, C., *The Divine Relativity*. New Haven: Yale University Press, 1948.

—, *Man's Vision of God and the Logic of Theism*. Hamden: Archon Books, 1964.

294 *Does God Suffer?*

Harvey, A.E., *Renewal through Suffering: A Study of 2 Corinthians.* Edinburgh: T & T Clark, 1996.
Haughton, R., *The Passionate God.* New York: Paulist Press, 1981.
Haynes, S.R., 'Christian Holocaust Theology: A Critical Reassessment,' *Journal of the American Academy of Religion* 62/2 (1994):553–83.
Hebblethwaite, B. and E. Henderson (eds), *Divine Action.* Edinburgh: T & T Clark, 1990.
Hefling, C.C., 'Reviving Adamic Adoptionism: The Example of John Macquarrie,' *Theological Studies* 52 (1991):476–94.
Hellwig, M., *Jesus, the Compassion of God: New Perspectives on the Tradition of Christianity.* Wilmington: Michael Glazier, 1983.
Helm, P., *Eternal God: A Study of God Without Time.* Oxford: Clarendon Press, 1988.
Hengel, M., *The Atonement: A Study of the Origin of the Doctrine in the New Testament.* London: SCM, 1981.
—, *The Cross of the Son.* London: SCM, 1986.
Henninger, M., *Relations: Medieval Theories 1250–1325.* Oxford: Clarendon Press, 1989.
Henry, M., *On Not Understanding God.* Dublin: The Columba Press, 1997.
Herbstrith, W., *Edith Stein: A Biography.* San Francisco: Ignatius Press, 1992.
Heron, A., *The Holy Spirit.* Philadelphia: Westminster Press, 1983.
Heschel, A., *The Prophets.* New York: Harper & Row, 1962.
Hill, W., 'Does the World Make a Difference to God?' *The Thomist* 38 (1974):146–64.
—, 'Does God Know the Future? Aquinas and Some Moderns,' *Theological Studies* 36 (1975):3–18.
—, 'In What Sense is God Infinite? A Thomistic Perspective,' *The Thomist* 42 (1978):14–27.
—, 'Two Gods of Love: Aquinas and Whitehead,' *Listening* 14 (1979):249–64.
—, *The Three-Personed God.* Washington, DC: Catholic University of America Press, 1982.
—, 'The Historicity of God,' *Theological Studies* 45 (1984):320–33.
Holte, R., 'Spermatikos Logos,' *Studia Theologica* 12 (1958):109–68.
Hooker, M., *Not Ashamed of the Gospel: New Testament Interpretation of the Death of Christ.* Carlisle: The Paternoster Press, 1994.
Horbury, W. and B. McNeil (eds), *Suffering and Martyrdom in the New Testament.* Cambridge: Cambridge University Press, 1981.
House, F., 'The Barrier of Impassibility,' *Theology* 83 (1980):409–15.
Hryniewicz, W., 'Le Dieu Souffrant?: Réflexions sur la notion chrétienne de Dieu,' *Eglise et Théologie* 12 (1981):33–56.
Imhof, P. and H. Biallowons (eds), *Karl Rahner in Dialogue: Conversations and Interviews 1965–1982.* New York: Crossroad, 1986.
Jacob, E., 'Le Dieu Souffrant, un Thème Théologique Vétéro-testamentaire,' *Zeitshrift für die Alttestamentliche Wissenschaft* 95 (1983):1–8.
Jantzen, G., *God's World, God's Body.* London: Darton, Longman & Todd, 1984.
Jenkins, D.E., *Still Living with Questions.* London: SCM, 1990.

Jenson, R.W., *Systematic Theology*, Volume 1: *The Triune God*. Oxford: Oxford University Press, 1997.

John Paul II, *Salvifici Doloris* (1984).

—, *Reconciliatio et Paenitentia* (1984).

—, *Dominum et Vivificantem* (1986).

—, *Redemptoris Missio* (1990).

—, *Veritatis Splendor* (1993).

—, *Fides et Ratio* (1998).

Johnson, E., *She Who Is*. New York: Crossroad, 1993.

Jonas, H., 'The Concept of God After Auschwitz: A Jewish Voice,' *The Journal of Religion* 67 (1987):1–13.

Jüngel, E., *The Doctrine of the Trinity: God's Being is in Becoming*. Grand Rapids: Eerdmans, 1976.

—, *God as the Mystery of the World: On the Foundation of the Theology of the Crucified One in the Dispute Between Theism and Atheism*. Edinburgh: T & T Clark, 1983.

—, *Theological Essays*. Edinburgh: T & T Clark, 1989.

Kamp, J., 'Présence du Dieu Souffrant,' *Lumiére et Vie* 25 (1976):54–66.

Kantzer, K. and S. Gundry (eds), *Perspectives on Evangelical Theology*. Grand Rapids: Baker, 1979.

Kasper, W., *Jesus the Christ*. London: Burns & Oates, 1975.

—, *The God of Jesus Christ*. New York: Crossroad, 1984.

Kehl, M. and W. Loser (eds), *The Von Balthasar Reader*. New York: Crossroad, 1982.

Kelly, A.J., 'God: How Near a Relation?' *The Thomist* 34 (1970):191–229.

—, 'Trinity and Process: Relevance of the Basic Christian Confession of God,' *Theological Studies* 13 (1970):393–414.

Kelly, J.N.D., *Early Christian Doctrines*. London: Adam & Charles Black, 1968.

Kereszty, R.A., *Jesus Christ: Fundamentals of Christology*. New York: Alba House, 1991.

Kirn, A.G. (ed.), *Selected Papers*. Toronto: Pontifical Institute of Mediaeval Studies, 1967.

Kitamori, K., *Theology of the Pain of God*. London: SCM, 1966.

Kittel, G. (ed.), *Theological Dictionary of the New Testament*. Grand Rapids: Eerdmans, 1965.

Kolakowski, L., *Metaphysical Horror*. Oxford: Oxford University Press, 1988.

Kondoleon, T.J., 'The Immutability of God: Some Recent Challenges,' *The New Scholasticism* 58/3 (1984):293–315.

Krempel, A., *La Doctrine de la Relation chez Saint Thomas*. Paris: J. Vrin, 1952.

Krenski, T.R., *Passio Caritatis. Trinitarische Passiologie im Werk Hans Urs von Balthasar*. Freiburg: Johannes Verlag, 1990.

Kretzmann, N., *The Metaphysics of Theism: Aquinas's Natural Theology in Summa Contra Gentiles I*. Oxford: Clarendon Press, 1997.

Küng, H., *The Incarnation of God*. New York: Crossroad, 1987.

Kuyper, L.J., 'The Suffering and the Repentance of God,' *Scottish Journal of Theology* 22 (1969):257–77.

LaCugna, C.M., 'The Relational God,' *Theological Studies* 46 (1985):647–63.

Lambrecht, J. (ed.), *Hoelang Nog en Waarom Toch? God Mens en Lijden.* Leuven/Amersfoort: Acco, 1988.

Lambrecht, J. and R.F. Collins (eds), *God and Human Suffering.* Louvain: Peeters Press, 1990.

Lampe, G.W.H., *God as Spirit.* Oxford: Clarendon Press, 1977.

Lang, U., *Studies in the Christology of John Philoponus and its Place in the Controversies Over Chalcedon.* Oxford: D.Phil. dissertation, 1999.

Leaman, O., *Evil and Suffering in Jewish Philosophy.* Cambridge: Cambridge University Press, 1995.

Lee, J.Y., *God Suffers for Us: A Systematic Inquiry Into a Concept of Divine Passibility.* The Hague: Martinus Nijhoff, 1974.

Leo XIII, *Divinum Illud* (1897).

Lilla, S.R.C., *Clement of Alexandria: A Study in Christian Platonism and Gnosticism.* Oxford: Oxford University Press, 1971.

Livingstone, E.A. (ed.), *The Oxford Dictionary of the Christian Church*, third edition. Oxford: Oxford University Press, 1997.

Loewe, W., 'Two Theologians of the Cross: Karl Barth and Jürgen Moltmann,' *The Thomist* 41/4 (1977):510–39.

Lösel, S., 'Murder in the Cathedral: Hans Urs von Balthasar's New Dramatization of the Doctrine of the Trinity,' *Pro Ecclesia* 5/4 (1996):427–39.

Louth, A., *The Origins of the Christian Mystical Tradition.* Oxford: Clarendon Press, 1981.

Lucas, J., *The Future.* Oxford: Oxford University Press, 1989.

Lyonnet, S. and L. Sabourin (eds), *Sin, Redemption, and Sacrifice: A Biblical and Patristic Study.* Rome: Biblical Institute Press, 1970.

Maas, W., *Unveränderlichkeit Gottes: Zum Verhältnis von griechisch-philosophischer und christlicher Gotteslehre.* Munich: Schönigh, 1974.

MacGregor, G., *He Who Lets Us Be: A Theology of Love.* New York: Seabury Press, 1975.

Macquarrie, J., *In Search of Deity: An Essay in Dialectical Theism.* London: SCM, 1984.

—, *Jesus Christ in Modern Thought.* London: SCM, 1990.

—, *Christology Revisited.* London: SCM, 1998.

Marcel, G., *The Mystery of Being, I: Reflection and Mystery.* London: The Harvill Press, 1950.

Maritain, J., *A Preface to Metaphysics.* London: Sheed & Ward, 1939.

—, 'Quelques Réflexions sur le Savoir Théologique,' *Revue Thomiste* 69/1 (1969):5–27.

Marshall, I.H., *Jesus the Saviour.* Downer Grove: InterVarsity Press, 1990.

Martin, R., *The Suffering of Love.* Petersham: St Bede's Publications, 1995.

Mascall, E.L., *Existence and Analogy.* London: Libra Books, 1966.

—, *He Who Is.* London: Libra Books, 1966.

—, *Theology and the Gospel of Christ.* London: Darton, Longman & Todd, 1977.

—, *Whatever Happened to the Human Mind?* London: SPCK, 1980.

May, G., *Creatio Ex Nihilo: The Doctrine of 'Creation out of Nothing' in Early Christian Thought.* Edinburgh: T & T Clark, 1994.

McCabe, H., *God Matters.* London: Geoffrey Chapman, 1987.

McGill, A., *Suffering: A Test of Theological Method*. Philadelphia: Westminster Press, 1982.

McGrath, A.E., *The Genesis of Doctrine: A Study in the Foundation of Doctrinal Criticism*. Grand Rapids: Eerdmans, 1997.

McGuckin, J., *St Cyril of Alexandria: The Christological Controversy*. Leiden: E.J. Brill, 1994.

McIntyre, J., Review of Moltmann's *God in Creation* in *Scottish Journal of Theology* 41 (1988):267–73.

—, *The Shape of Soteriology*. Edinburgh: T & T Clark, 1992.

—, *The Shape of Pneumatology*. Edinburgh: T & T Clark, 1997.

—, *The Shape of Christology* (Second Edition). Edinburgh: T & T Clark, 1998.

McWilliams, W., 'Divine Suffering in Contemporary Theology,' *Scottish Journal of Theology* 33 (1980):35–53.

—, *The Passion of God: Divine Suffering in Contemporary Protestant Thought*. Macon: Mercer University Press, 1985.

Meijering, E.P., *God Being History*. Amsterdam: North-Holland Publishing Company, 1974.

Mellert, D., *What is Process Theology?* New York: Paulist Press, 1975.

Metz, J.-B., *The Emergent Church: The Future of Christianity in a Postbourgeois World*. New York: Crossroad, 1981.

—, 'Suffering Unto God,' *Critical Inquiry* 20 (1994):611–22.

—, *A Passion for God: The Mystical-Political Dimension of Christianity*. New York: Paulist Press, 1998.

Meunier, B., *Le Christ de Cyrille D'Alexandrie: L'Humanité, Le Salut et La Question Monophysite*. Paris: Beauchesne, 1997.

Meyendorff, J., *Christ in Eastern Christian Thought*. Crestwood: St Vladimir's Press, 1975.

—, *Byzantine Theology: Historical Trends and Doctrinal Themes*. New York: Fordham University Press, 1979.

Milbank, J., *The Word Made Strange: Theology, Language and Culture*. Oxford: Blackwell, 1997.

Minns, D., *Irenaeus*. London: Geoffrey Chapman, 1994.

Molnar, P., 'The Function of the Trinity in Moltmann's Ecological Doctrine of Creation,' *Theological Studies* 51 (1990):673–97.

—, 'Moltmann's Post-Modern Messianic Christology,' *The Thomist* 56/4 (1992):669–93.

Moltmann, J., *The Crucified God*. London: SCM, 1974.

—, *The Trinity and Kingdom of God*. London: SCM, 1981.

—, *God in Creation: An Ecological Doctrine of Creation*. London: SCM, 1985.

—, *The Way of Jesus Christ*. London: SCM, 1990.

—, *History and the Triune God*. London: SCM, 1991.

Moore, J.F., 'A Spectrum of Views: Traditional Christian Responses to the Holocaust,' *Journal of Ecumenical Studies* 25/2 (1988):212–24.

Moore, S., 'God Suffered,' *Downside Review* 27 (1959):122–40.

Morris, T.V., *The Logic of God Incarnate*. Ithaca: Cornell University Press, 1986.

—, (ed.), *The Concept of God*. Oxford: Oxford University Press, 1987.

—, (ed.), *Philosophy and the Christian Faith*. Notre Dame: University of Notre Dame Press, 1988.

Moule, C.F.D., *The Origin of Christology.* Cambridge: Cambridge University Press, 1977.

Mozley, J.K., *The Impassibility of God: A Survey of Christian Thought.* Cambridge: Cambridge University Press, 1926.

Mühlen, H., *Die Veränderlichkeit Gottes als Horizont einer zukünftigen Christologie.* Münster: Aschendorff, 1969.

Muller, E., 'Real Relations and the Divine: Issues in Thomas's Understanding of God's Relation to the World,' *Theological Studies* 56 (1995):673–95.

Muller, R.A., 'Incarnation, Immutability, and the Case for Classical Theism,' *Westminster Theological Journal* 45 (1983):22–40.

Murray, J.C., *The Problem of God.* New Haven: Yale University Press, 1964.

Musurillo, H. (ed. and trans.), *From Glory to Glory: Texts from Gregory of Nyssa's Mystical Writings.* Crestwood: St Vladimir's Press, 1979.

Nestorius, *Liber Heraclidis*, trans. *The Bazaar of Heracleides*, Driver, C.R. and L. Hodgson (eds). Oxford: Clarendon Press, 1925.

Neville, R., *God the Creator: On the Transcendence and Presence of God.* Chicago: The University of Chicago Press, 1968.

Newman, J.H., *Essay on the Development of Christian Doctrine.* Harmondsworth: Penguin, 1974.

Nicolas, J.-H., 'Aimante et Bienheureuse Trinité', *Revue Thomiste* 73 (1978):271–87.

—, 'La Souffrance de Dieu?' *Nova et Vetera* 53 (1978):56–64.

Norris, R.A., *God and World in Early Christian Theology.* London: Adam & Charles Black, 1966.

—, 'Christological Models in Cyril of Alexandria,' *Studia Patristica* 13 (1975):255–68.

—, 'The Problem of Human Identity in Patristic Christological Speculation,' *Studia Patristica* 17/1 (1982):147–59.

—, (ed.), *Lux in Lumine.* New York: Seabury Press, 1966.

Oben, F.M., *Edith Stein: Scholar, Feminist, Saint.* New York: Alba House, 1988.

O'Collins, G., *Interpreting Jesus.* London: Geoffrey Chapman, 1983.

—, *Christology.* Oxford: Oxford University Press, 1995.

O'Donnell, J., *Trinity and Temporality.* Oxford: Oxford University Press, 1983.

Ogden, S., *The Reality of God.* New York: Harper and Row, 1961.

O'Hanlon, G.F., 'Does God Change? H.U. von Balthasar and the Immutability of God,' *The Irish Theological Quarterly* 53(1987): 161–83.

—, *The Immutability of God in the Theology of Hans Urs Von Balthasar.* Cambridge: Cambridge University Press, 1990.

O'Keefe, J.J., 'Impassible Suffering? Divine Passion and Fifth-Century Christology,' *Theological Studies* 58 (1997):39–59.

—, 'Kenosis or Impassibility: Cyril of Alexandria and Theodoret of Cyrus on the Problem of Divine Pathos,' *Studia Patristica* 38 (1997):358–65.

Origen, *Contra Celsum*, trans. H. Chadwick. Cambridge: Cambridge University Press, 1953.

—, *On First Principles*, trans. G.W. Butterworth. Gloucester: Peter Smith, 1973.

O'Rourke, F. (ed.), *At the Heart of the Real.* Dublin: Irish Academic Press, 1992.

Osborn, E.F., *Justin Martyr.* Tübingen: Mohr, 1973.

—, *The Philosophy of Clement of Alexandria.* Cambridge: Cambridge University Press, 1975.

Ouellet, M., 'The Message of Balthasar's Theology to Modern Theology,' *Communio* 23 (1996):286–99.

Owen, H.P., *Concepts of Deity.* London: Macmillan, 1971.

Pailin, D., 'The Utterly Absolute and the Totally Related: Change in God,' *New Blackfriars* 68 (1987):243–55.

Pannenberg, W., *Basic Questions in Theology,* Vol. 1. London: SCM, 1971.

—, *Systematic Theology,* Vol. 1. Grand Rapids: Eerdmans, 1991.

Papal International Theological Commission, *Select Questions on Christology* (1981).

—, *Theology, Christology, Anthropology* (1983).

Paul VI, *Evangelii Nuntiandi* (1975).

Pelikan, J., *The Christian Tradition: A History of the Development of Doctrine 1: The Emergence of the Catholic Tradition (100–600).* Chicago: University Press of Chicago, 1971.

Philo of Alexandria, *The Works of Philo,* trans. C.D. Yonge. Peabody: Hendrickson Publishers, 1993.

Pinnock, C., R. Rice, J. Sanders, W. Hasker and D. Basinger, *The Openness of God: A Biblical Challenge to the Traditional Understanding of God.* Carlisle: The Paternoster Press, 1994.

Pittenger, N., *The Word Incarnate.* Welwyn: James Nisbet and Co., 1959.

—, *God in Process.* London: SCM, 1967.

—, *Process Thought and Christian Faith.* New York: Macmillan, 1968.

—, *Christology Reconsidered.* London: SCM, 1970.

Pius XII, *Mystici Corporis* (1943).

Pollard, T.E., 'The Impassibility of God,' *Scottish Journal of Theology* 8 (1955):353–64.

Power, N. and F.K. Lumbala (eds), *Concilium: The Spectre of Mass Death.* London: SPCK, 1993.

Prestige, G.L., *God in Patristic Thought.* London: SPCK, 1952.

—, *Fathers and Heretics.* London: SPCK, 1968.

Quinn, J., 'Triune Self-Giving: One Key to the Problem of Suffering,' *The Thomist* 44 (1980):173–218.

Rahner, K., *Theological Investigations,* Vol. 28. New York: Crossroad, 1983.

Reichmann, J.B., 'Immanently Transcendent and Subsistent Esse: A Comparison,' *The Thomist* 38/2 (1974):335–43.

—, 'Aquinas, God and Historical Process,' *Tommaso d'Aquino nel suo settimo centenario,* Vol. 9, pp. 427–36. Napoli: Edizioni Dominicane Italiane, 1978.

Richard, L., *The Mystery of Redemption.* Baltimore: Helicon, 1965.

Richard, L., *What Are They Saying About the Theology of Suffering?* New York: Paulist Press, 1992.

Rivière, J., *The Doctrine of the Atonement: A Historical Essay.* London: Kegan Paul, 1909.

Roth, R.J. (ed.), *God Knowable and Unknowable.* New York: Fordham University Press, 1973.

Rousseau, M., 'Process Thought and Traditional Theism: A Critique,' *The Modern Schoolman* 62 (1985):45–64.

Rubenstein, R.L., *After Auschwitz: History, Theology, and Contemporary Judaism*, second edition. Baltimore: The Johns Hopkins University Press, 1992.

Runia, D.T., *Philo in Early Christian Literature*. Assen: Van Gorcu, 1993.

Russell, J.M., 'Impassibility and Pathos in Barth's Idea of God,' *Anglican Theological Review* 60/3 (1988):221–32.

Sabourin, L., *Christology*. New York: Alba House, 1984.

Sandmel, S., *Philo of Alexandria*. New York: Oxford University Press, 1979.

Sarot, M., 'De Passibilitas Dei in de Hendendaagse Westerse Theologie: Een Literaturoverzicht,' *Kerk en Theologie* 40 (1989):196–206.

—, 'Patripassianism, Theopaschitism, and the Suffering of God: Some Historical and Systematic Considerations,' *Religious Studies* 26 (1990):363–75.

—, 'Auschwitz, Morality and the Suffering of God,' *Modern Theology* 7/2 (1991):135–52.

—, *God, Passibility and Corporeality*. Kampen: Kok Pharos Publishing House, 1992.

—, 'Suffering of Christ, Suffering of God?' *Theology* 95 (1992):113–19.

—, 'Divine Compassion and the Meaning of Life,' *Scottish Journal of Theology* 48/2 (1995):155–68.

—, 'Pastoral Counseling and the Compassionate God,' *Pastoral Psychology* 43 (1995):185–90.

—, 'Divine Suffering: Continuity and Discontinuity with the Tradition,' *Anglican Theological Review* 78/2 (1996):225–40.

Schaff, P. (ed.), *Ante-Nicene, Nicene and Post-Nicene Fathers*. Reprinted Edinburgh: T & T Clark, 1989.

Schnackenburg, R., *Jesus in the Gospels*. Louisville: Westminster/John Knox Press, 1995.

Sellers, R.V., *The Council of Chalcedon*. London: SPCK, 1961.

Shea, N., 'Atrocities Not Fit to Print,' *First Things* 77 (1997):32–35.

Sia, S., 'The Doctrine of God's Immutability: Introducing the Modern Debate,' *New Blackfriars* 68 (1987):220–32.

Siddals, R., 'Oneness and Difference in the Christology of Cyril of Alexandria,' *Studia Patristica* 18/1 (1985):207–11.

—, 'Logic and Christology in Cyril of Alexandria,' *Journal of Theological Studies* NS 38/2 (1987):341–67.

Slusser, M., *Theopaschite Expressions in Second-Century Christianity as Reflected in the Writings of Justin, Melito, Celsus and Irenaeus*. Oxford: D.Phil. dissertation, 1975.

—, 'The Scope of Patripassianism,' *Studia Patristica* 17/1 (1982):169–75.

Smith, H., 'Has Process Theology Dismantled Classical Theism?' *Theological Digest* 35/4 (1988):303–18.

Sobrino, J., *Christology at the Crossroads*. London: SCM, 1978.

Sokolowski, R., *The God of Faith and Reason*. Notre Dame: University Press of Notre Dame, 1982.

Sölle, D., *Suffering*. Philadelphia: Fortress Press, 1975.

Solomon, N., *Judaism and World Religion*. London: Macmillan, 1991.

Sponheim, P., 'Transcendence in Relationship,' *Dialog* 12 (1973):264–71.

Staniforth, M. (ed. and trans.), *Early Christian Writings*. London: Penguin, 1968.

Stead, C., *Philosophy in Christian Antiquity*. Cambridge: Cambridge University Press, 1994.

Steen, M., 'Jürgen Moltmann's Critical Reception of K. Barth's Theopaschitism,' *Ephemerides Theologicae Lovanienses* 67/4 (1991):278–311.

Stein, E., *The Science of the Cross: A Study of St John of the Cross*. Chicago: Henry Regnery, 1960.

—, *On the Problem of Empathy*. The Hague: Martinus Nijhoff, 1964.

—, *Life in a Jewish Family*. Washington, DC: ICS Press, 1986.

—, *Essays on Woman*. Washington, DC: ICS Press, 1987.

—, *The Hidden Life: Essays, Meditations, Spiritual Texts*. Washington, DC: ICS Press, 1992.

Studer, B., *Trinity and Incarnation*. Collegeville: The Liturgical Press, 1993.

Sullivan, J. (ed.), *Blessed by the Cross: Five Portraits of Edith Stein*. New Rochelle: Catholics United for the Faith, 1990.

Surin, K. 'The Impassibility of God and the Problem of Evil,' *Scottish Journal of Theology* 35 (1982):97–115.

—, 'Theodicy?' *Harvard Theological Review* 76 (1983):225–47.

—, *Theology and the Problem of Evil*. Oxford: Basil Blackwell, 1986.

Swinburne, R., *The Coherence of Theism: Revised Edition*. Oxford: Oxford University Press, 1993.

—, *The Christian God*. Oxford: Oxford University Press, 1994.

Sykes, S.W. (ed.), *Sacrifice and Redemption: Durham Essays in Theology*. Cambridge: Cambridge University Press, 1991.

Sykes, S.W. and J.P. Clayton (eds), *Christ, Faith and History*. Cambridge: Cambridge University Press, 1972.

Talbert, C.H., *Learning through Suffering: The Educational Value of Suffering in the New Testament and in its Milieu*. Collegeville: The Liturgical Press, 1991.

Taliaferro, C., 'The Passibility of God,' *Religious Studies* 25/2 (1989):217–24.

Tanner, K., *God and Creation in Christian Theology*. London: Blackwell, 1988.

Taylor, V., *Forgiveness and Reconciliation: A Study in New Testament Theology*. London: Macmillan, 1946.

—, *The Atonement in New Testament Theology*. London: Epworth, 1958.

—, *Jesus and His Sacrifice*. London: Macmillan, 1959.

Terrien, S., *The Elusive Presence: Toward a New Biblical Theology*. San Francisco: Harper & Row, 1978.

Thompson, W.M., *The Jesus Debate*. New York: Paulist Press, 1985.

Torrance, T.F., *The Mediation of Christ*. Edinburgh: T & T Clark, 1992.

—, *The Christian Doctrine of God: One Being Three Persons*. Edinburgh: T & T Clark, 1996.

Tracy, D. and E. Schlüsser Fiorenza (eds), *Concilium: The Holocaust as Interpretation*. London: SPCK, 1984.

Tracy, T. (ed.), *The God Who Acts*. University Park: The Pennsylvania State University Press, 1994.

Trigg, J.W., *Origen: The Bible and Philosophy in the Third-Century Church*. London: SCM, 1983.

Turner, H.E.W., *The Patristic Doctrine of Redemption*. London: Mowbray, 1952.

——, 'Nestorius Reconsidered,' *Studia Patristica* 13 (1975):306–21.

van Beeck, F.J., '"This Weakness of God's is Stronger" (1 Cor. 1:25): An Inquiry Beyond the Power of Being,' *Toronto Journal of Theology* 9/1 (1993):9–26.

Vanhoutte, J., 'God as Companion and Fellow-Suffer,' *Arhivio di Filosofia* 56,1–3 (1988):191–225.

Vann, G., *The Pain of Christ and the Sorrow of God*. London: Blackfriars, 1947.

Vanstone, W.H., *Love's Endeavour, Love's Expense*. London: Darton, Longman & Todd, 1977.

Varillon, F., *La Souffrance de Dieu*. Paris: Le Centurion, 1975.

Vatican Council II, *Lumen Gentium* (1964).

——, *Gaudium et Spes* (1965).

——, *Ad Gentes Divinitus* (1965).

Vawter, B., *This Man Jesus*. London: Geoffrey Chapman, 1975.

von Balthasar, H.U., *Mysterium Paschale*. Edinburgh: T & T Clark, 1990.

——, *Explorations in Theology III: Creator Spirit*. San Francisco: Ignatius Press, 1993.

——, *Theo-Drama IV: The Action*. San Francisco: Ignatius Press, 1994.

——, *Theo-Drama V: The Last Act*. San Francisco: Ignatius Press, 1998.

von Hügel, F., *Essays and Addresses on the Philosophy of Religion*, second series. London: J.M. Dent & Sons, 1926.

Wainwright, A.W., *The Trinity in the New Testament*. London: SPCK, 1962.

Walsh, B., 'Theology of Hope and the Doctrine of Creation: An Appraisal of Jürgen Moltmann,' *Evangelical Quarterly* 59 (1987):53–76.

Walsh, J. and R.G. Walsh, *Divine Providence and Human Suffering*. Wilmington: Michael Glazier, 1985.

Walsh, W.J., *A History of Philosophy*. London: Geoffrey Chapman, 1985.

Ward, K., *Religion and Creation*. Oxford: Clarendon Press, 1996.

Ware, K., *The Humanity of Christ*, The Fourth Constantinople Lecture. London: Anglican and Eastern Churches Association, 1985.

Watson, G., *Greek Philosophy and the Christian Notion of God*. Dublin: The Columba Press, 1994.

Webster, J., 'Jürgen Moltmann: Trinity and Suffering,' *Evangel* Summer (1985):4–6.

——, *Eberhard Jüngel: An Introduction to His Theology*. Cambridge: Cambridge University Press, 1986.

——, *Theological Theology: An Inaugural Lecture*. Oxford: Clarendon Press, 1998.

Weinandy, T., *Does God Change?: The Word's Becoming in the Incarnation*. Petersham: St Bede's Publications, 1985.

——, 'Toward Overcoming the Spirit of Resentment in a Polarized Church,' *New Oxford Review* 57/9 (1990):14–17.

——, *In the Likeness of Sinful Flesh: An Essay on the Humanity of Christ*. Edinburgh: T & T Clark, 1993.

——, *The Father's Spirit of Sonship: Reconceiving the Trinity*. Edinburgh: T & T Clark, 1995.

—, 'The Case for Spirit Christology: Some Reflections,' *The Thomist* 59/2 (1995):173–88.

—, 'Gnosticism and Contemporary Soteriology: Some Reflections,' *New Blackfriars* 76 (1995):546–54.

—, 'The Soul/Body Analogy and the Incarnation: Cyril of Alexandria,' *Coptic Church Review* 17 (1996):59–66.

—, 'The Human "I" of Jesus,' *The Irish Theological Quarterly* 62/4 (1996/97):259–68.

Welch, L., 'Logos-Sarx? Sarx and the Soul of Christ in the Early Thought of Cyril of Alexandria,' *St Vladimir's Theological Quarterly* 38 (1994):271–92.

Wendebourg, D., 'Chalcedon in Ecumenical Discourse,' *Pro Ecclesia* 7/3 (1998):307–32.

Wesche, K.P., 'The Union of God and Man in Jesus Christ in the Thought of Gregory of Nazianzus,' *St Vladimir's Theological Quarterly* 28/2 (1984):83–98.

—, 'The Christology of Leontius of Jerusalem: Monophysite or Chalcedonian? *St Vladimir's Theological Quarterly* 31/1 (1987):65–95.

Westermann, C., *What Does the Old Testament Say About God?* London: SPCK, 1979.

Wheeler Robinson, H., *Suffering Human and Divine.* New York: Macmillan, 1939.

Whitehead, A.N., *Religion in the Making.* London: Cambridge University Press, 1926.

—, *Process and Reality.* New York: Free Press, 1979.

Widdicombe, P., 'Athanasius and the Making of the Doctrine of the Trinity,' *Pro Ecclesia* 6/4 (1997):456–78.

Wiesel, E., *Night.* London: Fontana/Collins, 1972.

Wiesenthal, S., *The Sunflower: On the Possibilities and Limits of Forgiveness,* revised edition. New York: Schocken Books, 1997.

Wiles, M., *God's Action in the World.* London: SCM, 1986.

Wilken, R.L., 'Tradition, Exegesis, and the Christological Controversies,' *Church History* 34 (1965):123–45.

—, *Remembering the Christian Past.* Grand Rapids: Eerdmans, 1995.

—, 'St. Cyril of Alexandria: The Mystery of Christ in the Bible,' *Pro Ecclesia* 4/4 (1995):454–78.

—, St Cyril of Alexandria: Biblical Expositor,' *Coptic Church Review* 19/1–2 (1997):30–41.

Williams, D.D., *What Present-Day Theologians Are Thinking.* New York: Harper & Row, 1952.

Williams, R., '"Person" and "Personality" in Christology,' *Downside Review* 94 (1976):253–60.

Willis, E.D., *Calvin's Catholic Christology.* Leiden: E.J. Brill, 1966.

Winter, M., *The Atonement.* London: Geoffrey Chapman, 1995.

Wolfson, H.A., *Philo,* 2 Vols. Cambridge: Harvard University Press, 1947.

Woollcombe, K.J., 'The Pain of God,' *Scottish Journal of Theology* 20 (1967):29–48.

Wright, J.H., 'Divine Knowledge and Human Freedom: The God Who Dialogues,' *Theological Studies* 38 (1977):450–77.

—, 'The Method of Process Theology: An Evaluation,' *Communio* 6/1 (1979):38–55.

—, 'Roger Haight's Spirit Christology,' *Theological Studies* 53 (1992):729–35.

Young, F., 'A Reconsideration of Alexandrian Christology,' *Journal of Ecclesiastical History* 22/2 (1971): 103–14.

—, *From Nicaea to Chalcedon.* London: SCM, 1983.

—, *Sacrifice and the Death of Christ.* London: SCM, 1983.

Index of Names

Adams, R.M., 133
Adelman of Brescia, 257
Alston, W., 133
Anastos, M., 178–181, 187
Anderson, J.F., 131
Andressen, C., 85
Anselm, 28, 129
Apollinarius, 34, 35, 175, 176, 178, 184
Aquinas, T., 13, 21, 24, 77, 84, 114–117,
    120–127, 129–144, 151, 152, 159–161,
    164, 165, 174, 183, 207, 208, 209, 219,
    222, 223, 226, 229
Aristides, 88
Aristotle, 44, 71, 72
Arius, 33–35, 175
Athanasius, 34, 176, 190, 199
Athenagoras, 88
Attfield, D.G., 16, 154
Augustine, 10, 28, 115, 118, 129, 139, 151,
    221, 253, 258
Aulén, G., 215

Baillie, D.M., 215
Baker, J.R., 25
Barnard, L.W., 86, 87
Bartel, T.W., 198
Barth, K., 12, 13, 62, 123, 161, 212, 215,
    219
Basil the Great, 30
Bassler, J.M., 40, 48
Batstone, D.B., 286
Bauckham, R., 2, 3, 6, 8, 10, 13, 18, 19, 21,
    41, 46, 173, 174
Baum, G., 286
Baxter, A., 198
Bebis, G.B., 180
Blocher, H., 22
Blumenthal, D.R., 286
Boff, L., 5
Bonhoeffer, D., 6, 285
Bouyer, L., 265
Bracken, J., 22
Bradshaw, D., 131
Braine, D., 117, 121, 126, 128, 131, 133,
    135, 137

Brandsma, T., 285
Brantschen, J.B., 5
Brasnett, B.R., 3, 13, 15, 16, 62
Brigg, C., 97, 100
Brinkmann, B.R., 4
Brown, R.E., 173
Bulgakov, S., 14
Burnley, E., 10
Burrell, D., 120–122, 124, 132–137, 143,
    144, 161, 167, 204

Cain, C., 19
Calvin, J., 151, 185, 187, 188
Cantalamessa, R., 13, 183
Cessario, R., 215
Chadwick, H., 74, 77, 81, 178, 195
Chestnut, R., 180, 187
Childs, B., 48, 56, 57
Clark, K.J., 8
Clark, S.B., 215
Clarke, W.N., 136
Clement of Alexandria, 95–97
Clément, O., 37
Cobb, J.B., 22
Cohen, A., 286
Cohn-Sherbok, D., 286
Cone, J., 5, 25
Congar, Y., 139
Cook, D., 158, 160, 161
Copleston, F., 71
Cousin, E.H., 22, 23
Creel, R., 14, 38, 133, 158, 164
Cross, R., 208
Crouzel, H., 97
Culpepper, R., 215
Cyril of Alexandria, 34, 35, 177–185, 187,
    190–206, 209, 210

Daniélou, J., 92, 100, 265
Davies, B. 120, 124, 134, 158, 164
Delp, A., 285
de Lubac, H., 257
de Margerie, B., 138, 139, 170
Deneken, M., 16, 20
Dillistone, F.W., 215

Dillon, J., 74
Dodds, M., 120, 123–125, 127, 134, 143, 144, 159–161, 164, 168, 204
Dorner, I.A., 13, 20, 21, 61, 62, 161
Dunn, J.D.G., 173, 212, 222
Dupré, L., 254

Edwards, M., 81, 85, 87
Edwards, R.B., 20, 62, 75
Enright, R., 275
Eutyches, 185, 204

Fairbairn, A.M., 1
Farrow, D.B., 154
Farmer, D.H., 285
Fiddes, P., 2, 9, 10, 12, 13, 15, 19, 21, 22, 155, 215
Fitzgibbons, R.P., 275
Flemington, W.F., 256
Foster, P., 21
Frankenberry, N., 156
Fretheim, T.E., 9, 56, 58, 62

Galot, J., 10, 11, 18, 116, 137, 154, 163, 173, 210, 211
Galvin, J.P., 215
Gaybba, B.P., 10, 17
Geach, P.T., 130
Gervais, M., 204
Gestrich, C., 148
Gillet., L. 10
Gillon, L.B., 124, 134, 135, 144
Gilson, E., 120–122
Goetz, R., 1, 2, 157, 241
Goitein, S.D., 59
Goodenough, E.R., 74, 85, 87
Gould, G., 195, 205
Graef, H., 282
Grant, C., 10, 20
Grant, R., 69, 72, 74, 85, 87, 90, 99
Greer, R., 178–180
Gregory the Great, 243
Gregory of Nazianzus, 115, 116, 177, 185, 221
Gregory of Nyssa, 116, 185, 221
Griffin, D., 22, 23, 25, 156, 241
Grillmeier, A., 35, 175, 178, 180, 183, 190
Grisez, G., 46, 124, 131, 132, 135, 144, 152, 165
Groves, P., 57
Gunton, C., 22, 27, 119, 156
Gutiérrez, G., 5

Haight, R., 199

Hall, D.J., 9
Hall, S.G., 115
Hallman, J., 19, 21, 24, 74, 75, 79, 86, 94, 96, 99, 103, 104, 202, 203
Hanley, B., 285
Hanratty, G., 83, 120, 124, 135, 157, 168
Hanson, A.T., 255
Harnack, A., 20
Hartshorne, C., 22, 24
Harvey, A.E., 255
Haughton, R., 5
Hayes, S.R., 286
Healy, N., 257
Hegel, G.W.F., 13, 155
Hefling, C.C., 199
Hellwig, M., 5
Helm, P., 124, 134, 158, 163
Hengel, M., 215
Henninger, M., 130, 136
Henry, M., 46, 56
Herbstrith, W., 282
Heron, A., 139
Heschel, A., 8, 59, 64–68
Hill, W., 115, 127, 137, 138, 143, 156, 161, 167, 168, 204
Holte, R., 85
Hooker, M., 230, 254
House, F., 10
Hryniewicz, W., 14

Ignatius of Antioch, 176, 280
Irenaeus, 90–95, 176

Jacob, E., 9
Jägerstätter, F., 285
Jantzen, G., 5, 24
Jenkins, D.E., 10
Jenson, R.W., 27
John Paul II, 28, 36, 152, 169, 201, 217, 219, 224, 225, 243, 250–252, 255, 258, 259, 262, 265, 266, 272, 277, 278, 280, 281, 283, 286
Johnson, E., 5, 11
Jonas, H., 286
Jones, D.R., 215
Julian of Norwich, 257
Jüngel, E., 12, 13, 15
Justin Martyr, 74, 85–88, 108, 176

Kamp, J., 10
Kasper, W., 53, 115, 119, 173
Kelly, A.J., 137
Kelly, J.N.D., 35, 115, 179, 180, 190
Kereszty, R.A., 173

Kitamori, K., 4, 5, 25
Kittel, G., 40
Kolakowski, L., 8
Kolbe, M., 285
Kondolean, T.J., 124, 137
Krempel, M., 130
Krenski, T.R., 13
Kretzmann, N., 161, 165
Küng, H., 8, 13, 20, 62
Kuyper, L.J., 7

Lactantius, 106, 107
LaCugna, C.M., 5
Lampe, G.W.H., 199, 279
Lang, U., 182, 185
Leaman, O., 286
Lee, J.Y, 5, 8, 9, 13, 14, 15, 17, 20, 21, 25
Leo the Great, 204, 205
Leo XIII, 246
Leontius of Byzantium, 185
Leontius of Jerusalem, 203
Lilla, S.R.C., 97
Loewe, W., 12
Lösel, S., 13
Loughlin, G., 27
Louth, A., 37
Lucas, J., 8
Luther, M., 151, 185
Lyonnet, S., 215, 221, 222

Maas, W., 20
MacGregor, G., 10
Macquarrie, J., 13, 199
Mann, W.E., 124
Marcel, G., 31
Maritain, J., 31, 36, 166, 167
Marshall, I.H., 173
Martin, R., 286
Mascall, E.L., 120, 131, 137, 138, 163
May, G., 75, 76, 87, 89, 91
May, W.F., 2
McCabe, H., 124
McFague, S.A., 24
McGill, A., 2, 276, 278
McGrath, A.E., 174
McGuckin, J., 179, 180, 190, 195, 196, 205
McIntyre, J., 139, 154, 156, 215
McWilliams, W., 5, 23, 25
Meijering, E.P., 13
Mellert, R., 22
Metz, J.-B., 5, 157, 277, 286
Meunier, B., 190, 193–195, 201, 203
Meyendorff, J., 151, 185
Milbank, J., 24

Minns, D., 90, 91, 93
Molnar, P., 154
Moltmann, J., 1, 3–5, 8, 9, 11, 12, 15–18,
    20, 21, 23, 25, 154, 157, 161, 226, 282
Moore, J.F., 286
Moore, S., 204
Morris, T.V., 189
Moule, C.F.D., 173
Mozley, J.K., 2, 13, 75, 99, 111, 112
Mühlen, H., 14
Muller, E., 130, 131
Muller, R.A., 162, 188
Murray, J.C., 52, 55, 122

Nestorius, 34–35, 175, 177–181, 185, 187,
    192, 203
Neville, R., 131, 137
Newman, J.H., 30, 36
Nicolas, J.-H., 163, 167
Norris, R., 91, 95, 103, 180, 191, 195, 197,
    200
Novatian, 104–106

Oben, F.M., 282
O'Collins, G., 173
O'Donnell, J.J., 17, 21, 154
Ogden, S., 22, 25, 156
O'Hanlon, G.F., 13
O'Keefe, J.J., 178, 180, 191, 203
Origen, 97–100, 107, 182, 221, 257
Osborn, E.F., 74, 87, 97
Ouellet, M., 13
Owen, H.P., ix, 38, 124

Pailin, D., 22
Pannenberg, W., 11, 19, 20, 21, 50, 62,
    115, 130
Paul of Samosata, 182
Paul VI, 249
Pawlikowski, J., 286
Pelikan, J., 35, 85, 115, 178
Peter of Blois, 271
Phelan, G., 121
Philo, 19, 69, 72, 74–82, 95, 113
Pinnock, C., 8
Pittenger, N., 22, 25, 156
Pius XII, 245
Plato, 70–72, 87, 143
Plotinus, 71, 143, 147
Pollard, T.E., 13, 15, 17, 19, 20, 62, 75
Prestige, G.L., 109, 111, 181
Putz, E., 285

Quinn, J., 138, 144, 162, 167

Rahner, K., 149, 157
Ramsey, P., 2
Reichmann, J.B., 121, 122, 134, 144
Rice, R., 61, 62
Richard, Lucien, 5, 8, 18
Richard, Louis, 215
Ritschl, A., 20
Rivière, J., 215
Robinson, P., 187
Romanides, J., 196
Rose, M., 40
Rousseau, M., 156, 157
Rubenstein, R.L., 286
Runia, D.T., 85
Russell, J.M., 12

Sabourin, L., 173, 215
Sandmel, S., 74
Sanders, J., 74–76
Sarot, M., 1–4, 10, 11, 16, 17, 24, 38
Schnackenburg, R., 173
Scullion, J.J., 7, 40
Sellers, R.V., 179
Selling, J. 157
Severus of Antioch, 185
Shea, N., 282
Sia, S., 2
Siddals, R., 201
Slusser, M., 176
Smith, H., 156
Sobrino, J., 5
Sokolowski, R., 132, 137, 143, 144
Sölle, D., 5
Solomon, N., 286
Stead, C., 74
Steen, M, 2, 4, 5, 8, 11, 12, 21, 157
Stein, E., 282–286
Studer, B., 35
Suchocki, M.H., 22
Sullivan, J., 282
Surin, K., 4, 10
Swinburne, R., 8, 20, 62, 133, 161, 189

Talbert, C.H., 271
Taliaferro, C., 13
Tanner, K., 135
Taylor, V., 215
Terrien, S., 52, 57
Tertullian,100–105,107,182,183,185,212
Theodore of Mopsuestia, 187
Theodoret of Cyrus, 186, 187
Theophilus, 89–90
Theresa of Calcutta, 252
Thompson, W.M., 173

Torrance, A., 12, 16, 18, 20
Torrance, T.F., 10, 16, 18, 21, 62, 211, 219, 224
Tracy, T., 132, 133
Trigg, J.W., 100
Turner, H.E.W., 179, 180, 187, 215

van Bavel, T.J., 10, 21
van Beeck, F.J., 5, 8, 62, 83, 112
Vanhoutte, J., 4, 22, 157
Vann, G., 16
Vanstone, W.H., 10
Varillon, F., 10
Vawter, B., 15
von Balthasar, H.U., 13, 62, 67, 119, 140, 163, 212, 217, 219, 227
von Hugel, F., 3, 160

Wainwright, A.W., 115
Walsh, B., 154
Walsh, J. 244, 270, 271
Walsh, R.G., 244, 270, 271
Ward, K., 8, 11, 20, 62, 155, 161
Ware, K., 212
Watson, F., 27, 74
Webster, J., 13, 27, 154
Weinandy, T., 22, 35, 37, 117–120, 130, 136, 137, 156, 163, 175, 176, 181, 186, 197, 198–200, 207, 209, 211, 212, 216, 241, 275
Welch, L., 190
Wendebourg, D., 199
Wesche, K.P., 180, 185, 203
Westermann, C., 46, 48
Wheeler Robinson, H., 10, 16, 20
Whitehead, A.N., 22, 23
Wickham, L., 195, 197
Widdicombe, P., 176
Wiesel, E., 3, 282
Wiesenthal, S., 275–276
Wiles, M., 132
Wilken, R.L., 83, 104, 178
Williams, D.D., 1
Williams, R., 211
Willis, E.D., 188
Winter, M., 215
Witte, J., 188
Wolfson, H.A., 74
Woollcombe, K.J., 18
Wolterstorff, N., 10
Wright, J.H., 137, 157, 199

Young, F., 190, 195, 215

Index of Subjects

Aristotelianism, 73–74, 79, 109
Auschwitz/Holocaust, x, xii, 3, 4, 25, 159, 285

Body of Christ, 244–259

Councils/Synods,
  Antioch (268–9), 182
  Nicea (325), 34, 115, 176, 200
  Constantinople I (381), 115
  Chalcedon (451), 34, 35, 197–198, 200, 203, 207, 209
  Lateran IV (1215), 129
  Florence (1438–45), 129
Creation (act of), 87–88, 91, 109–110, 112, 129–144, 155, 207
The Cross: The Glory of Man, 281–282

Development of Doctrine, 27–30, 36–7
Docetists, 175–176, 185

Enuma Elish/Epic of Gilgamesh, 147
Evil: the privation of good, 151–152

Forgiveness, 274–275

God,
  Actus Purus (immutable and impasible), 120–127, 207
  All Holy, 49–52
  Anger, 89–90, 98, 101–103, 106–107
  Arguments on behalf of God's passibility/suffering,
    The contemporary milieu, 2–6
    The Hebrew conception of God, 6–14
    The Incarnation, 14–19
    Contemporary Philosophy, 19–25
  Attributes, 72–73, 75–78, 85, 88–89, 95, 101–102, 106, 110
  Change of mind(anger, forgiveness, repentance, etc.), 59–61
  Creator: 46–48, 50–52, 69–70, 72–73, 85, 88, 91–93, 105, 108–110, 129–138
  Divine impassible love/compassion/

mercy/grief (fully in act) and human suffering, 160–168
  Does not suffer, 152–158
  Ethical immutability, 61–63, 161–162
  Immutability/mutability, 75–77, 97, 101, 103, 105–106, 110, 132–134
  Impassibility/passibility, 38–39, 78–79, 85–86, 89–90, 93–100, 103, 107, 110–112, 153
  Names, 52–53
  Oneness, 42–54, 50–52, 69–70, 94, 97
  Passion (goodness, compassion, love, etc.), 58–59, 78–79, 93–96, 98–100, 106–107, 110–112, 126, 144, 160–168
  Pathos: 64–68
  Present and Active, 53–55, 113, 134–136, 145–146
  Savour, 45–46, 50–52
  Suffering of God, 168–170
  Transcendence/Immanence: 41–42, 55–57, 80–82, 86–87, 95, 108, 113, 136–137, 144–145
  Utterly relational, 127–129
  The Wholly Other: 46, 53–54, 59, 63–65, 76, 113, 132–133
Gnoticism/Gnostics, 90–93, 108, 147

Human love and suffering, 159–160

Kenoticism, 186

Jesus,
  Creator, 73–74
  Communication of idioms, 174–206, 208
  Esse personale, 206–208, 212
  Incarnation, 173–174, 199
    Assuming sinful flesh, 211–213
    'Becoming' as personal/existential, 197–199
    Soul-body analogy and model, 182–190, 199, 203
  Human 'I', 209–211
  Mia physis formula, 192–196
  Suffering/passible as man, 199–206

309

Manichaeism, 147,
Monophysitism, 185–186, 192, 197

Pantheism/Panentheism, 21–25, 135, 154
Patripassianism, 16–18, 176
Platonism, 19–21, 44, 48, 55, 74, 79–80,
    85, 95, 97, 109, 147, 150, 156
Process Philosophy/Theology, 21–25,
    154–157, 241

Sin as the cause of suffering, 147–152
Soteriology,
    Assuming our condemnation, 216–220
    Becoming a new creation, 236–238
    Life in Christ, 238–242
    Models of redemption, 214–215
    Offering an atoning sacrifice, 220–225
    Putting to death sinful humanity,
        225–226
    Resurrection, 226–229
        Bodily resurrection, 234–236
        Vindication of Jesus, 229–234
Suffering,
    And the Eucharist, 259–260
    And Christian groaning, 266–268
    And God's Discipline and Education,
        268–171

And personal sin, 262–266
Caused by the sins of others, 271–281.
For the sake of the Gospel, 278–281
Sharing in the resurrection of Christ,
    246–252
Sharing in the sufferings of Christ,
    277–278
The risen Christ shares in human
    suffering, 252–259
Stoicism, 74, 106
Supernatural acts, 132–133

Theology,
    Problems and Mysteries, 30–35, 37–38
    The Contemporary Mindset, 35–36
Trinity,
    Creator, 138–144
    Persons of the Trinity as subsistent
        relations fully in act (verbs),
        114–119, 145–46
    Persons of the Trinity immutable and
        impassible, 119–120, 146
    Persons of the Trinity utterly relational
        to creation, 127–129, 140–143,
        145–146
    Persons of the Trinity do not suffer,
        157–158

CPSIA information can be obtained
at www.ICGtesting.com
Printed in the USA
LVHW031716240919
632131LV00013B/230/P